Dr. Strangelove's America

Dr. Strangelove's America

society and culture in the atomic age

Margot A. Henriksen

university of california press

Berkeley   Los Angeles   London

The publisher gratefully acknowledges permission to reprint the following:

Lyrics from "Imagine" by John Lennon. Copyright © 1971 Lenono Music. All rights administered by Sony Music Publishing, 8 Music Square West, Nashville, TN 37203. All rights reserved. Used by permission.

"Dream Deferred" from *The Panther and the Lash* by Langston Hughes. Copyright © 1951 by Langston Hughes. Reprinted by permission of Alfred A. Knopf, Inc.

Excerpt from "Lunch in a Jim Crow Car" from *Collected Poems* by Langston Hughes. Copyright © 1994 by the Estate of Langston Hughes. Reprinted by permission of Alfred A. Knopf, Inc.

University of California Press
Berkeley and Los Angeles, California

University of California Press
London, England

Copyright © 1997 by the Regents of the University of California

Library of Congress Cataloging-in-Publication Data
Henriksen, Margot A.
    Dr. Strangelove's America : society and culture in the atomic age / Margot A. Henriksen.
        p.   cm.
    Includes bibliographical references and index.
    ISBN 0–520–08310–5 (alk. paper)
        1. United States—Civilization—1945– 2. Cold War—Social aspects—United States. 3. Atomic bomb—Social aspects—United States. 4. Atomic bomb—United States—Moral and ethical aspects. I. Title.
    E169.12.H49   1997
    973.9—dc21   96–39460
                                                                          CIP

Printed in the United States of America
1 2 3 4 5 6 7 8 9

HERBERT F. ZIEGLER AND
ALEXANDRA L. ZIEGLER

MY COMFORTS IN THE APOCALYPSE OF LIFE

Contents

Acknowledgments

Despite the declared end to the cold war, the issues central to that conflict—especially the development, use, and impact of the atomic bomb and atomic technology—still provoke controversy and confusion in America. In the early and mid-1990s, numerous reports of previously secret atomic projects from the 1940s and 1950s have been unveiled, including the government's deliberate dropping or releasing of radioactive material between 1948 and 1952 (to see how it moved) and the feeding of radioactive food to dozens of retarded teen-aged boys for a decade (1946–1956) to study the human digestive process. The Smithsonian's National Air and Space Museum's planned exhibit to mark the fiftieth anniversary of the atomic bombings of Hiroshima and Nagasaki and its initial inclusion of material critical of those bombings aroused a storm of protest and resulted in a drastically scaled-down exhibit—suggesting at the very least the absence of national agreement over the meaning of those bombings and a national unwillingness to confront the unsavory aspects of World War II. These stories of radioactive experimentation and the debate over the role of the *Enola Gay* in World War II are reminders of the dangers and divisions that have afflicted America since the development and use of the atomic bomb and atomic technology. *Dr. Strangelove's America* is also a remembrance of the damage and cultural schisms attached to living with the bomb and the cold war.

A number of students and scholars have helped to shape my perceptions of the atomic age and many people and institutions have made this book possible, although I of course remain responsible for its contents. Most of those who have influenced my writing must by necessity remain nameless, particularly the long list of students in both Berkeley and Hawaii who have, through their cynicism or their tolerance of the atomic age and its bizarre popular culture, contributed greatly to my own understanding of the bomb's place in American society and culture. I would like to acknowledge, however, the special contributions of Carol Alberti, Joseph Campos, Carolyn Ching, Ava DeAlmeida, Nancy Diamond, Korey House, Sharon Shaw, Naoko Shibusawa, and Stephen Whittaker.

Many others have offered advice and insights on the atomic age, scholars and strangers alike, but I want to thank Allan M. Winkler especially for his incisive and intelligent suggestions and for his careful and critical reading of my manuscript. I also benefited from Ronald Walters's comments on my early work, and I am grateful as well for the moral support of Richard Immerman while he was at the University of Hawaii. Louise McReynolds has also been a supportive friend and colleague. Helping to refine my understanding of atomic age America most thoroughly, though, were those with whom I worked at the University of California at Berkeley: James H. Kettner, Leon F. Litwack, and Michael P. Rogin. They all have my deepest appreciation. I am notably indebted to Jim Kettner for his never-ending support, his expert counsel, and his selfless friendship and dedication. Leon Litwack has served as an eloquent and gracious model for the best scholarship and the best teaching, and he has been an inspiration to my career in history from my days as an undergraduate at Berkeley. His vision of history, informed by a respect and appreciation for alternative cultures and for cultural resistance to human oppression, has shaped my own view of life and history.

The researching and writing of this book would have been impossible without the aid of several generous grants. I am grateful to the Mabelle McLeod Lewis Memorial Fund and the MacArthur Foundation for their grants, which enabled me to complete most of the research for this study. A University of Hawaii Research Relations grant allowed me to undertake additional research at the Library of Congress Motion Picture, Broadcasting and Recorded Sound Division. The staff at the Motion Picture and Television Reading Room was incredibly helpful, and I am especially grateful for the assistance of film and television research librarian Rosemary C. Hanes.

I would also like to acknowledge the gracious efforts expended by those with whom I have worked at the University of California Press. I am especially appreciative of the support rendered by Stanley Holwitz, and I am grateful as well for the assistance offered by production editors Michelle Bonnice and Michelle Nordon and copy editor Amanda Clark Frost. They have made *Dr. Strangelove's America* a better book, and for that I am grateful.

Last, I would like to thank the many friends and relatives who have offered selfless support and encouragement through the long process of researching and writing. I would especially like to express my appreciation to my parents, Barbara and Paul Henriksen, for their long years of sustenance and patience; they brought me into the world during the age of anxiety and helped me see my way through it. I would also like to acknowledge my gratitude to my good friend Jeffrey Bass, who in reading, editing, and reformatting my manuscript made invaluable contributions. I cannot adequately thank my husband and colleague, Herbert F. Ziegler, for his generous emotional and intellectual support. This book is dedicated to Herb and to our daughter Alex, with gratitude.

preface

DR. STRANGELOVE'S AMERICA

or how americans learned to stop worrying and live with the bomb

With the controlled splitting of the atom, humanity, already profoundly perplexed and disunified, was brought inescapably into a new age in which all thoughts and things were split—and far from controlled.

—Time, *"The Bomb"* (1945)

he connection between revolutionary technological change and revolutionary cultural change which is only symbolically suggested in Stanley Kubrick's film *Dr. Strangelove or: How I Learned to Stop Worrying and Love the Bomb* (1964) is openly demonstrated in Kubrick's other spectacular film from the 1960s: *2001: A Space Odyssey* (1968). The opening sequences of this latter film feature ape-men in the process of discovering, ultimately with a flash of sudden, intelligent insight, the more "advanced" uses of the bones that litter their feeding and scavenging grounds. These ape-men learn to wield the bones as tools and, more precisely, as weapons for fighting and killing. Representative of the first true "human" leap in the intelligent understanding of how to control and shape the environment (whether by using these tools for the hunt or for the capturing and defense of territory), the ape-men's application of this primitive tool technology is then connected to the revolutionary advances in human culture and civilization which stemmed from this earliest of technological sparks. An ape-man throws his new tool of conquest and control up into the air and the spinning bone fades into the high-technology image of a space ship traversing the expanse of the universe—a testament to humanity's vastly increased sphere of knowledge and progress.[1]

While *2001: A Space Odyssey* posits the idea that a mysterious and extraterrestrial "black monolith" is responsible for such revolutionary human leaps of understanding, there have been many this-worldly demonstrations of the relationship between technological progress and change and its accompanying cultural progress and change. The Neolithic revolution in agricultural and irrigation technology formed the basis for the equally revolutionary human development of civilization and its urban culture. The revolution in printing technology that began in the mid-fifteenth century certainly contributed to the short- and long-term fueling of religious and political rebellions in Western Europe by providing for popular dissemination of ideas and information. And the mass technology of industrialization also influenced the cultural revolt of "modernism": just as assembly lines broke down manufacturing processes into distinct and separable parts, putting an end to unity or wholeness, so too did the culture, in disassembled cubist paintings and in the fractured prose and perspective of modern literature and poetry.

Given a conjunction between revolutionary technological change and revolutionary cultural change, it seems only reasonable to expect that an invention as revolutionary as the atomic bomb wrought an accompanying cultural revolution, particularly in the American culture that had created this new weapon and technology. It was certainly clear from the very earliest descriptions of the atomic bomb that its technology was indeed revolutionary and unique. Brigadier General Thomas Farrell witnessed the first atomic explosion at the Trinity test, held on July 16, 1945, in the desert of New Mexico, and the awestruck human recognition of the unprecedented change represented by this new bomb filtered into his description of the blast:

The effects could well be called unprecedented, magnificent, beautiful, stupendous and terrifying. No man-made phenomenon of such tremendous power had ever occurred before. The lighting effects beggared description. The whole country was lighted by a searing light with the intensity many times that of the midday sun. It was golden, purple, violet, gray and blue. It lighted every peak, crevasse and ridge of the nearby mountain range with a clarity and a beauty that cannot be described but must be seen to be imagined. It was that beauty the great poets dream about but describe most poorly and inadequately. Thirty seconds after the first explosion came first, the air blast pressing hard against the people and things, to be followed almost immediately by the strong, sustained, awesome roar which warned of doomsday and made us feel that we puny things were blasphemous to dare tamper with the forces heretofore reserved to The Almighty. Words are inadequate tools for the job of acquainting those not present with the physical, mental and psychological effects. It had to be witnessed to be realized.[2]

The same sense of the bomb's revolutionary new power and its auguring of an "indescribable" dawn of a revolutionary new era in human history characterized some of the early American responses to the atomic bombings of Hiroshima and Nagasaki. In an issue celebrating the end of World War II, brought to its conclusion by these stunning new atomic weapons, *Time* magazine stated its own understanding of the shattering impact of the atomic bomb—an impact that suggested the very revolution in physics which had produced the bomb: "With the controlled splitting of the atom, humanity, already profoundly perplexed and disunified, was brought inescapably into a new age in which all thoughts and things were split—and far from controlled."[3] Despite these early statements confirming the bomb's revolutionary character and the culture's expectations for revolutionary change in this new era, however, no such revolutionary change engulfed American culture in the resulting atomic age, at least not until the early 1980s—or so at any rate is the contention of those scholars and social commentators who have addressed the issue of the bomb's place in American society and culture. Regarding the first four decades of the atomic age, most scholars and commentators have apparently agreed with the pronouncement delivered by Albert Einstein, who bemoaned the absence of revolutionary human change in the early years of the atomic age. Suggesting that any early cultural awareness of the bomb's revolutionary nature had dimmed, Einstein noted, "The atomic bomb has changed everything except the nature of man."[4]

According to firsthand observers like Albert Einstein and more temporally distanced commentators alike, the atomic bomb somehow broke the pattern whereby scientific and technological revolutions forge similar revolutions in the nature of human civilization and human culture. This vision of the atomic bomb's unrevolutionary impact on culture and society is particularly evident in historical evaluations of atomic age America, where it is generally held that the atomic bomb stirred little response, let alone a revolution, until the most recent era in America's past. Not until the 1980s, when there arose signs of an organized and widespread antinuclear activism in America, did scholars begin to recognize an atomic awakening in culture and society. The few scholars who have addressed the atomic culture of America have reached substantial agreement on the essential apathy and unresponsiveness of atomic age America. In their work *Indefensible Weapons: The Political and Psychological Case against Nuclearism* (1982) Robert Jay Lifton and Richard Falk saw no break in America's "universal numbing" to nuclear weapons until the early 1980s:

> In the early 1980s something extremely important has happened to nuclear weapons. They have begun to emerge from the shadows. While they have been among us since World War II, it is only now that they have become psychologically and politically visible to the common man and woman. They are no less dangerous to us; they are in fact more dangerous than ever. But it is no longer possible, we believe, to reinstate the universal numbing

that has so long maintained such distance between them and us, and at so great a cost.[5]

Social critic Jonathan Schell argued the same point in *The Abolition* (1984). He noted that only recently had Americans started to face the peril of their age: "In the last few years, much of the public, having very largely ignored the nuclear peril for almost four decades, has been discovering a different faith."[6] And in one of the first contemporary historical works to focus on the culture of the bomb, *By the Bomb's Early Light: American Thought and Culture at the Dawn of the Atomic Age* (1985), Paul Boyer likewise concluded that, after a brief and initial period of atomic age activism ending in 1949–1950, apathy and a dull acceptance of the bomb characterized the American cultural response to the bomb:

> For a fleeting moment after Hiroshima, American culture had been pro-
> foundly affected by atomic fear, by a dizzying plethora of atomic panaceas
> and proposals, and by endless speculation on the social and ethical implica-
> tions of the new reality. By the end of the 1940s, the cultural discourse
> had largely stopped. Americans now seemed not only ready to accept
> the bomb, but to support any measures necessary to maintain atomic
> supremacy.[7]

This lack of "cultural discourse" on the bomb was similarly identified even in a work exclusively dedicated to examining representations of the bomb and nuclear war, Paul Brians's *Nuclear Holocausts: Atomic War in Fiction, 1895–1984* (1987). Brians commented that "Hiroshima has had nothing like the literary impact of other great military events," and he claimed therefore that comparatively little nuclear fiction appeared in print—and that when it did, it did not enjoy a large audience.[8] He inferred from his analysis that "nuclear war must be the most carefully avoided topic of general significance in the contemporary world."[9]

Only one historical treatment of the atomic age challenged this vision of almost complete American apathy about the bomb before the 1980s. In *Life Under a Cloud: American Anxiety about the Atom* (1993), Allan M. Winkler not only supported the idea that "the atomic bomb revolutionized American life" but also discovered multiple "waves" of American antinuclear activism.[10] In speaking of the atomic arousal of the 1980s, he pointed out:

> But this was not the first wave of anti-nuclear protest. American critics of
> atomic policy, more than any of the world's citizens, had been in the fore-
> front of the protest movement in launching a series of earlier attacks on

policies they felt threatened world stability. They had challenged the tests that made "fallout" a household word in the 1950s. They had questioned the defense policy that resulted in near-cataclysmic confrontation in the Cuban missile crisis in the 1960s. And now in the 1980s they were speaking out once again.[11]

Life Under a Cloud provided a necessary corrective to the historical image of a quiescent America before the 1980s, but it tended nevertheless to stress the episodic and limited nature of antinuclear activism. According to Winkler, in the wake of each period of activism, "after marginal success, anti-nuclear activism disappeared."[12] By focusing on more organized forms of protest and on the changes they brought about in American strategy and policy, *Life Under a Cloud* did not center its analysis on the continuing cultural discourse and change that accompanied the bomb's emplacement within American society.[13] As did the 1980s as a whole, the fiftieth anniversary in 1995 of the atomic bombings of Hiroshima and Nagasaki provided another historical moment of engagement with the atomic bomb and its place in American society. A plethora of scholarly studies and popular think-pieces addressed the efficacy and morality of the American decision to drop atomic bombs on Japanese cities, but the debate aroused in 1995 centered around the Smithsonian's National Air and Space Museum's proposed exhibit of the *Enola Gay*, the B-29 that dropped the atomic bomb on Hiroshima. The original script for the exhibit acknowledged the often contentious historical scholarship on the American decision to use the atomic bomb, and even the minimal amount of criticism conveyed in this survey of historical interpretation provoked a backlash from those groups desirous of maintaining the "official narrative" about the decision: that it had ended the war and saved hundreds of thousands of lives.[14]

Protests by veterans, the American Legion, members of Congress, and other groups prompted a drastic revision and simplification of the exhibit at the Smithsonian, effectively cutting off dialogue about the significance and meaning of America's decision to use the bomb at the conclusion of World War II. While the focus of dispute in 1995 was the decision itself, some scholars recognized the broader implications of this controversial commemoration. In their work *Hiroshima in America: Fifty Years of Denial*, Robert Jay Lifton and Greg Mitchell commented that Hiroshima, and by extension the atomic bomb itself, "remains a raw nerve," and the historian Barton Bernstein connected the battle royal at the Smithsonian to a larger "culture war" in the United States.[15]

Along with Hiroshima and the controversy at the Smithsonian, the bomb's contested place in American society activated great discomfort and provided evidence of a cultural struggle. The initial scholarly recognition of American sensitivity to the bomb located this sensitivity almost exclusively in the 1980s, when atomic apathy apparently evaporated. The works of history and social criticism published in the 1980s and early 1990s were themselves signs of the rising nuclear activism and atomic interest of these years—an atomic activism and interest aroused by President Ronald Reagan's reinvigoration of the cold war (through his references to the Soviet Union as an "evil empire") and re-vival of nuclear adventurism (through his Strategic Defense Initiative or "Star Wars" policies). This cultural responsiveness was also spurred by Europe's grow-ing peace movement and antinuclear radicalism, and a similar and increasing American concern about nuclear weapons did find impressive expression in the culture, thereby giving real credibility to the claims of these historians and commentators. The nuclear-freeze movement symbolized the organized anti-nuclear forces gaining support in these years, and the spate of books, television shows, and films produced during these years indicated the real cultural arousal of the 1980s, as evidenced in written works on "nuclear winter" and in propos-als for disarmament as well as in visual presentations of the nuclear peril like *The Day After* (1982) and *Testament* (1984).[16]

For all this compelling evidence of nuclear activism in the 1980s, however, it is neither historically nor culturally accurate to portray the 1980s as the first true years of America's atomic awakening or the preceding four decades as years of simple cultural silence, apathy, and acceptance of the atomic bomb. To so categorize atomic age American culture is to ignore the real, if often obscure connection between the revolutionary character of the bomb and the revolu-tionary character of atomic age American culture, a connection suggested both in *Time*'s recognition in 1945 of the bomb's instigation of a new era of uncon-trolled schisms and in Stanley Kubrick's acknowledgment in 1964 in *Dr. Strange-love or: How I Learned to Stop Worrying and Love the Bomb* of the bomb's central role in fomenting the kind of countercultural rebelliousness that characterized America throughout the 1960s. This study of Dr. Strangelove's America thus focuses not on the most visible evidence of the American atomic awakening in the 1980s but on the previously established and often less visible but nonethe-less "revolutionary" connection between the bomb and the culture which set the patterns of response later seen in the 1980s. My analysis of American soci-ety and culture reveals an understanding of atomic age culture whose revolu-tionary forms of expression matched the revolutionary technological changes represented by the atomic bomb.

To uncover the cultural changes associated with the atomic bomb, it is nec-essary to abandon the measures for atomic awakening and revolt adopted by most other scholars.[17] For those social critics who see "universal numbing" and apathy as characteristic of atomic age America, the standard for nuclear response and awareness is perhaps unnecessarily high: the existence of organized antinuclear movements and groups whose goals include the immediate abolition or international control of all nuclear weapons and the creation of some form of world government. While such explicitly constituted groups and goals certainly signal a revolutionary understanding of the bomb's radical potential for cross-national destruction, they are also too stringent a standard by which to gauge American cultural responsiveness in the atomic age. The relative absence of such groups and goals in the four decades before the 1980s does not denote an equal absence of cultural change in these decades, and it is through the explicitly changed forms of cultural response and expression that the revolutionary impact of the atomic bomb can be measured. Americans learned to live with the bomb, but they did so through the mediation of often radically changed forms of culture and with an often radically changed understanding of life in the atomic age.

Time magazine's consideration of the atomic age, "in which all thoughts and things were split—and far from controlled," actually hinted at the most important cultural tension that resulted from the "controlled splitting of the atom." Two contrasting and conflicting "revolutions" in culture occurred in this new era of schisms. First, the very acceptance and absorption of the atomic bomb into American culture, representative of the general cultural consensus that formed around the bomb and the accompanying cold war imperatives of life, compelled a revolution in American values and expectations. The atomic bomb and postwar atomic diplomacy symbolized the overturning of America's long-standing policy of isolationism which eschewed the "corruption" of world politics and entangling alliances. The new consensus that formed around America's position of postwar power and prominence and around the atomic bomb's role as provider of security and safety was thus emblematic of revolutionary change in America's cultural understanding of life and politics in the atomic age. Second, in conjunction with—but in opposition to—this new system of atomic power politics, there arose an alternative culture of dissent, a rebellious counterculture that conflicted with the culture of consensus and its new understanding of life with this revolutionary weapon of death and destruction.

While my examination of Dr. Strangelove's America is shaped by an appreciation for the revolutionary changes associated with the bomb's absorption into the culture and with the development of an accompanying culture of atomic consensus, I focus on the often quieter and less visible development of the atomic age culture of dissent that grew in the years following Hiroshima and Nagasaki. The split or tension in American culture represented by these two opposing postwar cultural visions proved the prescience of *Time*'s view of this age as an era "in which all thoughts and things were split—and far from controlled." These images of uncontrollability—creative cultural images and themes of chaos, disorder, and disjunction—provide the cultural materials for this portrait of postwar America. Against the dominant culture of consensus and its vision of a new order of atomic security, defense, and prosperity, my cultural study of postwar America highlights the changed forms of cultural expression which challenged the serenity and order of the atomic consensus with a new cultural "chaos" that mirrored the disruption of matter achieved in the technology of the atomic bomb.

The relationship between the split cultures of consensus and dissent is a reciprocal and reactive one, for both the revolutionary cultural absorption and rejection of the bomb reflected previous patterns of cultural accommodation and resistance to change. The culture of atomic consensus adapted to the bomb by stressing the American tradition of optimism and its secure belief in progress and technology; the culture of dissent questioned the emplacement of the bomb within American culture and society by refocusing the traditional moral qualms and doubts that had long accompanied America's political and cultural development. Such cultural tension in America had obviously existed previously, and the conflict between the American order of optimism and stability and the American sensibility of decay and disintegration had in fact been strained quite harshly in the years immediately preceding the atomic age. Both the Great Depression and World War II had disrupted America's ordered system and world view, so the culture was therefore primed both for a search for new stability and for expectations of continued chaos. In his depression-era novel *Miss Lonelyhearts* (1933) Nathanael West provided an image of man and culture shaped by the despair of the depression and conveyed this sense of perpetual struggle between order and chaos:

> Man has a tropism for order. Keys in one pocket, change in another. Mandolins are tuned G D A E. The physical world has a tropism for disorder, entropy. Man against Nature . . . the battle of the centuries. Keys yearn to mix with change. Mandolins strive to get out of tune. Every order has within it the germ of destruction.[18]

While both the Great Depression and World War II intensified cultural perceptions of the chaos threatening America's order, the atomic bomb served as the most symbolically appropriate carrier of this tropism for disorder. The culture of dissent which arose in the atomic age shaped its expressions to such atomic disorder, challenging America's tropism for order with its understanding of the atomic chaos that in fact was the "germ" of destruction within the postwar American order. If culture, an admittedly amorphous entity, is characterized, like man, by a battle between order and disorder, then it is the culture's struggle against order that serves as the central feature of my evaluation of Dr. Strangelove's America. My analysis of America's postwar culture from the 1940s to the 1970s examines the popular cultural products reflective of this dissociation from the American search for order and consensus as the products of a counterculture that signaled an awareness of the radical changes imposed by the atomic bomb and its absorption into American life.

Even though the atomic age cultures of consensus and dissent evolved from similar American traditions, the atomic bomb shaped this split American culture in distinct and unique ways. The atomic bomb became the unifying symbol of American safety and security in the culture of consensus, its distinctive changes perhaps best evidenced in America's new foreign policy, in its new system of internal and international security, and in its new and affluent cold war economy. At the same time the bomb became the disunifying symbol for American insecurity, immorality, insanity, and rebelliousness in the culture of dissent, and its distinctive changes are perhaps best seen in the new forms of cultural expression which demonstrated the dark disorder and destruction that came from living with the bomb. While more traditional forms and means of communication, whether film, television, novels, or essays, also exhibited cutural dissent, it was in particular the new cultural products and genres—film noir and roman noir, science fiction films, pulp crime literature, beat poetry, rock 'n' roll, and black humor—that illustrated the revolutionary and explosive cultural impact of the atomic bomb.

The nontraditional forms of culture created in the atomic age conformed to the disorder of the age, and the changes over time in the nature of these nontraditional forms of expression pointed both to the evolutionary qualities of the atomic age cultural revolution and to the evolutionary quality of the cultural balance achieved between consensus and dissent. In the early decades of the atomic age, the 1940s and 1950s, the cultural consensus regarding the atomic bomb was fairly secure. In this atmosphere of atomic acceptance most voices of dissent and many dark visions of atomic age life were by necessity allusive, ephemeral, and only metaphorically suggestive of the disruption caused by the bomb. Film noir, with its disturbing themes and distorted view of a modern American life characterized by alienation, danger, corruption, and mental illness, was a genre attuned to these years of quiet and often purposefully obfuscated dissent. By contrast, beginning in the late 1950s and extending into the 1960s and early 1970s the atomic consensus began to fragment and the culture of dissent became more open and vocal in its protests. Black humor, which combined the "darkness" associated with the film noir sensibility of the earlier years of dissent with the rambunctious and iconoclastic laughter associated with the fearless rebelliousness of the sixties protests, signified this overt radicalizing shift in the culture of dissent as well as the changing balance between consensus and dissent in atomic age culture. Stanley Kubrick's *Dr. Strangelove* was emblematic of the new openness in the cultural dissent and its spirit of black humor; the film thus forms the central symbolic product of revolutionary cultural dissent in America's atomic age.

The subversive laughter of *Dr. Strangelove* betokened an era of catharsis and awakening in which cultural dissent enlivened its response to match the equally enlivened thermonuclear activism of the consensus culture—a consensus activism reflected in the Berlin crisis, the bomb shelter craze, and the Cuban missile crisis of the early 1960s. The changing times then were central to the evolving nature of cultural dissent in America, as was the cultural understanding of time itself, particularly the cultural evaluation of America's recent past and its spawning of a new and dangerous atomic age system of power. In the early years of the consensual culture's dominance the culture of dissent only allusively revealed its recognition of the corruption and destruction stemming from the recent past and its creation of an atomic system of power. A representative film noir production from this era, *Sunset Boulevard* (1950), indicates the assimilation of film noir in atomic age life and the chaotic changes that resulted from this new atomic system of power.[19]

The film opens with a view of Sunset Boulevard, a street of dreams in Hollywood, California, and the perfect setting and paradigmatic symbol for America's illusions about itself. The camera pans to a bustling crime scene on this street, the swimming pool of a grandiose old mansion inhabited by the aging silent film star Norma Desmond. Floating dead in the pool, Jay Gatsbylike, is Joseph C. Gillis, the protagonist and narrator of this story. In classic film noir fashion Joe tells his story from the dead, from his face-down-in-the-pool perspective, and his breaching of the boundary between life and death reflects the blurred line between the two in this era of confusion. Norma Desmond, a woman enveloped in the deluded past of her long lost film career, has killed Joe for trying to escape her decayed world and for trying to force her to face the less comforting present reality of life.

An extended flashback (characteristic of film noir technique and the genre's obsession with the immediate past) explains how Joe ends up dead in Norma's pool. A struggling movie writer whose career has temporarily hit the skids, Joe by chance turns into the driveway of Norma's "grim Sunset castle" and agrees to stay and revise a screenplay written by this aging ex-star.[20] Once ensconced in Norma's world, Joe comments on its bizarre quality, his views of both the mansion and Norma resonating with death, disintegration, and delusion. Of her Sunset palace he says, "The whole place seemed to have been stricken with a kind of creeping paralysis, out of beat with the rest of the world, crumbling apart in slow motion." Joe is amazed as well at Norma's obsessive attachment to her glorious past, shrines to which clutter the mansion where she comfortably hides from reality. Joe metaphorically alludes to all delusions about an exalted past when he considers the futility of forcing Norma to face reality:

> You don't yell at a sleepwalker. He may fall and break his neck. That's it. She was still sleepwalking along the giddy heights of a lost career. Plain crazy when it came to that one subject—her celluloid self. The great Norma Desmond. How could she breathe in that house so crowded with Norma Desmonds? The plain fact was she was afraid of that world outside. Afraid it would remind her that time had passed.

Joe performs as Norma's kept man, her lover, and as Norma ensnares Joe more firmly, Joe sees more clearly her melancholy madness, particularly obvious in her unrealistic expectations for a successful return to the screen. Forever trapped in her past glory and success and forever convinced of her greatness, Norma reacts violently when Joe decides to break out of her world and stage his own return to the real world. Traumatized into a glassy-eyed and delusional trance, Norma follows Joe outside with her gun and shoots him three times, the force of the bullets plunging Joe backward into the swimming pool. Joe continues his narration from this perspective, describing the film's opening scene with the police and news media proceedings going on around him. After being photographed, his body is fished out of the pool and Joe wryly points out, "Funny how gentle people get with you once you're dead." He also notices how gentle life had become to Norma. Sitting in silent shock, she is aroused only by the rolling of the newsreel cameras that have come to film her arrest. The cameras were rolling once again for Norma Desmond. As she faces the cameras for one last demented close-up, Joe concludes that "the dream she had clung to so desperately had enfolded her."

Living in a decayed world of illusion had resulted in death and madness for Joe Gillis and Norma Desmond, and the fate of these characters suggested the disordered quality of life seen in film noir as well as the evaporation of the American dream and the American order that the bomb had presumably secured. At the beginning of *Sunset Boulevard* Joe had sardonically evaluated the cost of his dreams and desires: "The poor dope. He always wanted a pool. Well, in the end he got himself a pool, only the price turned out to be a little high." The price of American dreams of safety and security and the cost of American desires for an atomic order also threatened to be too high according to this amorphous culture of dissent. The themes expressed in film noir and its disquieting style, while certainly not limited only to film noir, provide the focus for the first two parts of this study. Such images and visions of the corruption of the past and present, of madness, of guilt, of sleepwalking delusion and dehumanization, and of decay and death suggestively indicate the culture of dissent's awareness that America's recent past promised no dawn of a new age but the sunset of all life, innocence, and sanity.

In contrast to this bizarre if quietly changed understanding of atomic age life and the recent past reflected in the early culture of dissent, there emerged by the early 1960s a loud and explicit awareness of America's apocalyptic peril. The dark and sardonic tone of *Sunset Boulevard* was replaced by the representative black humor of *Dr. Strangelove or: How I Learned to Stop Worrying and Love the Bomb,* and the root cause of America's peril and disintegration was openly identified by the culture of dissent: the atomic age system of power and politics and the culture of consensus that sustained it. No metaphoric images of death, insanity, and decay were necessary in the sixties to revise the cultural understanding of the cold war and its consequences. *Dr. Strangelove's* focus on the nuclear establishment and its fomenting of Armageddon symbolize the culture of dissent's shift to open criticism of the past and present consensual atomic system. The apocalyptic ending of *Dr. Strangelove* as well as the film's refusal to abandon its dark laughter even in the face of apocalypse denote the end of the fear and intimidation previously exercised by the culture of consensus. The final section of my work deals with this overt challenge to the culture of atomic consensus and highlights the moral and political awakening suggested in the fearless laughter and imagination of these years.[21]

The black humor of *Dr. Strangelove* evinced the mixture of nihilism and good spirits which matched the destructive and creative potential of atomic chaos. The radical new ethos of the comic-apocalyptic sensibility signaled a shift in the balance between cultural consensus and cultural dissent, and the rebelliousness contained in the culture of the 1960s and early 1970s instigated a tense battle over the authority and legitimacy of America's culture of consensus and the powerful figures of the American establishment who shaped it. The culture of dissent revised its perceptions of the past that had given rise to this atomic age system of power, exposing the immorality and the insanity of a system with such a potential for annihilation. The cavalcade of demented and demoralized characters in *Dr. Strangelove,* from General Jack D. Ripper and Major King Kong to General Buck Turgidson and Dr. Strangelove himself, exploded the mythic rationality and security of the American establishment and the atomic values first forged in the American atomic past of the Trinity test site, Hiroshima, and Nagasaki.

The dissenting culture's changing evaluation of America's past was much like the atomic age itself, "split—and far from controlled," and this disunity underscored the evolving and increasingly powerful nature of dissent from the 1940s to the 1970s. In this schizophrenic era Americans learned to live with the bomb, but they also learned to live with the revolutionary cultural changes and tensions that accompanied the bomb's absorption into their society. By exacerbating these tensions and by stressing the "germ of destruction" within the American atomic order, the culture of dissent helped to attenuate that germ of destruction and to provide the patterns of dissent which became so visible in the 1980s. *Dr. Strangelove's America: Society and Culture in the Atomic Age* thus examines the evolutionary development of this radical culture of dissent, from its origins in the immediate postwar years to its flowering in the atomic age awakening of the 1960s, a culture that was distinctively shaped by *Dr. Strangelove or: How I Learned to Stop Worrying and Love the Bomb.*

part 1

KNOWING SIN

the vertiginous end to american innocence

> When I was that young girl, I saw on the news films the
> Parisian people, with tears streaming down their faces,
> welcoming our GIs. They were doing what I wanted them
> to do. When the Holocaust survivors came out, I felt we
> were liberating them. When the GIs and the Russian sol-
> diers met, they were all knights in shining armor, saving
> humanity. I believed in that. . . . World War Two was just
> an innocent time in America. I was innocent. My parents
> were innocent. The country was innocent.
>
> —Nancy Arnot Harjan, from
> "The Good War": An Oral History of
> World War Two

nnocence has an indeterminate, subjective quality; the assumption or the shedding of the mantle of innocence often becomes the prerogative of individual moral judgment, rendered in desire or dread by those embracing or rejecting their nation's sense of purity. Americans, however, have throughout their history been in substantial agreement on the goodness and innocence of their mission in the New World. From its discovery and settlement America has been defined in opposition to Old World corruption and evil, and at no time did the contrast between the Old and New Worlds seem more striking than at the conclusion of World War II. The success of the American experiment, manifested in its material splendor, contrasted with the ruin and rubble of Europe; the achievement of the American spirit was embodied in the generosity and idealistic humanitarianism of a still young nation that had helped to free an older civilization from its own tyranny. As much of the war-torn world lay in desolation and shock, America bustled with the health and high spirits that accompany success and victory. The New World appeared ascendant, its promise fulfilled.

In the waning days of World War II Americans basked in the glow of having won a hard-fought victory for the forces of good against the forces of evil. As those days passed, though, some of the glow of victory began to dim; the clarity of the distinction between the forces of good and evil became clouded, the purity of America's role in the war and in the postwar world became sullied. American uneasiness with success and American fears about the cost of achieving the American dream have proved as constant as America's innocent belief and faith in its expansive mission, and ebullient postwar America found no immunity from the nagging worries that had plagued generations of achieving and optimistic Americans.

Colonial Puritans tamed a wilderness, conquered Native American tribes, spread their settlements, and prospered, only to fret in jittery jeremiads about the loss of faith and the guilty sins that resulted from such material success. Citizens of the young republic and later Manifest Destiny nationalists subdued a continent and stretched to the horizon the bounteous farms of America's yeomen—coming close to realizing Thomas Jefferson's republican ideal of an agrarian utopia—only to tremble and despair like James Fenimore Cooper's Leatherstocking at the diminishment of nature, the closing in of the frontier, and the festering growth of venal cities, those sores on the body politic. Northerners fought the Civil War to preserve the Union and its budding industrial-capitalist order against the undemocratic slave system only to recoil in the decades following the war at the idea of true black freedom, only to shrink from the social chaos and the democratic outcasts produced by the industrial order (whether radicalizing workers, immigrants, child laborers, or disgruntled and forgotten farmers), only to retreat in fear from the burgeoning technology and inventiveness that formed a part of the essential character of America, that very hellish American dynamo of which Henry Adams warned.

The twentieth century, for all its wondrous scientific and technical advances, has not evaded these dark American concerns about progress and success. This century, in fact, has witnessed the flourishing of fear, for it marks the era when humanity's capacity for destruction and violence equals humanity's capacity for dreaming and hoping. The Great War laid to rest many illusions about the innocence of man, with its trench warfare and its no-man's-land strewn with the muddy bodies of decaying youth. The horror and the meaninglessness of such slaughter sickened many, and American faith and optimism seemed at times as crippled as the defeated Woodrow Wilson and his League of Nations.

Yet even the disillusion of World War I was temporary, a malaise that affected only a sensitive minority of Americans. Through all these American generations, those who doubted and dissented from the American dream and those who questioned the cost of America's mission have represented only a relative few alienated from the mainstream of American optimism. Throughout their history Americans have shown an uncanny ability to overlook, overcome, or absorb those disturbing elements in their midst which more dispassionate observers might have used to pierce the armor of American innocence and optimism. America's bright faith in the future outshone and outlasted the doubts of each generation, and in *The Great Gatsby* F. Scott Fitzgerald gave voice to the continuing seductiveness of American dreams in the aftermath of World War I.

Despite Jay Gatsby's ghastly demise, Fitzgerald's narrator Nick Carraway was left with a grudging admiration for Gatsby's dream, however grandiose his illusions, however blind the innocence that allowed him to pursue his heart's desire, even at the cost of his life. As Carraway muses over the meaning of Gatsby, his thoughts are drawn to the very enchantment of the American vision of the "fresh, green breast of the new world" and to Gatsby's somehow attractive—and archetypically American—belief "in the green light, the orgiastic future that year by year recedes before us. It eluded us then, but that's no matter—tomorrow we will run faster, stretch our arms further. . . . And one fine morning we— So we beat on, boats against the current, borne ceaselessly into the past."[1] Like Jay Gatsby, Americans had refused and would continue to refuse to relinquish their confidence in that orgiastic future, no matter how hard their faith pushed them against the current of reality.

Looking back to the era that had produced Fitzgerald—the years immediately preceding and including World War I—an eminent American historian claimed to have discovered the end of American innocence. Henry May, in *The End of American Innocence: A Study of the First Years of Our Own Time, 1912–1917,* declared the death of that older American civilization that had clung to a simple order, Progressive ideals, and an undefiled and unerring vision of progress.[2] According to May, prewar social, political, and artistic challenges and finally the war itself crushed such innocent notions of simplicity, idealism, and progress and dirtied America's self-image. This older civilization was, in the words of Ezra Pound, "an old bitch gone in the teeth," "a botched civilization."[3] However correct May's conclusions, however final Pound's assessment, these were not finales that Americans seemed inclined to applaud or to accept. Whatever wounds World War I and its disruptions inflicted upon America and its sense of virtue soon healed. Not even the trauma of the Great Depression and World War II could completely extinguish the hopes and expectations of Americans; indeed, the suffering and sacrifices of those years seemed to purify the nation, purging America of its sins and excesses. Emerging from the chrysalis of depression and war, America was reborn into a new and different world, poised to reformulate and refine its regenerate mission for the postwar world.

The abandonment of American innocence in the wake of World War I thus has limits, in spite of the persuasiveness of May's argument. Claims for the abrupt end of a godly and righteous American world view have a tendency to underestimate the recuperative powers of American faith and optimism. Such claims also overlook the ability of the dominant American culture to affirm the virtuous American way of life—with its brash confidence in the goodness of democracy, opportunity, and free enterprise—and to absorb, counter, or blunt most doubts about the course of American democracy and progress. Moreover, any assertion about the cessation of American innocence misses the tentative and almost cyclical quality of these moments of American self-doubt, these continual expressions of guilt, and these intermittent laments about the lost simplicity of American life.

The repetition of this cycle of reclaiming and rejecting an untainted image of America in the years following World War II revealed that Americans themselves had perceived no such absolute break with innocence in the earlier part of the twentieth century. World War II engendered widespread admiration and acclamation, such as that of the young American girl who so sentimentally embraced the goodness of the American GIs and their irreproachable achievements—the liberation of Paris, the freeing of Holocaust survivors, the joining with Soviet soldiers to save humanity. Americans adopted the guise of knights in shining armor, reveling in this time of pride, innocence, and happy endings.

Yet even the young girl of World War II, so convinced of the innocence of these years, experienced a certain discomfort in the wake of the war. Her animated approval of America included the atomic bombing of Hiroshima, but in the aftermath of war an uncertainty challenged her belief in American innocence. On a family vacation in the Sierras during the week of the bombing, she recalled her reactions and her later ruminations:

> In the middle of it came August 6, the bombing of Hiroshima. The war was over. This wonderful new bomb had ended it all. I remember my father organizing everybody in camp, he was so happy the war was over. He had everybody dancing the Virginia Reel. . . . Within a week or two, bit by bit, it sank in. Seventy thousand or a hundred thousand or two hundred thousand civilians? It came as a shock after seeing so many war movies with the Japanese portrayed as militaristic brutes. To see women, children, and old innocent civilians brutally burned. And Nagasaki! Two of them? As the war came to an end, I was totally blown away by how quickly our former enemies became our friends and how quickly our former friends became our enemies. I couldn't understand that. I began to ask, What was it all about?[4]

Intoxicated by its newfound power, prestige, and prosperity, America effectively suppressed many such plaintive questions about its use of power. Nonetheless, this undercurrent of dubiousness was born of a long ambivalence in American culture about the cost and consequences of American success and the exertion of American authority. And this American ambivalence had never been more sharp than in the new atomic age, when America's power and promise had reached such dizzying heights. America's nascent atomic age culture of dissent fed upon the tension within the culture regarding America's triumphant yet potentially threatening sense of power, preying upon those long-standing fears about the cost of attaining an American ascendancy.

The atomic bomb defined postwar American power and shaped the cultural tensions of the late 1940s and 1950s. The bomb centered the debate about American innocence and guilt, and it served as the symbol around which the cold war culture of dissent formed, however multifaceted those forms of dissent became in the years following World War II. The very first expressions of American guilt issued from the lips of those most responsible for the creation of the atomic bomb, the nuclear physicists working on the Manhattan Project. The July 16, 1945 Trinity test of the first atomic bomb inspired comments that resonated with a sense of both cosmic and personal wrongdoing. J. Robert Oppenheimer let his mind's eye wander to a line from the Bhagavad Gita: "Now I am become Death, the destroyer of worlds."[5] Oppenheimer also felt a visceral approval of the reaction of one of his colleagues, who turned to him in the moment of success and uttered: "Now we are all sons of bitches."[6]

These early flowerings of American guilt among select Manhattan Project scientists blossomed more fully after Hiroshima, Nagasaki, and the war's end. Oppenheimer became the most visible and outspoken proponent of remorse when he publicly vented this sense of guilt in his controversial statement: "The physicists have known sin."[7] He elaborated on this knowledge of sin in a postwar speech in which he described the physicists' reactions to the Trinity explosion: "When it went off, in the New Mexico dawn, that first atomic bomb, we thought of Alfred Nobel, and his hope, his vain hope, that dynamite would put an end to wars. We thought of the legend of Prometheus, of that deep sense of guilt in man's new powers, that reflects his recognition of evil, and his long knowledge of it."[8] The first mushroom cloud had conjured thoughts of the wicked powers and destructive potential of man in its sophisticated audience, and this awestruck group of scientists formed a vanguard to warn humanity of the perils of the bomb and to argue against its further development and use.

In spite of the historic and mythic allusions in these scientists' perceptions of guilt and evil, nuclear physicists instinctively sensed the more radical dashing of innocence accomplished by their recent creation. The splitting of the atom and the harnessing of that basic power of the universe far surpassed both dynamite and fire in potential evil, and the shock of this recognition in the New Mexico dawn, on a stretch of desert named so appropriately the Jornada del Muerto, lent an urgency to the early efforts of the scientists to educate Americans about the moral and political dangers of atomic power.

The shock of the development and success of the atom bomb also prompted vertigo and confusion. A number of observers of the Trinity test expressed conflicting emotions; Manhattan Project physicist Philip Morrison recalled "a feeling of awe and wonder and dismay and fear and triumph, all together."[9] Elation and depression both characterized the responses of some of the scientists, creating a rupture in consciousness that deepened with the bomb's wartime use in Hiroshima and Nagasaki. The scientists' doubts about the beneficence of their creation were all the more painful and poignant for coming at the very moment of their accomplishment, a moment that left the scientists reeling with both delight and despair. Years of painstaking and self-sacrificing labor had resulted in awe-inspiring success and had contributed to the swift conclusion of the Pacific war, yet some scientists lamented that they felt a spinning emptiness, as if they had stepped into a vortex of their own making.

The atom bomb shook the foundations of the physical and psychological universe. As natural daylight replaced the searing light produced by the blast, there emerged a hazy sense among physicists that mankind had finally overstepped that fragile boundary between conquering nature for the benefit of future humanity and conquering nature at the risk of human survival. The tightrope that science and technology had long walked was now excruciatingly taut, and henceforth mankind teetered on the brink of annihilation. The scientists' faces reflected this dark recognition on the trip back from the Trinity test; physicist Stanislaw Ulam, who had not seen the test, surveyed their countenances: "You could tell at once they had had a strange experience. You could see it on their faces. I saw that something very grave and strong had happened to their whole outlook on the future."[10]

Many among the scientists attempted to regain their balance and to expiate their sense of sin by working to prevent the realization of that corrupted future they feared. After the war scientists organized to promote the international control of atomic energy, and they spoke to communities about their remorse and their reservations regarding the continuing and unilateral American development of atomic weapons. Of course, not all scientists became so politically engaged in questioning the virtue of American atomic policies and scientists were not the only forces in American culture apprehensive about the country's control of such lethal power. But the scientists' quick acknowledgment of sin and their recognition of the corruption inherent in atomic power and of the uncertain future guaranteed by that power propelled them into setting the moral tone for the culture of dissent in the late 1940s and the 1950s. The fate of some of these scientists and the overall failure of this relatively organized opposition to atomic expansion also revealed America's indifferent or hostile pattern of response to such opposition and prompted the birth of a more disorganized and diffuse but persistent culture of dissent.[11]

For all their intelligence and for all the force of their moral suasion as creators of the atom bomb, the physicists faced an antagonistic or unresponsive population. Each voice confessing a knowledge of atomic sin was drowned in a chorus of atomic approbation; near universal American celebration had greeted the atomic bombing of Hiroshima, especially among soldiers. According to merchant marine Frank Keegan: "We were in the Hebrides when we heard about the huge bomb that decimated Hiroshima. We said, Thank God that's over. A hundred thousand, two hundred thousand Japanese? Too bad. It's over, that's what it meant. Nice goin', Harry. You did it to 'em, kid. That's how guiltless I was. He saved our lives, he terminated the goddamn thing."[12] Harry Truman likewise had little patience for atomic guilt; after a meeting with a self-reproaching Oppenheimer, Truman exploded angrily, in words that recalled the scientists' self-assessment at Trinity and that prefigured Oppenheimer's later complete fall from governmental grace, "I don't want to see that son of a bitch in this office ever again."[13]

The resilience of American faith and optimism in the postwar years buttressed Americans against ethical attacks on the atom bomb, and the immediate rise of the Soviet Union as America's preeminent cold war enemy closed pragmatic American minds to the moral conundrums posed by the new weapon. The Soviet Union came to assume all the evil characteristics at first associated with a lost American innocence in the atomic age, thereby purifying America, if only in contrast; the bomb thus became America's best defense against the spreading corruption of international communism. Those who disputed the chasteness and correctness of America's atomic dream received increasingly harsh treatment, particularly because the nation's security seemed so dependent on an atomic arsenal. In an atmosphere at best indifferent, at worst persecuting, the scientists' messages of warning and fear were ignored.

The scientists' plans and dire prophecies may have been dismissed, but the cause of their concerns remained: the atom bomb and its symbolic representation of a vast and deadly increase in American power. American power and authority also increased domestically as a result of the bomb and the government's efforts to protect its atomic secrets from internal subversives. The exponential increase in American power and the temptations inherent in such power formed the core concern of the culture of dissent that emerged in the forties and fifties; the organized opposition offered by the scientists may have gone but the fears and doubts about America's ability to maintain an ethical balance in exercising such power persisted. Confronted with the widespread and popular affirmation of an atomic America, however, these discordant views of American power and purity appeared intermittent and often ambiguous, overwhelmed by the more confident culture of consensus.

While Americans continued to cloak themselves in the goodness and innocence they had won for themselves in World War II, the culture of dissent pricked the conscience of America, exploiting the uneasy ambivalence that had always accompanied American achievement. The ruling motifs of the culture of dissent punctuated the cultural consciousness of the 1940s and 1950s: guilt and innocence (and the blurring of the two), confusion, corruption, betrayal, the profligacy of power and authority. The culture of dissent kept near the surface of American awareness its warnings about the evil that resided in knowledge and power, warnings peculiarly trenchant in an atomic era fraught with multiplying possibilities of destruction. Like the best among past American voices of rebellion, this new atomic age culture of dissent failed to achieve a significant revision of America's dream, but it did succeed in perhaps limiting the more nightmarish potentialities contained within that dream.

Throughout its history America has always been resistant to admitting an end to that fresh innocence first proclaimed in the Puritan vision of a shining city upon a hill. At the end of World War II Americans were especially reluctant to yield to such suspicions because their nation was tantalizingly close to realizing all the promise embodied in that vision; America stood at the top of the world, invincible and righteous. But the culture of dissent did not let America forget that its new prominent position commanded peril as well as promise. It is perhaps no coincidence that historian Henry May declared the end of American innocence from the vantage point of the atomic age. Written in the late fifties, *The End of American Innocence* gained much force because its message was one that still awaited absorption by the larger American culture. Critical of America's nostalgic attachment to the "inveterate optimism" of the nineteenth century, May noted that for America

> its least successful periods have been those like the immediate present, times of false complacency that caricature the old confidence. . . . The end of American innocence was part of a great tragedy, but it was not, in itself, an unmitigated disaster. Those who look at it with dismay, or those who deny that it happened, do so because they expect true stories to have a completely happy ending. This is the kind of innocence American history must get over.[14]

That Americans still refused to throw off their innocence is clear by the frustrated tone of May's conclusions, but Americans in the atomic age were never able to suppress those perplexing doubts that had been born along with the atomic bomb in the New Mexican desert. The atom bomb and the cold war wrought significant changes for America, and the simple innocence and happy ending provided by World War II seemed difficult to maintain in the newly complex and quickly changing world. In too few years the idealistic hope captured in the rapt image of American and Soviet soldiers as "knights in shining armor, saving humanity" was crushed. The cold war and the arms race twisted and reduced superpower imagery into much less romantic terms; by 1953 Oppenheimer ominously pictured the United States and the Soviet Union as "two scorpions in a bottle, each capable of killing the other, but only at the risk of his own life."[15] A happy ending in such a conflict seemed doubtful, and the culture of dissent attempted to bring a reluctant atomic age America to this realization.

one

TOP OF THE WORLD

the corrupting contours of the cold war

> *"Cody Jarrett. He finally got to the top of the world. And it blew right up in his face."*
>
> —White Heat *(1949)*

usy readjusting to life in peacetime, Americans had little time or reason to consider the new ironies attached to life in the atomic age. Delivered from the deprivations of the Great Depression and the war, Americans reveled in the rewards offered in this new American century: affluence, consumer products, the opportunity to build new dreams and a better world for their children. America's victorious participation in World War II had rescued Americans from want and opened up a whole range of rich possibilities; an ex–New Deal relief worker commented on the vast changes in American material well-being brought about by the war, changes all the more striking when contrasted with the condition of the rest of the world:

> While the rest of the world came out bruised and scarred and nearly destroyed, we came out with the most unbelievable machinery, tools, manpower, money. The war was fun for America. . . . I'm not talking about the poor souls who lost sons and daughters in the war. But for the rest of us, the war was a hell of a good time. Farmers in South Dakota that I administered relief to, and gave 'em bully beef and four dollars a week to feed their families, when I came home were worth a quarter-million dollars, right? What was true there was true all over America. New gratifications they'd never known in their lives. Mass travel, mass vacations, everything else came out of it. And the rest of the world was bleeding and in pain.[1]

The war had placed America in a position of world superiority, and that superiority stretched beyond material wealth to encompass a moral graciousness toward that bruised and scarred world. The world was bloody and pained, but it was a freer place; America had helped to secure that increase in freedom and would continue to protect this liberty. In his *Memoirs* Harry Truman expressed his postwar hopes for the world: "We had won the war. It was my hope now that the people of Germany and Japan could be rehabilitated under the occupation. The United States . . . wanted no territory, no reparations. Peace and happiness for all countries were the goals toward which we would work and for which we had fought." He stressed the unique and unselfish American spirit guiding his hopes: "No nation in the history of the world had taken such a position in complete victory. No nation with the military power of the United States of America had been so generous to its enemies and so helpful to its friends."[2]

America stood in a position of material and moral supremacy, and for Americans peace and prosperity no longer lurked just around the corner—they were reality. In the early months and years following the war Americans did not hesitate to affirm filmmaker Frank Capra's celluloid dictum: "It's a wonderful life." Capra's affectionate view of America, refined in the 1930s, did not seem out of place in the early postwar era, and in his 1946 *It's a Wonderful Life* he rekindled that burning faith in the triumphant goodness of middle-class American society. In the character of George Bailey and in the setting of Bedford Falls Capra presents a composite picture of the American values and the American way of life that the United States had fought to defend during the war: small-town friendliness, family, home-ownership, a modest but comfortable living, and human compassion and caring. George and his small building and loan business have kept these dreams and this spirit alive in Bedford Falls, and when they are threatened with ruin by the cruel town banker, George—and the audience—are given the opportunity to see what America would be without such virtues. George's "guardian angel" reveals to him the poverty, meanness, and violence of a world without George Bailey, and George snaps out of his suicidal despair and embraces the wonderment of life—even his troubled life. And in this era of happy endings, the happiest sort of ending is provided by Capra: the entire town rallies in support of George and saves him from ruin, thereby preserving the sanctity of American goodness.[3]

In the aftermath of the war President Truman acted to preserve peace and prosperity and to ensure the survival of the American way of life so beautifully and sentimentally portrayed in Capra's film. In a nation so lately traumatized by the depression and the surprise attack on Pearl Harbor, security became the basic and completely understandable goal of United States policy. Truman announced this dual domestic and international program in a speech to the nation on the day that formally commemorated America's final victory, V-J Day:

Victory always has its burdens and its responsibilities as well as its rejoicing. But we face the future and all its dangers with great confidence and great hope. America can build for itself a future of employment and security. Together with the United Nations, it can build a world of peace founded on justice and fair dealing and tolerance. . . . From this day we move forward. We move toward a new era of security at home. With the other United Nations we move toward a new and better world of peace and international goodwill and cooperation.[4]

To attain domestic and world security, Truman later offered to Americans a "Fair Deal" to replace the New Deal and to foreign nations "fair dealing." These fair dealings with foreign powers would issue from the American position of strength and moral certainty, though, for Truman was also concerned to uphold the sanctity of American goodness in this new world. He stated in a foreign policy address in October 1945: "The foreign policy of the United States is based firmly on fundamental principles of righteousness and justice. In carrying out those principles we shall firmly adhere to what we believe to be right; and we shall not give our approval to any compromises with evil."[5] In order to ensure America's position of strength and security and thus to avoid any compromise with evil at home or abroad, Truman moved to consolidate and institutionalize the economic and military power of the United States government.

In his Fair Deal Truman pushed to extend or at least preserve the social and economic protections first established in the New Deal, a task made difficult by the rising forces of conservatism now shaking off the apathy that had paralyzed them during Roosevelt's reign. Truman let it be known that the government would continue its enlarged role in American life, and the extended provision of GI benefits and the expansion of the 1935 Social Security Act were just some examples of how the government and its solidified bureaucracy would help to guarantee American social and economic comfort. But the real focus for increasing the security of America was the military; the building up of military power would not only help to preserve international peace but would also help to maintain prosperity and employment at home. Fighting the resurgent and conservative power of isolationism, Truman urged America toward an active international role and toward a vigorous expansion of peacetime military strength. The United States' participation in the United Nations formed a part of this plan, but America's program for international and military strength became increasingly dependent on the atomic bomb.

Soon after assuming the presidency and well before the atomic bomb had been tested, Truman was informed that "the bomb might well put us in a position to dictate our own terms at the end of the war."[6] American policymakers rarely deviated from this early conviction of atomic invincibility, and when the successful Trinity test of the bomb surpassed all expectations in its devastating power, atomic diplomacy became an integral part of American foreign policy. By using the atomic bombs on Hiroshima and Nagasaki the United States sought to end the war as quickly as possible, but it also sought to present a dramatic image of American power to the world—and especially to the Soviet Union. The bomb seemed a sure means for protecting peace and freedom in the postwar world, particularly against the increasingly suspect actions of the Soviet Union and its massive Red Army in Eastern Europe, and America acted to protect its prized possession in a web of secrecy and safety.[7]

Even before the war had officially ended, Truman expressed his concern about atomic weapons and the necessity of preserving America's atomic advantage. In *Year of Decisions* he commented that

> we now had to find some way to control this new force. The destruction at Hiroshima and Nagasaki was lesson enough to me. The world could not afford to risk war with atomic weapons. But until a practical and foolproof method of control could be found, it was important to retain the advantage which possession of the bomb had given us. In other words, it was now more than ever necessary to guard and maintain the secrecy of the bomb.[8]

Truman accordingly issued such orders, and he noted that "vigilance at the various installations of the Manhattan District was intensified."[9] Secrecy was at a premium, because, as Truman worried, "atomic force in ignorant or evil hands could inflict untold disaster upon the nation and the world."[10] In the following year the Atomic Energy Commission was empowered to oversee the control and development of atomic energy, and the Crossroads series of atomic bomb tests took place on the Bikini atoll. President Truman had assured Americans and the world that the United States intended "to make the new force of atomic energy into a weapon for peace," but the rigid guarding of America's atomic monopoly, the quick institutionalizing and bureaucratizing of America's atomic capabilities and policies, and the continued development and refinement of atomic weapons gave no such assurance of peace.[11]

What the expansion of the atomic program did assure to Americans was the changed nature of America's place in the world. Slowly and somewhat grudgingly, Americans absorbed the first lesson of their atomic age education: this was a very different world from that which had existed before the war, a world in which preparation for peace became indistinguishable from preparation for war, a world in which atomic bombs were considered "weapons for peace." There could be little relaxation of wartime vigilance in this new world, and there could be no return to American isolationism—no matter how strong the American impulse to withdraw from the world, no matter how unshakable a habit American isolationism had become. America had no protection in this world save a strong human and technological preparedness; the splendid geographic separation that had traditionally kept America safe from the turmoil and corruptions of the Old World had been lost for all time. This was the message Harry Truman tried to convey when he recommended a program for universal military training to Congress on September 6, 1945. Truman recounted his arguments for a "prepared soldier-citizenry": "I pointed out that the latent strength of our untrained citizenry was no longer sufficient protection and that if attack should come again, as it did at Pearl Harbor, we could never again count on the luxury of time with which to arm ourselves and strike back." And he emphasized the reason for this new and perpetual vigilance: "Our geographic security was forever gone—gone with the advent of the atomic bomb, the rocket, and modern airborne armies."[12]

Such a revolutionary departure from past American policies ensured resistance to these lessons, and Congress summarily rejected Truman's call for peacetime conscription. The tide of world events, however, supported Truman, and the chaos of a world threatened by disease, poverty, and an expanding Soviet sphere of influence impelled America toward interventionism and military preparedness. The postwar Soviet Union with its vast army of soldiers, its large territorial gains and potential for further conquest, and its alien ideology and totalitarian form of government stood as the only power that could knock America off its perch at the top of the world, the only power that could seriously threaten America's vision of a postwar world shaped in its own image. A war-torn world swarming with displaced and destitute persons was perceived as vulnerable to the revolutionary doctrines of Soviet communism, and such vulnerability imperiled America: the only way to preserve the security of a free and pure American way of life in an era of lost geographic isolation was to create a world amenable to American ideologies.

Truman's message of preparedness and interventionism found a warmer reception as Soviet intransigence and aggression revealed the inadequacies of the American response. The chill had never completely vanished from Soviet-American relations, not even during the years of cooperation during the war, and the growing tension between the two nations became obvious as the war in Europe neared its end. The already emergent cold war gained real definition when the Soviets refused to relinquish control over Eastern Europe and the "iron curtain" fell across Europe. Americans digested Truman's teachings more fully as the Soviet Union and the spread of international communism made the attainment of American security more and more difficult and as the Soviets effectively challenged America's ability to dictate the terms of postwar peace. The Soviet Union, by working to frustrate America's quest for its own happy ending in the reconstruction of the world, became the very embodiment of the evil Truman had sworn to fight. A crusading America now prepared to combat and contain that evil.

Truman's formulation of the Truman Doctrine in March 1947 formalized the cold war and finalized the revolutionary shift in American policy which the atomic bomb had fomented. The doctrine enunciated the philosophic justification for expanding and exercising the power and influence America wielded by virtue of its monopoly on the bomb. Truman crafted an American conception of the cold war world which precluded any other response than the one he offered: a limitless American defense of freedom whenever and wherever it was threatened by the enslaving forces of communism. Truman spoke gloomily of a world frighteningly and dangerously but clearly divided between the purveyors of good and evil, light and darkness. Conjuring all the drama of this universal struggle, Truman made it imperative that every nation "choose between alternative ways of life." He left no doubt where a righteous America stood in this crisis: "I believe that it must be the policy of the United States to support free peoples who are resisting attempted subjugation by armed minorities or by outside pressures."[13] Having cleaved the world into diametrically opposed camps, Truman committed America to a policy of containing the communist camp and defending the democratic camp against contamination; in this world there was no middle ground, and Truman reiterated his pledge to brook no compromise with evil.

While Truman proposed his doctrine in a specific response to the deteriorating situation in Greece and Turkey, the Truman Doctrine served to legitimize the overall consolidation of the limitless American power deemed necessary for American security. In its implementation the Truman Doctrine branched out into solid and permanent forms. American economic and military aid was sent to countries threatened internally or externally, and the Marshall Plan offered generous aid to Western Europe in order to stave off the kind of collapse that could weaken the democratic world. The United States pushed for the democratic reconstruction of its recent enemies, West Germany and Japan, as yet another way to contain the spread of communism. The passage of the National Security Act in July 1947 codified the prestige and presence of the military in America and symbolized the vast changes in the postwar American world view. The Department of Defense replaced the more limited and defined War Department, signaling the need for vigilance and preparation to maintain national security; the Joint Chiefs of Staff gained greater status, a National Security Council was created to aid the president, and the Central Intelligence Agency was formed to gather information and intelligence from around the globe. The CIA was soon to gain the power to launch covert anti-Soviet and anticommunist operations as the cold war heated up.

Any opposition that Truman confronted in forging this new program soon dissolved in the face of volatile world events and Soviet expansionism. A bewildering succession of communist advances and successes in the final years of Truman's administration shocked Americans and spurred Congress to pour money and manpower into America's national security apparatus; the 1948 communist coup in Czechoslovakia, the Soviet blockade of Berlin and the resulting American airlift, the permanent division of East and West Germany, the 1949 Soviet explosion of the atomic bomb, the fall of China to communism, and the Korean War all buffeted America's confidence in its national security and broke down any remaining barriers to an unrestricted cold war struggle against the powerful tide of communism. These cold war events, sobering and at times traumatic—as in the dual 1949 punch of the Soviets' attainment of the A-bomb and the communist revolution in China—served to stiffen American resolve to maintain its position of supremacy in the world. There was no retreating from evil in this new world, so the American government solidified its power to fight the cold war on its two fronts: the military and foreign policy front and the home front, where wartime loyalty—now defined as 100 percent anticommunism—became an integral part of America's quest for security.

Once America had determined to take an active role in the postwar world, isolationist and peacetime traditions collapsed. Entangling alliances were formed, first with participation in the United Nations and then with the North Atlantic Treaty Organization. The military preparedness formerly reserved for wartime persisted throughout these cold war years of limbo between war and peace: Congress approved universal military training; the building of atomic arsenals escalated; agreement on the development of the hydrogen bomb was reached in the wake of the Soviet A-bomb explosion; and the Strategic Air Command was organized to oversee and control America's airborne atomic defenses. These military and political defenses against communism found a domestic parallel in the internal security measures adopted by the government to ensure the containment of communism within the United States. Particularly concerned about protecting America's atomic secrets, the government established an investigatory apparatus designed to detect all risks to its atomic and national security.

The House Committee on Un-American Activities (HUAC) was revived, President Truman ordered a loyalty investigation of federal employees, his attorney general issued a list of subversive organizations, Congress passed legislation aimed at outlawing and punishing the Communist party and its adherents, the Federal Bureau of Investigation scrutinized the lives of Americans engaged in apparently suspicious behavior or associated with subversive ideas and organizations, and congressional committees like those led by Senator Joseph McCarthy followed suit. The United States government assumed unprecedented and widespread powers to intrude on the privacy of its citizens, and Americans learned yet another atomic age lesson: the restriction of civil rights accepted as a temporary necessity during the crisis of war had become a feature of life in this purgatory between war and peace; cold war America demanded the loyalty and unity expected of a wartime population. Given Americans' attachment to their innocent way of life and their confidence in America's mission, few Americans objected to these new demands on their loyalty, particularly when justified in the name of national security.[14]

When Harry Truman left office in 1953, he was accused by many—particularly those conservative Republicans who had been out of power for two decades—of having bungled the job of maintaining American security: the Soviets had uncovered the secret of the atom bomb, China had fallen to the communists, the Korean conflict was bogged down, and Truman had unceremoniously relieved General Douglas MacArthur of his duties there. The Republicans leveled pointed criticisms, but in the Republican administration that followed Truman there was no detour from the atomic age patterns of response established by Truman. Truman had been greeted by the crises of an unpredictable postwar world, but he had succeeded in fashioning the revolution in American values and goals deemed necessary for ensuring the security and supremacy of the United States; he had presided over the aggregation of power deemed necessary to forswear any compromise with communist evil, abroad or at home. Truman guided America through the bumpy transition to superpower status which affluence and atomic invincibility had created, and when Dwight D. Eisenhower took office he presided over a population relatively accustomed to America's new power and position.

If Americans felt any anxiety about the righteousness of America's power and position in the world, the election of Eisenhower certainly helped to soothe them. The general's military expertise calmed any doubts about America's security in the world; Eisenhower's revered military status in itself symbolized the prestige and presence of the military in American society, and his World War II heroism infused American policies with the aura of goodness and innocence that had issued from that war. President Eisenhower fulfilled his campaign pledge to end the war in Korea, and while he confronted certain cold war crises, his two administrations enjoyed an era of relative peacefulness. The style and rhetoric of Ike's government differed from Truman's, but the essential substance of containment and security remained unchanged. The smiling, confident, and fatherly face of Eisenhower presented a picture of American power and authority that Americans respected and trusted. As mediated by the serenity and goodness of Eisenhower, Americans learned to live comfortably with the power that protected and secured their way of life.

The majority of Americans comforted themselves with the real benefits that their nation's status provided them, and they therefore remained relatively insensible to the ironies that attended America's new position of world power. The culture of dissent in the late 1940s and 1950s, however, did pay attention to the not very pretty ethical inconsistencies in America's new way of life in the atomic age. Truman vowed no compromise with evil and he built and exercised American power in order to forestall any tainting of American innocence, but the culture of dissent illuminated the many compromises with evil involved in the very process of building and exercising that American power. In order to fight a larger evil—increasingly embodied by the Soviet Union—America cut moral corners, and the culture of dissent registered its awareness of the ironic tarnishing of American values which resulted from America's attempt to protect the purity and primacy of those values.

Filtering through the products of popular culture in these years was a vague sense that the search for security entailed corruption of American ideals and traditions. Whether relying on deadly and apocalyptic A-bombs for its power, allying with former enemies against former friends, or scrutinizing citizens' lives in order to gauge loyalty, the United States seemed to be paying a high ethical price for its fight against evil. The culture of dissent saw the figures and symbols of American authority as tainted and the American way of life as no longer innocent. Success and supremacy bought at the cost of morality and idealism appeared hollow; the crisp distinctions between innocence and guilt, good and evil, had blurred, and "knowing sin" became the disillusioning way of life in the America envisioned by the culture of dissent.

In 1949, the year America gained cold war maturity and committed its resources to the long-term struggle against a Soviet communism much strengthened by the atomic bomb and its Chinese comrades, the culture of dissent presented an image of America that reversed the heart-warming and virtuous vision of American life in *It's a Wonderful Life*. In a celluloid counterpoint to Capra's confident statement of American goodness, *White Heat* offered an iconographic catalog of the culture of dissent's concerns about the perils of atomic age America's dreams of power. No tale of the small-town friendliness and middle-class ideals that epitomized America's postwar way of life, *White Heat* presents a story of America's darker and more violent inheritance.

The action opens with a swift, organized, and efficient train robbery by the brutal Cody Jarrett gang; the gang absconds with $300,000 in federal currency and in the process of getting away Cody Jarrett shoots and kills—coldbloodedly and at point-blank range—two train employees who could have identified him to the police. The band of criminals hides out in the mountains of California, waiting for the heat to cool, and Cody's personality reveals itself as the restless gang holes up in a cabin. Cody is a tough, hard, and intelligent leader, and he has the brains and the murderous intensity needed to foil both the G-men and his rivals for leadership within the gang. His one weakness is that he suffers from intermittent episodes of insanity, a sort of white heat shooting through his brain, and he must depend on his mother to help him through his seizures. Ma, an integral and equally tough member of the gang, soothes Cody through his fits (an inherited family problem of mental illness); she builds his strength and encourages his leadership, repeating their goal and their measure of success: "Top of the world, son."[15]

Cody's gang finally moves on to Los Angeles, but treasury agents investigating the train robbery have identified Cody as the mastermind behind the heist and murder, so the manhunt begins. Ma, Cody, and his wife Verna are trapped at a motel by the treasury agent in charge of this case, Philip Evans, but Cody manages to wound Evans and they escape the ensuing police chase by pulling into a drive-in movie. There Cody explains his ingenious plan to evade arrest and the gas chamber: he will confess to a robbery in Illinois, committed by Cody's prearrangement at the very same time as the train robbery, and thereby elude certain death by serving a two-year state sentence. Ma is left in charge of the gang while Cody leaves to carry out his plan, and she and Verna uphold Cody's story when questioned by Evans and the police. When the newspapers announce Cody's surrender, the feds realize his intentions and concoct their own sneaky plan. Evans sends an undercover agent into the prison to get close to Cody and discover the workings of the gang's network, particularly the manner in which they fence their stolen money.

The undercover agent, Hank Fallon—or Vic Pardo as he will be known in prison and in Cody's gang—is experienced in this kind of criminal role playing, but he is warned of Cody's dangerous mental fits; Evans cautions him about

Cody's instability, but he also suggests that Fallon/Pardo try to replace Cody's mother as his confidant. While constantly on the alert for prisoners who might recognize him as a cop, Fallon/Pardo finally succeeds in getting close to Cody by saving Cody's life in a prison murder plot arranged by "Big Ed" from Cody's gang, who is attempting a takeover of both the gang and Cody's wife, and then by comforting Cody through one of his fits. This fit was brought on when Ma visited Cody and told him she would take care of Big Ed so that Cody would be "back on top of the world" when he got out of prison. Given Cody's fear for Ma's life in her upcoming conflict with Big Ed, he cannot wait out his two-year sentence, so he plans an escape with Pardo. Pardo, of course, arranges the break with the feds, ensuring that their getaway car is equipped with an "oscillator" tracking device so that their movements can be followed and Cody's criminal network captured. On the day of the planned escape, however, Cody is informed by a new inmate that Ma is dead. Cody goes berserk. Screaming and kicking, he is taken away and placed in a straitjacket.

Pardo calls off the feds, so he is completely on his own when Cody nonetheless manages their escape that night; another prisoner smuggles a gun to Cody and he takes control of his cell and the guards and the psychiatrist who has come to examine him. He has Pardo and others—including the man who tried to murder him for Big Ed—brought to him and they escape with the psychiatrist and his car. Once back in control, Cody revives and sets off to revenge Ma's murder with Pardo as his sidekick. Embroiled completely in Cody's world, Pardo stands by and watches Cody murder and pillage; Cody pumps bullets into the car trunk containing his would-be murderer from the prison, "giving him some air" when he complained of the trunk's stuffiness, and Pardo can do nothing. He is likewise acquiescent when Cody finally catches up with Verna and Big Ed. The betrayal in this criminal world is clear: Verna and Big Ed had betrayed Cody (Verna had shot Ma in the back for Big Ed); when Cody found Verna, she blamed Big Ed for Ma's murder, and Cody gunned down Big Ed and kicked his lifeless body down the stairs. Pardo nonetheless deepens his involvement in Cody's criminal affairs, becoming—like Ma before him—Cody's partner.

Pardo has maintained his ties with Cody in order to uncover Cody's money "manager," and he gets his chance when Cody unveils his next grandiose robbery scheme: the gang will steal the cash from a large chemical plant safe by entering the plant in a modern-day Trojan Horse, a gas truck reconstructed to carry men in its tanks. Pardo meets Cody's co-conspirator in this crime, "the trader," the money-fencing genius behind Cody's crimes—a businessman who uses his respectability to cover his criminal activity. Having acquired all the information wanted by the feds, Pardo rigs an oscillator from the parts of a broken radio in order to alert Evans and his men to the chemical plant robbery. The ever-watchful feds catch on to Pardo's signal and the final conflict between Cody and the feds takes place at the chemical plant. The plant is surrounded by massive numbers of heavily armed law enforcement officers, and the equally well-armed gang prepares to fight. Pardo is finally fingered as a "copper" by one of the criminals operating inside the plant, but in spite of being cracked on the skull, Pardo makes it outside to Evans, tells him where to pick up "the trader," and then carries on the hunt for Cody.

The chemical plant becomes the scene of a chaotic battle between the feds and the gang. After many deaths on both sides, the battle reduces to Cody fighting off all the law, led by Evans and Pardo/Fallon. Cody climbs to the top of a huge chemical storage tank, and sweating, laughing, and going seemingly mad, he taunts them to "come and get me." The sharpshooters are warned against wild shots that might ignite the volatile chemicals, but the rifle shots fired by Fallon are hitting their mark: Cody is badly wounded, but he seems impossible to kill. Perched atop his globe-shaped tank, Cody again takes control. He fires the bullets that explode the tank, and as he yells "Made it, Ma! Top of the world!" he is spectacularly engulfed in a succession of mushrooming and fireballing clouds, a white heat of his own making. As they watch the expanding and fiery explosions, Evans and Fallon make their concluding remarks. Evans mutters, "Cody Jarrett." Fallon finishes the thought: "He finally got to the top of the world. And it blew right up in his face."

White Heat presented a plethora of images and themes that would resonate throughout the postwar culture of dissent. The corruption of power, whether criminal or legal, formed one new and confused concern. Cody Jarrett served as a symbol for a kind of criminal antihero, a corrupted chaser of the American dream, but a dreamer nonetheless. He rose to the top of the world through murderous means, but he achieved success by hard work, intelligence, and initiative, and he overcame (at least for a time) the obstacle of illness to achieve power, wealth, and fame. In this dark vision of the American way, the methods needed to get to the top were criminal and subversive: Cody Jarrett needed them, his respectable businessman partner needed them, and law enforcement officials needed them. The distinction between the good guys and the bad guys seemed unclear as criminal gangs mirrored the bureaucratic efficiency and organization of government law agencies and as officers of the law disguised themselves as criminals and engaged in the same underhanded methods employed by the underworld: infiltration, informing, betrayal. Power and success in themselves took on a subversive and criminal aspect, and the price of achievement could be death, moral and physical. The grotesque irony of Cody's arriving at the top of the world only to find self-destruction and fiery annihilation may have seemed cosmically correct given Cody's criminality, but the message carried moral overtones for atomic age America. Cody's miniapocalypse had the very look of atomic annihilation.

The film noir imagery of *White Heat* revealed a materially and morally changed America. The expanded presence of law and order forces was obvious, as was their increasing reliance on sophisticated technology to control the lives of Americans. The oscillator, the mobile tracking equipment in their specially outfitted automobiles, and their instantaneous radio communications all testified to the growing presence of technological power in America's security forces and in the society in general. Nowhere present in *White Heat* was the America of friendliness, trustworthiness, and kindness. This was a violent and confused society: friends betrayed friends, a wife betrayed her husband, an enemy befriended the enemy and then betrayed him; lying and deception were rampant, as were the death and brutality that resulted from the exercise of power. And there was no happy ending in this dark America, only the ironic annihilation of a man who had climbed to the pinnacle of power.

America's atomic age culture of dissent presented a different and more disturbing set of icons to Americans in the late 1940s and 1950s, challenging the more beneficent and innocent imagery found in mainstream American expressions. Dark and destructive symbols of power, as in *White Heat,* pervaded this more dubious American mindset; apocalyptic explosions, corrupt representations of power, and nightmare versions of the American way of life accentuated the fears and tensions that accompanied America's rise to atomic invincibility. These cultural qualms about the morality and goodness of America were revealed early in the cold war through reevaluations of America's participation in World War II and the resulting cold war. Images of war, military power, and technological and scientific prowess became subject to tones of ambivalence, remorse, depravity, and guilt. Beginning with such critical views of World War II and its aftermath, the culture of dissent questioned the morality of an American base of power built on compromise with evil.

Writer William Styron placed the war and its aftermath at the center of the forces shaping the world-weary view of his peers. For *Esquire* magazine in 1968 Styron attempted to define his generation, in a manner similar to that of F. Scott Fitzgerald, as "those of us who approached our majority during World War II, and whose attitudes were shaped by the spirit of that time and by our common initiation into the world by that momentous event." He added, "For a slightly earlier generation the common initiation was the Spanish Civil War;

for us it somehow simultaneously ended and began when Harry Truman announced the destruction of Hiroshima."[16] In contrast to World War I, which left "America and Americans generally intact," as Fitzgerald had noted, World War II had a more devastating impact, as Styron pointed out: "Our generation was not only not intact, it had been in many places cut to pieces."[17] He talked of those who had "died like ants in the Normandy invasion" and those who had "met ugly and horrible deaths on the hot coral and sands" of Iwo Jima and Tarawa. Then he turned to his own representative experience:

> I was lucky and saw no battle, but I had the wits scared out of me more times than I could count, and so by the time the bomb dropped on Hiroshima, thus circumventing my future plans (I was on my way [to the front]; "You can figure that four out of five of you will get your asses shot off," I can recall some colonel telling us, as he embroidered dreamily about the coming invasion of the Japanese mainland), an enormous sense of relief stole over my spirit, along with a kind of dull weariness that others of that period have recalled.[18]

Styron further defined this weariness of his generation as a sort of trauma: "I think most of us were in a way subtly traumatized . . . not only by what we had been through and by the almost unimaginable presence of the bomb, but by the realization that the entire mess was not finished after all: there was now the Cold War to face, and its clammy presence oozed into our nights and days." Give the multifaceted shocks of the war, the bomb, and the cold war, Styron offered this conclusion regarding his generation: "When at last the Korean War arrived, some short five years later (it was this writer's duty to serve his country in the Marines in that mean conflict, too), the cosmos seemed so unhinged as to be nearly insupportable. Surely by that time . . . we were the most mistrustful of power and the least nationalistic of any generation that America has produced."[19]

Certain American actions in the years after World War II clearly gave those sensitive to America's moral purity reason for mistrust. Having arrived at the heights of moral prestige, America seemed at times all too ready to stumble. As the war in Europe wound down, for example, American military intelligence officers were assigned to protect, provide money for, and prepare means of escape for upper-echelon Nazi officers and war criminals. Such infamous and brutal Nazi murderers as Klaus Barbie, the "Butcher of Lyons," were aided by the American government in order to obtain inside information on the Soviet Union and the Red Army. Some of the American soldiers involved in these operations felt sickened by their work. As one intelligence officer who gathered information from Barbie commented: "How this guy was helped to escape, by the Americans, is beyond my comprehension."[20]

While the American aiding and abetting of Nazi war criminals may have been beyond this intelligence officer's moral comprehension, it was not beyond his military understanding. In the months and years following the war the United States government and military had quickly moved to guard against the strength of the Soviet Union, even if such moves entailed a rather shocking reversal of wartime loyalties and animosities. This same intelligence officer watched in amazement as the same Soviets who had "saved our ass because they killed so many more Germans" immediately became America's enemy; in American maneuvers in Germany in the years after the war, the enemy was explicitly identified:

> Instead of calling the enemy the Red Army or the Blue Army, which we did in Louisiana and Texas, we actually called them the Russian aggressors. That struck me so severely. All of a sudden, four years after the war, we've picked them as our future enemy. . . . At first the GIs were a little stunned by it. But if that's what we gotta do, we gotta do it.[21]

The cold war imperative against Soviet aggression resulted in manifold compromises with the evil that had been Nazi Germany, a Germany that now promised to transform itself into a democratic ally against communism. Nazi war criminals found salvation and new life through a variety of American policies. German scientists who had developed the deadly Nazi war technologies—like Wernher von Braun, developer of the V-1 and V-2 rockets—were sent to the United States and mined for their knowledge (the Soviet Union also took possession of Nazi scientists it had captured). The cold war also ultimately affected the outcome of many of the war crimes trials held at Nuremberg. Designed to punish Nazi war crimes and atrocities, these trials soon felt the cold war pressure to minimize punishment in order to expedite reconciliation with Germany. After the first showcase trial involving the major names in the annals of Nazi horror, the majority of whom received the death penalty, the climate in Germany changed. Telford Taylor, chief American prosecutor at twelve of the Nuremberg trials, explained the shift in attitude:

> With the first trial successfully concluded, the whole climate of the occupation zone changed. The iron curtain came down, the cooperative administration of Occupied Germany had broken up. Came the Berlin airlift and great hostility between the Eastern and Western powers. The sentiment toward Germany, politically and militarily, began to change a great deal.

We wanted Germany on our side. That attitude, I think, affected the sentencing in the remaining trials. Quite a lot of death sentences were given out, chiefly to SS officials who were directly responsible for the Jewish exterminations. A great many of those sentences were pending when General Clay left as head of Military Government of Occupied Germany. John McCloy, who took his place as High Commissioner, commuted a great many of those death sentences. There were only five who were executed after that.[22]

The same sense of a confused shifting of alliances also characterized some responses to the conflict in Korea. Journalist Mike Royko remembered the disillusion he suffered as a result of the war, "our first embarrassing war." He wondered, "What is this? I didn't know anyone who was in Korea who understood what the hell we were doing there. We're here to stop the commies? Hell, when you looked at the way South Korea was run—I saw Koreans beaten to death by the Korean police."[23] Royko also felt uncomfortable about the new loyalties demanded in Korea:

> We were over there fighting the Chinese, you know? Christ, I'd been raised to think the Chinese were among the world's most heroic people and our great friends. . . . I was still mad at the Japs. The Japanese are now our friends, our pals. I'm going from Japan to Korea, where I'm supposed to fight the Chinese, who are now our enemies. A few years earlier, I was mad at the Japanese and I was supposed to love the Chinese. Now I gotta love the Japanese and hate the Chinese. That's when I decided something's wrong.[24]

Besides presenting a faith-shattering confusion about American friends and enemies in this rapidly changing world, the Korean War as well helped to dampen the glorious image of the American military. Royko felt personally shamed: "I remember coming back from Korea, the hostility, the indifference. I was almost embarrassed being in Korea because we didn't win. We cut a deal. We got a draw. We had failed where our older brothers had won."[25] Others noticed how the Korean conflict sapped the notion of goodness and innocence in war that had persisted from World War II; one veteran traced the end of American innocence to the years of the Korean War: "I think everybody still felt good about the war in '47, '48, '49. One wonders: could Truman have unilaterally committed American troops to Korea unless there had been the lingering romance of the Second World War? I rather doubt it. I think things began to sour and innocence end in, say, 1952 and 1953, as the Korean War dragged on."[26]

At least by the time of the Korean War, then, a group of American dissenters had recognized the vanishing of their easy faith in the goodness and innocence of America and its uses of power. In 1946 and 1947 a number of films were released that hinted at the sinister survival of Nazism and its anti-Semitism, but now the setting was America. Not only had World War II not snuffed out racist fascism, but such fascism and racism now threatened America from within. The 1946 film *The Stranger,* which presented an infamous Nazi war criminal living comfortably and undetected in a welcoming small-town community, seemed the logical product of America's lenient treatment of Nazis at the end of World War II. The frightening premise of *The Stranger* revealed the ease with which such evil could insinuate itself into innocent and idyllic American life. Even though an investigator from the Allied War Crimes Commission is hot on the trail of this Nazi criminal, it is clear that the Nazi has experienced little difficulty in gaining acceptance in America: he has found a job teaching and he marries the daughter of a liberal Supreme Court justice on the day the investigator arrives in town. He has established a "perfect cover" for awaiting the "next war," the next Nazi strike, so the investigator's job entails getting the new bride and her family to recognize the Nazi for what he is. The investigator and the wife's family work particularly hard to get her to face the truth: she is "shielding a murderer"; her husband was the "commander in charge of one of the more efficient concentration camps" and the conceiver of the policy of genocide. She is assured that Nazis "look like other people and act like other people when it's to their benefit," but she remains incredulous, horrified at the thought of having married a Nazi. Her father convinces her that she has "innocently married a criminal," and in the end they capture the Nazi, who dies in the struggle, maintaining to his death: "I followed orders . . . I only did my duty . . . I'm not a criminal."[27] While the Nazi in *The Stranger* met his just fate and was exorcised from the small town he had corrupted, the fear of infiltrating evil lingered. Alfred Hitchcock's *Notorious* (1946) also focused on the Nazi presence in America. The film opens with the conviction for treason of an influential Nazi in Florida, and even though the Nazi's daughter expiates her family's evil by working with American intelligence forces against a network of Nazis in South America, the persistent fear of Nazi corruption provides the context for the film.[28] American adherence to a self-serving and misanthropic fascism also marked the character of Harry Lime in *The Third Man* (1949). Harry Lime inhabits the shadowy criminal world of occupied Vienna, exploiting the profit potential opened by the conflicting zones of occupation.

He became a dealer in stolen penicillin, a rare and much needed commodity in the postwar world; he diluted the drug in order to increase profits and then sold it to the ill—pregnant women, gangrene-infected soldiers, children—who died from using it.

Lime has feigned his own death in order to elude capture for his crimes. An old American friend discovers the truth—that Lime is alive and that he is a crooked, murdering racketeer—and he confronts Lime on Vienna's giant ferris wheel. Lime looks condescendingly down on the people below and tells his idealistic friend that "the world doesn't make any heroes," that "no one thinks in terms of human beings." Lime feels absolutely no remorse for the deaths he has caused, and he rejects the concepts of brotherhood and democracy. To him human beings are simply the "dots" they appear to be from the vantage point of the ferris wheel:

> The dead are happier dead. They don't miss much here, the poor devils. . . . In Italy, for thirty years under the Borgias they had warfare, terror, murder and bloodshed, but they produced Michelangelo, Leonardo da Vinci, and Rembrandt. In Switzerland they had brotherly love and five hundred years of democracy and peace. And what did they produce? The cuckoo clock.[29]

The authorities, aided by Harry's friend, finally hunt down and kill Harry Lime in the dank sewers of Vienna, a fitting place of death for this modern rodent.

The popular culture's attention to the issue of anti-Semitism in the United States suggested that fascism could also infect the attitudes of Americans at home. The fate of the millions of Jews caught in the machinery of Hitler's "final solution" made the continued presence of anti-Semitism in America particularly repugnant, and two 1947 films held America up for criticism: *Gentleman's Agreement* and *Crossfire*. While *Gentleman's Agreement* exposed the insidious barriers against Jews in American society as well as the often unconscious prejudices Americans held against Jews, *Crossfire* tackled the more virulent anti-Semitism that also existed within American culture. *Crossfire* painted a dark portrait of a veteran, seething with the hate that the war had released, who spews anti-Semitic venom: "I don't like Jews, and I don't like anyone who likes Jews."[30] He proves this hatred by killing a Jew and by framing another veteran who had been befriended by the Jew. He considers all Jews to have been shirkers during the war, and he continues to kill in order to protect himself against those who could prove his guilt to the police. The film emphasizes the horror of this man's crime: the murdered man had been a good soldier, discharged after having been wounded on Okinawa; the murder resulted from "ignorant prejudice" and hate—and, as a policeman says, "Hating is always the same. Always senseless."[31] A combined force of veterans and policemen finally trap the guilty anti-Semite. When he tries to flee, the police gun him down. The policeman in charge of the case voices the film's moral in responding to a veteran's query, "Is he dead?": "He was dead for a long time. He just didn't know it."[32] While *Crossfire* excoriated the inhuman quality of anti-Semitism, it was a film as much about the troubled lives of returning World War II veterans as it was a film about moral corruption in postwar American society. As the morally compromising actions of postwar America were inspiring fears in the culture of dissent about the spread of evil, the widespread representations of veteran discontent and deviance were suggesting how little good had come from the war and how little innocence remained for these human symbols of America's military power. War itself—even a universally accepted "good war" like World War II—was beginning to be viewed as a monumental compromise with evil for all involved, forever altering the outlook of those exposed to the power and terror of war and death.

The popular culture abundantly documented the malaise of World War II veterans: their sense of being tainted by the war and their loss of naiveté; their own mistrust of themselves and the power they wielded over life and death in the war; and their difficulty in readjusting to civilian life after having participated in and witnessed the deadly horrors of war. Little of the ebullience expected from "knights in shining armor" returning from righteous battle characterized the postwar images of veterans in popular culture. Rather, these veterans reflected the ethos of Styron's generation—weary, traumatized, unhinged.[33] Not only did the veteran whose venom had been exacerbated by war murder a Jew in *Crossfire* but the veteran framed for the murder proved a perfect patsy because of his postwar depression and confusion. He had been drinking heavily and wandering around town forlornly and he had trouble remembering his actions and making sense of anything, including his own life, after the war. Filled with self-hate and jittery "postwar blues," he asks a buddy: "Has everything suddenly gone crazy? . . . Or is it just me?" His buddy assures him that this anxiety is common: "No, it's not just you. The snakes are loose. Anybody can get them."[34]

In the year following the war *The Best Years of Our Lives* brilliantly captured the disquiet that afflicted those returning to a bewildering life in America. The film tells the story of three veterans from the same hometown: Sergeant Al Stephenson, a banker and family man before the war; Captain Fred Derry, a bombardier during the war now returning to his night-clubbing wife; and the sailor Homer Parrish, a severely wounded soldier who returns with trepidation to his family and fiancée because of his disfigurement—in place of his hands he now wears hooks. Each veteran comes from a different background, but each experiences uncertainty and a real fear of alienation on coming home to American "normalcy." Resonant with shared emotion is Al's comment: "It feels like I'm hitting a beach . . . "[35] And each indeed experiences a rude and discomforting homecoming. Al comes home to face his son's rattling on about Hiroshima and his schooling on atomic energy and the need to control it "or else," Fred cannot even locate his partying wife, and Homer's family is squeamish about his hooks. They all wind up at a bar that night, drinking to drown their problems, and the only solace to be found is in the bar owner's sardonic advice to his nephew Homer. He calms Homer by telling him to give his family time to adjust, that all will settle down unless there is another war: "Then none of us will have to worry because we'll all be blown to bits the first day. So cheer up, huh?"

The America to which these men have returned is not a friendly or human place. Al's bank calls him the first day he is back, and the swiftness of his expected transition rankles him: "Last year it was 'Kill Japs,' this year it's 'Make money.'" Al tries to use his position at the bank to help GIs get loans for buying farms and homes, but the bank balks at their lack of collateral, so Al must make impassioned pleas about fighting for "the little man" in the face of the bank's hardness. Fred suffers terrifying nightmares about his bombing missions in the war and he cannot find a good job because of his limited work experience: "I only dropped bombs." His wife shows little sympathy for his problems, and she leaves him after he discovers her with another man in their apartment. Fred then loses his demeaning job as a soda jerk when he punches a customer who had taunted the still maladjusted and moody Homer about the war— Homer had lost his hands "for nothing," the radicals in Washington had forced America into the war, where "we fought the wrong people."

In this hard and uncaring America the lonely and disfigured Homer, the solitary and jobless Fred, and the disgruntled Al all feel like misfits or discards. While the love of their families and their women (Homer marries his fiancée and Fred strikes up a romance with Al's daughter) will ultimately help reconcile them to this new world, it is nonetheless a world of far less optimism and hope that they join. In one of the most dramatic concluding scenes Fred wanders through a vast field of dismantled aircraft from the war; it is at once a graveyard and a junkheap, and it seems to reflect the condition of postwar veterans. Fred finds a job here, even though that job becomes emblematic of the lost glory and glamor of the war and its veterans: he will help to tear up the planes so that the materials can be used to build prefabricated houses.

The physical and psychological deformities of returning veterans formed the themes of numerous postwar films. In *Till the End of Time* (1946) the problems of veterans add up to a distinctly antiwar statement. Veterans have lost their legs and their youth, they have silver plates in their skulls from head wounds, and they have the shakes and war fatigue. A legless veteran mourns, "I'm twenty-one and I'm dead," and another sums up the rage of veterans: "Anyone who talks about another war is out of his mind."[36] In films produced during the years of the Korean War, veterans appear as violently disturbed men. *Where the Sidewalk Ends* (1950) revealed the truth about a murdered war hero: he was involved with the criminal underworld and he beat his wife. In *Niagara* (1953) a veteran who had spent time at "an Army hospital, mostly psycho," brutally kills his beautiful wife—who had been plotting his murder—and then plummets in his boat over the falls. *Suddenly* (1954) came out just after the Korean War and the film featured the veteran-as-assassin. Johnny, poised to assassinate the president, talks of his past to those around him: he was a war hero of sorts, he won a silver star and killed twenty-seven Germans. He feels himself a patriot as a result of his war heroism, and the war had given him self-respect because when carrying a gun "you are a sort of god," you are "somebody." Johnny implies that his experience with the American military and his war-honed expertise with guns have made him the assassin he is: "They taught me to kill. I liked it."[37]

The weariness and cynicism and even the murderous impulses that affected veterans in the postwar years continued to find representation in the culture of dissent throughout the cold war years, casting a shadow over the good and innocent images of war and warriors that World War II had produced. Into the mid-1950s and beyond veteran malaise and guilt still nagged at the consciences of ex-servicemen. Tom Rath, "the man in the gray flannel suit," could not shake his memories of the war, even when immersed in his public relations career and suburban life-style. In his novel Sloan Wilson shows how Tom Rath's war experiences float unresolved in his mind, diminishing the quality of his present life. Tom cannot forget the seventeen men he killed, one of whom was only an eighteen-year-old German youth, and he cannot forget the Italian woman with whom he had an affair and by whom he has an illegitimate child. Tom is a man traumatized by the war and his past: "How curious it was to find that apparently nothing was ever really forgotten, that the past was never really gone, that it was always lurking, ready to destroy the present, or at least to make the present seem absurd."[38]

These images of the lost glory and goodness of the war and these visions of the persistent agony of the war for those who lived it diminished American confidence in war and the military and challenged the cold war policy of preparedness. Beyond the doubts raised in portraits of veterans, the culture of dissent also offered clear critiques of the military and its power. In an era that celebrated and embraced the military and its authority—to the point of electing one such military authority figure to the presidency in 1952—certain postwar novelists, filmmakers, and artists created a cast of military characters and a set of antiwar images that called into question the morality, goodness, and efficacy of military authority figures. Norman Mailer's 1948 antiwar novel, *The Naked and the Dead,* was one of only a few World War II American novels published in the years immediately following the war, a fact that suggests both the complex and sacred nature of the war. Belying the image of the war as a simple struggle between good and evil was the complexity, ambiguity, and horror of the war, making it difficult to render in prose (or film for that matter). Moreover, given the suffering that some Americans had experienced, assessing the war seemed an unenviable and even inconsiderate task, especially in a society so convinced of its war heroism. In this atmosphere Mailer nonetheless succeeded in crafting an unflattering account of military life in the Pacific theater. While reminiscent of earlier American novels on the idiocy and meaninglessness of war, particularly a novel like Ernest Hemingway's *A Farewell to Arms, The Naked and the Dead* stands apart. Earlier American novelists had attacked wars about which Americans genuinely and openly felt remorse and scorn, but Mailer took on the one war sacred to most Americans and introduced the moral corruption that reduced World War II to the level of more profane wars.

Mailer opens *The Naked and the Dead* with an image of the one incontrovertible reality of all war, from which World War II certainly had no exemption—death: "Nobody could sleep. When morning came, assault craft would be lowered and a first wave of troops would ride through the surf and charge ashore on the beach at Anopopei. All over the ship, all through the convoy, there was a knowledge that in a few hours some of them were going to be dead."[39] Mailer's naturalistic descriptions of soldiers' deaths make them seem matter-of-fact and therefore all the more horrifying for their sheer numbers and frequency; in the course of the novel the implied meaninglessness of such constant death becomes stated fact in the description of a purposeless patrol that costs the lives of many and the morale of all. Mailer reveals the moral corruption of war by showing man stripped naked and made ugly by war: the romance of the war evaporates as soldiers poke through fields of dead and swollen Japanese soldiers and rob them of their gold teeth, as men express their terror of fighting and dying, as the ethnically mixed troops slur one another and allow their battle anxiety and hostility to spill over into their own relations, and as a tyrannical superior officer orders a perilous mission with little concern for the risks incurred by the soldiers.

Mailer populates *The Naked and the Dead* with a variety of comically mediocre and dangerously totalitarian military officers, none of whom seems capable of exercising power effectively. The most dangerous and morally suspect officer is General Cummings, the officer who orders the unnecessary and ill-fated patrol. Cummings is an archconservative, and he and his methods are linked to the very fascism America is fighting. In a conversation with his liberal subordinate, Cummings speaks approvingly of the coming era of reaction: "You're a fool if you don't realize this is going to be the reactionary's century, perhaps their thousand-year reign. It's the one thing Hitler said which wasn't completely hysterical."[40] On his fictional island of Anopopei Mailer concocts a microcosm of war and its players: power-mad and ruthless generals or officers only stumblingly or luckily successful and a variety of weak, strong, cruel, and compassionate soldiers who nonetheless all come to see the futility of war and life after the endless repetition of muddy death and bloody fear. Mailer's description of the survivors of the patrol expresses his account of the war and its impact:

> The patrol was over and yet they had so little to anticipate. The months and years ahead were very palpable to them. They were still on the treadmill; the misery, the ennui, the dislocated horror. . . . Things would happen and time would pass, but there was no hope, no anticipation. There would be nothing but the deep cloudy dejection that overcast everything.[41]

Mailer's profane view of World War II was followed by a series of portraits in films and novels about equally unromanticized military characters. *From Here to Eternity,* the 1951 James Jones novel and the 1953 film, presented Schofield barracks in 1941 Hawaii as a place of petty and grand violence, as a harbor for unhappy and dissatisfied souls, and as a setting for the selfish vices and autocratic cruelty of the corrupt Captain Holmes.[42] *The Caine Mutiny*—both the 1951 Herman Wouk novel and the 1954 film—featured the startling character of Captain Queeg, an apparently paranoid and even cowardly navy captain who is relieved of his command during a typhoon by junior officers who fear for the safety of the *Caine.* The junior officers had been encouraged in their suspicions about Queeg's sanity by a manipulatively intellectual and morally insincere officer familiar with the jargon of psychiatry, but when the navy convenes a court-martial of the mutineers this officer abjures all responsibility and denies knowledge of any mutinous actions aboard the *Caine*. While Queeg may have deserved a better fate than mutiny and the humiliation of the court-martial, the captain's spectacular breakdown under cross-examination (particularly as played by Humphrey Bogart in the filmed version) certainly presented a bizarre and tormented image of a naval officer; the intellectual coward was simply an officer beneath contempt.[43]

Mister Roberts (1955) held up for scorn a wartime cargo ship captain whose blustering cruelty to his men is made all the more ugly by its contrast with the compassion and self-sacrifice of Lieutenant Roberts.[44] *The Bridge on the River Kwai* (1957) served as a parable of the multiform madness of war. The setting is a World War II Japanese camp for prisoners of war, and two opposing views of military survival are embodied in the two major characters: the cynical American naval commander Shears, who believes strictly in survival, without heroism but with individual initiative (including schemes for escape), and the British officer, Colonel Nicholson, who adheres strictly to the rules and who believes in order and decency at all costs (because escape is messy and means almost certain death, he does not even consider it). The contrast between the two is established immediately: a sloppy Shears who has just been burying dead prisoners watches as Colonel Nicholson brings his ragged and weak men into the camp whistling and in strict formation—a seeming idiocy given the hot sun and their weakened condition. When Nicholson next insists that the Japanese commander adhere to the Geneva convention, then being violated at the camp, Shears comments: "Those kind of guts can get us all killed."[45]

Shears manages to escape from the camp and Nicholson carries on his battle of wills with the Japanese commander over the convention. Nicholson finally wins because the commander needs his cooperation in order to build a strategically important bridge over the adjacent River Kwai. Nicholson tackles this job with zeal, seeing it as the means of keeping order and discipline among his men. He seems blind to the fact that his "efficiency project" amounts to a kind of collaboration with the enemy. In his obsession with order and pride he cannot see how the previous chaos and sabotage better served the Allied war effort. In the meantime Shears has been talked into participating in an elite Allied commando mission to sabotage the bridge—against his cynical survival instincts. As the mission proceeds, conflict develops between Shears and another Nicholsonesque British officer, the commando leader, and Shears states his objections to their world view: while the Nicholson types believe in dying with courage, Shears sees the point as "how to *live* like a human being."

The comparative value of these opposing views comes to naught in the final confrontation at the bridge. The Allies have timed the sabotage of the bridge to coincide with the first Japanese train over the bridge; an observant Nicholson sees the suspicious wires and amazingly alerts the Japanese commander. The saboteurs cannot believe Nicholson's treachery, and Nicholson only realizes his treason when he sees Shears and his men dying in their attempt to complete their mission. The ruthless commando leader, fearing that his men may be captured alive, then fires a shell in the direction of Shears, his men, Nicholson, and the detonator. The blast throws a shocked and now cognizant Nicholson onto the detonator and the bridge explodes. From above the scene, as a horrified British medical officer witnesses these violent deaths and the bridge's destruction, he utters the film's message about all war: "Madness. Madness."[46]

These antiheroic views of war and the military challenged mainstream patriotism and trust in authority characteristic of cold war America. American popular art in the 1950s also contributed to this war weariness with its demythologized artistic reinterpretations of two of America's most sanctified symbols of war, partriotism, and authority: George Washington and the flag. Larry Rivers's *Washington Crossing the Delaware* (1953) offers a confused and blurry remaking of the heroic Emanuel Leutze painting of the same name (1851); the modern painting purposely renders Washington indistinct, not the stoic in full control but a more human and less mythic idol.[47] The more realistic chaos of war is reflected in the painting's lack of definite lines and brush strokes. Such an interpretation of one of America's most beloved presidents and generals resonated with particular force in the Eisenhower years, and more such portraits appeared in popular art.

Roy Lichtenstein had painted an earlier and even more primitive version of *Washington Crossing the Delaware* (ca. 1951) in which Washington appears distinctly undignified and almost childishly drawn, and Edward Kienholz revived this humorous and absurdist representation of Washington in his 1957 *Washington in Drag,* a colorful and abstract portrait that flaunted the tradition of stodgy and respectful portraits of American heroes.[48] Also subject to reinterpretation during the cold war years was that paramount symbol of America and its patriotism, the flag. Leading the artistic reexamination of the flag as the quintessential American icon (a reexamination that would flourish in the 1960s) was Jaspar Johns, whose series of paintings on the flag challenged the sacred representation of this cherished symbol. Johns's flag works—*Flag* (1955), *Flag on Orange* (1958), and *Three Flags* (1958), for example—question the potency and unity implied in the flag by weakening its stark simplicity and boldness: the flag is pencil-colored, dull, lifeless, overpowered by a bright orange background or reduced to a limitless sameness and conformity by receding, overlapping, repetitious images.[49]

Tarnished symbols of American military and moral authority spread through the culture of dissent and registered a dark awareness of the moral compromises the United States had made in its cold war rise to power. Lurking behind these diverse and critical images of the military, the war, and a defiled America was that new and aweful American icon of power: the atomic bomb. Fears and doubts about the ethics of American power reverberated with an added intensity as a consequence of the new apocalyptic potential of American military and political power. In spite of the many imperatives against doing so, the culture of dissent spoke against this atomic corruption of American power and American authority, finding in the bomb a cohesive symbol for America's cold war compromise with evil. The culture of dissent, like William Styron, found the defining moment for the loss of morality and innocence of America in the World War II atomic experiment: "It somehow simultaneously ended and began when Harry Truman announced the destruction of Hiroshima."[50]

two

VERTIGO

the unhinged moral universe of cold war america

> "When man entered the atomic age, he opened a door
> into a new world. What we eventually find in that new
> world, nobody can predict."
>
> —Them! *(1954)*

he American atomic annihilation of Hiroshima and Nagasaki nourished the belief of William Styron's generation that the cosmos had suddenly come unhinged, and this atomic destruction generated much of that sense of guilt and mistrust of American power which found expression in the rebellious popular culture. Writer Frank Conroy noted this guilt and doubt in his discussion of his own "silent generation" and the forces that shaped the consciousness of those growing up in the 1950s. In "America in a Trance" Conroy considers the influence of the bomb:

> It goes without saying that the effects of the bomb on the American mind were profound. We who were children at the time, with our childlike sensitivity to mystery, magic, and the unknown, with our social antennae fully extended to pull in all sorts of information, regardless of its usefulness . . . were perhaps most deeply affected. We felt exhilaration at the indisputable proof that America was the strongest power on earth, apprehension because the power was mysterious, and most significantly we felt guilt, secret guilt that verged on the traitorous, guilt we could not possibly talk about. Our political apathy later, as college students in the Eisenhower years, seems to me to trace directly to our inability to reorganize those simple, propagandistic concepts of democracy and political morality which had been our wartime heritage, and which the bomb had rendered untenable.[1]

That very exhilaration that most postwar Americans felt about America's atomic power made expressions of guilt and remorse about the atom bomb seem traitorous, a blow against the simple and innocent values that World War II had secured. For this reason most Americans accepted the bomb openly, or at the very least they accepted it in silence and apathy. It was for this reason also that the scientists' organized antibomb sentiment failed to find a wide audience. Having just fought a world war for the protection of a particular American way of life, nationalistic Americans were not inclined to express sympathy for the scientists' internationalist ideas about the control of atomic energy and atomic weapons. Plans for world government or the international control of atomic energy—whether generated by nuclear scientists or United States and United Nations proposals like the Acheson-Lilienthal Report and the Baruch Plan— found little support from Americans or from the suspicious governments of the United States and the Soviet Union.[2] The failure of these far-sighted plans did not mean, however, that all moral qualms and mistrust of atomic power evaporated. The sense of knowing sin and the fear of the evil of atomic knowledge first expressed by select scientists received sympathetic hearing in the cold war culture of dissent (even if scientists themselves were sometimes treated with little sympathy). The doubt-filled products of popular culture questioned President Truman's notion of the atom bomb as a "weapon of peace" and instead focused on the evil repercussions of America's policy of atomic invincibility, from its capacity for apocalyptic destruction to its incompatibility with those "concepts of democracy and political morality which had been our wartime heritage."

Physicist Philip Morrison, who had devoted years of labor to the Manhattan Project, corroborated Frank Conroy's view of the bomb's distortion of democratic political morality. According to Morrison, America's postwar atomic arsenals, their institutional support systems, and their unimaginable scale of destructiveness constituted the evil legacy of World War II:

> This is the legacy of World War II, a direct legacy of Hitler. When we beat the Nazis, we emulated them. I include myself. I became callous to death. I became willing to risk everything on war and peace. I followed my leaders enthusiastically and rather blindly. . . . We fought the war to stop fascism. But it transformed the societies that opposed fascism. They took on some of its attributes.[3]

While there is a certain measure of dramatics in such a statement, the United States government's reliance on atomic weapons with their potential for genocide and the government's obsession with protecting its atomic secrets did support the charge that America had learned to emulate its enemies in order to fight them—from Hitler's callousness about death to the Soviet Union's maintenance of domestic tranquillity through the repression of its populace. A film like The Stranger, with its fear of infiltrating fascism and war criminality, took on an added dimension of horror for atomic age America: that stranger could be America itself.

The idea that the atomic bomb and its use constituted a crime against humanity and reflected an American callousness toward death infused the products of postwar culture. In *Hiroshima*, his moving treatise on the immorality of the atomic bomb, John Hersey uses an angry Japanese survivor's words to convey the criminality of the bomb's use: "I see . . . that they are holding a trial for war criminals in Tokyo just now. I think they ought to try the men who decided to use the bomb and they should hang them all."[4] More effective an indictment than even these words, however, were the simple and horrifying descriptions of the bomb's devastation which Hersey recorded from six Hiroshima survivors. Hersey's account of Hiroshima appeared a few weeks after the first anniversary of the bombing in the *New Yorker* (31 August 1946) and was thereafter republished in book form (it was a best-seller). Given the distance of a year, time for rehumanization and regained sensitivity after the deadening war, and given the human and individualized portraits drawn in *Hiroshima*, Hersey's work became one of the most effective cultural challenges to mainstream America's sense of righteous atomic power.

Disputing the widely accepted military rationale for America's bombing of Hiroshima, Hersey presents the story of Hiroshima as one cosmically removed from any military purpose, any moral rationale. Challenging the notion of Hiroshima as a "military target," Hersey tells his story through the eyes of six witnesses who little resembled the fanatic Japanese warriors who occupied a fixed place in the American imagination. Here instead were six ordinary civilians—women, children, doctors, religious men—whose lives were forever altered. It was certainly no coincidence that Hersey chose these specific victims, but his strategy effectively revealed the decimation of innocent civilians which accompanied the "military" use of the atomic bomb.

The blinding flash of light and succeeding blast interrupted the mundane morning chores and habits of Hersey's six survivors; in a split-second the atomic bomb forever charged their lives with horror. Burned into their consciousness—and the consciousness of Hersey's readers—were the horrors wrought by the bomb; they "wondered how such extensive damage could have been dealt out of a silent sky."[5] The damage and death were surreal: thousands upon thousands of dead, thousands of dying, vomiting, horrendously burned humans. A charnel house smell of death pervaded the city, whipped up and spread by bizarre atmospheric conditions: fires, windstorms, huge radioactive rain drops, an eerie, dusty darkness. The dead and the living became almost indistinguishable; the survivors, helpless amidst overwhelming death, were numbed zombies, feebly attempting when possible to comfort the thousands dying excruciating but quiet deaths. And the horrors for the living lingered, their lives forever diminished by what they witnessed, their bodies long suffering the aftereffects of radiation.

Hersey's cataloging of these terrors through their impact on the lives of specific individuals gave his account of Hiroshima the human dimension that had been absent from antiseptic official versions of the bombing, and *Hiroshima* conveyed a clear sense of remorse about the consequences of the atomic bomb.[6] Hersey concluded that America had used Hiroshima as a sort of scientific laboratory, its inhabitants "the objects of the first great experiment in the use of atomic power, which (as the voices on the short wave shouted) no country but the United States, with its industrial know-how, its willingness to throw two billion gold dollars into an important wartime gamble, could possibly have developed."[7] While few Americans felt quite the same despairing and cynical revulsion (particularly given the continuing rage over Pearl Harbor), Hersey's widely read work gave Americans a rare look into the human horror of the atom bomb and helped to shape that inchoate American awareness of the bomb's potential.[8]

Official and semiofficial justifications for the bombing of Hiroshima and Nagasaki countered the moral criticism of views like Hersey's, especially as these justifications coincided so closely with the popular American understanding of Hiroshima and Nagasaki. But even the most persuasive and eloquent among these defenses, ex-secretary of war Henry L. Stimson's 1947 "The Decision to Use the Atomic Bomb," ended with a note of remorse and a plea to contain the evil of the bomb and all war:

> The face of war is the face of death; death is an inevitable part of every order that a wartime leader gives. The decision to use the atomic bomb was a decision that brought death to over a hundred thousand Japanese. No explanation can change that fact and I do not wish to gloss it over. But this deliberate, premeditated destruction was our least abhorrent choice. The destruction of Hiroshima and Nagasaki put an end to the Japanese war. It stopped the fire raids, and the strangling blockade; it ended the ghastly specter of a clash of great land armies. In this last great action of the Second World War we were given final proof that war is death. War in the twentieth century has grown steadily more barbarous, more destructive, more debased in all its aspects. Now, with the release of atomic energy, man's ability to destroy himself is very nearly complete. The bombs

dropped on Hiroshima and Nagasaki ended a war. They also made it wholly clear that we must never have another war. This is the lesson men and leaders everywhere must learn, and I believe that when they learn it they will find a way to lasting peace. There is no other choice.[9]

In spite of such pleas for atomic moderation, American policymakers refused to see their choices as so clearly limited. Faced with the cold war and an aggressive Soviet Union, the United States chose first to strengthen its atomic arsenal and then in the urgent and frantic atmosphere surrounding the Soviet atomic explosion to develop the hydrogen bomb as a new counterforce against the Soviets. The hydrogen bomb exponentially increased the destructive and genocidal potential of America's weapons arsenal, and the physicists involved in the Atomic Energy Commission (AEC) decision on the hydrogen bomb futilely attempted to block this new nuclear compromise with evil. In 1949 the General Advisory Committee to the AEC, led by J. Robert Oppenheimer, strenuously objected to the development of the "super bomb." The majority report of the committee stated its opposition:

> We base our recommendation on our belief that the extreme dangers to mankind inherent in the proposal wholly outweigh any military advantage that could come from this development. Let it be clearly realized that this is a super weapon; it is in a totally different category from an atomic bomb. The reason for developing such super bombs would be to have the capacity to devastate a vast area with a single bomb. Its use would involve a decision to slaughter a vast number of civilians. . . . If super bombs work at all, there is no inherent limit in the destructive power that may be attained with them. Therefore, a super bomb might become a weapon of genocide.[10]

The minority opinion report objected to the hydrogen bomb even more vehemently; physicists Enrico Fermi and I. I. Rabi insisted that "it is necessarily an evil thing considered in any light" and they urged "the President of the United States to tell the American public, and the world, that we think it wrong on fundamental ethical principles to initiate a program of development of such a weapon."[11]

While the public had little access to these ethical arguments, at least until the hydrogen bomb was tested and until Oppenheimer lost his security clearance in part as a result of his moral qualms about the H-bomb, an uneasiness about the decaying political morality associated with America's quest for atomic invincibility did surface in certain corners of the culture. The government's compromise with atomic evils led to certain ethical compromises in the government's relations with its citizens. In order to protect its atomic policies and secure those policies from widespread criticism, the government engaged in secrecy and deception, instituting internal security programs that captured spies and all sorts of communist allies and quieted atomic dissenters. The government had legitimate security concerns in this new world, but its pursuit of internal security and atomic secrecy went beyond the bounds of reason, creating an atmosphere of suspicion that eventually also encompassed the government and its security forces.

By the time Eisenhower took office in 1953, it appeared that the government's atomic policies had corroded its sense of honesty and democratic decency. In a January 1953 advisory group report to Eisenhower on the possibility of disarmament, the scientists' group, led again by Oppenheimer, argued that too many nuclear weapons already existed and that the American people needed to be made aware of the dangers of these weapons. Oppenheimer called for "Operation Candor," in which "candor on the part of the officials, the representatives, of the people of their country," was forthcoming.[12] "Operation Candor" explicitly deplored the government's failure to share information with the public, and even though Eisenhower seemed open to atomic honesty, he nonetheless resisted true candor. Impressed by Oppenheimer's image of "two scorpions in a bottle" and by the mutual and massive destruction implicit in any atomic confrontation between the United States and the Soviet Union, Eisenhower nonetheless did not want the full and despairing truth known; he did not "want to scare the country to death. Can't we find some hope?"[13]

Eisenhower opted for a compromise between candor and hope, and he delivered his "Atoms for Peace" speech to the United Nations in December 1953. The speech addressed the deadly cold war scenario in which "two atomic colossi are doomed malevolently to eye each other indefinitely across a trembling world," but Eisenhower also put forth a tentative plan for an international agency that would stockpile uranium and fissionable materials in order "to serve the peaceful pursuits of mankind," in order "to serve the needs rather than the fears of mankind."[14] Eisenhower enunciated a message of peace and he promised that the United States would "devote its entire heart and mind to find the way by which the miraculous inventiveness of man shall not be dedicated to his death, but consecrated to his life."[15] Despite good intentions little resulted from this plan, which went the way of most early plans for international control of atomic energy. Eisenhower's administration stopped talking of candor or "atoms for peace."[16]

The government's quick return to a confidential policy was evident after the March 1954 hydrogen bomb tests on Bikini atoll. The Bikini blasts proved twice as powerful as expected and a Japanese fishing boat—ironically named the *Lucky Dragon*—lying well outside the stated danger zone was coated with the ashes of radioactive fallout. The burned and contaminated crewmen arrived in Japan complaining of illness, and when their radiation sickness was diagnosed and the cause discovered, the resulting furor forced the American government to respond. Washington, however, offered duplicitous arguments and denials. Popular periodicals like *Newsweek* and *New Republic* reported on the *Lucky Dragon* and the government's equivocation, the *New Republic* leveling its sights particularly on Lewis Strauss, head of the Atomic Energy Commission, who had made an official statement on the *Lucky Dragon:*

> But, said Strauss, reports on the range of dangerous radioactivity were exaggerated; the *Lucky Dragon* must have been "well within" the forbidden area, and its crewmen obviously had been burned by a chemical fall-out, not poisoned by a radioactive one. This has remained the official American attitude, although every fact so far uncovered shows it to be a willful minimization of a new danger which must eventually condition all thinking about both the use of and defense against the super-bomb.[17]

The same governmental reluctance to admit to any problem of atomic ethics, and the same governmental arrogance about protecting atomic and hydrogen weapons contributed to government attempts to ensure the internal security of atomic age America (for example, Lewis Strauss believed the *Lucky Dragon* to be a "Red spy outfit").[18] When the "Hiroshima Maidens" came to America, the government kept uncomfortable watch. Norman Cousins, editor of the *Saturday Review of Literature* and peace activist, and Kiyoshi Tanimoto, a Hiroshima minister and survivor of the atomic bomb (and one of the six survivors in Hersey's *Hiroshima*), had cooperated to organize the transportation of twenty-five young women from Hiroshima to the United States in 1955; these young Japanese were all disfigured as a result of the atomic bombing of Hiroshima and they came to America for corrective plastic surgery. The Hiroshima Maidens were housed in host homes around the New York area, and their presence in America had something of the impact of Hersey's *Hiroshima*. A woman who had proudly worked along with her husband on the Manhattan Project at Oak Ridge recalled her encounter with the Maidens: "You know what happened to us? We were living in New Canaan, Connecticut, and Norman Cousins brought over some Hiroshima Maidens. Weekly, we were confronted with these deformed, burned women. I would see them at the supermarket and think, My God, this thing I felt so smug about did this. Sometimes I cry . . ."[19]

The government's concern over the adverse propaganda of the Maidens and its aversion to the guilt stirred by their presence revealed itself in the information exchanged between Japan and America on the subject of Kiyoshi Tanimoto and his humanitarian mission with the Maidens. American officials in Japan sent Washington secret telegrams and diplomatic messages about Tanimoto and his potential communist sympathies. One telegram reduced Tanimoto's cause of peace and healing to the atomic security issues of so much concern to America:

> EMBASSY–USIS SHARE WASHINGTON CONCERN LEST HIROSHIMA GIRLS
> PROJECT GENERATE UNFAVORABLE PUBLICITY. . . . TANIMOTO IS LOOKED
> UPON HERE AS SOMETHING OF A PUBLICITY SEEKER. MAY WELL TRY TO
> TAKE ADVANTAGE OF TRIP TO RAISE FUNDS FOR HIROSHIMA MEMORIAL
> PEACE CENTER, HIS PET PROJECT. DO NOT BELIEVE HE IS RED OR RED-
> SYMPATHIZER, BUT HE CAN EASILY BECOME SOURCE OF MISCHIEVOUS
> PUBLICITY.[20]

A similar cynicism and suspicion about Tanimoto and the Maidens marked a secret message sent from Ralph J. Blake, American consul general in Kobe: "The Reverend Tanimoto is pictured as one who appears to be anti-Communist and probably sincere in his efforts to assist the girls. . . . However, in his desire to enhance his own prestige and importance he might ignorantly, innocently, or purposefully lend himself to or pursue a leftist line."[21]

The kind of scrutiny leveled at the Reverend Tanimoto and the Hiroshima Maidens became a systematic function of the internal security network in the United States, and Americans from all walks of life experienced the government's power to investigate their pasts and their beliefs, particularly if those pasts and those beliefs were believed to impugn or imperil the sanctity of America's atomic arsenal or simply to irritate the ruling cold war forces of conservatism and patriotism. An insistence on law and order became the domestic means to internal security and to protection against internal atomic or communist subversion. When the Soviets exploded their atom bomb in 1949, the law and order forces gained greater influence in American society. The government shrouded the Soviet attainment in suspicion, somewhat arrogantly assuming that the Soviets had achieved their atomic explosion only as a result of the information provided by spies who had infiltrated America's centers of defense and science. A newly strident anticommunist paranoia invigorated the already well-established and vigilant internal security forces, and the security network geared up to ferret out those responsible for giving away the A-bomb secret.

Law and order rhetoric and action escalated in the 1950s. Senator Joseph

McCarthy screamed such fear into Americans, exclaiming: "One Communist with a razor blade poised over the jugular vein of this nation or in an atomic energy plant can mean the death of America."[22] The Americans most likely to become the objects of this law and order movement were those who had at one time belonged to the Communist Party of America (or groups deemed sympathetic to it), but even liberalism became suspect in this atmosphere of fear. According to a 1955 army pamphlet, *How to Spot a Communist,* a "predisposition" to discuss civil rights and peace was one way to spot American infidels.[23] Questioning government methods of achieving atomic security became impolitic; the understandable anxiety of local residents about the fallout from a nearby Nevada test site prompted only disdain from a Nevada senator, who labeled their fears "Communist-inspired scare stories."[24]

Given these pervasive fears and vaguely defined criteria for suspicion, the government's law and order forces duly uncovered a variety of security risks to the United States. The internal security network broadcast stunning revelations of American treachery and deception, and Americans perceived the necessity of absolute loyalty in this era, especially when those charged with disloyalty or dissent received such harsh treatment for their rebellion. The House Committee on Un-American Activities (HUAC) launched a highly publicized attack on the idols of America in its investigation of liberal Hollywood. Those members of the film community who had joined or sympathized with the Communist party (or its causes, or with the Hollywood Ten and their First Amendment defense) came under direct attack. The nation watched as movie stars, directors, and screenwriters cringed in front of or clashed with the committee—either cooperating with the committee by informing on their friends and colleagues, and thereby saving their careers, or refusing to cooperate with the perceived immoral and undemocratic process and thereby losing their careers through the informal but widespread blacklist.[25] A Communist party organizer from this era in Hollywood whose husband's career as a theatrical agent was halted by thirteen years on the blacklist described HUAC's intentions in Hollywood as something less than purely security-oriented: the committee's goal was "to silence" the liberal, vocal, and highly visible members of the "communications business."[26] She maintained that there was no subversion in the content of Hollywood films and that in any case uncovering subversion was not the point for committee members: "They wanted to set the stage for the Cold War, and they really wanted to frighten the American people, and they did a masterful job in that direction."[27] HUAC's investigation of Hollywood succeeded in frightening the film establishment and as a result silenced many of the voices of open criticism and dissent in the film world. A number of the producers, writers, and directors who had worked or who would work on films belonging to the culture of dissent found themselves attacked, out of work, or unable to receive proper credit and payment for their craft. For example, Edward Dmytryk, the director of films like *Till the End of Time* and *Crossfire,* and Adrian Scott, producer of *Crossfire,* were both members of the Hollywood Ten, uncooperative witnesses who were ultimately jailed for their refusal to cooperate. Even though Dmytryk finally testified, thereby regaining his livelihood, others so blacklisted stood fast and could only work under pseudonyms or without credit, as did Michael Wilson on *The Bridge on the River Kwai.*[28]

The internal security forces also helped to secure silence, support, and protection for America's atomic policies through its prosecution of atomic spies and atomic security risks. The most infamous and controversial case of spying involved Julius and Ethel Rosenberg, who were arrested in 1950 and then executed by electric chair on June 19, 1953, for transmitting atomic secrets to the Soviet Union. The Rosenberg case became all things to all people. Conservatives found justification for their policies of security vigilance and retribution for the Soviet Union's attainment of the atom bomb, and liberals and communist sympathizers around the world found evidence of America's increasing brutality and antidemocratic actions. The judge in the Rosenberg case, Irving R. Kaufman, laid the blame for both the Soviet A-bomb and the Korean War on the Rosenbergs and did not hesitate to send them to the electric chair. World opinion found the United States' execution of the Rosenbergs cruelly wrong, and the French philosopher Jean-Paul Sartre accused America of fascism for having carried out "a legal lynching that has covered a whole nation in blood."[29] Regardless of their guilt or innocence, the Rosenbergs did seem to bear the brunt of America's atomic paranoia. While few Americans were inclined to trust the Rosenbergs and their supporters, some Americans did see the execution as vindictive and some acknowledged truth in Julius Rosenberg's 1951 letter to Ethel, in which he noted that "our case is being used as a camouflage to paralyze outspoken progressives and stifle criticism of the drive to atomic war."[30]

Perhaps more troubling to Americans and more reflective of America's atomic paranoia was the ignoble fate of J. Robert Oppenheimer, the father of the atom bomb. When President Eisenhower issued an executive order requiring more stringent security checks of federal employees in April 1953, Oppenheimer's file was reviewed; the Atomic Energy Commission then informed Oppenheimer that his security clearance would not be renewed. Even when Oppenheimer had started work on the Manhattan Project, American security officials had been aware of his prewar radical political affiliations and his close ties to Communist party members and organizations. What seemed to make the difference in the 1953 security check was Oppenheimer's outspoken remorse and his moral opposition to the hydrogen bomb. AEC chairman Lewis Strauss personally passed Oppenheimer's file to President Eisenhower. In 1949, as a member of the AEC, Strauss had been angered by Oppenheimer's and the physicists' moral qualms about the H-bomb, and so reported this to Truman in his recommendation to proceed with the development of the hydrogen bomb. Strauss argued against such ethical considerations—"A government of atheists is not likely to be dissuaded from producing the weapon on 'moral' grounds"[31]— apparently oblivious to what his statement implied about America.

On the basis of this presidential review Oppenheimer's security clearance was challenged and he was forced to attend a hearing before an AEC personnel security board in order to defend himself against charges leveled. The only substantial charge against Oppenheimer which issued from the post-Manhattan Project era involved his moral opposition to the hydrogen bomb. In listing the accusations against Oppenheimer, K. D. Nichols, the general manager of the AEC, noted that "it was further reported that in the autumn of 1949 and subsequently, you strongly opposed the development of the hydrogen bomb; (1) on moral grounds . . ."[32] Nichols went on to suggest (unfairly and incorrectly) that Oppenheimer's opposition to the H-bomb had continued after Truman's decision to proceed with development and that it had slowed progress on the weapon. The public became aware of the nature of the charges against Oppenheimer as popular magazines covered Oppenheimer's 1954 security hearing. *Time* not only noted the effect of Oppenheimer's negative recommendations on the H-bomb but also mentioned in its clipped account of his life that he "had fits of depression about moral correctness of developing atomic bomb, and remarked: 'The physicists have known sin.'"[33]

Even though many influential American politicians and scientists testified to Oppenheimer's loyalty (vice-president Richard Nixon believed Oppenheimer was "a loyal American," but Joseph McCarthy stated that Oppenheimer should have lost his clearance "years ago"), Oppenheimer was stripped of his security clearance in the summer of 1954.[34] In rendering his final recommendations not to reinstate Oppenheimer's clearance, K. D. Nichols claimed that Oppenheimer's "opinions" did not affect his decision. While it is true that other factors contributed to finding Oppenheimer a "security risk"—the damaging and self-serving testimony of the physicist Edward Teller, the increased cold war tensions after Korea, and the Soviet attainment of the hydrogen bomb, for example—it is also true that Oppenheimer's ethical criticism and political activism concerning atomic and hydrogen weapons had made him expendable to the United States government. In Nichols's words:

> In regard to Dr. Oppenheimer's net worth to atomic energy projects, I believe, first, that through World War II he was of tremendous value and absolutely essential. Secondly, I believe that since World War II his value to the Atomic Energy Commission as a scientist or as a consultant has declined because of the rise in competence and skill of other scientists and because of his loss of scientific objectivity probably resulting from the diversion of his efforts to political fields and matters not purely scientific in nature. . . . He is far from being indispensable.[35]

Oppenheimer's fall from grace had all the makings of a tragedy: the physicist behind the atom bomb who had become a widely recognized cultural hero, the man who had struggled with his own conscience about those very accomplishments achieved in the name of America and its wartime and cold war security, felled by his morality and cast out by the government he had served so well and so long, the human detritus of that new and tarnished American political power structure that could not tolerate criticism in its drive toward atomic invincibility. The revocation of Oppenheimer's security clearance appeared the final ignominious defeat of the already disdained scientist antinuclear movement and the ultimate confirmation that any expression of atomic guilt would be deemed traitorous by the government.[36] No one appeared innocent in cold war America, not the father of the atom bomb, not the government that ostracized him. Like Cody Jarrett in *White Heat,* Oppenheimer had reached the top of the world only to have it blow up in his face. Mistrust of all forms of power seemed only prudent in this atomic age, whether the atomic power that Oppenheimer helped to create or the governmental power that helped to topple Oppenheimer from the top of the world.

The loss of innocence and the compromises with evil that accompanied America's embrace of the atomic bomb and its later incarnation, the hydrogen bomb, found reflection throughout the cold war culture of dissent despite the many obstacles to criticism. Cold war America witnessed the growth of a new film genre—science fiction—that centered much attention on atomic age concerns about the political morality and apocalyptic potential of atomic and hydrogen bombs. Created as products of this specific 1950s mindset, these films demonstrated the cold war fears and anxieties about America's pursuit of atomic superiority. Two science fiction films of 1951 introduced a number of the themes and images that characterized this genre, *The Day the Earth Stood*

Still and *The Thing*. While these two films approached the perils of the atomic age in distinct fashion, the two together revealed the atomic apprehension that marked the cold war culture of dissent, and each conveyed its own recognition of the omnipresent dangers associated with living under the threat of atomic annihilation.

The Day the Earth Stood Still opens with a view of the expanses of the universe. From the perspective of the galaxies and other planets, Earth seems a mere speck in the cosmos. And it is from this universal stance that the world's, and America's, atomic policies will be critiqued. The perspective belongs to Klaatu and his huge robot Gort, highly intelligent and vastly powerful travelers from another planet. When their spaceship lands (after having been frantically tracked by worldwide security and military forces) in the center of all that represents American power and the American way of life—on a baseball diamond in the center of Washington, D.C.—it sends a clear signal about the illusory superiority and security of America. The spaceship is immediately surrounded by the massive forces and armaments of the American military: troops, tanks, machine guns, hand weapons, and artillery are all trained on the ship. The paranoia and violence of the American military are shockingly apparent. Klaatu descends from his spaceship and announces, "We have come to visit you in peace, and with good will." He reaches into his spacesuit and removes a strange-looking device. As he begins to point it and demonstrate its workings, a trigger-happy soldier suddenly shoots Klaatu, who falls wounded along with his crippled device. The robot Gort appears and begins to melt down the weapons of the military, vaporizing them with a powerful beam emitted from his eye slot. As spectators scream and run off, Klaatu calls Gort off and explains the destroyed object to the army men who approach him: "It was a gift for your President. With this he could have studied life on the other planets."[37]

The moral and technological superiority of Klaatu and his world are demonstrated in a number of ways.[38] The military cannot gain access to the spaceship (which they try to invade) and they cannot analyze or comprehend the sophisticated material of which it is constructed. The doctors who examine Klaatu and his wound cannot believe the alien's recuperative powers and his clearly superior physical condition (as they light up their cigarettes). When a White House representative comes to talk with Klaatu, the superiority of his world becomes clear. Mr. Harley, the president's representative, conveys the president's "deepest apologies" for the shooting and then asks about Klaatu's mission on Earth. Klaatu has traveled five months and 250 million miles from another planet in order to deliver a warning to Earth; Earth's limitations and problems are then discussed in the exchange between Klaatu and Harley. Harley has trouble accepting Klaatu's explanation of his planet—"Let's just say that we're neighbors"—and Klaatu bluntly informs him: "I'm afraid that in the present situation you'll have to learn to think that way." Klaatu wants to meet with all world leaders at once, and Harley reveals the difficulty of thinking in neighborly terms even on Earth as he tries to get Klaatu to see the impossibility of such a meeting: "Our world at the present moment is full of tensions and suspicions. In the present international situation, such a meeting would be quite impossible." Harley elaborates on the "evil forces" causing trouble in the world, but he is interrupted by an impatient Klaatu who sweeps away all cold war tensions as petty in the face of the warning he must deliver: "I'm not concerned, Mr. Harley, with the internal affairs of your planet. My mission here is not to solve your petty squabbles. It concerns the existence of every last creature on Earth." Harley agrees to try to arrange such a meeting, but of course he and the president fail to succeed in the cold war world. Klaatu cannot comprehend the "stupidity" of Earth, because "my people have learned to live without [such stupidity]." Harley apologetically responds: "I'm afraid my people haven't. I'm very sorry. I wish it were otherwise."

Having failed to find an audience among government leaders, Klaatu determines to escape from his security imprisonment at Walter Reed Hospital and secure help from the civilian population. He has no trouble eluding the authorities, and dressed in civilian clothes he wanders undetected among other Americans (and this alien looks indistinguishable from them). Reports of his escape inspire hysterical fears of an invading spaceman and of a "menace from another world" that "must be destroyed." Television and radio reports spread such news and rumors while the mild-mannered Klaatu and the residents of the rooming house where he stays discuss the "monster." The suspiciousness of cold war Americans seems to overwhelm all reason. One boarder equates the spaceman with the Soviet communist threat: "If you want my opinion, he comes from right here on Earth. And you know *where* I mean." Amid these suspicions is one voice of reason, Mrs. Benson, who suggests that the spaceman may not be a menace, just afraid and in hiding: "After all, he was shot the minute he landed here." Mrs. Benson and her son Bobby become Klaatu's allies, first befriending him and then believing in his cause once it is revealed to them.

Klaatu spends a good deal of time with Bobby, whose father had been killed at Anzio during World War II. They sightsee together throughout Washington, D.C., and Klaatu's kindness and good intentions become obvious. When the two visit Bobby's father's grave at Arlington, Klaatu is honestly saddened and shocked at the mass graves: "Did all those people die in wars?" At the Lincoln Memorial Lincoln's words impress Klaatu and he decides that he needs to find another such "great man" to aid his mission. Bobby tells him about the great scientist, Professor Barnhardt (an Einstein look-alike), and Klaatu seeks his help in his mission to stop the threat posed by Earth, now that the planet has achieved a usable knowledge of atomic energy and can destroy the peace and security of the universe: "I came here to warn you that by threatening danger, your planet faces danger, very grave danger."

Klaatu has a solution to offer, but he must offer it to all nations at once. The professor agrees to help by calling a meeting of world scientists and intellectuals to listen to Klaatu. He determines to gather the great minds of the world together, not just scientists, because "we scientists are too often ignored or misunderstood." Klaatu stresses the urgency of this meeting, because with failure there is no alternative: "The planet Earth would have to be eliminated." Klaatu worries that "violent action" may be necessary, "since that seems to be the only thing your people understand." Professor Barnhardt suggests that Klaatu give a demonstration of his world's power in order to convince Earth of his urgency and seriousness. Exhibiting a higher compassion and morality than did America at the time of Hiroshima and Nagasaki (when suggestions for a warning technical demonstration of the bomb were rejected), Klaatu agrees. He contacts his planet and the demonstration of their immense power commences: all electricity on Earth is neutralized for half an hour (except where lives would be endangered by such a cessation); Earth stands still, dramatically illustrating the ultimate insecurity of the planet.

As Klaatu prepares for his meeting with the world's great minds, his real identity as the spaceman becomes known to Bobby, Mrs. Benson, and her boyfriend. Mrs. Benson has listened to Klaatu and supports his cause, but her selfish boyfriend decides to inform the authorities, despite her explanation of Klaatu's mission and its crucial importance to Earth. The boyfriend opts for the self-aggrandizement of being the "big hero" who captures the spaceman: "I don't care about the rest of the world." Tension escalates as the race against capture begins; Mrs. Benson helps Klaatu, but he is nonetheless shot and killed by the military while on his way to the meeting. By prearrangement with Klaatu, Mrs. Benson goes to Gort and delivers a message from Klaatu. Gort retrieves Klaatu's body and revives him with the spaceship's superior technology. The great minds of the world are gathered outside the spaceship and the reborn Klaatu finally delivers his message and his warning:

I am leaving soon and you will forgive me if I speak bluntly. The universe grows smaller every day and the threat of aggression by any group, anywhere, can no longer be tolerated. There must be security for all, or no one is secure. Now this does not mean giving up any freedom, except the freedom to act irresponsibly. Your ancestors knew this when they made laws to govern themselves and hired policemen to enforce them. We of the other planets have long accepted this principle. We have an organization for the mutual protection of all planets and for the complete elimination of aggression. The test of any such higher authority is of course the police force that supports it. For our policemen, we created a force of robots [like Gort]. Their function is to patrol the planets in spaceships like this one and preserve the peace. In matters of aggression, we have given them absolute power over us. This power cannot be revoked. At the first sign of violence they act automatically against the aggressor. The penalty for provoking their action is too terrible to risk. The result is we live in peace, without arms or armies, secure in the knowledge that we are free from aggression and war—free to pursue more profitable enterprises. Now we do not pretend to have achieved perfection. But we do have a system, and it works. I came here to give you these facts. It is no concern of ours how you run your own planet, but if you threaten to extend your violence, this earth of yours will be reduced to a burned-out cinder. Your choice is simple: join us and live in peace, or pursue your present course and face obliteration. We shall be waiting for your answer. The decision rests with you.

Klaatu and Gort then take off in their spaceship, leaving Earth to ponder its irresponsible atomic violence with its inherent threat of obliteration. In *The Thing* "the thing . . . from another planet" lands on the North Pole, again warning the world of the perils attached to irradiated "things" that fall from the sky. Air force personnel, along with a curious reporter in search of a story, are sent to investigate a flying saucer reported by the North Pole scientific expedition led by Dr. Carrington, an atomic scientist who had been at Bikini. They first suspect the Soviets: "Could be Russians. They're all over the Pole, like flies." But at the North Pole site the combined air force and scientist team uncover the flying saucer and its occupant, "a man from Mars." The saucer is destroyed in the process of removal from the ice (much to the chagrin of the air force men, who finally had proof for the rash of flying saucer and UFO sightings reported all over America but dismissed by the air force as "a mild form of mass hysteria"), but the ice-encased man/thing is recovered and taken back to their base.[39] Conflict arises between the military men and the scientists about what to do with the Thing; the air force captain insists on waiting for higher orders against the scientists' wish to examine it, but the conflict is moot once the Thing escapes from its ice and radio interference (radiation-provoked?) prevents communication with the higher air force authorities.

The air force men arm themselves and pursue the Thing, which proves its violence in attacking the base's dogs; bullets do not appear to hurt the Thing and it eludes them, but it had lost an arm in the struggle with the dogs, so the scientists can study its nature. Dr. Carrington examines the Thing's tissue and describes it as some sort of awe-inspiring vegetable matter, a sort of "super carrot" that Dr. Carrington immediately senses is a superior form of life. The reporter Scotty comments, "an intellectual carrot. The mind boggles," and the strange atomic scientist Carrington goes on to rave about how the mind should boggle at such superior evolution. Unlike human evolution, the Thing's "development was not handicapped by emotional or sexual factors." Dr. Carrington's attraction to this emotionless form of life, not to mention his sinister, bearded appearance and resemblance to Lenin, seems to link him to an attraction to communism, but little is made of such politics in the battle that ensues with the Thing.

It becomes clear that the radioactive Thing is a killer that thrives on human blood (the military track its movements and its murders with geiger counters); it appears to be the advance force of outer space podlike forms of life bent on conquering Earth in order to feed off humans. The air force men insist on killing this murderous vegetable and its already growing offshoots, but they have to fight not only this superbeing but the protective Dr. Carrington: "Remember, it's a stranger in a strange land. The only crimes involved were those committed against it. . . . All I want is a chance to communicate with it." As the Thing continues its rampage, the military men become increasingly irritated at Carrington and his potentially destructive scientific curiosity. They set a trap to kill the Thing, and Carrington interferes for the last time. He gives an impassioned, if insane, plea for the knowledge that can be gained from the thing: "Knowledge is more important than life; we've only one excuse for existence: to think, to find out, to learn. It doesn't matter what happens to us, nothing counts except our thinking. We've fought our way into nature, we've split the atom." An air force man interrupts Carrington here to inject some atomic reality about the scientific "accomplishment" of splitting the atom. He challenges, "Yes, and that sure made the world happy, didn't it?"—a question that meets with the approval of all around him.

Carrington persists. He states that "we owe it to the brain of our species to stand here and die, without destroying a source of wisdom," and he then proceeds to sabotage the trap. He approaches the Thing in order to communicate with it, he tells it he is a friend, and the Thing unceremoniously bashes the doctor. The air force men then succeed in destroying it. With the radioactive presence of the Thing removed, they can finally get radio messages out, and the reporter Scotty is allowed to tell the story and deliver the warning. He reports: "Here at the top of the world a handful of American soldiers and civilians met the first invasion from another planet." He describes their success in destroying the Thing, but he concludes with a dire warning: "I bring you a warning. Everyone of you listening to my voice. Tell the world. Tell this to everybody, wherever they are. Watch the skies. Everywhere. Keep looking. Keep watching the skies."

Despite their different approaches and tones, both *The Day the Earth Stood Still* and *The Thing* illustrated a distrust of America's atomic power and a questioning of America's sense of righteousness. In whatever guise—whether as atomic bombs or as irradiated outer space vegetable pods—the ultimate effects of atomic power were danger, death, and destruction; moreover, atomic America was neither morally nor militarily invincible. The films did offer certain images of atomic age ambivalence: scientists were both revered and reviled, the military acted both crudely and heroically, atomic technology was both criticized and celebrated: while atom bombs came in for critique, other technologies—including the atomic-powered engines of Klaatu's spaceship—were seen as beneficent and necessary. Also converging in ambiguity were the mutual anxieties over atomic annihilation and Soviet invasion or infiltration: Klaatu could have been construed as a subversive Russian invader for some suspicious Americans (especially easy to assume since subversive communists took the guise of "normal" Americans), and the Thing had all the characteristics of those emotionally controlled and atheistic communists. This merging of antiatomic and anticommunist fears—particularly in the form of attack or invasion from outside forces, often tainted with radiation—became a relatively standard device in cold war science fiction films, and the representation of anticommunist anxieties helped to make the identical representation of atomic anxieties more acceptable to scrutinizing studios and law-and-order committees (see *Invaders from Mars* [1953] and *Invasion of the Body Snatchers* [1956] as classic examples of these merging themes).[40]

Regardless of the ambiguity and ambivalence of science fiction films of the 1950s, the films delivered an overriding message of atomic insecurity: from "here at the top of the world," as the reporter Scotty noted, Americans now needed to "watch the skies" incessantly. America's superior power could not prevent the infiltration of evil, and the cold war science fiction films made clear that such evil could take the form of total annihilation. Images of mass destruction, atomic fireballs, and worldwide nuclear death punctuated both science fiction films and literature; these icons of apocalypse, whether mushroom clouds, smashed urban centers, hysterical, panicked, and fleeing mobs, or scenes of mass death, appeared in a cavalcade of films and novels: *The War of the Worlds* (1953), *The Beast from 20,000 Fathoms* (1953), *Them!* (1954), *20,000 Leagues under the Sea* (1954), *Godzilla* (1956), Nevil Shute's *On the Beach* (1957), and Walter B. Miller, Jr.'s *A Canticle for Leibowitz* (1959).

That man, specifically American man, was morally responsible for the incidents of mass destruction formed one of the most potent themes of the science fiction genre. Numerous films metamorphosed America's atomic policies, particularly its extensive testing of atomic and hydrogen bombs, into cosmic wrongs, crimes against both man and nature. *The Beast from 20,000 Fathoms* contains the entire spectrum of atomic age scare scenarios, and responsible for all the fear is an American A-bomb test at the North Pole that awakens a prehistoric sea serpent. The film opens with the atomic test, and the blast is shown in all its brilliance: there is a flash, a huge explosion, and the mushroom cloud and fireball rise magnificently as ice at the North Pole is crushed and blown and as frozen snow and glaciers tumble. Two scientists observing the test exchange reactions; one comments that "each time one of these things go off, I feel as if I'm helping to write the next chapter of Genesis"; the other, with more prescience, replies, "Let's hope we're not helping to write the last chapter of the old."[41]

The latter scientist's fear seems to be coming true when it is discovered that the atomic blast has released and revived a prehistoric monster. A lone scientist has sighted the monster and he has great difficulty getting people to believe him; he is even placed under psychiatric evaluation for what is considered "traumatic shock." This nuclear physicist nonetheless gets the help of paleontologists and he identifies the primordial monster. He gains greater credibility when "sea serpent" attacks are reported all along the eastern coasts of Canada and the United States, and he is completely vindicated when the monster begins to wreak destruction all over New York City. As the creature knocks down buildings, crushes cars, and stands firm against the National Guard, waves of terrified New Yorkers run in panic. The newspapers proclaim this the worst disaster in New York history, blaring headlines like "Monster Death Toll Mounts." Civil defense shelters are opened to the public as the rampage worsens, physical acts of destruction followed by the spread of primordial and plaguelike germs. The nuclear physicist finally figures a way to kill the monster that his atomic testing had revived: shoot it with radioactive isotopes. The monster is killed by a variation of the atomic technology that had regenerated him. As the monster's carcass lies burning on Coney Island, America seems safe—at least until the next atomic test.

In *Them!* a similar scenario provokes the appearance of giant and deadly ants: the Alamogordo site of the first atomic bomb test has produced mutant ants that are beginning to spread from their desert habitat. A local police officer, an FBI man, and a father-daughter team of scientists, with the massed presence of America's military forces, unravel this mystery and seek to destroy these sinister atomic threats. When the scientists have difficulty convincing the military of the threat, they make it clear that this could be the end of the world. The adeptness of ants (like communists?) at aggression, industry, social organization, and savagery could make these Alamogordo ants the rulers of the world; if they are not stopped, says one of the scientists, "man as the dominant species on the planet will be extinct within a year's time."[42] While the forces of science, security, and militarism (the very forces that created and maintained atomic power) ultimately destroy "them," the Alamogordo ants, the film ends on a note of real atomic uncertainty. The FBI man wonders, "If these monsters got started as a result of the first atomic bomb in 1945, what about all the others that have been exploded since then?" A scientist's reply exposes the new mystery of this era: "Nobody knows . . . When man entered the atomic age, he opened a door into a new world. What we eventually find in that new world, nobody can predict."

The Japanese film *Godzilla* also focuses on the unpredictable, horrible, and morally evil results of America's hydrogen bomb testing in the Pacific. These H-bomb tests have revived Godzilla, another prehistoric monster, which rampages through Tokyo. The particular horror of *Godzilla* is its eerie and realistic recalling of Hiroshima and the *Lucky Dragon* incident, a connection made explicit by one of the characters witnessing Godzilla's annihilation of Tokyo. He comments: "First Nagasaki. Now I have to be in Tokyo when this happens."[43] Masses of injured and dead Japanese fill the streets and hospitals of Tokyo, and the city itself lies in fiery and awful ruin before Godzilla is finally destroyed (by yet another scientist). While there is again a fair element of atomic ambiguity in these mutant monster films—particularly in that science is both responsible for causing and curing the atomic and hydrogen horrors—their sensibility to guilt and remorse and their recognition of the crime against nature and man that is the essence of atomic and hydrogen bombs coalesce into an effective indictment of the atomic base of American power.

Throughout the cold war years promilitary and proatomic bomb and strategic defense films were produced to encourage support for America's defenses and to discourage the kind of doubts expressed in the culture of dissent. In 1952

Above and Beyond hailed the heroic role of Paul Tibbets, Jr., the pilot of the *Enola Gay*, who prepared his crew to drop the atomic bomb on Hiroshima. In 1955 *Strategic Air Command* glorified the role of "the boys that drop the A-bomb" and applauded the sacrifices made by these men who kept the peace and committed their lives to SAC. And in 1957 *Bombers B-52* offered the same praise for the air force personnel who kept "the B-52 combat ready" each and every day and in doing so helped to maintain America's long-range nuclear air capability.[44] In spite of the patriotic ethos of these films, they could not match the science fiction genre on a visceral level, and even these proatomic films gave off glimmers of doubt about military ruthlessness and the perils of the bomb. Paul Tibbets's doubts are highlighted the night before his mission to Hiroshima. He discusses his doubts in a letter to his mother, Enola Gay: "Maybe I'm scared of the idea of dropping one bomb that can kill thousands of people. It's a hard thing to live with, but it's part of my job and I've got to do it. . . . But I think mostly I'm scared for my sons and their world. I'm scared of what can happen if this thing we're unleashing tomorrow doesn't stop this war and all others."[45]

Even though there was mass support in American culture for America's atomic arsenal, the concerns raised in the science fiction films and novels about the dark ethics and dangers of America's atomic powers cast a shadow over the mainstream culture's generally blithe acceptance of America's quest for atomic invincibility. Lingering in the cold war culture of dissent was the confrontation with "that deep sense of guilt in man's new powers that reflects his recognition of evil, and his long knowledge of it" that the physicists had confronted in the deserts of New Mexico when they witnessed the Trinity test of the first atomic bomb.[46] Science fiction films and novels mirrored Oppenheimer's sense of knowing sin, and the deadly temptations of scientific knowledge both revealed to man and warned him of his essential moral weakness in the face of such temptation.

A scientist who believes fervently in the "sacredness of life," to the point where he would not harm anything, "not even a fly," ends up violating his own life-loving precepts in *The Fly* (1958). He becomes so caught up in his experiments for the Air Defense Ministry—experiments involving the transportation of matter through a disintegration-integration chamber—that he destroys and monstrously changes life. He accidentally kills the family cat in the chamber, and then in a hasty test he transports himself through the device, along with an unobserved fly. Their molecules mix and he turns into a half-human, half-fly mutant. When all attempts to right this wrong fail, he realizes that his research and equipment must be demolished and that he too must die: "There are things man should never experiment with. Now I must destroy everything, all evidence, even myself. No one must ever know what I discovered. It's too dangerous."[47] The scientist in *The Fly* succeeds in ridding the world of his dangerous knowledge, but in *A Canticle for Leibowitz* Walter B. Miller, Jr., poses more difficult questions about the destructive nature of knowledge and the destructive nature of man's use of knowledge. The novels opens after a "Flame Deluge," nuclear holocaust on a high order, which has wasted the world, leaving isolated remnants of humanity. Struggling against these new Dark Ages and the reaction against knowledge is a small order of monks, the order of Leibowitz, who protect what little knowledge and what few books and papers remain. Over the course of hundreds of years mankind once again learns the uses of destructive knowledge, and the world attains an Age of Enlightenment much like the one that preceded the Flame Deluge. The monks still exist to preserve knowledge, but the secular control of knowledge threatens another Flame Deluge; the monks monitor radiation levels from their abbey and become aware that "Lucifer is fallen." The Reverend Father of the monks despairs over this cycle of annihilation: "Listen, are we helpless? Are we doomed to do it again and again and again? . . . *Are we doomed to it, Lord, chained to the pendulum of our own mad clockwork, helpless to halt its swing?* This time, it will swing us clean to oblivion, he thought."[48]

The Reverend Father still hopes that man has learned from the past and that war will be averted before it results in another Flame Deluge.

Brothers, let us *not* assume that there is going to be war. Let's remind ourselves that Lucifer has been with us—this time—for nearly two centuries. And was dropped only twice, in sizes smaller than megaton. We all know what *could* happen, if there's war. The genetic festering is still with us from the last time Man tried to eradicate himself. Back then . . . maybe they didn't know what would happen. Or perhaps they did know, but could not quite believe it until they tried it. . . . They had not yet seen a billion corpses. They had not seen the still-born, the monstrous, the dehumanized, the blind. They had not yet seen the madness and the murder and the blotting out of reason. Then they did it, and then they saw it. Now—*now* the princes, the presidents, the praesidiums, now they know—with dead certainty. They can know it by the children they beget and send to asylums for the deformed. They know it and they've kept the peace. Not Christ's peace, certainly, but peace, until lately. . . . Now they have the certainty. My sons, they cannot do it again. Only a race of madmen could do it again.[49]

But, of course, they do it again. As the Flame Deluge once again engulfs the world, the monks send off their last hope for life: a spaceship carrying children, some of the monks, and the knowledge that their order had protected for so long. Contained in this vessel of hope, however, is that very knowledge that has been misused by man each time he discovers and rediscovers it, and there is great uncertainty thus accompanying fallen man's flight to the presumed edenic security of space.

The persistent evil of nuclear knowledge and the threat of cyclical annihilation in the presence of such knowledge and in the absence of a regeneration of man's values and ethics formed one of the hard warnings of America's culture of dissent. In a society corrupted by America's knowledge of power and potential destruction, everyone seemed guilty and no one seemed innocent, and "the princes, the presidents, the praesidiums"—those in power who knew the destructiveness and yet continued to wield the weapons and protect their security against doubters—seemed the most guilty and corrupt. The cold war culture of dissent posited the idea that just as atomic evil was capable of spreading everywhere and attacking anyone, so too was the moral corruption associated with the government power that maintained and protected that atomic evil.

The secrecy, the deception, and the massive extension of domestic law enforcement agencies that the American government relied on for the protection of its atomic security and internal political purity had given rise to an atmosphere of guilt and suspicion which the culture of dissent twisted and used to describe the representatives of American power: the multitudinous law-and-order forces.[50] The distortion of America's democratic political morality that resulted from the excessive and intrusive presence of the government's internal security apparatus gave rise to images and symbols of corrupt and evil law-and-order men in many critical products of the counterculture. The presumed symbols of American purity and moral authority—the police, sheriffs, FBI men, detectives—were tinged with evil. In a security-conscious mainstream America that demanded atomic innocence and unblemished patriotism, there was no such innocence, only varying degrees of guilt and corruption.

Against the society of law and order demanded by American authorities, the culture of dissent opposed a society of evil and chaos. That such evil and chaos could penetrate the inner sanctums of American life and American power was demonstrated repeatedly in the 1950s films of Alfred Hitchcock. In *Strangers on a Train* (1951) criminal evil infiltrates both quaint small-town America and Washington, D.C., as the psychopathic murderer Bruno runs amok in these settings symbolic of innocent Americana. In *North by Northwest* (1959) Mount Rushmore becomes the site of a cold war struggle and acts of espionage.[51] These metaphoric invasions of evil into the heart of ordered American life found widespread representation in the cold war culture, whether in Hitchcock films, films noirs, Hollywood westerns, or the pulp crime novels that cold war Americans consumed. In the vanguard of this invading evil were American law enforcement officers, whose morals and methods rendered them indistinguishable from the criminals and communists they sought to thrust from the heart of American life.

Like *White Heat,* many cold war dissent films used a mirroring process that linked the criminal and police worlds: both were tightly organized systems and both used violent, underhanded tactics to achieve their goals. Bad cops, whether violent or on the take, corrupted their police departments, and the law-abiding citizens and businessmen who consorted with criminals lent an air of respectability to the criminal world. Film noir, another genre born specifically in the World War II and cold war years, paid particular attention to the corruption and blurring of the worlds of good and evil, of innocence and guilt, particularly as applied to criminals and cops. *The Asphalt Jungle* (1950) portrays the modern urban world as a place of dirt and predators where no one is to be trusted. The criminal gang that pulls a major heist of jewels is not only aided by a cop on their payroll but also by a respectable lawyer/businessman who agrees to fence the jewels to other "very respectable men." Both the dirty cop and the businessman try to double-cross the criminals, and one criminal informs on the others. While the criminals either die or are captured, their core community seems much more human than that of the larger respectable community of the city.[52]

Where the Sidewalk Ends (1950) reveals the blurring of cop and criminal identity within the personality of one tormented police detective. Detective Mark Dixon's corruption issues from his past—his father was a "hood," a "mobster"—and try as he has to overcome his history by becoming a policeman, Dixon still seethes with the anger and violence that characterize the criminal world. Dixon has accrued numerous citizen complaints about his excessive use of force, and he is warned by his superiors about his lack of control. In his very next investigation he gets tough with a witness and in the fight he accidentally kills the man. His victim turns out to be a war hero, and Dixon covers up the evidence of his crime, becoming "half cop and half killer," becoming far more like his father than he ever dreamed possible.[53] The criminal, communist, and cop worlds all collide in *Pick Up on South Street* (1953) when a pickpocket lifts a piece of microfilm containing atomic secrets from the purse of the woman delivering the film to communist agents. The cops and the communists all go after the pickpocket, who treats each side with equal disdain. He remains unmoved by the patriotic rantings of the cops: "If you refuse to cooperate, you'll be as guilty as the traitors who gave Stalin the A-bomb." And the pickpocket reviles the communists as well; he only wants to bilk them of money: "I'll do business with a Red, but I don't have to believe one." The cops and the communists use the same methods of finding the pickpocket—criminal informants and go-betweens and constant surveillance (but the communists are more murderous than the cops; they kill uncooperative informants). While all the groups are confusingly blended here, it seems clear that once again the criminal community has the more developed moral code. The criminals sacrifice themselves for one another and they will not cooperate with the communists, yet they remain immune to the security mindset and "patriotic eyewash" of the cops.[54]

Yet another case of the confusion of government agents and criminals appears in the 1954 film *Suddenly.* The president of the United States has decided to make a brief stop in the small town of Suddenly, and the town therefore immediately fills up with state troopers, FBI men, and secret service agents. Assassins out to shoot and kill the president gain access to the home that provides the best shot at the president simply by disguising themselves as dark-suited, sober secret service agents. The crazed killers have no trouble adopting the mannerisms and demeanor of America's security forces, and it becomes almost impossible in the world of film noir to distinguish between the forces of good and evil, law enforcement and criminality.[55] This same difficulty attends the many pulp crime and detective novels produced during the 1950s. In the works of writers like Jim Thompson, Mickey Spillane, and Harry Whittington, the mentality and tactics of sheriffs, private detectives, and policemen merge with those of the criminals they hunt.

The 1952 crime novel of Jim Thompson, *The Killer Inside Me,* offers a spectacularly tarnished image of a small-town lawman in its antihero/protagonist Lou Ford. Lou is the folksy and chatty deputy sheriff of a small southwestern community; he also happens to be the schizophrenic killer for whom he and the other lawmen in the area are looking. Lou is responsible for the murder of the son of an influential citizen and a prostitute with whom the young man had become involved (as had Lou), and he goes on to kill those who suspect him or have information on him. Lou is a sick man, and his position as deputy sheriff shields him (at least for a while) from discovery. The absence of a distinction between law and order and criminal activity appears as stated fact in this novel. Lou himself explains. He prepares to strangle to death a trusting young man who can implicate him in the murders. The young man believes in Lou, the friendly and rather corny sheriff whom he considers a "square Joe." Lou disabuses him:

> "Am I?" I said. "How do you know I am, Johnnie? How can a man ever really know anything? We're living in a funny world kid, a peculiar civilization. The police are playing crooks in it, and the crooks are doing police duty. . . . It's a screwed up, bitched up world, and I'm afraid it's going to stay that way. And I'll tell you why. Because no one, almost no one, sees anything wrong with it. They can't see that things are screwed up, so they're not worried about it."[56]

The people around Lou certainly do not see how screwed up Lou is, at least until his murders have eliminated almost all other suspects but him. Their blindness may have resulted from their own corruption: Lou is only the extreme case of evil in a town filled with lesser evils—the wealthy man of the town is a bully and a corrupt employer; Lou beats his women and they are aroused by it (or so Lou concludes); many of the townsmen are capable of minor crimes and moral timidity. In the end the only power able to destroy Lou is Lou himself, and he does so. Cognizant of his own doom, he rigs his house for a vast explosion. When the authorities arrive to arrest him, he starts the fire and, like Cody Jarrett, dies in an apocalypse of self-annihilation: "And it was like I'd signaled, the way the smoke suddenly poured up through the floor. And the room exploded with shots and yells, and I seemed to explode with it, yelling and laughing and . . . and . . . "[57]

Mickey Spillane's immensely popular detective Mike Hammer never threatened self-destruction; he meted out the kind of brutal and violent "justice" due the criminals and communists of America, the kind of justice an effective police system should have rendered, repaying criminal atrocity with the same kind of atrocious force. In *Kiss Me Deadly* (1952) Mike Hammer helps a woman stranded on the road. They are attacked and Hammer's car is sent over a cliff in an attempt to kill the two. Hammer escapes but the girl dies and Hammer is being investigated by the police and the FBI. The feds had been watching the woman, who was to testify against the Mafia, and now Hammer is under suspicion. He wants revenge against the men who beat him, but the feds hamper him and search his place. Hammer resents the FBI and their persistence; some guilt will be found: "They won't give up until the day they die or I do because once the finger touches you it never comes away. There's no such thing as innocence, just innocence touched with guilt is as good a deal as you can get."[58] Mike's girl Friday, Velda, agrees with Mike's assessment of the end of innocence: "It's a funny world. Pure innocence as such doesn't enter in much nowadays. There's always at least one thing people try to hide."[59]

Whatever evidence of guilt Mike fears the FBI men will find, he objects to their intrusiveness, and he defies their authority and continues his search for the mafiosi who attacked him and killed the girl. In his progress toward uncovering and punishing the murderers, Mike makes use of the same kind of violence that the thugs employ. He beats and kills with impunity. The Mafia world he investigates is filled with the corrupt members of the powerful and respected society at large. Respectable party-goers at a Mafia party all become defiled: "I could spot faces you see in the paper often. Some you saw in the movies too, and there were a few you heard making political speeches over the air. Important people. So damn important you wondered about the company they kept because in each group were one or two not so important unless you looked at police records."[60] In a society as corrupt as is the Mafia ("The Mafia wasn't a gang, it was a government"), Hammer feels justified in using equally extralegal, harsh tactics; he becomes as effective a hit man as any Mafia thug when he single-handedly kills the men and a woman responsible for his beating and the girl's death.[61]

While private detective Mike Hammer fought the Mafia with the methods of the enemy, the policeman protagonist of Harry Whittington's *Forgive Me, Killer* (1956) compromised himself by working with the organized crime boss of his city: he was a dirty but rich cop on the boss's payroll. The novel opens with Lieutenant Mike Ballard embroiled in two controversial cases: the police investigation of him for graft and corruption and his own investigation of an old murder case, in which the man convicted and sentenced to death protests his innocence. The two cases come together as Mike determines to fight the charges against him by proving just how corrupt the whole system is: his crime boss respectably mingles with the police commissioner and other notables, and his crime boss is also the cold-blooded murderer responsible in that old murder case. Mike has difficulty proving the links between the establishment and the criminals because of a cover-up concocted by his enemies (both the police and the criminal network now), and he knows they are preparing him for a fall. He muses about his position while in a bar:

> I looked at my reflection in the beer glass. What would you do? I said to myself. You been riding a gravy train. This time there's trouble for keeps. You're not the first cop ever accepted graft, but every time they catch one, they yell like he's the only guilty one. People like to believe there's just one bad apple. They don't like to think about the barrel. They don't like to pay

cops a decent salary, either. They want them poor and honest. Or they want them dishonest. But the main thing is, they don't want to hear about it. It upsets them. So next to a guy that kills a cop, the crooked cop is tops on the list of bad eggs.[62]

Forgive Me, Killer accentuates once again the culture of dissent's focus on the doubling process that bound criminals and cops, extending that metaphoric expression of the mistrust of government power and morality that infected the counterculture in atomic age America. Whittington's novel also suggests a solution to such corruption: relinquish all claims to the kind of power that corrodes political and individual morality. Mike Ballard finds a form of redemption through self-sacrifice and through the love of a woman who helps regenerate his sense of ethics. He cleans up the corruption around him and within himself, then turns himself over to one of the honest policemen for judgment. He wonders, "How could love make me better now? I was a killer cop and a fugitive from the law."[63] But love does make him better, and he releases his claims to his rogue powers and to his freedom to be a fugitive from moral responsibility.

A similar sort of redemption from the guilt associated with wielding power was sought by the gunslingers in two of the more sensitive Westerns released in the early 1950s: *High Noon* (1952) and *Shane* (1952). These dramas told of a desire to relinquish the trappings of power and authority, a recognition of the often unethical violence demanded by the adoption of such power. That this moral was revealed through the most American and heroic of genres added a peculiar mythic weight to the message of renunciation as an act of conscience. *High Noon* serves as a particularly apt parable for this era of abusive power because its writer, Carl Foreman, crafted it consciously as a critique of the HUAC attack on Hollywood and as a critique of that community's failure to combat such undemocratic power (the town of Hadleyville in the film is thus Hollywood).[64] The sense of peril to any atomic age community is two-fold in this parable: not only can an outside destructive force threaten annihilation but an unresponsive and morally weak population can aid annihilation by accommodating that destructive power.

High Noon is in its essence a plea for individual moral responsibility and a plea for the preservation of American civilization. The film centers on the confrontation between the town marshal, Will Kane, and his dual opponents, his fellow townspeople and the outlaw gang headed by Frank Miller. Kane had been responsible for cleaning up the town of Hadleyville. He had ousted Miller and his gang, making sure the leader was jailed for his crimes, and he had made

Hadleyville a safe and peaceful place to live. The film's tension revolves around the return of Miller to Hadleyville after his release from jail. He is to arrive on the noon train in order to take his revenge on Will Kane. His gang of badmen has already assembled to await the train. In the meantime Will has embarked on a new life that will remove him from the concerns of law enforcement in Hadleyville. He has married Amy Fowler, a Quaker for whom he is relinquishing his position of power and violence. His new life is threatened, however, when the news of Miller's impending arrival disrupts the wedding.

Time is telescoped in *High Noon*. All the action takes place in the space of one Sunday morning, a morning that had started innocently enough with the marriage of Will and Amy. The disruption caused by Frank Miller's expected return to town quickens the pace and the sense of peril. The townspeople as well as Amy urge Will to leave town and run from the trouble, but Will ultimately refuses to abjure his responsibility (the new marshal had not yet arrived). He tries to rally the town against Miller and his gang, but the townspeople are cowed into a silence and inaction. Will seeks allies to no avail; he will face Miller alone, for even his bride has forsaken him for his return to violence and gunslinging. Time and movement seem frozen as the clock moves to strike the noon hour and as the train whistle signals Miller's approach. The shoot-out between the lone Will Kane and the Miller gang takes place on desolate streets. Kane, with the belated help of a repentant Amy, defeats and kills the entire gang. Disgusted by the violence and by the cowardice of the town, Will Kane drops his marshal's badge in the dusty street and he and Amy drive their wagon out of town toward a life of peace.

The film's ironic alliance of the rebellious individual of moral integrity with the symbol of law and order pointed criticism at America's system of security: HUAC-type officials were likened to a band of ruthless outlaws who provoked both chaos and cowardice; the iconoclastic marshal embodied ideal moral authority but discovered the worthlessness and thanklessness of such integrity in a corrupted world. The tarnishing of these ideals is apparent when Kane tosses his badge in the dust. In relinquishing his authority he recognized the contaminated nature of American political morality and affirmed Amy's vision of pacifism. Amy's father and brother had been killed in the Civil War; they had fought on the "right" side and they had died regardless. From this reality issued her strong belief: "I don't care who's right or who's wrong. There's got to be a better way for people to live." As Amy and Will left Hadleyville, that better way seemed more certain for Will's rejection of a violent position of authority.[65]

High Noon challenged the heroic image of law and order in a number of ways. A lawless band of bullies threatening the peace of a civilized community suggested the disruptive and repressive nature of America's internal security network. The townspeople's cowardice hinted at the effectiveness of the bullying tactics and at the ineffectiveness of individual moral strength when challenged. The susceptibility of this small town to evil and disruption reflected powerful doubts about the true security of any town. The film's obsessive attention to and compression of time—the very notion of an impending crisis culminating at "high noon" and the sense of time running out for civilization—emphasized the atmosphere of suspicion, urgency, and insecurity that accompanied life under the threat of atomic annihilation. The film's attention to the clock also provided a daytime equivalent to the scientists' atomic age symbol of crisis: the "doomsday clock" included in each issue of the *Bulletin of Atomic Scientists* (beginning with the June 1947 issue), where the hands of the clock moved closer to midnight as the world moved closer to the probability of annihilation.[66]

John Wayne labeled *High Noon* a communist film for its moral of relinquishing corrupt power. It was "un-American" for a marshal to drop his badge and quit, as Wayne explained: "It's the most un-American thing I've ever seen in my whole life. The last thing in the picture is old Coop [Gary Cooper, who played Will Kane] putting the United States marshal's badge under his foot and stepping on it."[67] While many Americans may have ignored or bristled at the implied criticism of America's political morality in *High Noon,* the culture of dissent persisted in its presentation of the doubts that accompanied America's rise to power and the ethical problems associated with exercising and maintaining that power. Shane, beleaguered by the horrible violence of his career as a gunfighter, drops out of the gunfighting arena. He works alongside a farmer and his family, but a cruel and repressive cattleman and his hired guns soon force Shane to abandon his newfound pacifism in order to protect the homesteaders, in particular the family that has befriended him. Shane defeats the evil forces disrupting the otherwise pastoral idyll of this western landscape, and he resists all temptation to stay, because staying in settled areas entails the fighting he has come to abhor. When the farmer's son Joey implores Shane to "come back," Shane tells him, "A man has to be what he is, Joey. He can't break the mold. I tried it, it didn't work for me. . . . There's no living with the killing. There's no going back. Right or wrong, it's a brand, and the brand sticks. There's no going back."[68] Shane cannot go back with Joey, and he imposes exile on himself. As he rides off wounded and alone, his only salvation seems a life of solitude, apart from the killing he can no longer abide.

Beyond the rejection of corruptible power, the cold war counterculture also questioned the ethics of methods employed by the state in its pursuit of internal security and law and order. The government's reliance on informers and its insistence that suspects called before committees and Congress "name names" and inform on friends and relatives came under questioning in the cultural works that upheld the traditional American disdain for self-serving squealers and stool pigeons. Arthur Miller's famous witch-hunting parable *The Crucible* (1953) honors individual conscience against mass hysteria, and Alfred Hitchcock's *I Confess* (1953) shows the moral heroism of a priest who maintains his vow of silence about a murderer's confession, even when his silence could result in his own conviction for the murder.[69] The anti-death penalty film *I Want to Live!* (1958), which told the true story of a woman unjustly executed by the state, targeted the state's capacity for cruel and unusual punishment or for punishing the innocent.[70]

The culture of dissent's criticism of law enforcement agencies and their methods was of course widely countered in the mainstream culture by idealized representations of the forces of law and order. America had absorbed the lesson of obedience to these security forces, and popular culture in the cold war years showed its support for law and order in America. American television screens flickered with an often humorless but seemingly obsessive interest in law and order, and shows involving the police, detectives, highway patrol officers, FBI agents, lawyers, and investigators filled the airways. Cold war television fare included *Lawbreakers, Highway Patrol, Perry Mason, Mr. District Attorney, King of Diamonds, I'm the Law, The Hunter, Martin Kane—Private Eye,* and *I Led Three Lives. I Led Three Lives* was based on the real-life exploits of protagonist Herbert A. Philbrick, "Citizen, Communist, Counterspy," and it featured a type of hero peculiar to these years: an informant for the FBI who infiltrates and informs on the Communist party in America.[71]

American films also sanctified the search for security and lionized law enforcement officials. The spate of anticommunist films produced in the late 1940s and early 1950s alerted Americans to the communist threat and to the effectiveness of the security forces' containment of this Red threat. Hollywood saw red in many of its anticommunist films—*The Red Menace, The Red Danube, Red Snow, Red Nightmare,* and *Red Planet Mars*—but it also released less colorful tales of communist iniquity: *I Was a Communist for the FBI, The Iron Curtain, My Son John,* and *I Married a Communist.*[72] While some cold war films and novels, along with *The Crucible* and *I Confess,* had castigated informing as a violation of ethics, these anticommunist films elevated informing and betraying friends or acquaintances to a patriotic and heroic duty. One of the most exquisite films produced during the 1950s, *On the Waterfront* (1954), eloquently argued the case for informing (even if it was a rather self-serving eloquence: many of those working on the film, especially its director Elia Kazan, had testified before HUAC and named names).[73]

Regardless of the intent of these positive images of law enforcement officers and their hunt for communists, such films and television shows helped to compound the confusion of good and evil and guilt and innocence in cold war American society. Even two staunchly anticommunist films that upheld the honor and glory of the anticommunist crusade in America—*I Was a Communist for the FBI* (1951) and *My Son John* (1952)—displayed elements of the ambiguity and corruption that marked America's quest for absolute internal security during the cold war.[74] Based on the experiences of FBI informant Matt Cvetic, *I Was a Communist for the FBI* featured a celluloid Cvetic who paraded around Pittsburgh as a communist agent while in fact working as an agent for the FBI. In *My Son John,* the uncovering of John Jefferson's communist affiliations also revealed the abnormalities in a presumably sacrosanct American family as well as the somewhat immoral tactics of the prying FBI. It was this type of meddling, duplicity, and role playing that suggested the seamier sides of the battle against communism in American society.

I Was a Communist for the FBI follows Matt Cvetic's career as a communist agent who has a job quite useful to the party. He is employed in the personnel department of Pittsburgh's North American Steel Company, and he uses his position to fire noncommunist workers and to hire communists. The film presents all the cynical notions about the Communist party current in the lexicon of anticommunism, including the idea that America's labor unions are riddled with communist infiltrators. In fact, according to the film, there are communists in all walks of American life, but especially in labor unions and schools. These communists, however, have no real desire to help the downtrodden in America. High-ranking communist officials live lives of luxury, swilling champagne and savoring caviar, while they merely exploit the masses for their own power and profit. The film shows workers, Jews, and blacks all being cruelly exploited by the communists. The film leaves no room for the possibility that there may be real causes for protest in American society; in particular it notes that there is no noncommunist motive for criticizing the workings of America's internal security bureaucracy. At one Communist party meeting a party big-wig discusses how the House Un-American Activities Committee has become "a danger to us."[75] Therefore a new order from Moscow insists that all party members ridicule the HUAC publicly. Members are to say that the "Un-American Activities Committee is a group of fat-headed politicians whose only aim is to crash headlines." The idea, according to this party leader, is that "we want them laughed at." In the universe of *I Was a Communist for the FBI* there is no need to question life in cold war America, and any such doubts clearly arise only as a result of communist inspiration.

While on a larger level Matt Cvetic's dualistic life as a communist and as an FBI informant offers no challenge to accepted contemporary values, his role does pose some difficult moral and psychological problems for Cvetic himself and for America as a whole. Cvetic suffers through his numerous communist meetings, even given their posh settings and the fabulous wines and foods, and he nearly winces when toasts are made "to comrade Stalin" and "to the Soviet Union." But Cvetic's real torture stems from the impact his double life has on his family and on his own self-image. In order to make his pose as a communist both realistic and safe, even his family must believe in his subversion. Cvetic stoically endures the disdain of his family, especially the venom of his brother, who variously calls him "a slimy Red" or "you dirty Red." Cvetic's brother has obviously rejected him; his son, when faced with the apparent truth of his father's communist ties, also rejects him; and Cvetic's mother actually dies thinking that her son is a traitor. Only the Cvetic family priest and the FBI know the "heroic" truth about Cvetic's life, but this does seem to be enough for Cvetic at times.

The pathos and ultimate heroism of Cvetic's life are stressed throughout the film, but it is clear in many ways that Matt Cvetic himself is unhappy about his role. He appears on occasion to recognize that his masquerade is as damaging as if he were really a traitor to his country. The distinction between patriotic informer and tortured enemy-of-the-state dims in *I Was a Communist for the FBI*. Cvetic himself, despite statements from the FBI that "he's quite a guy," registers the horror and pain of the anomalous position of being at once a Red and a red-blooded American hero. After his mother dies and his brother decks him at the funeral, Cvetic is left knowing that in reality he has no family except for the "slimy Commies." He begs the FBI to "wipe this Red smear off of me." Even though he has already served the FBI surreptitiously for nine years, the bureau men refuse his request at this time since they still need his services. Later, however, when he finally gets his chance to testify against his party comrades, his comment discloses the depths to which he had sunk as an informant for the FBI: "Thank God. Now I can crawl out of my rat hole and live like a man."

Cvetic's testimony in front of the House Un-American Activities Committee, where he exposes a "vast spy network" in America and where he likens the United States to a "slave colony" for the Soviets, appears to lift Cvetic out of his rat hole and into the embrace of his now proud brother and son. Still, the angst of his double life lingers, and the long-term corruption of his family life tarnishes his heroic actions. Matt Cvetic is no innocent, and the patriotic "good" he does for his country is masked in a veil of deception and deceit. Anticommunist justice prevails in *I Was a Communist for the FBI,* in spite of Cvetic's problems of identity and innocence, and it would again triumph in *My Son John.* Nonetheless, questions about the methods of the FBI and visions of communist evil within the American family again undercut the otherwise comforting conclusions of these films.

In this time of cold war paranoia the family (the "warm hearth") was meant to provide security in times of peril. It was also supposed to be America's best defense against communist subversion. *My Son John,* though, shows how even the most anticommunist and patriotic of families could fail to find such security or to escape infiltration by this foreign ideology. In fact, it is not difficult to see how the all-American Jefferson family has instead helped to encourage the disaffection of its son, John. On the surface the Jefferson family appears to be the perfect American family of the era. The father, Dan Jefferson, is a member of the American Legion and is thus by definition a strict anticommunist. He also teaches the "fundamentals" at a little red schoolhouse.[76] Two of his sons, Chuck and Ben, are high school football stars turned soldiers; they first appear dressed in their uniforms, ready to leave for their war service. And his wife, Lucille, pays heed to only two books: her cookbook and her Bible. As the film opens, these four are preparing to go to church. After church a farewell dinner is held for Chuck and Ben who are off to serve their country that very day. The patriotism of the Jefferson family thus seems irreproachable—until it is made clear that one member of the family, John, is missing from this domestic scene of service to church and country.

John's absence somehow exposes his subversion: he is not present to attend church or to see his brothers off to war. Throughout much of the film, in fact, John's communist leanings are only suggested in what was nonetheless the veiled language of the times. He "works in Washington" and he is the "bright one" in the family (his mother comments that "he has more degrees than a thermometer"). When John does come home, he spends more time with an old professor at the nearby Teachers' College than he does with his parents. Further, he pokes fun somewhat maliciously both at his father and at a priest whose sermon he was forced to endure. John is an intellectual, a sarcastic and irreverent one at that, and thus he is suspect even before his involvement with communists is firmly established.

John's alienation from his family does not always seem unwarranted; in fact, it seems almost a normal response to a rather stifling family situation. John's father is dull (he even admits, "I may not be bright") and he leaves himself open to his clever son's sarcasm. John's mother attempts to keep alive the smothering mother love she developed for a younger John (and she is presented throughout as a bit unbalanced, particularly when she is given pills by a doctor to prevent a breakdown when her two other sons leave for war). She is terrified that she and John are not close anymore, and she reminisces about the lullaby she sang to John when he was a baby (a "my son John" lullaby). John coolly reminds her that "boys do grow up" and that "I'm not a baby anymore," and she is hurt by this truth. The members of the Jefferson family see John's distance from them as unnatural, and his father will later point out that breaking up homes "is a Commie specialty." To the more dispassionate observer, though, it might seem that John's communist sympathies are the symptom rather than the cause of these unnatural family relations.

The crux of *My Son John* involves the Jefferson family's discovery of John's perfidy, and family relations are further strained as evidence of John's communist activities mounts. While the film reveals the shattering of the presumed sanctuary of cold war America, the family, it also raises questions about the morality and methods of the FBI. The Jeffersons already have their own doubts about John's political persuasion: his father wonders if John "is one of those guys" about which the American Legion should be alert, and his mother forces him to swear on the Bible that "I am not now or ever have been a member of the Communist party." It is, however, the visits of an FBI agent which confirm and deepen the family's suspicions, especially for Mrs. Jefferson. (Mr. Jefferson earlier recognizes that the Bible means nothing to communists, so he simply hits John in the head with the Bible.) Even though Mrs. Jefferson is mortified about John's potential communist associations, she is also quite upset at the means used by the FBI to gain access to her family and to her own thoughts on her son.

Seeking information on John, the FBI engineers a minor car accident with Mr. and Mrs. Jefferson as a way to open and then maintain contact with the family. FBI agent Steadman visits Mrs. Jefferson under the ruse of presenting a bill for his flattened fender, and he gets Mrs. Jefferson talking about the family and John. When he later returns and reveals his true identity, Mrs. Jefferson expresses her disgust with his methods. He acknowledges "that our methods are very often criticized by certain sources because we're after them day and night," and he defends his methods because the "innocent" never really mind such FBI intrusion. Mrs. Jefferson refuses to talk to him further. Instead, she goes off to Washington to confirm her growing belief in John's treason. She returns home with proof of his guilt, and, when John follows her to retrieve this evidence, the FBI man (who is now following her as well) arrives in the nick of time to save her from John's violence. Mrs. Jefferson finally admits her son's guilt, becoming something of an informant against her own son for the FBI: "Take him away. He needs to be punished."

Mrs. Jefferson suffers a collapse, however, because of the strain. In the midst of her breakdown, John escapes through a window, and the FBI must carry on its hunt for John on its own. The search for John resumes in Washington, D.C. Against the backdrop of America's national monuments, John undergoes a transformation. He calls the FBI to give himself up, and the FBI men tell him to "use whatever free will you have left" to get to their office, to "give up. Name names." John is then gunned down in front of the Lincoln Memorial by vengeful communists, preventing his defection, but John nonetheless redeems himself even in death. Having earlier been chosen to deliver a speech to his alma mater's graduating class, he has recorded a repentant message meant to serve as a warning to others. John's speech is played from an empty podium and the point is pure anticommunism. John's voice intones that freedom only exists in America, and he warns of the perils of intellectualism—its boldness, its defiance of family values. The recorded John goes on to pronounce the danger and salvation of the era: "The eyes of Soviet agents are upon you. It is not too late to save yourselves." A recovering Mrs. Jefferson approves her dead son's words, praying that these young Americans "forget what he did and remember what he said."

The film thus ended on the proper note of antiintellectual remorse and anticommunist triumph (John notes in his speech that the only proper degree for him was "a warrant for arrest"), but the film also managed to convey the corruptive elements of the cold war search for security—for the family and for the FBI. In both *My Son John* and *I Was a Communist for the FBI* traitors appeared within the family (whether masked as FBI informants or not) and family life was thus defiled. In both films the FBI relied on morally ambiguous if not completely deceptive practices (whether disguising FBI informants as communists or FBI agents as mild-mannered victims of car accidents). The films may have presented a clear-cut anticommunist vision, but little else was clear-cut. Family members could not be trusted, and neither could the FBI. No one was left pure: sons were communists, mothers were informants, and fathers were both.

The same confusion that characterized films like *I Was a Communist for the FBI* and *My Son John* also influenced the larger popular culture's treatment of the crusade against communism. On film and on television FBI agents masqueraded as communists, communists disguised themselves as normal Americans, and Herbert A. Philbrick in *I Led Three Lives* masked himself as all three.

In such a society, detecting all-American families from families infiltrated by communists, friends from enemies, cops from criminals, FBI men from communists, the innocent from the guilty, became practically an impossibility. In this suspicious culture Mike Hammer seemed right: "Innocence touched with guilt is as good a deal as you can get." The message that America's atomic age culture of dissent delivered was that American innocence was lost. In a nation that relied on politically and morally corrupt forms of power—the atom bomb itself or the internal security authorities that protected it—no one was innocent.

The United States's quest for atomic invincibility and a secure position of world superiority in order to avoid any compromise with the evil of the Soviet Union had compromised America in both human and moral ways. The suspiciousness about communist evil had been internalized and generated widespread suspicion of the existence and prevalence of American evil. The extent to which America's rather paranoid search for security had turned on its own citizens was evident in accusations that did not even spare those in the top positions of government power. The measure of America's fall from the grace and innocence of World War II lay in the tarnishing of that group of politicians who had helped to guide America through the hardships of the depression and the difficulties of the war. The humanist and innovative liberalism of New Deal Democrats became suspect in this harder cold war America, and many New Dealers in government found themselves accused and ostracized for an idealism out of place in the atomic age.

When Telford Taylor, a New Dealer and the chief American prosecutor at the Nuremberg trials, returned to Washington, D.C., after having been out of the country for seven years, he expressed shock at the changes that had taken place:

> I'd been away from home seven years and was out of touch with things
> politically. I thought Washington was still the way I'd left it in 1942. By
> 1949, it was a very different place. I had left Washington at a time when
> it was still Roosevelt, liberalism, social action, all these things. When
> I came back in the late forties, the Dies Committee . . . the cold war.
> I was a babe in the woods. I didn't know what hit me.[77]

When Taylor later criticized Senator McCarthy for his unethical tactics, he was denounced in Congress: "Instead of having been the avenging angel of justice at Nuremberg, I was denounced as a red."[78] It was precisely Taylor's type of liberal innocence that the literary and political commentator Leslie Fiedler declared at an end in the early 1950s.

In his 1955 *An End to Innocence: Essays on Culture and Politics* Fiedler analyzed the extent to which the popular front and New Deal liberalism—especially because of its dalliance with the experiment of Soviet communism—had been deemed guilty and corrupt in the more realistic years of the cold war, which gave a cynical and retrospective recognition to the criminal aggressiveness of the Soviet Union. Alger Hiss, one of those New Dealers who had occupied a top position in the government, served as the symbol of all that was now perilously wrong with the innocent liberalism of yesteryear. Fiedler argued that American liberalism had to come to terms with the evil of the Soviet Union and accommodate itself to the anticommunism that now uncovered the past guilt of liberals like Hiss.[79] According to Fiedler:

> American liberalism has been reluctant to leave the garden of its illusion; but it can dally no longer: the age of innocence is dead. The Hiss case marks the death of an era, but it also promises a rebirth if we are willing to learn its lessons. We who would still like to think of ourselves as liberals must be willing to declare that mere liberal principle is not in itself a guarantee against evil; that the wrongdoer is not always the other—"they" and not "us"; that there is no magic in the words "left" and "progressive" or "socialist" that can prevent deceit and the abuse of power. It is not necessary that we liberals be self-flagellants. We have desired good, and we have done some; but we have also done great evil. The confession in itself is nothing, but without the confession there can be no understanding, and without the understanding of what the Hiss case tries desperately to declare, we will not be able to move forward from a liberalism of innocence to a liberalism of responsibility.[80]

America's innocent liberalism did for the most part adjust itself to the imperatives of the cold war and the atomic age; liberals and Democrats became indistinguishable from conservatives and Republicans in their anticommunism and support for internal security, and they acquiesced as many government employees were purged for suspicious liberalism or for past associations. The innocent and humanitarian liberalism that had served as the guiding spirit of America in World War II did come to an end in the crusading cold war culture of resurgent conservatism, and in ending it helped to create an atmosphere even more conducive to America's morally compromising search for atomic security and internal political purity. In this guilt-ridden and suspicious atmosphere, however, idealistic and progressive New Dealers were not the only high government officials to find their positions at the top imperiled by charges of treason and corruption.

The 1952 presidential elections made painfully clear the corroded reputation of Democrats in the cold war culture; Republican campaign slogans referred to "twenty years of treason" and "K^1C^2"—Korea, Communism, and Corruption. President Truman's administration and his Fair Dealers endured the humiliation of allegations of corruption (graft, bribery) and communist-coddling. Even espousing a rabid anticommunism did not prevent charges of treason, as evidenced not only in Truman's case but also—and more stunningly—in the case of Senator Joseph McCarthy. As a result of the Army-McCarthy hearings—which, being nationally televised, helped to stir widespread revulsion at McCarthy's sinister and innuendo-oriented methods of investigation—McCarthy and his career as the preeminent anticommunist in America lay in defeat and ruin. McCarthy, censured by his congressional peers for unbecoming conduct, faded from national view for having finally attacked the one institution more sacred than the internal security network: the military. As government officials, including the likes of President Truman and Joseph McCarthy, joined the ranks of Americans stripped of their innocence and pushed from the top of their professions, it seemed that no one was above suspicion in America. Being on top—whether as a nuclear physicist like J. Robert Oppenheimer, as a crazed criminal like Cody Jarrett, or as a nation like the United States at the end of World War II—was no guarantee against a fall from grace and innocence.

Throughout the late 1940s and 1950s the cold war culture of dissent kept insistently, if ambiguously and allegorically, before the eyes of the American public its visions of the corruption and dangers that issued from America's new position of world power. Exploiting that long-standing American ambivalence about the cost of attaining and maintaining that glorious standard of American success, the culture revealed to Americans the rising moral and political costs accrued during America's assent to the pinnacle of world power.

The various products of the early atomic age culture of dissent had focused on uncovering the multiform evils of cold war America, and the master of lost innocence, Alfred Hitchcock, created the filmed images of lost innocence that perhaps best portrayed the confusion and corruption that characterized life in this new era. In *Vertigo* (1958) Hitchcock captured not only the chaos of life in America but also the deadly and dizzying guilt involved in climbing to the top. The malady of vertigo proves to be a darkly enchanting and fitting metaphor for morally uncertain postwar American life, and Scotty Ferguson, the protagonist, is the perfect tormented representative of the struggle to get to the top. In the opening of the film the policeman Ferguson is involved in a rooftop chase. During this precarious chase, Scotty loses his balance and slips off the high roof. He clings by his fingers to the roof ledge, but when another police-man tries to help Scotty, the rescuer loses his balance and falls to his death. Scotty is rescued, but the converging traumas of his near-death and the other man's horrible fall have left him weak with guilt, its symptom vertigo. Scotty quits the police force in order to rest and recuperate, but he is soon to discover that his psychophysical affliction may well be a normal operating reaction to a world filled with whirling death, deception, and evil.[81]

Scotty lives in San Francisco, a setting designed to heighten the comparison of Scotty's malady and the vertiginous quality of a morally uncertain world. The hills, the steep and winding streets, the narrow alleys, and the churning waters of the bay all lend an ominous air to life in the city, a sensation that only increases when Scotty begins to roam all over San Francisco on a private case of detection. Gavin Elster, an old friend of Scotty's, is concerned for the mental health of his beautiful wife, Madeleine. She has become possessed by her distant past and has started to haunt the old San Francisco spots of her dead ancestor, the "mad" Carlotta, who ended her life by suicide. Gavin wants Scotty to watch over Madeleine and prevent her from coming to harm. Scotty is immediately captivated by Madeleine and her mystery; he follows her, keeping her under constant surveillance, and soon saves her from a suicide attempt. Having met face-to-face, they now wander the city together and fall in love. Madeleine re-mains obsessed by Carlotta and despite her love for Scotty she feels a compul-sion to repeat Carlotta's descent into insanity and death. When she is drawn to a mission church outside of San Francisco, she runs madly to the top of the church tower—up a narrow and high set of stairs that Scotty cannot climb because of his vertigo—and jumps off, killing herself as Scotty stands by helplessly.

Scotty is plunged into guilty despair over Madeleine's death, the second death for which he feels responsible. He enters a hospital for melancholia, suf-fering terrifying flashbacks. Scotty's face, and particularly his eyes, express all the horror of his condition and all the depths of his melancholy. Yet although the detective Scotty has had his eyes open, he has failed to recognize the clouded nature of his perceptions. Madeleine had been Scotty's ideal—the embodiment of love, the symbol of his dreams and desires—and her image had blinded him. When he leaves the hospital, he wanders the city listlessly; he awakes from his trance only when he finds a Madeleine look-alike, Judy Barton. He comes to life in making her into Madeleine's double.

In searching once more for his ideal, Scotty is again blind to reality. Un-known to Scotty (but not the audience) Judy is in fact Madeleine. In a plan replete with deception and cruelty, Gavin Elster and Madeleine/Judy had con-spired to kill the real Madeleine for her money. Judy had posed as Madeleine to entrap Scotty and set him up as the perfect fall guy to witness the suicide. Knowing Scotty would not be able to climb to the top of the church tower, Gavin had waited at the top with the real Madeleine's body, which he threw off to simulate suicide. Judy wants to tell Scotty the truth, but she loves him and does not want to lose him. She reluctantly lets him make her into the replica of the Madeleine she had been. Just when they both appear to be happy together, Scotty's vision clears: he recognizes one of Judy's necklaces as a necklace Madeleine had worn and the truth dawns on him. He drives Judy to the mission church tower for a final confrontation, and she divulges the truth as Scotty drags her up the stairs to the top of the tower. Scotty has broken through both the internal and external manifestations of his vertigo, but as he does so his world crumbles again: a noise in the tower frightens Judy, she turns, stumbles, and falls to her death. As Scotty stands at the top of the tower, free of his vertigo, looking down, his world is once again empty, his ideal lost.

In *Vertigo* Scotty Ferguson inhabits a world of moral and physical danger, and it is no coincidence that firm grips and firm footing come only with difficulty. His world makes it all too easy to fall: rooftops and church towers are perilous places; human relations, marked by deception, betrayal, selfishness, and blindness, are equally perilous; ideals and dreams are ephemeral, empty, cruel illusions. Scotty Ferguson reached the top of the world—in his hard climb up those stairs of the tower—only to find his dreams shattered. This vertiginous world of lost innocence and lost ideals, a film image wonderfully, if despairingly reflective of William Styron's image of a cosmos "so unhinged as to be nearly insupportable," also mirrored America's fall from the glory and innocence of World War II.

It seems at least possible that the culture of dissent's message of the dizzying moral mistrust of power reached an audience among mainstream Americans. At least one influential American appeared to have arrived at conclusions similar to those of this more rebellious culture. In his farewell address to the nation President Eisenhower expressed his own sense of vertigo at the powerful heights and ethical depths that America's militarism had wrought in the United States. In his January 17, 1961, address he delivered his famous warning against the growing power of the military-industrial complex:

This conjunction of an immense military establishment and a large arms industry is new in the American experience. The total influence— economic, political, even spiritual—is felt in every city, every state-house, every office of the federal government. We recognize the imperative need for this development. Yet we must not fail to comprehend its grave implications. . . . In the councils of government we must guard against the acquisition of unwarranted influence, whether sought or unsought, by the military-industrial complex. The potential for the disastrous rise of misplaced power exists and will persist. We must never let the weight of this combination endanger our liberties or democratic processes.[82]

Eisenhower's words displayed a subtle recognition of the compromises with evil America had made in its decision to seek atomic invincibility, and his warning quietly reflected the loss of American political and moral innocence engendered by the massive militarism of cold war America. Eisenhower's warning belatedly corroborated the warnings that the culture of dissent had put forth throughout the late 1940s and 1950s, but this warning would be repeated by American youths coming of age in the 1950s. These youths, like America itself, were less innocent. They were more aware of the sometimes schizoid disjunction that existed between America's maintenance of an atomic invincibility—through the military-industrial complex—and America's maintenance of any democratic political morality. Taken very much to heart was Eisenhower's prediction of an unhappy ending for America if its military madness persisted.

part 2

PSYCHO

the emergence of a schizoid america in the age of anxiety

America I've given you all and now I'm nothing.
America two dollars and twentyseven cents January 17,
*   1956.*
I can't stand my own mind.
America when will we end the human war?
Go fuck yourself with your atom bomb.
I don't feel good don't bother me.
I won't write my poem till I'm in my right mind.
America when will you be angelic?
When will you take off your clothes?
When will you look at yourself through the grave?
When will you be worthy of your million Trotskyites?
America why are your libraries full of tears?
America when will you send your eggs to India?
I'm sick of your insane demands.

   —Allen Ginsberg,
   "America" (1956)

You shake my nerves and you rattle my brain
Too much of love drives a man insane
You broke my will, but what a thrill
Goodness gracious great balls of fire.

   —Jerry Lee Lewis,
   "Great Balls of Fire" (1958)

merican youths, like other Americans, lost their innocence and their balance in the new atomic age. Despite their parents' noble attempts to shelter them and despite their parents' generous provision of the material comforts of life, few middle-class youths coming of age in the 1950s harbored grand illusions about their long-term security in the cold war world. By the time Jerry Lee Lewis raucously begged "C'mon baby, drive me crazy" in his rock 'n' roll hit "Great Balls of Fire," the younger generation had long since signaled its cultural and psychological disaffection from the idealized and complacent America of its elders. Taboo-breaking, silence-shattering young rebels arose throughout the fifties to flout the social sanctions of cold war American life with their "deviance." Wild ones, rebels without causes, the beat generation, juvenile delinquents, and hip-swinging rock musicians exploited the expressive and behavioral freedom allowed to maladjusted youth in an otherwise conformist society. Against the constraining "insane demands" of cold war America, they exerted the liberating force of their own crazed questioning of America and its strange and conflicting life of material wealth and spiritual poverty, atomic apathy and atomic anxiety.

The language and forms of madness, alienation, and anxiety suffused the youth culture of the 1950s, revealing not only the nervous uncertainty and excited discontent of the young but also the insecurity and disorder exhibited by an entire culture of anxiety in postwar America. Innocence was not the only commodity lost in America's rise to atomic supremacy and cold war power. Also disappearing was any calm or sense of security or sanity. Rebel youths were not the only Americans bearing witness to their country's physical and psychological peril, but as the first generation of children denied the wonderment and naiveté usually cherished in the innocence of youth—as the initial group of Americans to live most if not all of their lives in the atomic age—their troubled testimonies leveled the most pointed charges against America's atomic search for security. Less inured to life's terrors than were their depression and World War II–era parents, these young Americans were more susceptible to the anxieties of the atomic age and were therefore more outraged by the insensibility to danger than characterized the older and seemingly more complacent America. Like the culture of dissent to which it belonged, rebellious youth culture recognized the unnerving irony of America's atomic quest for safety and security: it made life less secure, less safe.

In his 1951 novel *The Catcher in the Rye* J. D. Salinger introduced Americans to the cultural and psychological landscape of the age of anxiety. Through his troubled adolescent protagonist, Holden Caulfield, Salinger illustrated the depressing insecurity that ate away at many of the young in postwar America. Already crowned by a head of hair streaked with gray at the age of seventeen, Holden tells his tale of "this madman stuff that happened to me" from a sanitarium.[1] Holden has suffered a nervous breakdown, and he recounts in an intensely personal narrative the conditions that contributed to his madness: his low tolerance for the phoniness and perversity of those around him, particularly the adults around him, and the death and uncertainty troubling his young life—Holden's older brother D. B. faced death throughout World War II, his younger brother Allie died of leukemia, and a schoolmate leaped to his death from a dorm window. Holden's story begins as he is being kicked out of his fourth private school, and he explains his malaise and failure in two ways. He cannot adjust to the phoniness surrounding him: "I can't stand that stuff. It drives me crazy. It makes me so depressed I go crazy."[2] And he cannot muster much concern for his future: "Oh, I feel some concern for my future, all right. Sure. Sure, I do. . . . But not too much, I guess. Not too much, I guess."[3]

Holden's futureless world is filled with dreams of death and suicide, and the everyday concerns of normal life and school seem inconsequential by contrast. As Holden wanders around New York City, he finds no protection against the profound insecurity and uncertainty he feels; he is alone and lonesome and his nerves are frayed to the breaking point. He seeks comfort in two divergent solutions to the crisis he experiences. In a world threatened by war Holden cannot accept the idea of war or service in the army, so he determines to end the uncertainty from the start: "I swear if there's ever another war, they better just take me out and stick me in front of a firing squad. . . . Anyway, I'm sort of glad they've got the atomic bomb invented. If there's ever another war, I'm going to sit right the hell on top of it. I'll volunteer for it, I swear to God I will."[4] Yet in this world that acquiesces to such threats to children Holden contrarily desires to live in order to protect the children. He tells his younger sister Phoebe of his vision of salvation:

> Anyway, I keep picturing all these little kids playing some game in this big field of rye and all. Thousands of little kids, and nobody's around—nobody big, I mean—except me. And I'm standing on the edge of some crazy cliff. What I have to do, I have to catch everybody if they start to go over the cliff—I mean if they're running and they don't look where they're going I have to come out from somewhere and *catch* them. That's all I'd do all day. I'd just be the catcher in the rye and all. I know it's crazy, but that's the only thing I'd really like to be. I know it's crazy.[5]

Guilty and grief-stricken over his inability to prevent his younger brother's death and in need of his own catcher in the rye, Holden nonetheless attempts to keep his little sister safe. The ultimate futility of his efforts will push him over that crazy cliff. Holden visits her school and discovers "Fuck you" signs scrawled on the walls. He protectively rubs them out but then finds one scratched into the wall: "It wouldn't come off. It's hopeless, anyway. If you had a million years to do it in, you couldn't rub out even *half* the 'Fuck you' signs in the world. It's impossible."[6] As he later waits for Phoebe at the museum of natural history, in the Egyptian tomb, he comes face-to-face with this impossibility and with the anxious reality of the atomic age. Weak, dizzy, and under an increasing emotional strain, Holden retreats to the tomb as a place of calm and rest:

> I was the only one left in the tomb. . . . I sort of liked it, in a way. It was so nice and peaceful. Then, all of a sudden, you'd never guess what I saw on the wall. Another "Fuck you." It was written with a red crayon or something, right under the glass part of the wall, under the stones. That's the whole trouble. You can't ever find a place that's nice and peaceful, because there isn't any. You may *think* there is, but once you get there, when you're not looking, sombody'll sneak up and write "Fuck you" right under your nose.[7]

Unsuccessful in his quest for a place of peace and safety, overwhelmed by his helplessness in the fight against death and danger, alienated from the phony and perverse confidence of the adult world, exhausted by his attempts to sidestep the world's impersonal cruelty—to erase all evidence of those "Fuck you" signs—Holden collapsed. A nervous breakdown was the only truly human response to such a world, but, as Holden would have to learn in his sanitarium, the age of anxiety insanely demanded the phoniness and perverse denial of reality that could torture psyches like his.

Much of the popular history of the age of anxiety can be recorded from the asylums, sanitariums, and mental hospitals that filled the cultural terrain of cold war America, a saga filtered through the minds of the nervous, the neurotic, the deviant, and the violently insane. Young minds were not the only minds disturbed by postwar life, and the popular culture of cold war America overflowed with images of behavioral deviants and psychological delinquents of all sorts and all ages. In *Sunset Boulevard* (1950) Hollywood writer Joe Gillis commented that "psychopaths sell like hotcakes," and his statement only confirmed the culture's already established obsession with psychological confusion. This trend culminated at the end of the decade in Alfred Hitchcock's 1960 film *Psycho,* which featured the exquisitely crafted portrait of the young schizophrenic, Norman Bates. On the surface Norman appeared to be a kind, quiet, attentive, normal young man. Beneath the veneer, however, Norman was a psychopathic mess, tortured by guilt and violent impulses. The psychiatrist who finally diagnosed Norman's split personality explained his insanity in simple terms: "When the mind houses two personalities, there is always a conflict."[8] The schizoid malady of this exemplar of the age of anxiety also explained the divided and contrary cultural mind of postwar America.

In the aftermath of Hiroshima and America's successful splitting of the atom, *Time* magazine espied "a new age in which all thoughts and things were split."[9] In spite of the political, social, and cultural unity yearned for in these years of atomic and internal security, the American mind found no exemption from the new age's tendency toward schism. Like Norman Bates, postwar America revealed two cultural personalities in conflict. Struggling under the surface serenity and outward security of the mainstream cold war American mind was an unstable and paranoid underground American psyche in a state of panic. Challenging the culture of confident calm was the counterculture of nervous anxiety. The cold war consensus was split by this persistent cultural conflict and by the disruption of family and community life by the maladjusted and the discontented. The pressures exerted upon atomic age Americans to adjust to the nation's new world power status created fissures that rent the cultural consciousness of the United States.

Just as the culture of dissent exacerbated the tensions in postwar America about the moral and political corruption accompanying America's rise to power, so too did it inhabit these fissures and thereby raise doubts about the real psychological and physical security of Americans in this era of atom bombs and cold war confrontations. From the time of Hiroshima and Nagasaki the American government and mainstream culture had assured Americans of their safety, but insidious fears had also arisen with the advent of the atomic age. Some commentators noted as early as October 1945 that the atomic bomb and an atomic arms race could provide the impetus "for a world-wide nervous break-down."[10] The dominant American culture actively encouraged acceptance of life in the atomic age and in doing so fostered the development of the "double life" led by Americans in this anxious age. Americans were enticed into return-ing to normalcy in spite of the abnormal perils of the postwar world, and only a concerted atomic apathy and ignorance ensured their sense of calm security. Largely denied by the American government and by the majority of Ameri-cans was that other, insecure, anxious life that resulted from acknowledging the dangers of the atomic age. The culture of dissent attempted to prod Americans into an awareness of their double life and the dangers that came equally from denying or acknowledging the perils of modern life.

By focusing on psychological disturbances or on the deviance and discon-tent of America's young, both the mature and youthful manifestations of the culture of anxiety exposed a nervous and disunified America. The culture of dissent suggested that living comfortably with the bomb carried a disruptive and dehumanizing cost. Seeking consensus and conformity for the purposes of se-curity threatened to destroy any sense of democratic community, and deaden-ing emotions in order to enjoy the safety provided by atomic defenses menaced the human capacity to feel anything at all. The culture of dissent, by breaking convention and relying on nontraditional forms of expression and bizarre char-acters, urged Americans to recognize danger and to react. Allen Ginsberg's con-frontational "Go fuck yourself with your atom bomb" and his unconventional free verse aimed to stir controversy and rage, and Jerry Lee Lewis's absorption of the language of anxiety and atomic fireballing into his sexually suggestive lyrics cut through the emotional serenity of the age. The culture of dissent counseled Americans to feel and therefore to retain their humanity, even if staying human entailed pain and panic.

three

DUCK AND COVER

civil defense and existential anxiety in America

"By all means, provide some tranquilizers to ease the strain and monotony of life in a shelter."

—*1950s civil defense film*

ost Americans opted not to feel or express pain and panic, at least not openly or obviously, in the early years of the cold war. While the confident serenity of postwar American life could have been in itself a sign of atomic neurosis, an unnatural obliviousness to reality, it was also in part a sign of the effectiveness of America's internal security network and its promotion of a reality of secure and contented conformity. But for the most part America's calm consensus was a measure of the faith and hope that Americans carried with them in the wake of World War II. A sanguine belief in the future survived the war; as one ex-navy man remembered of the war: "There was a feeling of optimism. It will be a better world—afterwards, you know."[1] Americans, particularly the expanding white middle class, took advantage of their nation's affluence and abundance and strove to build a better world for themselves and their children, a world safe from the difficulties they had known in their own lives. After the war years and the early intense years of the cold war, when Americans' attention was preoccupied by the volatile and violent outside world, Americans voluntarily retreated to the peace and security of their more limited family and community lives. "Togetherness" and the safety and security connoted in that image of unity became the motto of postwar America.[2]

Through the late 1940s and 1950s Americans settled comfortably into their lives of prosperity and normalcy. The world seemed a safe place. Eisenhower reassured Americans and the world that atoms were for peace, and in 1953, with the end of the Korean War, Stalin's death, and the resulting easing of world tension, America shifted toward a more peaceful coexistence with its cold war foes. President Eisenhower maintained a pose of world and domestic serenity and he exuded carefree American optimism. He told the nation, "Everybody ought to be happy every day. Play hard, have fun doing it, and despise wicked-ness."[3] Americans followed the advice of their smiling and confident president and they found happiness and comfort in the new pleasures and possibilities of postwar life. In a growing suburban society, families cocooned themselves in calm and unvarying tract home communities in places like Levittown, Pennsylvania. American men sought economic security in jobs in large corporations, enjoying the prestige and corporate safety symbolized by their gray flannel suits and providing the income that allowed their wives and children to play hard and have fun.

Americans discovered much of their fun in the cornucopia of the consumer culture and in the technological wizardry of visual mass culture. Supermarkets, credit cards, and large new-model cars with flashy fins tempted American consumers, and the new technology of television became an increasingly important part of everyday life. Families laughed together in their living rooms at the antics of Milton Berle, Jack Benny, and Amos and Andy, and they regularly watched *Your Show of Shows, The Honeymooners,* and the *Ed Sullivan Show*.[4] American children participated in the creation of "fads," wearing Davy Crockett hats or whirling Hula-Hoops. Slightly older American youth of college age engaged in equally arcane crazes, like stuffing telephone booths and attending 3-D movies. American films of all sorts still attracted large audiences, and no matter what the plot, the backgrounds showed American affluence and presented widespread and happy evidence of American well-being. It took a trip to Italy for an otherwise cynical American commentator to see how American films expressed the confidence of America. Considering Italians' images of America, Leslie Fiedler discussed the dazzling impact of films in the early 1950s:

> But the movies provide other Americas, too. Americas of luxury: the oversize purring automobile, the long-legged girl, the penthouse towering above the swarming streets; and it is the movies in their endless repetition that are decisive in the end. . . . What is hard to see at home, where we are oppressed by the real vulgarity and triviality of our ordinary films, is the exuberant confidence they manage to convey to a society as anxious and unstable as Italy's.[5]

American films celebrated and highlighted the country's material wealth, and for many Americans the better world they had envisioned after the war had arrived, both on screen and in reality. They had worked to shelter their children and shower them with the products of their affluence. And in large measure they had succeeded in insulating their children and themselves from the dangerous outside world. Television's small screen also documented the American success in fulfilling Ike's dictum to "be happy every day." In the many family shows on 1950s television, such as *The Adventures of Ozzie and Harriet, Father Knows Best,* and *Leave It to Beaver,* which premiered respectively in 1952, 1954, and 1957, Americans saw their lives of contented conformity and family togetherness both reflected and positively reinforced.

Reflecting American society of the baby boom and suburban sprawl, television upheld the family as the unifying center of values and as the firm base of American security. This world focused itself internally, particularly on the lives of the children—whether David and Ricky Nelson in *Ozzie and Harriet,* Betty ("Princess"), Bud, and Kathy ("Kitten") Anderson in *Father Knows Best,* or Wally and Theodore ("Beaver") Cleaver in *Leave It to Beaver.* Rarely if ever did outside political or social issues and controversies impinge on the domestic security of these comfortable homes. Nestled in suburban neighborhoods of small-town America, these family homes harbored and comforted their inhabitants, and the gentle guidance of parents solved whatever minor problems their children caused by their rambunctiousness. Parental authority was wise, necessary, and beneficent and parents taught their children to be responsible and honest citizens.[6]

Above all else in this television world, family life and family rules were consistent and unchanging. Roles were clearly defined. Fathers, especially Jim Anderson and Ward Cleaver, left and returned home from their jobs at regular times, and mothers ceaselessly nurtured the family, contentedly inhabiting their modern, appliance-filled kitchens at all hours of the day. With little more than the harmless troublemaking of a Beaver to shatter the serenity of family life (except for Ricky Nelson's testing of behavioral boundaries with his rock 'n' roll singing), these television families presented a glowing image of loving family unity. The Nelsons, the Andersons, and the Cleavers were cold war paradigms of propriety and satisfaction; the children accepted their parents' values and seemed destined to grow up using their parents as secure models for their own future patterns of behavior.[7]

Given the affluence and affection that protected the fictional and real families of America during these years, there was little apparent cause for youthful disaffection from these patterns of life. Like their elders and like their younger siblings, college students of these years appeared to have adjusted easily to the quiet pleasures of cold war American life, pursuing their degrees and their careers with silent dedication and good-hearted fun. In "America in a Trance" Frank Conroy indicated how closely young Americans mirrored the quiescence of their parents and of Ike's America in general:

In college we were named. The Silent Generation. The Apathetic Generation. There was no doubt about it. The sleepy Eisenhower years. America in a trance, drifting leisurely through a long golf game while the clouds gathered. Among students it was hard to find a rebel, virtually impossible to find a Marxist, a mystic, a reformer, or indeed, anyone who felt very strongly about anything.[8]

Americans of all ages enjoyed the comforting sense of having created a better world. A lackadaisical indulgence in the playful pleasures of American life seemed only natural, as did a studied apathy about any issue that might inhibit Americans' everyday happiness.

Despite the soothing quality of life under President Eisenhower, there was something unnerving and unnatural about the placidity of America during the 1950s. Even though Americans watched their president set the national mood of play and fun—Ike was widely photographed grinning, outfitted in his golf clothes, playing scrabble with Mamie at Camp David, dabbling with his painting—they also watched as Eisenhower presided over an increasingly dangerous and destructive atomic and hydrogen arsenal.[9] Eisenhower's budget-conscious "New Look" for military and foreign policy relied almost exclusively on strengthening and developing America's nuclear stockpile. Secretary of State John Foster Dulles talked of "more bang for the buck," "massive retaliation," and "brinksmanship," rhetoric and policy that belied the outward calm of Eisenhower's administrations. The New Look policy kept atomic and hydrogen bombs regularly and fearfully in the public eye, suggesting that America's trance resulted as much from shock as from contentment.[10] The policy sent a mixed message to Americans about their real safety in the atomic age. When Dulles explained the policy for *Life* magazine in the mid-1950s, he stressed its riskiness. He noted, "You have to take chances for peace, just as you must take chances in war," and he defended going to the very verge of nuclear war to attain the nation's goal: "If you try to run away from it, if you are scared to go to the brink, you are lost."[11] Brinksmanship impelled America to the edge of war with its every decision, elevating each cold war flare-up, whether in Korea, Vietnam, or the Formosa Straits, to the status of a nuclear war scare. Each publicized test of an atomic or hydrogen bomb and each cold war showdown informed Americans of their danger in a world on the brink. The surface serenity of Americans seemed at times nothing less than an insane denial of reality.

Eisenhower's administration may have sent out conflicting information on American security, but a mixed message had reached Americans from the dawn of the atomic age. The American government and the culture at large promoted America's peaceful atomic intentions and hopes from the beginning of the atomic age, and Truman established an atomic and military bureaucracy whose sole purpose involved the protection and defense of the United States and its democratic allies. Yet in spite of these pledges of American security and in spite of the early American monopoly on the atomic bomb, the destructive potential of the bomb—and the lack of any defense against it—nonetheless inspired anxiety in segments of the population. Immediate concerns included the psychological damage that might result from this sense of atomic insecurity. In 1947 psychiatrist Jules Masserman contended that in the presence of the atom bomb "no sentient man or woman can really find peace of mind and body."[12] The writers of the 1948 *The Challenge of Atomic Energy* feared that worry about the bomb would promote such selfish and hedonistic philosophies as "Eat, drink and be merry" and "Why save for the 'rainy day'—spend, for there may be no tomorrow!"[13] And in the same year Joseph Barth published *The Art of Staying Sane,* noting that "many people are already minor neurotics, worrying about the falling atom bomb."[14] A physician who had studied the effects of radiation after the Bikini atom bomb test notified Americans of the reality of the atomic age in the title of his best-selling 1948 book, *No Place to Hide.*[15]

Hiroshima and Nagasaki, the Bikini test, and the government's own statements about the vast power of the atom bomb all provided early evidence for the psychological and physical danger of living with the bomb, but the most consistent forum for the presentation of Americans' vulnerability belonged to the promoters of civil defense. Whether sponsored by the government or by independent groups of scientists or schoolteachers, discussions about civil defense measures emphasized the tremendous destructive potential of a nuclear weapon for an unprotected society.[16] Even though some Americans had expressed fears of atomic destruction and the need for civil defense before 1949, the debate over civil defense gained force and added urgency after the Soviet atomic explosion in September of that year and again after the American and Soviet hydrogen bomb tests in the years between 1952 and 1954. From 1949 each new development in atomic weaponry (for example, the perfecting of the intercontinental missile) and each discovery of new dangers (for example, the lethality of radioactive fallout) fueled the controversy about America's lack of defense against atomic attack. Civil defense programs foundered with the exponential increase in the destructiveness of atomic and hydrogen bombs and missiles, but remaining at the heart of each proposal for civil defense was the concept of shelter: the shelter of a school desk for children in "duck and cover" drills, the shelter of physical distance provided in evacuation plans, or the sanctuary of underground blast and fallout shelters. By riveting attention on the need for shelter, particularly underground shelter, civil defense produced an expressive metaphor for a society divided: normal and unconcerned inhabitants above ground and cowering denizens of chambers of fear and worry underground.

Plans for civil defense explicitly recognized the split nature of life in the atomic age and openly addressed issues usually relegated to the quietly anxious mind of America, issues that most Americans had managed to shield themselves from in their lives of affluent consumerism. The notion of needing civil defense on an everyday basis was a relatively novel idea for Americans habituated to peace and geographic security, and civil defense therefore served for many Americans as an introduction to a new, potentially violent, and insecure way of life: Americans were in grave danger from atomic attack and from their own apathy about that danger; human life was devalued and threatened at all times, for sudden attack, the possibility of death, even a complete apocalypse, was omnipresent. Survival mandated facing these dangers and preparing for retreat underground.

Although Americans in the early 1950s realized that it would take the Soviets years to match the American atomic arsenal and pose a serious military threat, the Korean War helped to stir up the debate over civil defense, especially given the possibility of America's using the atom bomb in that war, and early discussions of American domestic defenses revealed the vast physical and psychological changes that already seemed necessary given the escalating American/Soviet confrontation. In September 1950 the *New Republic* reprinted an article from the *Bulletin of Atomic Scientists* written by Eugene Rabinowitch, editor of the *Bulletin,* entitled "The Realities of Atom Bomb Defense." Rabinowitch argued that the only effective defense against atomic attack entailed a massive geographical reorganization of America's major industries and war production centers. In order to prevent easy and decisive Soviet strikes against America's economic and military forces, vulnerable in their congested city settings, these centers of power would have to be dispersed throughout the country. Industry concentrated in urban centers was a perfect target, so the main thrust of civil defense would involve protecting America's productive capacity by removing it from such vulnerable areas. Admitting this primacy of production forced a recognition of the reduced value of human life in the equations of civil defense. Rabinowitch pointed out this new and psychologically difficult reality:

In the discussion of civil defense in America emphasis is laid on reducing the casualties of an atomic attack. This is natural in a humanistic civilization which considers the individual as its highest value. However, the grim reality is that in the case of a massive atomic attack the main problem will be, not how to save the greatest number of lives, but how to prevent the heartbeat of the nation from stopping. . . . Not the death of millions, but the disorganization of industry and transportation, will be the main threat to our survival. In the next war, civilian casualties will be considered in the same light as military casualties have been in past years.[17]

Even though Rabinowitch confronted Americans with one "grim reality" of the atomic age—the increasing inconsequence of human life—he tempered his message with the reassurance that civil defense preparation of this sort would deter the Soviet Union from risking an attack. He stated that "if the emphasis on maintenance of productivity, rather than on reduction of casualties, seems to be an inhuman approach, let us remember that the first purpose of preparations to meet an atomic attack is to make this attack less likely."[18] This widely reprinted article (and the intensified interest in civil defense it both reflected and aroused), besides revealing the lowered status of individual life, also signaled a sort of American fatalism. The atomic bomb and atomic arms race were now seen as permanent features of life in this age, and civil defense now replaced the international control of atomic energy and other peaceful proposals as the only—if much less effective—means for survival.

Rabinowitch himself symbolized the scientists' shift toward atomic pragmatism after their failure to achieve a more lasting and moral opposition to the bomb. A chemist on the Manhattan Project and one of the founders of the *Bulletin,* Rabinowitch reminded his readers that "the *Bulletin of Atomic Scientists* owes its existence to the conviction of the scientists that the invention of atomic weapons has made another total war the suicide of civilization" and that the scientists believe "there is no defense" against the bomb.[19] While not retreating from these positions, Rabinowitch had nonetheless accepted the grim realities of the atomic age and offered the only advice left for a society committed to the bomb: "measures to decrease the destructiveness of an atomic attack."[20] As America in general came to accept the permanence of the atomic age and the permanence of the cold war and its balance of atomic terror, proposals for civil defense gained greater attention and served as barometers of America's fluctuating sense of insecurity.

In the tumultuous wake of the Soviet atomic explosion and the beginning of hostilities in Korea *Newsweek* commented that "the big debate was whether

America should use the A-bomb. But what happened if somebody used it on us?" According to the magazine, America's civil defenses were in a mess: "Not a city or a state was ready to take an atomic attack."[21] A week later *Newsweek* still complained that "while the whole country jittered about lack of preparation in case of atomic attack, the civil defense program was still in the talk stage in Washington last week."[22] Given the aroused public anxieties and the clear paucity of civil defense programs at this time, President Truman pushed to establish the Federal Civil Defense Administration (FCDA) in the waning days of 1950, although the FCDA was not actually constituted until January 12, 1951.[23] In these early "jittery" years Americans learned all about civil defense from the FCDA, the scientists, and popular magazines—why it was necessary, what forms it would take, and how Americans needed to behave to make it work. In the process they also learned just how unprotected they were.

In its December 18, 1950, issue *Life* magazine published an in-depth article called "How U.S. Cities Can Prepare for Atomic War." The introduction to the piece captured the tense mood of the nation: "As the Russian-sponsored armies of Communist China smashed southward through Korea last week the growing likelihood of World War III posed a threat to this nation which its cities and civilians have never had to face before. War with Russia would be atomic war. And U.S. cities are the most destructible targets in the world."[24] The article proceeded to describe the destruction and panic that would accompany an atomic attack, a feature that became a mainstay of civil defense proposals and articles:

> The particular vulnerability of big American cities to atomic weapons
> stems from a combination of two factors: the intense congestion of the
> cities and the immense destructive power of the bomb. . . . First would
> come the immediate and total devastation of a large area, with casualties
> running into the hundreds of thousands. This would be the initial blow,
> terrible enough in itself, yet possibly less terrible than what would follow.
> Transportation would be paralyzed, power and water cut off, food supplies
> destroyed. The people would abandon the city in disorganized, panic-
> ridden flight. . . . In all, the indirect effects of the burst could well be more
> disastrous than its initial destruction, for the great city would act as a great
> explosive, triggered by the lesser explosion of the bomb itself.[25]

Critical of the government's inadequate planning for civil defense, *Life* devoted this article to a plan created by MIT professor Norbert Wiener which would solve the problem of urban vulnerability to atomic attack and postbomb panic.

Like Rabinowitch's proposal, Wiener's plan focused on the need to decentralize urban areas and to create "life belts" and "safety zones" around cities in order to facilitate escape and provide a destination and shelter for evacuees. The plan had the advantage of encouraging the trend to suburbanization; indeed, the "safety zones" that bordered the escape highways bore an uncanny resemblance to suburbia: "Nearby land will be reserved as parks and made ready for large tent cities which could quickly be erected to shelter the refugees. Supermarkets, suburban homes, and small businesses would be permitted to grow up near the life belt to supplement the emergency rations and housing set up for a fleeing population."[26]

Life made the specific connection between civil defense and suburbia, and the magazine saw the useful wartime and peacetime applications of Wiener's plan. Not only would it provide strengthened defense against atomic attack but "in peace it would expand and accelerate the current trend of many city dwellers toward the suburbs and help relieve the traffic congestion which plagues most U.S. cities."[27] Civil defense plans like these suggested a particular atomic age rationale for the American retreat to the suburbs, and such plans helped to taint the otherwise innocent and safe quality of life in the suburbs. While the suburbs were seen as somewhat protected from the initial terrors of an atomic blast (at least until the H-bomb and its radioactive fallout revised this vision of suburb safety), they nonetheless reflected the insecurity of the age in their potential roles as sanctuaries for the bombed out and psychologically dislocated survivors of urban atomic war.

Civil defense proposals revealed an awareness of the vast psychological problems that would accompany an atomic attack, and one Los Angeles psychiatrist offered some ideas about mental civil defense. The *Science News Letter* on January 27, 1951, highlighted Dr. Kurt Fantl's plans for what he termed "mental first aid," which included preparing "trailer first-aid stations for emergency treatment of mental casualties."[28] Dr. Fantl suggested that these first-aid trailers "be equipped to provide restraint for acute cases as well as quick sedation to quiet over-strained nerves."[29] Besides these measures, the psychiatrist urged preatomic war precautions against panic through the provision of shelters and through education of the public—albeit a necessarily calming sort of education:

> Panic may be prevented before disaster strikes by providing adequate shelters and lighting them with flashlights, and by education. The education should be provided carefully so that it will not create the panic it is intended to prevent. Informing the public of dangers without a master plan to help each individual to find an actual place in the defense may actually create panic.[30]

Civil defense proponents walked a fine line between educating and panicking the population, and it was at least in part the frightening aspects of atomic war and civil defense that prompted American apathy or disdain for civil defense. In a 1953 article for the *Bulletin of Atomic Scientists* Murray S. Levine (chairman of the New York Committee on Atomic Information) addressed the issue in "Civil Defense *vs.* Public Apathy." In doing so he challenged Americans to face the realities of the atomic age, but he also gave them every fearful reason for maintaining their illusions. Levine saw in civil defense a means for bringing an otherwise disunified and apathetic America together; he noted: "I do not want you to feel, after a look at the grim realities, that civil defense is a gloomy task—a job which implies hopelessness. . . . It might, on the contrary, be a means through which America faced realities, and in facing them develops a unity from the grassroots to the top levels of government—it might be a powerful means of achieving spiritual unity as well as physical strength."[31] In presenting the "grim realities" to Americans, however, Levine outlined a seemingly hopeless situation:

1. There is no defense against the atomic bomb as a bomb; and General Vandenberg, Chief of the Air Force, has emphasized that our air defense can not hope to stop more than three out of ten bombers sent against us. Russia is separated from us by only four hours flying time.

2. An attack might come without warning—it might come some Sunday, as did Pearl Harbor, or during a holiday period in which our civilian life is dislocated.

3. The rules of war in the atomic age have been changed—the time to prepare strength against war brought to our factories and our backyards must be now, before the attack is mounted. Tomorrow, or the day after an attack, is too late.[32]

In the face of this world made unsafe by the bomb, Levine urged Americans to shed their complacence, their ignorance, and their apathy. He stressed the urgency of ridding America of its selfishness and its mania for secrecy as the first step toward a unified and defended nation. Levine pointed out the need for information and education to combat ignorance, and he asked for an abolition of the secrecy practiced by the FCDA and the government: "Secrecy has become a mania with us; and it is foolish to carry it to the extremes to which we have gone. Russia knows of our hydrogen potentialities; someday she will make a hydrogen bomb herself; we cannot prevent her from doing it. But we can, and we have, arranged things so that our own people stumble blindly into the hydrogen age."[33] Beyond government openness about weapons and civil defense, Levine counseled Americans to re-create the kind of selfless neighborly spirit that helped Londoners through the bombings of World War II:

> Also we have developed in the U.S. in recent years, an appalling attitude in which a man considers it his chief duty to "look after himself first." The miracle of London is that once under attack people did not think only of saving their own skins—they learned to react, even under fear of death, to help others—to save others, and to save their city and their country. We will not have civil defense here until we rouse that spirit.[34]

Levine concluded his article by admitting the distressing character of civil defense and life in general in the atomic age, yet he held out hope for America's regeneration if the dangers were confronted in unison: "Civil defense, to many people, is a boring or a depressing subject. Anyone who has faced the realities of the atomic bomb—as I have at Bikini— . . . must admit it is depressing that we live in such a world. But from our peril I honestly believe we might find a creative unity."[35] Levine's optimism about creative atomic unity seemed misplaced as Americans continued "to stumble blindly into the hydrogen age." Not even the American government expressed a unified position on civil defense. While persistently conducting tests and publicizing the damage wrought by American bombs, the government wavered about spending the money necessary to ensure the safety of its citizens.

On March 30, 1953, *Newsweek* reported on an atomic test used by the FCDA "to thus remind the American public of what even a small A-bomb could do to a typical U.S. community," but the magazine also quoted a study that estimated the cost of achieving effective civil defense measures against such A-bombs at $42 billion or $43 billion.[36] In the cost-conscious Republican administration of Eisenhower, such spending seemed highly unlikely, but *Newsweek* stated the no-win character of the situation: "The study posed a double-edged question to the Administration: Can the U.S. afford to make such an outlay; and can it afford not to?"[37] The government opted not to approve the funds for a thorough civil defense program, and popular periodicals continued to bemoan the lack of government consistency and spending. The *Bulletin of Atomic Scientists* documented the actual decline in civil defense spending between 1952 ($153.6 million) and 1953 ($79.6 million), and the *New Republic* complained that "our civil defense program is lagging."[38] The divisions in attitude on civil defense, on its cost and its necessity, intensified and expanded as

America fully entered the hydrogen age after the March 1954 hydrogen bomb tests at the Bikini atoll in the Pacific.

In its coverage of the H-bomb blasts at Bikini—blasts frighteningly more powerful than expected—*Newsweek* included a cartoon that summed up the impact of the hydrogen bomb. The world is pictured with one arm covering its eyes and the other shaking hands with a representative of mankind, who carries with him "the ultimate super bomb." As the nearby planets plug their ears, the world says to mankind: "It was nice knowing you."[39] The H-bomb's potential for annihilation prompted yet another contrary division in civil defense attitudes. On one hand, the hydrogen bomb made civil defense seem even more urgent and necessary, and on the other, it made any defense seem inadequate and any chance of survival negligible. *Newsweek* called attention to the latter viewpoint. Its special section on the H-bomb opened with a somber statement: "If you live in a strategically important city, the odds against your survival in an H-bomb war would be about a million to one. If you live in the country, your chances obviously would be better. But wherever you live, much of what you live for would be destroyed."[40] After sifting through the horrible information on the H-bomb and assessing the slow progress made in civil defense to date, *Newsweek* concluded its report by stating the dire reality of the hydrogen age: "All the reports and all the statistics added up to one grim conclusion: In an atomic attack, the front would be everywhere. Every home, every factory, every school might be the target. Nobody would be secure in the H-bomb age."[41]

The *Newsweek* story also gave some space to official government recognition of the necessity for an intensified and reformulated domestic defense program in light of the H-bomb. The magazine noted: "Taking stock of the nation's defense situation, officials conceded last week that American cities were vulnerable to attack by enemy bombers and that, if successfully attacked with the latest type of H-bombs, their populations would be virtually exterminated."[42] The head of the FCDA, Val Peterson, vowed to pursue the new civil defense policy of "mass evacuation" with alacrity, because few options were left: "We think that if a hydrogen bomb is exploded over your city, there is only one way you can be certain of saving your life, and that is not to be in the city."[43] Others also lobbied for an accelerated program of civil defense and evacuation, and Eugene Rabinowitch pressed for dispersal of the population once again, slamming the government for its inaction. In a June 1954 editorial in the *Bulletin,* he lambasted American officials for these delays and at the same time vented his anger at the mistreatment concurrently being suffered by Oppenheimer in his security hearing:

A distinguished panel is considering, at this writing, whether the development of the thermonuclear bomb in America has been (as some allege) delayed by eighteen months; and, if so, whether this delay has been caused by ulterior, unpatriotic motives. Nobody seems, however, to be alarmed by the procrastination in another area, at least as important for our national preservation and the prevention of aggression as the hydrogen bomb—the reduction of America's vulnerability to atomic attack.[44]

Rabinowitch insisted that America's lack of security was not of recent origin: "The danger has been brought into new, sharp relief by the great fireball of the hydrogen blast, but has not been created by it." He noted the existence of peril from 1945, when, in the absence of world government or international control, scientists had recommended the dispersal of cities as a solution to cities becoming "death traps, and invitations for attack or blackmail." Rabinowitch ridiculed America's "miserly" development of civil defense, and he termed "suicidal" the advice to duck into shelters. He expressed annoyance that "it has needed the sight of the three-mile-wide Eniwetok fireball of 1952 on the nation's screens, and the scare of the still bigger Bikini blast of 1954, to make the idea of mass evacuation of endangered cities a legitimate subject of discussion."[45] While pleased at America's newfound attention to civil defense and evacuation, he nonetheless pointed out the limitations of evacuation plans and pushed for the more permanent solution of dispersal. Rabinowitch listed the many scenarios that could prompt "false alarms" and send millions marching back and forth between the cities and their evacuation areas, and he thus urged the national planning and coordination of dispersal: "Otherwise America will soon be a hamstrung giant, subject to neurotic fear in every crisis, open to blackmail, and inviting actual attack by promise of an overwhelming success."[46]

When the dangers of radioactive fallout became public knowledge in the months after the H-bomb test in Bikini—spectacularly illustrated in the case of the *Lucky Dragon*—even Rabinowitch's dispersal plans for civil defense were rendered inadequate. Civil defense options once again had to be revamped in the face of this new peril to human life (the presence and danger of fallout were known before the H-bomb blasts, but the power and range of the thermonuclear weapons and their fallout now increased significantly).[47] In conjunction with evacuation and dispersal, fallout shelters now assumed mandatory status in civil defense planning. Even though Ralph Lapp outlined in minute detail "the vertiginous, almost exponential, rise in the hazards faced" as a result of the H-bomb and its fallout, he nevertheless saw progress being made in civil defense as a result of the increased dangers. According to Lapp, in an article originally published in November 1954 in the *Bulletin of Atomic Scientists,* "The year 1954 may well mark the turning point in our C.D. activities. One very favorable index is that more and more top advisors in the government are becoming serious about civil defense. More and more, it is becoming clear that the security of the home base is of paramount importance. In this security, civil defense must assume a high priority."[48]

While Lapp gave reason to hope for a better system of civil defense, he ended his analysis with a warning: "the new peril from radioactive fall-out is more than just a threat to civil defense—it is a peril to humanity."[49] Rather than stressing the need for a strengthened civil defense, the *New Republic* used the information provided by Lapp to question the security guaranteed by anything less than an abandonment of America's nuclear policies and arsenals. Repeating Lapp's prediction that "fifty super-bombs could blanket the entire Northeast USA in a serious-to-lethal radioactive fog," the magazine focused on how "highly vulnerable" the United States therefore was to a Soviet H-bomb attack. A series of challenging questions was posed:

> What will be the effect of vulnerability on US policy? Is talk of "massive retaliation" permissible any longer, even as a bluff? Has development of super-weapons already reached the point where their ultimate use is improbable unless a fascination with economizing leaves us so lacking in non-atomic military strength that we would be forced to counter any kind of attack in just one way, by initiating atomic warfare? And must not all of our ingenuity and that of our allies be applied without rest and regardless of setbacks and disappointments to the task of fashioning a formula for atomic disarmament?[50]

The contrary impulses affecting the discussion of civil defense in the era of the hydrogen bomb and radioactive fallout persisted throughout the 1950s. With the development and testing of intercontinental ballistic missiles (ICBMs), the civil defense debate continued divided, with some urging more stringent plans and others doubting the effectiveness of any defense against the swiftly arriving missiles. Some, like President Eisenhower, doubted the overall effectiveness of missiles. Although he supported American programs for missile development, he tried not to rise to the Democratic bait of a "missile gap" in the mid-1950s and he tried to calm fears about Soviet missile progress and the new threat posed by ICBM research and development. In 1956 he bet his life on American safety from Soviet missiles; he registered his certainty in his gambling statement, "I'll wager my life I can sit on any base we've got and in the next ten years the Russians can't hit me with any guided missile."[51] Even though skeptical about missiles, Eisenhower did recognize that missiles carried "a very great psychological value."[52] The continuing debate about civil defense in the late fifties showed the psychological impact of missiles and grew even more extremist after 1957 when the Soviets succeeded both with missiles and with the Sputnik satellite.

President Eisenhower's apparent lack of concern—and lack of spending—for crash programs on missiles and civil defense both reflected and reinforced the public apathy that was as persistent as the debate on civil defense. Civil defense defenders attacked public and government apathy equally and with greater stridency in the later 1950s, and they affirmed with greater fervor the American susceptibility to destruction that deepened with the passage of time and with increasingly sophisticated methods for delivering the ever-increasing numbers of nuclear weapons. *Life* magazine again insisted on the necessity of civil defense in its March 18, 1957, issue, featuring an elaborate "Scientific Blueprint for Atomic Survival." Included in the article were finely detailed drawings of what a truly sheltered America would look like: mazes of underground concrete tubes and shelters that would connect with and mirror life above ground, ever ready to swallow Americans in an atomic attack. These plans were encouraged by physicist Edward Teller, father of the H-bomb, and by civil defense expert and research engineer Willard Bascom, as each argued the necessity of providing shelter for every American. In order to convince Americans of the need for shelters, "a subject not willingly faced by most Americans," according to *Life,* Bascom brandished the facts of American insecurity and pestered Americans and the federal government to act or face evolutionary elimination.[53]

Bascom began his argument for shelters by demonstrating the absence of safety and security in unsheltered America. He delivered a point-blank message: "The means to annihilate our unprepared civilian population is already in the hands of our potential enemy. . . . Yet the bulk of our population is totally unprepared today to meet a war emergency." He stressed how this lack of defense weakened America's policy of massive retaliation: "A strong stand, with the threat of war it implies, may be meaningless if the enemy knows that our civilian population is virtually naked before an attack."[54] Bascom then outlined the growing threat posed by the newly developing systems for weapons delivery, and he pointed out that no one was safe with these new dangers:

> We must face the fact that there is no complete military defense against atomic attack. Complicated defenses will be invented and improved but

they will never be perfect. Nuclear explosives can be carried by planes, or, eventually, by missiles launched from submarines. In a few years intercontinental missiles capable of carrying the H-bomb may become a reality. The targets these might be aimed at cannot be predicted with certainty. . . . However, since the effects of the explosions are far-reaching and since we can assume that many bombs and missiles will widely miss their targets, everyone in the country will be in danger.[55]

Bascom examined the gruesome physical damage and the traumatic psychological effects for survivors of an attack, and he thereby created an anxious audience more receptive to his major argument. Bascom held that civil defense "must offer a promise of better and more secure living; it must be made an effective part of our war deterrent; it must be built into our way of life," and he definitively stated his point: "Permanent defense means shelters."[56] He charged the government with the task it had shirked for so many years: "The responsibility for this, as with all forms of national defense, rests with the federal government, which must provide the leadership, the over-all planning and much of the financing."[57] Bascom advanced proposals for shelters, and he illustrated his article with drawings of easy-to-install family shelters, costing about $400, and with pictures of the many "radiation detector" products available on the market. He concluded with a challenge to end American apathy and inaction on civil defense, noting that shelter proposals had long been ignored. He warned against avoiding reality any longer:

> Unfortunately, too many people seem to believe that if war comes some magic will intervene to save them and that they are not personally required to make troublesome and expensive preparations on their own behalf. Let us hope that they are right and that evolutionists did not have them in mind when they speculated that war is a eugenic process which eliminates those without a special will to live.[58]

In its May 25, 1957, issue the *Saturday Evening Post* also confronted Americans with their dangerous lack of psychological and physical preparation for an H-bomb war. The *Post* reported the findings of the National Research Council's Committee on Disaster Studies, which had been established "to determine the probable behavior of the American people during and after a thermonuclear assault." The committee of psychologists, sociologists, and anthropologists studied disasters in order to answer such questions as "How would the American people take the blow? Would we crumble mentally amid the heaps of blackened corpses? Would we have panic, looting, chaos? Or would we rise from the ruins and start rebuilding our civilization?"[59] The committee's answers to these questions were, according to the *Post,* "far from reassuring," because the committee found—as had Bascom—that Americans continued to ignore the dangerous reality of the atomic age: "One thing the committee has learned is that most Americans won't listen to warnings. They just won't admit to themselves that something awful may befall them."[60]

The magazine focused its attention on this American ability to ignore disaster warnings, even "the threat of nuclear attack itself." Repeated here was a story of the American insensibility to imminent attack:

> One morning in May, 1955, a flight of unidentified bombers was spotted approaching the California coast. The Air Force was so alarmed that it ordered a "warning yellow"—attack imminent—in the Oakland area. Sirens wailed throughout the city. Fortunately, it turned out to be a false alarm—the planes were actually SAC bombers. The residents of Oakland can be thankful they were. For a team of Survey Research Center interviewers later learned, to their dismay, that a mere three out of every twenty people had believed the sirens.[61]

(Reports like these were not uncommon; in its November 1957 issue *Harper's Magazine* likewise featured a story on a similar false alarm in Schenectady, New York. In the early morning hours of July 22, 1957, air-raid sirens mistakenly went off, but only one person in the city roused his family and evacuated. The others, including civil defense officials, had done what the mayor did: "He had rolled over and gone back to sleep."[62]) The committee connected this ignoring of danger to another major psychological reaction to disaster: losing "contact with reality" and existing "in a state of dazed indifference."[63]

The findings of the Committee on Disaster Studies revealed the many ways Americans could break down under the strain of nuclear disaster, particularly given their lack of preparation and their unwillingness to face reality. They would wander in a daze or would seem outwardly calm until they snapped—like one British air-raid warden had during the London blitz. He had served heroically and without problem until one morning when he saw a happy, prancing puppy. The warden looked closely and discovered "the puppy was carrying a child's hand in his mouth." The warden "cracked," and the committee foresaw more breakdowns in an H-bomb war: "Millions of children's hands and feet would be strewn about after an H-bomb. They'd play havoc with people's nerves."[64] The committee also feared that under these and similar shocks, all kindliness, helpfulness, and neighborliness would disintegrate. Studies of the plight of evacuees demonstrated this loss of human caring; small-town and rural Americans were expected to turn away "bombed-out city folk." Some midwesterners had already stated their intentions to interviewers: "We'll get machine guns if we have to, to keep those city people from using up our children's food and water."[65]

In spite of the committee's discovery of Americans' predisaster refusal to face reality and their likely postdisaster disposition toward breakdown, the committee held out hope "if we plan and prepare intelligently now—as individuals and as a Government."[66] The *Saturday Evening Post*'s coverage of the committee findings dramatically carried forward to the missile age the long-standing message of civil defense—face reality and prepare now. The committee had uncovered the positive fact that "no matter what affliction they undergo, the American people have faith in their future," but their report maintained that only with psychological and physical preparation could "these hopeful aspects overbalance the colossal destruction and shock of an H-bomb."[67] When Americans learned that the Soviets had attained a workable (as opposed to the earlier experimental) intercontinental missile, however, significant cynicism about the effectiveness of any form of civil defense arose once again. *The Nation* announced that "Civil Defense Is Dead" in its September 28, 1957, issue arguing that "the Soviet claim of having achieved a successful intercontinental missile has blown into limbo not only our present concept of civil defense, but the whole civil-defense idea."[68]

It was estimated that an ICBM could reach America from Siberia in thirty minutes, and the vastly reduced warning time thus effectively ended the possibility of mass evacuation as a viable form of civil defense. *The Nation* rather sarcastically discussed the calming effect of the missile: "Civil defense is dead, as of right now. And to all the people who have been worrying because the stumbling procedures of the Federal Civil Defense Authority left them uncertain and unprepared, the ICBM brings a paradoxical note of cheer: You don't have to worry any more."[69] While the ICBM, like the H-bomb before it, did have the effect of increasing American fatalism about civil defense, it also propelled some Americans to worry more and to clamor more for government action—especially when the Soviets' success with the ICBM was followed in short order by their triumph with Sputnik.

The Soviets launched this first satellite into space on October 4, 1957, and as a result President Eisenhower had to deal with an increasingly critical and nearly hysterical population. Eisenhower admitted being surprised by "the intensity of the public concern," and he had to deal with a kind of hostility to which he had seemed immune.[70] At a press conference held a few days after Sputnik, a reporter brusquely questioned Eisenhower: "Russia has launched an earth satellite. They also claim to have had a successful firing of an intercontinental ballistic missile, none of which this country has done. I ask you, sir, what are we going to do about it?"[71] While Eisenhower refused to display undue concern about the Soviet successes, he did affirm the "great psychological advantage" that the Soviet Union reaped as a result of its technological advances in missiles and rockets.[72] In spite of this Soviet advantage and in spite of strong public concern, however, Eisenhower resisted the widespread pressure to increase defense spending and institute a nationwide system of fallout shelters. His resistance opened him to criticism, but his calm reaction to this perceived crisis helped to limit the hysteria.

The lobbying for shelters continued by influential individuals and groups, including Edward Teller (as in *Life*'s "Scientific Blueprint" article), H. Rowan Gaither, Jr., of the Ford Foundation, who produced the Gaither Report, full of dire predictions about Soviet superiority and the resulting American insecurity, and Congressman Chet Holifield, who conducted a congressional study of radioactive fallout. In an interview with the *Bulletin of Atomic Scientists* Chet Holifield repeatedly chided both the Eisenhower administration and Congress for not appropriating the money for fallout shelters, which his study had convinced him were absolutely necessary for the nation's "effective" civil defense.[73] He laid much of the blame for America's lack of preparedness, however, squarely on the shoulders of Eisenhower:

> One of my chief concerns during the past few years has been to bring this
> problem to the attention of the American people and the Congress in the
> hope that the executive branch might wake up to its responsibilities before
> it's too late. I'm not sure that it is not already too late. . . . The next move
> is up to the President. He is the Commander-in-Chief and charged by
> the Constitution with the responsibility of protecting our nation against
> a foreign foe. I earnestly hope he acts quickly.[74]

Despite the pressure-filled and urgent atmosphere, Eisenhower did not act to increase defense and shelter spending. Some turmoil and criticism persisted, but the issues of the missile gap, the space race, and the building of shelters would not come to a head until the early 1960s, when a new president did decide to act. Eisenhower did not "wake up" to his civil defense responsibilities as others saw them, but his sleepy mood apparently fit the general mood of a people who could ignore the screaming sirens of a warning of imminent attack. The debate over civil defense which punctuated the cultural consciousness of America throughout the fifties made clear the division that existed in the society and culture between those expressing fear and insecurity and those exhibiting calm confidence or apathy about life in the atomic age. Apathy seemed to rule in America.

The outward tranquillity of America—reflected by Eisenhower, by glowing images of affluence and suburban safety in the mainstream popular culture, and by lamentations of civil defense proponents about Americans' ignorance of their danger—did not necessarily connote an absolute insensibility and unresponsiveness to the dangers of atomic age life. While Americans may have avoided the issue of civil defense out of lack of interest or blithe fatalism, they may also have avoided the debate because such a controversial issue involving criticism of government policies was not compatible with the one hundred percent patriotism demanded in this age of rigid internal security. The surface complacence of the Eisenhower years, perhaps in part artificially induced by the security network that promoted conformity, may also have been medicinally aided by the billions of tranquilizers ingested by Americans in the postwar era. Adding to the complexity and ambiguity of this era's surface calm was this new reality: mental health had become the number one medical concern in the nation.

Initially spurred by the many psychological problems soldiers suffered after World War II, the boom in patients for American psychiatrists and psychologists steadily increased into the 1950s. Mental hospital admissions between the years 1940 and 1956 almost doubled, and in 1956 mental patients accounted for the single largest percentage of occupied hospital beds. By 1956 Americans were consuming a billion tranquilizers per year.[75] Miltown and phenobarbital became household words, and the mid-fifties witnessed Vice-President Richard Nixon's proclamation of "Mental Health Week" from the steps of the Capitol.[76] (This major health issue appeared in the 1955 novel and 1956 film of *The Man in the Gray Flannel Suit*: protagonist Tom Rath got a public relations job involved with the national concern for mental health.) As the fifties came to a close, one-third of all prescriptions contained tranquilizers; even civil defense information films soothingly urged Americans to stock their shelters with pills: "By all means, provide some tranquilizers to ease the strain and monotony of life in a shelter."[77]

Civil defense films also suggested that much of America's psychological trouble was related to the bomb. A filmed cartoon strip featured a man afflicted with "nuclearosis"; the man could only think of the "awfulness of the nuclear bomb." He was "deaf" from the sound of it, "blind" from fear of it—his eyes were filled with mushroom clouds. The doctor treating the malady cured his patient with a nontranquilizing prescription: a fallout shelter to make him safe.[78] While civil defense tried to alleviate the psychological dislocation of the atomic age, it also helped to increase the mental anxiety. Civil defense widely disseminated information on America's lack of safety and security, and however practiced Americans were at ignoring the danger, they could not completely repress the psychological effect. Entire cities practiced evacuation drills, fallout shelter signs spotted the everyday urban landscape, and school children throughout the fifties were subject to a panoply of civil defense drills and educational films and demonstrations. While adult Americans might by all means use tranquilizers to combat the strain of life inside or outside of shelters, the children were captive recipients of the civil defense message.

American children perhaps felt the psychological impact of living in the atomic age most keenly, but their anxious experiences spoke of the larger cultural anxiety that impugned, if quietly and underhandedly, the tranquil reputation of postwar America. The civil defense debate revealed an America divided between the nervous and the calm (whether that calm was real or induced), and children were introduced to this split life through school drills, where fear suddenly intruded, then receded, where—as one educator put it—children were trained to become both "disaster-minded" and "competent to survive."[79] From the early 1950s children in school watched "Bert the Turtle" films and cartoons that illustrated the "duck and cover" drill and then participated in similar drills; they drew posters containing civil defense ideas and suggestions; they listened to lecturers who presented atomic information; and they observed their schoolmates give demonstrations on how to stock a shelter with the proper foods.[80]

As nuclear technology progressed, school children learned new drills for evacuation and removal to shelters, and school and safety journals urged schools to update their drills given new dangers. In the *School Board Journal* for August 1957 the director of training and education for the FDCA in Battle Creek, Michigan, counseled schools to strengthen their civil defense programs and to practice drills that met all forms of danger, from blast to fallout. He included pictures to illustrate such drills, from students in Marshall, Michigan, practicing "taking cover" in their school halls to Murphy High School students in Mobile, Alabama, taking part in a citywide school evacuation of the town.[81] The *Safety Education* journal in 1959 also advised schools to improve their "disaster preparedness curriculum" and to use the students as civil defense conduits to the community:

> Schools are a prime channel of communication between the local disaster program and the homes of the community. People need to be sold on civil defense, and many people have children in school. Whether the children

bring the disaster protection message home verbally or as take-home material, the schools are an effective agent for its distribution.[82]

The *Safety Education* article stressed the need for all schools to prepare shelter, especially in the era of ICBMs and H-bomb radioactive fallout: "Even isolated rural schools must be alerted to the fact that their isolation is no defense against such deadly shower, and, like schools in the primary target area, they must be prepared to set up a shelter program to safeguard their children against contamination."[83] The article prompted schools to take responsibility for spreading their civil defense knowledge, because "it would be a good thing if everyone became acutely uneasy about the jeopardy which surrounds children as a result of man's and nature's inhumanity to man."[84] School children from urban and rural areas, from grade school to high school, had experienced civil defense drills; while *Safety Education* insisted that the question schools had to answer for each child was "*how best can we teach him to survive?*" many children came away from their schools and their drills with a better understanding of their jeopardy than their survival.[85]

One mother of a baby boomer made an explicit connection between the 1950s drills and her son's malaise. In *"The Good War"* Marnie Seymour noted that "these postwar babies feel that they will not live out their lifetime to expectation. I have one boy. . . . He doesn't think there's any future. He's just one of the thousands of young people who grew up ducking under their desks in atomic bomb drills at school. Why would they think there's a future? All their lives they've heard about the bomb being dropped."[86] A student activist in the 1960s, Todd Gitlin also recalled the fright and dislocation he and his peers experienced as a result of the drills. He claimed that "whatever the national pride in the blasts that pulverized Bikini and Eniwetok atolls, whatever the Atomic Energy Commission's bland assurances, the Bomb actually disrupted our daily lives. We grew up taking cover in school drills—the first American generation compelled from infancy to fear not only war but the end of days."[87] He went on to describe the drills and their damaging psychological effects:

Every so often, out of the blue, a teacher would pause in the middle of class and call out, "Take cover!" We knew, then, to scramble under our miniature desks and to stay there, cramped, heads folded under our arms, until the teacher called out, "All clear!" Sometimes the whole school was taken out into the halls, away from the windows, and instructed to crouch down, heads to the walls, our eyes scrunched closed, until further notice. Sometimes air raid sirens went off in the wider world, and whole cities were told to stay indoors. Who knew what to believe? Under the desks and crouched in the hallways, terrors were ignited, existentialists were made. Whether or not we believed that hiding under a school desk or in a hallway was really going to protect us from the furies of an atomic blast, we could never quite take for granted that the world we had been born into was destined to endure.[88]

Confirming these personal and impressionistic accounts of the impact of civil defense drills on America's young are the findings from a more scientific survey of participants from these 1950s drills. Psychologist Michael Carey interviewed over forty young men and women who had been exposed to the drills and he compiled an account of their responses. Memories of the drills were clear and detailed, as were recollections of the childhood psychological impact:

> And participants remembered, as the initial phase of their response, a sense of a dreadful and mysterious entity known as "the bomb" or "the thing," which was so powerful it might even blow up the world. While they varied in how closely or strongly the bomb entered their fears, they had frequent dreams or fantasies of people and neighborhoods and cities destroyed by explosions and fires, with desperate efforts to reach the sanctuary of shelters or find family members—all of this often in the form of disjointed images of terror and destruction.[89]

Beyond nightmares of atomic terror and destruction, certain common perceptions resulted from this youthful exposure to the bomb and civil defense: an early confrontation with death, especially in the form of annihilation; a sense of life's "ephemeralism," and a predisposition to doubt the permanence of anything; a "perception of craziness" relating to the bomb, and a certain sort of cynicism about believing what one was told; a sometimes personal "craziness" that manifested itself in identification with the bomb, a desire for its use and "an end to anxious wondering"; and a widespread recognition of "the double life" being led, the general ignoring of the everyday peril in order to pursue everyday life by numbing oneself against danger—and feeling in general.[90] And all of these psychological effects contributed to a general problem: the difficulty in imagining "a human future."[91]

That the civil defense debate in 1950s America both expressed and exacerbated the tensions and insecurities that divided an anxious America from an apparently tranquil America seems clear in these accounts of the psychological troubles caused the young by 1950s school drills. Less psychologically hardened (or medicated) than their parents, young Americans in the postwar years were more susceptible to the fears induced by civil defense, but the anxious message of civil defense evidently found an audience beyond the young. Along with the torment of young psyches prompted by civil defense drills, Americans' mental health problems also belied any absolute reign of apathy and contented conformity in America. Adult and youthful manifestations of mental trauma indicated the psychological embedding of those anxieties and neuroses that civil defense proponents had helped to illuminate and promulgate in their discussions of America's atomic insecurity. The civil defense debate had openly shown Americans that their calm apathy and denial of reality were not appropriate responses to atomic age dangers; rather, the debate had affirmed that, in the absence of safety and shelter, mental distress—whether in the form of deep feelings of insecurity, paranoia, guilt, or paralyzing fear—was a correct and operative response. While the mainstream American culture of consensus and Eisenhower's politics of tranquillity continued to uphold the image of a secure and contented American society, the culture of dissent shifted its attention to this coexistent underground America of anxiety, where tranquillity and satisfaction dissolved into tension and conflict.

America's rebellious culture of anxiety presented an image of America in conflict with Eisenhower's America, an image of America already disrupted by the bomb—without the bomb having fallen. In this America the psychological damage and community disintegration predicted for a panicked, postatomic attack population already existed. The mentally disturbed or the demented were ever-present, as were generalized fears of insanity. Family and community relations were abnormally strained and divisive, and angry deviants and delinquents disrupted the serenity of everyday life in the city and in suburbia. No one and no place was safe from madness. Alienation, loneliness, and nervous disillusion seemed the norm in anxious America. Panic and paranoia often appeared warranted in this psychologically damaged America, an appropriate reaction to an unsafe world that tried to avoid recognizing its insecurity. And the dissenters who inhabited this postwar culture offered some of the most sane and critical commentary on the diminishment of life in an anxious and schizoid atomic age.

four

THE SNAKE PIT

america as an asylum

"You fools! You're in danger! . . . You're next, you're next!"

—Invasion of the Body Snatchers *(1956)*

iven the real dangers of the atomic age, some psychological imbalance—
paranoia, perhaps—might have been justified in an America only beginning
to adjust to the dangers of the cold war world. Nonetheless, Americans in
many cases appeared to be oblivious to the perils of this era. In the civil defense
debate that raged throughout the late 1940s and 1950s, many proponents of
civil defense bemoaned this lack of concern, seeing in American behavior signs
of mental disturbance: Americans were losing contact with reality. This divorce
from dangerous atomic age realities recognized by the advocates of civil defense found metaphoric representation on the April 5, 1954 cover of *Newsweek*
magazine.

The magazine's cover featured a picture of two beautiful and smiling young
women driving a convertible with its windows plastered with the stickers of
vacation spots and tourist destinations. This vision of carefree and freewheel-
ing vacationing was designed to advertise *Newsweek*'s special report "Spring-
Summer Travel." Sprawled above this image of a happy getaway and offering
a disconcerting contrast was a banner added to promote the magazine's other
special section: "THE BOMB: WHAT ODDS FOR SURVIVAL NOW?"[1] The inside
segment on the H-bomb informed readers that their odds against survival
were a million to one (if they lived in a major city). The vacationers' blithe insensibility to such dangerous odds—to the threat hanging directly over their
heads—symbolized America's overall psychological dislocation in the atomic
age.

That Americans discovered psychological torment in the early era of the
cold war is documented in the statistics on mental health during this era; that
this psychological torment was related to the atomic age and the cold war is
suggested rather convincingly in the work of historian Elaine Tyler May, whose

Homeward Bound: American Families in the Cold War Era (1988) demonstrated the connection between the personal and the political during this time period, particularly between family ideology and cold war ideology. She noted this, as well as the disjunction in historical images of cold war American life, in her introduction:

> The context of the cold war points to previously unrecognized connections between political and familial values. Diplomatic historians paint one portrait of a world torn by strife and a standoff between two superpowers who seemed to hold the fate of the globe in their hands. Sociologists and demographers provide a different picture of a private world of affluence, suburban sprawl, and the baby boom. These visions rarely connect, and one is left with a peculiar notion of domestic tranquility in the midst of the cold war that has been neither fully explained nor challenged.[2]

In the era of the cold war the family was meant to be a "psychological fortress" against "the hazards of the age," and thus, according to May, a "domestic containment" arose to match cold war containment in foreign policy and to enfold and blunt the otherwise obvious dangers of the time.[3] Domestic containment manifested itself in what May termed "a family-centered culture," which "was more than the internal reverberations of foreign policy and went beyond the explicit manifestations of anticommunist hysteria such as McCarthyism and the 'Red Scare.' It took shape amid the legacy of the depression, World War II, and the anxieties surrounding atomic weapons. It reflected the fears as well as the aspirations of the era."[4] For some Americans, however, the fears of the era could not be contained within the presumably idyllic family or the comfortable middle-class prosperity of postwar American life. Americans, with or without the family, sought a security that was for many ephemeral; as May concluded, "containment proved to be an elusive goal."[5]

Given the political difficulties associated with expressing fear and discontent in cold war America, Americans often turned to experts—particularly in the field of psychiatry—for help with the discontent and anxiety that they believed they should not be feeling.[6] What May termed "the therapeutic approach" to problems was adopted during this era, and it promoted the attainment of personal mental health and psychic well-being through individual analysis. May claimed that the therapeutic approach was "geared toward helping people feel better about their place in the world, rather than changing it. It offered private and personal solutions to social problems."[7] Because the anxieties and fears associated with the cold war and the atomic bomb could not ultimately be solved through long-term individual therapy, which May demonstrated as having "reached unprecedented popularity in the mid-1950s," an amorphous psychological anguish coursed through the culture of anxiety and dissent, registering the failure of "domestic containment" and the psychological fortress it had attempted to erect in America.[8] Signs of psychological disturbance, both in and outside of the American family, developed into signs of larger atomic age anxieties and mental distress. Domestic tranquillity existed as little more than a construct of American dreams and hopes in postwar America. The culture revealed a swath of psychological trauma that began at the very beginning of the atomic age, at the conclusion of World War II.

American soldiers returning from World War II were the first to exhibit the psychological agony that surfaced in the postwar culture of anxiety. Popular culture portraits of disillusioned veterans which filtered into the culture in the late 1940s not only signaled the end of the veteran's innocent and optimistic view of life but also the end of any sense of belonging or acceptance in peacetime America. Films like *The Best Years of Our Lives* and *Crossfire* examined these psychological difficulties and illustrated the terrible shock of readjustment that veterans underwent. Anger, violence, and depression were common, and one veteran tried to explain their feelings in *Crossfire:* "I think maybe its suddenly not having a lot of enemies to hate anymore. . . . Now we start looking at each other again. . . . We just don't know what to fight. You can feel the tension in the air. A whole lot of fight and hate that doesn't know where to go."[9] Much of this unfocused anger turned inward as depression or self-hate, and guilt about the war and its human destruction increased the veteran's inability to adust to a peace that seemed nearly as nerve-wracking as the war.

In one of his early postwar short stories, J. D. Salinger demonstrated the lengths to which veterans could be driven in their attempts to resolve their sense of dislocation. "A Perfect Day for Bananafish" focuses on a young married couple vacationing in Florida after the war. Muriel Glass is alone in her hotel room talking to her mother on the phone, and it is clear that her husband, Seymour, recently returned from the war, has suffered from his experience. Muriel's mother is concerned for Muriel's safety with Seymour, and she tells Muriel of her father's conversation with Seymour's psychiatrist: "Well. In the first place, he said it was a perfect *crime* the army released him from the hospital—my word of honor. He very *definitely* told your father there's a chance—a very *great* chance, he said—that Seymour may *completely* lose control of himself. My word of honor."[10] Muriel calms her mother with the information that there is a psychiatrist at their hotel, and Muriel and her mother move on to other less serious subjects of conversation. In the meantime, in a mental world far removed from Muriel and her mother, Seymour lies on the beach, wrapped in his bathrobe. In his conversation with a little girl on the beach Seymour seems distracted, his thoughts disjointed—no hotel psychiatrist will be able to help him. When he returns to his room, he reconciles his dissociation from his wife and his life:

> He glanced at the girl lying asleep on one of the twin beds. Then he went over to one of the pieces of luggage, opened it, and from under a pile of shorts and undershirts he took out an Ortgies caliber 7.65 automatic. He released the magazine, looked at it, then reinserted it. He cocked the piece. Then he went over and sat down on the unoccupied twin bed, looked at the girl, aimed the pistol, and fired a bullet through his right temple.[11]

Despair and dislocation were not restricted solely to those Americans who had been directly involved in the war. Besides inhabiting the mental wards of army hospitals, troubled characters in postwar novels and films checked into private manors and sanitariums for the mentally ill, insane asylums and state mental institutions, all of which become the settings for a display of widespread psychological disturbance. The culture of anxiety revealed the illness and instability of all sorts of Americans—from psychiatrists and Santa Claus to young wives, aging salesmen, corporate businessmen, criminals, and Hollywood movie stars. Like veterans, many of these mentally unbalanced Americans looked inward for the cause of their maladjustment, certain that in their contented and conformist society their discontent must come from within. Guilt, culturally evocative given America's reluctance to come to terms with its diminishing innocence after the war and Hiroshima and Nagasaki, pervaded the lives of the disturbed and had to be confronted if any cure was to be forthcoming. The culture of dissent presented in almost didactic fashion a parade of the psychologically damaged victims of the age of anxiety, inculcating the American consciousness with the language and methods of psychiatry and alerting Americans to the need to address their mental health in this troubled and nervous era.

In *Spellbound* (1945) Alfred Hitchcock used a line from Shakespeare's *Julius Caesar* as the film's epigraph: "The fault is not in our stars, but in ourselves."[12] In spite of the irony that since 1945 the "fault" for atomic age anxiety might very well have come from the bombs potentially falling from the stars (a possibility widely recognized in 1950s science fiction films, where danger often comes "out of the sky"), this notion of finding fault within oneself nonetheless gained currency in postwar American culture and helped to explain the growing fascination with psychology during these years. Finding fault within themselves in *Spellbound* were the psychiatrists and doctors themselves. The head of the Green Manors psychiatric institute is being forced to retire as a result of a nervous breakdown. His replacement turns out to be an amnesiac imposter riddled with guilt complexes—and a suspect in the murder of the man meant to be the real replacement. The female psychiatrist who helps to cure the amnesiac is considered by the others to be "cold," lacking in human and emotional experience. In uncovering the truth about the amnesiac the female psychiatrist employs the many techniques of psychoanalysis, from questioning the man about his past and his childhood to analyzing his dreams, memories, and associations. The amnesiac's mental obsessions are detailed, and his dreams, filled with weird and frightening symbols, are represented in a sequence of surreal Salvador Dali designs. The woman psychiatrist finds the keys to these symbols and unblocks his memory by discovering the cause of his guilt: his witnessing of the replacement's murder had triggered childhood guilt about his younger brother's accidental death and his own war guilt about killing: "I hated it. I hated the killing." (The amnesiac had been seeing the murdered psychiatrist for treatment of his war-torn nerves.) The culprit in the murder turns out to be the mentally broken head of the institute, and when confronted, he turns a gun on himself, resolving his insanity with finality.

While *Spellbound* rather ironically demonstrated the pervasiveness of psychological disturbance through its focus on psychiatrists as equally disturbed as their patients, the film reflected the culture's growing familiarity with psychiatric terminology, criminal insanity, and guilt as well as its obsession with personal mental health. *Miracle on 34th Street* (1947) also reflects this preoccupation. In this instance, the presumed "insane" was Santa Claus. When Kris Kringle joins the Macy's staff as the store's Christmas Santa Claus, his "unusual" behavior, like his fight against the "crass commercialism" of Christmas and his insistence on being the "real" Santa Claus, ultimately leads to his confrontation with the psychiatric forces of the store and the state. The mean-spirited and narrow-minded store psychologist decides that Kris has "latent maniacal tendencies" and argues that Kringle "should be placed in a mental institution."[13] Kringle's "maladjustment" in fact stems only from his belief in the wonders of the imagination (in an otherwise cynical age) and from his apparent but harmless delusion that he is Santa Claus. The Macy's psychologist nonetheless forces Kris to Bellevue Hospital for psychological testing. Feeling defeated by the cruelty and cynicism around him, Kris purposely fails the mental tests and is threatened with commitment to a state mental institution.

When Kringle's crusading friend and lawyer finds him at Bellevue, he is morose and listless, disillusioned by a world filled with types like the Macy's psychologist: "He's called normal, and I'm not. If that's normal, I don't want it." The Macy's psychologist clearly considered all forms of eccentric or different behavior signs of mental illness, but Kringle—with his friend's legal help in the court-ordered sanity hearing—will fight to prove that his kind of idealistic insanity is both necessary and beneficial in life. At the spectacle of the hearing, where Santa Claus is on trial for "lunacy," the kindness and the innocent wonderment of his world view are vindicated, as are his idealism and his nonconformity. In an American society that was becoming increasingly intolerant of unconventional behavior and beliefs, *Miracle on 34th Street* upheld the right to be different, even a bit crazy. The film also introduced a theme that sporadically appeared in the culture of dissent of the forties and fifties: that the insane were often more "sane" and human than those presumed sane. This lighthearted treatment of insanity soon darkened, however, as more serious concerns for America's mental health intensified (perhaps intensified in part by the pressures to conform exerted by the internal security network). As everyday Americans much less noteworthy than Santa Claus found themselves entering the Bellevues of America in greater numbers, the culture documented their discomfort.

The 1948 tour de force of American madness, *The Snake Pit,* crafted an image of America crowded with the insane. The film exposed the horrors and the deficiencies of America's mental institutions through its stunning recreation of life in a state asylum. The travails of the film's protagonist Virginia offered an in-depth account of one woman's descent into this psychological hell and at the same time pointed up the central role that psychiatry and asylums now played in the lives of vast numbers of troubled Americans.[14] In outward appearance Virginia seems a happy and untroubled young woman, but her story illustrates the mind's easy slide into a disturbing insanity. The film opens with a shot of Virginia's smiling face, which immediately contorts itself as she wonders where she is—in a zoo? a prison? She knows she is caged—bars and locks are everywhere. She is disoriented. She knows she is married, but she does not recognize her husband. Her psychiatrist, Dr. Kik, interviews her husband and learns that the recently married Virginia just suddenly cracked: one day she became crazed and picked up a knife to attack her husband. Her husband leaves her at the state asylum, and Dr. Kik will use all the methods of psychiatry to treat her.

Virginia is given shock treatment and medication, and she is psychoanalyzed by a sympathetic but all too busy Dr. Kik. Her progress is erratic, though, especially when she gets shuttled back and forth between various wards and a variety of cruel and overworked nurses. Finally she winds up in the "snake pit," a large, multilevel basement room swarming and crowded with the deeply insane and violently delusional. Being forced into this room awhirl with the sick, the violent, and the helplessly ill prompts Virginia to better health; she knows she has hit the bottom—she is with "animals," living "as if I was in a snake pit."[15] The work Dr. Kik had accomplished in uncovering her traumatic past finally breaks through her delusions (she suffered from a sense of guilt for the deaths of her father and her earlier fiancé and thus had difficulty loving her husband for fear of killing him too). Virginia slowly recovers, and the finely detailed methods of modern psychiatry are applauded. Nonetheless, the film's lasting images are of the multitudinous insane who overflow the space of the inadequately staffed and equipped state institution.

Psychological imbalance hit Americans from all areas of American life, from all socioeconomic groups. *The Snake Pit* demonstrated how an ordinary middle-class wife could suddenly break down, and in *Death of a Salesman* (1949) Arthur Miller showed the mental despair and collapse of the "small men" in America. An exhausted and aging salesman, forgotten by his company and by his sons—and by the American society at large—Willy Loman cannot quite come to terms with the failure of his dreams, whose fulfillment seemed the very promise and guarantee of American life. Willy's mind wanders but he clings to his delusions, vainly attempting to keep up his salesman's optimism. His son Biff becomes impatient with Willy's "craziness," but his mother defends her husband against the inhuman and destructive pressures of his life:

> "I don't say he's a great man. Willy Loman never made a lot of money. His name was never in the paper. He's not the finest character that ever lived. But he's a human being, and a terrible thing is happening to him. So attention must be paid. He's not to be allowed to fall into his grave like an old dog. Attention, attention must be finally paid to such a person. You called him crazy— No, a lot of people think he's lost his—balance. But you don't have to be very smart to know what his trouble is. The man is exhausted. . . . A small man can be just as exhausted as a great man."[16]

Willy Loman is more than a tired dreamer, and he plots suicide as a way out of his defeated life. His insurance policy makes him worth more dead than alive, but he worries about the cowardly nature of suicide. He overcomes his qualms by posing a question to himself: "Does it take more guts to stand here the rest of my life ringing up a zero?"[17] And Willy then puts an end to his empty life of dreams by crashing his car. The void that greeted Willy at the end of his life and career also swallowed up other disillusioned, unstable dreamers. *White Heat's* Cody Jarrett had his criminal quest for success disrupted by fits of mental illness, and, like Willy Loman, he ended his dreams in self-annihilation. In *Sunset*

Boulevard Norma Desmond had achieved stardom, success, and wealth, but she found only despair at the top. Joe Gillis had asked himself early on, "Was her life really as empty as all that?" Her suicide attempts, her melancholia, and her final descent into insanity offered a potently affirmative answer to his question.[18] The crazed and tormented close-up of Norma that concludes the film—her insane face staring directly at the audience—raised a twisted and tortured challenge to the image of calm American contentment in the prosperous postwar world.

Insanity could touch the losers and the winners in the American search for success; it could undermine the minds of ordinary, law-abiding citizens and the minds of criminals. In the fictional world of his 1950s crime novels Jim Thompson demonstrated the widespread engulfment of seemingly normal men in the confusion and violence of criminal insanity. After the once mild-mannered sheriff Lou Ford suddenly unleashes his violent schizophrenia in *The Killer Inside Me,* Lou reveals his own understanding of his condition and its genesis in childhood sexual traumas. As the narrator, Lou is able to draw his readers into an identification with him—during his crimes, his sickness, and now in his own self-diagnosis:

> I've read a lot of stuff by a guy—name of Kraepelin, I believe—and I can't
> remember all of it, of course, or even the gist of all of it. But I remember
> the high points of some, the most important stuff, and I think it goes
> something like this: " . . . difficult to study because so seldom detected.
> The condition usually begins around the period of puberty, and is often
> precipitated by a severe shock. The subject suffers from strong feelings of
> guilt . . . combined with a sense of frustration and persecution . . . which
> increase as he grows older; yet there are rarely if ever any surface signs
> of . . . disturbance. On the contrary, his behavior appears to be entirely
> logical. He reasons soundly, even shrewdly. He is completely aware of what
> he does and why he does it." That was written about a disease, or a condi-
> tion, rather, called dementia praecox. Schizophrenia, paranoid type. Acute,
> recurrent, advanced. Incurable. It was written, you might say, about— But
> I reckon you know, don't you?[19]

Captured for his crazed murder spree, Lou Ford is sent to the local insane asylum for a few days. When he is released right before his final suicidal and fiery confrontation with the law, he notices the signs on the highway near the asylum:

WARNING! WARNING!
Hitch-hikers May Be Escaped
LUNATICS![20]

In Jim Thompson's novels these signposts of the culture's lunacy are omnipresent, and between such warnings and the use of devices like first-person narration by schizophrenic minds the novels suggested how close insanity came to infiltrating the everyday lives of Americans.

A Hell of a Woman (1954) presented yet another Thompson antihero schizophrenic. Protagonist Frank Dillon is another of America's "small men"; he has a job as a door-to-door salesman and bill collector, and he is just barely getting by in his quest for a life of respectability. His life has consisted of a string of these unfulfilling jobs, yet he strives for success despite his loathing of this life:

> So you come to this town, and you see this ad. Man for outside sales and collections. Good deal for hard worker. And you think maybe this is it. This sounds like a right job; this looks like a right town. So you take the job, and you settle down in the town. And, of course, neither one of 'em is right, they're just like all the others. The job stinks. The town stinks. You stink. And there's not a goddamned thing you can do about it. All you can do is go on like those other guys go on. The guy giving haircuts to dogs, and the guy sweeping up horse manure. Hating it. Hating yourself. And hoping.[21]

Frank Dillon soon stops hoping and striving for respectability and slides into a life of criminal madness. As he drifts farther from his original self, he begins to tell his story through a persona that has become Frank Dillon's complete and crazed opposite: "Knarf Nollid."[22] Frank/Knarf's descent into insanity ends in an orgy of drugs, grotesque dismemberment, and death, the antithesis of his former hopes for a modest life of calm respectability.

Few characterizations of American insanity matched the criminal and nihilistic intensity of Jim Thompson's psychological portraits, but the popular culture mirrored Thompson's vision of an America populated with the frustrated and the lunatic. Insanity and nervousness had so spread in society that it attacked not only the small men and the criminally disturbed of America but also the very symbols of 1950s American respectability and normalcy. In Sloan Wilson's novel *The Man in the Gray Flannel Suit* (1955) and in the film *The Three Faces of Eve* (1957) psychological disturbances reached into the suburbs and into the minds of the most common representatives of American values: young white husbands and fathers and young white wives and mothers. By the mid-fifties the pressures of conforming to the cold war rules of behavior had started to crack America's surface calm.

Tom Rath, the man in the gray flannel suit, has on the surface a life of American contentment and success: he has a lovely wife and three children, they live in suburban comfort in Connecticut, and Tom is in the process of climbing the ladder to a better paying and more prestigious job in public relations. But neither Tom nor his wife Betsy is happy, and the opening line of *The Man in the Gray Flannel Suit* establishes this fact: "By the time they had lived seven years in the little house on Greentree Avenue in Westport, Connecticut, they both detested it."[23] They see the house as a "trap," and they are continually discontented; their lives have not been the same since Tom returned from the war. Tom is tormented by his war past—he has disrupting flashbacks and memories of the deaths he caused, including his accidental killing of his best friend, and he cannot forget his wartime Italian lover, Maria, whom he left pregnant. But not all of Tom's torment issues from the past. The present has pressures and fears all its own.

Some of the pressures of life are refracted in the new job Tom takes with the United Broadcasting Corporation. His boss Mr. Hopkins announces their project "to start a national committee on mental health," and he presses Tom with the need for the project: "Do you know that more hospital beds are occupied by the mentally ill than by all the cancer, heart, and polio patients put together?"[24] As Tom begins work on the project, he seems a likely candidate himself for one of those beds. Betsy rails at him to be more ambitious, make more money, buy a new house; she resents his postwar malaise and screams "You've got *no guts!*" when he is unresponsive to her material demands. She insists that "we're going to start living sanely," but Tom continues to be nervous and distracted by both the present and past. On his daily train commute to New York City the newspaper exacerbates his fears: "Tom opened his [newspaper] and read a long story on negotiations in Korea. A columnist debated the question of when Russia would have hydrogen bombs to drop on the United States." Tom tries to calm himself and to laugh off his anxiety: "What the hell is all the crisis about? he thought. After the whole damn war, why am I scared now? I always thought peace would be peaceful, he thought, and laughed."[25]

Tom cannot laugh off this sense of menace, however, and his worries are unnerving him, especially when triggered by his obsession with the war:

> The past is gone Tom thought, and I will not brood about it. I've got to be tough. I am not the type to have a nervous breakdown. I can't afford it. I have too many responsibilities. This is a time of peace, and I will forget about the war. . . . They ought to begin wars with a course in basic training and end them with a course in basic forgetting. The trick is to learn to believe that it's a disconnected world, a lunatic world, where what is true now was not true then; where Thou Shalt Not Kill and the fact that one

has killed a great many men mean nothing, absolutely nothing, for now is the time to raise legitimate children, and make money, and dress properly, and be kind to one's wife, and admire one's boss, and learn not to worry, and think of oneself as what? That makes no difference, he thought—I'm just a man in a gray flannel suit. I must keep my suit neatly pressed like anyone else, for I am a very respectable young man. I will have guts—I'm not the type to start crying now.[26]

Tom learns from an old war buddy that his lover Maria and the son she had by Tom need money, and his conscience burns. He, Betsy, and the kids had recently moved into a big house left him by his grandmother, and Tom returns home one day to the news that the town wants to use their tower for civil defense. Betsy explains that they want to use the top of the tower for sky watchers: "It's Civilian Defense—they're making a plan for Civilian Defense here. They want to use our tower for airplane spotters until they get a permanent place for themselves." Tom groans at the absurdity, then apologizes for his unenthusiastic response: "I'm just tired, and I don't like thinking about another war."[27] In his mental health project Tom is gaining the confidence of Mr. Hopkins, but he is being overworked and overstrained. Nonetheless, he clings to the money he earns as the only panacea in a world he finds both insane and insecure: "The important thing is to make money. . . . The important thing is to create an island of order in a sea of chaos."[28]

The disorder of his life and his mind still threaten Tom with collapse, so he finally decides to act to stave off his impending psychological crisis. He pulls back from taking greater responsibility at his job, and he discusses his rationale with a sympathetic Mr. Hopkins: "I'm not the kind of person who can get all wrapped up in a job—I can't get myself convinced that my work is the most important thing in the world. I've been through one war. Maybe another one's coming. If one is, I want to be able to look back and figure I spent the time between wars with my family, the way it should have been spent."[29] At the same time Tom takes greater moral responsibility for his past; he tells Betsy about Maria and their son, and after an emotional scene Betsy reconciles herself to the situation and begins to understand the trauma Tom experienced in the war. Tom and Betsy will send money regularly to Tom's son by Maria and their life together promises happiness now that Tom has honestly faced himself and his past. He has awakened from the gray flannel trance:

I really don't know what I was looking for when I got back from the war, but it seemed as though all I could see was a lot of bright young men in gray flannel suits rushing around New York in a frantic parade to nowhere.

They seemed to me to be pursuing neither ideals nor happiness—they were pursuing a routine. For a long while I thought I was on the side lines watching that parade, and it was quite a shock to glance down and see that I too was wearing a gray flannel suit.[30]

In the process of reaffirming the possibility of family happiness and personal optimism in this age of anxiety, Tom Rath had to reject the routines and conformity demanded in cold war America, and his family had to suffer a discontent quite out of keeping with the traditional suburban complacence reserved for the representatives of 1950s respectability.

In *The Three Faces of Eve* the strain of being a contented and competent wife and mother contributed to the shattering of a young woman's personality, and the idyllic image of small town family life was again tarnished by the intrusion of mental illness. This story of the disintegration of a "neurotic housewife's" personality is presented in part as a filmed documentary of a "true story of multiple personality."[31] A narrator explains the background and the treatments, but otherwise the progression of this young woman's collapse is traced through the character. "Eve White," a wife and mother living in a quiet Georgia town, begins to exhibit signs of illness after losing a baby. She has headaches and blackouts, and she often does things without having any memory of doing them. She goes for psychiatric help after she inexplicably tries to strangle her daughter Bonnie with a cord. At the psychiatrist's office Eve's husband Ralph is angry and unsympathetic about his wife's "crimes" and bizarre behavior, despite Eve's plea, "I didn't do it." When Eve talks with the doctor alone, she simply wonders, "Am I losing my mind? . . . Am I?" As this mild, sweet, and submissive woman answers the doctor's questions, she indicates that she hears voices, voices urging her to do things like leave her husband. Eve suddenly gets a headache and a different woman emerges: "Eve Black," a sexy, playful, aggressive, and much freer woman, owner of the voice telling the other Eve to leave Ralph and the perpetrator of those "crimes" of which Eve White has no memory. When the psychiatrist determines that this is a true case of multiple personality, he commits the Eves to a state mental hospital and begins his work to reintegrate the personality.

The dual personalities stabilize after being introduced to one another, and the doctor allows the Eves to leave the hospital and live in town to work and continue treatment—but apart from Ralph and Bonnie. While never explicitly stated, it seems clear that Eve White's sometimes brutal and demanding husband is at least exacerbating her psychological difficulties. He is confused and ignorant about psychiatry, and when he sees her in town he states that he does not believe in "this multiplied thing." He wants her to leave with him, but Eve White refuses. She will stay alone and in sessions with the doctor until she is well, even if Ralph leaves her. Eve Black later emerges and sexually teases Ralph, promising to leave town with him. When he finds her soon after in a bar, drinking and flirting with other men, he beats her. The action at this point skips forward two years, and Eve White is divorced from Ralph (at least a partial acknowledgment of his cruel role in her illness). In spite of his absence, though, the Eves are little better. The doctor uses hypnosis on them, convinced that the key lies in a submerged childhood trauma. As he gets closer to the trauma, the two Eves both get weaker and a third personality, "Jane," comes forth.

Jane shows signs of being the integrated, healthy personality of the Eves, but she has no memory—it can only be provided by uncovering the earlier trauma. With the collaboration of the Eves, the doctor gradually uncovers the truth: as a screaming and terrified young girl, Eve was forced by her mother to kiss her dead grandmother, and her personality had started to split from that moment on. Between this early frightening confrontation with death and the daily pressures of her own life as mother and wife, Eve had disintegrated. Facing the trauma allows Jane to replace the Eves and to become capable once again of normal family life. She marries a kind man a few years later and regains custody of her daughter Bonnie. Jane seems destined to enjoy finally a tranquil family life, having left behind her the schizoid Eves and their terror of death and marriage. This fact-based story of a personality torn apart by the trials of her past and present, however, disputed America's myth of safety and sanity in marriage, the family, and suburbia.

Beyond individualized portraits of the insane, the anxious, and the schizophrenic, the culture of dissent also demonstrated the wider family and community disintegration that followed from these more personal and self-contained forms of mental instability. The tensions that had contributed to personal breakdowns contributed as well to the breakdown of human relations in the family and the community. Both *The Man in the Gray Flannel Suit* and *The Three Faces of Eve* tangentially illustrated how emotional damage corroded more than just the mind of the afflicted. Eve had physically threatened the life of her daughter, and her marriage and family life fell apart as a result of her confused condition. In *The Man in the Gray Flannel Suit* Tom's wife Betsy makes clear how Tom's depression desiccated their lives: "We haven't had much of a life together. . . . We've learned to drag along from day to day without any real emotion except worry. We've learned to make love without passion. . . . We don't really care enough to fight anymore, do we? I haven't even cried for months. I think I've forgotten how to cry."[32]

The 1956 film version of *The Man in the Gray Flannel Suit,* while less explicit about the cold war tensions that upset Tom, offers a dramatic visual frieze of the alienation that infected suburban lives in this era. When Tom returns home one evening, his three children are in the living room watching television. He greets them with "Good evening, children" and not one responds or moves. The camera lingers on this sad picture of a father overlooking his uncommunicative children, their eyes and attention riveted on the inanimate and dissociative marvel of communications technology.[33] The atmosphere of loneliness, suspicion, nervousness, paranoia, hatred, and violence which characterized the culture of anxiety derived from the pressure of living in a society threatened by atomic attack or communist infiltration and from the tension of living in a society where others were not to be trusted, where anyone might be a spy, an informer, or a lunatic.

The spreading mental disorders and emotional alienation that undermined postwar America found vivid representation in select areas of the visual arts, which helped to establish the early symbols of the disconnection that split the cultural mind and community of America. Before existential despair led to his suicide in 1956, painter Jackson Pollock dripped and splattered his agony in chaotic patterns over his canvases. This abstract expressionism admitted little order or control in these bold and disturbing paintings, in which Pollock released the confused energies of the "unconscious mind." In paintings like *One (#31, 1950)* (1950) and *Convergence* (1952) Pollock created messy and violent metaphors for the American condition, using unsettling and unconventional artistic methods that stirred controversy and provoked condemnation.[34] The depths of American fear and alienation appear in less abstract imagery in the art work of George Tooker. In his 1950 *The Subway* Tooker portrayed an eerie and despairing urban underground of furtive souls. Iron bars, stairways, barred stairwells and turnstiles, and receding corridors imprison the immobilized occupants of this subway station, and their trapped faces express the terror and suspiciousness of the age. Women cast frightened glances and indistinguishable men look coweringly over their shoulders or lean in anguish against the walls. Frozen in this space is a human still life of the fear and unhappiness of a disunified, deadened, lost American community.[35]

In his postwar cartoon drawings for the *New Yorker* Charles Addams presented only darkly humorous images of the emotional and physical violence that literally killed the conjugal relations of husbands and wives. Collected in his 1950 book *Monster Rally* were somber cartoons of marriage and murder. One cartoon pictures a wife comfortably seated in the living room, reading with a box of chocolates next to her. As her husband approaches from the rear, she comments without looking at him: "Now, don't come back asking me to forgive you." The husband, however, has no such reconciliation in mind. In one hand he carries a hatchet and in the other a bag, apparently for carrying out her body.[36] In a less overtly violent frame a despairing husband has attempted suicide by hanging from the living room light fixture, but he has clumsily caught his arm in the noose as well. He wife looks in and remarks: "For heaven's sake, can't you do anything right?"[37] In another macabre cartoon a wife's murder of her husband has been grotesquely eased by the convenience of the consumer culture, as she explains to the police interrogating her:

"I disconnected the booster from the Electro-Snuggie Blanket and put him in the deep-freeze. In the morning, I defrosted him and ran him through the Handi Home Slicer and then the Jiffy Burger Grind, and after that I fed him down the Dispose-All. Then I washed my clothes in the Bendix, tidied up the kitchen, and went to a movie."[38]

The psychological alienation and emotional sickness that infused these products of the visual arts also suffused the popular films and novels of America's postwar dissenting culture. The 1949 film *House of Strangers* presented an image of the family which thoroughly undercut its postwar American role as the center of stability and values. In this family sons turn against the father, the father turns against them, and the sons turn against one another. The wife and mother bemoans this house of "no love, just hate," and the father declares, "I have no sons. I have strangers."[39] The image of the family home occupied by betraying strangers and the accompanying vision of family stripped of its normalcy and security appeared with alarming regularity in the 1950s culture of anxiety. In his 1951 film *Strangers on a Train* Alfred Hitchcock carried forward this theme of human and family estrangement as the film focused on the disruption of life caused by all sorts of psychological, sexual, and behavioral oddities.

Strangers on a Train opens with the crisscrossing of the fates of two apparently opposite men. Bruno Anthony and Guy Haines accidentally bump into one another on the train, and Bruno's world of darkness, lunacy, and death impinge on Guy's world of light, order, and vitality. Guy is a well-known tennis player and Bruno has followed his career, so when they conveniently meet, Bruno attaches himself to Guy. As they talk it becomes clear that Bruno is strangely disturbed—he is an effete, wealthy, restless young man who bristles with dangerous nervous energy. It is also clear that Guy's life is not as light and carefree as befits a rising tennis star and young politician. He is unhappily married to an unfaithful and bitchy wife who is pregnant by another man. He is traveling to see his wife, Miriam, in order to obtain a divorce, which would free him to marry the daughter of the senator for whom he works in Washington, D.C. Bruno has heard of Guy's social troubles from the gossip columns, so he proposes a mad scheme to Guy: they should switch murders, with Bruno killing Guy's wife and Guy killing Bruno's father, whom Bruno despises. Bruno "reasons" that since neither has a motive for the other's murder, capture would be difficult. Guy simply brushes off Bruno and his idea as a rather sick joke.

But Bruno was not joking. After Bruno learns that Guy's wife refused him the divorce (and Guy's own angry reaction involved threatening "to strangle" her), Bruno goes to find Miriam; he follows her and strangles her. He returns to Washington, D.C., to inform Guy, who is horrified. He calls Bruno a "maniac," but there is an element of truth in Bruno's accusation that "you wanted it."[40] As the two face each other in this tense night meeting, in a dark recess outside of Guy's apartment, their interrelatedness is suggested by the half-light, half-dark shadows cast over them. Bruno's insanity and Guy's guilt have merged and Guy's previously sane and calm existence has been corrupted. The police immediately suspect Guy for the murder, but without any solid evidence they simply put round-the-clock surveillance on him. Guy's suddenly paranoid and suspicious world is made even more uncertain by the persistent Bruno, who follows Guy, pressing him to fulfill his part of the bargain by murdering his father. Guy tries to elude both Bruno and the police in order to figure a way out of his dilemma, but in the meantime his troubles disturb the lives of the senator's family members. Fear, suspicion, and mistrust invade all aspects of their daily lives as Guy behaves strangely and as the police and Bruno interrupt their serene routines.

The abnormal and unconventional aspects of family and emotional life that surround Guy—his adulterous and cruel wife, the girlfriend who dates him even though he is a married man, for example—pale in contrast to the abnormality in Bruno's family. Bruno is a psychopathic murderer who also shows signs of sexual confusion, hinted at in his understated attraction to Guy and in his overstated hatred of his father. His mother is a flighty woman who indulges Bruno but remains oblivious to his illness, and his father is a hard and brutal man who, while cognizant of Bruno's madness, does little but threaten to put him in restraints. Guy tries and fails (foiled by Bruno) to tell Bruno's father that he has a "lunatic son," and Guy's girlfriend, once informed of the truth by Guy, tries but fails to get Bruno's mother to control her dangerous son. Bruno's madness and his destruction of life end only with his death in the final confrontation with Guy and the police. Bruno's demise takes place at the scene of Miriam's murder—a small-town amusement park—and the carnival atmosphere that reigns during this climactic battle between Guy and Bruno suggests the whirling uncertainty and danger that could destroy life at any time and at any place. While proof of Guy's innocence finally emerges from this mayhem and he can resume a more normal life, his world view has been forever altered by his collision with guilt and insanity. In the film's final scene Guy is again on the train when a kindly minister recognizes him—in a manner similar to Bruno's initial meeting with Guy. Guy abruptly turns away, having learned to mistrust even the most seemingly benign stranger.

The psychological, sexual, and emotional disturbances that undermined the life of the family in *Strangers on a Train* also surfaced in other cultural documents from the 1950s. *Strangers on a Train* belonged in Hitchcock's cycle of films noirs, a genre that adapted perfectly to the presentation of the insanity and emotional instability so apparent in America's anxious culture. Film noir was especially suited to revelations of family and community discord simply because the noir world itself was one of betrayal, uncertainty, and degradation designed to expose the failure of all human relations. In *Strangers on a Train* the amusement park served as a metaphor for the chaos ready to engulf the inhabitants of this nervous era and to darken the sunny lives of American families. *The Big Carnival* (1951)—another product of this genre—employed similar settings and themes.

In *The Big Carnival* the discredited New York reporter Charles Tatum finds himself stranded in the rather exotic and isolated town of Albuquerque, New Mexico, where Indians and cowboys still wander the streets. He has been fired from eleven jobs as a result of libel suits, drinking problems, and philandering, and his broken-down status is reflected in the condition of his car at the beginning of the film: it is being towed, along with Tatum, into town. Tatum stops at the local newspaper office seeking work and is hired by Mr. Boot, the owner and publisher of the *Albuquerque Sun Bulletin*. Tatum's plan entails waiting in Albuquerque for the big news story that will propel him to fame and fortune once again. Waiting for his big story in a small town proves difficult for Tatum, however, and time passes excruciatingly slowly. He has been at the paper a year and he is beginning to feel as if he were serving a "life sentence," as if "I'm stuck here . . . stuck for good."[41] In the long run, though, it is Tatum himself who proves to be the difficulty as he regresses to the unethical behavior that had marked his past. Tatum not only disrupts the familial atmosphere of the small-town newspaper office but he destroys the family that becomes the subject of the big story he had so awaited.

Even before Tatum reveals the scope of his ambition, his cynical attitude clearly establishes the lengths to which he will go for his big story. He notes that "bad news sells best, 'cause good news is no news," and he asks a coworker to toss his cigar real far out of the window—"all the way to Los Alamos and BOOM! Now there would be a story!" While Tatum does not cause destruction on any such level, he does exacerbate the problems plaguing one family. On assignment to cover a "rattlesnake hunt" in the desert outside Albuquerque, Tatum exposes the snake within himself: he exploits the peril of a man trapped in a mountain cave-in, ultimately causing the man's death. Leo Minosa had become trapped in a cliff dwelling while hunting for the Indian curios he and his family sell at their roadside gas station/curio shop/café. Leo Minosa fears that the Indian spirits inside this sacred mountain—the Mountain of the Seven Vultures—are punishing him for violating their burial ground. It is, however, very much the this-worldly vulturism of Tatum that causes Minosa's death and the disruption of his family.

Having surveyed the situation and spoken to Minosa (by crawling as close as possible to the cave-in site), Tatum determines to sensationalize the Minosa tragedy in order to salvage his career. He links the Minosa story to an earlier, Pulitzer Prize-winning saga of a man trapped in a cave for eighteen days. Tatum hopes Leo can last a week in his confinement so he can milk the story for all it is worth. The trusting nature of the Minosa clan, particularly Leo and his father, accentuates the baseness of Tatum's acts. The father constantly thanks Tatum for the efforts he is making on Leo's behalf, and Leo clings to his moments of contact with Tatum as he suffers a living entombment. Leo's mother, though, places her faith in a power higher than Tatum, praying incessantly to a God who is clearly not listening. Leo's wife Lorraine is as much a cynic and opportunist as Tatum, and she makes clear that life in the Minosa family was not all that rosy, even before Leo's spectacular accident. To an extent, then, Tatum only accelerates a destructive process already in motion, but this dark twist in their family life only deepens the sense of basic human incompatibility revealed in the film.

Lorraine tries to use Leo's absence as an opportunity to flee her unhappy life, and she prepares to depart on the next bus, unconcerned for Leo's fate. Tatum forcefully persuades her to stay, not only because of the money to be made from the gawkers already arriving to witness this human interest story but also because he wants the story that way. A grieving wife—however insincere—makes the story "read better." In agreeing to stay Lorraine rather fatalistically comments, "There are three of us buried—Leo, me, you." She turns out to be exactly right. Tatum has so orchestrated the story and manipulated the participants and observers that the affair is transformed into a circus sideshow threatening the life of Leo and testing the humanity and morality of Tatum and Lorraine. Tatum is so concerned with intensifying the pathos and suspense of the story (and thus his own journalistic glory) that he subjects Leo to several extra days of confinement in order to heighten the drama—Tatum has rejected the direct method of extracting Leo in favor of a longer, more flamboyant method. As the tension of getting Leo out before he suffocates escalates, this usually quiet and remote desert spot erupts into the fever-pitched "big carnival." The Minosa café is flooded with local politicians, tourists, and journalists, all of whom Tatum controls because he controls the story. The Minosas are raking in cash from this windfall. Hordes of visitors are clogging the roads around the Mountain of the Seven Vultures, and there are rows of cars and tents to transport and house these prying guests. First a radio station and then television cameras are set up to broadcast the latest updates on Leo. Mobs of the curious continue arriving by special train and by car, buying the ice cream and balloons being hawked, and paying the $1 admission charge. Lost amid all this hoopla is any real concern for Leo's predicament as this carnival atmosphere exposes the worst elements of human nature. The sightseers disclose their morbid fascination with the tragedies of others, and Lorraine and Tatum reveal their degradation in exploiting and betraying Leo.

From the beginning there has been some sort of magnetism between Tatum and Lorraine, an attraction based on their mutual hard-heartedness and cynicism. Their relationship is tinged with a violence from the start. Early on, Lorraine comments to Tatum, "I've met a lot of hard-boiled eggs, but you're twenty minutes." But this hard man has been responsible for spectacular earnings for the Minosas, $1,000 in a single day. Lorraine thanks Tatum and makes sexual advances, but he slaps her hard, giving her the look of despair needed for Leo's wife in his story. He tells her to "go on back and peddle your hamburgers," and he later orders her to attend a rosary for Leo. She coldly states, "I don't go to church. Kneeling bags my nylons," but she finally consents to make an appearance. She warns Tatum, saying, "Don't ever slap me again." These two barren souls nonetheless consummate their relationship, completing the cycle of disloyalty to Leo. Tatum and his story have violated all ethics: his manipulation of the story undermines the journalistic standards promulgated at the *Albuquerque Sun Bulletin,* where a sign reads (to Tatum's discomfort) "Tell the Truth"; his affair with Lorraine makes a mockery of the trusting relationship Tatum has developed with the trapped Leo, who lets Tatum know how he cherishes Lorraine and is fighting to live until their five-year wedding anniversary. On that date, however, Leo loses the will to live. Gasping for breath, he conveys his one wish, that Lorraine receive the anniversary gift he has purchased for her. Tatum promises Leo to deliver the shabby fur piece to Lorraine, but when he does, she throws it to the floor. Aware that Leo is dying, Tatum reacts violently to Lorraine's insensitivity to the gift and the hope it represents for Leo. Tatum strangles Lorraine with the fur and in the struggle she stabs him with a pair of scissors. Badly wounded, Tatum—now realizing the horror of his deeds—proceeds to make Leo's last hours on earth as comforting as possible. He tells Leo how pretty Lorraine looks wearing the fur and he brings a priest to the cave-in site so that Leo can have his confession heard and receive last rites. When Leo dies, Tatum finally takes responsibility for his actions. He announces to the crowd that Leo is dead and tells them to go home: "The circus is over." The fame and fortune Tatum had found in his big story are also over. Leo's death does not provide the appropriate ending for such a tale, and Tatum is fired from the high-paying New York job he had procured as a result of the story. The carnival surrounding Leo and Tatum disappears as rapidly as it had appeared, and Lorraine awaits the same bus that she had tried to take before. The elder Minosas are left heart-broken. Tatum tries to tell the real story—that he murdered Leo Minosa—but the only ones listening are those already sickened by his ethics, his boss and a coworker from the *Sun Bulletin.* He notes to his ex-boss Mr. Boot that he is a "thousand dollar a day" man in the newspaper business, but concludes, as he lies dying from the stab wound, "You can have me for nothing."

The absence of any human kindness or love in *The Big Carnival* and the violence and corruption of human relations constituted a grim characterization of family and community life not uncommon in the culture of these years. The film held up a distorting mirror to the traditional comforts of home, family, and community. Rattlesnakes and vultures roamed this world where human beings were trapped, buried alive, or suffocated. While Tatum's perfidy did not have the brilliantly insane tinge of Bruno's actions in *Strangers on a Train,* its impact was equally devastating to those it touched and its cultural symbolism was equally bleak. Neither strangers like Tatum nor family members like Lorraine could be trusted, and humans disclosed a deep capacity for insensitivity and morbidity. There was no God to save Leo Minosa, nor were there angry spirits of dead Indians to cause or to prevent the snuffing out of his life. Chaos ruled in a universe without meaning, substance, or human fulfillment.

While *The Big Carnival* presented a peculiarly nihilistic portrait of human relations, it was certainly not the only film to do so. Another film noir from the 1950s, *Clash by Night* (1952), also focused on the tangled web of human relations that undercut the happier picture of cold war family togetherness. *Clash by Night* also held up a distorting mirror to American society, but in this instance it was a woman who shattered traditional expectations. Women in film noir largely tended to step well outside the traditional moral boundaries of wife, mother, and homemaker, and as a result there was a rather liberating quality to these films. Such films suggested the dissatisfying and unrealistically demanding nature of postwar gender roles—a dissatisfaction well hidden in the otherwise contented family images of the fifties—but they also further convoluted America's vision of family solidarity. In *Clash by Night* Mae Doyle is coming home after a ten-year absence, but her conception of home and marriage confound mainstream ideas on the subject and promote the type of dangerous family disruption so inimical to fifties ideals. Mae returns to her oceanside hometown a disillusioned, tough woman. She is home without the riches she wanted, and she has lived a sordid life that included an affair with a married man. She admits she had "big ideas" and got "small results" and she is not particularly happy to be home. As she notes, "Home is where you come when you run out of places."[42] Given Mae's discontent and restlessness, she is unlikely to find solace in her old hometown. In fact, her own destructive tendencies reassert themselves and cause the very turmoil and pain a supportive woman is meant to soothe.

Two local men, good friends, compete for Mae's attentions in *Clash by Night*. Jerry is a sweet, hard-working, down-to-earth man who could be the type of man Mae believes she wants: "a man who isn't mean and doesn't hate women," a man "to beat off the world when it tries to swallow you up." Earl, in contrast, is the type of man who has appealed to Mae in the past and given her those "small results." There is an exciting if dangerous edge of violence to their interaction, and Mae seems to sense this threat. She decides to marry Jerry and forget Earl, but she does not have many illusions about her capacity to be the kind of wife Jerry wants. She warns Jerry that she is "all wrong" for him, that she is "bad" for him. She knows she will not make a good wife because she is a woman "never satisfied," but she succumbs to Jerry's pressure and to her own need for "a place to rest." Jerry and Mae marry, settle down, and have a baby daughter, but it is not long before Mae bristles at her domestication and lack of fulfillment. An equally unhappy Earl and Mae are thrown together by circumstance during Mae's time of darkness and Earl recognizes her despair: "You're born and you'd like to be unborn." They couple in their desperation and in their tumultuous affair seem to find the satisfaction both had been missing in their lives. Mae has learned in her life with Jerry to "expect nothing, hope for nothing," but she wants more—she wants love. Even though she believes she has found this with Earl, she cannot bring herself to leave Jerry when he discovers the disloyalty of his wife and friend. Earl insists that if Mae leaves Jerry and the baby the two of them will be "free," but Mae understands that people like her and Earl have always made others suffer, have always walked out on their responsibilities. Mae goes back to Jerry and he takes her back, but their future is anything but certain. Mae has just admitted to Earl when he asks about love that she "doesn't know the word anymore." And her idea of home carries great force even at the end of the film. Perhaps Mae has just run out of places to go.

Clash by Night made clear that home did not always offer the sanctuary promised in America's cold war culture, and a character like Mae Doyle suggested that women and wives did not always serve as the bastions of trust and morality in this unsettled age. While film noir provided the culture with a genre expressive of such emotional betrayal and family disintegration, the presentation of distorted family and community relations was not limited to films like *Strangers on a Train, The Big Carnival,* or *Clash by Night.* Other products of the culture of the 1950s showed American homes that housed deceit, violence, and betrayal and the abnormal family relations that made trusting family members as dangerous as trusting strangers. In Jim Thompson's novel *A Swell-Looking Babe* (1954) an adopted son's oedipal attraction to his mother prompts him to destroy his father's life and career in a fashion peculiar to this era: he signs his father's name to a petition defending free speech, an act considered subversive and criminal, especially for a schoolteacher. While he is reluctant to admit the deviant impulses behind his act, Dusty Rhodes does on some level understand the destruction he has caused:

> The Free Speech petition . . . Well, the old man had reacted exactly as he thought he would about that. He wasn't sure that he hadn't signed. In any event, he would not deny that he had and thus indirectly damn a cause he had believed in. He had stood pat, and, of course, the school board had promptly booted him out of his job. And with his failing health, the blow was almost fatal. *But no. NO—Dusty almost shouted the word. That wasn't the way it was. It had worked out that way, but he hadn't planned it. A street-corner solicitor had offered him the petition, and he had signed it . . . without even thinking*

of the consequences. He had signed it simply William Bryant Rhodes, because there had not been enough space to add the Jr. (That was the only reason.) And he definitely had not faked his father's signature. Dad had taught him how to write. It was only natural that their signatures should be very similar.[43]

Dusty's mental defenses against the psychosexual truth behind his actions are shattered by a lawyer who deduces the son's motive. He insists that Dusty knew the consequences of his action: "You've lived in this town all your life— you know how people think here, how they'd react to a thing like this Free Speech business. You grew up in a school-teacher's family, and you know what a teacher's problems are." He also confronts Dusty with his oedipal intention: "You knew the old man was sick and that a blow like this one could easily kill him. And that's what you wanted, wasn't it? *You wanted him dead!"*[44] Dusty never gained the object of his lust, and the lawyer ensured that he paid for ruining his father's life. Unresolved themes involving the perversion of family trust and love continued to fascinate the counterculture. Vladimir Nabokov's 1955 novel *Lolita* addresses the controversial subject of pedophilia, or "nymphet love," a condition sympathetically explicated by its remorseful practitioner, Humbert Humbert, who has defiled the childhood of his step-daughter Lolita. In the pseudoscientific foreword written by the pseudoacademician "John Ray, Jr., Ph.D.," Nabokov presents an age of anxiety justification for *Lolita:*

> As a case history, "Lolita" will become, no doubt, a classic in psychiatric circles. As a work of art, it transcends its expiatory aspects; and still more important to us than scientific significance and literary worth, is the ethical impact the book should have on the serious reader; for in this poignant personal study there lurks a general lesson; the wayward child, the egoistic mother, the panting maniac—these are not only vivid characters in a unique story: they warn us of dangerous trends; they point out potent evils. "Lolita" should make all of us—parents, social workers, educators—apply ourselves with still greater vigilance and vision to the task of bringing up a better generation in a safer world.[45]

Humbert Humbert, "the panting maniac," had a history of mental instability and breakdown, not to mention a long-term predilection for young girls. When he enters the suburban female household of the Haze family as a summer boarder, he falls helplessly in love with the widowed Mrs. Haze's twelve-year-old daughter Lolita. Thus begins his true fall into the "madness" of nymphet love, which he describes in lusty and rapturous terms:

What drives me insane is the twofold nature of this nymphet—of every nymphet, perhaps: this mixture in my Lolita of tender dreamy childishness and a kind of eerie vulgarity, stemming from the snub-nosed cuteness of ads and magazine pictures, from the blurry pinkness of adolescent maidservants in the Old Country (smelling of crushed daisies and sweat); and from very young harlots disguised as children in provincial brothels; and then again, all this gets mixed up with the exquisite stainless tenderness seeping through the musk and the mud, through the dirt and the death, oh God, oh God. And what is most singular is that she, *this* Lolita, *my* Lolita, has individualized the writer's ancient lust, so that above and over everything there is—Lolita.[46]

Humbert, however, will come to regret his rapturous lust. He marries Mrs. Haze in order to remain close to Lolita, and when Mrs. Haze rather fortuitously dies in an accident he becomes father, lover, and corrupter of his young Lolita.

Even though Lolita is no innocent—Humbert insists "it was she who seduced me" and "I was not even her first lover"—and even though Humbert's physical lust is tempered by his transcendent romantic love for Lolita, Humbert suffers for his ruination of Lolita's life.[47] On their aimless travels throughout the United States, where Humbert's illicit love stains every little town and motel, Humbert is tormented by jealousy and guilt—he believes they are being watched and followed by some shadowy persecutor or detective. He suspects his own sanity, but in the end his fears prove correct: Lolita runs off with another man, Claire Quilty, who queerly resembles Humbert and who has indeed been tracking them. When Humbert learns this truth a few years later from a much changed Lolita (she is pregnant and married to a younger man), he determines to kill Quilty, who has metamorphosed in Humbert's mind into the very representation of Humbert's lust, the lust that destroyed Lolita's life. Humbert realizes that Lolita "had been deprived of her childhood by a maniac," and, "lucidly sane, crazily calm," Humbert goes after Quilty to atone for this crime.[48]

He confronts Quilty with a gun, and in their struggle the merging of Humbert, Quilty, and their lust is clear: "We fell to wrestling again. We rolled all over the floor, in each other's arms, like two huge helpless children. He was naked and goatish under his robe, and I felt suffocated as he rolled over me. I rolled over him. We rolled over me. They rolled over him. We rolled over us."[49] Humbert succeeds in killing both Quilty and his own lust, but he is left with an aching sadness for what Lolita had lost. As he waits for the police to capture and arrest him after Quilty's murder, he remembers a time when he stood atop a hill and heard the rising and ringing voices of children at play: "I stood there listening to that musical vibration from my lofty slope, to those flashes of separate cries with a kind of demure murmur for background, and then I knew that the hopelessly poignant thing was not Lolita's absence from my side, but the absence of her voice from that concord."[50] Despite his poetic acts of atonement—the killing of Quilty and the writing of the story of Lolita—Humbert senses the impossibility of repairing the torn fabric of childhood and family life. This sort of depressing awareness filtered into a larger cultural recognition of the damage done to family and community life in the age of anxiety.

While the surface sexual repression of 1950s culture usually kept these more open expressions of psychosexual deviance obscured (and *Lolita* was in many cases misunderstood and banned), the culture of dissent did highlight the many ways in which emotional perversion and violence disrupted family and community life. Building on the dark view of human nature and the abnormality of family life which he had established in *Strangers on a Train,* Hitchcock produced a body of mid-1950s films that captured the insecurity of everyday life and the corrosion of love and sanity that degraded human relations. The apartment house courtyard setting that formed the backdrop to *Rear Window* (1954) provided voyeuristic access to an emblematic community of America's lonely, alienated, and violently discontented. The film's protagonist, L. B. "Jeff" Jeffries, is a professional voyeur—a photojournalist—and the photographic proof of his adventurous career is evident throughout his apartment, including a picture taken of that special icon of this age, the mushroom cloud of an atomic explosion. *Rear Window* focuses on the prevalence of surveillance in American culture, but Jeff's surveillance of his neighbors uncovers not political subversion but the sad subversion of American contentment and community.[51]

Jeff has a broken leg, sustained while on assignment, and he is confined to his apartment for weeks. With little else to occupy his time, he has taken to watching the lives open to his view from his rear window, which overlooks a courtyard surrounded by other apartment buildings. In this New York sultry summer the neighbors' lives are glimpsed through the curtains and windows, and what they reveal has very little to do with the 1950s America of security and comfort. There is the tormented and frustrated music composer who despairs over his work; there is the couple who shower all of their love and attention on a little dog; there is "Miss Torso," a dancer who must fend off the lewd and unwanted advances of men; there is "Miss Sculptress," another woman alone who creates distressing pieces of abstract art; and there is perhaps the loneliest and unhappiest of them all, "Miss Lonelyhearts," an aging woman who searches unsuccessfully for companionship and love. There are also the Thorwalds, the noisiest and most violent of these discontented souls, who bicker incessantly and present a depressing portrait of marriage.

The nurse who visits Jeff daily warns him against his spying, noting that "we've become a race of peeping toms" and assuring him that only "trouble" will come from his peeping. She tries to get him to think about his girlfriend Lisa instead, but he is as confused and dissatisfied with love as his neighbors. The nurse contends that love has become too "intellectualized" and too "psychoanalyzed" now and the result is "lonely people." Both her points are prescient, as this enclosed community exudes its despairing loneliness. And then violence brings the trouble of which she warned. Thorwald murders his wife, cuts up her body, and carries it out of the apartment, and Jeff has witnessed enough of his actions to be suspicious. As he and Lisa increase their surveillance, the emotional debilitation of the community seems acute, with Thorwald's brutal murder just the most extreme manifestation of this disintegrating human community. While the revelation of Thorwald's crime and his climactic attempted murder of Jeff, acted out at the rear window, will help to bring members of this community together, the original vision of a deep alienation and violence in human relations lingered in Hitchcock's fifties films.

In *Dial M for Murder* (1954) a husband enraged by his rich and beautiful wife's affair with another man cunningly plots to have her murdered. When she kills the attacker, he frames her for murder. While her innocence is discovered just before her scheduled execution, this once vibrant woman has lost her color and liveliness, having been catapulted into a gray and emotionally deadened world.[52] A normal American family has a North African vacation terrifyingly shattered in *The Man Who Knew Too Much* (1956). The couple becomes embroiled in an international assassination plot, their son is kidnapped to ensure their cooperation, and the wife has to be heavily tranquilized in order to deal with this sudden loss of security.[53] *The Wrong Man* (1956) tells the true story of a man's world collapsing when he is wrongly accused, arrested, and tried for a crime committed by a criminal "double." He learns the horrifying fallacy of the police claim that "an innocent man has nothing to fear" when his wife suffers a complete breakdown under the pressure. The psychiatrist tells him that his wife is lost in a "maze of terror": "She knows she's in a nightmare, but it doesn't help her to know."[54]

When the innocent man is finally cleared, he goes joyously to the mental institution to tell his wife that "this awful nightmare we've been through, it's all over!" He hopes for a sudden cure with this good news, but his wife is unresponsive. She regards her husband and the world with the kind of blank, emotionally dislocated stare that was steadily becoming the trademark of this age of anxiety.

Empty and lifeless eyes that registered the emotional disintegration of living in a nightmarish world peered out from the art work of George Tooker and from the films of Alfred Hitchcock, but the classic 1950s science fiction films provided perhaps the most spellbinding imagery of the community disruption and dehumanization that characterized life in the atomic age. While Hitchcock films and other dramatic motion pictures revealed a violent and uncertain world in which paranoia or fear could be considered "normal" reactions to the amorphous and often unrecognized dangers to family and community relations, *Invaders from Mars* (1953) and *Invasion of the Body Snatchers* (1956) presented the metaphoric images that chillingly captured the surreal quality of debased human relations in this era that forcefully called for a human alertness against this growing dehumanization.[55]

Invaders from Mars begins with a quaint but modern family scene: at 4 A.M. young David and his scientist father are studying a nebula through their telescope when David's mother comes out to shoo them into bed. A little while later David looks out his window and sees a bomblike blast and flash of light and he witnesses the landing of a spaceship, which descends into a nearby sandpit. David rushes in and rouses his father, who assures him that it is "all your imagination," and David is sent back to bed. But David's father tells his wife that he will investigate—the area David pointed out is near the "secret plant" where the father works. When he has not returned by morning, his worried wife calls the police. The police search the sandpit and find evidence of David's father's presence, a dropped flashlight and shoe, but the police are suddenly sucked into the pit, presumably as David's father had been. David's father nonetheless soon reappears at home, but he seems a completely different man. He looks the same, but he is stern, grouchy, and hostile. His eyes are blank and his actions are robotic, and he strikes David when the boy asks about the strange puncture wound at the base of his neck. The policemen also return and they too have marks on their necks. The policemen and David's father plot conspiratorially, and David suspects that something horrible is happening at the sandpit. He watches the sandpit suck in people and spit them out mysteriously changed (his father soon takes his mother to the pit as well), and this confirms David's fear that something is "taking over" people, even though they retain their normal external appearance.

David frantically tries to find someone who will believe his fantastic tale. The people he warns think the boy's father ought to be called to deal with this clearly disturbed child. Horrified at this "threat," David goes to the police but notices that the police chief also has a mark on his neck. He retreats, only to be caught by another policeman, to whom he screams, "Please don't let my father get me!"[56] This policeman calls a doctor for this "really scared" kid, and after David checks the neck of this doctor and finds no mark, he tells her all about the pit and the changes it causes in people. After consulting with a scientist colleague from the secret plant who assures her that David is a bright and sane young boy, the doctor joins with David and the scientist to unravel the mystery of the pit. From the information provided by David and the scientist about the nature of the secret plant, they discover the truth: Martians have landed in the pit in order to sabotage the "atomic rocket" that is being constructed at the plant, an atomic rocket that will be used in space to destroy any potential attacker and that therefore constitutes a threat to Mars. According to the scientist, the Martians are acting in "self-defense"; they are taking over the minds of those involved in the rocket project in order to destroy the atomic device.

David, the scientist, and the doctor decide the Martian spaceship must be destroyed. They realize the once-human automatons can be saved by surgically removing their neck implants (before they explode and kill the implantee), and David's parents are reclaimed by this surgery. They then gather military help and place explosives in and around the pit and the spaceship. After a terrifying struggle with the Martians inside the ship (into which they had been sucked), they manage to escape and await the explosion. Just when it seems the ship will get away undamaged, the explosion goes off and engulfs the ship. At this moment, though, David wakes up—this has all been a horrible nightmare. He rushes to his parents and rouses them to see if they are all right. They convince him that he has been dreaming, that they are fine. David returns to his room. But this action begins an exact repetition of the scene that had begun the film and David's nightmare. As he looks out his window a little after 4:00 A.M., he witnesses the arrival of a spaceship in the sandpit.

The circularity of the plot of Invaders from Mars suggests that young David is forever trapped in this nightmare world of Martian invaders, secret atomic rockets, and dehumanized automatons, doomed to awaken to danger only to have his parents ignore his warnings. Even if this frightening scenario exists only in David's fertile imagination, David's life and dreams have nonetheless been disrupted by the fear of atomic attack and invasion which threatened the security of all Americans. The Martian-created zombies that were mere shadows of their human counterparts resembled the brutal and emotionless communist infiltrators of the cold war American imagination, but those who suffered this dehumanization were also those most closely associated with the secret atomic rocket so potentially destructive of human life. Deadened to the inhumanity of their technology and partakers in the secrecy that the development of this technology required, these dehumanized atomic workers served as age of anxiety symbols for the diminishing quality of human life and human relations. David's fright and hysteria were signs of his rebellion against this danger to humanity, signals of his reluctance to ignore this threat to his family and the community at large.

Like *Invaders from Mars, Invasion of the Body Snatchers* presents its story in circular fashion. The film begins and ends with a distraught Dr. Miles Bennell in a hospital loudly protesting his sanity to a psychiatrist: "Will you tell these fools I'm not crazy before it's too late. . . . *I am not insane!*"[57] In the interval between these hospital scenes of Miles's panic, he is allowed to explain how he ended up in this hospital being examined by a psychiatrist. His tale of the horror that destroyed the community of his hometown Santa Mira unfolds in an extended flashback. Miles recounts that he had been out of town and that when he returned the town was in the midst of some sort of "mass hysteria." His nurse and receptionist inform him of the many patients anxious to see him, and Miles soon discovers the bizarre nature of their complaints. Young Jimmy Grimaldi is brought to see Miles because he is hysterical—he does not believe his mother is his mother and he screams, "Don't let her get me!" Miles sedates Jimmy and sends him with his grandmother for the rest that will supposedly calm his "delusion." Miles's ex-flame Becky has also recently returned home (both she and Miles have been recently divorced from their spouses, offering yet more cultural evidence of the contemporary destruction of relationships), and she informs Miles of her cousin Wilma's similar delusion that Uncle Ira is not Uncle Ira. Miles goes to see Becky's cousin, who discusses the change in Uncle Ira: "There's something missing. . . . No emotion, none—just the pretense of it." Even though Miles considers this spreading delusion as rather strange and inexplicable, he nonetheless tells Wilma that "the trouble is inside you." He recommends she visit a psychiatrist.

Wilma asks, "Miles, am I going crazy?" He reassures her that "even these days it isn't as easy to go crazy as you might think," but the anxiety of the age seems the only reasonable explanation for this epidemic of madness. Miles and Becky run into the town psychiatrist later that evening, and he suggests that this "strange neurosis" and "epidemic mass hysteria" are the result of worrying, "worry about what's going on in the world, probably." Even though the outbreak of mass hysteria is seen as somehow "normal" for 1950s Americans,

Miles and Becky become increasingly suspicious about the real cause of this sudden insanity in Santa Mira. Their suspicions are confirmed when Miles's friends Jack and Teddy call him to examine a "body" found in their house. When this lifeless body starts to take on life and the characteristics of Jack as he falls asleep, the two couples piece together what is happening: strange pods adopt the external forms of the humans they replace while the humans sleep, thus explaining the "hysteria" about people not being who they really are and suddenly changing overnight.

As the two couples attempt to alert authorities to this menace, they realize a conspiracy is afoot. Those already taken over by the pods are spreading the takeover—placing pods near their friends and relatives to facilitate the change and protecting themselves against those who suspect the truth. Miles and the others are isolated in a Santa Mira almost completely invaded by the pod people, and they determine to escape and to obtain outside help. They congregate at Miles's house to plan their escape, and Miles speculates on the pods' origins: "So much has been discovered in these past few years that anything is possible. It may be the result of atomic radiation on plant life or animal life. Some weird alien organism. A mutation of some kind. It's fantastically powerful, beyond any comprehension, malignant." What they do recognize is the destruction of human life and love, caring and compassion. Those "podified" have lost the capacity to feel anything, and they are driven to make all others exactly like them. The podified town closes in on these four, stopping them from phoning for help or from fleeing. Pods are being placed near them at every opportunity, so the four take to running, each couple trying a different escape route.

In the midst of relentless pursuit by the pod people, Miles and Becky share a calm moment in hiding. They must prod each other to stay awake, however, for sleeping means waking up as "something evil and inhuman." Miles philosophically discusses how this takeover has only speeded up the process of dehumanization he has already witnessed. He tells Becky, "In my practice, I've seen how people have allowed their humanity to drain away. Only it happened slowly, instead of all at once. They didn't seem to mind." When Becky says, "But just some people, Miles," Miles corrects her: "All of us, a little bit. We harden our hearts, grow callous. Only when we have to fight to stay human do we realize how precious it is to us, how dear." The need to fight for their humanity becomes even more imperative as they witness the townspeople preparing to export pods all over the country. Miles is horrified: "It's a malignant disease spreading through the whole country." Even Jack and Teddy have succumbed, and the podified Jack helps the others to capture Miles and Becky.

They try to convince them to give in to the pods and their tranquillity. The podified psychiatrist argues that "less than a month ago, people were nothing but problems. Then, out of the sky came a solution." The seed pods had drifted in from outer space and taken root in a farmer's field, and those already transformed celebrate the fact: "You're reborn into an untroubled world."

Miles rebels against this defeatist philosophy and notes that this untroubled world is one in which "everyone is the same. What a world." He objects to losing his human capacity for love when the psychiatrist explains the "benefits" of "podism": "There's no need for love. . . . Love, desire, ambition, faith. Without them, life's so simple." Miles and Becky fight and escape, running for the highway and for access to the outside world. Sirens go off warning the podified town to chase down these two threats, and hundreds of podified townspeople mechanically pursue Becky and Miles. Miles and Becky elude them by ducking into a cave, but when Miles goes outside to check on the area, he comes back to a podified Becky who tries to seduce him into this human oblivion. Terrified at this last loss, Miles frantically dashes for the highway. On the highway, he screams at the cars and their drivers, "You fools! You're in danger! . . . They're here already! You're next, you're next!" The scene then shifts back to Miles at the hospital, still frantic, trying to convince others of his sanity. He yells, "Don't just sit there measuring me for a straitjacket, do something!" but the psychiatrist and the hospital aides are more inclined to fetch restraints. They believe Miles is insane—until they hear the news of a truck accident, in which strange pods had spilled all over the highway outside of Santa Mira. As the psychiatrist picks up the phone to inform and warn the FBI, relief floods Miles's face.

Unlike young David in *Invaders from Mars,* Miles is able to break out of his podified, insane world and find other humans who will heed his warnings of advancing dehumanization. Merging in *Invasion of the Body Snatchers* were the mainstream cultural fears of communist infiltration and the more rebellious but mirroring cultural fears of the deadened emotions and decaying humanism that were growing in conformist atomic age America. These pods that fell "out of the sky," perhaps products of "atomic radiation," resembled atomic and hydrogen bombs in their cigarlike shape, and they found easy prey in the symbolic small-town America of Santa Mira, in those sleepy Americans who neglected to fight for their humanity and who embraced the easy conformist and consensus solution offered in the "untroubled world" of podism. *Invasion of the Body Snatchers* promoted as preferable even the hysteria and panic Miles felt, his almost insane, solitary individuality, his crazed clinging to his capacity for human love. The human community of Santa Mira had forfeited its humanity for con-formism and emotional comfort, leaving only a nearly insane Miles Bennell to sound the alarm about America's weakening grasp on its humanity and to warn of America's lack of safety and security: "You fools! You're in danger!"[58]

Invaders from Mars and Invasion of the Body Snatchers dramatized the culture of dissent's recognition of the dangers menacing Americans in the atomic age. Paramount among these dangers was the disruption of a true community life. Insanity, emotional violence, betrayal, and a growing insensitivity to the dam-age wrought by living such an anxious and insecure life resulted in a schizoid society. In the culture of anxiety's America the double life of Americans found concrete representation in the many body doubles that appeared throughout these years, whether in the form of the apparently normal person who har-bored a psychopathic abnormality, the once sane and sentient individual who descended into quiet, colorless insanity, the living and feeling humans who mutated into brutal and emotionally blank zombies, or the diverse and caring members of a community who were converted into conformist, compassion-less, and dehumanized replicas of their former selves. Facing this army of som-nambulant Americans were the few remaining holdouts against this easier, emo-tionless life of debased conformism, and their voices of anguish were raised in rebellion against the madness.

While Invaders from Mars and Invasion of the Body Snatchers offered the most stunning metaphoric imagery of the "malignant disease" overspreading Amer-ica, an awareness of the cultural and psychological damage resulting from life in this era was not restricted to such products of popular culture. In articles writ-ten during these same years Lewis Mumford, one of America's most respected critics of society and culture, also warned of the insanity, the divisiveness, and the dehumanization that accompanied life in an increasingly scientific, tech-nological, and mechanical society and culture. His 1953 essay "Social Conse-quences of Atomic Energy" pointed to the dangerously schizoid and irrational nature of atomic age life:

The period in which we live is characterized by strange inner contradic-tions. . . . The most rational procedures of science now have as their end product in the human economy wholly irrational goals. . . . On one hand, our national government withholds from its citizens the knowledge needful to make sound judgments on military policy; but at the next moment the same authorities warn us that with the instruments now available, the price of victory in another war might be the extermination of the human race: a curious conception of military success. . . . And as long as our present knowledge continues to expand the sphere of the irrational and the pathologically automatic, the survival of man, to say nothing of his development, is plainly threatened.[59]

Mumford stressed equally Americans' lazy obliviousness to these irrational perils as part of the general threat to life. He noted: "The dangers of our present situation would not be so great had our responses to it been alert and timely. Even now, we should probably be able to mobilize enough political wisdom to provide a minimal basis for the necessary co-operations and safeguards, if only we could throw off the sleepwalker's insulation from reality that characterizes our collective conduct."[60] Mumford specifically argued here for an awakening among scientists as a first step toward "social responsibility and sanity," and he discussed the necessity of abandoning the scientific claim to objectivity, with its traditional lack of concern for the social consequences of its discoveries. He urged world scientists to pool knowledge and evaluate the moral and human consequences of atomic power before its application (actions they had not taken before they invented the atomic bomb and had not done with sufficient force afterward), because "cosmic power plus moral nihilism is, as Henry Adams had vigilantly predicted, a formula for general disintegration."[61]

In a 1956 piece, "Post-Historic Man," Mumford's sleepwalking imagery and Henry Adams-inspired fears of disintegration escalated into a vision of modern man that matched the dehumanized, robotic visions of man presented in *Invaders from Mars* and *Invasion of the Body Snatchers*. Mumford speculated on the end result, already partially visible, of civilization's continuing to develop along its "anti-organic" and "anti-historic" lines, lines represented by capitalism, mechanization, bureaucracy, and totalitarian government, lines leading toward the rule of "deliberately depersonalized intelligence" and toward the reign of post-historic man: a creature immune to desire, a creature bent on death and destruction.[62] Mumford indicated how the modern era was rushing toward its posthistoricism and how man was rapidly coming to resemble the machine, which already symbolized the loss of his more human and instinctual nature:

During the present era . . . man's nature has begun to undergo a decisive final change. With the invention of the scientific method and the depersonalized procedures of modern technics, cold intelligence, which has succeeded as never before in commanding the energies of nature, already largely dominates every human activity. To survive in this world, man himself must adapt himself completely to the machine. Nonadaptable types, like the artist and the poet, the saint and the peasant, will either be made over or eliminated by social selection. All the creativities associated with

Old World religion and culture will disappear. To become more human, to explore further into the depths of man's nature, to pursue the divine, are no longer proper goals for machine-made man.[63]

According to Mumford, the most convincing evidence of the coming of post-historic man was the evolution of modern war "into systematic and unrestricted extermination: in other words, genocide." He asked: "Is it an accident indeed that all the triumphs that point to the emergence of post-historic man are triumphs of death?" And he decided: "The will to deny the activities of life, above all, to deny the possibility of its development, dominates this ideology; so that collective genocide or suicide is the goal of the effort." The supreme symbol for the achievement of intelligence and for this impulse toward genocide/suicide, of course, was the splitting of the atom: "But to what end was this consummate feat of the intelligence directed? What in fact prompted the final decision that enabled man to start the process of atomic fission? We all know the answer too well: its object was the production of an instrument of large-scale destruction and extermination."[64]

The ramifications of this posthistoric lust for the machine, for human death and disintegration, on society and culture found reflection in the rapid declension of human diversity and desire. Uniformity and monotony constituted the goals of a mechanized society, and therefore the wildness and individuality of both nature and humanity became victims to a taming control and standardization. The urbanization of America produced such a controlled environment, according to Mumford, and his description of "uniform man" seemed evocative of those 1950s Americans seeking to escape their problems in conformity in suburbia:

If the goal of human history is a uniform type of man, reproducing at a uniform rate, in a uniform environment, kept at constant temperature, pressure, and humidity, living a uniformly lifeless existence, with his uniform physical needs satisfied by uniform goods, all inner waywardness brought into conformity by hypnotics and sedatives, or by surgical extirpations, a creature under constant mechanical pressure from incubator to incinerator, most problems of human development would disappear.[65]

In a posthistoric society all human problems, indeed all signs of humanity, would disappear, for in such a society "man becomes a machine," forced to strip himself of all human attributes, because "all his past achievements and memories, all his urges and hopes, all his anxieties and ideals, stand in the way of this transformation." Mumford saw this transmutation to posthistoric man as well on its way in American society:

Sympathy and empathy, the ability to participate with imagination and love in the lives of other men, have no place in the post-historic methodology; for post-historic culture demands that all men should be treated as things. Humanly speaking, post-historic man is a defective, if not an active delinquent, in the end a potential monster. The pathological nature of his defect has been concealed by his high intelligence quotient. Disguised in commonplace ready-made clothes, seeming to express equally commonplace, matter-of-fact opinions, these monsters are already at work in present-day society. Their characteristic activities—such as their preparations for "ABC" warfare [atomic, biological, and chemical]—are as irrational as their actions are compulsive and automatic. The fact that the moral insanity if not the practical futility of these preparations has not produced a general human recoil is a sign of how far the development of post-historic society has already gone.[66]

Mumford made clear that what "is post-historic is also post-human."[67] While mainstream American society and culture did not recoil from the insanity of the atomic age, the culture of dissent—whether represented by Lewis Mumford, Alfred Hitchcock, or science fiction filmmakers—did rebel against the declining sanity and humanism of the era. Regardless of the real or metaphoric form given to these posthuman "monsters," the culture of dissent announced their presence in the culture of anxiety and measured their destruction or disruption of the psychological and physical security of Americans, if only in allusive and imaginary ways. The creative chaos and psychological disorder that distinguished the culture of dissent from the calm and complacent culture of Eisenhower's America challenged the dehumanizing conformity and unifying standardization demanded in an age of cold war consensus and reflected the darker reality of an America divided and disturbed by life in an anxious world. The culture of dissent pushed Americans to recognize the diminution of human values and relations resulting from their refusal to face reality. The culture also urged Americans to fight for their humanity and to feel the pain and panic appropriate to life in the atomic age.

five

WILD ONES

youths in revolt against adult America

"You're tearing me apart!"
—Rebel Without a Cause *(1955)*

he one group of postwar Americans least able to deny reality and to block out their fears were the young of America, those children and young adults, like David in *Invaders from Mars* and Holden Caulfield in *The Catcher in the Rye,* who were emotionally and psychologically susceptible to atomic nightmares and atomic insecurities. By focusing on the psychological troubles of America's young and by highlighting the social deviance and rebelliousness of American youth, the culture of dissent illuminated the social and psychological disruption that characterized life in the age of anxiety. The prevalence of youthful discontent called into question the efficacy of the "psychological fortress" built by American families during the cold war.

The existence of wild and rebellious youth undermined the hopes that parents and the larger cold war culture had for their children and themselves. Children and parenthood had gained stature and responsibility in the atomic age, at least according to one observer. In a 1946 article for *American Home* Louisa Randall Church stressed the new significance of parenthood and children in this era:

> On that day in August 1945, when the first atomic bomb fell on Hiroshima, new concepts of civilized living, based on the obligations of world citizenship . . . were born. Out of the smoke and smoldering ruins arose a great cry for leadership equipped to guide the stricken people of the world along the hazardous course toward peace. On that day parenthood took on added responsibilities of deep and profound significance. . . . Surely, in all history, the parents of the world were never so challenged! However, there is a defense—an impregnable bulwark—which lies in meeting the world's desperate cry for leadership. Upon the shoulders of parents, everywhere,

rests the tremendous responsibility of sending forth into the next generation men and women imbued with a high resolve to work together for
everlasting peace. . . . The new philosophy of child guidance makes of
parenthood not a dull, monotonous routine job, but an absorbing, creative
profession—a career second to none.[1]

In *Homeward Bound* Elaine Tyler May commented on Church's point of view
and its significance in the cold war years, and at the same time she elaborated
on the meaning of children and parenthood in this era. According to May, "procreation in the cold war era took on almost mythic proportions. The writer
[Church] . . . articulated the fundamental principle of postwar parenthood:
children were a 'defense—an impregnable bulwark'—against the terrors of the
age. For the nation, the next generation symbolized hope for the future."[2]

Continuing her analysis, May made clear just how many expectations were
attached to children and parenthood in America:

But for individuals, parenthood was much more than a duty to posterity;
the joys of raising children would compensate for thwarted expectations in
other areas of their lives. For men who were frustrated at work, for women
who were bored at home, and for both who were dissatisfied with the
unfulfilled promise of sexual excitement, children might fill the void.
Through children, men and women could set aside the difficulties of their
sexual relationships and celebrate the procreative results. In so doing, they
also demonstrated their loyalty to national goals by having as many children
as they could "raise right and educate and be a benefit to the world," in the
words of one postwar father. Rather than expressing a retreat into private
life, procreation was one way to express civic values.[3]

Children thus appeared as an integral part of domestic containment and the
presumed security and comfort that it brought—to both parents and the nation. If children were meant to embody such weighty expectations and if parenthood was meant to be one of the most profound responsibilities of the
atomic age, then cold war American society may have been sorely tested by its
children's and its parents' inability to live up to such expectations.

In the counterculture, the children so presumably secure in these middle-
class suburban homes dedicated to civic values were in actuality disaffected,
alienated, and critical of the world their parents' generation had created. In
other words, the young were not so much a bulwark against the terrors of the
atomic age but rather were mirrors for the very terrors and familial divisions
that clouded life in this era. While still a clearly minority voice in cold war

America, rebel and delinquent youth exposed yet another growing division in the culture and society of this schizoid era, a generational split that represented the further disintegration of the American consensus. Those who were least able to protect themselves from the madness and dangers of the age, however, were also those most mentally and morally capable of assessing and expressing the disunity and discontent that belied the calm sanity and unified complacence of Eisenhower's older America.

By the mid-1950s the culture of dissent had documented the extensive psychological disturbance and community disintegration that characterized life in this age. In these same years the culture demonstrated how America's children also became victims of the era's insanity and hysteria. Madness crossed generational lines, and portraits of disturbed and violent children revealed an awareness of the spreading moral and psychological corruption of a society that offered little protection or sanctuary for its young. William March's 1954 novel *The Bad Seed* (also made into a popular 1954 play and 1956 film) and the 1956 film *Storm Center* telescoped not only the culture's concern about the inability of parents to protect their children from danger but also the culture's rising fear that parents (and the world they had created) were responsible for the danger and the madness that destroyed their children's peace of mind. By the mid-1950s even children came to resemble the inhuman monsters that so metaphorically symbolized the damage wrought by living in the atomic age.

In *The Bad Seed* eight-year-old Rhoda Penmark's mask of sweetness is torn away to reveal a truly amoral character. This story of a child's criminality and deviance revolves around the debate in psychology and criminology about the origins of evil: is it inherited or a product of the environment? The case is made in *The Bad Seed* for genetics—Rhoda appears to have inherited "the bad seed" from her mother's mother, who also began her career as a mass murderer in her youth. Still, the 1950s American environment seems to have shaped Rhoda's psychological and moral imbalances. In this era of mass consumption and extravagant materialism Rhoda is greedy and envious of others' possessions; her most sincere revelation of character, otherwise hidden beneath a well-mannered appearance of childish innocence, occurs in what her mother calls "Rhoda's acquisitive look."[4] The action in the novel begins at the end of the school year and Rhoda has just learned that she has not won the school penmanship medal. Her fury and selfishness begin to emerge: "I don't see why Claude Daigle got the medal. It was mine. Everybody knew it was mine . . . It was mine . . . The medal was mine . . . It was mine . . . The medal was mine."[5]

Rhoda's mother Christine finds such aspects of Rhoda's behavior disturbing—along with Rhoda's too perfect, too controlled, and too mature actions—

and she accompanies Rhoda to the school picnic in order to talk to Rhoda's teachers. The teachers are unwilling to let Mrs. Penmark know just how feared Rhoda is at school, and Christine leaves Rhoda at the picnic without having her concerns calmed. As she leaves, she overhears the conversation of two men on the street, and their evaluation of the age seems to set the stage for Rhoda's emergent evil:

"I was reading the other day," said the taller of the two, "that the age we live in is an age of anxiety. You know what? I thought that was pretty good—a pretty fair judgment. I told Ruth about it when I got home, and she said, 'You can say *that* again!'"

"Every age that people live in is an age of anxiety," said the other man. "If anybody asks me, I'd say the age we live in is an age of violence. It looks to me like violence is in everybody's mind these days. It looks like we're just going to keep on until there's nothing left to ruin. If you stop and think about it, it scares you."

"Well, maybe we live in an age of anxiety *and* violence."

"Now, that sounds more like it. Come to think about it, I guess that's what our age is really like."[6]

Christine ruminates on this conversation and appears to come to a partial understanding of Rhoda's and the world's essential ailment: "It seemed to her suddenly that violence was an inescapable thing that lay, like a bad seed, behind kindness, behind compassion, behind the embrace of love itself. Sometimes it lay deeply hidden, sometimes it lay close to the surface; but always it was there, ready to appear, under the right circumstances, in all its irrational dreadfulness."[7] Christine's husband is out of town, so when she comes to terms with Rhoda's violence, she has to do it on her own. In the meantime, she spends time with her friends and neighbors, Monica and Emory Breedlove, an aging sister-brother team who represent the culture's obsessions with psychology and death. Monica psychoanalyzes everyone (including the apartment building janitor Leroy, whom she pegs as "a schizophrenic with well-defined paranoid overtones"), and Emory and his friend Reginald Tasker, a crime writer, constantly discuss brutal and ingenious mass murderers. At lunch with these three, after facing a barrage of psychological questions and listening to information on infamous criminals, Christine falls into a state of reverie about Rhoda's "oddities" and her own vague past.[8]

Christine recalls the many problems she has had with Rhoda and she lists

Rhoda's deficiencies: she is "a fluent and most convincing liar," she is "a thief," she has "no capacity for affection, either, being concerned only with herself," and she is the embodiment of greed: "But perhaps the thing that was most remarkable about her was her unending acquisitiveness. She was like a charming little animal that can never be trained to fit into conventional patterns of existence."[9] Besides worrying about Rhoda, Christine worries over her own past and her distant memories of some dread. She discovers with some investigation that she was adopted and that in reality she is the only living relative, the daughter, of an unrepentant and cold-hearted killer. This knowledge of her past makes her feel responsible for Rhoda's crimes, which she soon discovers. She had passed on "the bad seed" of violence to Rhoda. The fertility of Rhoda's bad seed becomes immediately apparent as Christine's reveries are broken by a radio news report about a child's death at the school picnic—Claude Daigle, winner of the coveted penmanship medal, had drowned in a lake near the picnic site.

While Christine is reluctant to admit the depths of Rhoda's violence and greed, she soon uncovers the truth. At first upset at Rhoda's exposure to death at such a young age, Christine then notes Rhoda's callousness about Claude's death. Rhoda comments to the janitor Leroy, "Why should I feel sorry? It was Claude Daigle got drowned, not me." Other hints of Rhoda's responsibility in Claude's death soon arise.[10] School officials indicate some involvement on the part of Rhoda, who had badgered Claude about the penmanship medal throughout the picnic, and they ask that Rhoda not return to their school. Christine now has grave suspicions about her daughter, even though Monica Breedlove tries to brush off Rhoda's dismissal from school with a defense of Rhoda's nonconformity: "The truth of the matter is, Rhoda is much too charming, too clever, too unusual for them! She isn't like those simpering little neurotics who believe everything that's told them, and never have an original thought of their own."[11] But Christine knows of the violent underside of Rhoda's "nonconformity," and she recalls past incidents of death involving Rhoda (as the only witness)—Rhoda had thrown a puppy out of a window (she said it accidentally fell) and had stayed "dispassionately watching" the dying dog from the window, and Rhoda alone had witnessed the "accidental" death of a neighbor, an old woman who had promised to leave Rhoda a coveted crystal ball in her will.[12] When Christine finds the penmanship medal in Rhoda's room, she realizes that her daughter is a murderer. None of these deaths had been accidents.

Christine confronts Rhoda with the medal and Rhoda finally admits to killing Claude as well as the old woman. In her sickly sweet manner Rhoda cajoles her mother, "Oh, I've got the prettiest mother! I've got the nicest mother!" and she pleads with her not to let anyone hurt her. Horrified, guilt-stricken, and increasingly unnerved, Christine tells Rhoda she will protect her—she feels it her parental duty "to protect her against the cruelty of the world"—but she is trying to formulate some way to end Rhoda's reign of terror.[13] In the meantime, Leroy has been taunting Rhoda about Claude's death, and when he stumbles onto the truth, Rhoda kills him by setting fire to the basement room where he sometimes slept. Unhinged by Rhoda's remorseless murderous impulses, Christine decides to put a decisive stop to it all: she will kill Rhoda and then herself. She destroys the collected evidence of her past and Rhoda's crimes so as not to corrupt and ruin her husband; she gives Rhoda an overdose of sleeping pills and then blows her brains out with her husband's gun.

Rhoda, however, does not die. Neighbors had tried to get in touch with Christine and Rhoda for a worried Monica Breedlove, who had then come over to check on them. They broke in and rushed Rhoda to a hospital. Her father returns home, but he cannot comprehend why Christine did such a thing. Neither can the neighbors, who comment of Rhoda, "She's such an innocent child in many ways." They comfort Mr. Penmark with the fact that "at least Rhoda was spared. You still have Rhoda to be thankful for."[14] Rhoda is alive and free, secure in large part because of her effective disguise as an innocent child. When investigating the phenomenon of mass murderers, Christine had talked with crime writer Reginald Tasker, who warned her against being fooled by a "normal" veneer: "The normal are inclined to visualize the multiple killer as one who's as monstrous in appearance as he is in mind, which is about as far from the truth as one could well get. He paused and then said that these monsters of real life usually looked and behaved in a more normal manner than their actually normal brothers and sisters."[15] Christine had learned to see the monster in Rhoda, but that clear vision died with her, leaving her "bad seed" still comfortably disguised and able to pursue her monstrous desires.

Even though Rhoda had inherited her evil from the older generation, that evil manifested itself in a deadly material greed that seemed to fit the affluent age in which she lived. In the film *Storm Center* the environment of modern society is clearly indicted for a young boy's madness. But he too inherited his deviance from his father and from the entire adult community that promulgated the repressiveness of the cold war era. *Storm Center* presented a cold war parable about the evil ramifications of America's anticommunist hysteria, particularly its disruption of any democratic community spirit and its poisoning of young minds with hate and violence. The film focuses on the experiences of a small town librarian, Mrs. Hull, and her favorite young customer, Fred Slater, once the city council orders that a book—*The Communist Dream*—be taken from the library's shelves.[16]

Both Mrs. Hull's and Fred's love of books is well established at the beginning of the film. Mrs. Hull was responsible for getting the library built twenty-five years ago, and she tells young Fred, who spends most of his time at the library reading, that "the secrets of the world are on these shelves and they're all yours to discover." Fred's intellectualism becomes especially apparent at home, where, with his face buried in books, he endures the condemnation of his ignorant, anti-intellectual father. Fred's father likes beer, not books, and he is annoyed at having a son who "stuffs himself with words." Mr. Slater grabs a library book from Fred's hands and tears it in the process. When he goes to Mrs. Hull to explain, he complains about Fred's excessive reading—he wants a son who will play baseball instead. Mrs. Hull defends Fred and his intelligence and distinctiveness, and she urges Mr. Slater to "value that difference. We put far too much stress on conformity in this country."

Mrs. Hull learns just how much stress on conformity there is when she is asked by the city council to remove *The Communist Dream* from the library. The council calls it "pure Red propaganda" and the council members tell her of citizen complaints they have received about the book. She agrees that it is "a preposterous book," but she points out its value in showing readers just how preposterous communism is. She refuses on principle to remove any book. They tempt her with the promise of a new children's wing for the library, so she reluctantly agrees to remove the book. When actually faced with doing so, however, she changes her mind and keeps the book in the library, defending her action to the council in an impassioned argument against censorship. They ask her, "What do you want to do, turn the library into a propaganda agency for the Kremlin?" She responds with a plea to keep America different from the Soviet Union: "Tell me, would they dare keep a book praising democracy in a Russian library?"

In the face of her refusal to remove the book, the young firebrand on the council, Mr. Duncan, gets tough in his questioning of her: "Are you familiar with the Council for Better Relations with the Soviet Union? . . . the American Peace Mobilization? . . . the Voice of Freedom Committee?" Mrs. Hull admits having joined these organizations during the war, and Duncan smears Mrs. Hull as a participant in "communist front" organizations. Mrs. Hull reacts: "I resent your questions and your implications. . . . I am not a communist. I never was a communist. I detest communism." Mr. Duncan persists. He claims, "I didn't say you were a communist," but he insists, "You were a dupe once, you could very well be again." By tainting Mrs. Hull's liberal past, Mr. Duncan succeeds in frightening the council. The council members are worried about reelection, and Duncan's anticommunist hysteria about Mrs. Hull and his insistence on the removal of *The Communist Dream* persuade the council to act. The council fires Mrs. Hull, who is then ostracized by almost the entire community. Young Fred is distraught and confused at losing his friend and librarian, and in his confusion he becomes susceptible to the anticommunist cant of his father. When Fred's sympathetic mother explains his distress—he feels "betrayed" by Mrs. Hull—Fred's father condemns Mrs. Hull: "That's right. She did. She betrayed everybody. . . . She belonged to a dozen commie outfits, it said so right in the paper. . . . She even gave me some of that pinko talk—too much conformity in this country!"

Fred, like the rest of the community, is succumbing to hate and hysteria. Martha, Mrs. Hull's old assistant at the library and also the fiancée of Mr. Duncan, visits Mrs. Hull for advice about the now "strange and hostile" Fred. Mrs. Hull blames the repressive atmosphere of the town, noting how "frightening" it is that Fred's love of books has turned to hate under the pressure. Martha is beginning to feel the guilt and evil of what has happened, and her disgust grows as the anticommunist hysteria grows. Duncan decides to run for higher political office in the state legislature on his anticommunist, anti-Mrs. Hull platform. He discusses his designs with a group of people at a club, and while one young woman defends Mrs. Hull (she has difficulty picturing this elderly librarian as "a beaver working for the Kremlin"), another woman speaks for the community when she supports the anticommunist cause: "After all . . . we can't be blind to what's going on. H-bombs, brainwashing, boys like Sam here still being drafted, their careers interrupted." Nonetheless, a small contingent in the community is starting to regret its treatment of Mrs. Hull, a regret that will spread when the hate being fomented in Fred explodes.

Fred is having nightmares, visions of snakes coming out of books and Mrs. Hull yelling. His father explains to Fred that dreams come from somewhere— he thinks Mrs. Hull and the books she gave Fred poisoned him. He tells Fred that she worked for years "to fill those shelves with poison" and that all "they" want is to "smash and destroy, smash everything we've ever built up in this country." Having absorbed this hateful message, Fred screams hysterically at Mrs. Hull when he encounters her at a public ceremony: "You're a communist! You don't belong here!" The townspeople and some of the councillors begin to feel shamed by this outburst by a child, especially when as a consequence of the hysteria and repression the disturbed Fred sneaks into the library and sets it on fire. As the community watches the library go up in flames (the camera lingering on the destruction of revered classics, including Shakespeare and "The Story of Jesus"), Martha turns in disdain from her ex-fiancé Mr. Duncan, ridiculing his earlier claims that no damage came from his brand of politics. She succinctly sums up the destruction: "One little boy was turned into a lunatic." The films ends as a vehement and fist-clenching Mrs. Hull, returned to her post, vows to rebuild an inviolate library: "And if anybody ever again tries to remove a book from it, he'll have to do it *over my dead body.*"

Such portraits of violent and deviant children were perhaps reflective of an older generation's guilt about the unsafe world it had willed to its unprotected children, but these images of children joining the parade of "inhuman monsters" that inhabited the culture of anxiety began to take on slightly different connotations as America's young took a more active and vocal stance in America's culture of dissent. While revealing the culture's generalized concerns for the anxiety that damaged even the children in atomic age America, these culturally symbolic deviant children also signaled the emergence of uncontrollable and nonconformist youths disdainful of their parents' world.

While Rhoda in *The Bad Seed* and Fred in *Storm Center* turned into monsters of destruction, they did not resemble the silent, deadened adult monsters of cold war culture. The deviant children screamed their discontent and acted out their disturbance; they broke through the boundaries of conventional behavior and they squirmed out from under parental and societal control. Few of the culture's anarchic youth compared in intensity with the warped Rhoda and Fred, but the delinquents and rebels who appeared with greater regularity in the mid- and late fifties did contest the conformist values of their parents and society at large. In the cultural expressions produced by, for, and about the expanding youthful population of America, young Americans were pictured in pursuit of a more creative alternative to the older generation's apathy and social irresponsibility. Looking into the deadened and dehumanized stares of their elders, the eyes of the young brimmed with emotion—love, hate, despair, even pain. Young Americans reaching adolescence and young adulthood by the later 1950s fought for their humanity; their fight often lacked coherence and consistency, but from this creative disunity came an enlivening challenge to the sterile cold war values that had drained that elder America of its spiritual and mental health.

The flowering of deviant youth culture took place in the mid-1950s, but throughout the early postwar years the counterculture emitted signs of a nascent conflict between the older and younger generations in America. In a variety of films, dramas, and novels the young not only recognized the failings of an older generation's ideas but also rejected the values of their elders, often in violent, cruel, and self-destructive ways. An emergent delinquent youth culture had begun to form in the years following World War II, and films like *Red River* (1948) focused attention on the generational battle of wills and on the distinctively different character of the young. The story of the first cattle drive on the Chisholm Trail provides the setting for a contest of leadership between cattleman Thomas Dunson and his younger partner (whom he had raised as a son), Matthew Garth. Dunson's brutal and authoritarian manner contrasts with Matt's more compassionate and reasoned outlook, and Matt ultimately wins the loyalty of the men and ensures the success of the cattle drive by virtue of his restraint and kind-heartedness. When the angry Dunson catches up with Matt, Matt refuses to draw his gun, and the force of Matt's "too soft" heart—his love—triumphs over Dunson's violence, and the two are reconciled.[17]

As portrayed by the young Montgomery Clift, Matthew Garth introduced emotional and vulnerable character traits to the traditionally strong and unbending male role. This youthful challenge to the hardened emotions and violent strength of older authority figures (the superpatriot and ultraconservative John Wayne played Thomas Dunson) persisted and intensified in the 1950s, as did the growing association of the young actors with their rebellious and compassionate characters. In *The Boy with Green Hair* (1948) another youth fights the destructiveness of his elders and the violence of the world with his unconventional message of peace. This American boy had been left a war orphan when both his parents were killed doing war work in London. One day he wakes up to find his hair has turned green. He is confused by this transformation and suffers the derision and suspicions of all around him until he learns the reason for his green hair. He has a vision in which war orphans from all around the world praise his hair as a symbol of spring and hope and convince him that his hair gives him the notoriety necessary for delivering the message of all war orphans: that war is bad for children. The orphans beg him to tell everyone, Russians and Americans, to make no more war, and no more war orphans.[18]

Spurred by this vision, the boy takes pride in his hair and begins to deliver his message of peace. The community around him becomes uncomfortable; the boy's grandfather finally succumbs to the town's pressures and takes the boy to have his green locks shorn. The boy stoically submits, but as his hair is cut, tears roll down his cheeks. Those watching the haircut grow solemn, as if witnessing a crime, and the mortified grandfather admits: "I feel ashamed." Angry at the betrayal and cynicism of those around him, the boy runs away, but he finally decides to carry on his fight, to make people believe. His grandfather finds him and brings him home to wait for his green hair and its message of peace to regrow.[19]

Not all young rebels were so idealistic and pacifistic, however, and in *Rope* (1948) two young men express their disgust for societal values through murder and Nietzschean nihilism.[20] These two brilliant intellectuals commit murder in order to demonstrate that "murder can be art too," that "the power to kill" involves creativity and artistry. They strangle their friend David with a piece of rope, and the act makes them feel "alive." Considering themselves far above "ordinary men," they do not feel bound by conventional law and morality, and these two young men demonstrate the sickness that could be expressed in a half-deadened society that made feeling alive difficult. After strangling David, the dominant member of the duo notes that "the Davids of this world merely occupy space. . . . But he was a Harvard undergraduate, maybe that makes it justifiable homicide." They then stuff David's body in a large chest and serve dinner and drinks from the covered chest to the victim's friends and relatives arriving for a prearranged party. The "artistry" of their murder is destroyed when their crime is discovered by one of their guests, but the use of violence as a means to break through the timid conventionality and apathy of the age lived on in the culture of dissent.

Extreme and often violent emotional and physical outbursts by the young seemed one of the few effective ways to shatter the complacence of older America. Arthur Miller's *Death of a Salesman* (1949) charts the demise of Willy Loman, but it also traces the devastating generational confrontation between Willy and his son Biff. Biff embodies many of Willy's hopes and dreams for the future; he had been a high school football star and the light of Willy Loman's life, but Biff has not fulfilled his potential. Willy continues to place faith in Biff, but even he recognizes the truth in his moments of lucidity: "Biff Loman is lost. In the greatest country in the world a young man with such—personal attractiveness, gets lost."[21] The truth Willy cannot quite face is his own role in Biff's failures.

Willy had so filled young Biff with his grandiose dreams and expectations that Biff's whole world fell apart when he discovered Willy's betrayal of their mother and the family dreams. On the verge of going to college on a football scholarship, Biff unexpectedly follows Willy on one of his sales trips to Boston and finds his father with a woman in his hotel room. Dazed by his father's perfidy and unmoved by his father's plea of loneliness, Biff stands there weeping, his love, respect, and faith crushed: "Don't touch me, you—liar! . . . You fake! You phony little fake! You fake!"[22] Biff drops out of school and life, living a purposeless life of low-paying menial jobs and minor criminal acts. Biff had rebelled against Willy's phony values and had realized the emptiness of Willy's dreams, and now, home years later, he tries to get Willy to see the truth behind all the delusions that Willy has maintained despite Biff's slap in his face. Biff simply wants Willy to acknowledge, as Biff has, Biff's nothingness. Willy comes to see the centrality of his Boston affair in ruining his son's life, but he bristles against taking the blame and he accuses Biff of "spite." In return Biff attacks all of Willy's delusions:

> Pop! I'm a dime a dozen, and so are you! . . . I am not a leader of men, Willy, and neither are you. You were never anything but a hard-working drummer who landed in the ash can like all the rest of them! I'm one dollar an hour, Willy! I tried seven states and couldn't raise it. A buck an hour! Do you gather my meaning? I'm not bringing home any prizes any more, and you're going to stop waiting for me to bring them home! . . . Pop, I'm nothing! I'm nothing, Pop. Can't you understand that? There's no spite in it any more. I'm just what I am, that's all. . . . Will you let me go, for Christ's sake? Will you take that phony dream and burn it before something happens?[23]

Willy preferred death to the complete abandonment of his dreams, but his choice was firmly rejected by his son Biff. At Willy's funeral Biff concludes, "He had the wrong dreams. All, all, wrong." And a younger American generation came to agree with Biff's assessment of the phony and deluded dreams of that older American generation.[24] Holden Caulfield in *The Catcher in the Rye* likewise lost emotional and psychological control when trying to come to terms with the phoniness of the adult world; like Biff he wandered lost in a futureless world that seemed to offer only nervousness and nothingness. The youthful rebellion against the values of the older generation and against the conventional life of mainstream America increasingly reflected a sort of existential curiosity—and despair—about life's meaning and purpose. The youthful search for an alternative to this emptiness often entailed rebellion against all accepted values and all order and convention. Whether expressed in the vague criminality of a disillusioned Biff Loman or in the prescient insanity of an unhinged Holden Caulfield, the growing delinquency of America's youth exhibited an active alienation from the form and meaning of life prescribed by parents.

If the early 1950s witnessed the transition to the unfocused but all-encompassing rebellion of America's young, then the cultural attention to the rising "problem" of juvenile delinquency marked this shift. In Jim Thompson's 1953 novel *The Criminal* teenager Bob Talbert is accused of raping and murdering a girl from his suburban neighborhood. While his innocence or guilt is never clearly determined, his case betrays the community's fears about delinquent and disturbed youths. Bob's father makes clear the shocking ease with which unimaginable juvenile crime could enter one's life:

> You hear about some fifteen-year-old boy killing a neighbor's girl—raping and strangling her, and you think, well, I'm pretty well off after all. My boy may be a little wild but . . . *but Bob was never really wild; he was just all boy, I guess, just about average* . . . but my boy would never do a thing like that. That could never happen in our family. . . . Your wife couldn't turn gray overnight, and your fifteen-year-old couldn't do what that other fifteen-year-old did. The idea is so crazy that—well, you just laugh when you think about it. And then . . . [25]

The town newspaper decides, against accepted journalistic ethics in such cases, that "there's been too much hush-hush about these juvenile criminals. We've got to call a halt, and this is the ideal time to begin."[26] The reporter sent to collect information for this sensational story is wary of smearing a youngster, particularly when he goes to interview Bob and he recognizes how life has changed for the young:

> The kid was about on a par with a good many teenagers I've seen. They aren't watchful exactly. They aren't exactly sullen. There is rather a look of resigned hopefulness about them: they look as though no good can possibly come to them, albeit they would certainly welcome a little and are rightfully entitled to it. I do not recall that kids looked that way in my day. I think it must be the times, this age we live in, when the reasons for existence are lost in the struggle to exist.[27]

The reporter nonetheless does his job and discovers that almost everyone in town has a bad word for Bob Talbert and teenagers in general. The townspeople, including Bob's parents, display a willingness to believe a teenager capable of such a crime, and an employee in a soda fountain across from Bob's school sums up the community's attitudes about teens. According to the reporter, "The guy who ran [the soda fountain] was a cranky old bastard who was convinced that the younger generation was hell-bound on a handcar. No respect for their elders. . . . None of 'em were any good. Not a danged one."[28]

In this spiritually depleted world where "the reasons for existence are lost in the struggle to exist," American youths had begun to look for fulfillment in a variety of antisocial and deviant forms of behavior. The 1953 film *The Wild One* pictured this fifties transformation of rebel youth and presented the call-to-arms of young Americans discontented with the accepted norms and values of adult American society. The film, depicting a young motorcycle gang's rampage through a small town, warned in its opening, "This is a shocking story," but the portraits of these rebel youths—particularly Marlon Brando's portrayal of the leader Johnny—appealed to the growing restlessness of young Americans.[29] When the hoodlum members of the Black Rebels Motorcycle Club ride loudly and menacingly into this town, having just left the open road and yet another town where they had been "looking for trouble" with the "squares," they wreak havoc. In the local bar Johnny responds to the questions of a local girl and in doing so voices the new credo of the young. When she asks, "Where are you going after you leave here?" he responds in a manner that foreshadows the beat generation: "We're just gonna go . . . You just go . . . The idea is to have a ball." And when she wonders, "Hey Johnny, what are you rebelling against?" Johnny answers with the question being posed by many young Americans in the 1950s: "What've you got?"

The youthful impulse to go, to move, to seek something, and the young impetus for an all-encompassing rebellion infused the delinquent youth culture that expanded from the mid-1950s forward. Against the ordered purposeful-ness, the stasis, the silence of their elders, the young flaunted their mobility, their stridency, their emotionalism, and their search for a spiritual and existen-tial way out of an unfulfilling, ugly, unsafe world. Emblematic of the vocal and mobile expressions of youth was the new philosophical and musical "beat" that increasingly captured the tones of the youth culture's rejection of America's un-emotive stance in a troubled world. Two 1955 films announced the arrival of the forces that generated the emotional and spiritual charge of the young. In *Rebel Without a Cause* and *The Blackboard Jungle* delinquent youth culture em-braced the beat persona and morality (as exemplifed by James Dean) and the emergent rhythmic beat of rock 'n' roll music, both of which symbolized the spiritual and emotional awakening of the beat generation and rebel youth in general. The boundlessness of the rebellion reverberates in the title *Rebel With-out a Cause,* where the lack of motive portends a generalized malaise and dis-content with the nameless deficiencies of life. Nonetheless, parents and their values constitute the focal point of reaction in *Rebel Without a Cause*; the teen-agers protest the meaningless human relations that characterize the loveless, weak world of their elders. Of the three troubled young characters—Jim, Judy, and Plato—seventeen-year-old Jim Stark, portrayed by James Dean, most strik-ingly catches the angst and anger of the young. In an opening scene at the police station a drunk Jim mimics a police siren with a loud and despairing wail that exposes the inarticulate rage of the young.[30]

This early scene at the police station introduces the trio. It is late Easter night, and all three teenagers have been brought to see a juvenile officer for various infractions—Jim for public drunkenness, Judy for wandering around late at night, and Plato for shooting puppies. They are all suffering from alienation, loneliness, and a sense of betrayal and abandonment by their parents, and they are searching for love, belonging, and a sense of direction in life—which their parents are incapable of providing. Judy's father considers her a "dirty tramp," so she runs with a wild gang. Yet her discomfort is also tied directly to the era in which she lives. Judy's difficulty with her father—and by implication much youthful trouble with parents in general—is attributed to the troubled times of cold war America. When Judy leaves the dinner table distraught at yet another of her father's rejections of her affection, the father claims, "I don't know what to do. All of a sudden she's a problem." Judy's mother calms him, claiming, "She'll outgrow it. It's just the age." Judy's brother then interjects: "The atomic age!"

While all of the young characters in *Rebel* are affected by the atomic age, Plato's problems are the most severe and they speak to the failure of the family ideal in the 1950s. Plato's parents are divorced, his father has abandoned him, and his mother travels constantly, leaving the disturbed child in the care of a housekeeper. (The juvenile officer sincerely suggests that he see a psychiatrist.) Jim has become for his parents a convenient object of battle and an easy excuse for their problems, and his budding juvenile delinquency seems a venture into the manhood and emotional fulfillment he cannot find at home with his weak father and domineering mother.

When Jim's parents arrive to pick him up from the police station, their confrontation establishes the deepening divide between the generations in 1950s America. Unable to comprehend Jim's rebelliousness, his father wonders about the material and consumer comfort of his son, "Don't I give you everything you want?" When Jim coolly responds, "You buy me many things," he conveys the emptiness of the older generation's materialistic conception of security and fulfillment in which the more important emotional and psychological needs remain unmet. As his parents fall to bickering over him, Jim releases his torment in a flood of bitter and despairing emotion: *"You're tearing me apart!"* Finding none of the solace and guidance he needs, Jim has to work his own way free to love, meaningfulness, and adulthood, and *Rebel Without a Cause* centers on Jim's struggle to find a way to live in this troubled and lonely world.

Jim's family has just moved into a suburban neighborhood of Los Angeles and the next day is his first at a new high school. The test of his manhood and morality comes in his involvement with the tough gang at his school, the Wheels, the gang to which Judy belongs. On a field trip to a planetarium that day Jim becomes embroiled in a contest of courage with the gang's leader, Buzz; this more immediate danger is framed by the larger universal insecurities to life expressed in the lecture given at the planetarium. As the high school students sit in the dark watching the planetarium's visual representations of the universe and its eventual destruction, the lecturer speaks in terms that betoken the apocalyptic fears of the age:

> And while the flash of our beginning has not yet traveled the light years into distance, has not yet been seen by planets deep within the other galaxies, we will disappear into the blackness of the space from which we came, destroyed as we began in a burst of gas and fire. The heavens are still and cold once more. In all the complexity of our universe and the galaxies beyond, the Earth will not be missed. Through the infinite reaches of space, the problems of man seem trivial and naive indeed. And man, existing alone, seems to be an episode of little consequence.

Plato, sitting near Jim during this show, had ducked his head at the fearful images of annihilation, and a friendly and soothing Jim tells him, "Hey, it's all over. The world ended." Plato looks up at the planetarium lecturer and asks Jim: "What does he know about man alone?" But once outside, before they can deal with such a question, Buzz starts to heckle Jim and knifes a hole in one of the tires on Jim's car. Plato warns Jim about the Wheels, but Jim cannot ignore Buzz's action and the taunting about being "chicken." Jim and Buzz have a knife fight and Jim grudgingly earns a certain amount of respect from Buzz. They set up a later battle for that night—a chicken run in stolen cars. When Jim goes home, he seeks his father's advice about what to do: he does not want to be "chicken" yet he knows the danger involved in such a car stunt. Jim sees his situation as involving a point of honor, and he asks his father: "What do you do when you have to be a man?" His indecisive and confused father has no answer to Jim's demands for moral help. Jim leaves and goes to the high bluff where he and Buzz are scheduled to face off.

At the bluff Buzz explains the chicken run to Jim—each drives a car toward the precipice and the last one to jump before the car crashes over the bluff and into the ocean wins. Buzz admits to Jim that he likes him, and Jim asks why then the chicken run? Buzz's "we gotta do something" response exudes the delinquent/beat attitude of "kicks" and action for action's sake, the attitude that expressed the youthful desire to feel alive and to do so through antisocial and thrill-seeking acts (whether stealing the cars for the chicken run or risking the danger of driving the chicken run). Judy and Plato are there to watch, and as they talk it is clear that Plato has from brief acquaintance idealized Jim into his best friend, inventing in his own mind a deeper and more secure friendship that speaks of his loneliness and need for love. Even Judy starts to warm to Jim, beginning to overcome her cool Wheel attitude and her loyalty to Buzz. In the wake of this tragic test of courage—Buzz gets trapped in his car and dies when he cannot get out before the car hurtles over the bluff—these three are brought together to find what meaning and comfort in life they can.

After Buzz's death, the trio leave together, and Jim's sensitive and compassionate nature becomes apparent. He takes Judy home and shows concern for her well-being. When Plato pleadingly urges Jim to come home with him because he wishes Jim was his father and because "I don't have many people to talk to," Jim says "Who does?" He kindly shrugs off Plato's strange paternal needs and assures him he will see him tomorrow. Jim then goes home to tell his parents of the accident and to ask once again for the kind of spiritual guidance and comfort that they have always denied. Jim wants to go to the police to take responsibility for his actions: he is involved. His parents try to quash his moral sensibilities and stop him from admitting involvement or taking responsibility. His father exclaims, "You can't be idealistic all your life!" and his mother argues against going to the police and being the only one implicated. In the stormy argument Jim screams the need for involvement, for social and moral responsibility, for facing reality without evasion: "But I am involved! We're all involved! Mom! A boy was killed! I don't see how we can get out of that by pretending it didn't happen!" When his mother decides they will now have to move once again, Jim strenuously objects and confronts his mother with the truth: "No! You're not tearing me loose any more. . . . You're not going to use me as an excuse again, Mom. Every time you can't face yourself you want to move and you say it's because of me or the neighborhood or some other phony excuse. Now I want to do one thing right and I'm not letting you run away." Jim begs his father for strength—to stand up to his mother and support Jim's moral stance. When his father hesitates Jim lunges for him and tries to strangle him in a burst of rage, then runs wildly away. He goes to the police but is ignored and leaves without confessing. Buzz's gang friends nonetheless believe he has talked and are after him for being "chicken." Jim, Judy, and Plato—aware of this danger and eager to stay away from their homes—have taken refuge in a deserted mansion near the planetarium. Plato, having grabbed a gun from his mother's drawer, informs Jim and Judy about the mansion, his hiding place: "We're safe here. I hope." This is, of course, what each of these teenagers seeks, a sense of safe and secure love, a sanctuary from the confusion and pain of their lives. Their parents having failed them, they look to one another for this emotional safety, and here they will find it, at least temporarily. Jim and Judy act the protective parents of the lonely and loveless Plato, and they find that elusive love with one another. Jim wondrously and quietly tells Judy, "It's not going to be lonely, Judy. Not for you and not for me." Judy responds in the newfound amazement of love: "All the time I've been looking for someone to love me and now—I love somebody. And it's so easy."

This moment of love and safety does not last. Their refuge is invaded by Buzz's gang and the police, and in his fear Plato loses control, shooting at gang members and at Jim in his confusion and anger: "I don't want you for my father!" Plato in his pain and despair clings to the wall of the mansion, moaning "Save me, save me," and Jim tries to do just that. A shocked and dazed Jim follows Plato as he runs away to the planetarium, which is being surrounded by the police. Jim tells Judy that he recognizes Plato's needs: "He needed us . . . He was trying to make us his family." As the police shoot at Plato, Jim and Judy live up to their love and responsibility to Plato and go into the planetarium for him, despite the danger. Jim calmly speaks to the distraught Plato, who questions Jim sadly: "Jim, do you think the end of the world will come at night?" Jim replies, "No. At dawn," and then he works to convince Plato to surrender. He surreptitiously removes the bullets from Plato's gun, and he promises Plato, "There are a lot of people outside and they all want you to be safe." But as they get outside, Plato bolts, gun in hand, and he is shot dead by one of the policemen. Jim screams his opposition to this meaningless death—*"I got the bullets!"*—and he breaks down sobbing.

Jim learns through Plato's death the difficulty of keeping loved ones safe, but in making his effort he has wrought a transformation in his parents. His father steps forward to support Jim in the aftermath of the planetarium shooting, and he tells Jim, "You did everything a man could. . . . I'll stand up with you. Let me try to be as strong as you want me to be." The weeping Jim is helped by his humanized parents, and with his arm around Judy, they all leave for home. Jim's sensitivity and moral strength, while powerless to help Plato, nonetheless regenerate the survivors of this tragedy. While his is a world diminished by death and violence, Jim's life is a more pure and fulfilled one for his stance of involvement and responsibility: Jim has learned how to live as a man—"a man who can be gentle and sweet," as Judy had said. The character of Jim Stark was brought to life in all its tortured nuance by the young actor James Dean, a young man who displayed all the gentleness, sweetness, confusion, anger, and despair of his characters, a young man who captivated the hearts and souls of young, alienated America. Achieving mythic stature in youth culture on the basis of his brilliance in only three films (*East of Eden* and *Giant* along with *Rebel*) and on the basis of his spectacular and culture-shocking early death in a fiery car crash in 1955, Dean—and his film characters—represented the emerging personality and style of the beat generation.

In a 1958 *Esquire* article that explored and celebrated the beat revolution in values for 1950s Americans, John Clellon Holmes addressed the centrality of James Dean to the self-image of beat youth, a centrality that did not diminish with Dean's death. According to Holmes:

> A large proportion of this generation lived vicariously in the short, tumultuous career of actor James Dean. He was their idol in much the same way that Valentino was the screen idol of the Twenties, and Clark Gable was the screen idol of the Thirties. But there was a difference, and it was *all* the difference. In Dean, they saw not a daydream Lothario who was more attractive, mysterious and wealthy than they were, or a virile man of action with whom they could fancifully identify to make up for their own feelings of powerlessness, but a wistful, reticent youth, looking over the abyss separating him from older people with a level, saddened eye; living intensely in alternate explosions of tenderness and violence; eager for love and a sense of purpose, but able to accept them only on terms which acknowledged the facts of life as he knew them; in short, themselves.[31]

American youths intuitively understood James Dean: "They knew he was lonely, they knew he was flawed, they knew he was confused. But they also knew that he 'dug,' and so they delighted in his sloppy clothes and untrimmed hair and indifference to the proprieties of fame. He was not what they wanted to be; he was what they *were*." In life and in death James Dean was "beat": "He lived hard and without complaint; and he died as he lived, going fast."[32] Holmes also noted that Dean was a "Method" actor. The style, developed at the New York Actor's Studio, promoted emotional power by teaching actors to draw on their own experiences as sources of inspiration; the actor's task was to dig for "the essence of a character, his soul." Holmes called the Method "preeminently the acting style of the Beat Generation."[33]

Another raw and rebellious form of expression gained currency in the popular music of America. In the film *The Blackboard Jungle,* the first rock 'n' roll hit to reach the top of the popularity charts—Bill Haley and the Comets' "Rock Around the Clock"—was the anthem of the delinquent younger generation featured in the film.[34] The blaring sound and rocking beat of the music, the fast rhythms and the active lyrics—"One, two, three o'clock, four o'clock rock / five, six, seven o'clock, eight o'clock rock / nine, ten, eleven o'clock twelve o'clock rock / We're gonna rock around the clock tonight"—proclaimed the youthful discovery and creation of a music that matched the rebel spirit of their age. The film itself, focusing critical attention on the growing American problem of juvenile delinquency, announced its concern in a written opening statement: "Today we are concerned with juvenile delinquency—its causes—and its effects. We are especially concerned when this delinquency boils over into our schools. . . . We believe that public awareness is a first step toward a remedy for any problem." The film, however, stirred the very delinquency it sought to remedy, as its rock 'n' roll theme and its portraits of cool, criminal, and anti-authoritarian youth spawned theater riots and a general sensation throughout the country.[35]

The Blackboard Jungle centers on the attempts of a caring, liberal English teacher to inspire and communicate with his violent, alienated, racially mixed students, but the film also powerfully reveals the disturbed subculture of American youth. The adult explanations for the angry and uncontrolled behavior of these "wild animals" in their "jungle" involve the tensions and the troubles of the era: "Maybe the kids today are like the rest of the world: mixed up, suspicious, scared." According to the adults, this generation emerged from the war years, when parents were absent, when kids had "no church life" and "no place to go." One of the more criminally minded youths, Artie, has a different explanation for his antisocial actions: "A year from now, the army comes by and they say, okay Artie West, you get in a uniform and you be a soldier, and you save the world, and you get your lousy head blowed right off. Or maybe, maybe, I get a year in jail and maybe when I come out the army they don't want Artie West to be a soldier no more. Maybe what I get is *out*."

The English teacher succeeds in reaching his students, but like Jim Stark's parents in *Rebel Without a Cause,* the adult must learn from and listen to the young for answers. The lasting images of the violent energy of these delinquent youths, of their unbridled disdain for authority, overpowered this moderate compromise between youth and adult in any case, and the rock music that bracketed the film emitted the kind of energetic beat that rejected compromise with the adult world of smug complacence. Beginning in the mid-1950s the black and white pioneers of early rock 'n' roll fomented a musical and cultural revolution that attracted and incited the rebel young by its pulsing beat, its movement, sensuousness, and free emotional and physical expressiveness. While parents and the forces of authority reviled this raucous new music, legions of the young embraced the excitement expressed by the rising stars of rock 'n' roll: Chuck Berry, Little Richard, Fats Domino, Carl Perkins, Bo Diddley, Jerry Lee Lewis, Chubby Checker, Buddy Holly, and the Everly Brothers. But the man destined to become the "king" of rock 'n' roll, Elvis Presley, perhaps best exemplified the rebel beat that so aroused and energized the disaffection of American youth.[36]

After "Rock Around the Clock" first broke through the traditional boundaries of popular music, it was the music of Elvis Presley that confirmed the rebel presence of this taboo-shattering music in the culture of 1950s America. Between 1956 and 1960 Elvis charted fifteen number-one hits and twenty-three top-ten songs. His music, his persona, and his presentation of self and song encapsulated both the heights of delight and the despairing loneliness that youths alternately experienced in this schizoid age. Elvis's first number-one hit in 1956, "Heartbreak Hotel," revealed elements of his rock 'n' roll dualism; the song's driving, hard beat and its ebullient and moving rhythms express the exuberant sensibilities of the young, while its subject and lyrics speak of the aloneness and the depression of the failed search for love which so tortured the young in these years. The song begins with an image of the symbolic dwelling of lonely youth, the titled hotel on Lonely Street. In a quivering and emotional voice Elvis intones the deep pain of heartbreak, equating his loneliness with death. Elvis's Heartbreak Hotel is always crowded and everyone there suffers—guests, teary bellhops, and black-clad desk clerks. Elvis invites listeners to join these denizens of heartbreak, to walk down Lonely Street and feel such deadly sorrow.[37]

The sensual nature of Elvis's music was matched by his tempestuous public performances of his music. His suggestive movements conveyed all the uncontrolled passion that the rock 'n' roll beat aroused. As Elvis gained fame and mass exposure in television appearances throughout 1956, he became a controversial figure for his wild, sexy, gyrating performances of his string of hits, from "Hound Dog" and "Don't Be Cruel" to "Love Me Tender." The potency and energy of Elvis and his music led to his being billed in 1956 as "the nation's only atomic-powered singer," and this association not only hinted at the revolutionary potential barely restrained in rock 'n' roll but also ironically and unconsciously touched on the power of creative disunity that the atomic age produced along with the bomb.[38] Slyly associated with the boundless energy of the split atom, Elvis's success emphasized the cultural split that marked this age. In fact Elvis's provocative and unruly music and behavior opened him to widespread attack by the older generation and subjected him to local government surveillance and harassment.

In spite of the critics and adults who considered Elvis, his music, and his "voodoo acrobatics" to be corrupting the young of America—who in fact saw Elvis and all of rock 'n' roll as contributing to the problem of juvenile delinquency—Elvis defended the beat and dismissed charges of moral corruption.[39] He justified his wild movements: "I jump around because it's the way I feel. In fact, I can't even sing with a beat at all if I stand still." Weary of criticism, Elvis also downplayed his role in exacerbating delinquency, noting that he had been "blamed for just about everything wrong in this country."[40] Elvis and rock music clearly threatened the older generation and intensified parental fears about the rebelliousness of their children, and the delinquent young were attracted to Elvis's own deviance from the constraining standards of the era. Elvis did not moderate his music or his behavior (even though by technology Ed Sullivan's television studios could obscure his movements), and he continued to symbolize the youthful quest for movement, for feeling alive. And the young approved. In Eisenhower's America the young wore the "I Like Elvis" buttons that rivaled their elders' "I Like Ike" buttons.[41]

In the title of his 1957 hit "All Shook Up" Elvis offered a metaphoric musical statement about the impact of rock 'n' roll on the culture. This youthful musical shake-up of the culture countered the complacence of adult atomic age culture and expressed the painful disorder of young emotions which demonstrated the deeply felt humanity of the young. Against the adult culture's slide toward dehumanization, the rock 'n' roll culture posited a passion and love that reflected youth's lust for human life and emotion, whether that emotion entailed pain or pleasure. Unsettling but ecstatic pleasure was the subject of Elvis's "All Shook Up," and his musical sexiness—and the cultural focus on his pelvis, the force of life and sex—revealed the attachment to life. Elvis proclaims his love and its nerve-tingling effect in the song, and infuses that love with volcanic passion and physical yearning. A rapidly beating heart, chills, a tied tongue, and shaking insides convey his sense of being "all shook up" by love and lust.[42]

The exuberant sexuality and riotous rock 'n' roll that Elvis brought into youth culture began to diminish between 1958 and 1960 when he was drafted and served in the army for two years. His fulfillment of his patriotic duty muted his rebel image, which aided a more mainstream acceptance of him and his music. In 1960 Elvis was still aptly voicing the deep loneliness of the young in this tenuous world, and his hits included "Are You Lonesome Tonight?" and "It's Now or Never," which evoked heated sexuality and the potential evanescence of life in love: lovers could not wait in an era when life was so precarious. Tomorrow could be too late.[43] Nonetheless, in the late 1950s other rock 'n' roll singers had encroached on Elvis's singular popularity, and they helped to maintain the rebel spirit of the music. From Fats Domino's 1956 "Blueberry Hill" and the Big Bopper's 1958 "Chantilly Lace" to the Everly Brothers' 1957 "Wake Up, Little Susie" and Roy Orbison's 1960 "Only the Lonely," rock 'n' roll persisted in its loud presentation of the thrills, sexuality, vibrancy, and despairing aloneness of the American young.

The explosiveness of rock music, its wild yells and writhing, and its pounding rhythms continued to be expressed in Jerry Lee Lewis's 1957 "Whole Lotta Shakin' Goin' On" and 1958 "Great Balls of Fire," in the Isley Brothers' 1959 "Shout," and in Chubby Checker's 1960 "Twist." The rambunctious shouts, the low moans, and the use of slang and sometimes nonsensical words and phrases (as in Little Richard's 1956 "Tutti Frutti," for example) vocalized the young's alienation from the silence or the cold and inhuman rationalism of their elders as well as giving voice to the chaotic emotions and unquenchable desires for movement that had become such a part of the youthful dissent.[44] A rock 'n' roll star like Jerry Lee Lewis pleaded for—even demanded—the pure, instinctual drive for life, love, and sex. He did so in his raunchy whimpers—"Yeah, you can shake it one time for me / Shake it, baby, shake it / C'mon over, baby / A whole lotta shakin' goin' on"—or in his hard-driving, burning yelps—"Goodness, gracious, great balls of fire."[45] This sort of titillatingly crude and enlivening sexuality that emerged from the beat of rock 'n' roll piqued the young rebel spirit and prompted the kind of conservative, disgusted reactions among adults and authorities which only strengthened the rebel image of rock music, its singers, and its often riotous and hysterical audiences.

Newspapers around the nation asked of rock 'n' roll: "Music or Madness?" "Does Rock 'n' Roll Cause Delinquency?" (In 1956 Frankie Lymon and the Teenagers included in their lyrics, "I am not a juvenile delinquent.") Parents and the media attacked rock music, and the churches joined in the fight. The Reverend Jimmy Snow reviled the "beat" of rock 'n' roll that oozed with "evil feeling," and all sorts of critics condemned rock 'n' roll as "communist ideology" and as "obscenity and vulgarity." Southern racist conservatives feared that rock music was spreading the "corrupting" influence of black America. Secular authorities also cracked down on the music as local shows around the nation were canceled and banned. In 1958 the Jersey City commissioner for public safety announced the results of his investigation of rock 'n' roll shows: "We find that these programs are not for the good of the community, and that's why I ordered them banned." In the same year the United States government launched a harsh investigation of rock 'n' roll "payola" which destroyed the career of disc jockey Alan Freed, the disc jockey most responsible for popularizing rock music.[46]

The growing generational divide that rock 'n' roll helped to expose and enlarge was the larger product of the general youth culture that in the late 1950s became known as the "Beat Generation." Matching the cultural fervor and ferment expressed in rock 'n' roll were the imaginative and unconventional literary works and life-styles of the beats, particularly as represented by Allen

Ginsberg and Jack Kerouac, whose famous works *Howl* (1955–1956) and *On the Road* (1957) produced the innovative images of the young's vociferousness and antsiness. Kerouac characterized the young rebels in this cultural ferment as the "Beat Generation," and he became a somewhat reluctant spokesman for this group. In "The Philosophy of the Beats" John Clellon Holmes pointed out that Kerouac seemed to offer "at least some insight into the attitudes of a generation whose elders were completely flabbergasted"; he added, "Implicitly, rock and roll, drug addiction, juvenile delinquency, an amoral attitude toward sex and all the attendant phenomena that have characterized the modern young American in extreme seemed to be the primary preoccupation of Kerouac's characters."[47]

In their literature and poetry Kerouac and Ginsberg brought together the disparate threads of youthful American rebellion. As spokesmen for this generation, they excoriated the atomic age values that prompted their rebellious and spiritual search for a better way of life—a better way of life that subverted the older America's quest for safety and security through material comfort and mental conformity. In his analysis of the beats Holmes offered a long and insightful evaluation of the forces that shaped this generation and directed its quest:

> Perhaps all generations feel that they have inherited "the worst of all possible worlds," but the Beat Generation probably has more claim to the feeling than any that have come before it. The historical climate which formed its attitudes was violent, and it did as much violence to ideas as it did to the men who believed in them. One does not have to be consciously aware of such destruction to feel it. Conventional notions of private and public morality have been steadily atrophied in the last ten or fifteen years by the exposure of treason in government, corruption in labor and business, and scandal among the mighty of Broadway and Hollywood. The political faiths which sometimes seem to justify slaughter have become steadily less appealing as slaughter has reached proportions that stagger even the mathematical mind. Orthodox religious conceptions of good and evil seem increasingly inadequate to explain a world of science fiction turned fact, past-enemies turned bosom-friends, and honorable-diplomacy turned brink-of-war. Older generations may be distressed or cynical or apathetic about this world, or they may have somehow adjusted their conceptions to it. But the Beat Generation is specifically the *product* of this world, and it is the only world its members have ever known. It is the first generation in American history that has grown up with peacetime military training as a fully accepted fact of life. It is the first generation for whom the catch

phrases of psychiatry have become such intellectual pabulum that it can dare to think they may not be the final yardstick of the human soul. It is the first generation for whom genocide, brain-washing, cybernetics, motivational research—and the resultant limitation of the concept of human volition which is inherent in them—have become as familiar as its own face. It is also the first generation that has grown up since the possibility of the nuclear destruction of the world has become the final answer to all questions.[48]

According to Holmes, in spite of the forces pushing youth toward an exhausted despair, a tired cynicism was not the resulting or reigning motif of beat culture. Instead, the recognition of such doom stimulated an intense, extremist movement toward an answer to the question of this age: "How are we to live?"[49] While the answer to this question proved elusive and subjective, the creative search for the answer provided the means and the purpose for living a life that did not at all resemble the conformist, apathetic, immobile, and unfeeling life of America's older generation. The connotations attached to "beat," of being beaten down or indeed exhausted by the profanities of modern life and of being "beatified," living as a sentient, sanctified human capable of exulting at beauty and creativity amidst contemporary terror and madness, explained the chaotic, manic-depressive quality of the beats' fevered writings and lives and gave form to their often crazed quest for life's answers. When Allen Ginsberg heard the visionary voice that called him to his beat life and poetry, he explained it in the contrary terms that captured the literary philosophy of the beats; listening to the voice was "like hearing the doom of the whole universe and at the same time the inevitable beauty of all that doom."[50]

Ginsberg's *Howl* is a sprawling and chaotic poem that illustrates his visionary dualism. It is at once an expression of the apocalyptic forces eating away at the human spirit and, in its creative force and Whitmanesque scope, a violent protestation against the bonds constraining that human spirit. The free-form verse and uninhibited language and imagery of the poem battle against the debilitating and destructive forces of conventional society and evoke the boundless spiritualism and sexuality of the beat generation. Ginsberg begins his howl with a statement that conveys the hellish but living beat quest: "I saw the best minds of my generation destroyed by madness, starving hysterical naked, / dragging themselves through the negro streets at dawn looking for an angry fix, / angelheaded hipsters burning for the ancient heavenly connection to the starry dynamo in the machinery of night."[51] What follows is an extended catalog of the minds, actions, beliefs, and rebellions of these beats, a catalog that bristles with the same kind of dreamy imagery of the opening passage. Poverty, paranoia, hallucinations, self-destructive acts, suicide, mysticism, confusion, excitement, and constant movement prevail over the mental and geographic landscape of America, from those "with radiant cool eyes hallucinating Arkansas" to those "who vanished into nowhere Zen New Jersey," from those "who loned it through the streets of Idaho seeking visionary indian angels" to those "who disappeared into the volcanoes of Mexico."[52]

Along with these all-encompassing and hallucinatory visions of beat life are blunt and open images of the sexuality and pungency of those beats

> who copulated ecstatic and insatiate with a bottle of beer a sweetheart a package of cigarettes a candle and fell off the bed, and continued along the floor and down the hall and ended fainting on the wall with a vision of ultimate cunt and come eluding the last gyzym of consciousness, who sweetened the snatches of a million girls trembling in the sunset, and were red-eyed in the morning but prepared to sweeten the snatch of the sunrise, flashing buttocks under barns and naked in the lake.[53]

Ginsberg's exposure of the beat drug culture, his widespread adoption of brutal and explicit sexual and body imagery, his use of obscenity, and his reliance on violent images all batter against the conventions and respectability of an American culture and society that in reality subverted the niceties of life and a respectfulness for life in a far more shocking and brutal manner.

In fixing blame for the destruction of the best minds of his generation, Ginsberg asks: "What sphinx of cement and aluminum bashed open their skulls and ate up their brains and imagination?" He answers with "Moloch," a symbolic hungry deity of death who resembles the destructive and dehumanized America that demanded too high a human sacrifice for its existence:

> Moloch! Solitude! Filth! Ugliness! Ashcans and unobtainable dollars! Children screaming under the stairways! Boys sobbing in armies! Old men weeping in the parks! Moloch! Moloch! Nightmare of Moloch! Moloch the loveless! . . . Moloch whose mind is pure machinery! Moloch whose blood is running money! Moloch whose fingers are ten armies! Moloch whose breast is a cannibal dynamo! Moloch whose ear is a smoking tomb! . . . Moloch! Moloch! Robot apartments! invisible suburbs! skeleton treasuries! blind capitals! demonic industries! spectral nations! invincible madhouses! granite cocks! monstrous bombs![54]

In the "Footnote to Howl" Ginsberg opposed the beatitude of all life and things against the cold and mechanical deadliness of Moloch and in doing so he expresses the spiritual exuberance and amorphous human love that had arisen in the beat generation to combat the older America of Moloch. This spiritual ebullience concludes *Howl* and contrasts with its earlier demonism:

Holy! Holy! Holy! Holy! Holy! Holy! Holy! Holy! Holy!
Holy! Holy! Holy! Holy! Holy! Holy!
The world is holy! The soul is holy! The skin is holy! The nose
is holy! The tongue and cock and hand and asshole holy!
Everything is holy! everybody's holy! everywhere is holy!
everyday is an eternity! Everyman's an angel![55]

America's corruption of the holiness of life prompted the beat generation to seek spiritual regeneration through a confused, dangerous, and fast way of life that promised escape from—or at least an evasion of—the encroaching rationality and destructiveness of an unenlightened America. Whether through drugs, mysticism, sex, jazz, or sheer kinetic movement, the beats kept their minds and bodies open to the disordered perceptions and nimble activity that allowed them to sidestep the spiritual trap of convention and conformity.

The hyperactive and disordered form and tone of *Howl* exhibited Ginsberg's commitment to movement and fluidity and showed clearly how the poem formed a companion piece to Jack Kerouac's novel *On the Road*. In one of the lines in *Howl* Ginsberg precisely mirrored the frantic driving and traveling that suffused Kerouac's novel. When he described those beats "who drove cross-country seventytwo hours to find out if I had a vision or you had a vision or he had a vision to find out Eternity," Ginsberg illustrated the sort of visionary quest pursued by the characters in *On the Road*.[56] Through his narrator Sal Paradise and through Sal's "madman" idol, Dean Moriarty, Kerouac illuminates the ceaseless youthful quest for the spiritual and emotional fulfillment that was so elusive in this threatening age. Sal and Dean are the symbolic rebel youth of America: they are fatherless (Sal's father is dead and Dean's abandoned him when young) and they are therefore on their own in search of direction and salvation in life. Their search takes them in all directions and to all places, from East to West, from New York and New Jersey to San Francisco and New Orleans, back to the East and south to Mexico. The very process of this frenetic road trip promoted the self-discovery and the visionary existentialism that provide them with a way to live in an otherwise deadened world.

Even though narrator Sal Paradise is looking for a way to live, it is clear that he is also looking to avoid its alternative: the way of death so omnipresent in America. Dean Moriarty and the road are the cure for Sal, which he announces in his opening lines: "I first met Dean not long after my wife and I split up. I had just gotten over a serious illness that I won't bother to talk about, except that it had something to do with the miserable split-up and my feeling that everything was dead. With the coming of Dean Moriarty began the part of my life you could call my life on the road."[57] Dean's craziness and energetic life force as well as the road help to shake Sal out of his lethargy, and Sal explains his attraction to Dean in terms that reveal his awakening desire for life: "The only people for me are the mad ones, the ones who are mad to live, mad to talk, mad to be saved, desirous of everything at the same time, the ones who never yawn or say a commonplace thing, but burn, burn, burn."[58] Having been inducted into "the whole mad swirl" of Dean's "insanity," of the road's excitement, of the young's unquenchable curiosity about the world and self, Sal recounts his voyage and shares his newfound knowledge: that the sheer force of individual energy and movement seems at times enough to hold back the world's onrushing moral and human decay.

As Sal takes to the road to pursue Dean and to collect experiences for his writings, he feels as if he is embarking on a holy mission: "I could hear a new call and see a new horizon, and believe it at my young age."[59] He sets out for the West, and on the way he sees the loneliness and beauty of America and he learns the fatigue and the joyousness of life on the road. He meets Dean in Denver and enmeshes himself in the craziness of life and people he finds there. According to Sal, "everything was so crazy," "the whole universe was crazy and cockeyed and extremely strange," and "they were amazing maniacs."[60] But Sal sees in this insanity a saving presence, "rising from the underground, the sordid hipsters of America, a new beat generation that I was slowly joining."[61] Sal continues his journey throughout the West, and even though the road reveals the vast desolation and sickness of life, it also uplifts the spirit with its access to the wonderment and wildness of life. The necessity of the road, of movement, seems especially apparent to Sal when he arrives back East and is again struck by the death-tinge of stationary urban life:

> Suddenly I found myself on Times Square. I had traveled eight thousand miles around the American continent and I was back on Times Square; and right in the middle of rush hour, too, seeing with my innocent road-eyes the absolute madness and fantastic hoorair of New York with its millions and millions hustling forever for a buck among themselves, the mad dream—grabbing, taking, giving, sighing, dying, just so they could be buried in those awful cemetery cities beyond Long Island City.[62]

The frantic mad dream of Dean and the road—even as lonesome, tiring, and depressing as it could be—nonetheless seems preferable to this grabbing and pushing vision of American life. Sal soon takes off again with Dean. Dean's madness intensifies over time, and while there is a debilitating aspect to his nonstop craziness, there is also a creative and liberating aspect to his franticness. Sal notes the disturbingly uncontrolled character of Dean's madness: "He had become absolutely mad in his movements; he seemed to be doing everything at the same time. It was a shaking of the head, up and down, sideways; jerky, vigorous hands; quick walking, sitting, crossing the legs, getting up, rubbing the hands, rubbing his fly, hitching his pants."[63] From such frenetic movement, however, flow the visionary insights and revelations that come to Sal in his travels and adventures with Dean, from listening to jazz and smoking marijuana and feeling "that everything was about to arrive—the moment when you know all and everything is decided forever" to experiencing the sheer delight of the road, where "the only thing to do was go," where they could fulfill "the one and noble function of the time, *move.*"[64]

Whatever the problems of the road, "the purity of the road" and the openness of travel allow Sal to have flashes about the spiritual unity of life: "I knew like mad that everything I had ever known and would know was One."[65] For this beat generation the road is life, and for Sal, Dean is the essence of Beat: "He was *BEAT*—the root, the soul of Beatific."[66] And Sal finally follows this beat, and this beat life, on the grandest of road trips, to Mexico. Clinging to Dean's precept that "the road must eventually lead to the whole world. Ain't nowhere else it can go, right?" they plan this ultimate trip. Sal "couldn't imagine this trip. It was the most fabulous of all. It was no longer east-west, but magic *south*," and Dean just enthused, "Man, this will finally take us to *IT!*"[67] As they reach Mexico, it indeed seems they find "it," that sought-after magic: "Behind us lay the whole of America and everything that Dean and I had previously known about life, and life on the road. We had finally found the magic land at the end of the road and we never dreamed the extent of the magic."[68]

Driving into Mexico, Sal claims, was "like driving across the world and into places where we would finally learn ourselves."[69] As they travel farther into the hot and tropical jungles toward Mexico City, "digging" the people, the smell, the drugs of Mexico, they start to become "one" with nature and weather; as Sal wondrously points out, "For the first time in my life the weather was not something that touched me, that caressed me, froze or sweated me, but became me. The atmosphere and I became the same."[70] Coming closer to their destination of Mexico City, to "the end of the road," that sense of aliveness started to dissipate, just as the thrills and self-knowledge of the road always began to dim and fade as the movement slowed. With this slowing down of the search came reminders of the more deadly reality they were moving away from. Sal experiences such a reminiscence as the car crests the high mountains from which they will descend to Mexico City:

> Strange crossroad towns on top of the world rolled by, with shawled
> Indians watching us from under hatbrims and *rebozos*. Life was dense,
> dark, ancient. They watched Dean, serious and insane at his raving wheel,
> with eyes of hawks. All had their hands outstretched. They had come
> down from the back mountains and higher places to hold forth their
> hands for something they thought civilization could offer, and they never
> dreamed the sadness and the poor broken delusion of it. They didn't know
> that a bomb had come that could crack all our bridges and roads and re-
> duce them to jumbles, and we would be as poor as they someday, and
> stretching out our hands in the same, same way.[71]

Having arrived at the end of their Mexican road, Sal and Dean lose their magic. Sal gets sick and languishes, and Dean leaves Sal alone to drive back to America. This beat life sinks from its giddy, tropical heights, and the end of this trip marks the essential end of Sal's story. When Sal makes his way back to the United States, he runs across "a tall old man with flowing white hair" in Texas who urges him to "*Go moan for man.*"[72] Part of the impetus behind the beat generation's frantic movement and frenzied howls had emerged from the desire to bewail the emptiness and emotionlessness of humanity and man's diminishing capacity to be human. Despite all the cross-country and international searching of these youth, the energy needed both to moan and to seek an alternative to "the land where they let the children cry" proved difficult to sustain over time.[73] The road, however, had provided a direction and a way of life for the beats, who wailed in rebellion and quested after the elusive but enticing fulfillment denied them in the eerily complacent society of atomic age America.

With its outlandish antisocial and taboo-breaking sensibility, the beat generation fostered an active and loud resistance to mainstream America's cultural traditions. The young used shock tactics to break through the cold war consensus; these wild ones, juvenile delinquents, rock 'n' roll singers, psychopathic children, and Beat writers railed with all the lively energy of their dissent against the anxious and deadened world they had inherited from their parents. In his poem "America" Allen Ginsberg had thrown down the gauntlet in his impudent advice to America: "Go fuck yourself with your atom bomb."[74] The new generation was tired and "sick" of atomic age America's "insane demands," and the rebel young asked America, as did Ginsberg, "America, when will we end the human war?"[75]

The destruction of psychological and physical sanctuary in America could not be indefinitely ignored or tranquilized away. By the end of the 1950s, on the cusp of a new decade in American history, the cultural and psychological ferment that had brewed beneath the surface tranquillity of Eisenhower's America began to emerge in more violent and open form. As Eisenhower turned the presidency over to John F. Kennedy, as this youthful president reinvigorated America and the cold war, and as the ever-growing younger generation continued its energetic rebellion, the insane reality of atomic age life became more difficult to tolerate. Alfred Hitchcock's 1960 film *Psycho* welcomed Americans to the 1960s and to a new American way of life.

Psycho's world of death is a microcosmic American world. The disintegration and slashing that had subverted America's psychological health and humanism are evident in the film's opening sequence, in which vertical lines segment the aerial view of Phoenix, and the venetian blinds of a hotel window slit the opening shots of Marion Crane and her lover Sam Loomis. These two characters establish the unhappiness of all who inhabit this world—an illusory world that nonetheless condemns as unreal and fanciful the idealized image of a contented and secure America. Marion and Sam are illicit lovers, stealing what little time together they can. Sam lives out of state, is divorced, in debt, and unable to provide for another wife, but Marion wants even the less-than-satisfying marriage Sam could offer in order to break out of her unfulfilling life. Stifled, they part company after this brief noon-hour tryst, and Marion returns to her work at a real estate office that also houses the unhappy.

When she arrives at the office, Marion has a headache; she is unsettled, unhappy, jittery. The other secretary offers her some of the tranquilizers she relies on in her everyday life. A client interrupts them, plunking down $40,000 in cash for a house, a wedding present to his daughter. He proclaims his theory of life and money: "You know what I do with unhappiness? I buy it off."[76] Buying this house for his daughter does not promise happiness—it simply prevents unhappiness. Marion decides she cannot shed her unhappiness through drugs, and she refuses the other secretary's offer: "You can't buy off unhappiness with pills." But she does seize the opportunity to try buying off her unhappiness with the client's $40,000. Entrusted to deposit it in the bank, she instead runs off with the cash in a desperate attempt to find some satisfaction in life, presumably with the debt-ridden Sam, toward whom she nervously drives.

Marion's flight from her unhappiness turns ominous, then nightmarish as she experiences guilt and panic. She encounters a suspicious law enforcement officer on the highway between Arizona and California. An oppressive, drenching rain beats down on the dark highway, and the slashing windshield wipers of her car foreshadow the cutting down of her desire and her life. To evade the downpour (and the law), she seeks refuge at the desolate Bates Motel, where the shy young proprietor, Norman Bates, checks her in—she is the only guest—and offers her a light supper at his house up the hill. While Marion is unpacking, she hears Norman's mother screaming at him for inviting a "strange girl" to the house. Soon after, Norman comes down from the gothic house with a tray of food for Marion. He apologizes for his mother, and as they talk during the supper Norman haltingly discusses his insane mother and his empty life. The loneliness and sadness of Norman's life complete the picture of unhappiness that describes everyone in this world.

Norman's life at the Bates Motel is a solitary one, and he explains his only hobby to Marion—he stuffs "dead things," mostly birds, and the evidence of his taxidermy clutters the motel parlor where they talk: stuffed birds stare from their perches around the parlor. When Marion wonders, "Is your time so empty?" Norman admits that the motel is a sort of trap, as is caring for his disturbed mother. But he sees no alternative in a world full of traps: "Do you know what I think? I think that we're all in our private traps. Clamped in them. And none of us can ever get out. We scratch and claw, but only at the air, only at each other. And for all of it, we never budge an inch." Marion suggests that Norman escape his trap by placing his mother in an institution, but Norman reacts with horror at the idea of a "madhouse," where "cruel eyes" would stare and study his mother. He calms himself and defends his mother: "She just goes a little mad sometimes. . . . We all go a little mad sometimes." Marion, realizing the madness of her escapade, affirms Norman's claim, and she decides to return to Phoenix, to her unhappy but sane life, early the next morning. She bids Norman good night and retires to her room next door for a shower and bed. As she undresses, Norman stares at her in quiet pleasure through a peephole in the parlor wall; when she goes into the shower, he retreats to his house.

Feeling relieved and cleansed by her decision to face her problems in Phoenix, Marion steps into the soothing and refreshing shower. As the water rains down on her, however, the shadowy figure of a woman enters the bathroom, pulls the shower curtain aside, and slashes at Marion's nude body with a steely knife. The knife plunges repeatedly into Marion's flesh (to the accompaniment of high-pitched, screeching violins), and when the murderer's bloody and explosive rage is spent, the figure retreats from the bathroom. In her last gasps of life Marion tries to rise from the tub; she grasps the shower curtain to pull herself out but the curtain snaps off its rod and Marion falls dead on the floor. Her blood swirls down the drain, this image dissolving into one of Marion's eyes—a stilled eye expressive of the emptiness of death.

The stillness after Marion's death is broken by Norman's cry of "Oh, God, Mother! Blood, blood!" Norman rushes to Marion's room and finds her dead. He immediately begins to clean up the bloody mess, protectively hiding the evidence of his mother's brutal murder. He places Marion and her belongings (including the money) into the trunk of her car and sinks it in a swamp behind the motel. While Norman relaxes, having fulfilled his duties as a son, Marion's sister Lila, Sam, and a private detective are just beginning to cooperate in an attempt to find Marion. The detective discovers the motel and evidence of Marion's presence there, and in spite of Norman's protests and evasions he insists on questioning Norman's mother, whom he sees in the window of the adjoining house. The detective sneaks into the house, where he too is brutally knifed to death, the blade stabbing into his eye and then his body. Sam and Lila follow up on the detective's clues when they do not hear from him, and they uncover the bizarre truth about Norman and his mother. Sam keeps Norman talking for a time at the motel while Lila enters the house to find Mrs. Bates, who in reality is merely a "stuffed" skeletal figure long-preserved by Norman. As Lila screams in horror at the empty, sunken eye sockets that confront her, Norman—dressed as his mother—crashes in with knife raised. Sam prevents more of Norman's murderous violence, and Norman is taken into custody by the authorities.

In the aftermath of the capture, the authorities piece together the story of Norman and his mother. Norman, in the ultimate act of oedipal jealousy—and rebellion—had murdered his mother and her lover. Guilt and loneliness drove him to dig up her body and preserve her, despite her decaying physical form. Norman had absorbed her parental authority into his personality, and the resulting conflict of the two personalities, fired by jealousy, hatred, and guilt, exploded in murder. As Norman sits quietly in an institutional room at the end of the film, the merger of Norman and his mother seems complete. Her voice is heard as Norman stares blankly out, lips tightly closed, and the face of Norman and the face of his mother's sunken skull appear to overlap in an image of death-in-life.

The microcosmic world of the Bates Motel suggested the triumph of despair and death in an insane age. This was a world of solitude and unhappiness, a world populated by the dead—Norman's mother, Marion Crane, the detective, and other murdered women—and by the living dead, Norman and all the other unhappy souls seeking to buy off unhappiness or to tranquilize themselves against reality. In the world of *Psycho* death came in a manner appropriate to the atomic age: suddenly and brutally. Marion Crane's murder recalled the terms and language of the civil defense warnings about being "virtually naked" to enemy attack, about avoiding the "deadly shower" of radioactive fallout. The suddenness with which death could triumph was one of the lessons of *Psycho* which Hitchcock meant to instill in the minds of the audience with the shower scene: "Death may appear at any minute."[77] The living dead, the tormented and dissatisfied inhabitants of *Psycho's* America, suffered a slower running down of life, like Norman Bates, whose caged despair and loneliness gradually built into violent and murderous schizophrenia. Over time Norman went more than "a little mad." He could not suppress the conflict between the two personalities which festered under his surface normality and politeness. Like Norman Bates's split personality, the schizoid psyche of 1950s America also revealed a conflict that could not remain trapped in an underground culture of dissent. In the 1960s American culture more openly recognized the atomic age reality of death and violence.

part 3

IS GOD DEAD?

an american awakening on the eve of destruction

I hope God is not a reader of Time.

—*1961 letter to* Time *magazine*

For instance, do you know the story about Father on the day they first tested a bomb out at Alamogordo? After the thing went off, after it was a sure thing that America could wipe out a city with just one bomb, a scientist turned to my father and said, "Science has now known sin." And do you know what Father said? He said, "What is sin?"

—*Kurt Vonnegut,* Cat's Cradle *(1963)*

Suburban survivors of Hiroshima described the blast as a "mighty first boom, like a locomotive followed by a long, loud train roaring past, fading gradually away to a murmur." Wrong. They describe only the ear's inaccurate report. For that mighty boom was only the first faintest murmur of an explosion that is still roaring down on us and always will be. . . .
For the reverberation often exceeds through silence the sound that sets it off; the reaction occasionally outdoes by way of repose the event that stimulated it; and the past not uncommonly takes a while to happen, and some long time to figure out.

—*Ken Kesey,* Sometimes a Great Notion *(1964)*

ou unlock this door with the key of imagination," announced Rod Serling in the introductory segment of his long-running television show, *The Twilight Zone* (1959–1964). A door floating against a black sky dotted with bright stars formed the backdrop for his narration, and Serling explained what lay on the other side of that opened door: "Beyond it is another dimension . . . a dimension of sound, a dimension of sight, a dimension of mind. You're moving into a land of both shadow and substance, of things and ideas. You've just crossed over . . . into the Twilight Zone."[1] Shattering glass, a disembodied and wide-open eye, Einstein's equation $E = mc^2$, and a ticking clock illustrated this bizarre new dimension of sound, sight, and mind found not only in the *Twilight Zone* but also in the questioning culture of early 1960s America. Emerging into the open were cultural concerns about atomic age America's morality and sanity which had been locked away in the underground cultural consciousness. One key to unlocking the American imagination was time, and the dawn of a new decade gave a new dimension to time in the atomic age.

Anxieties and doubts about atomic age America's political, moral, spiritual, and psychological well-being had bristled in reaction to the confident cold war cultural dictates throughout the 1940s and 1950s. But given little dissociative distance, Americans had learned to live with the bomb and with the legacy of World War II in all its understated terror and overstated triumph. Fears and insecurities were shunted aside, restricted to a covert culture that nonetheless brimmed with the allusive, iconographic, and amorphous images of the moral corruption and communal insanity, the death and violence, that accompanied life with the bomb. Caged by the larger mainstream culture of optimism, stability, and affluence and the pressures of internal security and community consensus, this subversive culture was explained as a product of normal and tempo-rary anxieties associated with postwar dislocation and readjustment.

By the early 1960s the cultural fog that had shrouded Eisenhower's America lifted, revealing the clear relation between the rebellious culture's vision of an immoral and insane America and America's immersion in the atomic age. A cul-tural time lag between seeing and understanding the reality of life with the bomb, between understanding and being able to express that knowledge freely, had denied recognition of the cultural fallout of the bomb. In his 1964 novel *Sometimes a Great Notion* Ken Kesey noted the temporal oddities in perception of the past, concluding that "the past not uncommonly takes a while to hap-pen, and some long time to figure out."[2] The cultural reverberations from the bomb finally sounded in the early 1960s—when the past happened for Amer-ica, when the nation entered something like the twilight zone of the atomic age. A new dimension of sight, sound, and mind allowed an awakened culture to figure out the past and to assess openly the political and moral ramifications of the "explosion that is still roaring down on us and always will be."[3]

The passage of time helped to demystify the past, particularly World War II and its atomic legacy. The immediate postwar culture had registered its aware-ness of the evils resulting from America's embrace of the atom bomb, and by the late 1950s America witnessed the first stirrings of the culture of dissent's open criticism. Yet while a vantage point fifteen years distant from the explo-sion of the atom bomb provided a gratifying perspective (fifteen years in the atomic age seemed an eternity), the changed setting also gave the culture a dif-ferent and more terrifying perspective from which to view the past. The stasis of the Eisenhower years had begun to break down at the turn of the decade, at the transition from the aging Eisenhower administration to the youthful Ken-nedy administration, and this break in continuity offered the cultural opportu-nity for a revolutionary departure from the enforced quiescence of the 1950s.

Eisenhower had presided over the most intense time-warp years of the 1950s. He had by sheer force of his personality kept in operation the cultural tradition that enshrined past values and virtues: simplicity and order in a conformist so-ciety, togetherness in family and community, conservatism about change and experimentation, and calm appreciation for World War II and for America's secure position of cold war world power. Eisenhower's attachment to an older, pre-atomic age vision of life had distinct advantages. While the internal secu-rity network curtailed doubters and dissenters, Eisenhower's attitudes quieted American concerns about the radical changes in atomic age life and encouraged Americans to overlook present dangers by clinging to a more time-honored, secure conception of life (nonetheless improved by the affluence of the cold war economy). Eisenhower's military restraint and experience prevented the eruption of hostilities with the Soviet Union and tempered potential nuclear hysteria. His confident and serene guidance of the United States and his measured maintenance of the cold war status quo made it easy for Americans to ignore the harsher realities of the age, but also contributed to a bottling up of dissenting forces, producing an explosion in the sixties.

By the end of his term in office in 1961 Eisenhower had awakened to the dangerous reality of the atomic age, as he clearly indicated in his warning about the military-industrial complex. But the hopes for change and awakening in 1960s American culture rested not with Eisenhower but with John F. Kennedy, who in his inaugural address severed America's association with Eisenhower and the immobile past he had come to represent: "Let the word go forth from this time and place, to friend and foe alike, that the torch has been passed to a new generation of Americans . . ."[4] Kennedy's youth, his vigor, his expansive idealism, and his quick and open intellect indeed augured a new cultural dimension for 1960s America. Released from the restraints of the forties and fifties, a rebellious culture emerged into an open forum of debate. HUAC and the internal security forces—while still active in this cold war society—no longer inspired the terror or compliance of past years, particularly for members of the younger generation coming of age in large numbers during these years. The energetic and experimental atmosphere of Kennedy's New Frontier in America gave new promise of freedom and change throughout American society. The past was opened to critical observation or to overt opposition. The recent American past—World War II, the cold war, and the development and growth of the atomic arsenal—revealed the genesis of the violent and deadly atomic age reality that Americans finally confronted in the early sixties. The ramifications of the United States's cold war militarism were evident in the increasing probability of thermonuclear warfare between the superpower nations.

The ebullient spirit and expectations for social and spiritual change attached to the Kennedy administration, then, were simultaneously subdued and challenged by Kennedy's own atomic adventurism. Kennedy helped to foment a cultural awakening with his vision of a New Frontier in American history, but he also helped to spread a radical discontent as he brought the nation to yet another new dimension of time: the eve of destruction. Fifteen years into the atomic age, the apocalyptic imagination merged with reality, the past collided with the present, and time seemed to be running out.

When President Kennedy rejected the substance and style of Eisenhower's leadership, he also jettisoned Eisenhower's moderation. Grasping the opportunity offered by the nation's post-Sputnik panic over declining American technological strength, Kennedy took the offensive in the cold war. He reinvigorated America's weapons and space programs, and he demonstrated a bellicose willingness to confront the Soviet Union—whether in Berlin or in Cuba. A young maverick in an increasingly volatile world, Kennedy upset the delicate cold war balance so carefully maintained by Eisenhower. Gone was the atomic concealment of the Eisenhower years; gone was the insensibility to atomic realities which had shielded Americans during the forties and fifties. Under Kennedy's leadership Americans came face-to-face with their Soviet foes for the first time, and for the first time America squared off against an enemy with a relatively equal capacity for atomic annihilation. Kennedy's public brandishing of America's atomic arsenal shattered the cold war silence of the later Eisenhower years and shook Americans out of a long sleep of avoidance.

The American government's wielding of atomic weapons and Kennedy's use of the presidency as a platform from which to alert the American public to the necessity of waging thermonuclear battle brought into the open the political and moral issues of the atomic age which had been closeted in the more complacent years of peaceful coexistence. While the majority of Americans continued to support the cold war military and foreign policies of the government, it became far more difficult to ignore the cultural eruption that accompanied this early sixties intensification of cold war risks. Just as the government broadcast its atomic intentions, so too did the counterculture directly attack the immorality and insanity of those intentions. The tensions and schisms that had quietly divided atomic age America increased in the sixties as positions polarized. Both a radicalizing cold warriorism and a radicalizing pacifism and humanism characterized this aroused America on the eve of destruction.

The early 1960s in America emerged as the setting for an atomic age moral and psychological catharsis. The postwar barriers against open aggression and open dissent broke down and America was forced to recognize the bomb's defining role in society and culture. As the government threatened the peremptory use of its nuclear arsenal, as strategists predicted "survival" for a sheltered United States in a thermonuclear war despite the instantaneous death of fifty million Americans, and as machine gun–toting anticommunist survivalists proclaimed death preferable to communism ("Better dead than Red"), the thin guise of America's purely defensive policy of nuclear deterrence crumbled. Resurgent cold warriorism had militated that moral and political leap over the "unthinkable" and disjunctive chasm between means and ends in atomic war.

For lost in the plans for this new confrontational nuclear strategy were the human and moral consequences of atomic adventurism.

Overt voices of dissent rose up in a new 1960s style of direct confrontation with the bomb and with the resulting moral problems. The rebel culture advertised the nation's moral debilitation by the atomic bureaucracy and its violent and deadly technological world view; in the process dissenters promoted a revolution in human values designed to counter the nation's slide toward amorality. While this cultural revolution manifested itself in a variety of ways—street demonstrations, sit-ins, satiric novels, bizarre television shows—and while this revolution encompassed a myriad of issues, some of which were only tangentially related to the bomb, like civil rights, the cultural revolt was unified in its quest to reinvigorate and redefine the human and moral precepts of atomic age life and seek alternatives to the moral bankruptcy and human destructiveness of America's cold war mindset.

In his novel *Cat's Cradle* Kurt Vonnegut, Jr. crafted a symbolic portrait of a nuclear scientist which captured the rising countercultural concern about the moral void that had swallowed Americans in this scientific and technological era. This scientist, a participant in the construction of the first atom bomb and the inventor of a chemical substance that ultimately ends all human life, is so immersed in his scientific work that he becomes insensible to its human and ethical consequences. Morally ignorant and ethically blank, he asks, "What is sin?" in response to another scientist's remark about knowing sin as a result of the Trinity test.[5] His simple question conveyed the amorality that characterized the proponents of America's atomic dream and engineered America's twilight ride to the eve of destruction.

Opposing the hard-nosed and pragmatic ethics of the American nuclear establishment was the dissenting culture's more human insistence on the sinfulness of nuclear ethics. At the conclusion of his inaugural address President Kennedy had appealed to Americans to do "God's work," with God's help: "With a good conscience our only sure reward, with history the final judge of our deeds, let us go forth to lead the land we love, asking His blessing and His help, but knowing that here on earth God's work must truly be our own."[6] During the years of the Kennedy administration and beyond, however, the very nature of God's work and God's role in America seemed difficult to determine. Fighting godless communism with the equally godless threat of atomic annihilation stirred a spiritual debate in America, with open questioning of the meaning of God, religion, and morality. At once reflective of the bomb's conflicting power to induce malaise and to inspire spiritual regeneration, the cultural conflict over God and the bomb signaled the cathartic emergence of the forces of a humanized morality—ethical forces that demonstrated the incompatible nature of God and the bomb and that challenged America to invent a peaceful and humanitarian spirit more conducive to life.

The moral awakening of America in the early 1960s revealed itself in the culture in many different ways, but *Time* magazine managed to encapsulate in a most dramatic fashion the new tone of spiritual questioning. In two articles published in 1961 and 1966 *Time* bracketed the most intense years of ethical debate and captured the character of the conflict that raged over American morality, God, and the bomb. In its August 18, 1961, issue the magazine ran a story entitled "Gun Thy Neighbor?" in its Religion section.[7] The article focused on a disturbing trend in the booming construction of bomb and fallout shelters: shelter owners were arming their shelters with machine guns in order to repel those Americans who remained unprepared for nuclear attack. The article crystallized the moral issues involved in the rising cultural debate about shelters that surfaced at the time of the Berlin crisis. One *Time* reader summed up the growing moral revulsion for the selfishness and violence the bomb had engendered: in a letter to the editor he stated that, for the sake of such gun-bearing shelter owners, "I hope God is not a reader of *Time*."[8]

By 1966 the moral challenge in American culture had escalated to incorporate an extensive questioning of the nature and relevance of God, of all spiritual and political authority. *Time* boldly chronicled the deepening search for life's meaning and purpose which embroiled the culture in the turbulent early years of this new decade, years that witnessed such a flourishing of deadly violence and rebellious uprising that the foundation for any belief in traditional faiths seemed to crumble. On its April 8, 1966, cover *Time* starkly posed the question that revealed the spiritual battle being waged in the culture: "IS GOD DEAD?"[9] By the time Americans saw this somber question staring out at them from newsstands across the nation, they had already experienced the kinds of trauma that had helped to formulate such doubts about God. Foreign policy crises, political assassinations, mass demonstrations, riots, and a new and direct American war in Vietnam had crushed consensus belief in the God-given American way of life. Out of this chaos there emerged a nihilistic malaise, a sense of God's inconsequentiality and irrelevance in modern America, and the feature article in *Time* discussed this depressing disappearance of God.[10] But also emerging from this ferment was a quest for alternative theologies and philosophies to replace overturned, corrupted belief systems of traditional authorities and to explore more innovative and humanist possibilities for faith in this age of catharsis.

Between the bomb shelter craze in 1961 and the dubious declaration of God's death in 1966, the counterculture openly addressed the spiritual dilemma of living with the bomb. An understanding of life's meaning in Dr. Strangelove's America was surfacing in the cultural consciousness of the 1960s. The crescendo was reached in Stanley Kubrick's 1964 film with the cathartic release of the repressed cultural rumblings about the bomb and its insane and immoral grip on the hearts and minds of Americans. *Dr. Strangelove* exemplified the cultural explosion that finally matched the power of the bomb. What *Dr. Strangelove* and the culture of the sixties brought to the cultural consciousness was open recognition of America's tenuous balance on the edge of apocalypse. From *Dr. Strangelove*'s thermonuclear vision of the end of the world to Barry McGuire's angry rock 'n' roll dirge, "Eve of Destruction" (1965), the culture of dissent looked unblinkingly at the apocalyptic peril that was the true legacy of the atomic age. The fear of human extinction threatened by America's atomic aggression in the sixties impelled a cultural revolution on many fronts, but the bomb—and the moral and political values that sustained it—symbolized the human and moral drift now recognized. In "Eve of Destruction" McGuire ominously warned, "If the button is pushed, there's no running away / There'll be no one to save with the world in a grave."[11]

Announcing the beginning of this cathartic challenge to the ingrained cold war patterns of atomic apathy and acceptance was the cultural debate prompted by the mass hysteria associated with the Berlin crisis and the bomb shelter craze of 1961. The bomb shelter craze made public both the government's seriousness about preparing for nuclear war and the culture's growing restiveness about the bomb and the government. The crisis atmosphere of 1961 provoked extreme responses on the part of atomic advocates and atomic dissenters, and the stage for the moral and political battleground of the 1960s was set. Becoming clear in the midst of this crisis were the tensions that had split the cultural mind and animated the civil defense debate of the 1950s, and rising from the tumult was a cultural impulse for spiritual regeneration emblematic of the larger cultural awakening in the sixties.

The bomb shelter craze and the Berlin crisis defined the nature of the cultural conflict that engaged America in the 1960s, and the turmoil of 1961 signaled America's move into a new dimension of atomic age sound, sight, mind—and time. The dawn of the new decade compelled a new understanding of the preciousness of time. In a 1960 religious tract entitled "Fifteen Years in Hell Is Enough" the Christian writer Harold Fey expressed the sort of moral and historical impatience that reverberated throughout the culture during the early years of this new decade. He argued for American unilateral nuclear disarmament and for an end to the religious silence on issues related to the bomb's morality. He sounded the call for a spiritual rebirth heard in the culture at the time of the Berlin crisis and beyond: "Fifteen years of suspension over the fires of nuclear hell is long enough. It is time for a change."[12]

six

TIME ENOUGH AT LAST?

the bomb shelter craze and the
dawn of America's moral awakening

> *"We must remember Hiroshima as well as Pearl Harbor."*
>
> —Gerard Piel,
> *"The Illusion of Civil Defense"* (1962)

few months before the Berlin crisis and the bomb shelter craze burst upon the panicked American public, a March 1961 editorial in *The Nation* declared that "the strangest psychological phenomenon of the twentieth century, transcending the frenzies and manias of the Dark Ages, is 'civil defense'— the notion that an H-bomb war could be conducted, on the home front, like World War II."[1] The editorial, entitled "The Great Illusion," denied the illusory power America claimed by virtue of the bomb and civil defense, protesting "that national power in the classic sense is now without meaning, that victory is unattainable, that war is no longer the supreme arbitrating force."[2] *The Nation* considered this disjunction between illusion and reality a characteristic of America's "political schizophrenia," and in a companion editorial, "Wanted— A Peace Movement," the magazine urged America to create a movement that would correct the country's "divorce from political realities."[3]

While the widespread discovery of America's political, moral, and psychological schizophrenia occurred during the era of the Berlin crisis, when opinions on nuclear power polarized, the signs of cultural change had been stirring since the late 1950s. The rumblings of dissatisfaction that now arose fed into the tumult that exploded in the early 1960s and provided a cultural bridge between the fifties and sixties. America's atomic complacence and consensus began to crumble as the result of surfacing activism. Tense events in the cold war gave rise to greater uncertainty in America; the country seemed more vulnerable and more in need of change and action. Eisenhower attempted to control this rising restlessness, but neither he nor Kennedy could relieve the sense of failure that resulted from technological and foreign policy setbacks of these years.

In 1957 the Soviets appeared to have the initiative in the weapons and space race with the success of their Sputnik and missile programs. Fidel Castro's revolution in Cuba in 1959 brought the specter of communism uncomfortably close to the United States, and relations between these neighboring states deteriorated rapidly. The Soviets downed an American U-2 spy plane with their surface-to-air missiles on the eve of a spring 1960 Paris summit between Eisenhower and Nikita Khrushchev, embarrassing the United States and ending any chance for substantive peace talks. The abortive Bay of Pigs operation against Cuba in April 1961 carried cold war misfortunes and the sense of American weakness into the Kennedy administration, as did the Soviet Union's triumph in space, when on April 12, 1961, Yuri Gagarin became the first man to orbit the earth. This succession of foreign policy and technology embarrassments promoted calls for American action and shifted cold war policy to a more extreme position. Democrats and Republicans alike pushed for a resumption of the American initiative. Kennedy formulated his "flexible response" for the military and he oversaw a massive expansion of America's nuclear and conventional forces. The Republican "radical right" contingent increased in strength as spokesmen like Senator Barry Goldwater emerged as leaders of an increasingly bipartisan resurgence of cold warriorism.

The forces backing a more aggressive stance in the cold war were countered by those now openly proclaiming the apocalyptic reality of cold war life. Proponents of what would come to be called the "Armageddon attitude" emerged,[4] opposing the claims of civil defense experts and contesting the widespread public trust in America's physical safety. This growing apocalyptic sensibility demonstrated an understanding of the human reality of nuclear war: that no one would survive or would want to survive. This Armageddon attitude openly challenged the dangerous illusions of power and supremacy harbored in the nation's new offensive nuclear strategy. Nevil Shute's 1957 novel *On the Beach* and Stanley Kramer's 1959 film version were most responsible for defining and dramatizing this sober, more realistic view of nuclear aggression.

On the Beach depicts the end of human life. The novel captures the meaninglessness of indiscriminate death and presents the tragic outcome of humanity's atomic apathy. After a vast nuclear war has completely destroyed all life in the Northern Hemisphere, the "survivors" in the Southern Hemisphere quietly await the death by radiation that inexorably arrives in the winds blowing from the irradiated north. In Australia, life goes on with eerie normalcy despite the knowledge of humanity's impending extinction—there is little hysteria, little panic, and absolutely no attempt to escape the deadly radiation. The meaninglessness and the unfairness of it all are the issues that the condemned men and women most clearly address. By the time the fate of humanity is sealed by the war and its exhaustion of every weapon in nuclear stockpiles, including the "cobalt" H-bombs that produce the especially deadly radiation, too little information remains to piece together the reason or the rationale for the war. It is clear, however, that no cause could have justified the end result and no reason had directed the war. From what information exists, experts hypothesize about the escalation that occurred in the confusion after the first nuclear exchanges. The purposelessness of the war and its resulting annihilation of all human life leave only an impotent sense of cosmic injustice, and this unfocused anger is expressed by a young Australian woman: "It's not fair. No one in the Southern Hemisphere ever dropped a bomb, a hydrogen bomb or a cobalt bomb or any other sort of bomb. We had nothing to do with it. Why should we have to die because other countries nine or ten thousand miles away from us wanted to have a war? It's so bloody unfair."[5]

Beyond the simple issue of unfairness is the more profound question of responsibility. No single specific country can be assigned blame for the war, but the responsibility for extinction is clear: it belongs to all those living in the atomic age who, mirroring the inhabitants of this fictional Southern Hemisphere, live their lives normally while under the threat of annihilation, patiently waiting to die this unnatural death without noise or protest. Shute indicated his position in the novel's epigraph and title, taken from T. S. Eliot's "The Hollow Men": "In this last of meeting places / We grope together / And avoid speech / Gathered on this beach of the tumid river. . . . / This is the way the world ends / This is the way the world ends / This is the way the world ends / Not with a bang but a whimper."[6] The world does end with a whimper in *On the Beach,* as the last living members of the human race die tidy and neat deaths (most take government-issued tablets to induce death when the radiation sickness debilitates them), but it is a didactic whimper. A dying married couple discusses what had happened to the world, and the young husband—responding to his wife's question: "Couldn't anyone have stopped it?"—delivers the novel's warning:

> I don't know. . . . Some kinds of silliness you just can't stop. . . . I mean, if a couple of hundred million people all decide that their national honour requires them to drop cobalt bombs upon their neighbour, well, there's not much that you or I can do about it. The only possible hope would have been to educate them out of their silliness.[7]

Nevil Shute's *On the Beach* was a persuasive example of the Armageddon attitude, and it began educating the public to the deadly human reality of nuclear war. An international best-seller, *On the Beach* and its vision of passive human extinction became part of the awakening cultural imagination in this era of changing perspectives.[8] Unlike most of the symbolic images of apocalypse in the culture of the 1940s and 1950s, *On the Beach* directly attributed annihilation to the use of nuclear weapons and blamed the human beings who had acquiesced to their development and planned use. There were no prehistoric atomic monsters, no dehumanized zombies, and no last-minute solutions by scientists and government officials to the threat of extinction. The willingness and the ability to face the blunt realities of atomic war became a distinguishing feature of this rebellious attitude within the culture, and other stark presentations of nuclear war followed in the wake of the novel and film *On the Beach.* A 1959 episode of *The Twilight Zone* focused on the nature and meaning of nuclear war and confirmed the existence of a new dimension of cultural understanding in America at the end of the decade. In "Time Enough at Last" Rod Serling buttressed Nevil Shute's arguments for an atomic age awakening.

"Time Enough at Last" charts the fate of Henry Bemis, a quirky but endearing bank teller who loves to read, as indicated by the bottle-thick glasses he wears. His avocation is thwarted by his mean-spirited boss and his hostile wife, both of whom prevent Henry from snatching precious minutes with his books. The only time Henry has for reading is on his lunch hour, during which he retreats to the privacy and solitude of the bank's underground vault. On one particular day he carries his lunch, a book, and a newspaper into the vault and settles in. As he glances at the newspaper headline—"H-BOMB CAPABLE OF TOTAL DESTRUCTION"—the glass face of his watch suddenly shatters and a forceful blast shakes the vault.[9] When Henry recovers from the shock, he makes his way out of the vault to discover a completely desolate world. Surveying the destruction and emptiness, he realizes that "they're all dead . . . everybody's dead," and he becomes increasingly distraught as he comprehends the lifelessness around him. He understands that the vault saved his life, but he also comes to know the worthlessness of living in such a dead world: "The thing of it is, I'm not at all sure that I want to be alive." Henry wanders dazed through the rubble of civilization while Rod Serling narrates this "tour of a graveyard." Serling's comments underline the futility of Henry's search "for a spark in the ashes of a dead world" and the completeness of the vaporization of life, where all the comfortable and normal institutions of modern life "lie at his feet as battered monuments to what was but is no more."

As in *On the Beach,* there is no relief from the horror of this H-bomb annihilation. Henry Bemis, a man who had so little time and so little solitude in his previous life, now has a glut of these so terrifying that he decides to end his torture by suicide. As he raises a gun to his temple, however, his eyes fall on the ruins of the public library—and Henry finds a scrap of solace. He searches the rubble for books and piles up his treasures. He organizes the books for the months and years to come, and he has his measure of happiness: "And the best thing, the very best thing of all, is there's time now. There's all the time I need and all the time I want. Time. Time. Time. Ah, there's time enough at last." Just as Henry expresses his joy, however, his glasses slip off and the thick lenses splinter on the pavement, crushing Henry's modest comfort in apocalypse. He is left weeping at this last ironic cruelty, and he murmurs again and again. "That's not fair. That's not fair at all." Even the slimmest glimmer of hope or happiness could not survive in the Hiroshima-like terrain of the Twilight Zone, and Rod Serling briskly summed up the hard fate of Henry in his closing narration: "Henry Bemis, now just a part of a smashed landscape, just a piece of the rubble, just a fragment of what man had deeded to himself."

The knowledge of what man had deeded to himself in the atomic age was coming into focus: death. The culture of dissent also began to reflect on the malaise connected with the death wish in America. In both *On the Beach* and "Time Enough at Last" humans were in essence already dead when the bomb finally dropped: they were morally and spiritually oblivious to the deadly atomic evil with which they lived; they were hardened against human compassion and unforgiving of the slightest eccentricities of their neighbors—as was clear in the treatment afforded Henry Bemis. The vision of a dehumanized population which had received symbolic treatment in the earlier years of the cold war carried forward into the late 1950s and early 1960s, and a fatalistic malaise was seen as seeping into American society. While the new critical culture worked to prod Americans out of their acceptance of the bomb, it also worked to reveal the extent of America's obsession with death.

A preoccupation with unnatural and early death was one of the strangest cultural phenomena of these years. Beginning with the late 1959 release of Mark Dinning's "Teen Angel," teenage death songs became a mainstay of the youthful musical scene, and into the early 1960s these songs registered the fascination that death held in the cultural consciousness of America, and especially in young America. "Teen Angel" reached the top of the charts in early February 1960, and its mass popularity indicated the cultural receptivity for this kind of morbidity among teenagers.[10] The song tells the story of "that fateful night" when the car stalled on the railroad tracks and the young girl, even though pulled out, insists on running back to retrieve the school ring given to her by her boyfriend. She dies as a result of her actions, transmuted into the "teen angel" to whom the song is sung—by her boyfriend. He plaintively wonders if his teen angel can see or hear him and, more important, if she still loves him. He ends his song on a note of despairing finality, recognizing that he will never again kiss his dead sixteen-year-old girlfriend, buried that day.[11]

"Teen Angel" incorporated the themes of accident and death-thwarted love that resonated through this genre. Trains and motorcycles, but especially cars, are the vehicles of death in these songs; like James Dean before them, these youths in song live and die fast, recklessly. In Ray Peterson's "Tell Laura I Love Her" (1960) Tommy dies horribly in a "twisted wreck" at a stock car race, where he had tried to win the prize money in order to buy Laura a wedding ring. Dickie Lee's "Patches" (1962) offers a tale of double suicide, the drastic solution two teens chose when their love is broken up by parents and social conventions (Patches was from "shanty town" and was therefore not acceptable to the boy's parents). When Patches is found dead, floating facedown in the river, the boy decides to follow her lead that night. In the 1964 hits by Jan and Dean ("Dead Man's Curve") and the Shangri-Las ("Leader of the Pack") the screeching and screaming of crashing cars and motorcycles pronounce more death for teenagers.[12] While teenage death songs do not issue from an explicit sensibility of the bomb's deadliness, their sensitivity to the prevalence and possibility of death (death usually caused by technology, albeit more benign everyday technology) and their presentation of a cruel world nonetheless hinted at growing morbidity among teenagers in America.[13]

Even though some communities tried to limit the spread of this teenage attraction to death by banning the songs from the radio, there were too many signs and too much evidence of morbidity in the culture for such measures to be effective.[14] In Walker Percy's novel *The Moviegoer* (1960–1961) the protagonist Binx Bolling presents an evaluation of his own life and of modern American society that conveys the deep moral confusion that tormented some Americans in this era. On a personal search to find meaning and to elude the omnipresent "malaise" suffocating him, Binx cannot escape the chaos or the impending catastrophe he senses, and he wonders at the lack of feeling in the everyday lives of those around him: "For some time now the impression has been growing upon me that everyone is dead. It happens when I speak to people. In the middle of a sentence it will come over me: yes, beyond a doubt this is death. . . . At such times it seems that the conversation is spoken by automatons who have no choice in what they say."[15] Hate is the only real and palpable expression of life, according to Binx, and he reads controversial liberal and conservative magazines to glean their mutual hatred of one another: "This hatred strikes me as one of the few signs of life remaining in the world. This is another thing about the world which is upside down: all the friendly and likable people seem dead to me; only the haters seem alive."[16]

Binx is not himself beyond such deadness; in fact, he suffers heartily from "the malaise": "What is the malaise? you ask. The malaise is the pain of loss. The world is lost to you, the world and the people in it, and there remains only you and the world and you no more able to be in the world than Banquo's ghost."[17] On his thirtieth birthday this lost Binx comes to terms with himself and his failed search, contemplating the despairing quality of life and humanity in this debilitated world:

Now in the thirty-first year of my dark pilgrimage on this earth and knowing less than I ever knew before, having learned only to recognize merde when I see it, having inherited no more from my father than a good nose for merde, for every species of shit that flies—my only talent—smelling merde from every quarter, living in fact in the very century of merde, the great shithouse of scientific humanism where needs are satisfied, everyone becomes an anyone, a warm and creative person, and prospers like a dung beetle, and one hundred percent of people are humanists and ninety-eight percent believe in God, and men are dead, dead, dead; and the malaise has settled like fall-out and what people really fear is not that the bomb will fall but that the bomb will not fall—on this my thirtieth birthday.[18]

Binx's understanding of the perversions of atomic age life, of the bomb's sickness in a professedly humanist and God-believing nation, exposes the dawning cultural recognition of humanity's contradictory and death-conscious comportment in this age. From this open confrontation with nuclear death and malaise arose the new cultural hope for moral change and regeneration. Norman Gottwald, professor of Old Testament at the Andover-Newton Theological School, discussed the signs of arousal in 1960 and at the same time argued for a quickened pace of action given the much weakened moral condition of man. Gottwald claimed that "everywhere men are awakening to the fact that ours is the first generation in an utterly new era," but he also noted in caution that "whether they are awakening rapidly enough is open to question—and apprehension."[19] He revealed an understanding of the time lag that had delayed the awakening, but he also recognized the urgency that accompanied the arrival of 1960:

Arthur Koestler calls 1960 the year 15 P.H. (Post-Hiroshima). He finds it natural that the full import of man's newly found ability to bring history to an end will take a long while to spread from the unconscious mind into the conscious levels of thought and finally into political policies. Others wonder if we can afford the time. They feel nervously for the pulse of the creature who spares no efforts to perfect the means and to multiply the possibilities for destruction.[20]

As the pulse of the "creature" grew ever more faint in the midst of resurgent cold warriorism, a new sense of time and a new sense of deadly nuclear realities contributed to raising awareness to the conscious cultural mind of America. Fueling the moral revolt that exploded in the 1960s were these cultural expressions of an activist and polarizing cold war debate in the late fifties and early sixties. The "political schizophrenia" that *The Nation* clearly perceived in March 1961 had become more apparent by the turn of the decade—just as Norman Bates's schizophrenia had surfaced in a moment of stress. The magazine searched for a sign that the schism between nuclear reality and illusion could be closed, and it discovered a modest basis on which to rest its desires for peace. *The Nation* pointed out: "If there is no effective peace movement, neither is there a war movement. The divorce from political realities has gone so far and no farther. The opportunity to influence the mass of citizens remains."[21]

While a small straw to grasp in this perilous age, the absence of a war movement in atomic age America had significant cultural meaning in a presumably apathetic population. The restraining influence of this neutral or even negative American response to cold warriorism became obvious as Americans' divorce from political realities reached its extreme in the hysteria surrounding first the Berlin crisis and then the Cuban missile crisis. Ironically for *The Nation,* it was precisely this intensification of America's schizophrenia that helped to promote a revolutionary cultural quest for a reinvigorated peace and morality—but it was a quest that gained momentum from the presence of a war movement that effectively ended the negative control that American apathy had exerted.

John F. Kennedy orchestrated an abrupt end to atomic apathy when he placed the power of the presidency behind a renewed and strengthened program of civil defense. On July 25, 1961, Kennedy addressed Americans on national television and urged the country to prepare for thermonuclear war by building family fallout shelters. The president and his government planned to provide all necessary information, as Kennedy indicated in his speech: "To recognize the possibilities of nuclear war in the missile age without our citizens knowing what they should do and where they should go would be a failure of responsibility. In the coming months I hope to let every citizen know what steps he can take without delay to protect his family in case of an attack."[22] In the months following Kennedy's speech massive amounts of civil defense information were distributed, shelter building reached its greatest peak, and panic was at an all-time high. Lending the sharp edge of hysteria to this unprecedented shelter craze was its origin in the Berlin crisis. The cold war atmosphere in America was now charged with the electrifying threat of war with the Soviet Union, and Kennedy had conveyed the seriousness of the threat with his admonition to the public to begin "without delay" the widespread building of fallout shelters.

Kennedy clearly linked the urgent need for shelters to the growing crisis in Berlin, a subject he also discussed in his July 25 speech. The anomalous position of West Berlin, enclosed by communist-controlled East Germany, constituted one of the more important unresolved issues from World War II. Since 1958 Soviet premier Nikita Khrushchev had been demanding a solution to the problem of West Berlin—and particularly to the problem of East German refugees flowing to freedom through the "escape hatch" of West Berlin—but the East-West confrontation over this issue did not reach frightening proportions until the summer of 1961. Both Kennedy and Khrushchev felt pressure from their countries to act without compromise to defend the interests of their nations in Berlin. Kennedy described the defense of West Berlin as central to the defense of freedom in Germany, Western Europe, and the "entire free world"; he therefore had to stand firm for free access to Berlin (especially after his failure in the Bay of Pigs).[23] Khrushchev bristled under the tensions aroused by Kennedy's vast expansion of the United States's military and nuclear capabilities and by the renewed boasts of American superiority. The exodus of East Germans to the West was a propaganda embarrassment that he could no longer tolerate. The belligerence of both the United States and the Soviet Union made credible the impending threat of a thermonuclear battle between the two nations.

While Kennedy steadfastly promoted the American ability and willingness to fight over Berlin, Khrushchev complained that "a military hysteria is now being drummed up in the United States."[24] He acted swiftly to quell the turmoil and solve the problem of refugees when he erected the Berlin Wall overnight on August 13, 1961. Tensions increased, however, in the following weeks when Khrushchev suddenly resumed nuclear testing, ignoring the informal Soviet-American moratorium on such testing that had been in effect since 1958. In a shocking show of strength meant to counter American claims of nuclear superiority, the Soviets detonated a series of bombs of unequaled megatonnage (the largest of which was a fifty-eight megaton bomb, three to five thousand times more powerful than the Hiroshima atomic bomb).[25] Kennedy now accused Khrushchev of "atomic blackmail," declaring, "What the Soviet Union is obviously testing is not only nuclear devices but the will and determination of the free world to resist such tactics and to defend freedom."[26] Americans envisioned Khrushchev as a ruthless warmonger, and *Time* magazine captured this spectacular and terrifying vision of Khrushchev on its September 8, 1961, cover: an angry and gesticulating Khrushchev framed by a giant billowing nuclear fireball.[27] The crisis dissipated gradually over the following months, but one result was an American population more intimately aware of the risks and the realities of life in the atomic age.

An alerted and active public was exactly what Kennedy had hoped for in delivering his July 1961 message on civil defense. In an earlier speech in May he had also promoted civil defense as insurance—"insurance, we trust, that will never be needed; but insurance which we could never forgive ourselves for forgoing in the event of catastrophe."[28] Disappointed at the lack of response to this backing of civil defense, Kennedy aimed in his July speech "to arouse the people, without creating undue alarm." An article in *Newsweek* discussed the president's expectations for his speech: "The President wanted a far greater public response to—and deeper understanding of—the basic problem than has so far been evinced." The article also pointed out the "biggest obstacles" to such a rousing civil defense response: "apathy, complacence, and sometimes contempt."[29] Delivered in the midst of the Berlin crisis, Kennedy's civil defense speech achieved a public response that exceeded all expectations, but it was mingled with as much alarm as it was with arousal. Nonetheless, the obstacles of apathy, complacence, and contempt came tumbling down, and the nation experienced a sort of mass hysteria peculiar to the atomic age.

The day after the president's July speech the *New York Times* assured everyone that Americans were "calm" and "confident" and that they were suffering from "no shock and no sense of panic."[30] The events of the next few days and months contradicted such assurances, however, and Americans showed every sign of panic and concern: thermonuclear war had become real. *Newsweek* opened its account of the postspeech reaction with a less calm and confident scenario:

The phones began ringing the morning after the President's speech. Some callers were belligerent. "Why are we so unprepared for nuclear attack?" one man demanded of the Office of Civil and Defense Mobilization. Others were anxious. "Mothers want to know if they should stockpile food," an aide at the New York City civil-defense office reported. "They're worried about their children. I don't remember as many calls in my ten years here." Spurred by the sense of deepening crisis over Berlin, the callers echoed a common theme: "What could be done, individually and collectively, to meet the unutterable horror of nuclear war?"[31]

Despite the public's fear and panic *Newsweek* considered the nervous interest in civil defense beneficial. According to the magazine, "This new concern was salutary: It helped to dispel some atomic-age mythology which held that the public was apathetic about shelters, that CD was a boondoggle."[32] Atomic age apathy about civil defense and nuclear war indeed appeared dispelled. The new respect for civil defense and the new hunger for information were revealed in the statistics: in the wake of Kennedy's speech twenty-two million copies of the Department of Defense pamphlet *The Family Fallout Shelter* were distributed, as were millions of copies of another government pamphlet, *Family Food Stockpile for Survival.*[33]

In this new atmosphere evidence emerged that quite a few Americans had already taken civil defense seriously. The Office of Civil and Defense Mobilization (OCDM) revealed that one million households had built shelters but had been too timid to admit to their preparedness in the previously cynical and complacent society. "They seem rare because most people are a little embarrassed about them," claimed an OCDM official.[34] Little timidity or embarrassment characterized the supporters and builders of shelters in the intense months of the bomb shelter craze when a kind of radical survivalist attitude accompanied a psychological and physical gearing up for war provoked by the Berlin crisis. After first discussing the late 1950s view that equated nuclear war with "a vaporized planet—charred, radioactive, lifeless," *Newsweek* reported that "another school of thought has emerged to challenge this dominant 'Armageddon attitude.'"[35] The magazine explained that "the new school holds that a nuclear war does not necessarily mean the complete and utter destruction of civilization," and it introduced the Rand Corporation's military theorist Herman Kahn as the spokesman for this new type of thinking that distinguished "degrees of awfulness" in thermonuclear war. The *Newsweek* article quoted Kahn on the pragmatic benefits of civil defense and its ability to guarantee survival for at least some Americans in the event of war: "If one says that it is not true that everybody is killed but that only 50 million people are, this does not mean that the speaker is implying that 50 million people are a small number, but that 50 million people are much less than 150 million."[36] A sort of cultural accommodation to the probability of thermonuclear warfare and an accompanying acceptance of the need for both an activist civil defense and a sanguine fatalism about the death of millions underlay much of this outspoken survivalist sensibility. Another sign of the rising seriousness in the preparation for war involved the stocking of shelters with controversial items: guns. This issue gained national prominence amidst the feverish interest in shelters when *Time* published the "Gun Thy Neighbor?" article a few weeks after Kennedy's speech.

The article presented as introduction the hardened words of a suburban Chicago resident, words that reflected the intensified survivalist intentions in America during the Berlin crisis:

> When I get my shelter finished, I'm going to mount a machine gun at the hatch to keep the neighbors out if the bomb falls. I'm deadly serious about this. If the stupid American public will not do what they have to to save themselves, I'm not going to run the risk of not being able to use the shelter I've taken the trouble to provide to save my own family.[37]

Time noted that "this kind of tough talk from a Chicago suburbanite last week had echoes all over the U.S., as the headlines spread uneasiness and the shelter business boomed," and the magazine discussed the manifestations and the morality of this new American "toughness."[38]

The article focused on the kind of preparations made by the Charles Davis family of Austin, Texas. A hardware dealer, Davis had constructed a well-stocked and well-armed shelter. He was equipped with four rifles and a .357 magnum pistol. A photograph of the intent and unsmiling Davis family in their shelter revealed their large stockpile of canned goods. Davis sealed his shelter with a four-inch-thick wooden door, explaining the precaution: "This isn't to keep radiation out, it's to keep people out." He also kept a tear-gas gun handy, in case the neighbors reached the safety of his shelter before he and his family did: "If I fire six or seven tear-gas bullets into the shelter, they'll either come out or the gas will get them."[39] *Time* made clear that it was not just individuals taking precautions against those unprepared hordes who would seek shelter in the event of an attack. Cities and towns on the distant outskirts of Los Angeles feared the mass of refugees that would issue from that metropolitan area, and they began formulating plans to fight off the refugees. A Las Vegas civil defense leader argued for the creation of a five-thousand-man militia to retard the Californians who would descend on Nevada "like a swarm of locusts," and the Riverside County civil defense coordinator suggested that all survival kits contain a pistol to fend off refugees from Los Angeles. He argued that "there's nothing in the Christian ethic which denies one's right to protect oneself and one's family."[40]

Time questioned "the guardians of the Christian ethic" on the ethics of shelter defense, and the religious leaders surveyed were divided on the subject. Their positions ranged from support for protecting one's shelter to a general condemnation of the immorality of nuclear war. The dean of a Baptist seminary believed that "if you allow a tramp to take the place of your children in your shelter, you are in error. A Christian has the obligation to ensure the safety of those dependent on him." But a Methodist minister argued that "the immorality takes place much earlier than when people are in their shelters. It occurs when people think they can protect themselves from an all-out nuclear war."[41] The reader response to the "Gun Thy Neighbor?" article was as split as the religious response. The letters to the editor included some amusing sarcasm, like the short note from a Los Angeles man who nominated shelter owner Davis for Neighbor of the Year, but most responses offered serious support for or opposition to the notion of using guns against shelterless neighbors.[42] While another Austin, Texas, man supported his fellow townsman Davis, proclaiming that "guns are a man's best friend," a Detroit woman described Davis as a "monster": "I have often pondered the advisability of a bomb shelter, wondering whether survival may not be the most horrible choice. If survival depends upon living with such monsters, Mr. Davis need not worry. I, for one, would not knock on his door."[43] The following week's batch of letters displayed the same divisiveness. A young Connecticut man admitted, "I was planning to get my parents to build a bomb shelter with a removable top that could double as a swimming pool." He changed his mind after reading about Davis: "After reading about the Davis family, I decided that it would be much better to die from the bomb's fallout than live in a world ridden with people who would gun down their neighbors."[44] A California woman defended Davis because of her family's experience with friends and neighbors after building a shelter: "For the most part we have met with smirks or polite indifference. Since we have spent our time and money to prepare for something we sincerely hope will never come, we would not hesitate to defend ourselves with guns if necessary against these same people who would be threatening our lives because of their ignorance."[45] Even though early opinion on the ethics of shelters appeared divided and even though it was this sort of moral debate that characterized an awakening American culture, the expressions of moral concern elicited as a result of the surging survivalist and war impulse nonetheless tended to be overshadowed in the early months of the shelter craze by the sheer hysteria of war fear and preparedness. Triumphant in these summer and early fall months was a sort of panicked but firm determination to come to terms with civil defense and the likelihood of thermonuclear war.

Between August and October 1961 Americans found themselves becoming accustomed to the rather bizarre accoutrements of civil defense and thermonuclear warfare. Popular periodicals and survival advertisements reported and promoted the shelter craze, and through these mediums the culture revealed the growing domestication of shelters and a wide variety of strange survival products and institutions. A *Life* magazine cover of September 15, 1961, featured a man outfitted in a ghostly-looking "civilian fallout suit"; the man has his arm and hand raised above his head, as if to physically repel the fallout, and the caption announced the magazine's major story: "How You Can SURVIVE FALLOUT."[46] The survival and shelter companies that capitalized on the craze advertised their products and helped to familiarize Americans with civil defense equipment. The "Surviv-All, Inc." company, like *Life,* urged the necessity of fallout suits in its advertisement for its $19.95 "decontamination suit." The advertisement described the suit's "vital features" (its vinyl material, its breathing devices, and its "unaided entry" and "unaided exit" features) as well as its economy features: "Although this suit is intended to be disposable after use, nevertheless where decontamination facilities exist, the suit can be cleaned and used again."[47]

Like Surviv-All, Inc., hundreds of private civil defense-oriented companies—like the "Peace-O-Mind Shelter Co." of Texas or California's "Nuclear Survival Corp."—advertised and displayed their products, whether in magazines, at state fairs, or at model home sites.[48] Just as shelter companies provided information and education to the frightened and curious public, so too did popular periodicals become educational tools for information-hungry Americans. In its September 15 issue *Life* devoted its attention to the Berlin crisis and, as indicated by its fallout suit cover, to survival via fallout shelters and other survival equipment. The magazine discussed the cold war setting and impetus behind the shelter craze and then turned into a veritable how-to book on shelter building. In its editorial "The Power and the Honor" *Life* insisted that America honor its commitment to defend freedom in Berlin, that America stand ready to fight—and be victorious—in any impending "hot" war:

> Darkness falls from the air. Khrushchev's nuclear debris over North America [the atmospheric radioactivity resulting from the resumed nuclear testing], on its way around the globe, redeclares the Cold War's ubiquity. His brutal intransigence on Berlin redeclares its seriousness. The Cold War may turn hot any week. We have been told that nobody can win that hot war—and there is still reason to hope and pray that it can be avoided. But the Berlin Crisis makes one thing clear, even to Americans who have long preferred not to face it. The Cold War will have a winner. And it will have a loser. Winner and loser may not be decided in Berlin. . . . But Berlin is one test of our readiness to fight for freedom, and that readiness is one qualification for victory in the Cold War.[49]

The editorial maintained that "Khrushchev must be aware that the American people are willing to face nuclear war for Berlin," and it proudly boasted of "our spontaneous boom in shelter-building" as proof of this willingness. The editorial referred readers to the issue's feature on shelters, and the magazine's encouragement to Americans to build shelters and survive was given the highest kind of endorsement in a letter from President Kennedy. He wrote upholding the intentions of *Life*'s shelter plans, and the letter served as the opening to the article "Fallout Shelters: A New Urgency, Big Things to Do—and What You Must Learn." After discussing the government's work in progress on civil defense (preparing and marking public buildings for shelters and improving warning systems), the president endorsed *Life*'s shelter program:

> I urge you to read and consider seriously the contents of this issue of *Life*. The security of our country and the peace of the world are the objectives of our policy. But in these dangerous days when both these objectives are threatened we must prepare for all eventualities. The ability to survive coupled with the will to do so therefore are essential to our country.[50]

Life, taking its cue from the president, stressed the urgency for shelters—an urgency that had overturned completely the past civil defense complacence of Americans. The magazine noted that as a result of Berlin and the Soviet nuclear tests, "the people woke up to the fact that they ought to be doing something to protect themselves," and it discussed the change represented by this awakening to civil defense:

> This was a new idea. For years, most people have had the fatalistic idea that it was no use trying to do anything about protection against a nuclear bomb. If the blast did not kill them, they felt, radiation certainly would. The man down the street with the backyard shelter was considered odd. But he is actually a solid, sensible man—and a responsible citizen.[51]

Life applauded the cultural transformation of shelter builders into respectable and responsible Americans, and it reinforced and rewarded such war preparedness with its optimistic assurances of survival in fallout shelters: "Prepared, you and your family could have 97 chances out of 100 to survive."[52]

Life's ideas and plans for shelters ranged from the rudimentary to the sophisticated. The magazine offered simple suggestions, noting, "If you want a rudimentary shelter, you can dig a cave in a hillside or build wooden double walls in your basement, filling them with dirt." It also displayed blueprints for four other types of shelters: the "simple room in the basement built with concrete blocks," the "big pipe in the backyard under three feet of earth," "a double-walled bunker for safety above ground," and "a $700 prefabricated job to put up in four hours."[53] *Life* included pictures of each of these shelters and illustrated both the actual assemblage and then complete stocking of the Kelsey-Hayes prefabricated shelter (to be mass-marketed by Sears, Roebuck and Co. that fall). The equipment was cataloged, including the air blower and filter, the "14-day supply of Multi-Purpose Food, water and vitamins," and the radiation meter. The Carlson family, whose father and son had demonstrated the erection of the shelter, was finally pictured in the shelter, each member of the family assigned his or her duties. The father looked after the heavy tools and emergency equipment, the mother oversaw "the larder of canned foods" and the supply of water, one daughter took care of the linens, the son kept the flashlights, transistor radio, and batteries in working order, and the other daughter served as "shelter librarian," stocking books and games (including the game "Life") to "help pass the time." Keeping the shelter more cozy was its color scheme: "The inside walls of the shelter are painted bright colors to add a note of cheerfulness and increase illumination."[54]

Life also documented the clever ways Americans accustomed themselves to the everyday reality of living with civil defense—like painting the interior of shelters. The "pioneers of self-protection in barnyard and patio" also camouflaged shelters by making them usable in normal life. An Illinois farmer housed and fed his cattle in a huge steel shelter that doubled as an atomic age barn, a Florida family made their shelter—replete with roof garden—a part of their patio, and a Texas teenager employed her family's backyard shelter as a makeshift "clubhouse" where she chatted on the phone with friends.[55] *Time* magazine also commented on the ingenious decorating advice and everyday comforts being provided for and by shelter owners, and this kind of cultural evidence spoke of the rapid incorporation of shelters into the everyday world of Americans. In Salt Lake City the daughter of a local civil defense official painted a large mural of nature—"a picture window"—on the wall of the family shelter, and a Jacksonville, Florida, millionaire's shelter was "equipped with an elevator, a pool table, and a keg of wine."[56] Virgil Couch of the Office of Civil Defense in Battle Creek, Michigan, argued that "civil defense must be part of the normal way of life. Like smallpox vaccination, we've got to get used to it and build it into the fabric of our lives." Americans finally appeared ready to follow such advice.[57]

Even as Americans began to show signs of accommodation to the ideas of war, shelter, and civil defense in general, accompanying signs of fear and panic also arose as a result of the Berlin crisis and the shelter boom. Unlike *Life,* which presented a calm and rational account of shelters and the American response, *Time* focused more attention on the fear evident in the early months of the shelter craze. While *Time* generally envisioned Americans as stoic and "resolved to face Communist pressure without yielding an inch," its September 29 issue nonetheless contained a portrait of panicked Americans:

Nikita Khrushchev's war of nerves was plainly having an effect on the U.S. citizenry. Across the nation last week, there was endless conversation about the threat of nuclear war. There was apprehension and an edge of sadness as men and women looked at their children and wondered about their chances of survival. There were the usual neurotics. In Chicago, public officials received a spate of calls from women complaining that their hair curlers were radioactive, from men suspicious of the olives in their martinis (Chicago Psychiatrist Milton A. Dushkin named the ailment "nucleomito-phobia"—fear of the atom). A motorcade of thirty food faddists set out from New York to find new, safe homes in the northern California town of Chico—blandly ignoring the fact that a Titan missile pad, which would presumably be a prime Soviet target, was less than seven miles from their sanctuary.[58]

Beyond revealing the kind of apprehension and seemingly "irrational" behavior of Americans, *Time*'s accounts of the shelter craze also conveyed the sense of how strange and extreme civil defense appeared to an America only just beginning to face the probability of thermonuclear war. Over two months after President Kennedy's speech *Time* reported that the subject of shelters was still preoccupying Americans, who discussed it everywhere: "At cocktail parties and P.T.A. meetings and family dinners, on buses and commuter trains and around office watercoolers, talk turns to shelters."[59] One Los Angeles man had difficulty getting used to the increasingly common sight of trucks carrying bomb shelters up and down the California highways; after watching a shelter-carrying flatbed truck rumble down Sepulveda Boulevard, he told *Time*: "It gives you a jolt, seeing that shelter going down the road. A year ago I'd have snickered."[60] The oddity of shelters was often matched by the sickly strangeness of some of the items deemed necessary for life in the shelter. Along with the radiation suits, the canned water, and the "Foam-Ettes—the Toothpaste Tablet You Can Use ANYTIME, ANYWHERE—WHEREVER YOU ARE, Even In a Family Fallout Shelter" that survivalists recommended, *Time* included in its list of items to stock "perhaps the most ghoulish shelter article": the "'burial suit,' a $50 polyvinyl plastic wrapper for anyone who dies in a shelter. It contains chemicals to 'keep odors down' and can be used as a sleeping bag by the living."[61]

Time made it clear that Americans were exhibiting not so much panic as "concern" and "strength," but the magazine also approvingly portrayed the extreme forms often taken by that concern and strength. In late September *Time* recorded how "last week just such strength expressed the nation's will in even more activist forms," and it proceeded to laud the growing membership and intense patriotism of the "Minute Man" organization:

> In Santa Barbara, 23 "survival groups" joined the "Minute Man" vigilante organization, swelled its membership to 2,400, enthusiastically began an elaborate program to train themselves as guerrilla fighters. They have caches of water in the California hills, 100 rounds of ammunition for every weapon they own. Their aim: to survive, and to fight the Russians if they should attempt to land in the U.S. after a nuclear attack.[62]

The extremist attitudes and actions prompted by the Berlin crisis and the shelter craze led to an escalating cultural debate over the ethics of shelters and nuclear war. While the robust supporters of cold war strength and preparation had seized the initiative in the early months of crisis—and this position remained the majority sentiment in the early sixties—those who opposed this sort of extremism started to express themselves openly. *Time,* as it had done in its earlier "Gun Thy Neighbor?" article, presented evidence of this intensifying cultural battle.

In the letters to *Time's* editor on the subject of shelters, the rigidity of American attitudes revealed itself clearly. Reflecting the lingering psychological effect of the surprise Japanese attack on Pearl Harbor, a number of writers offered enthusiastic support for American preparation. One letter proclaimed that "this time we will not be caught napping," and another announced that "it's good to read of Americans preparing for Pearl Harbor *before*—and not after!"[63] In stark contrast to such sentiments a psychology professor from the University of Maryland reviled *Time* for fomenting and spreading the hysteria about war and shelters:

> Race suicide, whether by H-bomb, fallout, or simple starvation in the months following successful survival of these, and destruction of the human cultural heritage are not justified by any issue now facing us, anywhere in the world. We must refuse to walk into the H-crematoria you are cajoling us into, in the name of the dubious semantics of "freedom."[64]

Time openly acknowledged the more formal debate taking place in the culture over the morality of nuclear war, a debate given new and urgent currency by the Berlin crisis and by America's public demonstration of its willingness to fight a thermonuclear battle. In its October 13 issue *Time* included a piece entitled "Aristotle & The Bomb: Red, Dead or Heroic?" which examined the recent debate among intellectuals on the question: "Can Western civilization use the horrible weapons of thermonuclear war to save itself, or would such a war destroy the very things the West stands for?"[65] *Time* first discussed the emotional and instinctual American acceptance of the necessity of fighting communism with nuclear weapons and offered the assurance that "behind the emotions and instinct lies a carefully reasoned moral case." The magazine made this "moral case" clear by stressing the views of philosophy professor Sidney Hook in its coverage of the intellectual debate over nuclear war. Presenting first the view of Harvard professor of history H. Stuart Hughes, who argued against nuclear war as a violation of Western principles and as an abrogation of the rule in war that ends should justify means (and no end could justify nuclear extermination), *Time* commented: "By any measurement, Hughes's arguments do not represent a large segment of U.S. public opinion, but they do epitomize much of the moral confusion the West has suffered in contemplating The Bomb." The article proceeded then to focus on what the magazine considered to be the less confused and more representative moral beliefs of Hook, who relied on Aristotle for his justification of risking all life in nuclear war. According to Hook:

> The West, buttressed in part by belief in immortality, whether as myth or fact, has always maintained that there are certain values more important than life itself. . . . It was Aristotle who said that it is not life as such, or under any conditions, that is of value, but the good life. The free man is one who in certain situations refuses to accept life if it means spiritual degradation. The man who declares that survival at all costs is the end of existence is morally dead.[66]

Even though other intellectuals pointed out that Aristotle had not considered "mass extermination" in his formula for gauging the good life, Hook stood firm in his belief that communist life was not the good life and that Americans had to remain "heroic" in keeping their anticommunist values more sacred than "life as such."[67]

While reflective of the mainstream cold war determination to fight that gained strength in the early 1960s, Hook's moral argument for nuclear war faced a more strident cultural challenge in the coming months, a challenge that viewed the Berlin crisis and shelter craze as productive of the "spiritual degradation" and moral death that Hook had ascribed to more peaceful points of view. In its cover story on shelters in late October *Time* indicated the sort of issue that helped to polarize positions in the waning days of acute crisis. While brushing aside the moral qualms raised, *Time* pointed out that "controversy still storms over one possible item of shelter equipment: guns."[68] What had given new impetus to the controversy about shelters and guns was the nationally publicized position taken by Father L. C. McHugh. Writing in late September for the Jesuit magazine *America,* Father McHugh had posited his "guidelines of essential morality at the shelter hatchway." He upheld the Christian right of self-defense as justification for "the use of violence to defend life and its equivalent goods," and he determined that it was "misguided charity" not to defend shelters with guns, because shelterless neighbors seeking entrance to shelters were "unjust aggressors." These aggressors could be "repelled with whatever means [to] effectively deter their assault," according to McHugh, without a violation of Christian ethics.[69]

Time included but downplayed the outraged reaction of the Reverend Angus Dun, Episcopal bishop of Washington, D.C., who labeled the use of guns against neighbors "utterly immoral."[70] The bishop explained his view of Christianity, guns, and shelters: "I do not see how any Christian conscience can condone a policy which puts supreme emphasis on saving your own skin without regard for the plight of your neighbor. Justice, mercy and brotherly love do not cease to operate, even in the final apocalypse."[71] While dismissed by *Time,* it was just Bishop Dun's sort of moral anger and spiritual concern for human brotherhood that was piqued by the Berlin crisis and bomb shelter craze. As the culture absorbed the meaning of the war and shelter panic and as the ability and need to maintain a thermonuclear bravado began to fade with the passage of the most tense moments of the Berlin crisis, critical evaluations of shelters and their ethics gained a greater public hearing. The renewed cold war imperative had created the atmosphere conducive to shelter and war activism in the early months of the craze, but a reinvigorated attraction to peace, morality, and humanism characterized—and helped to prompt—both the denouement of America's hysteria about shelters and the debut of a rebellious new atomic age spirituality.

Beginning in October and November 1961 and continuing well into 1962 the spiritual and human degradation associated with shelters and thermonuclear war became a paramount concern in the culture.[72] Men of religion, like Bishop Dun, were in the cultural forefront of the rising moral opposition to the "shelter hatch ethics" espoused by Father McHugh, and the religious outrage spurred by McHugh's shelter defense helped to inspire a more generalized cultural outrage.[73] The secular culture also poured forth reasoned and moral challenges to the values expressed in shelter building, shelter arming, and the hardened acceptance of thermonuclear warfare implied by those actions. In fact, certain doubts about the human and community efficacy of civil defense arose earlier in the secular culture. Even before October and November there were some signals of cultural aloofness from the shelter and war hysteria—an aloofness born from the contemplation of the more human consequences of thermonuclear war and shelter selfishness. From its earliest accounts of the shelter craze spawned by Kennedy's speech, *Newsweek* demonstrated a more reserved and skeptical attitude than did many of America's other popular periodicals. In its August 7 issue *Newsweek* asked in an article title, "Civil Defense: Who'd Survive?" and the article itself examined different schools of thought on civil defense, tempering the optimistic predictions for survival with the pessimistic expectations of the more dubious. Wondering about the society's ability to reconstruct itself after nuclear war, the magazine noted the positive attitude of theorist Herman Kahn: "Basing his thinking on the remarkable resiliency of the Nazi productive machinery after massive bombing, he believes the economy could be 'even more flexible than a salamander (which can grow new parts when the old ones are destroyed).'" *Newsweek*'s own thinking about the postwar scene was based on more human concerns:

> But families may prove less salamander-like. When the bombs begin to fall, the husband might be at work, the older children at school, and the young and the mother at home. Whatever the exact target or time of destruction, few families would likely be untouched. Kahn suggests that survivors will "put something together," perhaps in Vermont. But for the husband who has lost his family or for the wife without her children, that task of re-creation may require a supreme act of will—more will, indeed, than is required to insure that the "impossible" does not happen.[74]

Newsweek's sober and sensible conclusion contrasted sharply with other predictions of mass survival in a sheltered America, but other areas of the popular culture mirrored its focus on the human costs and losses of nuclear war. A topical episode of *The Twilight Zone* counted the crushing of the human and neighborly spirit as one of the costs of the bomb shelter craze. Aired on September 29, 1961, "The Shelter" told a story of community destruction in an era of shelters and air alerts. Serling introduced the episode with a plea for reason: "What you are about to watch is a nightmare. It is not meant to be prophetic, it need not happen, it's the fervent and urgent prayer of all men of good will that it never shall happen. But in this place, in this moment, it *does* happen. This is the Twilight Zone."[75] It may have been the Twilight Zone, but "The Shelter" addressed a problem current in America during the Berlin crisis: a neighborhood party for Doc Stockton is interrupted by a radio announcement urging citizens to go to their shelters as UFOs have been detected by radar; Doc takes his wife and son to their shelter, refusing entrance to his unprepared neighbors, who finish battering down the shelter door just at the moment when the radio signals that the alert was a false alarm. The neighbors face each other in shame, their relations forever destroyed. In his concluding words Serling delivered a Berlin crisis sermon: "No moral, no message, no prophetic tract, just a simple statement of fact: for civilization to survive, the human race has to remain civilized. Tonight's very small exercise in logic from the Twilight Zone."[76]

In a mere thirty minutes *The Twilight Zone* exposed the loss of human compassion embodied in shelter ethics.[77] This position gained added authority when ex-president Eisenhower delivered his authoritative statement about shelters on October 18, 1961. He told the press that he was opposed to the building of home shelters, and he made clear that he would not want to survive without the other members of his family: "If I were in a very fine shelter and they were not there, I would just walk out. I would not want to face that kind of world."[78] As many respected Americans, like Eisenhower and the numerous spokesmen for America's various religious denominations, expressed their deep reservations about shelters and the morality of survival in thermonuclear warfare, the cultural atmosphere became receptive to critical evaluation of America's new emphasis on civil defense. In November 1961 *Newsweek* and the *New York Times Magazine* published two articles that asked the same question, a question representative of the rising moral revolt against shelters and their ethics: "Are Shelters the Answer?" *Newsweek* began the debate in its November 6 article, "Survival: Are Shelters the Answer?" and anthropologist Margaret Mead's "Are Shelters the Answer?" in the November 26 issue of the *New York Times Magazine* carried it forward.

Newsweek set the stage for its questioning of shelter policies by describing the vast impact the shelter craze had made on America. According to the article, "less than six months after President Kennedy called for vigorous new civil defense programs, the nation is responding with a vengeance."[79] Gone was the old apathy and complacence of Americans: "The President's own eloquent statements about the duties of every man to provide for his family—plus Khrushchev's truculence over Berlin—have vaporized, as effectively as the latest Soviet superbomb, the old foot-dragging indifference." The magazine noted that "in place of apathy, however, there now exists a wild fallout of confusion, concern, commercialism, and misinformation," and it went on to show the human fallout of the shelter craze:

> There is evidence that the Administration policies, which seem to emphasize an every-man-for-himself approach, have succeeded in bringing out the worst side of human nature. Some citizens are behaving as if they were

cavemen already. A number of happy shelter owners have announced that they would gun down their shelterless neighbors if their refuge were threatened by overcrowding. . . . Ethics-in-the-shelter has become a subject of serious theological debate.[80]

Most "remarkable" and abhorrent to *Newsweek,* though, was how "the talk of shelters and protection has by some mad alchemy transmuted the unutterable horrors of thermonuclear war into a rather cozy affair." The magazine was most critical of *Life's* upbeat treatment of shelters and survival, and it condemned as having "no authority whatsoever" *Life's* blithe claim that ninety-seven out of every hundred could survive war if sheltered. *Newsweek* argued that "the facts of nuclear war, fallout, and shelter life are far more complex and sobering" than *Life's* portrayal, and the article addressed some of these darker facts.[81]

Newsweek first made clear that individual shelters were well beyond the financial means of many Americans: "For most homeowners, the $1,000-and-up price tags on shelters are apparently too steep." The magazine went on to raise doubts about other civil defense assumptions: optimistic appraisals of survival were a "fantasy" (physicist Ralph Lapp was quoted on this subject); shelters might save some individual lives, but they would not contribute to the overall survival of society as any sort of competent entity; and survival via shelters was itself based on "shaky premises."[82] Moreover, taken to its logical conclusion, a truly sheltered America would entail astronomical costs and outrageous changes in life-style. *Newsweek* pointed out that only a "mole-like life" would make shelters effective on an everyday basis, and the article quoted Norman Cousins of the *Saturday Review* to this effect: "Shelters . . . should have practically everything underground. Most important of all, we should move into them immediately, for there will not be time enough to get into them once the bombs fall."[83]

Newsweek ended its reevaluation of the sheltered life by asking, "Is there an alternative to the mole-like life?" The alternative offered involved arms control and disarmament, "tasks" that seemed "as monumental as going underground." Nonetheless, *Newsweek* found professor Seymour Melman, author of *The Peace Race,* who believed peace a good deal easier to achieve because "to me planning a 'good' shelter is like talking about an efficient design for Auschwitz." *Newsweek* concluded that whatever alternative America chose, "It must make its choice free of illusions." The magazine warned against the illusion of security in shelters:

The most important thing to understand is that there are no certitudes in the atomic age, however neatly the mathematicians make their calculations.

The most dangerous illusion is that shelters make nuclear war thinkable—that after the bombs have fallen the nation will climb out of its hole and go on with life as it has always been lived.[84]

Margaret Mead used her article to criticize shelters and to promote peace, but "Are Shelters the Answer?" went beyond the *Newsweek* analysis to show Americans how "the armed, individual shelter is the logical end" to the moral course America had taken since World War II. In her analysis of atomic age America she openly acknowledged the cultural concerns and fears about the community's political and psychological corruption which had previously remained restricted to that subterranean cultural consciousness. Mead opened her account of the bomb shelter craze by stepping outside of American culture and presenting the image of America as seen by foreign observers of the shelter hysteria. Western Europeans, according to Mead, were horrified at the American quest to build individual bomb shelters and defend them with weapons against their "less provident neighbors." To Europeans this was "one more example of Americans' inexplicable affinity for violence," and "set beside such terms as 'overkill' and 'megadeath,' the picture of members of the richest and most technically advanced country in the world regressing to a level lower than that of any savages, to the level of trapped animals, made Europeans shudder."[85] Mead then set forth the idea that captured both past and present moral qualms about America in the atomic age: "Perhaps the world did not have to wait for a nuclear war to bring about the physical dissolution of civilization: perhaps it was dissolving morally now."[86] Her evidence for this moral dissolution came directly from American culture during the Berlin crisis:

A clergyman sanctioned the right of a man to kill his neighbor in order to protect his own family—a right accorded to no member of a society which calls itself a society. A nation-wide television program, depicting the fictional response to an alert, showed a frantic group of neighbors battering down in violent rage a family's shelter which, once destroyed, could protect no one.[87]

Mead attributed much of this shelter selfishness to the American government, which by its promotion of individual shelters abrogated its communal defense promise and shattered any sense of community responsibility. Beyond the explanation of government error and beyond the excuse of "temporary hysteria," however, Mead argued that the type of American moral dissolution exhibited in the shelter craze was "symptomatic" of the more general and abiding changes in American attitude that had occurred since World War II.

Mead stated that "the fantastic, unrealistic, morally dangerous behavior in which citizenry and government have indulged in thinking about the shelter program was an expression of a much wider ethical conflict—one in which Americans have been involved ever since we dropped the first nuclear bomb on Hiroshima."[88] According to Mead, the atom bombing of Hiroshima ended both the era of American insulation from the world and the era of easy reliance on war to settle and defend national honor—because war meant risking "suicide" and "murder against all bystanders." As a result of Hiroshima, then, "we were no longer protected by fixed boundaries" and therefore "we extended our defenses around the world."[89] The expansion of post-World War II American interests led to a conflict in American society and culture and a contraction of the spirit that ultimately expressed itself in the selfish immorality of shelter ethics in 1961:

> Countering this centrifugal movement was the centripetal pull of fear and dread—dread of the danger of mass destruction with which mankind now must live, perhaps forever; dread of the strain of living always related to distant and still alien peoples and having somehow to assimilate their experiences, good and bad, to our own; dread of the vast population spurt that is already being likened to an atomic explosion; and closer to home, dread of the surging masses of young people, uneducated and unprepared for urban living, turning to drugs and crime; dread of our crumbling, dangerous cities. As American feeling was stretched to the utmost, moving even further outward, those who were ill-prepared to take these unexpected, giant steps turned inward. Drawn back in space and in time, hiding from the future and the rest of the world, they turned to the green suburbs, protected by zoning laws against members of other classes or races or religions, and concentrated on the single, tight little family. They idealized the life of each such family living alone in self-sufficient togetherness, protecting its members against the contamination of different ways or others' needs. . . . The armed, individual shelter is the logical end of this retreat from trust in and responsibility for others.[90]

Even though Mead saw the bomb shelter craze as symptomatic of a morally disturbing American self-centeredness, she saw the opportunity to use the debate about shelters as a starting point for stimulating a morally regenerated and more generous America, an America that would finally take moral responsibility in the atomic age. Mead recognized that "the debate about shelters has caused an upsurge of genuine, realistic concern about nuclear war," and she urged Americans to "refocus this concern into a greater understanding and acceptance of the responsibility carried by the nation which first invented the bomb and, so far, is the only one to have used it." From such concern could issue a mandate for peace—"a mandate for a national effort to invent ways to protect the peoples of the world from a war which might end in the extinction of the human species."[91]

The questioning of shelter morality, the fear of extinction, and the quest for peace and a rebuilt sense of human responsibility and community that issued from Mead's analysis of the bomb shelter hysteria found greater expression in the culture in the months following the article's November publication. As bomb shelters increasingly came to be seen as immoral, as the spiritual degradation associated with shelters and the acceptance of thermonuclear war came to be understood in the culture, the open and often contemptuous defense or display of shelters suffered a quiet demise. Americans no longer felt comfortable displaying their preparedness. No longer visible were the "He Who Laughs Last" signs that had earlier adorned the homes of proud shelter owners.[92] According to building contractors, Americans who still wanted shelters expressed "an almost universal insistence that their projects be secret." A shelter manufacturer in Milwaukee specifically advertised: "We use unmarked trucks."[93] While civil defense was relegated to underground cultural consciousness, the moral debate the shelter craze had inspired continued with little abatement. In the process of rejecting bomb and fallout shelters as unethical forms of sanctuary, the culture in the early sixties exhibited the moral courage that would serve as the hallmark of change in a spiritually awakened America.[94]

The ongoing cultural debate over civil defense was not, of course, characterized by a complete ethical rejection of shelters. Neither was it devoid of its share of ambiguity. Herman Kahn's *On Thermonuclear War* (1960) remained an influential text on the rational waging of nuclear war and on the advisability of shelters, which would be the determining factors in any "postwar state" where recovery was equated with the number of survivors. Kahn summarized his rational approach in his table 3, "Tragic but Distinguishable Postwar States,"[95] by contrasting the number of dead with the years necessary for "economic recuperation":

DEAD	ECONOMIC RECUPERATION
2,000,000	1 year
5,000,000	2 years
10,000,000	5 years
20,000,000	10 years
40,000,000	20 years

DEAD	ECONOMIC RECUPERATION
80,000,000	50 years
160,000,000	100 years

Kahn explained his intent:

Here I have tried to make the point that if we have a posture which might result in 40 million dead in a general war, and as a result of poor planning, apathy, or other causes, our posture deteriorates and a war occurs with 80 million dead, we have suffered an additional disaster, an *unnecessary* additional disaster that is almost as bad as the original disaster. If on the contrary, by spending a few billion dollars, or by being more competent and lucky, we can cut the number of dead from 40 to 20 million, we have done something vastly worth doing! The survivors will not dance in the streets or congratulate each other if there have been 20 million men, women, and children killed; yet it would have been a worthwhile achievement to limit casualties to this number. It is very difficult to get this point across to laymen or experts with enough intensity to move them to action. The average citizen has a dour attitude toward planners who say that if we do thus and so it will not be 40 million dead—it will be 20 million dead. Somehow the impression is left that the planner said that there will be *only* 20 million dead. To him is often attributed the idea that this will be a tolerable or even astonishingly enough, a desirable state![96]

In order to address the squeamishness of the "average citizen" about the millions to die in thermonuclear war, regardless of advance preparations, Kahn had subtitled his table "Will the survivors envy the dead?" He presumably relieved any qualms by assuring citizens that survivors need not envy the dead. And he at least inadvertently supported the above charges against planners by envisioning more than a tolerable life after nuclear war, emphasizing: "*Despite a widespread belief to the contrary, objective studies indicate that even though the amount of human tragedy would be greatly increased in the postwar world, the increase would not preclude normal and happy lives for the majority of survivors and their dependents.*"[97]

Given the continued power of such reasoned and optimistic appraisals of thermonuclear war in a sheltered America, even in the midst of rising opposition to civil defense, a certain amount of ambiguity crept into the popular culture treatments of thermonuclear scenarios. Robert Moore Williams's science fiction novel *The Day They H-Bombed Los Angeles* (1961) reflected at once this persistent optimism about a survivable nuclear exchange and at the same time the rising cynicism about the American government's motives and morals in all things atomic. As the novel opens the protagonist Tom Watkins reacts quickly "as an intolerably bright light flared in the sky."[98] His eyes swiftly scan the Los Angeles streets for civil defense markers: "Unless he reached the shelter quickly, Tom Watkins knew that he too might be just so much twisted human junk. He headed for the shelter, running all the way."[99] Once inside the shelter, Tom notes that "CD had done a good job. It had even added long wooden benches to sit on."[100] While the shelter has certain deficiencies (no food) and partially collapses in the late stages of the H-bomb attack, it nonetheless saves the lives of most of those smart enough or lucky enough to take shelter there during this attack, when three H-bombs are dropped on Los Angeles.

Inside the shelter it is generally supposed that this is a communist attack: "'That's a Commie sub firing missiles off the coast,' someone screamed. 'That's where the bombs come from. Them damned dirty Commies!'"[101] The error of this assumption becomes gradually clear, especially later when Tom and a few others attempt to escape the city. Ted Kissel, an FBI man also taking cover in this shelter, had already hinted to Tom that some sinister and "top secret" danger in the Los Angeles area had drawn masses of security forces to Southern California. Suspicions and fears grow as Tom, Ted, and their group try to exit town via the highway and find themselves barricaded—by machine-gun-wielding federal troops. A young woman in the group asks, "Why would Army troops be shooting our own citizens as they try to flee from disaster?" and the answer to this question emerges only when they return to the city and to the lab of Dr. Homer Smith.[102]

Smith, the employer of the young woman in Tom's group and coincidentally also a scientist in the American government's employ, has been engaged in work on that top-secret peril in the Los Angeles area. Once at the lab, though, it is the FBI man Kissel who pieces together the mystery of the H-bomb attack and the federal barricade:

> It was Ted Kissel who spoke. "I can tell you, I think," the FBI man said. "No foreign nation bombed us." Listening, Tom Watkins wondered what meaning Kissel's words could possibly have. A stir ran through the others. Smith's face showed signs of intense strain. "Those were our own bombs," Kissel continued. "They were dropped from our own bombers." In the big basement laboratory, the only sound was the hiss of gas moving through the jets of the lanterns. "I know none of you realize what has happened," Kissel continued. "I did not realize it until we found the barricades around the city, the examining stations being set up. This was the missing clue that explained what I had not dared guess before." He paused and took a deep

breath. "Our *own* government has ordered the destruction of this great city. It has done this in a desperate effort to destroy something that is here in this place, some menace so insidious that it can hardly be detected, so subtle that, so far as I know, it has eluded the efforts of our best brains to uncover it. This 'something' is so dangerous and deadly, with so much potential menace to the whole nation that our own government has been forced to take the horrible decision to destroy a whole city to eliminate this menace from our nation and from the world."[103]

In the days after Kissel outlines the government's responsibility for the bombing of Los Angeles, this group searches for a way to identify, attack, and destroy this menace (the H-bombs did not get rid of it), led of course by Dr. Smith. They also seek out news about their situation, despite Kissel's doubts about the kind of news that will be available: "What politician is going to admit he bombed a city and killed hundreds of thousands of his own people? The government that made such an admission would face revolution. If we had a radio, we'd hear a lot of stories, but the truth wouldn't be in any of them."[104] Kissel is nonetheless still quite upset when they do obtain a radio and hear a government news account of the "horrible accident" that had occurred in Los Angeles. The government urged the "utmost patience" in dealing with this accident. At this Kissel explodes: " 'Patience!' Ted Kissel's fist came down on the table top. 'Patience while they tell the country and the world the biggest lie in human history. This city was deliberately bombed. It was no accident!' "[105]

When Smith finally uncovers the nature of the menace, the government is seen as more than responsible for the H-bombing of Los Angeles; it is also apparently responsible for the menace itself. The basis for the deadly peril threatening Los Angeles and the world is a protein molecule "gone mad." Dr. Smith postulates the cause for this disastrous mutation:

"I don't know what drove this molecule mad. Perhaps neither I nor anyone else will ever know the truth." Fretfulness crept into the old doctor's voice. "Perhaps a cosmic ray plunged deep into the ocean and struck the heart of this molecule. A far more likely probability, however, is that the old atom bomb tests far out in the Pacific provided the hard radiation that brought about this change in the core of this protein molecule."[106]

This mad molecule had traveled the Pacific Ocean to the Los Angeles basin, where it then infiltrated the bloodstreams of humans, who provided "a far better breeding place than even the Pacific Ocean." The aberrant molecule has no concern whatsoever for its human host, and Dr. Smith explains the real danger of the resulting molecule-infested zombie:

> "This molecule has one quality which distinguishes it from all disease-causing bacteria. . . . It links itself to others of its kind. . . . With each linkage, each molecule has the strength and intelligence of two molecules. When these linked molecules take over the human brain and spinal cord, the molecules acquire not only their own massed intelligence, *but also the intelligence of the human being they have taken over!* Some time is apparently required for the mass molecule, and in a human being, it has become a gigantic thing, to grasp not only the emotional structure of a man but also to understand and control the symbolical system that expresses itself in the form of words. Once this mad massed molecule has taken over the brain and nervous system of a first class scientist, it will have all of his knowledge. If he is a physicist, working with reactors, it will know all about reactors and atomic power. If he is an engineer designing spaceships, it will know all about spaceships. . . . If the scientist knows how to make a hydrogen bomb, it will know how to make a hydrogen bomb. Considering that it has no morals of any kind, no regard for any other form of life, the prospect is truly appalling."[107]

Smith helps to avert the appalling future by concocting a vaccine against the molecule. The entire group, which had been fighting off zombie assaults for days, is finally rescued by the military. The novel ends with the promise of normal and happy lives for the survivors of the mutant molecule and the bombing of Los Angeles. *The Day They H-Bombed Los Angeles* recalled the science fiction products of the 1950s that envisioned atomic destruction in the form of mutants and zombies, and it promoted confidence, albeit an uneasy confidence, in the ability of civil defense and brilliant scientists to save America from any real apocalypse or atomic scourge. Dr. Smith had given voice to the formulaic cry of anguish, the claim that "none of this horror need have come about if man had not prodded nature." But *The Day They H-Bombed Los Angeles* subverted this traditional formula by suggesting that "they"—the others—were in fact America's own governmental forces.[108]

In spite of its optimistic outcome, *The Day They H-Bombed Los Angeles* inextricably linked the dropping of hydrogen bombs and the creation of an amoral menace to the American government and its nuclear policies. Ted Kissel had suggested that a "revolution" would follow the government's truthful admission that it had H-bombed Los Angeles. In the awakened culture of the early 1960s, this is precisely what did happen when the government more openly announced its atomic aggressiveness in the Berlin crisis, the bomb shelter craze, and the Cuban missile crisis. Contradictory evaluations of civil defense and atomic diplomacy still punctuated the cultural debate in the early 1960s, but even the expressions of support, however qualified, publicized some of the very issues that concerned critics of civil defense and atomic aggression: the irrationality of nuclear war, the amoral quality of all nuclear policies, including civil defense, and the government's responsibility for imperiling its own citizens by its atomic arrogance.

By late 1961 and 1962 the tide had turned against civil defense and individual fallout shelters, and a rebellious culture of dissent expanded on the ringing denunciation of shelters—and the accompanying values—that Margaret Mead and others had already begun. In the continued critique of shelters a new vision of life in America began to emerge, contrasting sharply with the image of life in a sheltered America. Both religious and secular forces constructed a vision of peace, sanity, and a more human morality—a new conception of society and culture that rejected the immorality and insanity of America's nuclear policies.

After the third hydrogen bomb had exploded over the city in *The Day They H-Bombed Los Angeles,* Tom Watkins had displayed a certain numbness about the efficacy of prayer in such horror. The overweight woman who had led the earlier praying in the shelter had died in this last thermonuclear explosion. Tom and another shelter denizen had dragged this woman and the other dead outside, and Tom dryly noted: "No prayers were said. The fat woman had been the prayer leader."[109] Later, when Dr. Smith asked him to say prayers for the success of the vaccine, Tom replied: "I used them all up long ago."[110] This sense of the uselessness or lost relevance of prayer and God in a thermonuclear world constituted a recurring theme in the culture of the 1960s, but many religious leaders and writers steadfastly maintained the necessity of God and religion in re-creating and reforming the spiritual life of atomic age America. Building on the religious awakening that had been stirred by the shelter debate and by Father McHugh's conception of "shelter hatch ethics," certain religious leaders spoke out against shelters and nuclear weapons in general, marshaling their considerable powers of moral suasion to the cause of a more human, sane, and moral world.

The 1961 collection of essays by religious writers in *God and the H-Bomb* (published in 1961 and released in paperback in 1962) offered a representative sample of Catholic, Jewish, and Protestant thinking on nuclear weapons. Theologians, professors of religion, ministers, and rabbis all sought alternatives to the current direction of America's nuclear policies, for—as the foreword stated—

"That our nation is in the throes of a moral collapse of serious dimensions is, apparently, no longer a debatable conclusion."[111] The bomb, of course, was named the immediate cause for moral collapse, and these writers tied America's moral rebirth and survival to vocal opposition to the bomb and its ethics. Bishop James A. Pike linked these concerns to the shelter debate in his simply titled essay, "Survival by Shelter or Sanity?"

Pike confirmed the increasing cultural trend toward polarization on civil defense and nuclear issues when he categorized two different schools of thought on survival: "It would appear that the protagonists on the problem of survival divide themselves into two general camps: those who feel that survival will be 'by shelter,' and those who still retain enough faith in the sanity of mankind to suppose that the nuclear war will never come."[112] Pike came down squarely on the side of sanity, but only after he condemned those pro-shelter types he variously termed "so-called realists" or "crackpot realists."[113] He rather clearly had Herman Kahn in mind when he resisted the numbers game of these realists:

> Advocates of the back-yard bomb shelter program suggest that if every home is provided with its own shelter, casualties in the first bombardment may be cut from eighty million to a mere twenty million. As one reads these figures, one cannot help wondering if any of these writers has bothered to stop and picture the carnage implied in the phrase "twenty million casualties." No disaster in history, of course (with the possible exception of Noah's flood), could be properly labeled a disaster in the face of such a figure as this.[114]

Having rejected survival by shelter, Pike argued for survival by sanity—a sanity that impelled a complete reinterpretation of America's cold war patterns of behavior. According to Pike, America had misconstrued the arena of cold war battle. It was not an arena of atomic diplomacy, threatened thermonuclear war, or civil defense: "In short, the cold war is a political, ideological, and economic war; it is not a shooting war, nor does Soviet Russia have any intention of making it this unless it must."[115] America was losing the ideological cold war by relying on its atomic arsenal and on its confrontational and militarist vision of the struggle. To this end, "The shelter mentality—and the trust in atom bombs—simply serves the Communist cause."[116] Pike urged America to shift its attention from bombs to "propaganda and people," a strategy already being successfully exploited by the Soviet Union. He counseled American believers in democracy and free enterprise to have "the courage of their convictions" and to use their principles to help "the poor, the downtrodden" of the world.[117] Pike fretted over the strength of America's courage ("with the building of backyard bomb shelters, the last of our courage would seem to have fled"), and he concluded with both hope and a warning: "There is still a real possibility that America can arise from the spirit which has gripped her for so long and take the position of world leadership which awaits her; but every proposal which involves nuclear weapons and bomb shelters removes us that much further from the possibility."[118]

In "The Road to Sanity" Jewish Agency executive Israel Goldstein mirrored Pike's concerns about the insanity of nuclear weapons, and his road to sanity, like Pike's, also led directly away from such weapons. Goldstein pressed for total disarmament and for a nurturing of the "concepts and instrumentalities of peace." As Goldstein stated of this path to peace: "This is the road of morality. This is the road of sanity."[119] Morality more than sanity was on the mind of Rabbi Samuel Dresner in "Man, God and Atomic War," and his solution to the atomic peril was simultaneously more simple and more radical than the solutions offered by his peers. His recommendation for change revealed an essentially ethical stance, and his program relied far more heavily on God than on any specific call for disarmament or repudiation of shelters and their ethics.

Dresner opened his essay with a powerful compendium of facts about man—which added up to an indictment. Noting that when all else fails, many individuals fall back on the idea that God will not let atomic destruction extinguish His own human creations, Dresner listed select facts of human history in order to challenge this idea and to answer the difficult series of questions that he himself posed: "But are we so sure that God wants to save us, even if He could? Are we so confident that we deserve being saved at all? Who dares declare that he knows the will of God?" There followed his catalog of human iniquity:

> Perhaps God has had enough of the human race. Perhaps He is fed up with us, disgusted with our killing, our hating, our wars, our treachery, our intrigue, our concentration camps and gas chambers, our Bergen-Belsens and Treblinkas, our Cains and Hamans, our Genghis Khans and Attilas, our Hitlers and Stalins, our miserable struggle for money and power and ego-satisfaction, with the filth and rottenness of our world and our lives. Perhaps He thought that the human race might learn in time from the suffering and tragedy which it encountered in the world and would, thereby—in a hundred years, a thousand years, three thousand years—become faithful to Him. But we did not.[120]

Dresner's tracing of humanity's faithlessness was not meant to cause despair but to serve as preparation for the acceptance of his solution to the corruption of the world and to the possible extinction of humanity through atomic destruction. Advance preparation would be necessary: "Neither military defense, international agreement or God's miraculous intervention is the solution we are seeking. But this does not mean that there is no solution. There *is* a solution to the problem of nuclear war and the possible end of human life. But it is a radical solution. It must be so. It can only be so. A radical situation demands a radical solution."[121] According to Dresner, "It is in the roots of the human being and the human situation that the solution lies. It is not a political formula, a diplomatic theory, a gospel of economics or a master plan for world government, but something which, on the one hand, reaches beyond them all and, on the other hand, is their foundation, the only real hope for their fulfillment."[122] Rabbi Dresner's solution was, of course, an absolute and immediate call for humanity to become faithful to God, "to choose the good way, to love the Lord and walk in His ways."[123]

Dresner's explication of the meaning and consequences of this choice revealed the radical and pressing nature of choosing "the good way." He emphasized that "whether or not men walk in God's ways—whether or not men are criminals or responsible citizens, tyrants or dedicated leaders, corrupt or decent, depraved or exalted—is literally a matter of life and death, of the very survival of the world." And he stressed the urgency of adopting his solution: "Either there will be a change in man's heart or there will be no man nor heart to change!"[124] Dresner insisted on the spiritual basis of his radical solution, contending that "nothing—*nothing*—is more relevant to the problem we face than the condition of the human spirit." He concluded by numerically listing the reasons and the requirements for his radical solution:

1. The machinery for instant death for all mankind is now in men's hands.

2. There is no defense.

3. Only the creation of a new society can prevent the use of the bomb and outlaw war.

4. A new society requires a new man who can only become so by revering God and walking in His ways.[125]

Secular counterculture may have questioned or ignored Dresner's method for building a "new society," but it did not challenge the urgency of working a change in man's heart at this critical point in the atomic era. There was, in fact, a great deal of congruence between religious and secular voices of dissent. The critical secular culture displayed the same sort of spiritual and moral orientation and exhibited as well a real affinity for the kind of existential awareness registered by a religious writer like Rabbi Dresner. Expressing the same sensibility that appeared in many cultural evaluations of shelter morality and American atomic aggression, Dresner commented on the human and philosophical realization of life's new meaning in this new era:

What the inescapable facts of our situation are forcing man to understand with merciless pressure is the very meaning of life itself. He soon comes to the solemn and frightening conclusion that life is not simply a game without rules, created solely for his pleasure. He understands that life must be taken *seriously.* That man's actions have *consequences.* That man may be *called to account* for his actions, by overwhelming disaster. That *man himself is only an experiment,* a possibility in time, a colossal gamble in joining the holy and the profane, heaven and earth, angel and animal, infinite and finite, a *divine experiment* with no guarantee of success; and it is precisely this experimental nature of man's existence, which the Bible has always taught, that men everywhere have suddenly become aware of.[126]

While God was not considered the only source of spiritual regeneration, the increasing recognition of humanity's experimental status in the world was certainly viewed by both the religious and secular culture as an alarming spur to America's moral awakening.

Secular forces, like the religious, had been prodded into awareness, and one of the most symbolic acts of arousal was the paid advertisement that ran in the *New York Times* on November 10, 1961. This advertisement was an "open letter to President Kennedy" signed by approximately two hundred members of the eastern university community. The letter began with the acknowledgment that academic concern over civil defense had emerged as a result of recent events and their threat to life: "We are deeply concerned by current developments in the field of civil defense. It appears to us that the prodigious energy of our people is being channeled into wrong directions for wrong reasons; and that a continuation of this trend may be extremely dangerous to the nation and to civilization itself."[127] The letter went on to oppose quite openly the entire program of civil defense, particularly on moral grounds and on the grounds that such a shelter program actually increased the likelihood of thermonuclear war and decreased the probability of real peace. The academic statement accused civil defense of promoting a "false sense of security" and analyzed the result: "By buying a shelter program that does not shelter, and thereby believing that we can survive a thermonuclear war, we are increasing the probability of war. This probability increases both because we may be more willing to 'go to the brink' if we think survival is possible and because we are less likely to devise and take any of the constructive steps which may ease tension and secure the peace."[128] The letter also critically revealed how the government-sponsored civil defense program raised "a number of basic moral issues,"

> such as the question of whether it is right to plan on "losing" our cities and the people in them, the question of defending private shelters against intruders, the question of abandoning millions of injured outside while the rest of us hide underground, the question of shelters for the wealthy vs. shelters for the poor or the apartment dweller, the question of the long term effect of a shelter psychology on the values of a democratic society.[129]

The letter noted that "a moral code does not exist in a vacuum. If we lose the structure of society we cannot hope to keep our moral values." In order to protect America's moral values, the letter urged the abandonment of civil defense and the adoption of "a positive program for peace with freedom." The letter then dramatically ended by asking President Kennedy "to lead the nation forward on a race towards peace."[130]

As more letters and articles on the subject of civil defense appeared, the same concerns for America's morality surfaced and provided growing evidence of the popular opposition to shelters. In a letter to the editors of *Science* magazine, responding to an earlier positive editorial on civil defense, an Arizona writer agreed with both secular and religious voices of dissent by curtly denouncing both "the folly and the selfishness of building a private fallout shelter" and "the insanity and immorality of atomic war."[131] Gerard Piel's article in the February 1962 issue of the *Bulletin of Atomic Scientists,* "The Illusion of Civil Defense" (adapted from a November 1961 speech), confirmed that such public anger and opposition to civil defense were real. Piel declared:

> Happily, it cannot be said that the fallout shelter movement has found wide popular acceptance. Apart from the inertia which any such pushing and shoving must encounter in a democracy, the effort has evoked suspicion and incredulity. Close-range contemplation of thermonuclear war has brought many citizens to the conclusion that civil defense is an illusion—a dangerous illusion because it increases the probability of war.[132]

In fact Piel, publisher of *Scientific American,* launched his own crusade against civil defense and the prospect of thermonuclear war. "The Illusion of Civil Defense" deflated the many optimistic myths about the survivability of nuclear war, including those put forth by rationalists: "Civil defense, it is said, increases markedly our ability to survive war if the war is fought by rational methods. But there is little reason to think that a real war will be fought by the rational strategies of the game theory that are supplied as inputs to a computer." Piel appealed to history for proof: "The experience of history suggests that the first exchange, if 'rational,' will trigger an unlimited escalation of violence, going on to the final exhaustion and destruction of the installed capacity for violence. We must remember Hiroshima as well as Pearl Harbor."[133]

Piel warned that "the escalation toward the ultimate catastrophe is already under way," and he charted the continuing development of new weapons and systems ("intercontinental pushbutton armaments") as part of this escalation and its danger: "The danger of the totally irrational accidental war must mount as control over these weapons becomes attenuated over constantly lengthening chains of command."[134] By describing further the characteristics of this escalation, Piel determined that its cost outweighed any potential protection:

> U.S. citizens are personally witness to this escalation, in the rising tide of callousness and brutality at home. It is to be seen, at the top level of government, in the writing off of Tucson and other cities by the siting of missile bases in their immediate environs. It erupts in an ugly way, at the middle level, in the vigilante league of Las Vegas and Bakersfield against the prospective flood of refugees from Los Angeles. It shames the nation before the world in the climax of American privatism that prescribes a sawed-off shotgun as equipment for the family fallout shelter. The civil defense program of our federal government, however else intended, must be regarded as a step in the escalation process.[135]

Piel asked America to break free from the illusory benefits of escalation and to face reality, especially in this volatile era: "The nations of the world must accept the truth that thermonuclear war cannot settle even the most irreconcilable conflict to anybody's satisfaction. With all due caution, at the present stage in the escalation of terror, governments must seek the settlement of political differences by peaceful means." He counseled all governments to stop the arms race and to pursue complete disarmament and the solution to all international conflicts—because "they must be settled before madness, stupidity, accident, or the arms race itself precipitates the war."[136]

Changing tactics in a second 1962 article Piel appealed to Americans not simply to dismiss the illusion of civil defense but to consider actively the possibility of peace. "On the Feasibility of Peace" (a version of a December 1961 speech), published in the February 23, 1962, issue of *Science,* took Piel's earlier analysis of America's nuclear situation a step further. He argued that the dismantling of America's war economy was the only true way to peace, and he hoped that his suggestion would find a more receptive audience now that the deadly truth about America's economic abundance had finally been revealed. Before 1961 and since 1941, according to Piel, Americans had acquiesced to the "formal installation of the war economy as the central institution of the U.S. economic system," in large part because of the full employment of luxuriant consumerism it allowed. Because the war economy "has never exacted any visible sacrifice of the domestic economy" (and in fact fueled the domestic economy) and because modern weapons did not exact much sacrifice in terms of young American soldiers, Americans felt free to bask in "the American celebration."[137] Piel pointed out how discomfiting it was "to recall at times that this age of abundance and adventure rested upon preparation for war. But if science and technology had in truth made war unthinkable, then the enjoyment of abundance and adventure might go on indefinitely."[138] Then Piel briskly announced, "This period in our history has now come abruptly to an end." He explained that the Berlin crisis and President Kennedy's pronouncement on civil defense had engineered this historical change, because "for the first time it was made clear to the American people that the assertion of their country's power abroad is now predicated upon their readiness to accept assault upon their home territory." Or, in more simple terms, Americans finally had to confront the fact that "the business of the war economy turns out to be war."[139] Given this historical perspective, Piel urged a reinvention of the American economy, and he did so for two compelling reasons. The first involved the current direction of the war economy, which, with plans for civil defense and thermonuclear war, was leading toward "a nightmare civilization": "a realm of underground subeconomies and subtopias that appear no more plausible and no less challenging to human ingenuity than a world without war."[140] The second reason concerned the changed historical perspective occasioned in 1961—the new perception of the war economy's corruption and the new perception that peace was indeed as plausible as thermonuclear war. The article's subtitle expressed Piel's view that "a world without war is no less plausible and no more difficult than a world built on thermonuclear threat." Piel challenged America to refashion its economy in peace.[141]

Piel suggested how the economy could be reoriented to preclude war and the accompanying losses in expenditure (shifting monies, for example, to labor and welfare, public health, and education), and he did so in order to answer the most basic question: "Can we live with peace?" According to Piel, "our society, with its enormous productive capacity, can find significant and fruitful final demands to take the place of the war economy. This lesson is in itself crucial to the recognition that peace is as feasible as war."[142] Also crucial to the possibility of peace was popular activism and an accompanying shift in social priorities: "It is up to the citizens to prepare the peace. Science and technology exploited in the cause of national power have brought mankind to this impasse. War cannot be eliminated from the life of nations until the genius that thus commands the forces of nature is committed in the cause of man."[143]

Such proposals resisting the nightmare civilization represented by civil defense and thermonuclear war and advocating a more humane society of peace signified the breadth of the attack on civil defense—an attack that ultimately succeeded in forcing the government to change and then abandon its plans for a privately sheltered America. In "On the Feasibility of Peace" Piel credited the "popular wisdom" in America that had already rejected civil defense and its peril (a peril that went "infinitely beyond fallout"), because "to accept the dubious protection of a fallout shelter is to accept that peril as a condition of existence."[144] The many accounts of the government's modified and then abandoned program of civil defense consistently invoked popular wisdom and popular opposition to shelters as the root causes for the government's troubles. In early January the Kennedy administration had turned to the concept of "community shelters" in an attempt to diffuse concern over individual shelters. The editor of the *Nation,* in introductory comments to an article already highly critical of even these community shelters, corroborated the impact of popular opposition on administration strategy: "The idea of government aid for the construction of private, family shelters collapsed under a barrage of public and legislative criticism. Now the Kennedy Administration has put forward its new plan: community shelters."[145]

The *Nation's* article on community shelters suggested that this form of civil defense would find almost as little popular support as had private shelters. Author Roger Hagan referred to a recent *San Francisco Chronicle* poll that showed only 5 percent supporting family shelters and a slightly higher but still low 19 percent favoring community shelters, "even if they were provided by the government."[146] Community shelters did in fact face the same sort of moral and popular scrutiny that had hampered the drive for private shelters, and Irving Brant's essay "Who Shall Be Saved by Shelters?" in the March 5, 1962, issue of the *New Republic* brought an ethical and humanist sensibility to bear against such shelters. Brant first set forth the problem:

President Kennedy's request for $450 million with which to begin a
federal-state system of public bomb shelters is running into the expected

discussion of necessity, effectiveness and cost. Since it is obviously impossible to protect everybody, everywhere, from the combined effects of blast, fire, heat, radioactive fallout, bone rot, degenerate mutation and all the other channels to oblivion that are being discovered from year to year, the real question is one of using the available means of preservation in the most useful and effective way.[147]

Brant argued that "when the issue is one of human survival, it ought to be looked at from the point of view of humanity as a whole," and he thus posed two questions, removing the civil defense debate from its specific American context: "Who shall survive? And who shall pay the cost of their survival?"[148] He answered the latter question first: "The cost of preserving the human race ought to be borne by the nations that have put it in peril," most obviously (but not exclusively) the United States and the Soviet Union. America was presumed to be the only nation able to pay, so while America was to bear the cost of human survival, its very responsibility for the peril removed the nation from consideration as a candidate for survival. In his long explanation of who should survive, Brant made a persuasive moral case against American survival by any form of shelter:

> If American dollars are to save the human race from obliteration, let them be spent to preserve people who had no share in creating the threat of extinction. For the past several months I have been in Mexico, traveling by automobile more than 4,000 miles within the borders of that country. Perhaps that has given me a new approach to the halls of Montezuma. . . . But with that bias allowed for, let us look at the Mexicans, as well as ourselves, in terms of ultimate value as sole survivors. Search for those who live sanely in a mad world, and who can be found to surpass our neighbors south of the Rio Grande? Who excels in human dignity or in the greatness of their heritage? However, in so diverse a world one must not be parochial. If not the Mexicans, find some other people still more worthy of survival. But let the choice be dictated by the survivors' harmony with the world they live in—the world of fields and forests, mountains and deserts, beasts and birds, sun and stars. And let the survival be a complete one: that of the land, the people, the culture, past, present and future; the survival of a body of men and women preserved as a whole and worthy to endure. Let not the future be the crawling existence of a shattered remnant of a people, and least of all the people—ourselves and others—who have not had the wit and morality to control the forces they brought into being.[149]

This kind of moral stance against the survival of Americans—Americans who were not living sanely in a mad world and who had neither the wit nor morality to control the forces of atomic destruction—fueled the continuing opposition to the government's policy of civil defense, whether based on family or public shelters. Civil defense obituaries kept appearing throughout 1962, and not even the Cuban missile crisis and its tension brought shelters back to life. The November *Bulletin of Atomic Scientists* surveyed the demise of civil defense through congressional appropriations, but it also listed adverse public reaction as the official cause of the death of civil defense. The *Bulletin* recorded that in the crisis summer months of 1961 Congress had approved an unprecedented $306.2 million for civil defense for the fiscal year 1962 (this compared with a total $532 million spent between 1951 and 1961). The *Bulletin* then charted the recession of this civil defense hysteria and its cause: "At the same time there sprung up a vigorous opposition to civil defense composed of peace groups, academics, students, scientists, religious organizations, and a few politicians."[150]

The rebellion against civil defense persisted in spite of administrative alterations, as the magazine pointed out: "In the face of general bewilderment and mounting opposition to civil defense, the administration announced that the civil defense program was going to be shifted to community shelters. It was hoped that such a program would settle the shoot-your-neighbor debate. . . . But the community shelter idea raised more questions than it answered."[151] According to the *Bulletin:*

> The administration and the Congress had not foreseen the furor caused by the civil defense issue. The general confusion, the anger, and the sharp divisions between neighbors, scientists, churches, and other organizations came as a disturbing surprise. As the turmoil mounted, some of the administration advocates of shelters began to doubt their value.[152]

When Kennedy requested $695 million for his fiscal 1963 civil defense program, the congressional response conveyed the impact of the public's rebellion against shelters: the House Appropriations Committee allotted a mere $80.5 million. As the *Bulletin* concluded, "The House reflected the mood of the country and returned to its previous anti-civil defense attitude."[153] The *New Republic* confirmed the still moribund status of civil defense in the wake of the Cuban missile crisis in the very title of its December 1, 1962, article: "Where's Civil Defense Now?" Writer Asher Brynes took note of the congressional and public rejection of shelters, and he reported the essential inconsequence of the Cuban crisis on civil defense:

> The last Congress cut 83 percent off the budget request of the Office of Civil Defense, after extensive polling in their constituencies. These Congressional polls showed that there was not a single district among those surveyed in which majority support for the Administration's modest fall-out shelter program existed. . . . Civil defense officials have reported much telephoning at the height of the crisis, and many requests for pamphlet materials, but practically no action of a substantial kind. This latter-day flurry over shelters moved few bricks, literally or figuratively, and mixed no mortar.[154]

Brynes sounded the death knell of civil defense with understatement: "It seems unlikely that the old fallout shelter programs will be revived."[155]

As early as June 1962 *Newsweek* magazine had claimed that civil defense officials were once again confronted with "the same old problem: Public apathy."[156] What became clear in the revolt against civil defense in the early 1960s, however, was the inadequate descriptive power of the term "apathy" when applied to the popular lack of support for shelters. Embodied in the popular opposition to and "apathy" about civil defense, perhaps only potentially for the 1950s but certainly for the 1960s, was the symbolic kernel of a cultural and moral revolution. In their vocal critique of bomb shelters, both religious and secular groups and individuals had offered alternative visions of a more sane, human, moral, and peaceful America. They scored the first unambiguous atomic age victory for the forces of dissent, diffusing the bomb shelter craze and forcing the dismantling of the government's civil defense program. The popular wisdom that rebelled against a sheltered America announced the kinds of moral and political questions that would be asked throughout the 1960s, if never again asked in the context of the now settled issue of civil defense.[157]

The Cuban missile crisis of October 1962 did not have the power to revive the banner of civil defense, but it did have the power to remind an awakening culture of the continued need for vigilance and dissent: the defeat of bomb shelters had not conquered the more generalized and ingrained patterns of cold warriorism, nor had it significantly altered the structure of the deeply rooted atomic bureaucracy. The Cuban missile crisis did not reinvigorate civil defense, but it did reinforce the dissenting culture's view of America's place in time and space—on the eve of destruction and at the edge of apocalypse. As America once again displayed its atomic machismo and as the thermonuclear threat was telescoped into a few short days of frightening tension, the issues of time and extinction assumed crucial importance in the culture. The message sounded by religious writer Harold Fey in 1960 in the earliest moments of the revolt against the moral drift of atomic age America retained its relevance in 1962: "It is time for a change."[158]

The film *The Day the Earth Caught Fire,* released in 1962, exhibited this sense of cultural impatience, and the urgency of freeing the world from the nuclear peril was its focus. The film opens with a shot of the deserted streets of London, a loudspeaker announcing the minutes as they tick away in some final countdown. A sweat-drenched reporter trudges alone through the empty streets, on his way to the newspaper office to file his story. He refers vaguely to the "corrective bombs" that have been detonated, and he notes that in minutes the world will know if this is "the end or another beginning, the rebirth of man or his final obituary."[159] As he fills in the details on this crisis, the film presents an extended flashback on the developments that led to this atomic age news bulletin.

The first sign that something was amiss on Earth was strange weather phenomena, beginning with floods and earth tremors. Ten days earlier the Americans had conducted one of the biggest bomb tests in history; the Soviets had just announced that they too had conducted nuclear tests at approximately the same time, and their test bomb had been 20 percent larger than the Americans' bomb. The coincidence of these tests is termed "the biggest jolt the Earth had taken since the ice age" in the newsroom of the *Daily Express,* and reporter Pete Stenning suspects a connection between the tests and the weather patterns. As massive antinuclear and prodisarmament protest meetings are held in London and as the bizarre weather turns dangerous in the form of paralyzing heat mists and cyclonic winds, Pete proves the tie between the tests and the weather: the tests had caused a "mutation" in the Earth's axis, which was rotating the Earth closer and closer to the sun.

Fires, drought, and great heat plague London and the rest of the world, and time begins to grow short for the planet: it is revealed that, if nothing is done, man will be "charcoaled" by the sun within four months. Water shortages and outbreaks of disease are already disrupting the fabric of everyday life when Britain's prime minister makes an emergency announcement to London and the nation. The prime minister reports that government leaders have agreed on a course of action aimed at halting the Earth's increasingly hot orbital course. Four of the most powerful thermonuclear bombs will be exploded in Siberia in an attempt to correct the imbalance in the earth's axis. He stresses that without this experiment there is "certain doom," but he is also compelled to admit that even this drastic experiment offers no guarantee.

As the time for the thermonuclear showdown approaches, a number of Londoners begin preparation for "the end of the world," living in a riotous and hedonistic fashion. Pete's girlfriend does not understand this "insane" behavior, so Pete explains: "A lot of people don't want to live, it's too difficult. They're tired, they're frightened. They'd rather it was all over than go on worrying, being frightened, losing a bit more hope every day. So they want it to finish." The possibility that the world might indeed be finished is left quite open as Pete brings his story to its conclusion. The countdown for the corrective bomb explosions is on, the fate of the world eerily suspended in time. The newspaper has prepared two alternate headlines, "World Saved" and "World Doomed," and the clocks in London are inching toward a fateful noon. Pete delivers a final sermon in his news bulletin as the world waits: "And if there is a future for man, insensitive as he is, proud and defiant in his pursuit of power, let him resolve to live it lovingly, for he knows well how to do so."

As the film ends the bells of London begin to ring—but the meaning of their tolling is purposely vague. Are the bells signaling "all's well" or are they tolling doom? Or are they simply marking the arrival of the critical noontide in the atomic age? If the bells did not resolve the world's suspension between doom and survival, the film certainly offered a clear-cut statement about the world's perilous balancing act at high noon in the era of thermonuclear weapons. The Cuban missile crisis, of course, echoed this suspenseful celluloid scenario, and during those few days in late October 1962 time seemed paralyzed by the possibility of thermonuclear extinction.

In a historical and personal account of the era, Todd Gitlin recalled the Cuban missile crisis and the transformation it wrought in perceptions of time: ". . . time was deformed, everyday life suddenly dwarfed and illuminated, as if by the glare of an explosion that had not yet taken place. Until the news was broadcast that Khrushchev was backing down, the country lived out the awe and truculence and simmering near-panic always implicit in the thermonuclear age."[160] *Newsweek* also reflected this emphasis on time in its account of the crisis. The magazine stated that "everything that happened on the surface took place in seven short days—seven days in which the world had to face up to the true terrors of its existence as it never has done before."[161] A young survivor of this tense and time-bending period in American history later testified how such a crisis could more permanently alter one's concept of life and time:

> When I was about ten years old (around the time of fallout shelter craze
> and the Cuban missile crisis), I remember going Christmas shopping with
> my mother, who naturally asked what I wanted that year. I don't remember

what I said, but I remember what I thought. "What's the difference? We're not going to live till Christmas anyway." Strange thoughts for a ten-year-old, although by the time Christmas actually arrived I'm sure I had managed to repress them. At any rate, periodically throughout my childhood I believed that I was never going to grow up.[162]

The short and therefore intense nature of the Cuban missile crisis undoubtedly strengthened the contemporary obsession with time and the meaning of existence in the thermonuclear world. The relatively brief duration of the crisis and its relatively quick resolution also explained the almost complete public support for Kennedy's handling of the crisis and the almost complete absence of any American protest over this most serious exercise in brinksmanship. Between October 22, when Kennedy made public the Soviet installation of "offensive" missile bases in Cuba and his intention to "quarantine" or blockade Cuba and thereby prevent Soviet ships from delivering any further weapons, and October 28, when Khrushchev sent his conciliatory letter promising to dismantle and withdraw the Cuban weapons, there was little time and little inclination—given the psychologically important location of Cuba—to organize any sort of opposition. While there was mass support for Kennedy's tough stance, people—like time itself—seemed paralyzed, as *Newsweek* recorded: "Throughout the nation, Americans hung by their radios and TV sets, and pressed up to television store windows. Transistor radios popped up on streets, in trains, even in theaters. There was the gnawing apprehension everywhere that this time might really be it."[163]

Despite the many declarations of an American victory in Cuba and of a triumphant cold war "win" for President Kennedy, there emerged in the immediate wake of the crisis a more enlivened sense of the dangers that had been risked and a more reasoned if grudging appreciation for Khrushchev's motives and ultimate moderation. *Newsweek* recognized that this had been "the greatest crisis since World War II" and pointed out how the crisis illustrated that a "showdown might 'escalate' into an apocalyptic nuclear war."[164] The following week in its article "The Lessons Learned," the magazine concluded: "Now the world can reflect on the profound and palpitating experience of what it is to be involved in the cold war, where miscalculation can lead to thermonuclear war."[165] *Newsweek* also reported on the lesson of this presumed victory: "Instinctively, the world felt it had been close to the nuclear brink, and that now was the time to seek paths to peace."[166]

It was Khrushchev who moved to edge the world away from the brink, and, even though he was widely viewed as also having pushed the world to the edge of war, he did find some (often reluctant) respect for his actions. The popular press, like *Newsweek,* also gave some coverage to the facts that called into question Kennedy's extreme reaction. Mention was made of the American missiles in Turkey that threatened the Soviet Union at close range, and *Newsweek* included the information that "oddly enough, there was some argument from the Pentagon in favor of ignoring the missile buildup in Cuba on the ground we've had missiles looking down our throat for a long time and that it makes no difference where they're fired from."[167] The text of Khrushchev's October 28 letter, widely circulated, seemed a model of sympathetic conciliation ("I understand very well your anxiety and the anxiety of the people of the United States . . ."), and at least in the eyes of some observers Khrushchev had gained the moral high ground with his letter and his decision to remove the missiles from Cuba. British philosopher Bertrand Russell claimed that Khrushchev's move had placed a "moral obligation" on Kennedy to work for peace with the Soviet Union.[168]

President Kennedy did speak of peace in his response to Khrushchev's decision, noting that "it is my earnest hope that the governments of the world can, with a solution of the Cuban crisis, turn their urgent attention to the compelling necessity for ending the arms race and reducing world tensions."[169] This sort of peace pronouncement was not enough to calm the still active culture of dissent. While apparently quiet during the Cuban crisis, the rebellious culture did not fade away. And the experience of Todd Gitlin, who became a leader of student activism in the 1960s, suggested that the Cuban missile crisis did in fact act as a spur to the continued cultural revolt. For Gitlin this crisis was the "public milestone" that "made radical politics appear necessary, even possible."[170] An increasing cynicism about the government's motives and methods and an increasing suspicion of the government's uses and justifications of power—like the "official myth" of the Cuban missile crisis—fueled such radicalism:

> This is supposed to have been the moment when the nuclear age proved viable. Apocalypse was, after all, averted. Kennedy resisted the counsel that would have bombed the missile sites or invaded Cuba; his precision was vindicated by Khrushchev's decision to withdraw his missiles. When the chips were down, the superpowers wised up. But the hindsight is pat, a luxury. Another ending was possible, the ending of all endings, and then we would not be alive, most likely, to challenge the official myth.[171]

The Cuban crisis helped to transform Gitlin from a participant in milder forms of activism (he was involved in the Harvard-Radcliffe peace group Tocsin) to an advocate of more direct forms of protest. He was inspired by Barrington

Moore, Jr., who, at a rally held during the crisis, issued the command for "destructive criticism of a destructive system."[172] Gitlin accepted this imperative for radicalism because he fully accepted the evaluation of the crisis by one of his fellow activists, Paul Potter: "What the crisis did was make clear the fact that American power had reached the point of *menace*. America had to be curbed."[173] Thus the reaction to the Cuban missile crisis and the popular opposition to civil defense and bomb shelters promoted the adoption by the culture of dissent of Rabbi Dresner's dictum "A radical situation demands a radical solution."[174]

seven

LAUGHTER AND A NEW MYTH OF LIFE

attacking the menace of the American system

> *"The enemy . . . is anybody who is going to get you killed, no matter* which *side he's on."*
>
> *—Joseph Heller,* Catch-22 *(1961)*

n the wake of the Cuban missile crisis a more radical and diverse rebellion grew in response to the menace of American power and to the menace of an American system that had absorbed the debased values associated with the bomb and the cold war. The spark of cultural rebellion born in the popular opposition to civil defense did not die during or after the Cuban crisis. The revolt expanded to encompass a broad range of issues that mirrored the larger concerns raised in the civil defense debate: the morality and sanity of America, the reliability and responsibility of the government, the fear of extinction and extermination, the quest for peace and a new society, with a regenerated sense of human history and of community and individual ethics. Both before and after the Cuban missile crisis signs of the more broadly based cultural revolution appeared with regularity, and indeed the beginnings of this more diverse rebellion had developed in conjunction with the popular revolt against civil defense.[1]

In the first years of the 1960s the concept of time—the understanding of the relationship of the past to the present and the future—obsessed the counterculture, both in the context of civil defense and the threat of thermonuclear war and outside that context. While the sense of time was crucial to the cultural understanding of these early years as a new era in history, a new understanding of the past equally characterized this dawning period of rebellion. The rebellious culture now reevaluated and rejected much of the recent American past—the past that was responsible for the evolution of the menacing system of American power. This very rejection of the past and its historical legacies reinforced the claim that the sixties marked a new era in American history, and even more positive reinforcement of this age's fresh perspective appeared in its adoption of new forms of political and cultural expression and action.

Ken Kesey wrote aptly in 1964 that "the past not uncommonly takes a while to happen, and some time to figure out." Even in the 1950s cultural commentator Lewis Mumford had suggested the great importance of breaking the spell of the past. In an essay written in 1956 he warned of the technological dehumanization of life in the atomic age, arguing that "the ability to select, to revaluate, and to rethink the past in terms of its further development in the future is what has given vitality to every true cultural renascence."[2] Rethinking the past became a hallmark of the cultural rebirth in the 1960s, and the critical revision of recent American history began in the earliest years of the decade. One of the first historical forces selected for reconsideration was anticommunism, particularly its manifestation in a powerful internal security bureaucracy. Because the forces of domestic security and 100 percent Americanism were largely responsible for the inhibition of political and cultural change in the 1940s and 1950s, they had to be challenged to allow the freedom of expression necessary in any cultural rebirth.

The culture of dissent attacked the internal security bureaucracy and its various by-products, like informing and loyalty oaths, with direct action and with more subtle, even satiric, portraits of its ethical dangers and ultimate inanity. On May 13, 1960, demonstrators, many of them students from nearby Berkeley, gathered in San Francisco to protest the hearings being held in City Hall by the House Committee on Un-American Activities. The participants in this anti-HUAC demonstration staged a sit-in, employing one of the new forms of direct action that young black civil rights activists had fashioned earlier that year.[3] This 1960 sit-in symbolically marked the end to America's historical acquiescence to the authority of internal security forces, and it gave notice that institutions like HUAC would no longer be able to operate in secrecy without facing some open and vocal challenges.[4]

The rebellious popular culture also provided evidence that the historic power of these forces had been broken and that their methods had been judged corrupt. The film *Spartacus*, released in 1960, demonstrated the declining power of internal security to intimidate. The film was directed by Stanley Kubrick (director of *Dr. Strangelove*) and the screenplay was written by—and openly attributed to—Dalton Trumbo, one of HUAC's first victims and one of those who had suffered long years of blacklisting by Hollywood. The blacklist had been broken by 1960, and the plot of *Spartacus* reflected in its backward glance at history an attack on HUAC's demands of loyalty and a condemnation of the moral cowardice of those who had succumbed to these expectations.[5] Suggestively set in the period of the late Roman Republic, when military dictators and imperial ambitions were destroying the republican institutions of Rome, the film promoted rebellion against a corrupt, repressive, and undemocratic system by glorifying the slave revolt led by the heroic Spartacus.[6]

Challenging the morality of a society that not only enslaves men and women but also trains select slaves as gladiators—who are then expected to fight against and kill their brothers in slavery—Spartacus turns his gladiatorial skills against the Romans. He welds together a loyal and formidable slave army that enjoys some early spectacular successes against the Romans before ultimately suffering defeat in their march on Rome. Amid the slaughtered bodies of their fallen comrades, the surviving slaves, including Spartacus, are taken captive. A Roman official promises to spare the slaves the death penalty by crucifixion, but only if they will identify—or inform on—Spartacus. In the most compelling scene of the film the slaves refuse to betray Spartacus, each slave in turn identifying himself as Spartacus. The chorus of "I'm Spartacus" resounds with the kind of moral strength and courage that had been conspicuously absent in the informerwitnesses who had appeared before HUAC.[7] The slaves, of course, all die by crucifixion for their loyalty to Spartacus and for their "disloyalty" to the state, but the finale of the film promises hope for the future. Before his death Spartacus warns the Romans that "millions" more will rise up against their decaying system, and he dies knowing that his son, who had escaped with his mother, will be raised free—free to keep alive Spartacus's memory and mission.

If *Spartacus* exposed in symbolic and subtle ways the immorality and corruption of the American imperial system and its internal security apparatus, Joseph Heller's *Catch-22* (1961) satirically attacked the insanity of that same system and its demands. Nominally set on an American military base in Italy during World War II, the novel nonetheless contains a segment on the "Glorious Loyalty Oath Crusade" which confirms its later composition and its participation in the rebellious historical revisionism of the early 1960s. Heller creates a brilliant parody of the security paranoia of the late 1940s and 1950s, showing the absurdity and petty politicism that underlay the obsessive patriotism of the cold war. The origins of the Glorious Loyalty Oath Crusade point out its absurdity and politicism clearly. Captain Black, upset that Major Major had received the coveted promotion to squadron commander, is bent on revenge. When other administrative officers comment that Major Major is "somewhat odd," Captain Black draws a further conclusion and determines a course of revengeful action:

Captain Black announced that he [Major Major] was a Communist. "They're taking over everything," he declared rebelliously. "Well, you fellows can stand around and let them if you want to, but I'm not going to. I'm going to do something about it. From now on I'm going to make every son of a bitch who comes to my intelligence tent sign a loyalty oath. And I'm not going to let that bastard Major Major sign one even if he wants to."[8]

Thus begins the Glorious Loyalty Oath Crusade, and it takes on the appearance of a religious crusade as the occasions for oath-signing, pledging of allegiance, and singing of the "Star-Spangled Banner" multiply endlessly under Black's doctrine of "Continual Reaffirmation." Officers and enlisted men in the squadron are expected to swear loyalty at all times of the day and for all sorts of action, from eating in the mess hall and getting a haircut to preparing for bombing missions. The impact and the meaning of the crusade are detailed:

> Without realizing how it had come about, the combat men in the squadron discovered themselves dominated by the administrators appointed to serve them. They were bullied, insulted, harassed and shoved about all day long by one after the other. When they voiced objection, Captain Black replied that people who were loyal would not mind signing all the loyalty oaths they had to. To anyone who questioned the effectiveness of the loyalty oaths, he replied that people who really did owe allegiance to their country would be proud to pledge it as often as he forced them to. And to anyone who questioned the morality, he replied that "The Star-Spangled Banner" was the greatest piece of music ever composed. The more loyalty oaths a person signed, the more loyal he was; to Captain Black it was as simple as that, and he had Corporal Kolodny sign hundreds with his name each day so that he could always prove he was more loyal than anyone else. "The important thing is to keep them pledging," he explained to his cohorts. "It doesn't matter whether they mean it or not. That's why they make little kids pledge allegiance even before they know what 'pledge' and 'allegiance' mean."[9]

To the other officers and men the Glorious Loyalty Oath Crusade becomes "a glorious pain in the ass," effectively ending the possibility for any quick and ordered military action, but the crusade is not halted until the elderly Major ___ de Coverley returns from Rome. Finding his way to the mess hall "blocked by a wall of officers waiting in line to sign loyalty oaths," the Major swats aside all oaths and pledges and orders the men to "Gimme eat." He then commands the mess to "Give *everybody* eat!" and the Glorious Loyalty Oath Crusade comes abruptly to an end.[10] Heller specifically documented both the pointlessness of continually demanded patriotism and the damaging administrative paralysis caused by the obsession with loyalty, but it was the more general tone of ridicule in the Glorious Loyalty Oath Crusade and in *Catch-22* as a whole that constituted the most effective cultural attack against the internal security bureaucracy, its parent system of menacing power, and the historical past that had produced them both.

The culture of dissent in the early 1960s exploited the subversive power of laughter against the American past and the American system of power, and the many variants of humor employed—from satire and ridicule to fantasy and irony—shared a single mood: black. The rise of a cultural imagination tinged with black humor or with a comic-apocalyptic sensibility signaled the rise of a new cultural consciousness and a new cultural understanding of history and authority. The buoyancy and the disdain of this cultural mirth in the early sixties broke the constraints of fear and intimidation that had curtailed free expression in the late forties and fifties and loosed the spirit of iconoclasm that complemented the dominant mood of the rebellious sixties. The nurturing of a laughing spirit was the nurturing of a radical spirit—a spirit without fear and without respect for the demands of consensus and conformity. Humor exposed and deflated the crazed and serious rationality of the cold war past and present, and the blackness of the humor stemmed from a recognition of what nonetheless ultimately lay under the laughable rationality: death. Black humor offered a subversive alternative world view to America in the 1960s as it uncovered the corruption and insanity that had accompanied America's rise to power since World War II. Black humor matched both the explosive power and the deadly nihilism of the atomic bomb, and it announced the dawn of the cultural revolution that also finally matched the transforming power of the bomb.[11]

Three cultural productions from the early 1960s launched the comic crusade against history and the system: Heller's *Catch-22,* Ken Kesey's *One Flew Over the Cuckoo's Nest* (1962), and John Frankenheimer's *The Manchurian Candidate* (1962). These works provided more evidence about the nature of the cultural rebirth by exposing the dark reality of the past and of all systems of authority. They also posited the need for alternatives to that past and those systems, both in their innovative structural forms and themes and in their concrete representations of the changed state of mind in the 1960s. Writers in the civil defense debate, like Margaret Mead and Gerard Piel, had identified World War II and the cold war as the points of American departure from a more peaceful and moral view of life, and the black humorist perspective concurred. In *Catch-22* Joseph Heller uses World War II as a backdrop to his novel's action in order to suggest that the war and the armed forces served as the generator of and the model for all such systems of authoritarian and bureaucratic control.

He simultaneously uses a nonlinear plot structure—along with a cast of often uncontrollable characters—to challenge the power and the rational or "logical" point of view of history and authority.

Time operates on a plane outside of ordered chronology in *Catch-22*, but it nonetheless has a logic that once again demonstrates how an understanding of the past often only becomes clear after the passage of time, as perspective is gained. Time in the novel belongs to the protagonist Yossarian, and events are constructed in relation to his consciousness and to his understanding of the facts as they become clear and meaningful to him. Yossarian is a bombardier for an American squadron based in the Mediterranean theater on the Italian island of Pianosa; he measures both war and time by the number of missions he has flown for America. The most significant moment in Yossarian's ultimate understanding of life occurs at the midpoint in his tour of duty, but this moment is not revealed in full—but only in brief flashes—until the end of the novel, when Yossarian's moral and human education allows him to absorb the meaning of the Avignon mission and Snowden's death. The phenomenon of déjà vu explains the nontraditional functioning of time in the novel—the delay between seeing and understanding something, when the meaning of a past event only appears lucid at a later point—and the novel's construction of time in turn provides a metaphor for the new understanding of history in the 1960s. Heller has his protagonist discuss this phenomenon with the chaplain of the squadron, to whom Yossarian "explained that déjà vu was just a momentary infinitesimal lag in the operation of two coactive sensory nerve centers that commonly functioned simultaneously."[12]

Heller also concocts another more evocative and colorful image of the inability to "see things as they really are": flies in the eyes. According to Orr, one of Yossarian's buddies, the pilot Appleby—the most gung-ho pilot of the squadron, who relished each mission with unquestioning patriotism—had these flies in his eyes:

> "Oh, they're there, all right," Orr had assured him about the flies in Appleby's eyes after Yossarian's fist fight with Appleby in the officers' club, "although he probably doesn't even know it. That's why he can't see things as they really are." "How come he doesn't know it?" inquired Yossarian. "Because he's got flies in his eyes," Orr explained with exaggerated patience. "How can he see he's got flies in his eyes if he's got flies in his eyes?"[13]

While the flies stayed in Appleby's eyes through much of the action in *Catch-22*, the flies had now lifted from the cultural eyes of America; the time lag in historical understanding had passed. The revised view of World War II presented in Heller's novel gave proof of this clear new view of the past.

The probability of death and an insane bureaucratic and moral corruption were the true legacies and meaning of World War II, and Yossarian learns both of these lessons in his wartime experiences. From the very beginning Yossarian takes the deadly peril of war personally and seriously, turning the idea of war's "impersonal" form of death on its head. In a debate with Clevinger he makes his point:

> "They're trying to kill me," Yossarian told him calmly. "No one's trying to kill you," Clevinger cried. "Then why are they shooting at me?" Yossarian asked. "They're shooting at *everyone*," Clevinger answered. "They're trying to kill everyone." "And what difference does that make?" . . . "Who's they?" he wanted to know. "Who, specifically, do you think is trying to murder you?" "Every one of them," Yossarian told him. "Every one of whom?" "Every one of whom do you think?" "I haven't any idea." "Then how do you know they aren't?" "Because . . . " Clevinger sputtered, and turned speechless with frustration. Clevinger really thought he was right, but Yossarian had proof, because strangers he didn't know shot at him with cannons every time he flew up in the air to drop bombs on them, and it wasn't funny at all.[14]

Yossarian "had decided to live forever or die in the attempt," and his lust for life fuels his sense of peril in war and in life.[15] An atomic age everyman, Yossarian is paranoid about his safety, to the point that he believes that "catastrophes were lurking everywhere, too numerous to count."[16] The forms of peril expanded without end for Yossarian. "There was Hitler, Mussolini and Tojo, for example, and they were all out to kill him," there were his superior officers and comrades who endangered his life, and there were even a multitude of diseases gunning after his health: "There were diseases of the head, diseases of the neck, diseases of the chest, diseases of the intestines, diseases of the crotch. There were even diseases of the feet." As Yossarian concludes: "There were billions of conscientious body cells oxidating away day and night like dumb animals at their complicated job of keeping him alive and healthy, and every one was a potential traitor and foe."[17]

Fulfilling and justifying Yossarian's—and the culture's—paranoia about the perils to life is the reality of death. As most of his friends and comrades die or mysteriously "disappear" in either a cosmic or bureaucratic sort of elimination, Yossarian comes to see the greatest threat as that which emanates from within America's own military system. Colonel Cathcart, the group commander, continually raises the required number of missions for Yossarian's squadron (far beyond the number required by air force headquarters) and continually volunteers the squadron for especially dangerous bombing runs, all for his own personal advancement in the military bureaucracy. He thus becomes, by Yossarian's definition, an enemy, and his concept of an enemy is hammered out in yet another exchange with Clevinger. Arguing about Cathcart's right to volunteer the men for a deadly mission and about the distinction between "winning the war" and "winning the war and keeping alive," Yossarian attacks Clevinger's pro-Cathcart, pro-winning the war point of view: "Open your eyes, Clevinger. It doesn't make a damned bit of difference *who* wins the war to someone who's dead." This battle of war wits ends with Yossarian's definition of the enemy:

> Clevinger sat for a moment as though he'd been slapped. "Congratulations!" he exclaimed bitterly, the thinnest milk-white line enclosing his lips tightly in a bloodless, squeezing ring. "I can't think of another attitude that could be depended upon to give greater comfort to the enemy." "The enemy," retorted Yossarian with weighted precision, "is anybody who's going to get you killed, no matter *which* side he's on, and that includes Colonel Cathcart. And don't you forget that, because the longer you remember it, the longer you might live."[18]

Clevinger did not remember, though, and Yossarian thus got the last word in their long string of arguments: "Clevinger was dead. That was the basic flaw in his philosophy."[19] Yossarian, however, does keep his definition of the enemy uppermost in his mind and he survives to witness the many ways in which the American enemy tries to control and thereby kill him. While it is Yossarian who is diagnosed as "crazy" by the military psychiatrist, it is the American military bureaucracy that appears more dangerously insane. Yossarian's form of insanity, as described by the psychiatrist Major Sanderson, seems in fact sane and reasonable. After determining that Yossarian's personality is "split right down the middle," the Major lists the symptoms of Yossarian's craziness:

> "The trouble with you is that you think you're too good for all the conventions of society. . . . Well, do you know what you are? You're a frustrated, unhappy, disillusioned, undisciplined, maladjusted young man!" Major Sanderson's disposition seemed to mellow as he reeled off the uncomplimentary adjectives. . . . "You're immature. You've been unable to adjust to the idea of war. . . . " "You have a morbid aversion to dying. You probably resent the fact that you're at war and might get your head blown off any

second. . . . " "You have deep-seated survival anxieties. And you don't like bigots, bullies, snobs or hypocrites. . . . " "You're antagonistic to the idea of being robbed, exploited, degraded, humiliated or deceived. Misery depresses you. Ignorance depresses you. Persecution depresses you. Violence depresses you. Slums depress you. Greed depresses you. Crime depresses you. Corruption depresses you. You know, it wouldn't surprise me if you're a manic-depressive!"[20]

The all-encompassing and controlling insanity of the military system on Pianosa is enunciated in the evolving concept of "Catch-22." The same sort of zany logic Yossarian uses in his arguments with Clevinger is adopted in the military's formulation of Catch-22, but it is a formulation that soon loses its humor. In its classic statement Catch-22 is invoked by Doc Daneeka as the explanation for his inability to ground Yossarian by reason of insanity. After discussing his own craziness, Yossarian shifts the conversation to Orr's case and receives his first real contact with Catch-22:

> Yossarian looked at him soberly and tried another approach. "Is Orr crazy?" "He sure is," Doc Daneeka said. "Can you ground him?" "I sure can. But first he has to ask me to. That's part of the rule." "Then why doesn't he ask you to?" "Because he's crazy," Doc Daneeka said. "He has to be crazy to keep flying combat missions after all the close calls he's had. Sure, I can ground Orr. But first he has to ask me to." "That's all he has to do to be grounded?" "That's all. Let him ask me." "And then you can ground him?" Yossarian asked. "No. Then I can't ground him." "You mean there's a catch?" "Sure there's a catch," Doc Daneeka replied. "Catch-22. Anybody who wants to get out of combat duty isn't really crazy." There was only one catch and that was Catch-22, which specified that a concern for one's own safety in the face of dangers that were real and immediate was the process of a rational mind. Orr was crazy and could be grounded. All he had to do was ask; and as soon as he did, he would no longer be crazy and would have to fly more missions. Orr would be crazy to fly more missions and sane if he didn't, but if he was sane he had to fly them. If he flew them he was crazy and didn't have to; but if he didn't want to he was sane and had to. Yossarian was moved very deeply by the absolute simplicity of the clause of Catch-22, and let out a respectful whistle. "That's some catch, that Catch-22," he observed. "It's the best there is," Doc Daneeka agreed.[21]

The final and most ominous statement of Catch-22 is delivered toward the end of the novel, when Yossarian is in a nearly destroyed Rome searching for the friends he and his squadron buddies had made at a whorehouse in the city. Having rushed there to help them, he is shocked to find them all gone. Only an old woman is left at the place, and Yossarian questions her as to why the girls were "chased away":

> "There must have been a reason," Yossarian persisted, pounding his fist into his hand. "They couldn't just barge in here and chase everyone out." "No reason," wailed the old woman. "No reason." "What right did they have?" "Catch-22." "*What?*" Yossarian froze in his tracks with fear and alarm and felt his whole body begin to tingle. "*What* did you say?" "Catch-22," the old woman repeated, rocking her head up and down. "Catch-22. Catch-22 says they have a right to do anything we can't stop them from doing." "What the hell are you talking about?" Yossarian shouted at her in bewildered, furious protest. "How did you know it was Catch-22? Who the hell told you it was Catch-22?" "The soldiers with the hard white hats and clubs. The girls were crying. 'Did we do anything wrong?' they said. The men said no and pushed them away out the door with the ends of their clubs. 'Then why are you chasing us out?' the girls said. 'Catch-22,' the men said. 'What right do you have?' the girls said. 'Catch-22,' the men said. All they kept saying was 'Catch-22, Catch-22.' What does it mean, Catch-22? What is Catch-22?" "Didn't they show it to you?" Yossarian demanded, stamping about in anger and distress. "Didn't you even make them read it?" "They don't have to show us Catch-22," the old woman answered. "The law says they don't have to." "What law says they don't have to?" "Catch-22."[22]

The crazed arrogance of power reaches its climax in this last pronouncement of Catch-22, but the immoral character of the military system takes other forms as well. The members of the military high command are concerned only for themselves and for the extension of their personal power. Heller describes Colonel Cathcart as a "valorous opportunist" who judges all actions either "black eyes" or "feathers in his cap," depending on whether they hinder or help his chances to achieve the only thing he truly cares about: the rank of general.[23] Cathcart raises the number of combat missions for Yossarian's squadron in his pursuit of higher position, hoping to attract the generals' attention, and he relies on yet another version of Catch-22 for his authority. Even though the air force requires only forty missions before the men can be sent home, Cathcart is allowed to extend this number (ultimately to eighty) because of the catch: "Catch-22 . . . says you've always got to do what your commanding officer tells you to."[24] This version of the catch also comes into play when the squadron is ordered on a mission that high authorities admit "is entirely unnecessary" and that the men believe is "cruel." The mission entails "bombing a tiny undefended village, reducing the whole community to rubble." The presumed intent of the bombing is to create a roadblock against German reinforcements, but the mission turns out to be simply an opportunity to demonstrate "bomb patterns" as they appear in aerial photographs (also admitted to be worthless by one of the generals). As a superior officer tells the major briefing the men: "'We don't care about the roadblock. . . . Colonel Cathcart wants to come out of this mission with a good clean aerial photograph he won't be ashamed to send through channels.'" The concern for the village inhabitants voiced by the men ("they won't even take shelter. . . . They'll pour out into the streets to wave when they see our planes coming, all the children and dogs and old people. Jesus Christ! Why can't we leave them alone?") carries no weight with their superiors.[25]

Another offshoot of this American wartime bureaucracy is the exercising of the capitalist imperative, as practiced by Milo Minderbinder. Milo parlays his position as mess officer into a more glorious role as head of M & M Enterprises:

Milo Minderbinder's planes flew in from everywhere. . . . The planes were decorated with flamboyant squadron emblems illustrating such laudable ideals as Courage, Might, Justice, Truth, Liberty, Love, Honor and Patriotism that were painted out at once by Milo's mechanics with a double coat of flat white and replaced in garish purple with the stenciled name M & M ENTERPRISES, FINE FRUITS AND PRODUCE. The "M & M" in "M & M ENTERPRISES" stood for Milo & Minderbinder, and the & was inserted, Milo revealed candidly, to nullify any impression that the syndicate was a one-man operation.[26]

Like Catch-22 and the military establishment, Milo's syndicate takes on an increasingly corrupt and deadly character as the profit motive above all else comes to rule Milo and his syndicate. Milo does business with the Nazis, and when German planes loaded with his goods land on Pianosa and are subsequently surrounded and threatened with confiscation by the Americans, Milo explodes:

"Is this Russia?" Milo assailed them incredulously at the top of his voice. "*Confiscate?*" he shrieked, as though he could not believe his own ears. "Since when is it the policy of the American government to confiscate the private property of its citizens? Shame on you! Shame on all of you for

even thinking such a horrible thought!" "But Milo," Major Danby interrupted timidly, "we're at war with Germany, and those are German planes."
"They are no such thing!" Milo retorted furiously. "Those planes belong
to the syndicate, and everybody has a share. *Confiscate?* How can you possibly confiscate your own private property? *Confiscate,* indeed! I've never
heard anything so depraved in my entire life." And sure enough, Milo was
right, for when they looked, his mechanics had painted out the German
swastikas on the wings, tails and fuselages with double coats of flat white
and stenciled in the words M & M ENTERPRISES, FINE FRUITS AND PRODUCE.
Right before their eyes he had transformed his syndicate into an international cartel.[27]

The international character of Milo's cartel completely undercuts the "normal" wartime divisions and alliances, and Milo does business with every nation
"but Russia, with whom Milo refused to do business."[28] The principles of profit
and private enterprise control Milo to the point that he contracts with both the
Germans and Americans to direct the same military maneuver; he will bomb a
German bridge for the Americans and direct the defensive antiaircraft fire for
the Germans at the same bridge. Milo has Yossarian's squadron bomb the bridge
and a man is killed on the mission. Amid Milo's constant refrain of "I didn't kill
him!" Yossarian tries—and fails—to make Milo see his responsibility for the
death. Milo asks, "If I can persuade the Germans to pay me a thousand dollars
for every plane they shoot down, why shouldn't I take it?" Yossarian responds,
"Because you're dealing with the enemy, that's why. Can't you understand that
we're fighting a war? People are dying. Look around you for Christ's sake!"
Milo, however, has his completely reasonable explanation ready, and it shows
his clear loyalty—to profit and capitalism:

> Milo shook his head with weary forbearance. "And the Germans are not
> our enemies," he declared. "Oh, I know what you're going to say. Sure,
> we're at war with them. But the Germans are also members in good stand-
> ing of the syndicate, and it's my job to protect their rights as shareholders.
> Maybe they did start the war, and maybe they are killing millions of peo-
> ple, but they pay their bills a lot more promptly than some allies of ours I
> could name. Don't you understand that I have to respect the sanctity of my
> contract with Germany? Can't you see it from my point of view?"[29]

Yossarian has growing difficulty seeing anything from Milo's point of view, especially once Milo's passion for profit reaches its heights in the mounting death

toll of the squadron. Milo contracts a second time with the Germans to bomb and strafe his own squadron ("Decent people everywhere were affronted, and Milo was all washed up until he opened his books to the public and disclosed the tremendous profit he had made"). And he is responsible for Cathcart's final raising of the number of missions to be flown, an act that leads directly to the death of twelve men in the squadron.[30] As Milo becomes more and more obsessed by a deadly capitalist ethic and less and less attached to a human and moral consideration for life, Yossarian becomes more and more alienated from the insanity and immorality of both Milo and the military system. Yossarian learns that death is the rational product of this bureaucracy in all its guises and he learns from death the very fragility of life, but his newfound knowledge spawns his rebirth as a more human and morally responsible man.

Beginning in fear and disillusion and ending in hope and discovery, Yossarian's wartime education teaches him to reject and rebel against all systems of authority. Yossarian first deserts God, then prepares himself to desert the corrupt system at Pianosa. Of God Yossarian asks, "Good God, how much reverence can you have for a Supreme Being who finds it necessary to include such phenomena as phlegm and tooth decay in his divine system of creation?" and "Why in the world did He ever create pain?" and then he slams the God he does not believe in as "a colossal, immortal blunderer! When you consider the opportunity and power He had to really do a job, and then look at the stupid, ugly little mess He made of it instead, His sheer incompetence is almost staggering."[31] Yossarian is intimately acquainted with this "stupid, ugly little mess" of a world, and his descent into this hell—in no small part aided by his immersion in the war system—forces Yossarian to choose either to succumb or to climb out. Having faced the intolerable threat of death through seventy-one missions and having suffered the death or disappearance of the majority of his buddies, Yossarian finally confronts the horror of it all and makes his renewing choice: desertion.

Toward the end of the novel Yossarian is AWOL in Rome and wanders the nightmarish streets, where he most clearly begins his transformation to a sort of modern, antiheroic secular Christ. Nauseated by the pain and inhumanity evident in every corner of Rome, "Yossarian quickened his pace to get away, almost ran. The night was filled with horrors, and he thought he knew how Christ must have felt as he walked through the world, like a psychiatrist in a ward full of nuts, like a victim through a prison of thieves. What a welcome sight a leper must have been!"[32] Yossarian had already begun his rebellion against the system—he had refused to fly any more missions after the twelve men were killed—and when he returns to the squadron after his hellish visit to Rome, he is offered a tempting deal by his superiors, who tell him: "We're sending you home."[33]

There is, however, a catch to their offer—Catch-22. They cannot send him home for refusing to fly more missions, particularly since his refusal is playing havoc with the men's morale. Yossarian blames the morale problems on his superiors for raising the number of missions, but they blame him for refusing to fly: "The men were perfectly content to fly as long they thought they had no alternative. Now you've given them hope, and they're unhappy. So the blame is all yours."[34] In order to remedy this situation, the superiors have a plan, one they know Yossarian will "loathe" since "it really is odious and certainly will offend your conscience," but one they know he will accept—in order to go home and to avoid a court-martial (for desertion of duty, being AWOL in Rome). The catch is that Yossarian must "like" them: they will promote him, give him a medal, and send him home a hero, but he must be their friend and thereby convince the other men in the squadron not to rebel. As they point out about the others: "They'll be easy enough to discipline and control when you've gone. . . . You know—this would really be wonderful—you might even serve as inspiration to them to fly more missions." Yossarian, fully aware that "it's a pretty scummy trick I'd be playing on the men in the squadron," agrees to their Catch-22.[35]

But Yossarian does not stick to the deal, for he undergoes the final trial in his journey of renewal: he comes to terms with that significant moment of past experience, Snowden's death on the Avignon mission. Fully sensitized and ready to absorb the message, Yossarian recalls and reveals the encounter with Snowden over Avignon—in detail and in normal chronological progression. Insistently urged by the pilot on the intercom to help the wounded gunner, Yossarian crawls to the back of the plane to aid Snowden. Bundled in his flak suit, Snowden lies on his back, whispering in a constant refrain, "I'm cold." Yossarian sees a gaping wound in Snowden's thigh, "large and deep as a football, it seemed." Yossarian composes himself, tells Snowden, "You're going to be all right, kid," and begins to attend to the wound with tenderness and thoroughness (despite the fact that Milo has taken all the syrettes of morphine— "What's good for M & M Enterprises is good for the country"). Yossarian becomes more confident as he fixes the wound, certain that Snowden will survive, but Snowden persists in his cry, "I'm cold." Snowden finally manages to indicate that Yossarian has focused on the wrong wound—and then he spills his message of life for Yossarian:

But Snowden kept shaking his head and pointed at last, with just the barest movement of his chin, down toward his armpit. Yossarian bent forward to peer and saw a strangely colored stain seeping through the coveralls just above the armhole of Snowden's flak suit. Yossarian felt his heart stop, then pound so violently he found it difficult to breathe. Snowden was wounded inside his flak suit. Yossarian ripped open the snaps of Snowden's flak suit and heard himself scream wildly as Snowden's insides slithered down to the floor in a soggy pile and just kept dripping out. A chunk of flak more than three inches big had shot into his other side just underneath the arm and blasted all the way through, drawing whole mottled quarts of Snowden along with it through the gigantic hole in his ribs it had made as it blasted out. Yossarian screamed a second time and squeezed both hands over his eyes. His teeth were chattering in horror. He forced himself to look again. Here was God's plenty, all right, he thought bitterly as he stared—liver, lungs, kidneys, ribs, stomach and bits of the stewed tomatoes Snowden had eaten that day for lunch. Yossarian hated stewed tomatoes and turned away dizzily and began to vomit, clutching his burning throat. . . . He turned back weakly to Snowden, whose breath had grown softer and more rapid, and whose face had grown paler. He wondered how in the world to begin to save him.[36]

There was, of course, no way for Yossarian to save Snowden. As Snowden voices his dying coldness again and again, Yossarian learns the lesson written in Snowden's fate:

> Yossarian was cold, too, and shivering uncontrollably. He felt goose pimples clacking all over him as he gazed down despondently at the grim secret Snowden had spilled all over the messy floor. It was easy to read the message in his entrails. Man was matter, that was Snowden's secret. Drop him out a window and he'll fall. Set fire to him and he'll burn. Bury him and he'll rot like other kinds of garbage. The spirit gone, man is garbage. That was Snowden's secret. Ripeness was all.[37]

It was too late to save Snowden, but Snowden's message prompts Yossarian to save himself and to protect his newly won human and moral spirit. Yossarian backs off from his deal with his superiors immediately after coming to an understanding of Snowden's secret; he may have to live within the limits of life as taught by Snowden, but he does not choose to live within the man-made confines of the immoral and insane military system on Pianosa. He decides to desert—to break out of the enclosed world of Catch-22.

Yossarian argues about his options with Major Danby, but insists: "Don't talk to me about fighting to save my country. I've been fighting all along to save my country. Now I'm going to fight a little to save myself. The country's not in danger any more, but I am."[38] The chaplain confirms both the feasibility and the miraculous possibilities of desertion for Yossarian when he rushes to tell Yossarian the news about the "miracle" of Orr. Presumed missing or dead since his last crash, Orr had instead made his way alive and well to Sweden (Yossarian now realizes that Orr's other crashes had been practice and that Orr had rowed to Sweden according to plan). Inspired by what the chaplain calls "a miracle of human intelligence and human endurance" and given hope by this demonstrated alternative to staying within the system, Yossarian exults in his plan of escape. He knows he is not running away from his responsibilities— "I'm running *to* them"—and he knows how impossible the journey to Sweden will be—"But at least I'll be trying." Major Danby tries to convince Yossarian of the danger and difficulty: "I mean it, Yossarian. You'll have to keep on your toes every minute of every day. They'll bend heaven and earth to catch you." Yossarian promises to keep on his toes, and when Danby warns him, "You'll have to jump," Yossarian jumps—to his freedom and to his new life of human and moral responsibility.[39]

At a point near the end of the novel Milo lectures Yossarian on the dangers of his rebellion against the system: "Morale was deteriorating and it was all Yossarian's fault. The country was in peril; he was jeopardizing his traditional rights of freedom and independence by daring to exercise them."[40] Daring to exercise these rights—plus the right of dissent—fed into the moral and political code of the 1960s, and it was the fictional Yossarian's kind of example that illustrated the possibilities of opposition and alternative states of mind. It was possible by the early sixties to exercise imagination and the right of dissent, to see a different version of history, a version that transformed cold war rationality into all-encompassing malignant American arrogance. Heller's antiheroic and darkly humorous reinterpretation of World War II and its legacies promoted an appreciation both for this acknowledgment of American arrogance and for the necessity of eluding and renouncing the dangerous future that such arrogance promised. A more human and moral vision of the meaning of life and history in the atomic age appeared: Man is perishable matter.

The spirit of dissent let loose in *Catch-22* also coursed through Ken Kesey's novel *One Flew Over the Cuckoo's Nest,* if in a less grandiose historical context. The representative "system" in *One Flew Over the Cuckoo's Nest* is not the World

War II military bureaucracy but a mental institution, which equally symbolizes the systemic insanity and repression that had bound America since the war. The main character and narrator of the novel, Chief Bromden, has been a patient in the ward since World War II, and a clear connection between the war and his "illness" is made: the fear and the "fog" that first engulfed the Chief in the war are re-created in the mental institution, particularly in the "Shock Shop" that "treats" patients with electroshock therapy (EST). The terror and control of the war system have been transformed in the Chief's eyes into the "Combine," another enclosed system bent on "adjusting," rationalizing, and organizing all human behavior to fit smoothly into the conforming patterns of the Combine. His ward in the mental institution is just one element of the Combine, and it is managed by the "Big Nurse," Nurse Ratched. The Chief uses an industrial metaphor to describe the workings of the Combine, which captures precisely the human limitations of the system:

> The ward is a factory for the Combine. It's for fixing up mistakes made in the neighborhoods and in the schools and in the churches, the hospital is. When a completed product goes back out into society, all fixed up good as new, *better* than new sometimes, it brings joy to the Big Nurse's heart; something that came in all twisted different is now a functioning, adjusted component, a credit to the whole outfit and a marvel to behold.[41]

The Chief ultimately opts to remain "twisted different" and to resist becoming a "functioning, adjusted component," and he is aided in his escape from the system by his very ancestry. Like Yossarian, who claimed an Assyrian background, the Chief is an outsider. His status as half American Indian allows him a place beyond the mainstream and beyond the mainstream acquiescence to the Combine. He is also helped in his escape by the arrival of Randle P. McMurphy, whose fate encapsulates the novel's thread of apocalyptic black humor. While the Chief perceives the operation of the Combine in all its minute features, down to the invisible electronics in the pills the patients are forced to take, it is McMurphy who disturbs and thereby invigorates the ward and it is McMurphy who sacrifices himself to save the others on the ward, including the Chief, from the Combine. The Chief, again like Yossarian, is reborn and renewed by his decision to live outside the system. In effect, both of these characters mirrored the direction of cultural rebellion in the early 1960s.

Before McMurphy's appearance at the mental institution, both the Chief and the ward had been enveloped in the blinding, suffocating "fog" produced by the Combine. The Chief realizes how the fog machine functions, because he had first seen it during World War II: "I know how they work it, the fog machine. We had a whole platoon used to operate fog machines around airfields overseas. Whenever intelligence figured there might be a bombing attack, or if the generals had something secret they wanted to pull—out of sight, hid so good that even the spies on the base couldn't see what went on—they fogged the field."[42] He believes the Combine bought one such fog machine from army surplus, and "they" are using it for similar purposes—to keep the men on the ward lost, to keep the men from seeing the secret operations of the Combine. The depth of the Chief's withdrawal into the fog is indicated by his behavior: he wanders aimlessly with a broom, sweeping the ward, pretending to be deaf and dumb. The Chief, despite his gigantic stature (approximately six feet, seven inches), comports himself as a small and mute man lost in the fog. McMurphy, however, comes along to free him and to restore his size, his sight, and his voice.

The image of the lifting of a blinding fog that had prevented a clear view of reality resembled the "flies in the eyes" imagery of *Catch-22* and suggested the same sort of historical revision. The craziness of America's recent past is hinted at in McMurphy's own description of his insanity. Trying to convince the others on the ward that he is in fact the "psychopath" the authorities claim, he tells them, "I'm so crazy I admit to voting for Eisenhower."[43] From this introduction of McMurphy and from his wild and rebellious challenges to the rule and authority of Nurse Ratched and the Combine, it becomes clear that McMurphy is indeed something "twisted different," something outside the ordinary tide of history and culture, something outside the control of the Combine. The Chief recognizes the threat that McMurphy poses to the Combine as a new admission and as an uncontrollable character: "You never can tell when just that *certain* one might come in who's free enough to foul things up right and left, really make a hell of a mess and constitute a threat to the whole smoothness of the outfit."[44] By fouling up the routine and the control of the Combine, McMurphy dispels the fog and exposes the origins of the threat: the Combine and the American system it represents.

McMurphy's kinetic personality is the key to the dismantling of the Combine, and his rebellious character is exemplified in his quick laughter. McMurphy's free spirit, the force of his laughter, and the instructional power of his actions combine to rouse the Chief from his small, safe silence, a fact the Chief points to at the outset of his retelling of this story: "I been silent so long now it's gonna roar out of me like floodwaters and you think the guy telling this is ranting and raving my *God;* you think this is too horrible to have really happened, this is too awful to be the truth!"[45] It is McMurphy's final confrontation with the Combine that lends an element of horror to the Chief's tale and a blackness to the humor. But it is McMurphy's laughter that frees the Chief from his silence and the system: "He stands there waiting, and when nobody makes a move to say anything to him he commences to laugh. Nobody can tell exactly why he laughs; there's nothing funny going on. . . . It's free and loud and comes out of his wide grinning mouth and spreads in rings bigger and bigger till it's lapping against the walls all over the ward. . . . This sounds real. I realize all of a sudden it's the first laugh I've heard in years."[46]

McMurphy explains the meaning and the necessity of laughter to the other inmates in the institution. He chides them for their fear of Nurse Ratched, noting, "I never saw a scareder-looking bunch in my life than you guys." He accuses them of being even too "scared to open up and *laugh*," and then he teaches them the danger of losing mirth:

"You know, that's the first thing that got me about this place, that there wasn't anybody laughing. I haven't heard a real laugh since I came through that door, do you know that? Man, when you lose your laugh you lose your *footing*. A man go around lettin' a woman whup him down till he can't laugh any more, and he loses one of the biggest edges he's got on his side."[47]

The Chief knows why McMurphy feels such urgency about laughter—"he knew you can't really be strong until you can see a funny side to things"—but he also knows that the others need time to overcome the years of Combine-indoctrinated fear, a fear McMurphy had evaded in his life.

McMurphy laughs, sings, and otherwise challenges the order established by Nurse Ratched, and he is evidently "out of control," not subject to the fog and fear of the Combine. The Chief guesses that "the Combine missed getting to him soon enough with controls," in large part because—like the beats of the 1950s—McMurphy had kept on the move:

Maybe he growed up so wild all over the country, batting around from one place to another, never around one town longer'n a few months when he was a kid so a school never got much a hold on him, logging, gambling, running carnival wheels, traveling lightfooted and fast, keeping on the move so much that the Combine never had a chance to get anything installed. Maybe that's it, he never gave the Combine a chance.[48]

Having lived outside the Combine's control, McMurphy shows the others how to do so, by his laughter and by his actions. He protects the weak against the Big Nurse, he gains extra privileges for the inmates, and he urges them to keep hope and to see the other possibilities in life. In a debate about how to escape from the institution, McMurphy decides that the quarter-ton control panel in the tub room is heavy enough to crash through the mesh screen over the window. The others only argue the obvious reality: it is too heavy for anyone to lift. McMurphy bets them he can do it, and when he fails he nonetheless leaves an inspiring lesson: "But I tried, though. . . . Goddammit, I sure as hell did that much, now, didn't I?"[49]

Under McMurphy's guidance, the others—including the Chief—are beginning to try. The Chief realizes what McMurphy is doing, "trying to drag us out of the fog," and he notes the gradual but complete triumph of McMurphy: "There's no more fog any place."[50] They all look to McMurphy, "full of a naked, scared hope," and McMurphy lives up to that hope. The Chief drops his deaf and dumb act with McMurphy, and McMurphy promises to help the Chief get "big" again—to reach his full power and to prove it by moving the control panel in the tub room. McMurphy arranges a trip outside of the institution and the residents begin to taste a sort of liberation. Outside of the mental hospital, one of the inmates senses the power of insanity when he uses it to intimidate a passerby. He exults: "Never before did I realize that mental illness could have the aspect of power, *power*. Think of it: perhaps the more insane a man is, the more powerful he could become."[51] The Chief, while exultant, has his sense of freedom tempered by his disquieting recognition of the Combine's power both inside and now outside of the ward. Not having circulated in the environs of Portland or in the Pacific Northwest since his admission to the hospital, the Chief is struck by the Combine's external transformation of the land—the land he had known in its more natural state in his childhood with his Columbia River tribe. The Chief describes an American system that felt the threat of insanity or laughing nonconformity:

All up the coast I could see the signs of what the Combine had accomplished since I was last through this country, things like, for example—a *train* stopping at a station and laying a string of full-grown men in mirrored suits and machined hats, laying them like a hatch of identical insects, half-life things coming pht-pht-pht out of the last car, then hooting its electric whistle and moving on down the spoiled land to deposit another hatch. Or things like five thousand houses punched out identical by a machine and strung across the hills outside of town, so fresh from the factory they're still linked together like sausages, a sign saying "Nest in the West Homes— No Dwn. Payment for Vets," a playground down the hill from the houses, behind a checker-wire fence and another sign that read "St. Luke's School for Boys"—there were five thousand kids in green corduroy pants and white shirts under green pullover sweaters playing crack-the-whip across an acre of crushed gravel. . . . All that five thousand kids lived in those five thousand houses, owned by those guys that got off the train. The houses looked so much alike that, time and time again, the kids went home by mistake to different houses and different families. Nobody ever noticed.[52]

Even though both the Chief and McMurphy have the depressing knowledge that life is threatened by more than just the Big Nurse ("It's not just the Big Nurse by herself, but it's the whole Combine, the nation-wide Combine that's the really big force"), this knowledge does not stop them from battling that element of the Combine within their grasp: Nurse Ratched and the mental institution's controlling and deadening conformity.[53] After their trip to the outside world, the tempo of McMurphy's rebellion and the Chief's rebirth quickens. The Chief has regained enough of his size and strength to move the control panel in the tub room, and he joins McMurphy when a physical fight with the cruel hospital attendants breaks out. McMurphy and the Chief, tagged as "disturbed" patients, are sent for treatments at the Shock Shop, and thus begins the final showdown and resolution of the confrontation with the Combine. While the two will survive and in fact grow stronger as a result of their electroshock therapy, their contrasting fates are nonetheless foreshadowed in the early description of the Combine's most naked forms of control—EST and lobotomy.

One of the more experienced patients explains EST for McMurphy, and the imagery prefigures both the sacrifice to be made and the salvation attained:

"The Shock Shop, Mr. McMurphy, is jargon for the EST machine, the Electro Shock Therapy. A device that might be said to do the work of the sleeping pill, the electric chair, *and* the torture rack. It's a clever little procedure, simple, quick, nearly painless it happens so fast, but no one ever wants another one. Ever . . . You are strapped to a table, shaped, ironically, like a cross, with a crown of electric sparks in place of thorns. You are touched on each side of the head with wires. Zap! Five cents' worth of electricity through the brain and you are jointly administered therapy and a punishment for your hostile go-to-hell behavior, on top of being put out of everyone's way for six hours to three days, depending on the individual. Even when you do regain consciousness you are in a state of disorientation for days."[54]

The other extreme form of treatment, lobotomy, is described as "chopping away the brain" and "frontal lobe castration."[55]

The life and laughter that will eventually be sucked out of McMurphy are absorbed by the Chief, who will make good on McMurphy's sacrifice by breaking free of the Combine. The EST session for the Chief is a catharsis and signals his renewed strength; the EST session for McMurphy is the beginning of his final self-sacrifice and signals the ebbing of his strength. The Chief recalls all the fear and horror of EST as he is shot with electricity—"The machine hunches on me. AIR RAID"—and his mind experiences a bewildering welter of memories.[56] But the Chief is now stronger, and rather than submit to the posthaze of EST, he fights it: "I couldn't remember all of it yet, but I rubbed my eyes with the heels of my hands and tried to clear my head. I worked at it. I'd never worked at coming out of it before. I staggered toward the little round chicken-wired window in the door of the room and tapped it with my knuckles. I saw an aide coming up the hall with a tray for me and knew this time I had them beat."[57] The Chief recognizes the significance of his exertion: "And when the fog was finally swept from my head it seemed like I'd just come up after a long, deep dive, breaking the surface after being under water a hundred years. It was the last treatment they gave me."[58]

The Chief's transformation is sealed when he returns to the ward before McMurphy, who, while maintaining his wild reputation and good spirits, is receiving a series of shock treatments. As he enters the ward the Chief notices the changed attitudes toward him: "Everybody's face turned up to me with a different look than they'd ever given me before. Their faces lighted up. . . . I grinned back at them, realizing how McMurphy must've felt these months with these faces screaming up at him." He responds to their questions about McMurphy, and the Chief's (and the ward's) new strength is confirmed:

I told them all I could, and nobody seemed to think a thing about me all of a sudden talking with people—a guy who'd been considered deaf and dumb as far back as they'd known him, talking, listening, just like anybody. I told them everything that they'd heard was true, and tossed in a few stories of my own. They laughed so hard about some of the things he'd said to the nurse that the two Vegetables under their wet sheets on the Chronics' side grinned and snorted along with the laughter, just like they understood.[59]

Laughter continues to ring out in the ward, and McMurphy arrives back "foot-working into the day room like a boxer into a ring, clasping his hands over his head and announcing the champ was back." He tells them that he is "fulla piss an' vinegar, buddies; they checked my plugs and cleaned my points, and I got a glow on like a Model T spark coil," but the Chief has noticed the strain in

McMurphy and they all notice that the Big Nurse is maneuvering for a final epic struggle with the rebellious McMurphy. They want him to escape, but he does not—and the struggle ensues. One of the patients commits suicide as a result of the Big Nurse's torment, and Nurse Ratched blames McMurphy, accusing him of "gambling with human lives—as if you thought yourself to be a *God!*"[60] McMurphy snaps and attacks the Big Nurse, strangling her, and the Chief reasons that there is no stopping this man who had in fact become a god to the residents of the mental hospital:

> We couldn't stop him because we were the ones making him do it. It wasn't the nurse that was forcing him, it was our need that was making him push himself slowly up from sitting, his big hands driving down on the leather chair arms, pushing him up, rising and standing like one of those motion-picture zombies, obeying orders beamed at him from forty masters. It was us that had been making him go on for weeks, keeping him standing long after his feet and legs had given out, weeks of making him wink and grin and laugh and go on with his act long after his humor had been parched dry between two electrodes. . . . Only at the last—after he'd smashed through that glass door, her face swinging around, with terror forever ruining any other look she might ever try to use again . . . —only at the last, after the officials realized that the three black boys weren't going to do anything but stand and watch and they would have to beat him off without their help, doctors and supervisors and nurses prying those heavy red fingers out of the white flesh of her throat as if they were her neck bones, jerking him backward off of her with a loud heave of breath, only then did he show any sign that he might be anything other than a sane, willful, dogged man performing a hard duty that finally had to be done, like it or not.[61]

At the end McMurphy issues a death-rattling cry, "a sound of cornered-animal fear and hate and surrender and defiance," and he is taken off for the brain-chopping operation that stifles life and laughter forever.[62] McMurphy did not win the physical struggle with the Big Nurse, for she recovers and comes back to the ward. But he did win the larger battle with the controlling Combine power she represents, for her power is broken and the inmates break rebelliously free: "She tried to get her ward back into shape, but it was difficult with McMurphy's presence still tromping up and down the halls and laughing out loud in the meetings and singing in the latrines. She couldn't rule with her old power any more. . . . She was losing her patients one after the other."[63] Most of the patients leave or transfer out of her much reduced jurisdiction, but the

Chief waits for McMurphy. The lobotomy has made him a vegetable and those left on the ward conclude, "That ain't him." The Chief wonders what should be done, revealing how deeply he has absorbed the spirit and the message of McMurphy's life: "I watched and tried to figure out what he would have done. I was only sure of one thing: he wouldn't have left something like that sit there in the day room with his name tacked on it for twenty or thirty years so the Big Nurse could use it as an example of what can happen if you buck the system. I was sure of that."[64] Acting from his renewed spirit and strength, the Chief suffocates and kills "it," the McMurphy that was no more. Using the very method McMurphy had shown him, the Chief then flees the mental institution and the Combine, accomplishing the "impossible": he hurls the control panel through the window of the tub room. He runs and will keep running, through the countryside and through the lost lands of his Indian tribe, to remain beyond the reach of the Combine: "I remember I was taking huge strides as I ran, seeming to step and float a long ways before my next foot struck the earth. I felt like I was flying. Free."[65] The Chief, like Yossarian, had leapt for his life and had escaped the controlling conformity and lifelessness of the system. The Chief, unlike his equally fictional counterpart from the 1950s, Holden Caulfield, did not end up confined in the mental institution. Both *The Catcher in the Rye* and *One Flew Over the Cuckoo's Nest* are narrated from a psychiatric hospital, but the Chief—like the culture in the 1960s generally—was able to identify the real source of insanity and paranoia: it came from within the troubled system, from within the corrupt institution, not from within the "twisted different" individual.

That it was the outside world, the system, that created or demanded "insane" behavior is evident in the Chief's explanation for his deaf and dumb act: "But I remembered one thing: it wasn't me that started acting deaf; it was people that first started acting like I was too dumb to hear or see or say anything at all."[66] Whether in the hospital, the army, or school, the Chief had been ignored. Reborn and renewed, he no longer tolerated the system's refusal to see or listen to him, and his kind of demand to speak and be heard multiplied in the culture of the sixties. The Chief spoke of the dangers of the all-powerful Combine, justifying the type of paranoia that informed the very first line of *One Flew Over the Cuckoo's Nest,* "They're out there." The enemy was "within"—it was the American system itself and those who ran it.

This same sensitivity to the "enemy within" characterized *The Manchurian Candidate.* The novel by Richard Condon, published in 1959, and the film by John Frankenheimer, released in 1962, both investigate the fate of an American war hero brainwashed by Chinese and Russian communists during the Korean

War, but it is the film that gives a peculiarly dark, complex, and comedic aspect to the story.[67] The time of the film's release, October 1962, also provided an atmosphere more charged and primed for a dramatic revision of cold war history. Given the demonstration of America's thermonuclear bravado in the Cuban missile crisis, the film's message about an internal American menace seemed pregnant with contemporary meaning.

The Manchurian Candidate revamped and parodied the simplistic modes of cold war logic, which divided America and the world between the forces of democratic patriotism and the forces of international communism. The film's ironic premise is that the representatives of anticommunism and 100 percent Americanism are in fact operatives and stooges for the communist powers. Liberal fears about the damaging nature of McCarthyism are openly inflated here, illustrating once again the culture's discovery of the enemy within. The "enemy" in this case is deep within the American political system, and the danger resides within the bosom of one well-known American family. Senator Iselin, his wife, and his stepson Raymond Shaw act out the two-pronged communist plot against America. At the urging and direction of his ambitious wife, Senator Iselin has made his name and his political career on the issue of anticommunism, using the method of witch-hunting. His wife's son, Raymond, is a highly decorated hero of the Korean War. These irreproachable Americans serve as vehicles (albeit somewhat unwittingly, since Mrs. Iselin is the only self-conscious traitor) for the forces of communism and, in doing so, collapse any neat cold war distinctions.

While the relations and loyalties of these characters only become clear at the end of the film, the peril embodied in these characters is evident from the beginning. Even before Mrs. Iselin is unmasked as the "Red queen" directing the actions of her husband and son, the brutal and inane anticommunism of Senator Iselin is presented as more corrosive than any form of communism. Raymond despises his demagogic stepfather for his transparent and insincere political opportunism, and the liberal Senator Jordan gives voice to the obvious point in his denunciation of "Iselinism": "I think if John Iselin were a paid Soviet agent he could not do more to harm this country than he's doing now."[68] The irony that Iselin is in fact in the hands of communists contributes to the film's black humor, as does Iselin's anticommunist buffoonery. The film satirizes McCarthy's propensity for spewing forth lists and exact numbers of communists in the government by having Johnny Iselin announce a constantly varying number. He first reveals that he has a list of 207 communists in the defense department, then he puts forth a series of decreasing and increasing totals. His numbers game is being directed by his wife, and she makes it clear that there is no evidence for these "exact" numbers, save to convince America of the communist threat. Iselin, pictured as something of an idiot, nevertheless insists that they settle on one number. After looking at a Heinz condiment bottle, he determines that there are 57 communists in the government.

The ironic political and familial relationships in the film are compounded by the anomalous position of Raymond Shaw, the other "patriotic" threat to America. Returning from Korea in 1952, Raymond is a war hero. His mother tries to capitalize on Raymond's fame to further Iselin's political career, but Raymond rejects this sort of manipulation for both emotional and political reasons. He hates both his mother and his stepfather and violently disagrees with their brand of politics. Having distanced himself from this branch of the communist plot, Raymond is unknowingly still very much a part of that plan. While in Korea, Raymond and his patrol group had been captured and brainwashed by communist experts. The communists programmed Raymond to be an assassin, a killer without memory or conscience. The communists in fact brainwashed the entire patrol because, even though Raymond was their most prized subject, the others had to believe the fabricated story of their loss and rescue in order to explain their temporary absence from the war and to provide eyewitnesses to Raymond's equally fabricated heroics. Raymond becomes open to suggestion when in his programmed trance, which is triggered by playing solitaire and turning up the queen of diamonds (the symbolic "Red queen"). A demonstration of this process takes place at the end of the patrol's Manchurian captivity when, in scenes awash with dark comedy and horror, Raymond cold-bloodedly kills two members of the very patrol he will be credited with heroically saving. In this final session before communist officials, the patrol members are under the spell of mind control. They believe they are attending the meeting of a ladies garden club, listening to a lecture on hydrangeas, and their demeanor reflects both the bored disinterest and the exquisite politeness natural and requisite among such genteel ladies. The comic surrealism of the incongruity is stressed in the film's constant shifting of perspective, when the illusion of the ladies club competes with the reality of the gallery of uniformed communist officials. The surrealism turns horrific when Raymond, having been entranced by the order to play solitaire and expose the queen of diamonds, is told by a communist official to kill two of the patrol soldiers. With all the calm etiquette befitting a performance in front of club women, Raymond first strangles one to death and then cold-bloodedly shoots the other through the forehead, all while the other patrol members look on without a trace of understanding or concern.

The success of Raymond's programming having been demonstrated so thoroughly, the communists release the patrol to spread the imaginary and brainwashed version of their war adventure. Raymond is patently a time bomb waiting to go off under communist direction, and thus the danger of both Raymond and the Iselins is apparent from the beginning. The precise nature of their threat, however, is not revealed until the end of the film, when the iniquitous elements of the plot come together. The communists have concocted an elaborate eight-year plan, and they patiently wait out the passage of time between Raymond's initial programming in 1952 and the climax of the plot in the presidential elections of 1960. In the interim Senator Iselin and his wife have whipped their anticommunist fervor into the kind of political power that ensures Johnny Iselin a place on the party's ticket as the vice-presidential candidate. Raymond's skills as an assassin, having been kept fresh by test trances and test killings, are to be used to propel Iselin—and thus the senator's wife, the communist agent—into the presidency. Raymond will be instructed to kill the party's presidential candidate at the party convention, and the Iselins will exploit the tragedy and catapult themselves into the top positions of power in America.

What ultimately complicates and foils the completion of this communist plot is the unraveling of the brainwashing, particularly among the other members of Raymond's patrol. The one patrol member most responsible for disrupting the orderly workings of the plot is Captain (later Major) Ben Marco, the intellectual career army officer who has been having terrible nightmares about his wartime past. The nightmares, of course, are the visions of what had really happened in Korea: Ben remembers Raymond Shaw murdering two patrol members in front of numerous communist officials. By working with the other patrol members, including Raymond, and by challenging the patriotic credentials of the past and of an American war hero, Ben quashes the power of the brainwashing and figures out what really happened. Spurred by the small and incomprehensible fabrications in the story of the patrol—for example, every member of the patrol praises Raymond, saying on cue, in conditioned rote, when questioned about Raymond: "Raymond Shaw is the kindest, warmest, bravest, most wonderful human being I've ever known in my life," when in reality all despised Raymond who, by his own admission, was not a "lovable" character—Ben ferrets out the complete facts of the deception and begins to deprogram Raymond.

The political convention in 1960 opens as Ben is in the midst of breaking down Raymond's mental defenses and gaining the inside information on the communist plot, including the identification of Raymond's mother as the key American agent. When Raymond leaves Ben but does not report back as arranged, the success of Raymond's deprogramming does not seem at all assured.

It is thus not clear under whose orders Raymond is acting when he arrives—armed—at Madison Square Garden for the convention. Ben searches for Raymond at the convention, but Raymond is already poised to shoot from his assassin's perch high up in the convention hall. His sights are on the stage, where he can see both the presidential candidate and the Iselins. As Ben spots Raymond, he rushes toward him but he is too late—shots have already been fired. It is, however, the Iselins who have been assassinated. Believing himself the only one capable of stopping the ambitious Iselins with their nefarious connections, Raymond has killed them; he then turns his gun on himself, effectively erasing all American elements of the communist plot and all traces of the past they represent. Ben extols Raymond for giving his life for his country, assessing the meaning of Raymond's final assassination: "He freed himself at last."

The Manchurian Candidate's exposé of the brainwashed cold war mentality gained added symbolism from the presence of corrupt parental figures. Authority, whether residing in political or parental forces, was found to be threatening, and this type of authority—the enemy within—had to be repudiated. The Manchurian Candidate presented with this theme a slick and satiric reversal of the images that had filled the screens in the anticommunist films of the 1950s. Not only were the representatives of anticommunism seen as the true threat to America but the very symbol of American purity—the mother—was also put forward as instigator of the peril. Whereas in a film like My Son John (1952) the all-American mother turns her intellectual communist son over to the authorities in a show of true patriotism, The Manchurian Candidate comedically exploded the easy myths and bizarre sexuality of such cold war scenarios. The strange and understated Freudianism of earlier cold war films evolved into sardonically explicit sexuality in The Manchurian Candidate, where the "Red queen" harbored openly incestuous lust for her tortured son.[69] The presumed cold war stereotype of the normal American family found little support in this film.

Other easy myths of the cold war disintegrated under the satire of The Manchurian Candidate. The usual communist "suspects," liberals and intellectuals, were more heroes than villains in this film. But the film ultimately allowed no facile judgments at all, as what might be termed smug liberalism came under attack as well. While liberal fears about anticommunism and the erosion of American rights and freedoms seemed confirmed, the film also upheld the reality of the communist threat. The patriotic facade of anticommunism was ripped off, but there was no simple retreat to the dualistic thinking of the cold war. In the end the film collapsed all distinctions between anticommunism and communism: both systems emerged as examples of political repression. By dealing a deathblow to all such easy assumptions, The Manchurian Candidate cleared the cultural path to a new vision of the cold war and its dangers, internal and external.[70]

Certain historians concurred with the revisionism implicit and explicit in these works of black humor. Daniel Bell's 1962 article "The Dispossessed," for example, reflected the same cynicism about the historical direction of anticommunism. Discussing the emergence in 1961–1962 of a "radical right" contingent of out-of-power and status-paranoid Republicans, Bell identified a new historical and political trend:

> Something new has been happening in American life. It is not the rancor
> of the radical right, for rancor has been a recurrent aspect of the American
> political temper. Nor is it just the casting of suspicions or the conspiracy
> theory of politics, elements of which have streaked American life in the
> past. What is new, and this is why the problem assumes importance far
> beyond the question of the fight for control of a party, is the ideology
> of this movement—its readiness to jettison constitutional processes and
> to suspend liberties, to condone Communist methods in the fighting of
> Communism.[71]

Bell identified different factions of this radical right, including the "fringe movement" of survivalism that surfaced during the civil defense and bomb shelter craze, and he decried the growing official acceptance of such extreme anticommunism:

> What is uniquely disturbing about the emergence of the radical right
> of the 1960s is the support it has been able to find among traditional com-
> munity leaders who have themselves become conditioned, through an
> indiscriminate anti-Communism that equates any form of liberalism with
> Communism, to judge as respectable a movement which, if successful, can
> only end the liberties they profess to cherish.[72]

While both professional historians and cultural revisionists of the black humor school cited evidence of the growing menace in the American system, it was the cultural force of black humor that broke the restraints of the past with the most radical spirit. Sharing something of the film noir and roman noir sensibility so prevalent in the late forties and fifties, the products of black humor in the early sixties—whether *Catch-22, One Flew Over the Cuckoo's Nest,* or *The Manchurian Candidate*—exposed the dark, irrational, alienating, and godless character of postwar life and history. But, unlike their more somber predecessors in the culture, these characters did not remain trapped. The eyes cleared, the fog lifted, and the brainwashing was overcome, freeing them to break out and speak out against the system's defects, freeing them to ridicule, to reject, and to demolish the residual restraints against active opposition. The internalized fears of insanity and the oblique criticisms of American corruption in the earlier cold war culture were now externalized and could be openly attributed to the menacing American system that was the true legacy of the post–World War II American past.

In revising the historical image of the American system, whether through the symbolic military bureaucracy of *Catch-22*, the emblematic social system of the mental hospital in *One Flew Over the Cuckoo's Nest*, or the representative cold war political enterprise in *The Manchurian Candidate*, the many and powerful voices of black humor indicated the breadth of the early sixties cultural revolution. Lewis Mumford had noted the necessity of rethinking the past for any "true cultural renascence," and the radical comic-apocalyptic visions of these works had reinterpreted the past at least in part to promote the creation of a better future. Rejecting the official rational explanations of the American past, however, constituted only one way of rethinking history. Reexamining past events and their relevance for the present also formed part of the process of historical revision. One historical event in particular gained new exposure in the early 1960s—the Holocaust. The issues raised in any understanding of Nazi Germany's "Final Solution"—from basic human morality and individual willingness to participate in the extermination of human beings to the definition of criminal state authority and the meaning of obedience to such authority—found a new currency and applicability in America's new age of thermonuclear peril.

A myriad of questions relating to the Holocaust received increased attention in the culture of the 1960s, in large part because of the Israeli capture, trial, and execution of Nazi war criminal Adolf Eichmann, but also as a result of aroused fears of nuclear extermination. In conjunction with the historical revisionism of black humorists, the refocused interest in Nazi Germany and its death camps seemed to indicate that only now were the human and moral difficulties of World War II open to real cultural and historical examination. Modern culture was finally coming to terms with the human and moral conundrums that derived from World War II and the cold war—from the atomic bomb and the death camps to the development of dangerous bureaucratic systems of organization and control. The renewed attention to the Holocaust, like the enlivened protest against civil defense and like the sardonic critiques of America's system of power, was another indication of the moral awakening in American culture, signaling once again the presence of an ongoing search for an alternative human future to replace the destructiveness of the past.

While the general cultural interest in issues related to the Final Solution, especially the issue of moral responsibility, was reflected in the press accounts of Eichmann's capture and trial and in the release of a film like *Judgment at Nuremburg* (1961), the focus on the Nazis and the Holocaust was also related to other revived human and moral concerns. The relevance of the Holocaust was explicitly tied to life in the atomic age, especially by those in the early 1960s pushing for a moral overturning of society in the nuclear era. In his foreword to *God and the H-Bomb* Steve Allen saw in the "sin" of America's nuclear policies "an example of our moral insensitivity that cries out for attention, the same sort of attention that the world all too belatedly gave to the Nazis' extermination of millions of Jews."[73] In order to confront Americans with the brutal amorality of the atomic bomb, Allen argued by Nazi analogy:

The Nazis are regarded as animals in human form because they gassed, shot or burned perhaps as many as six million Jews. Today the people of the United States are quite prepared, if provoked, to actually burn alive *hundreds* of millions of innocent men and women, young and old. I deliberately put the matter in such blunt terms because it is long past time to do so and because there is apparently no other way to start people thinking of the moral questions raised by nuclear weapons.[74]

Another welding of American and Nazi morality occurred in Kurt Vonnegut's *Mother Night* (1961), which treated the intertwining of Nazi and American roles in the spirit of black humor. Using the devices of absurdity and exaggerated circumstance, Vonnegut suggested correlations between American and Nazi methods and actions in World War II. He thereby undermined the historical American conception of the war as a "good war" and American claims to moral superiority vis-à-vis the Nazis by equating these supposed "enemies." Recalling the rather vague postwar fears about Nazi survival and infiltration in America and the issue of America's aiding Nazi war criminals, *Mother Night* presents the "Confessions of Howard W. Campbell, Jr.," an American turned Nazi propagandist who was in reality a secret American agent.[75] Serving the Americans secretly, Campbell had served the Nazis openly and well, becoming the most effective voice for the Nazi mentality and war effort. The clouded morality attached to Campbell's double life provides the dark and comedic twist to the novel as *Mother Night* traces Campbell's postwar fate—a fate that pointedly mirrored (however distorted by black humor) that of Eichmann.

While clearly modeled on the writings being undertaken by Adolf Eichmann at the time of his trial in Israel, the "Confessions of Howard W. Campbell, Jr." differ from their nonfictional counterpart in two important respects.

First, Howard Campbell is an American, and this brings the issues of moral responsibility and war criminality into a specifically American context. Second, Campbell is a morally sensitive human being, and unlike Eichmann he ultimately admits to and acts on his sense of human and moral responsibility for his war crimes. In the fictional "Editor's Note" to the "Confessions" Vonnegut-as-editor reproduces Campbell's rededication to his "Confessions," and the new dedication reveals Campbell's understanding of his "crime": "This book is rededicated to Howard W. Campbell, Jr., a man who served evil too openly and good too secretly, the crime of his times."[76] This dedication also gives definition to Campbell's own explanation for how he could have become such an extremely successful propagandist for the Nazis. While imprisoned in Israel, having listened once again to the tapes of his Nazi radio broadcasts, Campbell confesses his reaction and diagnoses the moral malady of his times: "The experience of sitting there in the dark, hearing the things I'd said, didn't shock me. It might be helpful in my defense to say that I broke into a cold sweat, or some such nonsense. But I've always known what I did. I've always been able to live with what I did. How? Through that simple and widespread boon to modern mankind—schizophrenia."[77]

This modern schizoid ability to live with evil, a sickness easily associated with Eichmann types and Germans of all kinds during the Nazi regime, is suggestively centered on atomic age Americans in the guise of Howard Campbell. Living in Germany with his German wife before the start of the war, Campbell is recruited by the Americans in 1938 for his ultrasecret mission as Nazi defender of the faith/American agent. His "real" job for the Allied war effort is known only by three people—his contact (the "Blue Fairy Godmother," according to Campbell), a high-ranking military officer, and the man Campbell refers to in his broadcasts as "Franklin Delano Rosenfeld."[78] These were the only three in the world who knew, or would ever know, the "good things" Campbell did; to the rest of the world, during and after the war, he remained the vicious Nazi radio personality and escaped war criminal. Reluctant to admit having created and used an American Nazi, a means of highly questionable morality, the American government evades responsibility for Campbell, except to save him from death at the end of the war. He is "disappeared" from Europe and repatriated to New York where he lives in relative anonymity (despite using his own name) until his surrender to Israeli agents as an "American" war criminal in 1961.

Even though Campbell was warned about the loneliness and the difficulty of his spy mission ("'To do your job right,' my Blue Fairy Godmother told me, 'you'll have to commit high treason, have to serve the enemy well. You won't ever be forgiven for that, because there isn't any legal device by which you can be forgiven'"), Campbell nonetheless comes to have serious misgivings about his role in the war.[79] At the end of the war Campbell's German father-in-law makes a damning indictment of Campbell. No longer caring about his suspicions of Campbell as a potential spy, the father-in-law tells Campbell why: "Because you could never have served the enemy as well as you served us. . . . I realized that almost all the ideas that I hold now, that make me unashamed of anything I may have felt or done as a Nazi, came not from Hitler, not from Goebbels, not from Himmler—but from you. . . . You alone kept me from concluding that Germany had gone insane."[80]

Back in America Campbell is still associated with his Nazi past, especially once his identity becomes known publicly. He is contacted by the Aryan lunatic, Dr. Lionel Jones, publisher of the *White Christian Minuteman* and author of *Christ Was Not a Jew.* He discusses Dr. Jones in his "Confessions" in order to distinguish himself from a true racist, but all such distinctions seem to blur. He states why he talks about Jones: "In order to contrast with myself a race-baiter who is ignorant and insane. I am neither ignorant nor insane. Those whose orders I carried out in Germany were as ignorant and insane as Dr. Jones. I knew it. God help me, I carried out their instructions anyway."[81] This sort of remorse and this sort of purposeful blending of those insane orders—Germany's and America's—lead Campbell toward a rejection of all systems and all absolute faiths and toward an acceptance of his own moral responsibility for serving evil too well.

In explaining the circumstances behind Israel's desire to place him on trial, Campbell ruminates on both the public evil and the private immorality of any "unquestioning faith":

The Republic of Israel stepped up its demands for me, encouraged by rumors that I wasn't an American citizen, that I was, in fact, a citizen of nowhere [no American official could or would admit knowledge of Campbell]. And the Republic's demands were framed so as to be educational, too—teaching that a propagandist of my sort was as much a murderer as Heydrich, Eichmann, Himmler, or any of the gruesome rest. That may be so. I had hoped, as a broadcaster, to be merely ludicrous, but this is a hard world to be ludicrous in, with so many human beings so reluctant to laugh, so incapable of thought, so eager to believe and snarl and hate. So many people *wanted* to believe me! Say what you will about the sweet miracle of unquestioning faith, I consider a capacity for it terrifying and absolutely vile.[82]

The dangers of "unquestioning faith" multiplied when associated with what Campbell exposes as the "totalitarian mind," the symbol for the blind and insane systems of all-encompassing belief that characterized the modern age. Like the Chief in *One Flew Over the Cuckoo's Nest,* Howard Campbell uses an industrial-mechanical metaphor to describe the totalitarian mind,

> a mind which might be likened unto a system of gears whose teeth have been filed off at random. Such a snaggle-toothed thought machine . . . whirls with the jerky, noisy, gaudy pointlessness of a cuckoo clock in Hell. . . . The dismaying thing about the classic totalitarian mind is that any given gear, though mutilated, will have at its circumference unbroken sequences of teeth that are immaculately maintained, that are exquisitely machined. . . . The missing teeth, of course, are simple, obvious truths, truths available and comprehensible even to ten-year-olds, in most cases. The willful filing off of gear teeth, the willful doing without certain obvious pieces of information—. . . . That was how Rudolf Hoess, Commandant of Auschwitz, could alternate over the loudspeakers of Auschwitz great music and calls for corpse-carriers— That was how Nazi Germany could sense no important differences between civilization and hydrophobia— That is the closest I can come to explaining the legions, the nations of lunatics I've seen in my time.[83]

Having absorbed the lesson of his double life and the lessons of modern life—of serving evil, of relying on the boon of schizophrenia, of inclining toward unquestioning faiths and totalitarian minds missing the teeth of simple moral truths—Howard Campbell is thrown back on himself. He denies allegiance to any country or system and he takes on himself the duty of adjudicating guilt. Awaiting trial in the Israeli prison, he receives a letter from his "Blue Fairy Godmother," who, against orders, reveals his true identity and offers to testify about Campbell's "real" role in the war. Campbell, however, is beyond such absolution. He condemns himself to death in an act of personal moral responsibility, despite the freedom represented by the letter: "So I am about to be a free man again, to wander where I please. I find the prospect nauseating. I think that tonight is the night I will hang Howard W. Campbell, Jr., for crimes against himself. I *know* tonight is the night."[84]

Campbell's suicide, and *Mother Night* as a whole, represented the kind of aroused moral conscience that characterized the "moral rearmament" taking place throughout American culture in the early 1960s. In a conversation with a man in a bar Campbell had been introduced to such a new movement, the

"Moral Rearmament movement," which believed in "absolute honesty, absolute purity, absolute unselfishness, and absolute love."[85] While this movement had "unquestioning" elements that might have made him wary, Campbell wished the movement "all the luck in the world."[86] The sixties cultural treatments of the Nazis and the Holocaust underlined the need for a restructured and refined moral confidence precisely because such a confidence had been so lacking in Germany during the war—and was feared to be equally lacking in America in this age, when people were finding it so hard to laugh and so easy to snarl and hate. The importance of the Eichmann case, as indicated by *Mother Night*'s use of it as well as by Hannah Arendt's account of it in *Eichmann in Jerusalem* (1963–1964), derived from the urgent desire to avoid the Eichmann example in an era so analogous to that of the Nazis and the Holocaust.

In specific references to Eichmann in *Mother Night* Vonnegut addressed the necessity of stopping the spread of Eichmann's type of morally blank conscience. Campbell has a passing acquaintance with Eichmann in an Israeli prison, and, in a conversation with Eichmann, Campbell sidesteps Eichmann's offer of advice. Eichmann tells Campbell to "relax . . . just relax," and Campbell dryly responds, "That's how I got here."[87] Vonnegut probes the pitfalls of such moral relaxation in the discussion following this initial exchange between war criminals, illuminating their differing moral character. Campbell begins their debate with a question:

"Do you feel that you're guilty of murdering six million Jews?" I said. "Absolutely not," said the architect of Auschwitz, the introducer of conveyor belts into crematoria, the greatest customer in the world for the gas called Cyklon-B. Not knowing the man for sure, I tried some intramural satire on him—what seemed to me to be intramural satire. "You were simply a soldier, were you—" I said, "taking orders from higher-ups, like soldiers around the world?" Eichmann turned to a guard, and talked to him in rapid-fire Yiddish, indignant Yiddish. If he'd spoken it slowly, I would have understood it, but he spoke too fast. "What did he say?" I asked the guard. "He wondered if we'd showed you his statement," said the guard. "He made us promise not to show it to anybody until it was done." "I haven't seen it," I said to Eichmann. "Then how do you know what my defense is going to be?" he said. This man actually believed that he had invented his own trite defense, though a whole nation of ninety some-odd million had made this same defense before him. Such was his paltry understanding of the God-like human act of invention. . . . As a friend of the court that will try Eichmann, I offer my opinion that Eichmann cannot distinguish between right and wrong—that not only right and wrong, but truth and falsehood, hope and despair, beauty and ugliness, kindness and cruelty, comedy and tragedy, are all processed by Eichmann's mind indiscriminately, like birdshot through a bugle. My case is different. I always know when I tell a lie, am capable of imagining the cruel consequences of anybody's believing my lies, know cruelty is wrong. I could no more lie without noticing it than I could unknowingly pass a kidney stone. . . . The only advantage to me of knowing the difference between right and wrong, as nearly as I can tell, is that I can sometimes laugh when the Eichmanns can see nothing funny.[88]

Eichmann's lack of imagination or sense of humor contributed to his under-developed moral consciousness, and it was this gross disparity between the too ordinary man and his all too extraordinary actions in the Holocaust that caused Vonnegut to call him "the bureaucratic Genghis Khan" and that caused Hannah Arendt to subtitle her examination of the Eichmann trial "a report on the banality of evil."[89] "Normal" modern man's capacity for evil propelled Eichmann into the exalted position—in Vonnegut's eyes—of "Man of the Century," and there was, of course, something seriocomic about such banal evil.[90] The incongruous blending of an ordinary man and his incomprehensible, unprecedented crimes encompassed essential elements of black humor and pointed to the real horror of the Eichmann example. Eichmann was no inhuman or insane master of terror; he was a plodding bureaucrat who nonetheless found within himself the capacity for great evil, the capacity to participate in the slaughter of six million Jews without guilt or remorse. In the form of Adolf Eichmann and the morally upside-down world of Nazi Germany, reality had become so bizarre, awful, and surreal as to be almost funny—at least for those with the moral imagination to see the dark humor and the equally dark warning contained in the banality of evil.

Like Vonnegut, Hannah Arendt was able to see the comedic aspects of Adolf Eichmann. She went to Jerusalem to report on the trial for the *New Yorker* (her reports appeared in the magazine in 1963 and then were reprinted in book form in 1963 and 1964), and she discovered in Eichmann's very use of language the roots of his banality and comedy. She noted that Eichmann spoke in nothing but tired, mundane clichés, a habit Eichmann explained to the court: "Officialese is my only language." Arendt elaborated on his comment and provided background information about Eichmann's amoral world view:

But the point here is that officialese became his language because he was genuinely incapable of uttering a single sentence that was not a cliché. . . .

The longer one listened to him, the more obvious it became that his inability to speak was closely connected with an inability to *think,* namely, to think from the standpoint of somebody else. No communication was possible with him, not because he lied but because he was surrounded by the most reliable of all safeguards against the words and the presence of others, and hence against reality as such.[91]

The "macabre humor" that often resulted from Eichmann's slogan-ridden language and his protective tunnelvision (he interpreted the events of the Final Solution according to his career and his advancement in the SS, with little regard for what those events entailed for the victims or for what they meant to his Israeli audience, for example) detracted from the image of Eichmann as an example of pure evil. It was hard, according to Arendt, to take Eichmann seriously:

These habits of Eichmann's created considerable difficulty during the trial—less for Eichmann himself than for those who had come to prosecute him, to defend him, to judge him, and to report on him. For all this, it was essential that one take him seriously, and this was very hard to do, unless one sought the easiest way out of the dilemma between the unspeakable horror of the deeds and the undeniable ludicrousness of the man who perpetrated them, and declared him a clever, calculating liar—which he obviously was not.[92]

She discussed Eichmann's ludicrousness:

Despite all the efforts of the prosecution, everybody could see that this man was not a "monster," but it was difficult indeed not to suspect that he was a clown. And since this suspicion would have been fatal to the whole enterprise, and was also rather hard to sustain in view of the sufferings he and his like had caused to millions of people, his worst clowneries were hardly noticed and almost never reported. What could you do with a man who first declared, with great emphasis, that the one thing he had learned in an ill-spent life was that one should never take an oath ("Today no man, no judge could ever persuade me to make a sworn statement, to declare something under oath as a witness. I refuse it, I refuse it for moral reasons. Since my experience tells me that if one is loyal to his oath, one day he has to take the consequences, I have made up my mind once and for all that no judge in the world or any other authority will ever be capable of making me swear an oath, to give sworn testimony. I won't do it voluntarily and no one will be able to force me"), and then, after being told explicitly that if he wished to testify in his own defense he might "do so under oath or without an oath," declared without further ado that he would prefer to testify under oath?[93]

The "unspeakable horror" of Eichmann's deeds overshadowed in the end the comedic aspects of his character, and the horror in fact deepened as a result of his character. His inability to admit responsibility for his actions and his inability to provide evidence of even an elementally functioning conscience made his banality far more threatening than humorous. Here was a moral everyman, sincerely confused by the charges of guilt and complicity in the murder of six million Jews. As a lieutenant colonel in the SS, considered a "Jewish expert" and in charge of transportation, Eichmann had helped to organize the systematic "emigration" (expulsion), concentration, and then mass deportation of Jews to be exterminated. He insisted on the distinction between transporting and murdering Jews, and he denied involvement in any murder of Jews: "With the killing of Jews I had nothing to do. I never killed a Jew, or a non-Jew, for that matter—I never killed any human being. I never gave an order to kill either a Jew or a non-Jew; I just did not do it."[94]

The malfunctioning of Eichmann's conscience and sense of human responsibility, however, was clear. He was fully cognizant of the Final Solution (and the reality behind the euphemism), and he fulfilled his duties efficiently. His conscience, such as it was, was calmed by the fact that "no one protested, no one refused to cooperate." As Arendt summed up, "As Eichmann told it, the most potent factor in the soothing of his own conscience was the simple fact that he could see no one, no one at all, who actually was against the Final Solution."[95] Just as Eichmann marched with the unimaginative majority in his clichéd language, so too did he march with the morally impaired majority in carrying out the policies of the Final Solution. At one point Arendt termed *Eichmann in Jerusalem* "my report on Eichmann's conscience," a report relevant not only to Nazi Germany. At issue was modern man's conscience and the ease with which it could be subverted or perverted in the modern bureaucratic state.

Complicating—but not reducing—Eichmann's individual responsibility for the Final Solution was the moral and structural setting that framed his actions. Eichmann, for example, was not alone in losing track of his conscience; Arendt determined that "from the accumulated evidence one can only conclude that conscience as such had apparently got lost in Germany, and this to a point where people hardly remembered it and had ceased to realize that the surprising 'new set of German values' was not shared by the outside world."[96] Furthermore, this "new set of German values," which transformed killing into a state duty, was promulgated and legalized by the government and put into operation by a large-scale, "impersonal" bureaucracy. The legal character of the Final Solution allowed Eichmann to dismiss his actions as "acts of state," and his position within a bureaucracy relieved him of any sense of personal responsibility for his actions (as Arendt noted of bureaucracy [the "rule of Nobody"], its nature "is to make functionaries and mere cogs in the administrative machinery out of men, and thus to dehumanize them").[97] In this sense, then, Eichmann became what Arendt called a "new type of criminal," one who "commits his crimes under circumstances that make it well-nigh impossible for him to know or to feel that he is doing wrong."[98]

Despite the perverted circumstances of time and place for Eichmann, the court in Jerusalem did not find these sufficient for absolving Eichmann of responsibility. Concluding that human beings are morally capable of distinguishing right from wrong and capable of resisting criminal values and a criminal state, the court sentenced Eichmann to death for his moral and human weakness. Arendt recognized at the center of the decision "one of the central moral questions of all time . . . the nature and function of human judgment." This moral question predominated in both Eichmann's trial and the Nuremburg trials, and Arendt explained the moral demand being made: "What we have demanded in these trials, where the defendants had committed 'legal' crimes, is that human beings be capable of telling right from wrong even when all they have to guide them is their own judgment, which, moreover, happens to be completely at odds with what they must regard as the unanimous opinion of all those around them."[99] Coincident with this faith in independent human judgment was the imperative to resist evil, no matter how unanimously voiced and acted, no matter how legitimized by state power. Countering the argument of some Germans about the uselessness of protest in Nazi Germany, where protest only resulted in "meaningless death," Arendt presented a compelling human case for noncompliance with evil:

> It is true that totalitarian domination tried to establish these holes of oblivion into which all deeds, good and evil, would disappear, but just as the Nazis' feverish attempts, from June, 1942, on, to erase all traces of the massacres—through cremation, through burning in open pits, through the use of explosives and flame-throwers and bone-crushing machinery—were doomed to failure, so all efforts to let their opponents "disappear in silent anonymity" were in vain. The holes of oblivion do not exist. Nothing human is that perfect, and there are simply too many people in the world to make oblivion possible. One man will always be left alive to tell the

story. . . . The lesson of such stories is simple and within everybody's grasp. Politically speaking, it is that under conditions of terror most people will comply but *some people will not,* just as the lesson of the countries to which the Final Solution was proposed is that "it could happen" in most places but *it did not happen everywhere.* Humanly speaking, no more is required, and no more can reasonably be asked, for this planet to remain a fit place for human habitation.[100]

A double-edged urgency to absorbing the lessons of Eichmann's absent conscience filtered into *Eichmann in Jerusalem.* Part of the necessity stemmed, of course, from the very ordinariness of Eichmann: "The trouble with Eichmann was precisely that so many were like him, and that the many were neither perverted nor sadistic, that they were, and still are, terribly and terrifyingly normal."[101] The easy predisposition to evil among normal men and women seemed even more dangerous given the other reason for urgency and watchfulness—the likelihood of the recurrence of the "unprecedented" and inhuman crimes of the Nazi era, a likelihood made more plausible by the existence of nuclear weapons. Arendt examined the "possibility that similar crimes may be committed in the future" within the specific context of the atomic age:

The reasons for this sinister potentiality are general as well as particular. It is in the very nature of things human that every act that has once made its appearance and has been recorded in the history of mankind stays with mankind as a potentiality long after its actuality has become a thing of the past. No punishment has ever possessed enough power of deterrence to prevent the commission of crimes. On the contrary, whatever the punishment, once a specific crime has appeared for the first time, its reappearance is more likely than its initial emergence could ever have been. The particular reasons that speak for the possibility of a repetition of the crimes committed by the Nazis are even more plausible. The frightening coincidence of the modern population explosion with the discovery of technical devices that, through automation, will make large sections of the population "superfluous" even in terms of labor, and that, through nuclear energy, make it possible to deal with this twofold threat by the use of instruments beside which Hitler's gassing installations look like an evil child's fumbling toys, should be enough to make us tremble.[102]

Coming together generally in the renewed cultural attention to Nazis and the Final Solution in the early 1960s and specifically in *Eichmann in Jerusalem* was the knowledge of what both the Nazi past and the atomic age present promised and threatened: mass extermination. Eichmann's example made imperative a moral awakening and a rebirth of moral imagination in this age because it had been "precisely this lack of imagination" that allowed Eichmann to face human extermination as a moral cipher: "He *merely,* to put the matter colloquially, *never realized what he was doing.*"[103] The Nazi and Eichmann analogy provided a number of historical warnings for America in the early 1960s, not the least of which was to realize always what one is doing. The imperative to exercise moral awareness and moral imagination also stemmed from this historical example, as did the dictum to resist compliance with a criminal and immoral state. The concurrent cultural recognition of the increasing menace of American power made the historical lessons of Nazi Germany all the more pertinent for those refusing to comply with the American system—through opposition to civil defense, through black humor, or through the sort of historical revisionism that found disturbing parallels between the Nazi past and the American present.

If the intensified thermonuclear peril of the early 1960s gave new relevance to Eichmann and the Final Solution, so too did the intensifying civil rights movement in America in these same years. The rising black agitation for civil rights was an integral part of the moral awakening taking place in America in the early sixties, and the movement set the example for civil disobedience in an oppressive state. The civil rights movement contributed to reshaping the American understanding of the recent past and of the menace within the system. Moreover, the civil rights movement gave new meaning to the problem of racism, a prime lesson of the Nazi past, and to the threat of extermination, so apparent in the precedent of the Holocaust and so implicit in the development of America's nuclear arsenal.

The early 1960s marked the emergence of a more radicalized and energized civil rights activism, but, like other forms of atomic age dissent, this sort of activism had roots deep in the American past. The history of black resistance to white control and repression can be traced to the arrival of the first slaves in America, but in the more recent past World War II had acted as the last in a long series of watersheds in the history of race relations in America. The demonstrated racism in the Nazi extermination of Jews and the racism often suspected to be at least latent in the United States's decision to use the atomic bomb against Japan certainly gave blacks a new perspective from which to view the everyday racism they faced in America, particularly in (but certainly not limited to) the segregated South. Black fears about the possibility of genocide in America provided an appalling measure of the menace perceived in white America, and these fears were voiced or demonstrated with regularity in the postwar culture.

World War II served as a long-term catalyst of black activism for a variety of reasons, but most poignant among these was the proof the war offered about the depth of Western racism and the breadth of the Western world's technological and destructive power. The Western powers' racism and destructiveness came together explicitly in the Holocaust and implicitly in the atomic bombings of Hiroshima and Nagasaki. One black soldier recalled in his memories of the end of the war the warnings he read in these terrible examples of white power:

And that's when we came to Buchenwald. I *think* it was Buchenwald. You begin to approach and the first thing you get is the stench. Everybody knows that's human stench. You begin to realize something terrible had happened. There's quietness. You get closer and you begin to see what's happened to these creatures. And you get—I got more passionately angry than I guess I'd ever been. I said, "Let's kill all the son-of-a-bitches. Kill all the goddamn Germans. Anyone who could do this to people, they're not worth livin'." On reflection, I know not all Germans did this. But my feelings were, how could they let others do it? This was the clincher for me. If this could happen here, it could happen anywhere. It could happen to me. It could happen to black folk in America. I guess more than any single event, it was this sight that crystallized my determination to do as much as I could to bring about some sanity in a very insane world. During the time I was in, I'd heard all sorts of anti-Semitic remarks from white gentiles. They'd come up to me and say, "Hitler was right about the Jews." I'd say, "Get away from me." I'm a quartermaster. Hell, I can cut off his goddamn food. Some of the Germans I met said, "Well, it won't be long before the United States and the Soviet Union will be at each other." What kind of insanity is this? V-E Day had now occurred. I was in Marseilles. We were being processed for the invasion of Japan. I got word through *Stars and Stripes* that an instrument had been dropped on Japan such as boggled my mind. A city had been devastated with one instrument the size of a golf ball. Most of the soldiers were elated. I was saddened. I wish we had gone and taken our chances. I sensed a new world I had never dreamed of. I went back to my bunk and lay there. What does this mean?[104]

The genocidal aspect of the war prompted both anger and fear, neither of which dimmed during the "insanity" of the early cold war years. The cold war itself stimulated enough international political pressure to force white America to reexamine its racial policies (given adverse Soviet propaganda about the status of blacks in America and the growing revolutionary action of blacks in Africa). In this atmosphere the Supreme Court pronounced its decision against school segregation in 1954 in *Brown v. Board of Education.* The combination of the cold war and direct black action for desegregation (in the Rosa Parks–inspired and Martin Luther King, Jr.–led Montgomery bus boycott in 1955–1956, for example) began to chip away the legal structure of segregation and racism in America. But discrimination against blacks continued in the later 1950s, and blacks no doubt felt the same anxieties as other Americans about atomic extinction as well.

The very language of white opposition to desegregation took on the cast of cold war militarism. Whites in the South offered "massive resistance" to black rights, and it should be no surprise that black southerners sometimes nervously interpreted civil defense as a threat of death rather than as a promise of survival. In 1957 the *Saturday Evening Post* reported a "shocking incident" that had taken place in Mobile, Alabama:

> During a scheduled civil-defense exercise a downtown section of the city was to be evacuated. But before the exercise began, a rumor started in the Negro districts that an atomic bomb was really going to be dropped. "They're going to kill all us Negroes so they don't have to go through with school desegregation," the rumor had it. A large number of Negroes accepted this as truth. They took to the roads, carrying their most precious belongings with them.[105]

Given the willingness of some blacks to envision the atomic bomb as an instrument of white supremacy, it is not surprising that many blacks chose to ignore civil defense for civil rights. Yet if the bomb sometimes symbolized a genocidal threat against blacks in the cold war years, it was also sometimes a rather powerful metaphor for the explosiveness welling up in the black community. In his postwar works black poet Langston Hughes hinted at and openly suggested this potent connection. Harlem becomes something quite like a bomb in his poem "Harlem":

> What happens to a dream deferred?
>
> Does it dry up
> like a raisin in the sun?
> Or fester like a sore—
> And then run?
> Does it stink like rotten meat?

Or crust and sugar over—
like a syrupy sweet?

Maybe it just sags
like a heavy load.
Or does it explode?[106]

In his "Lunch in a Jim Crow Car" Hughes makes the comparison evident and prepares for the imminent outburst of black activism—an outburst evident in the early 1960s: "Get out the lunch-box of your dreams. / Bite into the sandwich of your heart, / And ride the Jim Crow car until it screams / Then—like an atom bomb—it bursts apart."[107]

The acknowledgment of the perils for blacks in past and present white systems of power and the imperatives for black activism and self-protection coalesced in the early sixties. In *The Fire Next Time* (1962, 1963) James Baldwin recognized the historic and current impulses to action in the black community, and his work reflected in a more literary and historical fashion the explosive forces already evident in black activism in the early sixties (for example, in 1960, with young blacks staging a sit-in for the desegregation of the lunch counter at the Woolworth in Greensboro, North Carolina). Baldwin addressed the apocalyptic dangers fueling race activism and resulting from the "racial nightmare" in America, and the title of his book contained the warning of cataclysm to come if America did not experience a moral revolution:

If we—and now I mean the relatively conscious whites and the relatively conscious blacks, who must, like lovers, insist on, or create, the consciousness of the others—do not falter in our duty now, we may be able, handful that we are, to end the racial nightmare, and achieve our country, and change the history of the world. If we do not dare everything, the fulfillment of that prophecy, recreated from the Bible in song by a slave, is upon us: *God gave Noah the rainbow sign, No more water, the fire next time!*[108]

Baldwin's warning of the coming fiery apocalypse was itself prophetic given the rising black violence that followed white America's recalcitrance about reform, but Baldwin's cataclysmic view was not solely informed by the dangers to come. The increasing power and popularity of the Black Muslims had helped Baldwin envision a fiery future for America, but in explaining the changed perspective of blacks that allowed for the rise of the Black Muslims he also touched on other historical and apocalyptic forces that shaped the modern black understanding. Baldwin first held that the power of Black Muslims could only have arisen in the present because only recently—at approximately the time of World War II—had it even become "possible to believe in a black God." In the past, according to Baldwin, "to entertain such a belief would have been to entertain madness. But time has passed, and in that time the Christian world has revealed itself as morally bankrupt and politically unstable."[109] The most instructive revelation of such Christian bankruptcy, of course, came from Nazi Germany, which Baldwin pointed out:

> Again, the terms "civilized" and "Christian" begin to have a very strange ring, particularly in the ears of those who have been judged to be neither civilized nor Christian, when a Christian nation surrenders to a foul and violent orgy, as Germany did during the Third Reich. For the crime of their ancestry, millions of people in the middle of the twentieth century, and in the heart of Europe—God's citadel—were sent to a death so calculated, so hideous, and so prolonged that no age before this enlightened one had been able to imagine it, much less achieve and record it. . . . From my own point of view, the fact of the Third Reich alone makes obsolete forever any question of Christian superiority, except in technological terms.[110]

That black Americans took seriously the German revelation of moral bankruptcy and the white capacity for human extermination seemed clear in Baldwin's own reaction to the Holocaust. He noted that while "white people were, and are, astounded by the holocaust in Germany" because "they did not know they could act that way," blacks experienced no such shock: "But I very much doubt whether black people were astounded—at least, in the same way." Baldwin was personally confident that whites could and would "act that way," and the Holocaust thus looked like the future to Baldwin: "For my part, the fate of the Jews, and the world's indifference to it, frightened me very much. I could not but feel, in those sorrowful years, that this human indifference, concerning which I knew so much already, would be my portion on the day that the United States decided to murder its Negroes systematically instead of little by little and catch-as-catch-can."[111] Blacks also took seriously America's treatment of blacks during World War II, and this treatment—along with the Nazi example—spurred the kind of black consciousness necessary for the prevention of a repetition of history.

Baldwin recognized in World War II "a turning point in the Negro's relation to America. To put it briefly, and somewhat too simply, a certain hope died, a certain respect for white Americans faded."[112] The reasons for the demise of black faith in America were legion, but Baldwin focused on just a few: being called a "nigger" while in uniform by one's comrades and superiors, being assigned to the most menial tasks of war, being forced to watch German prisoners of war receiving more respectful treatment than black soldiers, being more socially free in foreign lands than at "home," where the returning soldier faced fruitless job hunting on segregated buses.[113] Both the Nazi precedent of human and racial extermination and the American betrayal of blacks in the military in World War II prompted the black loss of faith in America and the impatient black demand for change. But for all the impetus provided by World War II, Baldwin did not credit the war with providing the most compelling explanation for the changed consciousness of blacks. That dubious honor belonged to the same threat troubling the culture of the early 1960s: the threat of extinction.

In his analysis of the reasons for the upheaval in the black community and for the black community's search for alternatives to the "racial nightmare," Baldwin centered his attention on the atomic age:

> But, in the end, it is the threat of universal extinction hanging over all the world today that changes, totally and forever, the nature of reality and brings into devastating question the true meaning of man's history. We human beings now have the power to exterminate ourselves; this seems to be the entire sum of our achievement. We have taken this journey and arrived at this place in God's name. This, then, is the best that God (the white God) can do. If that is so, then it is time to replace Him—replace Him with what? And this void, this despair, this torment is felt everywhere in the West, from the streets of Stockholm to the churches of New Orleans and the sidewalks of Harlem.[114]

Disclosing the apocalyptic impulse behind black discontent and black activism in his discussion of the appeal of Black Muslims ("The white God has not delivered them; perhaps the Black God will"), Baldwin also presented an apocalyptic analysis that had wider application for the culture of dissent, black or white.[115]

The signs of the broad cultural revolution that arose before the Cuban missile crisis, while diverse, all shared the connective thread of opposition to the atomic age and cold war authorities of America, whether historical, political, or social, and they all shared the impatient sensibility of their age of thermonuclear peril. The multiform cultural movement for change found perhaps its most symbolic expression in a document produced by young college students in the summer of 1962. In the "Port Huron Statement" the student activists of the Students for a Democratic Society (SDS) pronounced their "agenda for a generation" and signaled the emergence of the broad revolt that would engulf atomic age America throughout the 1960s.[116] In the introduction to the statement the SDS clearly revealed the interrelatedness of the cultural concerns in the early sixties:

We are people of this generation, bred in at least modest comfort, housed now in universities, looking uncomfortably to the world we inherit. When we were kids the United States was the wealthiest and strongest country in the world; the only one with the atom bomb, the least scarred by modern war, an initiator of the United Nations that we thought would distribute Western influence throughout the world. Freedom and equality for each individual, government of, by, and for the people—these American values we found good, principles by which we could live as men. Many of us began maturing in complacency. As we grew, however, our comfort was penetrated by events too troubling to dismiss. First, the permeating and victimizing fact of human degradation, symbolized by the Southern struggle against racial bigotry, compelled most of us from silence to activism. Second, the enclosing fact of the Cold War, symbolized by the presence of the Bomb, brought awareness that we ourselves, and our friends, and millions of abstract "others" we knew more directly because of our common peril, might die at any time. We might deliberately ignore, or avoid, or fail to feel all other human problems, but not these two, for these were too immediate and crushing in their impact, too challenging in the demand that we as individuals take the responsibility for encounter and resolution.[117]

The students' arousal about these issues of racial inequality and the bomb's destructive threat was heightened by the sense of betrayal they experienced, having once imbibed the American dream. They saw "tarnish appear on our image of American virtue" when "the proclaimed peaceful intentions of the United States contradicted its economic and military investments in the Cold War status quo," and they felt "disillusion occur when the hypocrisy of American ideals was discovered"—discovered not just in America's paradoxical peaceful claims and warlike acts but also in the hollowness of America's first and best belief that "all men are created equal."[118] Their impulse to activism, to "encounter and resolution," however, was driven by the greatest betrayal of all: "Our work is guided by the sense that we may be the last generation in the experiment with living." Explicit in the "Port Huron Statement" was the urgency motivating the rising protests of the 1960s as well as the difficulties involved in conveying the pressing need for change to the "majority" in America:

But we are a minority—the vast majority of our people regard the temporary equilibriums of our society and world as eternally functioning parts. In this is perhaps the outstanding paradox: we ourselves are imbued with urgency, yet the message of our society is that there is no viable alternative to the present. Beneath the reassuring tones of the politicians, beneath the common opinion that America will "muddle through," beneath the stagnation of those who have closed their minds to the future, is the pervading feeling that there simply are no alternatives, that our times have witnessed the exhaustion not only of Utopias, but of any new departures as well. Feeling the press of complexity upon the emptiness of life, people are fearful of the thought that at any moment things might be thrust out of control. They fear change itself, since change might smash whatever invisible framework seems to hold back chaos for them now. For most Americans, all crusades are suspect, threatening. The fact that each individual sees apathy in his fellows perpetuates the common reluctance to organize for change. The dominant institutions are complex enough to blunt the minds of their potential critics, and entrenched enough to swiftly dissipate or entirely repel the energies of protest and reform, thus limiting human expectancies.[119]

The SDS committed itself to seeking and showing the alternatives possible in their America, and the students believed that something more hopeful underlay the consensus of fear and apathy in America. They asked two questions:

Some would have us believe that Americans feel contentment amidst prosperity—but might it not better be called a glaze above deeply felt anxieties about their role in the new world? And if these anxieties produce a developed indifference to human affairs, do they not as well produce a yearning to believe there *is* an alternative to the present, that something *can* be done to change circumstances in the school, the workplaces, the bureaucracies, the government?[120]

Just as the civil defense debate revealed deeper layers of meaning for "apathy," so did the SDS inject "apathy" with potential yearning for change. The SDS dedicated itself to nurturing this yearning for alternatives: "It is to this latter yearning, at once the spark and engine of change, that we direct our present appeal. The search for truly democratic alternatives to the present, and a commitment to social experimentation with them, is a worthy and fulfilling human enterprise, one which moves us and, we hope, others today." "The Port Huron

Statement" was, in effect, in its own words, "an effort in understanding and changing the conditions of humanity in the late twentieth century."[121]

The SDS proposed a number of alternatives for the American system, most notably a "participatory democracy" in which "we would replace power rooted in possession, privilege, or circumstance by power and uniqueness rooted in love, reflectiveness, reason, and creativity."[122] The same changes in the power structure would affect social and economic conditions in America, but basic and central to all political, social, and economic changes were the necessary and alternative values to be cultivated. The primacy of developing more human and idealistic values resulted from the SDS's intent to attack the ingrained American malaise inhibiting activism. The need to dispel the malaise became clear in its description:

> There are no convincing apologies for the contemporary malaise. While the world tumbles toward the final war, while men in other nations are trying desperately to alter events, while the very future qua future is uncertain—America is without community, impulse, without the inner momentum necessary for an age when societies cannot successfully perpetuate themselves by their military weapons, when democracy must be viable because of the quality of life, not its quantity of rockets.[123]

The creation and sharing of new ideals and morals constituted the SDS's option to contemporary emptiness.

The SDS certainly understood the reasons for the modern lack of faith and hope, and in this sense the students expressed the new historical understanding of these years. They noted that "doubt has replaced hopefulness—and men act out a defeatism that is labeled realistic." Discussing the causes for despair and the resentment against those willing to hope, they cited "the horrors of the twentieth century, symbolized in gas ovens and concentration camps and atom bombs, [which] have blasted hopefulness," concluding that "to be idealistic is to be considered apocalyptic, deluded."[124] Willing to risk such opprobrium, the SDS declared that "the first task of any social movement is to convince people that the search for orienting theories and the creation of human values is complex but worthwhile." The SDS then defined its values, first regarding human beings and second regarding human relationships. The students' expectations for human beings and human relationships promised to inspire the changed human heart needed for cultural revolution:

> We regard *men* as infinitely precious and possessed of unfulfilled capacities for reason, freedom, and love. In affirming these principles we are aware

of countering perhaps the dominant conceptions of man in the twentieth century: that he is a thing to be manipulated, and that he is inherently incapable of directing his own affairs. We oppose the depersonalization that reduces human beings to the status of things. . . . Men have unrealized potential for self-cultivation, self-direction, self-understanding, and creativity. It is this potential that we regard as crucial and to which we appeal, not to the human potentiality for violence, unreason, and submission to authority. . . . Human relationships should involve fraternity and honesty. Human interdependence is contemporary fact; human brotherhood must be willed, however, as a condition of future survival and as the most appropriate form of social relations. . . . Loneliness, estrangement, isolation describe the vast distance between man and man today. These dominant tendencies cannot be overcome by better personnel management, nor by improved gadgets, but only when a love of man overcomes the idolatrous worship of things by man.[125]

As a student organization the SDS envisioned students leading the social movement that would instill these new human values and implement the search for human alternatives to the American system of racial injustice and atomic terror. The group found reason for optimism in the fact that "in the last few years, thousands of American students demonstrated that they at least felt the urgency of the times" by participating in active protests for civil rights and against war. The significance given to these student uprisings had little to do with "success," according to the SDS:

The significance of these scattered movements lies not in their success or failure in gaining objectives—at least not yet. Nor does the significance lie in the intellectual "competence" or "maturity" of the students involved— as some pedantic elders allege. The significance is in the fact the students are breaking the crust of apathy and overcoming the inner alienation that remain the defining characteristics of American college life.[126]

Because the determination of the success or failure of student activism and of all forms of atomic age activism required time and resisted evaluation of their effectiveness along more conventional lines of judgment, the SDS's measure of significance proved accurate. For students and for the rebel culture of the early 1960s in general, it was success enough to smash the seemingly invincible framework of atomic age apathy and cold war consensus. Only from this fresh and open perspective could the human and imaginative alternatives to America's system of menace be proposed and tested.

The activist students in the SDS may have felt alone, a minority group experiencing the special urgency of the early 1960s, but they clearly had company in the rebel and popular culture of these years. Opponents of civil defense, historical revisionists, black humorists, and black agitators for civil rights all contributed to the challenge of the cold war status quo, and all exhibited the moral arousal and temperamental impatience appropriate to the times of thermonuclear peril. The variety of moral and political concerns expressed in the imaginative culture of these years constituted the basis for the widespread radicalized revolt that took place throughout the 1960s, particularly in the wake of the Cuban missile crisis. The grave situation that revealed itself in the years of the Berlin crisis and the Cuban missile crisis demanded the radical solutions gestating during those same crises. In the following years the counterculture dramatically exposed the smashed cold war consensus and the shattered status quo.

Devaluing and denigrating the ruling configurations of the cold war system and breaking the stranglehold of the status quo were the first steps in the process of rebuilding a new society and a new human culture. In an essay written in 1962, "The Human Prospect," Lewis Mumford reviled the American system of debased and dehumanized values, and he voiced concerns quite similar to those of the SDS. He too recognized the malaise and alienation of modern life and the need to restore "the human prospect" in America, a need all the more pressing given the sway of technology and standardization—the features of the American system which came under increasing attack after the Cuban missile crisis. In "The Human Prospect" Mumford described both the threat of this dehumanized technology and the human obligation to overthrow its powerful rule. He began by warning America, using the "explosive" language that appeared with regularity in the sixties:

> Unless we take the full measure of the dangers that confront us, with open eyes, we shall not summon forth the human energies that will be necessary to overcome them. The threat of wholesale nuclear extermination, on a scale that might mutilate even that part of the human race which escaped immediate destruction, is only the most spectacular example of the negative results produced by science and technics when they are divorced from any other human purpose than their own propensity to increase knowledge and power, and expand the use of their own special products in a fashion profitable to the producer. But we are in the midst of other explosions, other forms of destruction, actual, not just threatened, that will be just as fatal as long as they go in the present fashion: the population explosion, the

freeway explosion, the recreation explosion, the suburban explosion (or should one say the "slurban" explosion?) are all working toward the same blank goal—that of creating more and more featureless landscapes, populated by more and more featureless people. . . . All our dominant forces today now tend to cramp and dwarf our life, to automatize and increasingly dehumanize our activities, when they might be hugely increasing our actual wealth and our real enjoyment.[127]

Mumford pointed out how the preeminence of the machine in modern life had detracted from a more fulfilling and loving style of life. He noted that "our trouble, then, is not merely that we have fallen in love with the machine, and have treated it as a god. . . . Our trouble is that equally we have ceased to respect ourselves, just as we have ceased to love our neighbors and want to be near them." The purely "mechanical factors" of the machine, "standardization, mass production, automation, quantitative excesses," controlled American lives and deformed American memories of a more complete life: "So we constantly forget that all these capacities are beneficial only when they are at the disposal of a purposeful life that is itself more rich, complex, varied, individualized, stimulating, and humanly valuable: something different from a machine's existence." He concluded that "in their worship of the machine, many Americans have settled for something less than a full life, something that is hardly even a tenth of a life, or a hundredth of a life. They have confused progress with mechanization, and, lacking any will or purpose of their own, having lost any real religious faith or personal pride, they have let mechanization take command."[128]

The denaturalized life in America found its most intense expression in Mumford's admitted "caricature" of the typical American male who returns home after work, "where he finds a house and a wife in the midst of what is usually called ideal suburban surroundings":

a green ghetto, half natural, half plastic, also cut off from human contact, where his wife has for her chief daily companions in her solitude the radio set, the soap opera, the refrigerator, the automatic mixer, the blender, the vacuum cleaner, the automatic washing machine, the dishwasher, and, if she is lucky, the second car. They and their children finally, together or by turns, immobilize themselves before a television screen, where all that has been left out of the actual world, all their unlived life, flickers before their eyes, in images that give a faked sense of the realities they have turned their backs to, and the impulses that they have been forced to repress.[129]

Like others in the culture, Mumford believed that the time had come for change, that the need to shatter this plastic life was clear and urgent. He asked,

"Isn't it about time that we took a hard second look at this life of ours and faced the fact that if we go on acting this way, the human prospect will be increasingly dismal?" He answered in the affirmative: "The time has come to understand that mechanization without a corresponding humanization is monstrous: just as . . . power without purpose—the kind of power we now have in such abundance, power enough to exterminate the human race—is immediately destructive and suicidal, and ultimately impotent."[130]

Mumford argued that the whole pattern of modern life must change, and he was certain that

the answer to the problems of human organization and human control will not come from computers; the answers will come from men. And it will not come from the sort of men whom we have indoctrinated with the myth of the machine: the disoriented experts and specialists whose uncoordinated and lopsided efforts, uncorrected by the more humane wisdom of their peers, and untutored by historic experience, have produced the over-mechanized, standardized, homogenized, bureaucratized life that now surrounds us on every side.[131]

Offering more positive proposals for change, Mumford suggested that "we shall have to overthrow the myth of the machine and replace it with a new myth of life," a myth that embodied respect for nature and organic life and a belief in the human possibility of change and a myth that encompassed "a passionate religious faith in man's own capacity to transform and perfect his own self and his own institutions in co-operative relation with all the forces of nature, and, above all, with his fellow men."[132]

Mumford forthrightly announced that "the time has come for bold counterattack—and we may not have long to wait." His confidence in the coming revolution was based on the same faith expressed by the SDS: the arrival of "a new generation coming into the colleges." Mumford described these students as "no longer cagey conformists," and in them he envisioned the promise of the "new myth of life" that would do battle with the standardized and dehumanized consensus of the machine:

Though they have grown up in an age of violence and totalitarian conformity, they now challenge its brutalities and reject its compulsions; and their respect for themselves is greater than their respect for anything the machine, with or without their help, has created. They are still in all probability a minority; but the seed of life has ripened in them: if their elders do not betray them by surrendering even more abjectly than they have already done to the forces of disintegration and extermination, this generation will assume responsibility that too many of us still shrink from. They will overcome our passivities, overthrow our regimentations, and place the guardians of life once more in command. This is still an uncertain promise: but at least—and at last—it opens up a human prospect.[133]

The promise of American youth creating a new myth of life found fulfillment throughout the 1960s, but the cultural revolt against America's plastic and standardized patterns of life involved many groups and took many forms. Mumford treated with disdain the one "machine" that did reflect the growing disillusionment with America's cold war consensus: television. American youth broke through the crust of apathy and conformity to challenge the ruling standards and values of the American system, and television in the early and mid-sixties likewise illustrated America's break from any certain rules of life and behavior. Nonconformists and "oddballs" (not unlike Yossarian in *Catch-22* and the Chief and McMurphy in *One Flew Over the Cuckoo's Nest*) and bizarre representations of the American family were celebrated in the television culture of these years, revealing the extent to which the consensus of the 1950s had already been shattered. When on television a family like "the Munsters" replaced a family like the Cleavers in *Leave It to Beaver,* change was clearly in the air.

A more conflict-ridden and more diverse portrait of America had already appeared on the film screens of America, aided in large part by the reemergence of the socially conscious and "liberal" themes and issues that had been forsworn during the fifties. Films like *West Side Story* (1961) and *To Kill a Mockingbird* (1962) focused on racial tension and violence in America, showing a much darker side to the American dream. The films also pictured an America finally liberated from the ubiquitous presentations of "all-American" and all-white film topics and heroes. This attention to the "others" in America contributed to undermining what was considered to be "normal," and television took this new cultural trend of tolerance for diversity and difference even further. *The Twilight Zone* (1959–1964) provided the earliest indications of this openness to experimentation and nonconformity, as much in its conception as in its episodes. The show's imperative to exercise the imagination and to enter previously unexplored dimensions of sight, sound, and mind exemplified the expanding consciousness of the times.

The Twilight Zone's individual episodes reflected the culture's increasing acceptance of different forms of life, alien and human, but the show was most effective in its sympathetic treatment of downtrodden and eccentric human beings. In his introduction to "Mr. Bevis" (1960), for example, Rod Serling announced his admiration for the benignly crazed soul of Mr. Bevis:

In the parlance of the twentieth century, this is an oddball. His name is James B. W. Bevis. . . . Mr. Bevis is accident prone, a little vague, a little discombooberated, with a life that possesses all the security of a floating crap game. But this can be said of our Mr. Bevis: without him, without his warmth, without his kindness, the world would be a considerably poorer place, albeit perhaps a little saner.[134]

Serling adapted other themes significant for the sixties, including those revolving around the dangers of technology ("The point is that too often man becomes clever instead of wise, he becomes inventive but not thoughtful"), but it was *The Twilight Zone*'s respectful treatment of troubled and confused humans, of unusual and abnormal types, that most clearly overturned the culture's acceptance of the ultranormal role models portrayed in series like *The Adventures of Ozzie and Harriet, Father Knows Best,* and *Leave It to Beaver.*[135]

The most revealing trend in the television culture of the early and mid-1960s in fact concerned the changed image of the American family, for the families in this decade bore little resemblance to the Nelsons, the Andersons, and the Cleavers. The traditional nuclear family became on the whole a thing of the past as a variety of unconventional family units began to appear in the situation comedies of the sixties.[136] *Mr. Ed* (1961–1965) featured Wilbur and Carol Post with their surrogate son, the cynical and often rebellious talking horse, Mr. Ed (in this strange ménage à trois, Mr. Ed often caused jealousy and resentment on Carol's part, especially since he only talked to Wilbur). In *My Favorite Martian* (1963–1966) the familial group consisted of young reporter Tim O'Hara and his "uncle Martin," an alien from Mars, replete with retractable antennae. An oddly related bunch of uncultured and uncouth "hicks" (Jed, his daughter Elly May, Granny, and cousin Jethro) in *The Beverly Hillbillies* (1962–1971) invaded Beverly Hills after discovering oil and joining the ranks of the admittedly weird nouveaux riches. Astronaut Tony Nelson uncorked a bottle containing an ancient but beautiful and semisexual slave/genie in *I Dream of Jeannie* (1965–1970) and was thus forced to become her "master" in their home in Florida. And in perhaps the most unlikely scenario of all, Dave Crabtree discovered the reincarnation of his mother in a talking 1928 Porter in *My Mother the Car* (1965–1966).

These animal, alien, supernatural, and mechanical additions to families did not exhaust the imaginative mutations of families on television in the 1960s.

Also included were the rather magical or morbid variations on the family that appeared in the middle of the decade. Samantha Stephens struggled with the difficulties attached to her dual life as a powerful witch and as a conventional American housewife in *Bewitched* (1964–1972); her "mortal" husband, Darrin, insisted that she behave "normally" while her bevy of magically touched relatives urged her to use and practice her witchcraft. *The Munsters* (1964–1966) demonstrated a decidedly hybrid mix of monstrosity and humanity in the family, with father Herman resembling Frankenstein, mother Lily and Grandpa exhibiting all the qualities of vampires, and son Eddie looking rather like a young werewolf. Their gothic mansion on Mockingbird Lane had much in common with the cobwebbed castle dwelling of the other family featured in the "ghoul comedies" of the 1960s, the Addams family. The names of the family members and servants alone in *The Addams Family* (1964–1966) illustrated the morbid strangeness of the Addams household: Morticia, Uncle Fester, Lurch (another Frankenstein), Thing (a disembodied hand), Cousin Itt, and Pugsley—to name only some.[137]

If television served as any sort of cultural measure of consensus, then the highly unconventional families of these situation comedies indicated that there was no consensus in America in the 1960s. The nonconformists who populated television in these years represented distinct alternatives to the homogenized and indistinguishable television families of the 1950s, and the strict rules and boundaries of behavior evident in the 1950s crumbled under the barrage of the bizarre in the 1960s. There was an element of liberation in television's celebration of diversity and oddity, particularly when this open-mindedness of the sixties was contrasted with the controls and constraints on televised images in the fifties. It is quite possible that the unreality of families on television in the sixties was something of a backward-looking parody of the unreal demands for conformity made in the fifties, but the unreal elements of these families also suggested a darker truth about America. Lewis Mumford critiqued television's function in the dehumanized lives of those inhabiting the "green ghetto" of the suburbs, and it was precisely this dehumanization that these television shows emphasized.

The transmogrification of mothers into automobiles or vampires, of wives into prehistoric genies or extraterrestrially empowered witches, of uncles into Martians, of sons into horses or werewolves, and of fathers into Frankensteins certainly hinted at the less than human (or more than human) capacities of these sixties television families. These bizarre creatures were definitely not God's human creations. The situational humor of these shows and their contrast of inhuman and human lost some of its giddiness when examined in the context of the larger cultural concerns about America's debased and dehumanized values. While these television shows offered the freedom of nonconformity and diversity, they also reflected the increasingly inhuman quality of life in America. The varieties of life possible—human or not—seemed endless in these shows, but the shows at least vaguely warned that one of those possibilities was mutation into something less than human. Standardization and conformity certainly promised a less than human existence, but the dangers to human life did not dissolve simply as a result of the growing nonconformity of the sixties or as a result of the shattering of the cold war cultural consensus. Even rebels and nonconformists had to continue to fight for their humanity and for their human values.

The often understated and humorous critique of dehumanization and standardization contained in the family television programs of the early and mid-1960s was evident as well in popular art and literature. Pop art in the early sixties centered in part on the unnatural and mass-produced emptiness of American life, and a number of artists produced sardonic celebrations of such American "progress." In his essay "The Human Prospect" Mumford sarcastically described American bread as an illustration of the marvels of the machine; this technologically produced bread was a "devitalized foam-rubber loaf, laden with additives and substitutes, mechanically sliced for built-in staleness, that boasts of never being touched by human hand."[138] Like Mumford, American artists in the 1960s also envisioned food as a symbol for America's dehumanized and denaturalized standardization, and the envelopment by technology of the very staff of life—food—became a major theme of artists like Wayne Thiebaud, Claes Oldenburg, Tom Wesselmann, Robert Watts, and Andy Warhol. Rows of hot dogs, ice cream cones, lunch table foods, and pastry counter collections (1961–1964) filled the paintings of Thiebaud and stressed the leaden, regimented, and false appearance of the nonetheless pretty and plentiful foodstuffs of America. Claes Oldenburg's *French Fries and Ketchup* (1963) portrayed this fast-food product in massive globs of vinyl; he also constructed a huge ice cream cone from painted canvas and foam rubber in his *Floor Cone* (1962). He as well enfolded a group of ice cream bars in fake psychedelic fur in his *Soft Fur Good Humors* (1963).[139]

Artists like Thiebaud and Oldenburg responded not just to the gross materialism and consumerism apparent in affluent America but also to the lack of nutrition or natural quality in food items so overwhelmed by mass production and high-tech packaging. The profusion of identical products, the new-fangled invention of frozen TV dinners, the multiplication of fast-food chains and supermarkets all became subjects for the artists who perceived the absence of any real or human sustenance in the products of the food industry. Tom Wesselmann featured brand-name products like a can of Del Monte asparagus, a bottle of Wish-Bone Italian dressing, a box of Kellogg's Rice Krispies, and a package of "Lite-Diet" bread in his pop art *Still Life #24* (1962) and *Still Life #30* (1963). Robert Watts presented *TV Dinner* (1965) in lamination, with latex and paint, preserved forever in a shiny, thin plastic package.[140] Andy Warhol's visions of food—whether Campbell soup cans (1962) or Coca-Cola bottles (1962)—perhaps best exhibited the eternal sameness and unoriginality of edible American products. His seemingly endless series of cans and bottles signified the omnipresence of technological standardization in American society and culture, yet Warhol himself reveled in this American propensity for exact replication, developing a silkscreen stencil process to cover his canvases with hundreds of copies of the same image which mirrored the workings of the system of mass production.[141]

In a 1963 interview with Gene Swenson entitled "What Is Pop Art?" Warhol explained that he saw a metaphor for American life in the technological "sameness" he highlighted in his art. He rather eccentrically and ironically approved of the loss of human distinctiveness in modern America:

> Someone said that Brecht wanted everybody to think alike. I want everybody to think alike. But Brecht wanted to do it through Communism, in a way. Russia is doing it under government. It's happening here all by itself without being under a strict government: so if it's working without trying, why can't it work without being Communist? Everybody looks alike and acts alike, and we're getting more and more that way. I think everybody should be a machine.[142]

Nihilistically embracing a trend already apparent throughout the mechanized and dehumanized culture of cold war America (and simultaneously deflating any distinction between life in capitalist America and communist Russia), Warhol revealed the depths of the countercultural recognition of America's slide toward inhumanity and toward the "featureless" landscapes and people that Lewis Mumford feared.

Thomas Pynchon, in his black humor novel *V.* (1963) about a variety of searches for the meaning of life, corroborated the artistic argument about humanity's tendency toward a more inanimate form of existence. Pynchon uses the deadening impact of technology as a theme in his work, and one of his main oddball characters, Benny Profane, finds on his life's search a sobering vision of the human future. Profane works at Anthroresearch Associates and comes into contact with "synthetic humans" in the workplace:

Across one of the laboratory spaces, features lit Frankenstein's-monsterlike by a nightlight, facing Profane, sat SHROUD: synthetic human, radiation output determined. Its skin was cellulose acetate butyrate, a plastic transparent not only to light but also to X-rays, gamma rays and neutrons. Its skeleton had once been that of a living human; now the bones were decontaminated and long ones and the spinal column hollowed inside to receive radiation dosimeters. . . . Anthroresearch Associates was a subsidiary of Yoyodyne. It did research for . . . Civil Defense on radiation absorption, which was where SHROUD came in. In the eighteenth century it was often convenient to regard man as a clockwork automaton. In the nineteenth century, with Newtonian physics pretty well assimilated and a lot of work in thermodynamics going on, man was looked on as a heat-engine, about 40 percent efficient. Now in the twentieth century, with nuclear and subatomic physics a going thing, man had become something which absorbs x-rays, gamma rays and neutrons.[143]

SHROUD has a companion at Anthroresearch Associates, SHOCK ("synthetic human object, casualty kinematics"), who is used in test car crashes. When Profane engages SHROUD in conversation, he learns an unnerving lesson about humanity's drift toward the inanimate.[144]

SHROUD tells Profane that "Me and SHOCK are what you and everybody will be someday." Profane counters that "there are other ways besides fallout and road accidents," but SHROUD is ready with a response: "But those are the most likely. If somebody else doesn't do it to you, you'll do it to yourselves." Disturbed by SHROUD's message, Profane is even more disturbed by the fact that SHROUD can talk. He points out to SHROUD, "You don't even have a soul. How can you talk," and SHROUD offers him another lesson in cynicism: "Since when did you ever have one? What are you doing, getting religion? All I am is a dry run. They take readings of my dosimeters. Who is to say whether I'm here so the people can read the meters or whether the radiation in me is because they have to measure. Which way does it go?" Profane is a little stunned and only returns later to confront SHROUD: "What do you mean, we'll be like you and SHOCK someday? You mean dead?" SHROUD replies, "Am I dead? If I am then that's what I mean." Profane persists: "If you aren't then what are you?" SHROUD ends the discussion with the message of dehumanization so prevalent in the 1960s: "Nearly what you are. None of you have very far to go."[145]

In a culture that envisioned the suburbs as "a green ghetto, half natural, half plastic," the television family as half human and half alien, food as brand-name labels, foam rubber, and fake fur, and man as "synthetic human, radiation output determined," something was clearly awry with both the human and natural world. The culture of dissent increasingly set its sights on the bomb as the prime mover in the evolving mutations of human and natural life, making the same connection Pynchon did in associating synthetic humans, for example, with the irradiated products and the subatomic scientific outlook of the atomic age. These cultural concerns about dehumanization and denaturalization precluding a more human and naturally harmonious life created a more receptive atmosphere for attacks on the atomic menace of the American system. These cultural products reflected the generalized fear of personal and societal apocalypse, the fear that "none of you have far to go" in a perverse world no longer hospitable to human life.

Human nature and nature itself were so out of balance in modern America that Armageddon was certain to arrive—or so was the claim of Alfred Hitchcock's film *The Birds* (1963). Apocalypse was in the air literally and figuratively in *The Birds,* and Hitchcock gathered together the diffuse cultural fears about the imperiled human future in this bizarre vision of the end of the world. From the opening minutes the film establishes the oppressive, sinister presence of birds. Wheeling, screeching, chirping, cawing birds are everywhere. The opening shot of San Francisco shows a swarm of gulls circling overhead. The action focuses on a pet shop crammed with a variety of caged birds, an obvious reference to humanity's cruel incarceration of such "natural" creatures. Melanie Daniels, an impulsive socialite, and Mitch Brenner, a criminal lawyer, meet in this store, and Melanie pursues Mitch to his mother's home in Bodega Bay with a gift of a pair of love birds (a suggestive gift, nominally meant for Mitch's little sister, who is having a birthday party this weekend). Here in Bodega Bay the vanishing of any natural or human order is ominously illustrated.

When Melanie is returning across the bay, having surreptitiously delivered the birds to Mitch's home in her rented boat, she is attacked by a gull. Mitch observes the incident and rushes to her aid; as he is attending to the gash made by the gull, he comments, "It seemed to swoop down on you deliberately," and he exclaims: "That's the damnedest thing I ever saw."[146] The inhabitants of Bodega Bay thus receive a warning about flaws in the operation of the usually ordered natural universe. Strange and violent behavior, in fact, is not restricted to the birds—human relations also demonstrate serious disruption. Both Mitch and Melanie live essentially loveless and unsatisfying lives. Melanie was deserted by her mother, whereas Mitch is saddled with a possessive and cold mother who has ruled his life since his father's death. Mitch's career as a criminal lawyer also introduces the violent excesses of human behavior, as Mitch's sister Cathy explains to Melanie: "He has a client now who shot his wife six times. Six times. Can you imagine it? I mean, even twice would be overdoing it." Mitch's explanation for his client's crime heightens the sense of imbalance in human relations: his wife had switched the television channel while he was watching a ball game.

When the birds inaugurate their full-scale revolt, then, the suggestion has already been planted that humans have also revolted from a loving and harmonious relation with nature and with one another—in a certain sense the humans deserve their winged Armageddon. After a number of deadly bird sorties, including one at a farmhouse where the owner has his eyes pecked out in a grotesque and bloody mess and one at the schoolhouse where the children run away from the avenging birds in pandemonium, the townspeople, tourists, and Mitch and Melanie take shelter in "The Tides," a local seafood restaurant, awaiting the inevitable escalation of the bird attack. A discussion about the birds takes place and a feeling of doomed judgment against man fills the conversation. The neighborhood ornithology buff, Mrs. Bundy, downplays the destructive capacities of birds, saying, "Birds are not aggressive creatures. They bring beauty into the world. It is mankind, rather, who insists upon making it difficult for life to exist upon this planet." Her commentary is interrupted by the waitress, who shouts her order to the cook, underlining Mrs. Bundy's point and providing the birds with their motive: "Sam—three southern-fried chicken, baked potato on all of them." A drunk sitting at the restaurant's bar provides a more metaphysical explanation for the bird's actions, insisting that it is God's retribution: "It's the end of the world!"

Mrs. Bundy scoffs at this apocalyptic scenario: "I hardly think a few birds are going to bring about the end of the world." When Melanie informs Mrs. Bundy of the vast number and deadly intention of the birds, Mrs. Bundy points out that birds have been on the planet for 140 million years, asking: "Doesn't it seem odd that they'd wait all that time to start a war against humanity?" Hysteria begins to grow in the restaurant crowd. The birds have massed and they coordinate an attack right outside of the restaurant. The gas station across the street forms the center of activity; the cars and their drivers try to escape the birds' violence and in the confusion gas is spilled and ignited. A magnificent fireball rises above the station, with the camera offering a bird's-eye view of the destruction.

Outside the restaurant during the attack, Melanie finds refuge in a telephone booth that becomes in effect a glass cage—she is trapped within as the birds stare in, scratch, and smash into the booth. The natural order has collapsed, announcing nothing less than the end of the world. With the news that the bird war is expanding beyond Bodega Bay, Mitch and Melanie flee home and barricade the house. These defensive precautions prove inadequate, however, and when Melanie investigates the attic she discovers herself trapped in a swarm of beating wings and darting beaks. A dazed and devastated Melanie is rescued by Mitch, who then determines they must escape and seek medical help. As Mitch, his mother and sister, and Melanie quietly creep to the car during a lull in the attack, the view offered of the human future is not promising. All human life seems stilled and the birds are in possession of the land. Melanie, Mitch, and his family drive away nonetheless, headed for an uncertain future that may be as much a trap as Melanie's glass cage.

Hitchcock's description of his characters in *The Birds* as a group of "victims of Judgment Day" confirms the apocalyptic interpretation of the otherwise ambivalent ending to the film.[147] The film's ambiguities resulted from the one glimmer of hope that did remain at the end: love. Accompanying Mitch, Melanie, and the others as they fled Bodega Bay were the love birds that had set in motion the film's action. Their evident love, and the developing love between Mitch and Melanie, provide the only potential force for combating the power of the disrupted universe. The salvation represented by love, and by its attributes of affection and respect for life, became more generally recognized during the sixties and augured the strength of the new myth of life and laughter growing to combat the aberrant and menacing forces of the atomic age. The imperative to love and live and laugh was rendered particularly urgent by the unnatural and inhuman forces in America that also became more generally recognized during the decade. Judgment Day was upon America, and the harbingers of the end of the world—whether birds or atomic bombs—were evident throughout society and culture.

Hitchcock made a vague connection between *The Birds* and the bomb when he explained the message of the film as "don't mess about or tamper with nature." He then discussed how man had tampered with uranium-235 and commented, "Look what's happened."[148] François Truffaut, however, felt discomfort at ascribing the apocalypse to birds in the atomic age; in his interview with Hitchcock he pointed out that "since 1945, it's the atom bomb that has represented the ultimate threat to mankind, so it's rather disconcerting to suggest that the end of the world might be brought about by thousands of birds."[149] Whether Armageddon would be brought about by atomic bombs or birds was less important in these cultural rumblings about the corruption of man and nature than was the central, accepted fact: that human life was coming to an end or was at least changing so drastically that it was no longer recognizably "normal" or "human."

eight

JUDGMENT DAY

dr. strangelove's cultural revolution

"History! . . . Read it and weep."

—*Kurt Vonnegut,*
Cat's Cradle *(1963)*

mens of disaster abounded in American society in the early sixties, not just in the tense days of the Cuban missile crisis but also in the two years following the crisis. President Kennedy had commanded the nation through its closest brush with thermonuclear oblivion and soon thereafter suffered a terrifying death. Kennedy's assassination in November 1963 was yet another sign that something was horribly wrong in the natural and human order of life in America, and his assassination signaled to at least some cultural observers that America was indeed being "judged" for its propagation of a system of violent human degradation. The expectation of doomsday filtered into Malcolm X's response to Kennedy's death (as did the imagery contained in *The Birds*), which he expressed after giving a prearranged speech entitled "God's Judgment of White America." As the most visible and outspoken minister of the Black Muslims, Malcolm X delivered a typically provocative—and typically insightful—account of Kennedy's assassination. He repeated and explained his comments in his *Autobiography*:

> Many times since then, I've looked at the speech notes I used that day, which had been prepared at least a week before the assassination. The title of my speech was "God's Judgment of White America." It was on the theme, familiar to me, of "as you sow, so shall you reap," or how the hypocritical white man was reaping what he had sowed. The question-and-answer period opened, I suppose inevitably, with someone asking me, "What do you think about President Kennedy's assassination? What is your opinion?" Without a second thought, I said what I honestly felt—that it was, as I saw it, a case of "the chickens coming home to roost." I said that the hate in white men had not stopped with the killing of defenseless black

people, but that hate, allowed to spread unchecked, finally had struck down this country's Chief of State. . . . The headlines and the news broadcasts promptly had it: *"Black Muslims' Malcolm X: 'Chickens Come Home to Roost.'"* It makes me weary to think of it all now. All over America, all over the world, some of the world's most important personages were saying in various ways, and in far stronger ways than I did, that America's climate of hate had been responsible for the President's death. But when Malcolm X said the same thing, it was ominous.[1]

More ominous than Malcolm X's voicing of the obvious was the simple but frightening truth contained in his analysis. A climate of hate, a climate hostile to life, had engulfed America, and the menacing system that produced such violent hate found itself subject to all kinds of critical judgment—whether by the Black Muslims' God, by young students, black and white, or by satiric films and novels. Between 1963 and 1964 the apocalyptic imagination of the culture of dissent merged with the apocalyptic reality of a society confronted by events like the missile crisis and Kennedy's assassination, and the American system itself faced internal apocalypse and dissolution. The "Armageddon attitude" triumphed in the culture of dissent, and its triumph revealed equally the moral degradation of the atomic age and the burgeoning of the human and spiritual rebirth which would combat both the malaise and the menace of the system.

While the Cuban missile crisis and Kennedy's assassination made palpable America's proximity to Armageddon and America's climate of hate, it is somewhat ironic that the cultural catharsis of the atomic age took place during and after these events. President Kennedy had embodied the promise of change in America, and although he had done little to alter cold war patterns of thought and much to increase the terrors of cold war confrontations, he did evince in the aftermath of the missile crisis an apparently changed approach to life in the atomic age. A more sober and reflective leader after the missile crisis, Kennedy cooperated in easing overt tensions between America and the Soviet Union. Two concrete agreements aimed at avoiding any repetition of such brinksmanship were concluded in 1963, marking a rather clear retreat from Kennedy's previous belligerency. On June 20, 1963, the two countries affirmed the necessity of establishing a "direct communications link" between the United States and the Soviet Union, and the resulting "hot-line" provided the kind of instantaneous contact that could diffuse tension and prevent misunderstandings.[2] Less than two months later, on August 5, 1963, the two nations, along with Great Britain, signed the "Treaty Banning Nuclear Weapon Tests in the Atmosphere, in Outer

Space, and Under Water" and began to calm and retreat from the nuclear terror that had escalated during the Berlin and Cuban crises.

The partial test-ban treaty seemed particularly evocative of change because its ultimate goal was the banning of all tests and all weapons. The treaty stated that the signatories were "proclaiming as their principal aim the speediest possible achievement of an agreement on general and complete disarmament under strict international control in accordance with the objectives of the United Nations which would put an end to the armaments race and eliminate the incentive to the production and testing of all kinds of weapons, including nuclear weapons." The treaty further noted that the signing nations were "seeking to achieve the discontinuance of all test explosives of nuclear weapons for all time, determined to continue negotiations to this end, and desiring to put an end to the contamination of man's environment by radioactive substances."[3] The treaty succeeded only in limiting nuclear tests (underground testing remained permissible) but its expressed ideals suggested the possibility of a more peaceful future.[4] Kennedy's public pronouncements often emphasized the trend toward détente represented by these two Soviet-American agreements of 1963. In a speech at American University on June 10, 1963, Kennedy termed peace "the necessary rational end of rational men," and he expressed a respect for all human life which seemed renewed by the threat barely escaped in the missile crisis: "In the final analysis, our most basic common link is the fact that we all inhabit this planet. We all breathe the same air. We all cherish our children's future. And we are all mortal."[5]

The treaty's concern for protecting the environment from nuclear contamination and the respect for human life expressed in Kennedy's speech seemed to recapture the excitement and the promise of change that had long been associated with the young president and his formulation of the New Frontier and the Peace Corps. Yet Kennedy's assassination relegated to the realm of speculation any lasting determination of his sincerity in promoting peace. It is unlikely, however, that peace had become more probable even under the guidance of this more temperate Kennedy. Aggressive actions belied the words of peace both within the Kennedy administration and within the overlapping and succeeding Johnson administration, and expectations for change within the ruling cold war bureaucracy were betrayed. The Kennedy and Johnson administrations, along with the still vocal contingent on the radical right, gave every sign of perpetuating the cold war status quo, save for an innovative and presumably more moderate emphasis on fighting communism with the methods of "counterinsurgency" in the third world, where the threat of provoking a superpower confrontation like that in Cuba was much reduced. Even as the specially trained army guerrillas, the Green Berets, arrived in Vietnam to act as advisers and bolsterers of democracy, it was clear that nothing had yet undercut either the nuclear basis or the arrogance of America's cold war power and its unlimited application around the world.

A lively cold warriorism and a similarly lively nuclear build-up survived the missile crisis, and America's conception of its power and purpose—derived from atomic diplomacy and from the containment of communism—likewise escaped the crisis unscathed. The absence of any official rethinking of the cold war, let alone the absence of any official reversal of cold war policy, can be seen in the acceleration of the nuclear arms race after the Cuban missile crisis as well as in the expansion of America's military involvement in the increasingly direct, if undeclared, war in Vietnam.[6] American culture and politics, along with the government and military, reflected the resilience of cold warriorism and its deterrent instrument of choice, the bomb. Aware of the growing cultural restiveness about the bomb, General Curtis LeMay (chief of staff for the air force) approved the production of the film *A Gathering of Eagles* (1963), a glowing account of the military organization LeMay had recently headed, the Strategic Air Command.[7] Dedicated to the men of SAC, the film centers on the tough, disciplined, and dedicated personality required to do the job of nuclear preparedness. Elaborate drills and tense decision-making skills are highlighted, and the lead character, Colonel Jim Caldwell, a base commander, demonstrates the responsible and mature qualities of SAC leadership. While the anxiety of constantly being on alert causes personal problems, such problems pale before the necessity of doing the job. At the end of the film Jim's wife lovingly places the "red phone" (that can signal the commander at any time of the day or night) next to her husband, commenting, "You have to learn to live with these things in SAC."[8]

Science fiction writer Robert Heinlein one-upped *A Gathering of Eagles* by positing the idea that Americans could learn not just to live with, but to love, life with nuclear weapons and nuclear destruction. In *Farnham's Freehold* (1964) Heinlein promotes the kind of survivalist and anticommunist ethos that surfaced during the Berlin crisis and bomb shelter craze. Hugh Farnham and his family group are prepared with a sturdy bomb shelter when a crisis much like that of the Cuban missile crisis turns into a hot thermonuclear exchange. They survive nuclear war and, when they leave their shelter, find that they have been magically catapulted through time into an idyllic natural setting. Life after nuclear holocaust thus appears to have innumerable advantages for Hugh Farnham and his consort Barbara. Even as the bombs were dropping, they had discussed the "good genetics" of nuclear war—where only the intelligent and the prepared survive, or, as Farnham explains: "I've worried for years about our country. It seems to me that we have been breeding slaves—and I believe in freedom. This war may have turned the tide. This may be the first war in history which kills the stupid rather than the bright and able—where it makes any distinction."[9] Living then in a "genetically purified" and natural environment, however strangely they arrived there, makes Hugh and Barbara happier than they had ever been, and they revel in returning to nature and honing their survival skills in the wilderness. Though they have to contend with the futuristic rulers of this land (whom they soon encounter and who represent an amalgam of current cultural problems like civil rights and anticommunism: they are blacks who enslave whites), they are able to escape and rediscover their blissful postnuclear life in Farnham's flag-bedecked "freehold."

The American political scene also illustrated the high visibility and the heightened relevance of the cold war and the bomb, particularly in the 1964 presidential campaign and election. Barry Goldwater's nomination indicated that the more extreme or "rightist" elements in the Republican party had gained prominence, and Goldwater's association with a more vigorous and aggressive approach to communism and the cold war became a central issue in his contest with Lyndon Johnson. To some Americans Goldwater appeared as a radical rightist whose trustworthiness in overseeing America's nuclear arsenal was not at all assured, whereas Johnson and the Democrats—if only in contrast—presented a more reassuring image of liberalism and moderation, despite the nation's deepening involvement in Vietnam under Johnson's guardianship. Exploiting an approach that would become policy, particularly in the Vietnam era—that anything short of angrily threatening or actually using nuclear weapons constituted a limited, moderate, and even "moral" response to any cold war crisis—Johnson handily defeated Goldwater in the election. The cold war options offered by the two candidates were thus severely limited, and their differences were more of degree than kind. Both upheld the necessity of waging the traditional cold war battles, and both demonstrated their commitment to the policy of "containment." Only Goldwater, though, was willing to admit to the probability of American military escalation in Vietnam, and only Goldwater was willing to recognize nuclear escalation as the possibility it always was and would be in the atomic age.[10]

Given the rather carnival-like cold war atmosphere in America in 1963 and 1964, it is perhaps not so ironic after all that the culture's atomic age catharsis occurred during these years. President Kennedy may have legitimately believed that peace was "the necessary rational end of rational men," but neither he, nor Johnson, nor anyone involved in the cold war bureaucracy seemed to be pursuing such a rational end. The cultural revolution that crystallized in 1963 and 1964 was fomented by the oppressive presence of the bomb and the menacing system it represented. Dehumanization and, in the end, human extermination were characterized in the culture of dissent as the irrational ends of the irrational men who ran America's atomic bureaucracy. The bomb no longer served as the symbol for the cold war power that had unified a secure and safe America. Rather, the rebellious culture transformed the bomb into a symbol of social and cultural disruption, a symbol of technological triumph and human failure, and a symbol that now unified the culture of dissent and pronounced the arrival of America's judgment day.

Two central cultural products from these years sealed the connection between the bomb and the cultural rebirth it spawned, gathering together the diverse issues that had circulated widely during the early years of revolt against the degrading American system. Kurt Vonnegut's *Cat's Cradle* (1963) and Stanley Kubrick's *Dr. Strangelove or: How I Learned to Stop Worrying and Love the Bomb* (1964) encapsulated both the spirit and the substance of dissent in the 1960s, both relying on black humor to expose the deadly and irrational realities of life with the bomb. Vonnegut's novel and Kubrick's film attacked the historical legacy of the bomb and the cold war and acknowledged the dehumanization and the moral collapse that accompanied a system designed to promote the atomic bomb. These works portrayed the insanity and the enemy within the nuclear establishment, and they held up the Nazi paradigm for America in the atomic age, the deadly model of behavior that the counterculture connected to American nuclear policies in the sixties. Most important, both *Cat's Cradle* and *Dr. Strangelove* recognized the inevitable apocalypse as the irrational result of irrational policies. *Cat's Cradle* and *Dr. Strangelove* offered the ultimate denigration and devaluation of the system. Their metaphoric destructions of the system left only one option in a culture poised at judgment day: a revolutionary commitment to a new system and a new set of human and moral values.

The first chapter of *Cat's Cradle* is entitled "The Day the World Ended," and the protagonist Jonah explains its meaning, suggesting the bomb's central historical place in the revolutionary culture in 1963 and 1964: "When I was a much younger man, I began to collect material for a book to be called *The Day the World Ended*. The book was to be factual. The book was to be an account of what important Americans had done on the day when the first atomic bomb was dropped on Hiroshima, Japan."[11] Jonah soon admits that he never finished that book, but in fact *Cat's Cradle* is about "the day the world ended" and Jonah is the narrator of an apocalyptic tale. The atom bomb is not responsible for destroying the world on the day it ends, but the substance that does eliminate all life ("ice-nine") is intimately connected with the bomb and with one of the fictional creators of the bomb, Dr. Felix Hoenikker, "one of the so-called 'Fathers' of the atom bomb," according to Jonah.[12] Hoenikker and his twin inventions of mass death represent the depraved nexus of scientific and military values that instigate the end of the world, beginning on "the day when the first atomic bomb was dropped on Hiroshima."

Jonah's investigations of Dr. Hoenikker, originally undertaken as research for *The Day the World Ended,* allow him to witness the actual end of the world, and his investigations also introduce him to the religion—Bokononism—that shows him the strange connections between things, like between Hoenikker, the bomb, ice-nine, and the end of the world. Bokononism, though, does not teach him how to make sense out of such connections, because Bokononists define a "fool" as "anyone who thinks he sees what God is doing."[13] Jonah thus learns through Hoenikker about the deadened human morality that ends the world, and he thereafter learns through Bokononism that there is no spiritual understanding or religious solace possible in a world that commits suicide. Jonah does not need Bokononism, however, to understand the character of Felix Hoenikker, because Hoenikker's essential inhumanity is a subject that almost everyone agrees on. Hoenikker is already dead when Jonah decides to include him among the "important Americans" in *The Day the World Ended,* so he interviews those who knew Hoenikker in order to understand him and his activities on August 6, 1945. The image of Hoenikker that emerges suggests the general qualities needed for the promotion of Armageddon.

Jonah's first account of Hoenikker comes from Newt Hoenikker, the scientist's midget son, who responds to Jonah's queries with a long letter. In his letter to Newt, Jonah had explained that his book would "emphasize the *human* rather than the *technical* side of the bomb," but Newt can find little human in his father: "People weren't his specialty."[14] Newt does, however, provide an amusing description of his father's activities on August 6, 1945, and the irreverence in this depiction of Felix Hoenikker ultimately matches Hoenikker's own irreverence for human life. According to Newt, his father "was playing with a loop of string. Father was staying home from the laboratory in his pajamas all day that day." Absurdity and coincidence fill *Cat's Cradle,* and Newt's explanation of how his father got the string and what he did with it reflected a confluence of the two:

> It so happens I know where the string he was playing with came from. Maybe you can use it somewhere in your book. Father took the string from around the manuscript of a novel that a man in prison had sent him.

The novel was about the end of the world in the year 2000, and the name of the book was "2000 A.D." It told about how mad scientists made a terrific bomb that wiped out the whole world. There was a big sex orgy when everybody knew that the world was going to end, and then Jesus Christ Himself appeared ten seconds before the bomb went off. . . . My father never read the book, I'm pretty sure. . . . As I say, all he wanted from that manuscript was the string. That was the way he was. Nobody could predict what he was going to be interested in next. On the day of the bomb it was string. . . . Anyway, Father looked at that loop of string for a while, and then his fingers started playing with it. His fingers made the string figure called a "cat's cradle". . . . Making the cat's cradle was the closest I ever saw my father come to playing what anyone else would call a game. He had no use at all for tricks and games and rules that other people made up. In a scrapbook my sister Angela used to keep up, there was a clipping from *Time* magazine where somebody asked Father what games he played for relaxation, and he said, "Why should I bother with made-up games when there are so many real ones going on?"[15]

While the "real" games Felix Hoenikker played with the atom bomb and ice-nine constitute the focal point for the end of the world, the "made-up" game of the cat's cradle also becomes an increasingly important symbol for the absurdly deceptive and ultimately meaningless game of life—especially since that game ends as a result of a bizarre and purposeless series of "coincidences." The complexity and intricacy of life (also represented by the often strange and inexplicable connections or coincidences in life) are reflected in the complex geometric patterns of the cat's cradle, but those patterns do not reduce to any truth or meaning. This is the message of both the cat's cradle and the Bokononist religion, which stated this central absurdity in the very first sentence of the *Books of Bokonon*. According to the leader Bokonon, "All of the true things I am about to tell you are shameless lies."[16] Newt and Jonah discuss the cat's cradle later and the same lesson emerges. Newt has painted a cat's cradle and Jonah describes it: "It consisted of scratches made in a black, gummy impasto. The scratches formed a sort of spider's web, and I wondered if they might not be the sticky nets of human futility hung up on a moonless night to dry." Newt relates such human futility specifically to the cat's cradle: "He held out his painty hands as though a cat's cradle were strung between them. 'No wonder kids grow up crazy. A cat's cradle is nothing but a bunch of X's between somebody's hands, and little kids look and look and look at all those X's. . . . *No damn cat, and no damn cradle.*' "[17]

Propelling and shaping the darker tone of this otherwise laughable vision of the cat's-cradling life is the blank and deadly ethos of science and technology, as represented by Felix Hoenikker. In his letter to Jonah about his father's activities on August 6, Newt also includes some anecdotes that illustrate his father's human and moral void. Newt tells Jonah that his father "was one of the best-protected human beings who ever lived. People couldn't get at him because he just wasn't interested in people," and he illustrates this point with a story regarding his mother, who had died when Newt was born: "I remember one time, about a year before he died, I tried to get him to tell me something about my mother. He couldn't remember anything about her."[18] Newt concludes his letter to Jonah by recounting his father's reaction to the Trinity test of the atom bomb, particularly noting his father's response to another scientist's remark: "Science has now known sin." As Newt stresses: "And do you know what father said? He said, 'What is sin?'"[19]

The lack of human and moral concerns in the scientific and technological world view is again emphasized when Jonah travels to Ilium, New York, to interview Hoenikker's acquaintances and coworkers at the General Forge and Foundry company. Most notable among his interviewees is Dr. Asa Breed, the living counterpart to Hoenikker and the vice president of the research laboratory. Jonah had already heard a number of uncomplimentary things about both Breed and Hoenikker during the previous evening, which he had spent drunkenly in a local bar, so he is feeling a little cynical and critical when he meets Breed. This co-creator of the atom bomb tells Jonah of a man in Ilium who had killed twenty-six people in 1782, and he exclaims, "Think of it! . . . Twenty-six people he had on his conscience!" Jonah coolly responds that "the mind reels," but his disaffection from science becomes unmistakable as the interview proceeds:

> When I started to ask Dr. Breed questions about the day of the bomb, I found that the public-relations centers of my brain had been suffocated by booze and burning cat fur. Every question I asked implied that the creators of the atomic bomb had been criminal accessories to murder most foul. Dr. Breed was astonished, and then he got very sore. He drew back from me and grumbled, "I gather you don't like scientists very much. . . . All your questions seem aimed at getting me to admit that scientists are heartless, conscienceless, narrow boobies, indifferent to the fate of the rest of the human race, or maybe not really members of the human race at all."[20]

Insulted by such a portrait, Dr. Breed nonetheless proceeds to show himself, and Dr. Hoenikker, as "heartless, conscienceless, narrow boobies." He converses with Jonah about Dr. Hoenikker's last project, just one of many proposed by the military. According to Breed, "admirals and generals in particular" turned to Hoenikker for new weapons and solutions: "They looked upon him as a sort of magician who could make America invincible with a wave of his wand. They brought all kinds of crackpot schemes up here—still do."[21] The last scheme was proposed by a marine general, who was sick of having his men wade through mud, so he asked Hoenikker to discover a way to get rid of mud. Dr. Breed explains the supposedly theoretical solution found by Hoenikker, the crystal "ice-nine," the smallest amount of which would freeze the mud engulfing marines. From the beginning Jonah sees the dangerous ramifications of ice-nine, whereas Dr. Breed only envisions the scientific-military triumph. Jonah realizes that the seed of ice-nine would freeze not just the mud but all surrounding and connecting bodies of water, and when he asks Breed in confirmation if they would freeze, Breed exults: "You bet they would! . . . And the United States Marines would rise from the swamp and march on!"[22] When Jonah presses Breed about the never-ending chain of freezing that would follow, Breed admits that even rain would freeze, and he further admits what Jonah had immediately sensed about life without water: "When it fell, it would freeze into hard little hobnails of *ice-nine*—and that would be the end of the world!"[23]

The cooperation between science and the military which produced devices like the atomic bomb and ice-nine proved the charge of their indifference to the fate of the human race, and the inhuman and immoral results of this type of "pure research" call into question the rationality and the humanity of this system of scientific and military values. Dr. Breed defends "pure research," stating: "New knowledge is the most valuable commodity on earth. The more truth we have to work with, the richer we become." But this type of sentiment falls into complete disrepute in *Cat's Cradle,* as Jonah indicates in his response: "Had I been a Bokononist then, that statement would have made me howl."[24] The divorce between living human principles and scientific "truth" renders all claims to truth suspect. The final tarnishing of science and Dr. Felix Hoenikker in Ilium is voiced by Dr. Breed's disillusioned brother, who connects Hoenikker to guilt and death, not truth. Marvin Breed vents his rage at Hoenikker:

"I suppose it's high treason and ungrateful and ignorant and backward and anti-intellectual to call a dead man as famous as Felix Hoenikker a son of a bitch. I know all about how harmless and gentle and dreamy he was supposed to be, how he'd never hurt a fly, how he didn't care about money and power and fancy clothes and automobiles and things, how he wasn't like the rest of us, how he was better than the rest of us, how he was so innocent he was practically a Jesus. . . . But how the hell innocent is a man who helps make a thing like an atomic bomb? And how can you say a man had a good mind when he couldn't even bother to do anything when the best-hearted, most beautiful woman in the world, his own wife, was dying for lack of love and understanding. . . . Sometimes I wonder if he wasn't born dead. I never met a man who was less interested in the living. Sometimes I think that's the trouble with the world: too many people in high places who are stone-cold dead."[25]

These insights about the deadliness of both ice-nine and scientific "truth" work themselves out in reality on the island republic of San Lorenzo, where Jonah is sent—coincidentally—on assignment for a magazine; here he becomes acquainted with the surviving Hoenikker family and with Bokononism and faces the end of the world. The Hoenikker children, Angela, Frank, and Newt, are gathered on San Lorenzo because Frank—Major General Franklin Hoenikker—was soon to succeed the ailing ruler of San Lorenzo as leader of this poverty-stricken island. Through the Hoenikker children, Jonah learns of the existence of ice-nine, and he learns that the "father" of the atom bomb had also fathered the children whose irresponsibility with ice-nine ends the world. The children had divided their father's grain of ice-nine after his death and each had used the ice-nine for selfish advancement: Angela bought her husband with it, and his secret government research work for America was based on ice-nine; Newt had enticed an Eastern-bloc dancer with his ice-nine, and when she deserted him she took the ice-nine secret to the Soviet sphere of influence; and Frank had gained his position of power in San Lorenzo through his knowledge of science and ice-nine. Given this cold war scenario, it seems just a matter of time before catastrophe strikes.

Explaining and placing into perspective these events is the island's own religion, Bokononism. When Jonah discovers the truth about ice-nine and the Hoenikkers' uses of it, he provides the appropriate Bokononist commentary:

> And I remembered *The Fourteenth Book of Bokonon,* which I had read in its entirety the night before. *The Fourteenth Book* is entitled "What Can a Thoughtful Man Hope for Mankind on Earth, Given the Experience of the Past Million Years?" It doesn't take long to read *The Fourteenth Book.* It consists of one word and a period. This is it: "Nothing."[26]

He also quotes Bokonon more succinctly: "'History!' writes Bokonon, 'Read it and weep.'"[27] While Bokononism shows the despair of a world approaching

Armageddon, the conception of the religion also expresses the central tension of *Cat's Cradle* and the central tension of the atomic age. One of the major principles of Bokonon, the black holy man, was that of "dynamic tension," defined as "the belief of Bokonon that good societies could be built only by pitting good against evil, and by keeping the tension between the two high at all times."[28] Frank Hoenikker identifies the good and evil in Bokononism as he explains parts of the religion to Jonah. Jonah asks, "What *is* sacred to Bokononists?" and Frank informs him that only one thing is sacred: "'Man,' said Frank. 'That's all. Just man.'" Frank just as briefly sums up what Bokonon opposes: "He's against science."[29]

The tension between good and evil, between the sacredness of man and the supremacy of science, is obviously not taut enough in San Lorenzo, and it is the ugliness of these truths—that science, poverty, and death would triumph—that initially compelled Bokonon to formulate his religion. An itinerant seafarer, originally from Tobago and originally named Lionel Boyd Johnson, Bokonon, along with his companion, an American deserter from the marines named McCabe, had been shipwrecked on San Lorenzo. A resident of San Lorenzo fills Jonah in on what happened when these two took over:

> "When Bokonon and McCabe took over this miserable country years
> ago . . . they threw out the priests. And then Bokonon, cynically and play-
> fully, invented a new religion. . . . Well, when it became evident that no
> government or economic reform was going to make the people much less
> miserable, the religion became the one real instrument of hope. Truth was
> the enemy of the people, because the truth was so terrible, so Bokonon
> made it his business to provide the people with better and better lies."[30]

Bokonon has McCabe declare him an "outlaw" and the practice of his religion punishable by the "hook" in order to give "zest" to the religion and keep the tension high between the good human hope of his religion and the evil "truth" of life. As the apocalyptic events unfold in San Lorenzo, however, Jonah comes to understand the "cruel paradox of Bokononist thought": "the heartbreaking necessity of lying about reality, and the heartbreaking impossibility of lying about it."[31]

The tension between human good and scientific evil shifts in favor of scientific evil when the dying ruler of San Lorenzo ingests Frank's ice-nine in a novel form of suicide, and the ugly truth of the resulting apocalypse renders moot the issue of human sacredness. By a series of accidents the body of the iced-nine leader slips into the ocean waters off the island, setting in motion the freezing of the world's waters. Jonah, Newt and Frank Hoenikker, and some others survive the initial maelstrom of deadly ice-nine winds and waters, but this is nonetheless the day the world ends. At least Jonah finds no life broadcasting on the radio and he concludes: "This I assumed: tornadoes, strewing the poisonous blue-white frost of *ice-nine* everywhere, tore everyone and everything above ground to pieces. Anything that still lived would die soon enough of thirst—or hunger—or rage—or apathy."[32] Jonah had survived in an underground shelter, and when he emerges he investigates the island, looking for the dead or for the survivors. He makes his way to the top of the island's mountain, Mount McCabe, and he discovers thousands of dead bodies, all exhibiting the signs of self-induced ice-nine poisoning—their fingers were in their mouths, having first touched the ice-nine powder. A note, signed by Bokonon, was left as explanation:

> To whom it may concern: These people around you are almost all of the survivors of San Lorenzo of the winds that followed the freezing of the sea. These people made a captive of the spurious holy man named Bokonon. They brought him here, placed him at their center, and commanded him to tell them exactly what God Almighty was up to and what they should now do. The mountebank told them that God was surely trying to kill them, possibly because He was through with them, and that they should have the good manners to die. This, as you can see, they did.[33]

Jonah gasps at what Bokonon had done, stating "What a cynic!," but he is soon enough ready to take Bokonon's advice as well. He lives with Newt and the others for a few months (they melt ice-nine into water), writing his story—the final version of *The Day the World Ended*—that began with Hiroshima and concluded with San Lorenzo. His desire to live is sapped. He and Newt discuss this diminishing life impulse and relate it to their absent "sex urge." Jonah remembers a similar lesson in history:

> I recalled a thing I had read about the aboriginal Tasmanians, habitually naked persons who, when encountered by white men in the seventeenth century, were strangers to agriculture, animal husbandry, architecture of any sort, and possibly even fire. They were so contemptible in the eyes of white men, by reason of their ignorance, that they were hunted for sport by the first settlers, who were convicts from England. And the aborigines found life so unattractive that they gave up reproducing. I suggested to Newt now that it was a similar hopelessness that had unmanned us.[34]

Unlike the end-of-the-world scenario presented in the manuscript "2000 A.D.," the novel from which Felix Hoenikker had taken the string for his cat's cradle, there is no sex orgy and no last-minute appearance of Jesus before apocalypse. Human life is no longer sacred, no salvation is possible, and Jonah is ready to take Bokonon's advice.

Jonah wants to die, but he is haunted by a dream of his death, in which he is "climbing Mount McCabe with some magnificent symbol and planting it there." His problem is that he cannot think of an appropriate symbol, and this is where Bokonon proves useful. Jonah spots Bokonon on the road and asks him his thoughts. Bokonon replies: "I am thinking, young man, about the final sentence for *The Books of Bokonon*. The time for the final sentence has come." Bokonon's final sentence provides Jonah with the form of his symbol and the form of his death, and it concludes *Cat's Cradle:*

> If I were a younger man, I would write a history of human stupidity; and
> I would climb to the top of Mount McCabe and lie down on my back
> with my history for a pillow; and I would take from the ground some
> of the blue-white poison that makes statues of men; and I would make a
> statue of myself, lying on my back, grinning horribly, and thumbing my
> nose at You Know Who.[35]

Bokonon gives Jonah a suitable subtitle for *The Day the World Ended* in his formulation of "a history of human stupidity," and *Cat's Cradle* generally embodied the stuff of such history: the meaningless and irrational complexities of atomic age life and the irreducible patterns of "scientific truth" that masked the sacredness of human life and marked human extinction for inclusion on the last page of history. The "horrible grin" of black humor seemed the only possible response to the unbalanced but triumphant system of military and scientific values, particularly in a godless universe. Kubrick's *Dr. Strangelove* treated America's nuclear establishment to the same sort of nose-thumbing that Vonnegut delivered to both God and science. Both of these works of black humor shared the nihilistic sensibility of Bokonon's *Fourteenth Book*—that a thoughtful man can hope for nothing for mankind on earth—but the liberating laughter that emerged from the nothingness of this cultural Armageddon nonetheless prompted a revival of the "dynamic tension" between good and evil in American society in the sixties. The overt and rebelliously humorous recognition of the "evil" system of science and technology in the atomic age, nowhere better exposed than in *Dr. Strangelove or: How I Learned to Stop Worrying and Love the Bomb*, in itself helped to reinvigorate a dynamic tension in America between the forces of cultural dissent and the forces of the political and technological status quo.

The tension generated by *Dr. Strangelove* was apparent in the controversy aroused by the film and expressed in glowing and glowering reviews. Reviewers focused as much on how Kubrick made his points as on what points Kubrick made, in large part because the tone and the approach of the film contained the true indictment of the American nuclear system. According to Kubrick, he initially tried a serious treatment of his theme: the accidental launching of nuclear war and the resulting Soviet-American cooperation to thwart its full eruption. As he wrote the various scenes for the film, however, he discovered more comedy than drama and finally opted to present his scenario with black humor. As Kubrick pointed out at a later date, "How the hell could the president ever tell the Russian premier to shoot down American planes? Good Lord, it sounds ridiculous."[36] The apparent ridiculousness of an otherwise serious and plausible atomic age potentiality—accidental nuclear war and its manifold ramifications—thereby became the message and the method of *Dr. Strangelove*. The ultimate irrationality of living with the bomb dictated the temper of the film, thereby challenging the cherished seriousness and rationality of America's nuclear ethos and establishment.[37]

As Kubrick realized, the atomic age establishment could not be taken seriously, whether in reality or in film—a distinction that collapsed in *Dr. Strangelove,* as Kubrick indicated: "The greatest message of the film is in the laughs. You know, it's true. The most realistic things are the funniest."[38] While a tense debate took place over the film's message, its "realism," and its humor, it was precisely *Dr. Strangelove's* capturing of a higher and perhaps surreal "truth" about life in the atomic age that made critics uncomfortable and that made the film truly representative of the cultural rebirth. Its attention to accidental nuclear war and the profanity of the nuclear establishment summed up postwar cultural qualms about the corruption of American power and leadership and undermined the sacred cold war institutions of the bomb and its military and political bureaucracy. While exaggerated and caricatured, the portraits of the bomb and its promoters contained elements of realism, and the satiric treatment of the cold war in fact heightened cultural recognition of the inconsistencies, ironies, and dangers in the atomic age. With a revisionist, imaginative, iconoclastic vision symbolic of the cultural renaissance in the 1960s, *Dr. Strangelove* showed the previously disguised cold war reality for what it was: immoral, insane, deadly—and ridiculous.

While *Cat's Cradle* used the fantastical setting of San Lorenzo and the bizarre set of ice-nine circumstances to announce Armageddon as the irreducible and absurdly ugly truth of the atomic age, *Dr. Strangelove* leveled its sights on the nuclear establishment and on the embedded cold war mentality. In *Dr. Strangelove,* as in *Cat's Cradle,* there is the implication that there are "too many people in high places who are stone-cold dead."[39] Generally oblivious to the destructive nature of their policies and actions, these representatives of the cold war military and political elite have their deadened, perverted, or underdeveloped moral personalities expressed in their very names. Through such characters as the generals Jack D. Ripper and Buck Turgidson, Major King Kong, President Merkin Muffley, and Dr. Strangelove, the film's humor underscores the insanity, machismo, incompetence, and inhumanity increasingly associated with American leaders and their policies in this era. These outrageous lampoons of leaders expose the growing suspicion that irrational madmen, unresponsive to human life and captivated by deadly technology, had triumphed in America.

Drawn to exaggerate reality, the characters in *Dr. Strangelove* actually do symbolize cold war trends evident by the early 1960s—trends like the emergence of the radical right and the reinvigoration of cold warriorism. Their names are equally emblematic of the culture's recognition of the danger in those trends. The supremacy of technology and the declining value of human life, so intimately linked with America's thermonuclear bravado and its threatened extinction of all human life, are illustrated in the sexual orientation of these characters (which is also illustrated in their names) and in the various sexual symbols that punctuate the film. Only "strange" forms of love and sex are practiced by these American leaders, and the very propagation of life becomes associated with death: it is the bomb, and all forms of technology, that they love. The extremism of General Jack D. Ripper, manifested in his obsessive anticommunism or his misogyny and messianic insanity, is obvious in his name. His sexual abstinence from women ("I do deny them my essence") contributes to his paranoia and to his willingness to start in motion the nuclear holocaust.[40]

General Buck Turgidson shares Ripper's zealous cold warriorism, but he is ruled by his lusty desire to wield his male and military power—as is none too subtly suggested by his name's connotations. Turgidson is all swagger and he is dominated by low passions. From the very first he is associated with the "base" bodily functions of defecation and lust: he is in the "powder room" when he receives the call to come to the war room, and his bikini-clad "secretary" relays the message to him, their sex party having obviously been interrupted. While Turgidson later assures the secretary by phone that their relationship is more than just "physical" and that "I deeply respect you as a human being," it is clear that he considers women, and all human beings, as mere objects upon which to loose his passions and his power. The brutish characteristics of military men are also represented by Major King Kong, pilot of the pivotal B-52 in the film, yet his animalism is tempered by the technological objects of his affections: his plane and its H-bombs. When Major Kong rides the H-bomb to earth in one of the most stunning scenes in the film, the bomb becomes an extension of his sexuality and the connections between sex, death, and the bomb are sealed.

The military's deadly blending of sex and technology finds little effective opposition from its civilian political and scientific counterparts in the nuclear establishment. President Merkin Muffley's ineffectuality and effeminacy are revealed in the colloquially obscene references to female genitalia in his name, and he is incapable of the strong and decisive action needed to halt the growing military and technological madness around him. As director of weapons research and development, Dr. Strangelove is not inclined to halt the technological doomsday his scientific prowess has helped to make possible. Crippled, wheelchair-bound, and operating with a mechanical right hand, Dr. Strangelove appears incapable of love for anything but the deadly technological devices he himself so resembles; his stunted sense of morality and humanity is indicated by his past association with Nazism, traces of which are still evident in his present behavior and mentality. Dr. Strangelove's half-machine, half-Nazi character provides the crowning symbol for all these characters' inhuman and lifeless sexual perversions, and it is this basic human failure that advances *Dr. Strangelove*'s plot to its triumphant conclusion in a technological Armageddon.

Kurt Vonnegut proposed in *Cat's Cradle* that healthy or "normal" sexual desire disappeared in the atmosphere of hopelessness that surrounded the end of the world, and the characters in *Dr. Strangelove* also reflected this shift away from a human and loving sexuality. The mutation of sex into something associated with death, not life, is confirmed in the film not only by the characters and their names but also by the images of technology in the film. It is for the bomb and for its related technology that romance and sensuality are reserved. Kubrick emphasizes the culture's affection for this deadly technology in the camera's lingering glances at the complex technology of the B-52s and the "Big Board" in the war room as well as in the phallic shapes of the H-bombs so prominently featured. And the one act of "sex" that does take place in the film involves airplanes, not humans. The opening credits roll over footage of an in-air refueling of a bomber, the injection accompanied by soft and lyrical music that provides the romantic highpoint of the film.[41]

General Jack D. Ripper triggers the events that constitute the plot of *Dr. Strangelove*. The SAC base commander at Burpleson Air Force Base, he is the embodiment of paranoid anticommunism. He has convinced himself that the fluoridation of America's water is in fact a massive communist conspiracy to sap and impurify "our precious bodily fluids." His cold war mentality links the coincidental beginning of fluoridation in 1946 with the Soviet rise to power, and he inflates this convergence of events into a concerted communist plot to infiltrate the bodies of Americans. As he sneers to one of his aides, "How does that coincide with your postwar commie conspiracy?" Convinced of the communist threat, he orders the H-bomb-laden B-52s under his command to attack Russia. He prepares his base for an attack that may come in any guise, warning his soldiers to "trust no one," for of course it is American troops who arrive to stop this disturbed general's maverick thermonuclear attack on the Soviet Union. Forewarned about communist treachery, Ripper's troops obediently open fire on the advancing American soldiers, all the while expressing their admiration for these supposed Russians and their realistic disguises: "You've sure got to hand it to those commies." A pitched battle ensues between these American contingents, with heavy fire being exchanged under posters and billboards that proclaim the motto of the Strategic Air Command: "Peace Is Our Profession."

In the meantime President Merkin Muffley gathers his top military advisers and nuclear strategists in the war room. Led by the chief of the Joint Chiefs of Staff, General Buck Turgidson, these men discuss how and why General Ripper has single-handedly launched a potential H-bomb war. They discover that Ripper has exploited a putative "retaliatory safeguard" in America's nuclear policy whereby a lower-echelon commander has the power to order a nuclear strike in the event that a surprise enemy attack wipes out the regular chain of command. Turgidson begins to suspect that Ripper has "exceeded his authority," and when the president then questions the value of this supposed nuclear safeguard, Turgidson is forced to make another chagrined observation: "I admit the human element seems to have failed us here." The completeness of this human failure becomes apparent when General Turgidson explains Ripper's acts.

According to Turgidson, the president cannot recall the B-52s under Ripper's command because of an added safeguard. Once the planes are ordered beyond their fail-safe points, as Ripper had ordered them, the planes switch off all communications save those by a coded radio device—and only Ripper knows the three-letter code that would bring the planes back. Furthermore, no communication with General Ripper is possible because he has sealed off his base. Ripper had telephoned earlier, however, to inform his superiors of his intentions, and General Turgidson has the transcript of this conversation, which explains, at least to the president's satisfaction, the cause of Ripper's actions. Turgidson reads the transcript, in which Ripper suggests that an all-out nuclear attack be launched to support the "best kind of start" his planes are giving America. Ripper concludes: "God willing we will prevail in peace and freedom from fear and in true health through the purity and essence of our natural fluids." When Turgidson hesitatingly notes that "we're still trying to figure out the meaning of that last phrase," the president abruptly interrupts: "There's nothing to figure out, General Turgidson. This man is obviously a psychotic."

Having concluded that insanity impelled Ripper's actions, the president vents his rage on Turgidson. Blaming Turgidson for allowing this madman to gain such power, Muffley exclaims: "General Turgidson, when you instituted the human reliability tests, you assured me there was no possibility of such a thing ever occurring." Turgidson objects, stating, "I don't think it's quite fair to condemn a whole program for a single slip-up," and his insensitivity to the seriousness of this "single slip-up" becomes understandable when he suggests a course of action to the president. Reasoning along Ripper's lines, Turgidson proposes an all-out attack on the Soviet Union in order to prevent the inevitable Soviet retaliation when the Soviets make radar contact with the approaching American B-52s:

> If, on the other hand, we were to immediately launch an all-out and coordinated attack on all their airfields and missile bases, we'd stand a damned good chance of catching them with their pants down. Hell, we've got a five-to-one missile superiority as it is. We could easily assign three missiles per target and still have a very effective reserve force for any other contingencies. . . . We would therefore prevail and suffer only modest and acceptable civilian casualties from their remaining force, which would be badly damaged and uncoordinated.

When the president sternly reminds General Turgidson that "it is the avowed policy of our country never to strike first with nuclear weapons," Turgidson smugly reminds the president that "General Ripper has already invalidated that policy" and he goes on to offer a moving plea for a first-strike attack on the Soviet Union:

> Mister President, we are rapidly approaching a moment of truth, both for ourselves as human beings and for the life of our nation. Now truth is not always a pleasant thing. But it is necessary now to make a choice, to choose between two admittedly regrettable but nevertheless distinguishable post-war environments—one where you got twenty million people killed and the other where you got one hundred and fifty million people killed.

The president accuses Turgidson of considering "mass murder, not war," and the general replies: "Mister President, I'm not saying we wouldn't get our hair mussed, but I do say not more than ten to twenty million killed, tops, depending on the breaks." Muffley halts this discussion, insisting that he "will not go down in history as the greatest mass murderer since Adolf Hitler." He decides on another alternative: (1) an army attack on Burpleson Air Force Base in order to find Ripper and the three-letter code for recalling the planes, and (2) an agreement to cooperate with the Soviets in order to stop the planes from delivering their H-bomb loads.

President Muffley invites Soviet ambassador DeSadeski to the war room in order to coordinate the Soviet-American plans, and General Turgidson is livid at this "serious breach of security." He mutters "degenerate, atheistic commie" at the ambassador and gets into a physical brawl with the ambassador when he catches him secretly taking photographs of the war room with a miniature camera. The president breaks up the fight, shouting, "Gentlemen, you can't fight in here—this is the war room!"—and order is thus restored. The president and the ambassador then contact Soviet premier Kissof to inform him of the dire situation, using the advanced telephone equipment specially designed for these superpower crises. The crisis, however, is not diffused, in fact it is intensified. Kissof reveals another catastrophic complication: the Soviets have just installed a "doomsday machine" with the result that any single atomic explosion on Soviet territory will activate the device and initiate the destruction of "all human and animal life" on the planet.

The director of weapons research and development, Dr. Strangelove, enters the war room discussion when talk turns to the doomsday machine. While the doomsday machine represents the ultimate nuclear technology and the ultimate relinquishing of human control to safeguarded machines, Dr. Strangelove himself represents the ultimate dehumanized form, tinged with technological genocide. Crumpled in his wheelchair, constantly struggling with his quixotic metallic hand (which periodically and uncontrollably rises in a "Heil Hitler" salute), and speaking in the crisp Germanic accent that denotes his Nazi past, Dr. Strangelove is the appropriate spokesman for the doomsday machine.[42] The workings of the machine become clear in the discussion: once an atomic explosion sets off the machine, it triggers hundreds of atomic explosions tainted with "cobalt-thorium G," which in turn will envelop the earth in a deadly radioactive "doomsday shroud" lasting ninety-three years. Any attempt to disarm the doomsday machine will also result in its automatic triggering. A concerned President Muffley questions Dr. Strangelove about these automatic triggering mechanisms, asking if it is possible to create a device that is at once automatically triggered and yet impossible to untrigger. Dr. Strangelove responds:

Mr. President, it is not only possible, it is essential. That is the whole idea of this machine, you know. Deterrence is the art of producing in the mind of the enemy the *fear* to attack. And so because of the automated and irrevocable decision-making process which rules out human meddling, the doomsday machine is terrifying, simple to understand, and completely convincing.

What the doomsday machine has made completely clear is the absolute necessity of stopping each and every B-52—the failure to do so now means the end to all human life. Feverish attempts are made to accomplish exactly this. The three-letter recall code is finally discovered after the surrender of Burpleson Air Force Base and the suicide of General Ripper (the code is P-O-E, meaning either "Peace on Earth" or "Purity of Essence"), and the Soviets have shot down a number of the planes, so it appears for a time that all of the planes have either been recalled or destroyed. It turns out, however, that through a series of mishaps and through the ingenuity of Major Kong and his crew, one B-52 is still continuing on its apocalyptic mission. When Major Kong and his crew received their orders to proceed beyond the fail-safe point, they adjusted admirably to the task of fighting a nuclear war—at least once they had suppressed their complaints and their initial suspicions that this was either a joke or a "loyalty test." They stowed away their playing cards and *Playboy* magazines and got down to the task of reviewing their mission and surveying their survival kits. Donning his cowboy hat in preparation for "nuclear combat, toe-to-toe with the Russkies," Major Kong patriotically addressed his crew about their nuclear assignment and then cataloged the contents of their survival kits, which included rubles and gold, all sorts of pills (pep and sleeping pills, along with tranquilizers), prophylactics, packs of chewing gum, lipstick, nylons, and "one combination Russian phrase book and Bible." The survival kits did not provide any comfort once a Russian missile hit and damaged their B-52 (although Major Kong notes that "a fella could have a pretty good weekend in Vegas with all that stuff"), however, and the repercussions of this missile hit are the stuff of doomsday.

With its fuel system leaking and its sophisticated communications device destroyed by the Soviet missile, Major Kong's B-52 now glides onward in Soviet territory, operating outside the control of the cooperating Americans and Soviets. The B-52 cannot receive the recall code once its radio device is disabled, and the missile damage prompts Kong to fly the plane at an abnormally low altitude, which also allows it to escape Russian radar detection. Low on fuel, the crew decides to abandon the primary and secondary targets for their mission in favor of a closer site, and this thwarts the last-ditch efforts of the Soviet military forces, who are waiting at the original target sites. When yet another glitch in the machinery develops—the doors of the bomb bay will not open to release the H-bomb—it seems that Kong's B-52 rather fortuitously will not be able to complete its mission. But Major Kong rallies to "rescue" the mission, following orders to the bitter end. In one last burst of skill and dedication, Major Kong takes charge and descends into the bomb bay in order to open the jammed doors. He straddles one H-bomb, which has its name, "Hi there!" scrawled on it, and he assiduously works on the wires controlling the doors. As the B-52 flies over its target, a missile base, the bomb bay doors suddenly open and the H-bomb is released—with Major Kong aboard for the ride. Kong bronco rides the H-bomb to earth, yahooing, shouting with joy, and waving his cowboy hat wildly as he heads toward his death and toward the detonation of the doomsday machine. Major Kong's absurd laughter in the face of death encapsulates the very spirit of the film.

Also intensifying at the film's conclusion are the power and presence of Dr. Strangelove. As the world and all its forms of life near their end as a result of Major Kong's rodeo ride, Dr. Strangelove takes physical and philosophical prominence—symbolizing the final triumph of his and the others' strange and deadly love of the bomb. Once Strangelove realizes that the H-bomb explosion has activated the doomsday machine, he wheels his chair around to face President Muffley and his advisers and announces: "Mr. President, I would not rule out the chance to preserve a nucleus of human specimens. It would be quite easy, at the bottom of some of our deeper mine shafts. Radioactivity would never penetrate a mine some thousands of feet deep, and in a matter of weeks sufficient improvement in dwelling space could easily be provided." Having abruptly captured the attention of his audience with these remarks, Dr. Strangelove takes center stage and elaborates on his plan at the urging of those around him. Doomsday and the death of humanity provide a stimulating atmosphere for Dr. Strangelove. The deadened parts of his body and the deranged slant to his morality come alive in this milieu. He can no longer control himself either physically or mentally, and his Nazism bursts forth with impunity during his disquisition on mine-shaft living. When asked by the president if people could actually live in mines for one hundred years, Strangelove excitedly responds: "It would not be difficult, Mein Führer! Nuclear reactors could . . . I'm sorry, Mr. President. . . . Nuclear reactors could provide power almost indefinitely, green houses could maintain plant life, animals could be bred and *slaughtered* . . ."[43]

As Dr. Strangelove reverts verbally to his Nazi past, his mechanical hand and crippled body also perform in concert with their now enlivened memories of the Nazi world view. His hand persistently pulls his arm into a rigid Nazi salute and his body forces him into amazing contortions. Those around him ignore his struggles with his disobedient and not quite de-Nazified limbs as they are enchanted with the details of Dr. Strangelove's plan for life-after-doomsday—and it is a plan coolly and self-servingly designed to seduce this specific crowd. Computers would decide which Americans would descend into the mines (thereby freeing the reluctant president from having to make human decisions, particularly since he wonders aloud if those living in the mine shafts might not "envy" the dead), but Dr. Strangelove assures his audience that it would of course be "absolutely vital" that America's "top government and military men" take their places among the elect. He suggests that those living underground would "breed prodigiously," especially with little else to do, and he justifies this as a means of returning the gross national product to its present level within twenty years. There would be a ratio of ten females for every male, so monogamy would "regrettably" have to be abandoned ("a sacrifice required for the future of the human race," according to Strangelove, and a new feature of life that spreads an appreciative grin on General Turgidson's face). All the while he is explaining these characteristics of mine-shaft life, Dr. Strangelove is attempting to beat his unruly hand into submission and to control its urge to heil, but the hand finally rebels and clutches Dr. Strangelove's throat, momentarily strangling him.

As Dr. Strangelove recovers, Buck Turgidson raises questions about the military aspects of the plan. Steadfastly adhering to his cold war patterns of thought, he argues for stockpiling bombs in the mines in order to counter Soviet mine-shaft expansionism, and he bellows loudly: "Mr. President, we must not allow a mine-shaft gap!" Revived and enlivened, Dr. Strangelove exclaims, "I have a plan!" Triumphant in this atmosphere of death and madness, Dr. Strangelove haltingly rises from his wheelchair and takes steps toward the president, exulting in his newfound strength: "Mein Führer! I can walk!" The scene immediately shifts from this war room arena of Dr. Strangelove's miraculous cure to a panoramic scene of successive atomic explosions and mesmerizing mushroom clouds—a scene that effectively conveys, then silences and cancels the world of Dr. Strangelove. The film ends as the world ends and the apocalypse is accompanied by the incongruous and uplifting musical refrain of "We'll Meet Again Someday": "We'll meet again / don't know where, don't know when / but I know we'll meet again some sunny day. / Keep smiling through, / just like you always do, / till the blue skies drive the dark clouds far away."

There was no retreat from the crescendo of black humor and bleak nihilism at the end of *Dr. Strangelove,* as is evident in Kubrick's use of "We'll Meet Again Someday" as the musical serenade to America's Armageddon. Even apocalypse and the extinction of human life were subjects of the satire that ruled the film as a whole, and it was this complete commitment to both satire and nihilism that made *Dr. Strangelove* a cultural tour de force and a cultural center of controversy. Its blending of laughter and death spawned the celebration and the outrage over the film, and it was thus the nightmarishly funny tone and form of the film that thrust it into the culture's attention. *Dr. Strangelove,* particularly when taken in conjunction with *Cat's Cradle,* had tied together all of the culture's disparate atomic age concerns—from the fears and expectations of accidental nuclear war and human extinction to the revisionist interpretation of anticommunism as an insane and internal menace, from the recognition of the increased power and position of technology and militarism in American society and the accompanying dehumanization of that same society to the open understanding of America's system as an irrational and unworkable one, directed by leaders tinged with fascism, madness, and moral corruption.

The film relied on the "real" in many cases to point out the inconsistencies and ironies of America's cold war establishment: American troops fighting under the "Peace Is Our Profession" banner of the military organization that guarded America's most destructive war weapons, General Buck Turgidson repeating almost verbatim Herman Kahn's comparative death tolls in nuclear war, detailing the various ways in which SAC's otherwise infallible system of safeguards could fail and thereby render the system unsafe. Yet for all the exposure that *Dr. Strangelove* gave to the diverse and widely shared concerns of the aroused culture of the 1960s, it was the film's attitude toward those concerns rather than their simple presentation which aroused the debate and the dynamic cultural tensions that followed the film's release.

Dr. Strangelove was hailed as a cultural breakthrough and it was condemned as a sick, traitorous, and defeatist joke. An extreme polarity of views were expressed about the film and its method, with only a few cultural commentators walking a middle line between enthusiasm and horror. Joan Didion's comments about the film proved more the exception than the rule, as she treated the film with a fair amount of disinterest. In an article on Hollywood and the motion picture industry originally written for the *American Scholar* in 1964, she downplayed the "creativity" that had supposedly emerged in Hollywood with the rise of independent film producers, and she included Kubrick and *Dr. Strangelove* as evidence for this less-than-original "new" Hollywood:

Stanley Kubrick's *Dr. Strangelove,* which did have a little style, was scarcely a picture of relentless originality; rarely have we seen so much made over so little. John Simon, in the *New Leader,* declared that the "altogether admirable thing" about *Dr. Strangelove* was that it managed to be "thoroughly irreverent about everything the Establishment takes seriously: atomic war, government, the army, international relations, heroism, sex, and what not." I don't know who John Simon thinks makes up the Establishment, but skimming back at random from "what not," sex is our most durable communal joke; . . . the army as a laugh line has filtered right down to Phil Silvers and "Sergeant Bilko"; and, if "government" is something about which the American Establishment is inflexibly reverent, I seem to have been catching some pretty underground material on prime time television. And what not. *Dr. Strangelove* was essentially a one-line gag having to do with the difference between all other wars and nuclear war.[44]

While Didion realized that *Dr. Strangelove* mirrored the more generalized cultural trend to irreverence and "underground" disrespect for the establishment, she remained unimpressed by the film's peculiar mode of expression. Others, however, did not offer the same detachment in their evaluation of the film. In his review of the film, "The Strange Love of *Dr. Strangelove:* A Movie Review" (adapted from a sermon delivered at the White Plains Community Church on February 23, 1964), Homer Jack focused on the "treatment" of the film as the genesis for all the excitement and controversy: "Given the story and the cast, why all the enthusiasm, ask impatiently those who have not seen the film? The secret is in the treatment. A combination of melodrama, comedy, satire, and nihilism produce what has been widely called 'nightmare comedy.'"[45] Jack noted how numerous film critics had commented on *Dr. Strangelove's* "unblinking nihilism" and "sadistic humor," and in fact it was the black humor of the film that either attracted or repelled cultural commentators.

In her work on cold war films, *Running Time: Films of the Cold War,* Nora Sayre interjected a personal reminiscence about *Dr. Strangelove* that suggested the tone of positive film reviews and that expressed the sense of cultural freedom captured by the film. She pointed out that "laughing at death was a novel experience," recalling her own sense of liberation at watching the film:

After radioactive clouds enveloped the world at the end of *Dr. Strangelove,* one could leave the theater with the echo of Vera Lynn singing, "We'll meet again, don't know where, don't know when," reverberating in one's ears, oddly elated by a sense of possibility; a movie that defied the traditions of taste and subverted our institutions implied that the Fifties were finally fading. The concept of change had seemed remote to many of us who had grown up with the Cold War: accepting the norm had been the rondo theme of our education, and the future was expected to perpetuate the past. But parts of our culture were beginning to signal that passivity or stoicism need not be quintessential to the national character, and a film like *Dr. Strangelove* suggested that we owed reverence to no fixed authority— and that authority could even be disputed.[46]

The review of *Dr. Strangelove* in *Newsweek* also applauded Kubrick's satiric point of view. *Newsweek* saw the film as "outrageous," "side-splittingly funny," and as spilling over with "low clowning"; the reviewer believed that the humorous tone of the film made the film's message and Kubrick's points "all the sharper, all the clearer." The *Newsweek* review appreciated the treatment of the film and upheld the sense of freedom created by such a black sensibility: "Kubrick, and his biting bitter satire, stands as eloquent testimony not only to the possibilities of intelligent comment in film, but to the great freedom which moviemakers have, even if most of them have not dared to use it." The review approved the more "serious" message that resulted from the film and its laughter, the message "that human society is not yet so well organized as to be able to afford such dangerous toys as hydrogen bombs."[47] Lewis Mumford also recognized the serious message in *Dr. Strangelove,* hailing the film as "the first break" in America's "cold war trance." He connected the "crazy fantasy" treatment of the film to the very reality of America's nuclear policies:

> What has masked the hideous nature of our demoralized strategy of total extermination is just the fact that it has been the work of otherwise well-balanced, responsible men. . . . What the wacky characters in *Dr. Strangelove* are saying is precisely what needs to be said: this nightmare eventuality that we have concocted for our children is nothing but a crazy fantasy, by nature as horribly crippled and dehumanized as Dr. Strangelove himself.[48]

Opposing these glowing reviews of *Dr. Strangelove* and its black humor were angry statements like those voiced by Bosley Crowther, film reviewer for the *New York Times*. Crowther became an influential and representative spokesman for the harsh critics of *Dr. Strangelove,* and he strenuously objected to the film's satiric vision. He termed *Dr. Strangelove* the "most shattering sick joke I've ever come across."[49] While a cultural commentator like Lewis Mumford countered this charge, arguing that "what is sick is our supposedly moral, democratic country which allowed this policy to be formulated and implemented without even the pretense of open public debate," Crowther's comments nonetheless served as a gauge of negative opinions.[50] Even though Crowther admitted that *Dr. Strangelove* was "a devastating satire," he considered the film in general "a bit too contemptuous of our defense establishment for my comfort and taste." His distaste for the film grew clear in his further commentary. He believed that the film's "sportive speculation about a matter of gravest consequence seems more malicious than diverting, more charged with poison than wit" and he saw the film's "mordant satire" stemming more from "wild imagination" than from "basically rational truths."[51]

Crowther was simply unconvinced of any real "truth" in *Dr. Strangelove,* and he charged that Stanley Kubrick "goes beyond truths that are absurd and asks his audience to follow in a frightening and dangerous fantasy. He constructs a nightmare speculation upon an assumption of military and political flaws that are so fanciful and unsupportable by any evidence that they are beyond sober belief." Concocting "a terrible joke" about the atomic age and its terrors was intolerable to Crowther; it "is not only defeatist and destructive of morale. It is to invite a kind of laughter that is only foolish and hysterical."[52] Homer Jack noted that Crowther was not alone in being repelled by the film. He quoted Robert Brustein, who maintained that "conservatives will find [the film] subversive, liberals irresponsible, utopians bleak, humanitarians inhuman."[53]

But if Crowther found little redeeming value in the black treatment, in the "realism," or in the message of *Dr. Strangelove,* a reviewer like Homer Jack focused on exactly these issues in order to find the film's redeeming qualities. Jack openly wondered about the film's message, and he discovered one—one that derived directly from the film's insanity and nihilism:

> Is there, then, any message to this picture? If there is a message—and as *Time* suggests, "the message never quells the madness"—the message may be that the dehumanization of man results in the death of man. War is only the end of the line, the final dehumanization. This is much more than an anti-war film. It is a satirical onslaught against modern civilization and technology, using the war theme. This film is a protest against the mechanization of man and society to a point where Dr. Strangelove himself, as a symbol of this mechanization, takes charge—and triumphs. The message is that modern man and modern society are both—all—crazy.[54]

Jack recognized that the film's apocalyptic message, delivered without solution or escape, spawned much of the dissatisfaction with the film, whether it was liberal or conservative dissatisfaction. Jack, however, pinpointed the film's most redeeming feature: Kubrick captured truth and realism precisely in his lack of proffered solution. As Jack concluded: "Perhaps no moral, certainly no pat answer, is the best moral, the best answer. There is no obvious answer to the direction mankind is taking except to change direction."[55] *Dr. Strangelove's* conclusion in Armageddon and the resulting destruction of the system and values that had led to America's judgment day certainly pointed to the need for change, but the film signaled the demand for a change in its style as much as in its content. Beyond the imperative for restructuring or disposing of America's nuclear establishment and for rebuilding human values, there was also the imperative to demand change in a radical new fashion. The film's black humor, its satire and its nihilism, announced this second and equally important change in direction, as it suggested that a fearless, rebellious, and experimental mode of expression and action was arising in order to force America's change of direction in the atomic age.[56]

That it was this second imperative of change—the black voice of cultural revolution and antiauthoritarianism—that created the film's controversy and that aroused disturbed tensions in the culture became apparent on the release of two other films that also focused critical attention on America's nuclear establishment. Both *Fail-Safe* and *Seven Days in May* premiered in 1964 and both presented nightmarish scenarios about American life in the atomic age. While reflective of the cultural revolt against the bomb's central place in America, these two films did not generate the kind of debate that *Dr. Strangelove* did. *Fail-Safe* and *Seven Days in May* tarnished both military and political authorities, challenged the sway of power exercised by the nuclear establishment, and exposed the quality of human life in the atomic age. Neither film, however, approached these subjects with the satire and nihilism of *Dr. Strangelove,* and it was these films' varying attitudes about their subjects which distinguished them from *Dr. Strangelove* and prevented them from having the same revolutionary cultural impact.

Fail-Safe, both the film and the novel on which it was based, written by Eugene Burdick and Harvey Wheeler and published in 1962, was an effective critical account of America's nuclear bureaucracy and its profession of technological control and infallibility. In the preface to their novel Burdick and Wheeler took pains to express the serious truths contained in their fictional story:

This book is not an exposé. It does not purport to reveal any specific technical flaw in our defense system. Perhaps our charge may be considered more grave. For there is substantial agreement among experts that an accidental war is possible and that its probability increases with the increasing complexity of the man–machine components which make up our defense system. Hardly a week passes without some new warning of this danger by knowledgeable persons who take seriously their duty to warn and inform the people. In addition, all too often past crises have been revealed to us in which the world tottered on the brink of thermonuclear war while SAC commanders pondered the true nature of unidentified flying objects on their radar screens.[57]

The grave and socially responsible tone of the novel likewise characterized the film, and the contrast with *Dr. Strangelove* is particularly striking given *Fail-Safe*'s nearly identical scenario concerning accidental war.

The basic plots and premises of *Fail-Safe* and *Dr. Strangelove* are so similar that they share the "nightmarish" quality of the scenario. In the case of *Fail-Safe,* however, a real nightmare initiates the action. The film opens with black-and-white overexposed images of a bullfight; awaking from this recurring bad dream is a disturbed and sweaty General Black. He is convinced that once he sees and recognizes the face of the matador he will die—it will be the "end of me."[58] He vaguely knows that this sinister dream is connected to his work as an air force officer in a world of nuclear weapons and he believes the dream would end if he resigned his commission. But as a committed officer and a proponent of peaceful solutions, he prepares for work; he gets ready to leave his home and family in New York to attend a Pentagon war room meeting in Washington, D.C. By the end of the day, however, his nightmare will reassert itself and re-solve in exactly the disastrous fashion he so fears.

The working out of General Black's nightmare results from the American launching of accidental nuclear war, which, as in *Dr. Strangelove,* was made possible by the technological sophistication and flaws in the system of safeguards. Even before the crisis begins, there are signs of discontent with the present system of nuclear defense. At a SAC base for the advanced H-bomb-armed "Vindicator" planes in Anchorage, grumblings are heard from the lead pilot about how machines are taking over all operations. He is saddened by the fact that one "can't depend on people" but only on machines. At the SAC center in Omaha, a visiting congressman decries the modern state of operations in which "no one is responsible" in a system so dependent on technology. Divisions within the upper echelons of the strategic command are also registered during the Pentagon meeting with the secretary of defense (who happens to be handicapped, walking with the aid of arm-brace crutches), where General Black's arguments for peace and disarmament ("stop war, not limit it") are countered by the presumably more representative Professor Groeteschele, who urges a "speed-up" in plans for "limited" war with H-bombs. As these abstract complaints and debates take place, an alert is signaled from Omaha—an unidentified flying object is spotted and the Vindicator planes are sent to their fail-safe points by SAC. As concern grows about the UFO, it is finally identified as a commercial airliner flying off-course as a result of a power failure and high tail winds. The Vindicator planes waiting at their fail-safe points are recalled and the alert is terminated—until the SAC base in Omaha realizes that a group of Vindicators has not returned but has flown beyond the fail-safe point on its way to its ultimate target in the Soviet Union: Moscow.

An obscure and unidentified mechanical malfunction, a new Soviet program of radio-jamming, and the complex system of security safeguards combine to "explain" the behavior of the maverick Vindicator group: they had mistakenly received a "go code" for attack and they cannot be recalled by radio or by voice command because of Soviet jamming and because of the preestablished policy against receiving orders save by the "safeguarded" fail-safe box aboard the plane, which has already relayed the incorrect order to wage nuclear war on the Soviet Union. As the six Vindicators head for Soviet airspace, the developing crisis is tracked at SAC headquarters in Omaha and in the Pentagon war room, where the big boards register the progress of the planes, and at the deep underground shelter at the White House, where the president and his Russian translator communicate with the others and eventually with the Soviet premier as well.

A tense discussion takes place among all the various advisers to the president concerning the causes of this crisis and the possible responses. Even though it is eventually determined that mechanical failure is to blame for this "accidental" state of war, one military adviser wonders aloud about someone having gone "berserk." Suspicions are also leveled against the Soviet Union, but in the end General Black settles the issue by declaring that it "doesn't matter" whether it was "man or machine"—it is "our accident." As a civilian adviser to the Pentagon, Professor Groeteschele suggests that America "take advantage" of the accident, because he sees the accident as "our chance" to destroy the "Marxist fanatics" in the Soviet Union. This course of action is rejected, and despite the slim odds for success the president decides to send American fighter planes after the Vindicators. The fighter planes are ordered to shoot down the Vindicators, but they cannot catch the Vindicators, and the fighters finally flame out and crash into the ocean, killing all their crews. Given this failure, nuclear war with the Soviets is almost a certainty, for it is recognized that no matter what defenses the Soviets have, at least one or two of the Vindicators will get through to Moscow and drop a load of H-bombs.

The president decides at this point that he must communicate with the

Soviet premier to convince him of the accidental, perhaps preventable nature of this attack. He removes the complex "direct telephone" to the Kremlin from its storage place, unseals the equipment, and arranges it in working order. Operating against the deeply ingrained cold war suspicions between Soviets and Americans, the president finally manages to convey his message to the Soviet premier (aided in large part by the Soviet admission of complicity in the radio jamming that contributed to the "accident" and by the Soviet technology that allowed them to view the American attempt to shoot down their own Vindicators). While still keeping their own nuclear forces on alert, the Soviets agree to help in the attempt to stop the Vindicators. The president orders the SAC command center in Omaha to cooperate with the Soviets, giving them the information needed to break through Vindicator defenses and thus to destroy the American bombers.

Some extreme American reactions surface in the high tension of this situation. Professor Groeteschele remains adamant about striking hard at the Soviet Union, claiming to have learned this lesson from the history of the Nazis and the Jews. With curious logic he argues that just as the Jews should have met their Nazi destroyers with guns, so too should America fight back—first. General Black, however, suggests that Groeteschele's ideas are themselves more reflective of Nazism when he points out that there is "no difference" between the professor and "what he wants to kill." At Omaha, meanwhile, the men are having difficulty giving the Soviets the information that will kill their fellow American soldiers. Colonel Cascio, in particular, suffering from the strain of the situation, has a physical and mental breakdown. He refuses his superior's orders to relay vital information to the Soviets and then attempts to take command, calling his superior a "traitor." Cascio is convinced the whole "accident" is a Soviet trap, and his hysterical behavior is indicative of the strain affecting all American advisers.

The president, of course, endures more stress than anyone, but he is an efficient, quick-minded, and sure leader, making decisions and plans to avert escalation to a worldwide nuclear holocaust. While the Soviets track and destroy a number of the Vindicators, it becomes increasingly apparent that one Vindicator will make it to Moscow. In anticipation, the president sends General Black from the war room to an air base and warns him of the great "sacrifice" he may have to ask of him. The meaning of this mysterious sacrifice becomes clear as the final events unfold. One Vindicator is definitely on its way to Moscow, and, in order to prevent full-scale Soviet retaliation, the president offers to have an American Vindicator drop an equal number of H-bombs on New York City, thus exchanging one great American city for the one great Soviet city. He has thought out the elaborate plan, to which the Soviet premier—against the advice of his military men—has acceded. The American ambassador in Moscow is connected by telephone to both the president and the premier (who has abandoned Moscow), as is the Soviet representative to the United Nations in New York. When the ambassador's phone goes dead in the aftermath of the bombing of Moscow, the president will order General Black's Vindicator to bomb New York, and the Soviet representative's deadened phone will signal the destruction of New York to the Soviet premier.

As this scenario reaches its climax, there is much silence and seriousness at the horror of this all-too-plausible atomic age "accident." The human horror for General Black and the president is especially acute, because both General Black's family and the First Lady are in New York. In relatively heartless contrast, Professor Groeteschele begins a rational appraisal of the damage expected in New York, and, after calculating the number of dead at three to five million, he stresses the need to salvage the many corporate records stored in New York—for the salvation of the American economy. The president, though, has more human concerns in mind when he talks with the premier in the minutes before the cities are destroyed. The Soviet premier tries to find comfort in the rationale that this nuclear accident was "nobody's fault," but the president vehemently argues with him and urges change for the future. Showing some of the real emotional stress of the moment, the president addresses the premier: "Today we had a taste of the future. Do we learn from it or do we go on the way we have? What do we do, Mr. Chairman? What do we say to the dead?" When the equally emotional and drained premier responds that the lesson will be that "this will not happen again," a slight ray of hope emerges from the otherwise dark horror of the H-bombs dropping on Moscow and New York.

Because in *Fail-Safe* the bombs do fall. The president and the premier listen to the wrenching sounds of the phone line dying in Moscow, and then the action switches to General Black receiving his orders from the president. Black takes full responsibility for dropping the bombs on New York, relieving his crew of that torment, and then he injects himself with a suicide substance. As he drowses into death, he mumbles about the matador of his nightmare—and he voices the recognition: the matador is "me." His nightmare is resolved in the very terror and death he had foreseen, and the flashing still images of life in New York as it approaches its apocalypse are accompanied by the sounds of the bullfight that opened the film. Balanced against this nightmarish vision of the atomic age, however, is the limited scope of destruction and the unlimited prospect for change promised by the now sober and responsible leaders of America and the Soviet Union. They would now take human control of their nations and their defenses, for as the president had noted to the premier: "We're to blame, both of us. We let our machines get out of hand."

The scenario of accidental nuclear war in *Fail-Safe* clearly had significant parallels in *Dr. Strangelove,* but there were dramatic contrasts in tone and style as well. While their accounts of accidental nuclear war and the vulnerable human and mechanical fail-safe systems of the nuclear establishment are quite similar, the straightforward and serious approach of *Fail-Safe* contrasted markedly with *Dr. Strangelove's.* Certain governmental and military figures are presented as cruel or unreasonable (Professor Groeteschele and Colonel Cascio, most specifically), but there is no wholesale condemnation of the establishment in *Fail-Safe.* The heroes of the film are in fact the ranking civilian and military men, the president and General Black, who recognized the dangers of the nuclear system. Likewise, while there is horrifying devastation in the bombings of Moscow and New York, the cataclysm is not shown and it is not complete. There is no Armageddon in *Fail-Safe.*

The serious tone and restraint of *Fail-Safe* allowed Bosley Crowther to praise the film, and its contrast with *Dr. Strangelove* is evident in his comments. According to Crowther, *Fail-Safe* "does not make its characters out to be maniacs and monsters and morons. It makes them out to be intelligent men trying to use their wits and their techniques to correct an error that has occurred through over-reliance on the efficiency of machines."[59] For all that *Fail-Safe* received acclaim for its serious message and tone, however, not even the film's producer believed it carried the power of *Dr. Strangelove.* Max Youngstein was certain that his film was "good picture," but he was also certain that *Dr. Strangelove* was a "brilliant picture." Youngstein claimed, "It's as simple as that. . . . It was a brilliant type of black humor, so far ahead of its time."[60]

The same contrast between black humor and seriousness held for *Dr. Strangelove* and *Seven Days in May,* the other effective film critique of America's nuclear system released in 1964. The less threatening or combative quality of *Seven Days in May* was evidently known even before the film's release, as the film's director, John Frankenheimer, revealed. Commenting on Kennedy's helpfulness in the filming of *Seven Days in May,* Frankenheimer explained: "[Kennedy] loved it [*The Manchurian Candidate*], supposedly. . . . I never talked to him but I heard so. He loved it enough so that when my next picture, 'Seven Days in May,' was filming, he moved out of the White House for five or six days so we could shoot there. He went up to Hyannis Port."[61] While this action was perhaps simply reflective of JFK's cosmopolitanism and secure self-image, it may also have revealed Kennedy's change of heart regarding brinksmanship after the missile crisis. His cooperation in the filming of *Seven Days in*

May indicated that at least one major figure in America's establishment did not object to the critical portrait of atomic age America presented in the film.

Such cooperation may also have come easily because *Seven Days in May,* like *Fail-Safe,* did not offer a wholesale condemnation of America's system. Like *Fail-Safe, Seven Days in May* leveled criticism at certain American figures of authority and exposed the menace of a defense system based on nuclear weapons, but it did not render all authority or the entire system ridiculous or insane. What *Seven Days in May* did strikingly present was the extreme political, military, and cultural divisiveness of the bomb, and it did so through a plot that was significantly different from that of either *Fail-Safe* or of *Dr. Strangelove.* The focus of the film is the discovery and thwarting of a planned military coup in America, a coup led by a top American military figure as a result of the president's decision to conclude a peace and nuclear disarmament treaty with the Soviet Union. The opening scenes of the film capture the splintered American opinion about disarmament by showing a mixed demonstration outside of the White House. Half of the protestors carry signs in support of the president's plan ("Peace on Earth or No Earth at All") and the other half carry signs opposing his plan ("Ban the Treaty not the Bomb").[62]

President Lyman Jordan is concerned and a little bewildered by the opposition he faces, because he is absolutely certain that one day, without the treaty, nuclear war would in fact break out. The opposition forces are increasingly forming around the leadership of General James Scott, the chairman of the Joint Chiefs of Staff, who broadcasts his many reservations about the proposed treaty to a congressional hearing. He finds the treaty "naive" at its best and "gross negligence" at its worst; he does not believe in Soviet "trustworthiness" and he does believe in building weapons arsenals as deterrence. General Scott has transformed his rabid opposition to the treaty into a plan for concrete action: he is surreptitiously organizing a coalition of military and political men for an overthrow of President Jordan's government. General Scott's aide, Colonel Casey, begins to be suspicious of the general's actions, though, and his own investigations confirm his fears. He is alarmed by the general's drift into criminal and unconstitutional action, as well as by the general's growing popularity for his diatribes against the treaty and the "one-worlders." So he informs the president about this grave matter of "national security."

After a brief period of incredulity, the president and his advisers come to take Colonel Casey's fears seriously. The president assigns Casey and some of his trusted allies to investigate Scott and his cohorts. It becomes clear that General Scott and his men are in fact planning a coup, yet their thorough cover-up of their actions is inhibiting the collection of solid evidence. Eventually Casey and the others gather enough proof for the president to expose Scott to the public, and the president does in fact fight and win in this battle. He confronts Scott and is ultimately able to uphold the worthiness of the Constitution as well as the worthiness of his peace and disarmament treaty with the Soviet Union. He does not even blame Scott and his "lunatic fringe" conspirators for their actions. The president blames "the age, the nuclear age" for "the sickness of frustration" and for the "impotence" that it has imparted. By fighting for peace and disarmament in spite of opposition and in spite of the coup attempt, then, the president will work to heal the divisions and the frustrations of the age.

Although *Seven Days in May* looked at the nuclear establishment from a different angle, the film offered many of the same critical observations as did *Fail-Safe* and *Dr. Strangelove*. Certain Americans in positions of authority appeared as criminal or power hungry (General Scott, most obviously), and the atomic age emerged as the source of the dangers afflicting America. The seven days in May cleverly mirrored the intense time frame of the Cuban missile crisis, shifting the locale of the nuclear threat from the outside to the inside, and accented the same discovery of the "enemy within" seen in the other two films. Yet, as in *Fail-Safe, Seven Days in May* approached its subject with reason and responsibility, and there was no uniform dismissal of American authorities and the system they had created. The president and Colonel Casey provided the ideals and the hopes for peace in the political and military establishment in America and ultimately thwarted the forces primed for nuclear destruction and reactionary revolution.

Dr. Strangelove, Fail-Safe, and *Seven Days in May* all presented dark images of atomic age America in the mid-sixties and all three films contributed to the cultural understanding of the bomb's central role in shaping and damaging American society and culture. These films exposed postwar cultural suspicions, now verging on certainties, about the insecurity of life under an American nuclear system marked by corruption, insanity, arrogance, and inhumanity. The "rational" insensitivity to death and the fanatic and criminal usurpation of authority by American leaders, political and military, suggested their moral corruption. The mad extremism of cold warriorism and the crazy reliance on presumably "infallible" fail-safe devices and policies of deterrence conveyed the insanity of the system and its leaders. The conflicting attitudes toward peace and violence among the military and political elites, and the various stages of atomic destruction depicted—from *Seven Days in May*'s image of political divisiveness and nuclear age impotence to *Fail-Safe*'s devastation of Moscow and New York to *Dr. Strangelove*'s annihilation of all life—all emphasized the divisive power of the bomb.

These films posited a dubious faith at best in America's nuclear establishment, and each identified the enemy within America: the bomb and the system that sustained it. The image of America instigating atomic destruction on its own soil recalled the earlier portents associated with the self-annihilating drift of America—for example, the dire predictions made in *The Day They H-Bombed Los Angeles*, which postulated revolution once the American government admitted complicity in wreaking atomic destruction in America. While the American establishment in the mid-sixties avoided making any such admission, the culture of dissent had drawn its own conclusion about the apocalyptic direction of the American system. As a result, the American system and its leading figures of authority faced a cultural revolution that matched the force of the bomb.

However much *Fail-Safe* and *Seven Days in May* openly corroborated the cultural revolt against the nuclear establishment, it was *Dr. Strangelove* that led the cultural revolution. Only *Dr. Strangelove* attacked the entire American system and its cold war world view, and only *Dr. Strangelove* spoke with the mordant spirit that signaled the cultural disaffection from American authority and tradition and impelled a continuing change in direction, away from the Armgeddon that only *Dr. Strangelove* foresaw as the inexorable fate of an unchanged and unchallenged American establishment. In the end, it was *Dr. Strangelove's* vision that American history and culture accredited and it was *Dr. Strangelove's* black humor that captured the temper of the cultural revolution.

Like other black satires of the early 1960s, most particularly *Catch-22* and *Cat's Cradle, Dr. Strangelove* had perceived that the postwar American order had not been created or ruled over by rational, liberal, or humane men. The "human element" had indeed failed in cold war and atomic age Americ, and, contrary to Bosley Crowther's claims, "maniacs and monsters and morons" did appear to be in positions of power and authority in America. It was the satiric portrait of American leadership in *Dr. Strangelove*, not the balanced and responsible portrait in *Fail-Safe* and *Seven Days in May*, which anticipated the widespread and cynical ridicule of authority articulated by the rebellious culture of the later sixties.

The fight against authority and tradition took on diverse guises in the revolutionary culture of the 1960s, whether it was a battle waged by women, blacks, youth, or the peace and antiwar activists of the Vietnam era. In the cultural impulse to change direction, to create new systems of values, and to structure the new "myth of life" envisioned by Lewis Mumford, all authorities faced challenge. The first step—discrediting and demystifying the validity of the old system and its values—proceeded with a vengeance in the early 1960s as the culture of dissent exposed the deadly and violent underpinnings of power in America. One measure of the culture's success in challenging traditional authority can be traced in the fate of God and of American presidents in the later sixties and early seventies. Building on *Dr. Strangelove*'s liberating destruction of the mythic power of the nuclear establishment, the cultural revolt against authority extended to the highest spiritual and secular powers in America. In an era of moral malaise God seemed irrelevant and the traditional faith in the solace and authority of God faltered, as was strikingly portrayed in *Time* magazine's cover story of 1966, "Is God Dead?" And in an era no longer willing to trust in cold war traditions and solutions, the American presidents still immersed in that mentality faced the types of opposition destined to arise in a time of changing values and expectations. In 1969 and 1974, respectively, Presidents Johnson and Nixon left office in defeat and disgrace, in part victims of the immense "credibility gap" that disclosed the gulf between the corrupt values of the past and the regenerating values of the present and future. The presidents' brutal escalation of the war in Vietnam, their illegal investigations of and intrusions against domestic dissenters, and their embattled and paranoid behavior validated the culture of dissent's perceptions of the immorality and insanity of the cold war system and its leaders.

The language of "madmen" had been associated with cold war leaders since the time of the Cuban missile crisis, often applied by the leaders themselves, and madness thus came to describe the images of authority in America. During the missile crisis Khrushchev noted that only "lunatics" could instigate the mutual annihilation toward which both he and Kennedy were in fact headed; and while Lyndon Johnson and his supporters transformed Barry Goldwater's campaign slogan "In your hearts you know he's right" into "In your guts you know he's nuts," Johnson himself came to be seen as a "monster" and a "wild man" as his administration became embroiled in an increasingly unpopular war.[63] Nixon provided the best evidence of his own "madness" and immorality when he defined his foreign policy theory in Vietnam as "the Madman Theory," a theory he explained to his aide-de-camp, Bob Haldeman:

> I call it the Madman Theory, Bob. I want the North Vietnamese to believe that I've reached the point where I might do anything to stop the war. We'll just slip the word to them that, "for God's sake, you know Nixon is obsessed about Communists. We can't restrain him when he's angry—and he has his hand on the nuclear button"—and Ho Chi Minh himself will be in Paris in two days begging for peace.[64]

America's waging of the Vietnam War has been widely credited with inciting the mass cynicism about American authorities and the cold war system of thought and values, but the culture of dissent had emerged well before the worst excesses of the Vietnam War were evident—indeed, it had been building since Hiroshima and Nagasaki—and had clearly tied the awakening revolt to the preeminent and preexisting symbol of America's ills: the bomb.[65] The "madmen" leaders of America, like those portrayed in *Dr. Strangelove,* had their views shaped by the sense of invincibility that stemmed from the beginnings of the atomic age and the cold war, and, while these leaders would only threaten to use nuclear weapons in Vietnam, the American war in Vietnam was the long-term product of the American order that had begun in Hiroshima and Nagasaki.

Corroborating the central role of the bomb in shaping and reshaping American perceptions of power and authority was an invigorating if controversial trend in the writing of history. Generally termed *revisionism,* particularly in the historical fields related to American foreign policy and America's role in the origins of the cold war, this new school of history emerged in the late 1950s and blossomed from the mid-1960s, often posing critical reevaluations of American policies and motives in international relations. While revisionism is usually seen as an academic by-product of American disillusion stemming from the Vietnam War, the movement actually predated America's direct involvement in Vietnam and its demonstration of the folly of cold war containment policies.[66] One of the works of revisionism that made the greatest splash in academic circles was Gar Alperovitz's *Atomic Diplomacy: Hiroshima and Potsdam,* published in 1965.

In *Atomic Diplomacy* Alperovitz looked to the development and use of the atomic bomb during World War II for the explanation and illustration of America's abusive exercise of power in the cold war. Labeled the *enfant terrible* of revisionism for his iconoclastic thesis regarding the bomb and the cold war, Alperovitz argued that American leaders envisioned the bomb far more as a "political" weapon than as a military weapon for ending the war.[67] According to Alperovitz, both the promise (before its testing) and the reality of the bomb (demonstrated during the Trinity test, which was specifically timed to coincide with Truman's meeting in Potsdam) instilled an arrogance in American leaders about their ability to shape and dictate the terms of the postwar "peace." In the bomb Truman believed he had a "master card" to play in all foreign relations, and in order to make the most of this "card" American decision makers were determined to drop the bombs during wartime: not because the bomb was militarily necessary to end the war but because it was politically useful to their plans for the postwar world.[68]

The United States wanted to dominate the Soviet Union during the peace, and the bomb was the instrument of choice: it would intimidate the Soviets and it would particularly reduce their role in Asia once the war ended without their deep involvement—which the bomb could ensure. Alperovitz noted that American officials believed the Pacific war could be concluded by a Soviet declaration of war against Japan, a modification of the surrender terms offered to Japan (ensuring the emperor's position), or a combination of the two. The war was almost over, no invasion was seen as needed, yet the atomic bombs were nonetheless dropped on Hiroshima and Nagasaki. Alperovitz explains the significance of this decision, for which hundreds of thousands were killed:

> It is not my purpose to argue whether either or both of these measures would, in fact, have ended the war. What I wish to show is that American leaders *believed* such a result was likely. Hence, their decision to use the atomic bomb was made at a time when the best intelligence and military advice indicated there were other ways to end the war without an invasion. As will be shown, the bomb was used not because there were no alternatives, but precisely because American policy makers wished to avoid the political consequences of these alternatives.[69]

By positing base political motives for the use of the atomic bomb against Japan, Alperovitz destroyed the heroic myth about the bomb's place in ending World War II, and he tarnished the image of the American leaders who had chosen to wield the bomb politically and who had thereby delivered the first blow in the cold war. Alperovitz's exposure of the opportunism of American officials in their use of the bomb and their fostering of the cold war added academic and historical weight to the cultural disaffection that had already arisen in the culture of dissent, and *Atomic Diplomacy* as a whole pointed to the centrality of the bomb in the culture's growing rebelliousness.

Works like *Atomic Diplomacy* and *Dr. Strangelove* assumed significance in the cultural revolution of these years not just because they demonstrated how the sixties revolution was guided by the earlier and still coexistent atomic dissent but also because they conveyed the tone of the rebellion that was to follow. An irreverence for the traditions and myths of the past filtered through both of these products of the mid-1960s, and while there was an element of nihilistic malaise attached to the destruction of old systems and ideas, there was also an exhilaration evident in the free expression of such revisionist attacks on systems of authority and in the substitution of new explanations and new systems of beliefs. The cultural ferment of the 1960s and 1970s resembled the spirit of black humor and revisionism because it too exhibited such extremes: the extremes of nihilism and optimism, the extremes of spiritual malaise and spiritual regeneration.

The revival of the "Armageddon attitude," capped by *Dr. Strangelove*'s annihilation of all human life, helped to explain the tensions within America as a whole as well as within the culture of dissent. The sense that America was standing at an atomic age crossroads in the early and mid-1960s provoked conflicting responses and alternative interpretations of America's destiny. Just as *Dr. Strangelove*'s black humor embodied elements of a constraining nihilism and a liberating spirit of hilarity, so too did the rebellious culture of the sixties and early seventies. Visions of a violent and godless American nightmare contrasted with dreamlike visions of an alternative America of peace and humanism. While often posing diametrically opposed evaluations of the American prospect, the rebel culture's conflicting voices were unified by their goal: to change the direction of America on its "eve of destruction," whether by demonstrating the repercussions of America's present system or by creating the new values and the new myth of life meant to counter—or at least limit—America's dehumanized and demoralized slide toward Armageddon.

Whether exposing the violent spiritual crisis generated by America's system or whether bringing forth its nonviolent and spiritually regenerative forms of belief and action, the awakened culture of these years strove to keep taut the "dynamic tension" between good and evil that Vonnegut had proposed in *Cat's Cradle*. Challenging the "evil" of a destructive system with the "good" of its multifaceted opposition, the explosive cultural revolution contributed to the making of a better America. From the cultural chaos of the 1960s emerged the reshaped values and the revised patterns of cultural response that limited the potential of America's system of atomic arrogance. The very tension of the age demanded this change in direction, and in looking toward the future the rebel culture continued to feel the urgency of change that had characterized atomic age dissent in the early 1960s and that had signaled the beginning of the awakening.

Two different visions of America's "tomorrows," representing the persistent concern for the future and the conflicting spirit of rebellious dissent in the 1960s and 1970s, appeared in the culture around the time of *Dr. Strangelove*'s release. In a 1963 episode of *The Twilight Zone*, "No Time Like the Past," a disgruntled inhabitant of the twentieth century had tried to travel through time into the past first to correct and then to escape from the perils of atomic age life, which he described as "an exquisite bedlam, an insanity," a result of man's "bombs, fallout, his poisons, his radioactivity." Having failed to achieve his goal, however, he returns to the present determined "to leave the yesterdays alone, do something . . . do something about the tomorrows. They're the ones that count. Tomorrows, tomorrows. God, let there be tomorrows."[70] Turning away from the past and its destructiveness, changing direction and looking toward tomorrow—no matter how fragile—constituted one imperative in the cultural rebellion of the sixties, an imperative born of dreams and hope.

The other imperative was less optimistic, but it too added to the urgency for change. The fear that there would be no tomorrows expressed the malaise of the age and confirmed the necessity for altering cultural directions. In *Sometimes a Great Notion* (1963–1964) Ken Kesey has his young protagonist blame his unsettled outlook and his insecure life on the bomb's perversion of "tomorrows." He tries to explain to his sister-in-law why he finds no meaning in school or in his writing; he compares earlier generations with his own: "They had something we've lost. . . . They had a limitless supply of tomorrows to work with. If you didn't make your dream today, well, there was always more days coming, more dreams full of more sound and fury and future. . . . There was always tomorrow." When she asks in turn, "And there isn't anymore?" he elaborates on the uncertainty of his world:

> "Pretty likely, sure. But let's say Jack comes home unexpectedly, all miffed at the steel magnates, his back aching and his vigor gone, and finds Jackie and Barry making it in his rocking chair . . . then what? Or, say, Nikita has one vodka too many and decides what-the-hell, then what? I'll tell you. *Zap;* that's all it takes. The little red button and *zap.* Right? And this little button makes a definite difference in our world; in our generation, ever since we've been old enough to read, our tomorrows have been at the mercy of this button."[71]

The despair about the potential loss of tomorrows lent an edge of violence and terror to cultural rebellion in the late 1960s, just as the potential resurrection and salvation of those tomorrows lent an air of hope to the rebellion. It was just such contrasting forms of rebellion—full of hope or despair, peace or violence, optimism or nihilism/pessimism—that characterized the widespread cultural revolution spawned in the years surrounding the appearance of *Dr. Strangelove or: How I Learned to Stop Worrying and Love the Bomb.*

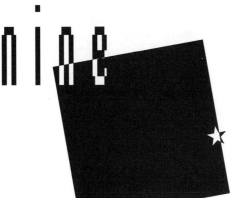

nine

GODLESS VIOLENCE AND TRANSCENDENT HOPE

the american nightmare exposed and contained

Mother, mother
There's too many of you crying
Brother, brother, brother
There's far too many of you dying.
You know we've got to find a way
To bring some lovin' here today
Father, father, father we don't need to escalate
You see, war is not the answer
For only love can conquer hate
You know we've got to find a way
To bring some lovin' here today.
Picket lines and picket signs
Don't punish me with brutality
Talk to me, so you can see
Oh, what's going on
What's going on . . .

> *—Marvin Gaye,*
> *"What's Going On" (1971)*

n a hot summer day, snippets of ominous radio broadcasts fill the sweltering city air—such is the opening to the film *Lady in a Cage* (1964). From a passing car radio is heard the beginning of a religious program: "We've been conquering polio and space, but what have we done about the devil?"[1] When the film's protagonist, the "lady in a cage," gets trapped in her home's elevator-cage during a power outage, she turns on her portable radio for news and hears the following bulletin: "Here in the city, the nude, decapitated body of a woman has been found in a cistern . . . " Suspended mid-air in the elevator she had had installed because of an injury, the lady in the cage is now immobile, a captive audience to the frightening pronouncements on the radio. She soon becomes a victim herself of this godless and violent universe, when a group of psychopathic young criminals invade her home, forever altering her expectations about a future of health and happiness.

Her previous conception of a secure life, already challenged by her debilitating injury, is now completely shattered as the marauding criminals ignore her pleas for help, instead ransacking her home and planning her murder. Against the lawless and inhuman disorder around her she screams, "I'm a human being, a thinking, feeling creature." As the terror escalates, however, she comes to the only reasonable conclusion: "Someone must've pushed the button, dropped the bomb." She turns the radio on to confirm her suspicions and finds no such news. But no radio confirmation is really necessary to understand from the chaos and threat of death around her that the bomb might as well have dropped. She now recognizes that she exists in a cruel and murderous world where no one stops to help a person in distress and, in fact, where almost everyone takes advantage of the weak and lonely. No help arrives for the lady in the cage, so she "helps" herself, becoming an "animal" like her attackers. She manages to escape with her life, but it will be a life of empty tomorrows. Falling in her escape from her cage, she reinjures herself and must drag herself outside to the street in search of the help that is not at all guaranteed to arrive.

The irrational and violent world presented in *Lady in a Cage,* a world in which "someone must've pushed the button, dropped the bomb," was just one of the many chaotic images of American life that appeared in the culture of the 1960s and 1970s. Reflective of the nihilistic malaise and violence spreading throughout America, such images confirmed the cultural recognition of the dying system of order and morality in America and suggested the bomb's metaphoric appropriateness for cultural chaos. Barry McGuire's rock 'n' roll tale of approaching apocalypse, "Eve of Destruction," likewise signaled the growing discontent of the sixties and soldered the connection between the bomb and the disintegration of America. As in *Lady in a Cage,* the image of "pushing the button" dominated the apocalyptic discourse in "Eve of Destruction," asserting that the future of the world was a "grave." The feelings of frustration, anger, fear, and disgrace propounded this message, as did the song's constant refrain about America's precarious balance on the eve of destruction.[2]

Both *Lady in a Cage* and "Eve of Destruction" conveyed the increasingly horrific quality of life in America, but "Eve of Destruction" specifically cataloged the manifestations and causes of America's disintegration into violence. "Eve of Destruction" suggested the fears about tomorrow which stemmed from official acts and forms of violence, from the bomb and the Vietnam War to the white hate visited on civil rights activists during the 1965 Selma march, but it also suggested the stirrings of violence in the temper and activism of the culture of dissent itself. With America perched on a perceived "eve of destruction," the culture of dissent took on the extreme characteristics of the time, including the violence that infected the establishment itself in these years. The anger and frustration evident in McGuire's song did not just spread throughout rock 'n' roll and its emergent form of "protest rock"—it spread throughout all elements of the rebellious culture. Believing that the American system promoted death and violence at home and abroad, this culture responded in kind, expressing both the despair and the anger of living on the brink of the apocalypse.

The escalation of violence in the American system, associated first with the bomb, particularly in the civil defense debate of the earlier 1960s, now became everyday reality as the omnipresent television cameras captured rampant American violence in Vietnam and on the streets of turmoil-ridden American cities. The culture of dissent's rejection of such an American system also escalated and radical rebellion against American authorities and traditions solidified under the banner of violent action and violent rhetoric. The cacophony of violence and death in these years prompted even more apocalyptic visions of America and, as both official and oppositional violence escalated, so too did fears for the future and doubts about the validity of traditional faiths and beliefs. As conflict and change eroded the old order of power and authority and as domestic dissent and the death toll in Vietnam increased, the resulting cultural disquiet and confusion did certainly seem emblematic of a society in which "someone must've pushed the button, dropped the bomb."

Announcing the generalized atmosphere of violence in America was the string of brutal assassinations that shocked the nation in the 1960s. These gunned-down leaders of America (whether associated with the establishment, as was John F. Kennedy in 1963, with transforming the establishment, as was Robert Kennedy in 1968, or with the diverse movement for civil rights, as were Malcolm X in 1965 and Martin Luther King, Jr., in 1968) had all been figures of hope and symbols of change in America. Their murders confirmed the presence of disorder in American society and culture and helped to destroy a certain hope and optimism in the nation. The insecurity and nihilism stemming from these shattered dreams and hopes saturated the culture as disillusion and violence infected and molded a variety of cultural and political responses throughout the late sixties and early seventies.

Increasing violence certainly characterized the American government's response to the worsening military and political situation in South Vietnam. Having acquiesced to, if not abetted, the assassination of South Vietnam's corrupt president Ngo Dinh Diem a mere three weeks before Kennedy's assassination, the United States thereafter worked to support the anticommunist war cause of South Vietnam through increasing involvement and escalating violence. Beginning with the Tonkin Gulf resolution in 1964 and the "Rolling Thunder" bombing campaign against North Vietnam in 1965, the United States government embroiled itself in South Vietnam's cause to the point that American troops, at their peak strength numbering over 500,000, were committed to fight and die in the jungles of Southeast Asia. American technology produced massive death and destruction, culminating in the Tet offensive of 1968 and the My Lai massacre, committed in 1968 and publicly exposed in 1969. Cities were destroyed in order to be "saved," napalm and white-phosphorous bombs defoliated the jungles and deformed Vietnamese peasants, and frustrated American soldiers, involved in an increasingly irrational and seemingly unwinnable war, vented their pent-up rage on the inhabitants of a small village, murdering hundreds of civilians, including women and children.

For a war that to some had been ill-advised from its very beginnings—ill-advised as a war whose conception was mired in the inappropriate, arrogant mindset of containment and in the cold war expansion of American spheres of influence and interest and ill-advised as an immoral interference into the internal politics of another and much smaller nation—the Vietnam War now possessed all the volatile ingredients for a crisis of conscience and culture stemming in large part from the unprecedented acts of violence being perpetrated by Americans in that war. The atrocities and the killing did not end in 1968 with Tet and My Lai, for President Nixon illegally and secretly expanded the air and ground war into Cambodia in 1969 and into the early 1970s. But incidents like My Lai brought home the American capacity for violence and "evil," which pointed out America's need to question its values. *Time* magazine expressed just such sentiments in its coverage of the My Lai atrocity, especially in the article "On Evil: The Inescapable Fact," in which Hannah Arendt's image of the "banality of evil" lent guilty resonance to the cultural trauma engulfing America:

> The banality of evil. Hannah Arendt's trenchant comment on Jerusalem's Man in the Glass Booth springs easily to mind in contemplating the appalling horror of Pinkville [My Lai]. The massacre of March 16, 1968, can be explained away as further proof, if any were needed, that war is indeed hell. Especially the Viet Nam war, with its peculiar frustrations, its bloody agonies, its nervous uncertainties about who and where the enemy really is. But to excuse My Lai on these grounds, or to argue that the enemy has done worse (as he has), is to beg a graver issue. The fact remains that this particular atrocity—a clear violation of the civilized values America claims to uphold—was apparently ordered by officers of the U.S. military and carried out by sons of honorable, God-fearing people. Inevitably, My Lai will be taken by some as a measure of American society. To certain critics of America, the massacre will be added evidence that the U.S. is an immoral, unprincipled and racist power; others will insist, with a shade more justice, that the action mocks the pious official rhetoric about saving Asia from Communist aggression in the name of humanity. The most pertinent truth, however, is less accusatory and more difficult for the U.S. to accept: it is that Americans as a people have too readily ignored and too little understood the presence of evil in the world.[3]

More pertinent even than "the presence of evil in the world," though, was the presence of evil within America and within the American past that put My Lai into perspective for *Time*. *Time* noted "Traditionally, evil has been something distant, Wholly Other, rather than an enemy within. When Rap Brown complained that 'violence is as American as cherry pie,' most Americans dismissed the charge as the aberrant nastiness of a Black Power fanatic." *Time* then proceeded to uphold Brown's notion of the "violence within": "But there is a dark underside to American history: the despoliation of the Indian, the subjection of the black, the unwise and probably unmoral insistence on the enemy's unconditional surrender that led to Hiroshima."[4] While *Time* argued for an almost existential American realization of humanity's flaws, the magazine did discuss the widespread and specific evil being recognized in America, particularly by the rebellious elements within American society:

> Today's young radicals, in particular, are almost painfully sensitive to these and other wrongs of their society, and denounce them violently. . . . To them: evil is not an irreducible component of man, an inescapable fact of life but something committed by the older generation, attributable to a particular class or the "Establishment," and eradicable through love and revolution.[5]

The violence in Vietnam, ultimately perpetrated by the establishment, according to the culture of dissent, did open American culture to a reevaluation, and the culture was found wanting. A soldier fighting in the Vietnam War confirmed this judgment when he contemplated the meaning of his acts in Vietnam. He found himself caught up in the brutality, sharing in inflicting torture on the enemy, and he discovered the enemy within himself and within his culture as well:

> The thing that I feel the worst about was that my own humanity was called into question, my own values, my own sense of myself as a moral, righteous person. I was defrocked. I was exposed as another barbarian along with all the rest. . . . The war took my measure. Not just me, but me and my culture. The culture had given me a framework, a point of reference for understanding myself, my religion and my parents, my background and all. And I was not that person.[6]

The measure of the culture that resulted from an evaluation of the Vietnam War and the entire "dark underside" of American history was not an inspiring or uplifting one, and the culture of dissent did in fact fight the "evil" of the establishment with love and revolution. But if violence constituted the measure and the legacy of the culture, it also became in the sixties one of the means by which such a legacy would be fought. The distasteful character of the American system, recognized both before and during the Vietnam War, faced a revolutionary challenge mixed with as much violence as love.

The many dissenting groups who felt distressed by the American system and its traditions developed a tendency toward violent expression and violent acts, revealing an extremism in thought and action that matched that of the system and of the age. Early in the decade women began to voice the sense of social, cultural, and political oppression they would express more forcefully in later years, and the images they used to describe the stifling place of women in a male-dominated society were characteristic of the rising vehemence in the rhetoric of cultural opposition. In Sylvia Plath's autobiographical novel *The Bell Jar,* published in the same year she committed suicide (1963), she portrayed a life of suffocating confinement, where a woman's possibilities were limited to the small space of a "bell jar."[7] In the same year Betty Friedan published *The Feminine Mystique,* which disclosed the unhappiness ("the problem that has no name") women suffered as a result of their idealized but ultimately degrading roles as "happy housewives." She likened the imprisoning suburban homes of such housewives to "comfortable concentration camps."[8] Such visions of exclusion formed a part of the rising radical rejection of the authorities and traditions responsible for such injustice.

Friedan's reference to concentration camps suggested the continuing relevance of the Nazi example in the 1960s, as did the comparisons prompted by My Lai later in the decade. Increasingly the culture of dissent gave evidence of having learned at least one of the moral lessons from that era: noncompliance and noncooperation with systems of evil. The rising tide of violent language and action was particularly noticeable in the civil rights movement and in student activism and the spreading antiwar movement. In conjunction with the Christian nonviolence of the civil rights activism associated with Martin Luther King, Jr., black radicals, both on organized and grassroots levels, demanded immediate empowerment and black respect, but they confronted the system in the way it best understood—with power and violence. Malcolm X, having rejected Christianity for the Black Muslims and their program of black nationalism, became the earliest spokesman for "black power" and provided a violent alternative to the nonviolent civil rights movement.

In a speech delivered in November 1963, his "Message to the Grass Roots," Malcolm X offered the simple observation that distinguished his outlook on black activism: "There's no such thing as a nonviolent revolution."[9] Anticipating the later famous dictum on violence delivered by black activist H. Rap Brown—that "violence is as American as cherry pie"—Malcolm X argued the necessity of using violence against a system that had no compunction against relying on violence:

If violence is wrong in America, violence is wrong abroad. If it is wrong to be violent defending black women and black children and black babies and black men, then it is wrong for America to draft us and make us violent abroad in defense of her. And if it is right for America to draft us, and teach us how to be violent in defense of her, then it is right for you and me to do whatever is necessary to defend our people right here in this country.[10]

Malcolm X's religion, one of the many alternatives that challenged the traditional sway of the Christian God in the 1960s, influenced his belief in the propriety of self-defense, violent or not, for blacks seeking a revolutionary change in status in America. According to Malcolm X: "There's nothing in our book, the Koran, that teaches us to suffer peacefully. Our religion teaches us to be intelligent. Be peaceful, be courteous, obey the law, respect everyone; but if someone puts his hand on you, send him to the cemetery. That's a good religion."[11]

The urgency behind black empowerment came in part from the murderous actions taken by the white resistance to black civil rights activism: the killing of civil rights workers, the water-hosings and dog attacks unleashed by southern state and local authorities, the bombing of a Birmingham church that killed four young black girls. In the face of such terror, given the widely perceived lack of governmental action and protection, many black activists found the idea of black power and armed self-defense understandably attractive. Vocal black power leaders like Stokely Carmichael and H. Rap Brown gained visibility with their messages of violence, as did the armed and radical organ of the black revolution, the Oakland-based Black Panthers. A more disorganized attraction to violent action and change spread in urban black communities, and the long, hot summers between 1965 and 1967 gave rise to major race riots that spread death and destruction from Watts to Detroit. The extent of black resentment and frustration was clear in these years, for, even as President Johnson's "Great Society" legislation was resulting in unprecedented improvements in the legal position of blacks in America (for example, the Civil Rights and Voting Rights Acts of 1964 and 1965), violent black activism intensified.

Student activism also escalated, and student demonstrations, increasingly focused on opposition to the Vietnam War, were more and more designed to provoke official violence—in order to illustrate as blatantly as possible the brutality of the American system both at home and abroad. Student activism grew from its earlier manifestations in the SDS program for "participatory democracy" and renewed human values and in Berkeley's campus-based free speech movement (1964) to include mass demonstrations against the system and the war being waged in Vietnam. Combining with other antiwar and peace activists, but still in the vanguard of such confrontational national actions, students often put themselves in danger in order to expose the violence of the system. At the 1968 Democratic convention in Chicago and at Kent State in Ohio in 1970, youths engaging in civil disobedience to the state were horrifyingly successful in provoking the wrath of the establishment. The adoption of violence among youth and students involved the radical "Weatherman" branch of the SDS, which, not content merely to challenge the system by exposing its propensity for violence, engaged in the rhetoric and action of violent revolution. In the spring of 1970 the Weatherman faction of the SDS issued a declaration that symbolized the violent direction of dissent in the culture:

> Tens of thousands have learned that protest and marches won't do it. Revolutionary violence is the only way. Within the next fourteen days we will attack a symbol or institution of Amerikan injustice. This is the way we celebrate the example of Eldridge Cleaver and H. Rap Brown and all black revolutionaries who first inspired us by their fight behind enemy lines for the liberation of their people. Never again will they fight alone.[12]

The language and stance adopted by the most radical elements of black and youth activism had been absorbed in part from the "war of liberation" in Vietnam that the American government was opposing, and "revolutionary" language also filtered throughout the medium of rock 'n' roll, which played such a big role in the cultural revolution in these years. Antiwar and peace themes had already gained exposure in the early and mid-1960s in the folk-rock music of artists like Peter, Paul and Mary, Bob Dylan, and Joan Baez, and protest rock, like "Eve of Destruction," revealed that it too participated in the trend toward radicalism and violence. Replacing the softer acoustic tones of folk-rock were the electric chords of psychedelic or acid rock, which in form and tone alone represented the rising force and rebellion of rock 'n' roll. Jimi Hendrix's screeching electric version of the "Star Spangled Banner" (1968) at Woodstock constituted a radical subversion of an "Amerikan" symbol, and numerous rock bands supported the demonstrations and radical dissent of the young by singing their approval in songs reflective of antiwar attitudes and violent action—whether it was the Beatle's "Revolution" (1968), the Jefferson Airplane's "Volunteers" (1969), the Rolling Stones' "Street-Fighting Man" and "Sympathy for the Devil" (1969), or Edwin Starr's "War" (1970).

When this rebel rock 'n' roll provided the accompaniment to real death and violence, however, as it did at the free concert at Altamont in December 1969, it seemed evident that the directed violence of the 1960s (whether directed by the American system or by the dissenters to that system) was spilling over into the kind of directionless and nihilistic violence that called all forms of violence into question. The Altamont concert, held on December 6, 1969, was a vehicle for the Rolling Stones. Having invoked the devil in one of their featured songs, "Sympathy for the Devil," the Rolling Stones and the massive crowd at Altamont witnessed a hellish display of death and violence. The volatile outlaw motorcycle group, the Hell's Angels, had been hired as "security" for the concert, but they instead provided terror, brutally beating members of participating bands (for example, the Jefferson Airplane) and members of the audience, and finally murdering a young concert-goer.[13] Violence was taking anarchic forms in the culture and society, and events like Altamont emphasized the glut of violence in America.

The violence that affected so much of American society and culture in the 1960s and 1970s, whether it was official, oppositional, or anarchic violence, at times seemed purposeless, meaningless, and nihilistic. And Altamont was not an isolated event in the culture. A few months earlier in 1969 another act of murderous violence highlighted even more fearfully the chaotic quality of life in this America. During the hot August of 1969 the bloody corpses of the rich and famous victims of the Manson family were discovered in mansions nestled in the hills of Los Angeles. The most famous among the slaughtered included the beautiful and pregnant Hollywood starlet, Sharon Tate (married to the film director Roman Polanski), the wealthy Abigail Folger (heir to the Folger Coffee fortune), and the equally wealthy couple, Rosemary and Leno LaBianca. This mass murder was a macabre affair, staged as a violent and revolutionary ritual. Amid wild speculation about the perpetrators of these executions, it finally emerged that the murders were the work of American youths under the control of a strange pseudorevolutionary, Charles Manson. Booked into prison as "Manson, Charles M., a.k.a. Jesus Christ, God," Charles Manson and his followers presented the hallucinogenic and insane flipside of the "cool" youth scene of drugs and rebellion, and their commission of the bloody Tate-LaBianca murders shockingly revealed the rage that had built up in this age of often confused revolution and bizarre religiosity.[14]

Joan Didion, as an autobiographer and social commentator, remembered the summers of 1968 and 1969 as ones of apocalyptic tension. In her essay "The White Album" (1968–1978) she suggested the hellish atmosphere in America during these years. In addition to the Manson murders, which culminated the orgy of violence in Southern California, Didion's perceptions were also shaped by a number of other disturbing events—from Robert Kennedy's assassination in Los Angeles to the many other random murders taking place in her own neighborhood, which had been dubbed a "senseless-killing neighborhood."[15] In recalling the reaction to the Manson murders, Didion captured the extent to which Southern California and America had become conditioned to and brutalized by senseless violence:

> I imagined that my own life was simple and sweet, and sometimes it was, but there were odd things going on around town. There were rumors. There were stories. Everything was unmentionable but nothing was unimaginable. This mystical flirtation with the idea of "sin"—this sense that it was possible to go "too far," and that many people were doing it—was very much with us in Los Angeles in 1968 and 1969. A demented and seductive vortical tension was building in the community. The jitters were setting in. I recall a time when dogs barked every night and the moon was always full. On August 9, 1969, I was sitting in the shallow end of my sister-in-law's swimming pool in Beverly Hills when she received a telephone call from a friend who had just heard about the murders at Sharon Tate Polanski's house on Cielo Drive. The phone rang many times during the next hour. These early reports were garbled and contradictory. One caller would say hoods, the next would say chains. There were twenty dead, no, twelve, ten, eighteen. Black masses were imagined, and bad trips blamed. I remember all of the day's misinformation very clearly, and I also remember this, and wish I did not: *I remember that no one was surprised.*[16]

This lack of surprise stemmed from the widespread expectation of death and violence already rampant in the culture, expectations that Didion had also held. She could not look at the "house blessing" hanging in her mother-in-law's house—which included the line "And bless each door that opens wide, to stranger as to kin"—because, as she explained, "so insistently did it seem to me the kind of 'ironic' detail the reporters would seize upon, the morning the bodies were found. In my neighborhood in California we did not bless the door that opened wide to stranger as to kin. . . . Charles Manson was the stranger at Rosemary and Leno LaBianca's door."[17] When Charles Manson and his followers so shockingly validated these expectations on August 9, 1969, there was then no surprise—only devastating acknowledgment. Didion summed up the reaction: "The tension broke that day. The paranoia was fulfilled."[18] America's violence prompted the kind of dark visions of America that Didion expressed, and she presented her own personal response to this summertime of senseless killing: "an attack of vertigo and nausea."[19]

Just as the violent dissent of the 1960s had trained its sights on the highest political authorities in America, so too the cultural malaise spread to a questioning of America's highest spiritual authority: God. Even before Charles Manson "a.k.a. Jesus Christ, God" had made mass murder and any image of such a "god" seem the harbinger of a paranoid and hellish future, another account of mass murder, Truman Capote's *In Cold Blood* (1965), analyzed the stark human and spiritual implications of such sudden, irrational death for America. Using the techniques of "new journalism," the blending of the form of fiction with the facts of nonfiction, Capote conveyed in his true story of mass murder the very rationale for "new journalism"—that in the sixties reality had become stranger than fiction. Journalism, therefore, as a genre of fact, had evolved into the new medium of reality. Capote highlighted the deadly drama of everyday American life in his account of a family's murder in Kansas, a murder that shattered the ordinary lives and community security of a representative American town. Capote touches on these themes in the introduction to his account:

> Until one morning in mid-November of 1959, few Americans—in fact,
> few Kansans—had ever heard of Holcomb. . . . Drama, in the shape of
> exceptional happenings, had never stopped there. The inhabitants of the
> village, numbering two hundred and seventy, were satisfied that this should
> be so, quite content to exist inside ordinary life—to work, to hunt, to
> watch television. . . . But then, in the earliest hours of that morning in
> November, a Sunday morning, certain foreign sounds impinged on the
> normal nightly Holcomb noises. . . . At the time not a soul in sleeping
> Holcomb heard them—four shotgun blasts that, all told, ended six human
> lives. But afterward the townspeople, theretofore sufficiently unfearful of
> each other to seldom trouble to lock their doors, found fantasy re-creating
> them over and over again—those somber explosions that stimulated fires
> of mistrust in the glare of which many old neighbors viewed each other
> strangely, and as strangers.[20]

It was less the murders and less the mutual suspicions the murders cast than the murder victims themselves who caused the American everymen and women of Holcomb to question the meaning of life in this violently disrupted world. The murder victims were the four members of the prosperous and universally loved and respected Clutter family: Herbert Clutter and his wife Bonnie, their sixteen-year-old daughter Nancy, and their fifteen-year-old son Kenyon. The Clutters were devout Methodists. They had no vices and few faults of any kind. The Kansas Bureau of Investigation (KBI) later concluded that "of all the people in the world, the Clutters were the least likely to be murdered." It was this incomprehensibility about their deaths that fed the sense of despair and fear in

Holcomb.[21] As one townswoman put it: "But who hated the Clutters? I never heard a word against them; they were about as popular as a family can be, and if something like this could happen to *them,* then who's safe I ask you?"[22]

The meaninglessness of it all tortured the residents of Holcomb and contributed to the desiccation of the town's faith and spirit. When neighbors gathered to clean the bloodied rooms of the Clutter farmhouse and to burn the blood-soaked furniture, they pondered this senseless destruction. A longtime friend of Herb Clutter's was particularly distressed because of all that Herb had accomplished: "Everything Herb had, he earned—with the help of God. He was a modest man but a proud man, as he had a right to be. He raised a fine family. He made something of his life." The difficulty, of course, came from trying to reconcile Herb's life with his death, and this difficulty Capote expressed: "But that life, and what he'd made of it—how could it happen. . . . How was it possible that such effort, such plain virtue, could overnight be reduced to this—smoke [from the burning detritus of the Clutter home], thinning as it rose and was received by the big, annihilating sky?"[23] A Holcomb schoolteacher summed up the dispiriting impact of the Clutter deaths:

> "Feeling wouldn't run half so high if this had happened to anyone *except* the Clutters. Anyone *less* admired. Prosperous. Secure. But that family represented everything people hereabouts really value and respect, and that such a thing could happen to them—well, it's like being told there is no God. It makes life seem pointless. I don't think people are so frightened as they are deeply depressed."[24]

These feelings of godlessness and depression did not dissipate when the murderers were apprehended; in fact, the perceptions of life's senselessness and disorder escalated. The murderers were not local people but strangers, ex-convicts who mistakenly believed (from the information given to them by a onetime prison cellmate who had worked for the Clutters) that Mr. Clutter kept large amounts of cash at the farmhouse. The Clutters had been killed for no reason, by people they did not know. The murderers had netted a profit of between forty and fifty dollars. The KBI agent in charge of the case concluded that "the crime was a psychological accident, virtually an impersonal act; the victims might as well have been killed by lightning. Except for one thing: they had experienced prolonged terror, they had suffered."[25] While it was discomfiting to consider the kind of "prolonged terror" of waiting to die that the Clutters had suffered and that everyone in this age of violence potentially faced, it was no less discomfiting to try to understand the murderous brutality behind such terror and death.

In Cold Blood focused as much on the murderers as on the victims. The existence of cold-blooded killers like Dick Hickock and Perry Smith compounded the sense of violent disorder in human relations and in the human conscience. While the Clutter crimes resulted from the volatile interaction between Hickock and Smith, it was Perry Smith who shotgunned or knifed each Clutter to death. His discussions of the murders, during the time of his trial and his incarceration on death row and up to the time of his execution, disclosed the awful sort of human distancing that America produced at its extreme. Perry Smith noted about Herb Clutter: "I didn't want to harm the man. I thought he was a very nice gentleman. Soft-spoken. I thought so right up to the moment I cut his throat." Smith displayed the same human and emotional dislocation when he described how he and Hickock felt after the murders had taken place: "I think we both felt very high. I did. Very high, and very relieved at the same time. Couldn't stop laughing, neither one of us; suddenly it all seemed very funny—I don't know why, it just did. But the gun was dripping blood, and my clothes were stained; there was even blood in my hair."[26]

Smith's chilling alienation from human beings was particularly disturbing because of its social roots in his past and in the character of society as a whole. He felt he had been mistreated all his life and he thought perhaps this mistreatment had influenced his killing of the Clutters: "They [the Clutters] never hurt me. Like other people [did]. Like people have all my life. Maybe it's just that the Clutters were the ones who had to pay for it." He was "devoid of conscience and compassion" and put his coldness about killing into the social context of America—the America that sanctified killing:

"Soldiers don't lose much sleep. They murder, and get medals for doing it. The good people of Kansas want to murder me—and some hangman will be glad to get the work. It's easy to kill—a lot easier than passing a bad check. Just remember: I only knew the Clutters maybe an hour. If I'd really known them, I guess I'd feel different. . . . But the way it was, it was like picking off targets in a shooting gallery."[27]

In America in the 1960s and early 1970s killing did seem inhumanly easy, as the frequency of mass murders suggested. A violent American society provided a fertile milieu for the life choices made by Perry Smith and Dick Hickock and their like, for they were not lonely or isolated perpetrators of this American-bred violence. On the eve of Smith and Hickock's murder trial, a local newspaper placed the trial in disturbing perspective in its editorial:

Some may think the eyes of the entire nation are on Garden City [the Kansas town where the trial was being held] during this sensational murder trial. But they are not. Even a hundred miles west of here in Colorado few persons are even acquainted with the case—other than just remembering some members of a prominent family were slain. This is a sad commentary on the state of crime in our nation. Since the four members of the Clutter family were killed last fall, several other such multiple murders have occurred in various parts of the country. Just during the few days leading up to this trial at least three mass murder cases broke into the headlines. As a result, this crime and trial are just one of many such cases people have read about and forgotten.[28]

Also confirming the increasing frequency of mass murder was the presence of the many companions of Smith and Hickock on death row in the Kansas State Penitentiary. One of their fellow death-row inmates had killed his parents with excessive zeal (his father was shot seventeen times), and another pair of young men had embarked on a "cross-country murder spree" because they both believed "the world was hateful, and everybody in it would be better off dead." One of these killers explained his world view in more detail, expressing the nihilism that constituted a growing threat in America: "It's a rotten world. . . . There's no answer to it but meanness. That's all anybody understands—meanness. Burn down the man's barn—he'll understand that. Poison his dog. Kill him."[29] While all these killers on the Kansas State Penitentiary's death row died by hanging, as Dick Hickock and Perry Smith did in April 1965, their executions did not snuff out violence in America. Violence and death escalated throughout the 1960s, and *In Cold Blood* had helped to explain the human and spiritual impact of such death and violence: it was like being told there is no God.

While less certain in its pronouncement of God's disappearance, *Time* magazine posed the question on the cover of its April 8, 1966, issue which transmitted most effectively the spiritual crisis overtaking America: "Is God Dead?"[30] Such an expression of spiritual doubt—extending to a questioning of God's very existence—was a potent symbol of the spiritual sickness that infected and continued to infect an America afflicted with the violent legacies of the atomic age and its corrupted spiritual and temporal authorities. Just as *In Cold Blood* presented the cultural context for understanding America's proliferating violence and the resulting sensibility of life's pointlessness, *Time*'s cover story suggested the cultural perimeters for the questioning of authority in the 1960s. They were elastic and near boundless perimeters that revealed the confusion of

American spirituality and the robustness of American skepticism about traditional faiths and authorities.

Time opened its article on God's probable demise by discussing the extent of the contemporary attack against God:

> Is God dead? The three words represent a summons to reflect on the meaning of existence. No longer is the question the taunting jest of skeptics for whom unbelief is the test of wisdom and for whom Nietzsche is the prophet who gave the right answer a century ago. Even within Christianity . . . a small band of radical theologians has seriously argued that the churches must accept the fact of God's death, and get along without him.[31]

The magazine explained this anomaly of "Christian atheists" by contrasting the beliefs of atheist theologians (represented by Thomas Altizer, William Hamilton, and Paul Van Buren) with those of Nietzsche. According to *Time*, "Nietzsche's thesis was that striving, self-centered man had killed God, and that settled that. The current death-of-God group believes that God is indeed absolutely dead, but proposes to carry on and write a theology without *theos*, without God."[32] While Christian theologians who rejected *theos* and pronounced the death of God served as the most extreme example of modern atheism and the modern challenge to traditional faiths, *Time* analyzed the profusion of "atheists" in modern life.

"Existential" atheists constituted just one brand of disbelief in modern society, and this group tended to be composed of writers. *Time* referred to Samuel Beckett (*Waiting for Godot*), whose "antiheroes" believed "that waiting for God is futile since life is without meaning," and the magazine also quoted French writer Simone de Beauvoir on her lack of faith: "It was easier for me to think of a world without a creator than of a creator loaded with all the contradictions of the world." The article focused on "another variety of unbelief" pointed out by a Jesuit theologian, "the atheism of distraction," which described "people who are just 'too damn busy' to worry about God at all." The last group of atheists *Time* examined were the "practical atheists," and it was this group that demonstrated the breadth of the spiritual malaise in modern America. Bristling against the uplifting statistic collected by pollster Lou Harris that 97 percent of all Americans believed in God was the less reassuring figure, also culled by Harris, that of these 97 percent, only 27 percent considered themselves truly or deeply religious.[33]

This low rate of genuine religiosity confirmed the suspicions of many clergymen "that all too many pews are filled on Sunday with practical atheists—disguised nonbelievers who behave during the rest of the week as if God did not exist." An absence of faith was attributed especially to the disillusioned young of America, as *Time* noted: "Particularly among the young, there is an acute feeling that the churches on Sunday are preaching the existence of a God who is nowhere visible in their daily lives." And, "speaking for a generation of young Roman Catholics for whom the dogmas of the church have lost much of their power," philosopher Michael Novak gave voice to an image of God that revealed the spiritual void of that concept: "I do not understand God, nor the way in which he works. If, occasionally, I raise my heart in prayer, it is to no God I can see, or hear, or feel. It is to a God in as cold and obscure a polar night as any nonbeliever has known."[34]

There were a number of reasons for the spread of atheism, in all its guises, and for the decline of true faith and religiosity, but perhaps the best reason was inadvertently forwarded in an obituary of God that Methodist students published to satirize the rising God-is-dead theology. According to these students, "God, creator of the universe, principal deity of the world's Jews, ultimate reality of Christians, and most eminent of all divinities, died late yesterday during major surgery undertaken to correct a massive diminishing influence."[35] It was in fact the diminishing influence of God that accounted for the rising varieties of atheism, as was evident in the images presented of God's irrelevance in the modern world. God had lost the power to influence, to explain, to inspire, or to comfort.

Time traced God's diminishing influence to two related features of modern life. The first involved the long-term changes associated with modernism: "Secularization, science, urbanization—all have made it comparatively easy for the modern man to ask where God is, and hard for the man of faith to give a convincing answer, even to himself."[36] Science in particular made inroads against mystical and metaphysical faiths by upholding the scientific method of direct observation, experimentation, and verification as the authoritative means to knowledge. The result was that "slowly but surely, it dawned on men that they did not need God to explain, govern or justify certain areas of life."[37] No longer needing God as a "prime mover" in the universe and no longer needing God as the source of knowledge, modern society also no longer considered God and His powers of retribution sufficient cause for faith and belief. God had lost the power to coerce faith and belief—and this perhaps was the definitive contribution of events in the most recent past, events also made possible by the rise of scientific prowess and scientific values.

As *Time* pointed out, "Faith is something of an irrational leap in the dark, a gift of God."[38] In the increasingly distant past, if all other means failed, the church compelled men and women to face that leap, to accept that gift: men and women were threatened with "everlasting punishment in hell" if they did not serve God. The fear behind this compulsion was gone, however, and the article looked to the recent historical past for the explanation of this change: "Unlike in earlier centuries, there is no way for churches to threaten or compel men to face that leap; after Dachau's mass sadism and Hiroshima's instant death, there were all too many real possibilities of hell on earth."[39] The scientific and technological advances that had rendered God irrelevant on a rational level, then, had also contributed to rendering God irrelevant on a spiritual level. The mass, instant death made possible by the rationalized machinery of Nazi death camps and the atomic bomb had made hell a part of everyday life and everyday memory, and the spiritual solace and terrifying authority of God dissipated in the shadow of the inhuman horrors of World War II's hells on earth: Dachau and Hiroshima.

Just a few months after the appearance of the *Time* magazine issue on God, another pronouncement on the declining prestige of traditional spiritual authorities stunned America. In the summer of 1966 a comment made by John Lennon of the Beatles received wide exposure in America. Reflecting on the charged atmosphere of spiritual change and the rebel atmosphere that the Beatles and their music had helped to shape and create, Lennon remarked, "Christianity will go. It will vanish and shrink. I needn't argue about that, I'm right and will be proved right. We're more popular than Jesus Christ right now."[40] The furor raised by Lennon's comments indicated that not all Americans were willing to forgo God, Jesus, and Christianity ("Beatles record bonfires" were held throughout the nation, denunciations of Lennon were made, and Lennon was forced to apologize).[41] Lennon's comments, however, as well as the *Time* article indicated that while traditional spiritual authorities were being questioned, such questioning did not necessarily result in a declaration of no faith or in a rejection of all faiths and spirituality.

Spiritual authorities and beliefs were being redefined and alternatives were being found—whether it was the alternative of the Beatles or the alternative of reformed or nontraditional forms of religion, including Christianity. The Christian atheists examined in the *Time* article did not abandon all theology; they sought a new theology without *theos*. Likewise, *Time* had also pointed to the different forms of spiritual solace and to the different forms of Christianity that maintained attractiveness, including psychiatry, Zen, drugs, and "new Christianity."[42] In describing the new Christianity *Time* showed how spiritual regeneration could emerge from spiritual malaise and doubt and how the reformation of religion stemmed from the cultural revolution occurring in these years: "In this new Christianity, the watchword is witness: Protestant faith now means not intellectual acceptance of an ancient confession, but open commitment—perhaps best symbolized in the U.S. by the civil rights movement—to eradicate the evil and inequality that beset the world."[43] God and religion had been an effective force of protest during the civil defense debate in the early sixties, and this type of redefined and activist spirituality continued to have power even in the years that witnessed the "death" of God. Questions about God, Jesus, and Christianity demonstrated cultural malaise and the growing disillusion with outmoded authorities, but these questions also illustrated the continuing search for new theologies, new spiritual authorities, and new moral values—all of which were designed to eradicate evil and to limit the "all too many real possibilities of hell on earth."

Another article published in the following year made the same connections for secular society and secular authorities. In August 1967 Senator J. W. Fulbright wrote an article for the *New York Times Magazine* called "The Great Society Is a Sick Society" in which he extended the analysis of America's malaise—and potential regeneration—to the social and political realm. The disillusioned senator not only saw too many real hells on earth but he also saw America's sickness stemming from the recent past—from the World War II era of death camps and atomic bombs. Fulbright went on to describe how his vision of "hell" derived from the two wars being fought in the Great Society and the debilitating conflict arising from them:

> Standing in the smoke and rubble of Detroit [after the 1967 riot], a Negro veteran said: "I just got back from Vietnam a few months ago, but you know, I think the war is here." There are in fact two wars going on. One is the war of power politics which our soldiers are fighting in the jungles of Southeast Asia. The other is a war for America's soul which is being fought in the streets of Newark and Detroit and in the halls of Congress, in churches and protest meetings and on college campuses, and in the hearts and minds of silent Americans from Maine to Hawaii. . . . The connection between Vietnam and Detroit is in their conflicting and incompatible demands upon traditional American values. The one demands they be set aside, the other that they be fulfilled. The one demands the acceptance by America of an imperial role in the world, or of what our policymakers like to call the "responsibilities of power," or of what I have called the "arrogance of power." The other demands freedom and social justice at home, an end to poverty, the fulfillment of our flawed democracy and an effort to create a role for ourselves in the world which is compatible with our traditional values.[44]

In opposition to the cultural trend of rejecting tradition, Fulbright argued for a fulfillment of America's traditions. But the traditions and ideals Fulbright wanted America to uphold and to live up to were not the cold war traditions being challenged by the rebel culture of the 1960s. Fulbright expressed disdain for those contemporary traditions that issued from World War II and the cold war, and his disdain stemmed from the recognition that it was in large part America's "arrogance of power" that was fomenting these dual and connected wars in America and preventing America from consecrating its democratic traditions and ideals. Contrary to the claims of the Johnson administration that America could afford "both Vietnam and the Great Society," Fulbright demonstrated the incompatibility of fighting an inhuman war abroad and attempting to improve human life at home: "Anxiety about war does not breed compassion for one's neighbors nor do constant reminders about the cheapness of life abroad strengthen our faith in its sanctity at home. In these ways the war in Vietnam is poisoning and brutalizing our domestic life. . . . The Great Society has become a sick society."[45]

The sickness spreading throughout America as a result of Vietnam had its origins in the world role adopted by America at the end of World War II, an imperial role that ultimately explained America's morally troubling predicament in Vietnam and the growing "war" at home against America's international and domestic violations of its democratic and egalitarian faiths. Because of choices made at the time of World War II, according to Fulbright,

> we are, almost, the world's self-appointed policeman; we are, almost, the world defender of the status quo. We are well on our way to becoming a traditional great power—an imperial nation, if you will—engaged in the exercise of power for its own sake, exercising it to the limit of our capacity and beyond, filling every vacuum and extending the American "presence" to the farthest reaches of the earth. And, as with the great empires of the past, as the power grows, it is becoming an end in itself, separated except by ritual incantation from its initial motives, governed, it would seem, by its own mystique, power without philosophy or purpose.[46]

Fulbright proposed that America look back to "old values," to "the idea, which goes back to the American Revolution, that maybe—just maybe—we can set an example of democracy and human dignity for the world." Fulbright believed that this goal of democracy and human dignity was the idea that was fueling the war at home, and he applauded the young and often radical critics of America for their rejection of America's new imperial tradition and for their adherence to the more humanist principles of America's past. He noted how and why these critics rebelled against the immoral power politics of the contemporary American system:

> They think that the methods of the past have been tried and found wanting, and two world wars attest powerfully to their belief. Most of all, they think that, in this first era of human history in which man has acquired weapons which threaten his entire species with destruction, safety and prudence and realism require us to change the rules of a dangerous and discredited game, to try as we have never tried before to civilize and humanize international relations, not only for the sake of civilization and humanity but for the sake of survival.[47]

Fulbright understood the urgency behind the cultural dissent on the home front because the image of America in the world had come perilously close to an inversion of its ideal image: "Both in our foreign affairs and in our domestic life we convey an image of violence. . . . America, which only a few years ago seemed to the world to be a model of democracy and social justice, has become a symbol of violence and undisciplined power."[48] Fulbright therefore applauded the rise of controversy and dissent in America, for he considered such rebellion a sign of health in an otherwise weakening society. About the "profound controversy" engulfing America, Fulbright noted: "This in a way is something to be proud of. We have sickened but not succumbed, and just as a healthy body fights disease, we are fighting the alien concept [imperialism] which is being thrust on us, not by history but by our policymakers in the Department of State and the Pentagon."[49] Fulbright credited the "remarkable younger generation" in America for leading this battle for health in America, and he thereafter discussed, as had the "Is God Dead?" article in *Time,* how hope and regeneration could emerge from an otherwise dispiriting recognition of society's illness.[50]

Fulbright despaired about the death and violence of America's two wars and about the "process of deterioration" these wars had instigated in American society. He saw the Vietnam War, though, as the key to the moral and social disintegration: "An unnecessary and immoral war deserves in its own right to be liquidated; when its effect in addition is the aggravation of grave problems and the corrosion of values in our own society, its liquidation is doubly imperative. Our country is being weakened by a grotesque inversion of priorities."[51] Coming forth to correct this inversion of priorities and morality was the rebellion of the young: "When the country sickens for lack of moral leadership, a most remarkable younger generation has taken up the standard of American idealism."[52] Fulbright defended the often radical actions taken by the young ("they are doing it [radical activism] in defense of traditional values and in protest against the radical departure from those values embodied in the idea of an imperial destiny for America"), and he expressed his admiration for "the spirit of this regenerative generation":

> The focus of their protest is the war in Vietnam, and the measure of their integrity is the fortitude with which they refuse to be deceived about it. By striking contrast with the young Germans, who accepted the Nazi evil because the values of their society had disintegrated and they had no moral frame of reference, these young Americans are demonstrating the vitality of American values. They are demonstrating that, while their country is capable of acting falsely to itself, it cannot do so without internal disruption, without calling forth the regenerative counterforce of protest from Americans who are willing to act in defense of the principles they were brought up to believe in.[53]

While Fulbright placed his faith in this "regenerative" generation, he nonetheless envisioned "the false and dangerous dream of an imperial destiny" as giving quite a battle for the "soul" of America. In his conclusion to "The Great Society Is a Sick Society," he contrasted two potential futures for America:

> It may be that the [imperial] challenge will succeed, that America will succumb to becoming a traditional empire and will reign for a time over what must surely be a moral if not a physical wasteland, and then, like the great empires of the past, will decline or fall. Or it may be that the effort to create so grotesque an anachronism will go up in flames of nuclear holocaust. But if I had to bet my money on what is going to happen, I would bet on this younger generation—this generation of young men and women who reject the inhumanity of war in a poor and distant land, who reject the poverty and sham in their own country, who are telling their elders what their elders ought to have known—that the price of empire is America's soul and that the price is too high.[54]

Always remaining a possible scenario for the tomorrows of America in this age of nihilism and violence were the flames of nuclear holocaust. But even in this era of malaise poised on the "eve of destruction," the hope for a regenerative change in the direction of the American system persisted.

While Fulbright saw the regenerative possibilities of the radical, often violent, actions of rebellious youth in America, the issue of violence in America remained at the center of controversy. The proliferation of violence on all levels of American life undoubtedly accounted for such confusion and for the understandable difficulty in distinguishing illegitimate from legitimate uses of violence. With the Vietnam War, violent protest demonstrations, riots, assassinations, and anarchic acts of mass murder, violence seemed inescapable, and no element of the culture seemed untouched by the excesses of these years. Reflective of this pervasiveness was the trend in filmmaking toward the use of brutal and realistic violence—a trend inspired to a great extent by *Bonnie and Clyde* (1967) but by no means limited to that film, which was followed by such films as *Easy Rider* (1969), *Butch Cassidy and the Sundance Kid* (1969), *Dirty Harry* (1971), and *The Godfather* (1972). It was the controversy surrounding *Bonnie and Clyde,* however, that exposed the extent to which violence had become a disruptive issue in America, and it was the evaluation of violence in *Bonnie and Clyde* that suggested how the culture reconciled deadly violence with the purposes of regeneration and life.[55]

On the surface *Bonnie and Clyde* was a rather simple tale of the romance and the crime spree of the semimythical but historical figures of Bonnie Parker and Clyde Barrow, two relatively small-time criminals who had nonetheless captured the antiheroic imagination of depression-era America. The re-created Bonnie Parker and Clyde Barrow of the 1960s also captured the imagination of America, not just for their acts against the symbols of the establishment (banks, law enforcement officers, and social mores) but also for their nihilistic joie de vivre: they knew their antisocial acts would result in death, yet they persisted in the face of this knowledge. The "blues" often overtook Bonnie as a sense of doom overwhelmed her. The poetry she wrote reflected her awareness of the ephemerality of their lives: "Someday they'll go down together; / They'll bury them side by side; / To few it'll be grief— / To the law a relief— / But it's death for Bonnie and Clyde."[56] The attitudes of Bonnie and Clyde in the film seemed attuned to an age of nihilistic malaise, as did the violence they inflicted and suffered.

The portrayal of violence, however, not the characters of Bonnie and Clyde per se, caused the uproar about the film. The violence appeared particularly brutal because it gradually grew in intensity and because it was consistently shown graphically—from Clyde's having to shoot a man in the face to the macabre dance of death that ended the film, with Bonnie and Clyde so riddled by the lawmen's barrage of bullets that their bloodied bodies jump from the force of the shots. The controversy the film aroused was evident in the battle waged by film critics, and once again the *New York Times*'s reviewer Bosley Crowther was in the vanguard of those attacking the film. He called *Bonnie and Clyde* "another indulgence of a restless and reckless taste and an embarrassing addition to the excess of violence on the screen"; he condemned its style as "wild jazzy farce melodrama."[57] Crowther so vehemently attacked the film, its subject, and its violence that other reviewers, like Andrew Sarris of the *Village Voice,* accused him of launching a "crusade" against the film, of pandering to the "lurking forces of censorship and repression" with his "inflammatory diatribes."[58]

Pauline Kael, film reviewer for the *New Yorker,* examined the controversial and troubling aspects of the film in a more dispassionate way, but she indicated in the first line of her review the confusion and concern raised by *Bonnie and Clyde:* "How do you make a good movie in this country without being jumped on?" Kael devoted a good bit of her review to the issue causing the controversy—violence—and she discussed both the reasons why it generated such a controversy and the reasons why such violence was, despite the protests, appropriate. Part of the "problem" with the violence derived from the alternating tone of the film itself. The film begins in a rather seriocomic fashion, showing a bumbling and laughable but attractive and rather innocent pair of criminals. Abruptly, however, once the couple engages in exchanges of gunfire and killing, the tone grows serious. Yet as the violence escalates, the couple never completely loses the aura of innocence, and this is one of the aspects of the film's violence that offended some, or so Kael suggested: "In a sense, it is the absence of sadism—it is the violence without sadism—that throws the audience off balance at *Bonnie and Clyde.* The brutality that comes out of this innocence is far more shocking than the calculated brutalities of mean killers."[59]

Brutalities committed by supposed "innocents" threw Americans off balance in the theater and in reality as well, as students and young soldiers in Vietnam proved their innocent capacity for violence. Ultimately the filmed reflection of reality in *Bonnie and Clyde* provided the best justification for its use of graphic violence. Having discussed other disquieting aspects of the film (for example, its sexual subtheme about Clyde's impotence), Kael addressed the subject of violence and its appropriateness:

> But people also feel uncomfortable about the violence, and here I think they're wrong. That is to say, they *should* feel uncomfortable, but this isn't an argument *against* the movie. Only a few years ago, a good director would have suggested the violence obliquely, with reaction shots. . . . In many ways, this method is more effective; we feel the violence more because so much is left to our imaginations. But the whole point of *Bonnie and Clyde* is to rub our noses in it, to make us pay our dues for laughing [in the earlier segments]. The dirty reality of death—not suggestions but blood and holes—is necessary. . . . Suddenly, in the last few years, our view of the

world has gone beyond "good taste." Tasteful suggestions of violence would at this point be a more grotesque form of comedy than *Bonnie and Clyde* attempts. *Bonnie and Clyde* needs violence; violence is its meaning.[60]

While critics of the film denounced its "glamorization" of violence and the "danger to public morality" it thereby posed, Kael stressed the film's extreme contrasts—its brutality and innocence, its laughter and its death—as the basis for the disturbance caused by the film.[61] In an age of extremes, everything, including life, had become devalued—a clear reflection of the nihilism overspreading America. Kael saw the development of black humor in film as a shaping force in these nihilistic cultural expectations and reactions, and it was in opposition to this cultural inclination to laugh at death that *Bonnie and Clyde* operated. In a long passage Kael credited *Dr. Strangelove* with having inculcated the counter-cultural values that *Bonnie and Clyde* modified—by teaching that there were limits to the ability to laugh at death:

> Movie audiences have been getting a steady diet of "black" comedy since 1964 and *Dr. Strangelove, Or: How I Learned to Stop Worrying and Love the Bomb.* . . . *Dr. Strangelove* opened a new movie era. It ridiculed *everything* and *everybody* it showed, but concealed its own liberal pieties, thus protecting itself from ridicule. . . . *Dr. Strangelove* was clearly intended as a cautionary movie; it meant to jolt us awake to the dangers of the bomb by showing us the insanity of the course we were pursuing. But artists' warnings about war and the dangers of total annihilation never tell us how we are supposed to regain control, and *Dr. Strangelove,* chortling over madness, did not indicate any possibilities for sanity. It was experienced not as satire but as a confirmation of fears. Total laughter carried the day. A new generation enjoyed seeing the world as insane; they *literally* learned to stop worrying and love the bomb. Conceptually, we had already been living with the bomb; now the mass audience of the movies—which is the youth of America—grasped the idea that the threat of extinction can be used to devalue everything, to turn it all into a joke. And the members of this audience do love the bomb; they love feeling that the worst has happened and the irrational are the sane, because there is the bomb as proof that the rational are insane. . . . It is not war that has been laughed to death but the possibility of sane action. . . . This is the context in which *Bonnie and Clyde,* an entertaining movie that has some feeling in it, upsets people. . . . Maybe it's because *Bonnie and Clyde,* by making us care about the robber lovers, has put the sting back into death.[62]

Beginning in laughter at the "innocent" escapades of Bonnie and Clyde and ending in their grotesquely violent deaths, *Bonnie and Clyde* stopped the laughter at death and halted the devaluation of life. The violence in *Bonnie and Clyde* and the violence throughout American society therefore contained a kernel of regeneration: it increased the perceived value of life and promoted the desire to protect it. While Pauline Kael distinguished between *Bonnie and Clyde*'s redemptive limits on laughter and *Dr. Strangelove*'s rather nihilistic lack of such limits, it was nonetheless the case that both films remained central to the understanding of the extremism and violence of this era and to the understanding of the regeneration emergent from such nihilistic violence. In *Dr. Strangelove* it was the threat of extinction (not the film itself) that devalued life, and there were clear limits, if unrecognized by Kael, to the laughter in *Dr. Strangelove*— the laughter and satire were essentially limited to the military, political, and scientific authorities responsible for that threat. The possibility of sane, rational action by those in positions in power was satirized because their "rational" and "sane" actions led to apocalypse. It is in fact this same recognition that limits the laughter in *Bonnie and Clyde* as well, and it is the "system" that murders Bonnie and Clyde and puts "the sting back into death."

The ending of *Bonnie and Clyde* is in its own way every bit as apocalyptic as the ending of *Dr. Strangelove,* and it is the brutal violence of the annihilation of Bonnie and Clyde by the forces of law and authority which rescues the antiheroic and "innocent" reputations of Bonnie and Clyde. This duo had engaged in ugly and unredeemable acts of violence, but in the end the law's horrifying slaughter of the two completely overshadowed any of those violent deeds.[63] In both *Bonnie and Clyde* and *Dr. Strangelove* the true locus of violence was the American system of law and authority. It was this recognition of the system's danger, of its annihilating power and violence, which accounted for the extremism in the cultural rebellion of the sixties and early seventies. The threat of extinction did indeed devalue everything—including the proscriptions against excessive violence and excessive laughter. At least in the culture of dissent such excesses of violence and laughter were directed at America's corrupt and deadly cold war system of power.

If young Americans had learned to "love" the bomb, as Kael suggested, it was because the bomb—largely through such rebellious statements as *Dr. Strangelove*'s—had become a clear and trenchant symbol for the insanity and the peril of America's system. Laughing fearlessly at the system and its figures of authority and learning to oppose that system and its authorities, often through violent action, were just two possibilities for "sane action" perceived during the cultural rebellion of the 1960s. *Dr. Strangelove* had suggested the impossibility of sane action under America's current system; by default the only possibility of sane action involved challenging that system and changing its apocalyptic direction.

Violence in America in the 1960s and early 1970s produced a debilitating malaise and sense of spiritual crisis in parts of the culture, but the spread of violence also instigated and contributed to the concurrent cultural rebelliousness and regeneration. Violence often took horrific form in these years, whether in the Manson murders or in Vietnam, but it was increasingly acknowledged that the American establishment was responsible for creating and encouraging this American nightmare. The indiscriminate nature of official American violence affected the culture as a whole and seemingly sanctified all uses of violence, however indiscriminate. While the culture of dissent's use of violence was problematic, if only because it conflicted with its proclaimed peaceful goals and became associated with rash and anarchic uses of violence, the recourse to violence was reconciled to the purposes of life and regeneration because of its rationale—to put the meaning back into death and the sacredness back into life, to end violence, and to change the deadly and inhuman direction of the American system of power.

The violence exercised by the culture of dissent had declared limits and purposes. Malcolm X, for example, succinctly defined the limits and purposes of violence when he claimed, "I'm not for wanton violence, I'm for justice." He explained the clear intent of his rebellious violence: "I *am* for violence if nonviolence means we continue postponing a solution to the American black man's problem—just to *avoid* violence. I don't go for non-violence if it also means a delayed solution. To me a delayed solution is a non-solution. Or I'll say it another way. If it must take violence to get the black man his human rights in this country, I'm *for* violence."[64] Violence was discriminate in Malcolm X's view, limited to forcing a solution to black discrimination in America and justified by its purpose of gaining black human rights. The youth and student groups relying on violence also so delimited their uses of violence by their goal: peace and the end of war. In 1969 a faction of the SDS proclaimed this goal under an illustration picturing the new brand of youthful antiheroes— urban guerrillas: "We are advocates of the abolition of war, we do not want war; but war can only be abolished through war, and in order to get rid of the gun it is necessary to take up the gun."[65]

However potentially misguided or misapplied, the rebel culture's advocation of violence found redemption in its limits and its purposes, and its goals of peace and human rights legitimately belonged to what J. W. Fulbright had termed "the regenerative counterforce of protest" against a violent system.

The recourse to violence seemed understandable and even necessary given the government's immersion in violence, and in the end the dissenting culture's use of violence succeeded like nothing else in exposing the government's dependence on violence.[66]

The historian Richard Hofstadter, in his evaluation of American violence, "Reflections on Violence in the United States" (1970), underscored this cultural recognition of the official spawning of an atmosphere of violence:

> Even in our day, I think it should be emphasized, the growing acceptance of violence has been unwittingly fostered from the top of society. The model for violence, which has rapidly eroded the effectiveness of appeals to non-violent procedures, has been the hideous and gratuitous official violence in Vietnam. And after having created and made heroes of such a special tactical force as the Green Berets, we should not be altogether surprised to find the Black Panthers wearing *their* berets and practicing close-order drill. It may be childishly irrelevant to cite the example of Vietnam as an answer to every reproach for domestic acts of force or violence, but there is in that answer a point of psychological importance that we should not overlook: now, as always, the primary precedent and the primary rationale for violence comes from the established order itself. Violence is, so to speak, an official reality.[67]

Beyond confirming the American government's role in fostering violence, Hofstadter also pointed out how the government's reliance on open violence contributed to weakening the legitimacy of the government. He reasoned that "no society exists without using force or violence and without devising sanctions for violence which are used to uphold just wars and necessary police actions." Yet he also signaled the trouble that came from excessive violence: "But the frequency and the manner in which official violence is used is of signal importance to the legitimation of the civic order. Any liberal democratic state is in danger of wearing away its legitimacy if it repeatedly uses violence at home or abroad when the necessity of that violence is wholly unpersuasive to a substantial number of its people."[68] The rising violence among dissenters in America, which worked to provoke and thus publicly disclose more official violence, illustrated the decreasing persuasiveness of the American establishment and its system of violence. While the tendency toward violence in the rebellious culture had contributed to the nihilistic visions of life in America, the same violence also carried within it a regenerative result: it exposed the illegitimate violence of the system and thereby created an atmosphere conducive to challenging violent authority and to creating more human and peaceful alternatives to that authority.

The disturbing edge of extremism and violence in the cultural dissent of these years, with its renewing and cathartic quality, gave added force to the contrasting form of radical cultural rebellion that also characterized the sixties and early seventies: the search for a new set of human and moral values and for a new myth of life. The cultural revolution in human and moral values offered peaceful and humanist alternatives to the nightmarishly violent values of the American system, and the rebellious culture's use of violence—however limited and purposefully directed—confirmed the necessity of this spiritual and moral rebirth, if only by demonstrating the extent to which violence had become a part of everyday life. Despite the apparent incongruity of these two forms of cultural protest, one stressing peace and the other violence, these two elements of dissent merged to complete America's awakening on the eve of destruction. Less contradictory than complementary, violent and peaceful expressions of protest coalesced to demand the overthrow of the ruling spiritual and political authorities in America.

If the awakened apocalyptic imagination in the America of excessive violence created visions of an America where "someone must've dropped the bomb, pushed the button," the equally awakened peaceful imagination of the rebellious culture constructed competing visions of harmony, respect, and peace. In *In Cold Blood* Truman Capote had suggested the fearful workings of the imagination in the sixties; as he noted, "Imagination, of course, can open any door—turn the key and let terror walk right in."[69] Imagination in the sixties and early seventies, however, also let in hope. John Lennon's ballad of peace, "Imagine" (1971), dreamed of a world without terror:

> imagine there's no heaven
> it's easy if you try
> no hell below us
> above us only sky
> imagine all the people
> living for today . . .
> imagine there's no countries
> it isn't hard to do
> nothing to kill or die for
> and no religion too
> imagine all the people
> living life in peace . . .

imagine no possessions
i wonder if you can
no need for greed or hunger a brotherhood of man
sharing all the world . . .
you may say i'm a dreamer
but i'm not the only one
i hope someday you'll join us
and the world will be as one[70]

The conflicting voices of dreamers and doomsayers were heard throughout the 1960s and 1970s, and these contrasting visions of American dreams and
American nightmares coalesced in the culture to redefine the perceptions of
America's future. The terror unleashed by the culture's apocalyptic imagination
was countered and limited by the human hope expressed in its peaceful imagination. In their contrasting visions of terror and peace, both Truman Capote
and John Lennon had made references to the sky, from the "big, annihilating
sky" of *In Cold Blood* to the "above us only sky" of "Imagine." This attention
to the sky, the open spaces above the earth, became a popular theme in the cultural imagination of these years, particularly as a means for envisioning America's future. From John Glenn's 1962 manned orbital flight around the earth to
the 1969 moon landing, space had served as a new frontier for America, and
whether in reality or imagination—as in Stanley Kubrick's *2001: A Space Odyssey* (1968)—space provided a setting for appreciating the awe-inspiring possibilities of humanity and the universe. But in the culture of the sixties and early
seventies space also became the imagined locale for the working out of two
radically different futures for America, two futures that nonetheless spoke to
the ultimate compatibility of the dissenting culture's nightmares and dreams.

The science fiction film *Planet of the Apes* (1968) envisioned a somber future
for Americans, whether in space or on earth. Astronauts traveling in both space
and time find themselves marooned in the far distant future on a planet as
bizarre as any they could have ever imagined. They experience the future as
pure horror and incomprehensibility as they discover the nature of life on this
strange planet: talking and thinking apes are in control while human beings are
mute, animalistic creatures. Evolution has been completely turned on its head
on "the planet of the apes," and Taylor, the one astronaut who survives his
ordeal with this ape society, decides to set out on horseback to explore this
planet and learn how and why apes evolved from men in this world. Not long
into his journey he discovers along the uninhabited seacoast the twisted remnants of the Statue of Liberty, and the sickening meaning of his discovery over-

whelms him. He now recognizes this mutant planet as his own earth forever altered and out of balance as a result of vast nuclear devastation. He screams in helpless anguish, "Damn you all to hell!"—now perfectly comprehending the ape society's dictums against man: "Beware the beast-man. Alone among God's primates, he will murder for sport. . . . He will make a desert of your lands."[71]

At the very beginning of *Planet of the Apes* Taylor had expressed no remorse at leaving behind the twentieth century, when man had made war on his brothers and allowed his neighbor's children to starve. He finds the future product of that twentieth century on the planet of the apes, where the violence and inhumanity of man in the atomic age had reduced the United States to a surreal wasteland. Yet even this macabre future does not represent the bleakest outcome of America's atomic legacy. The sequel to *Planet of the Apes, Beneath the Planet of the Apes* (1970), reveals that one mutant band of "intelligent" humans has survived, but these mutant humans inhabit an underground world devoted to worshipping the very vehicle of mutation on the planet of the apes: the bomb. They possess a "doomsday bomb" to which they pray: "Glory be to the bomb, and to the holy fallout. As it was in the beginning so it shall be in the end."[72] And so it is—for the atomic destruction that created the planet of the apes also destroys the planet of the apes. In a war between the mutant humans and the mutant apes, between two groups so apparently dedicated to death and violence, a mortally wounded and despairing Taylor detonates the doomsday bomb that destroys the planet of the apes and thus halts for all time, through apocalypse, the bizarre mutations of atomic age life.

While the *Planet of the Apes* films suggested yet another apocalyptic future, one extrapolated from the supremacy of the atomic bomb in America and from the bomb's perversion of natural and human relations, an alternative vision of the future in space postulated just the human and moral transformations needed to prevent the *Planet of the Apes* future. The science fiction television series *Star Trek* (1966–1969) at once confirmed the bleak human future promised by the atomic bomb and violent militarism and at the same time touted the human ability to overcome and avert the worst nightmares of that future through universal peace, cooperation, and brotherhood. At the beginning of each episode of *Star Trek* Captain James T. Kirk explains the mission of the United Space Ship *Enterprise,* and in doing so he expresses the kind of open curiosity and expansive imagination necessary not only for this fictional space travel but also for the culture's experimentation with new and alternative values: "Space—the final frontier. These are the voyages of the starship *Enterprise.* Its five-year mission: to explore strange new worlds, to seek out new life and new civilizations, to boldly go where no man has gone before."[73]

Star Trek's exploration of strange new worlds and search for new life and new civilizations provided the fictional means of creating an idealized and instructive image of the future. The USS *Enterprise* patrolled the galaxy two hundred years into the future, and those two centuries had witnessed many changes and advances in human culture and civilization. The *Enterprise* belonged to the United Federation of Planets, the governing body of a model and peaceful world. The federation preached a policy of peaceful coexistence among all member planets and upheld the principle of acceptance for the diverse beings and cultures found throughout the universe. The guiding creed of the federation was the "prime directive," which forbade intervention or interference into other societies and cultures. *Star Trek* thus postulated a future world quite different from that in the *Planet of the Apes*. The world in *Star Trek* was one of federation, cooperation, harmony, peace, and tolerance for all things different and unusual.[74]

Star Trek's glorious future, however, had derived from earth's violent and destructive past, a past not unlike that presented in *Planet of the Apes*. World War III had occurred on earth in the 1990s and its mass nuclear destruction and eugenics experiments, having almost destroyed all life on the planet, spurred the changes in the human heart and mind that led to the creation of the federation and its policies of peace. Having learned from the atomic age barbarism of their past, humans in the *Star Trek* future had moved beyond the need or desire for nuclear weapons, war, and conquest. The federation opposed equally the war, violence, inequality, and intolerance that had promoted conflict in the past. The bridge crew of the *Enterprise* symbolized the ideal international and interplanetary diversity and harmony of the federation: the *Enterprise* was guided by the all-American Captain Kirk; his second-in-command was Mr. Spock, an alien from the planet Vulcan; others included the communications officer, Lieutenant Uhura, a black African woman; the ship's Scottish engineer, Scotty; and two younger officers, the Asian Sulu and the Russian Chekov.

While there were rather clear contradictions and violations of the ruling spirit of the federation in the weekly episodes of *Star Trek* (the prime directive was often subverted and humans, like the energetic Captain Kirk, often had difficulty subduing their violent impulses), the lingering message of the series remained one of optimism and peace: all beings did have the capacity to overcome their history of violence and aggression. This message was not only the central theme of numerous episodes (for example, "The Devil in the Dark" in 1966–1967 and "Spectre of the Gun" in 1968–1969), but it was the key to the personality of the most fascinating character on the series, the alien Vulcan, Mr. Spock. In response to their planet's violent past, Vulcans had developed an aversion to violence and killing; in order to halt the violence the Vulcans had learned to suppress their volatile emotions and to reason with rigid logic for the principle of nonviolence. Mr. Spock appeared in *Star Trek* as an example of achieved peacefulness and intelligence, an example the emotional humans also strove to attain.

Because Mr. Spock was half-human and half-Vulcan, he represented the continuing struggle between the natural, if base, human instincts for violence and the higher learned instincts of nonviolence. The future as envisioned in *Star Trek* then was not so far removed from the present struggles in culture of the 1960s and 1970s, and *Star Trek's* vision of the future suggested not only the relationship between the apocalyptic and peaceful cultural imaginations of these years but also the extent to which the values of peaceful dissent had been absorbed in the culture. Recognized in *Star Trek* and in the dissenting culture in general was the ever-present possibility of human violence and atomic annihilation, like that portrayed in *Planet of the Apes*. But also recognized in *Star Trek* was the human willingness and ability to suppress and to limit those violent urges, a willingness and an ability made all the more urgent by the alternative: Armageddon. It has been claimed that television in the 1960s successfully avoided reflecting or spreading the cultural rebellion of these years, but a series like *Star Trek* was the very embodiment of rebellion and change.[75] The futuristic world view of *Star Trek* had absorbed the antiwar and civil rights sensibilities of the sixties, and the series owed its very conception to the changed attitudes of these years. Its optimistic vision of a future of human equality, harmony, and peace was shaped by the cultural revolution of the age, and television's dramatization of the very values that informed the rebelliousness of these years revealed the receptivity of America to cultural change.

Boldly going "where no man had gone before," *Star Trek* imagined a future life that offered an optimistic alternative to the violent future of death envisioned in *Planet of the Apes* and throughout the culture's apocalyptic imagination in general. It was the real and already changed cultural values reflected in *Star Trek,* however, which contributed to the building of this new myth of life in the 1960s and 1970s. The one man perhaps most symbolically responsible for stirring this cultural and moral rebirth and for creating the receptive atmosphere for the molding of a new myth of life was, of course, Martin Luther King, Jr. This recognized leader of nonviolent black activism for civil rights spoke of the power and persuasiveness of dreams of life, equality, and peace, and his "I Have a Dream" speech, delivered at the August 1963 March on Washington that marked the one hundredth anniversary of the Emancipation Proclamation, embodied the human hope that characterized the diverse dreams of change in the 1960s and early 1970s. Standing in the shadow of the Lincoln Memorial in Washington, D.C., King not only expressed his dream of an America of racial equality and human respect but also expressed the same sort of urgency that had fueled all the protest and rebelliousness of these years:

> We have also come to this hallowed spot to remind America of the fierce urgency of now. This is no time to engage in the luxury of cooling off or to take the tranquilizing drug of gradualism. Now is the time to make real the promises of democracy; now is the time to rise from the dark and desolate valley of segregation to the sunlit path of racial justice; now is the time to lift our nation from the quicksands of racial injustice to the solid rock of brotherhood; now is the time to make justice a reality for all of God's children. It would be fatal for the nation to overlook the urgency of the moment. This sweltering summer of the Negro's legitimate discontent will not pass until there is an invigorating autumn of freedom and equality.[76]

Imbuing nonviolent revolution and moral rebirth with the same radical intensity that characterized the more violent forms of protest, King promised that "the whirlwinds of revolt will continue to shake the foundations of our nation until the bright day of justice emerges."[77]

While King spoke eloquently of the legitimate black impatience for change, he nonetheless steadfastly adhered to his peaceful principles, urging blacks to continue their struggle for justice without recourse to violence or malice, no matter how much violence and malice they suffered from white racists. King counseled blacks to maintain their moral and human superiority:

> In the process of gaining our rightful place, we must not be guilty of wrongful deeds. Let us not seek to satisfy our thirst for freedom by drinking from the cup of bitterness and hatred. We must forever conduct our struggle on the high plain of dignity and discipline. We must not allow our creative protests to degenerate into physical violence. Again and again we must rise to the majestic heights of meeting physical force with soul force.[78]

King was aware of the difficulty of this task, particularly given white brutality, and he conveyed his understanding and his still paramount belief in the moral righteousness of nonviolence: "I am not unmindful that some of you have come here out of great trials and tribulations. . . . You have been the veterans of creative suffering. Continue to work with the faith that unearned suffering is redemptive."[79]

It was this "creative protest," nonviolent and humanist, born of suffering, that spurred and supported the dream of Martin Luther King. Despite all the trials and tribulations, King fervently believed in his dream, as he emotionally argued to his listeners: "Even though we face the difficulties of today and tomorrow, I still have a dream. It is a dream deeply rooted in the American dream. I have a dream that one day this nation will rise up and live out the true meaning of its creed, 'We hold these truths to be self-evident, that all men are created equal.'"[80] As he rhythmically chanted his refrain *"I have a dream today!"* he upheld a vision of hope and faith for the future:

> This is our hope. This is the faith that I go back to the South with. With this faith we will be able to hew out of the mountain of despair, a stone of hope. With this faith we will be able to transform the jangling discords of our nation into a beautiful symphony of brotherhood. With this faith we will be able to work together, to pray together, to struggle together, to go to jail together, to stand up for freedom together, knowing that we will be free one day. And this will be the day.[81]

In this most eloquent and urgent statement of cultural rebellion and spiritual rebirth, Martin Luther King demonstrated how effectively Christian activism was marshaled for the forces of moral and political change in America, even in an era of increasing nihilism and doubt, and he as well demonstrated the force of dreams—dreams of equality, brotherhood, and hope—in an era of increasing violence. While clinging to such dreams became difficult during the violent 1960s and early 1970s, particularly when the spokesmen for such dreams were ruthlessly assassinated, the culture of dissent, like King, kept such hope and faith alive. Martin Luther King's specific concern, of course, was civil rights, but his emphasis on finding and adopting the creative spiritual and human alternatives to the violence and brutality of the American system and its representative authorities influenced the entire counterculture that developed in the sixties to offer peaceful and humanist alternatives to the dehumanized and demoralized system of life and values in atomic age America.

The cultural imperative to keep dreams alive in this age of violence received widespread and often unexpected support. The popular culture of these years stressed the necessity of nurturing such dreams and fantasies. In between Martin Luther King's "I Have a Dream" and John Lennon's "Imagine" there appeared another statement of support for the protection of dreams of change. In his satirical novel *The Crying of Lot 49* (1966) Thomas Pynchon included an exchange between his protagonist, Oedipa Maas, and her psychiatrist, Dr. Hilarius, in which the psychiatrist urges Oedipa to cling to her "fantasy" (her belief that she has uncovered a "secret" underground society—filled with possibilities—that conflicts with the deadened American system as a whole). Through Dr. Hilarius, Pynchon defended fantasy precisely because of its capacity to inspire hope and life:

> "I came," she said, "hoping you could talk me out of a fantasy." "Cherish it!" cried Hilarius, fiercely. "What else do any of you have? Hold it tightly by its little tentacle, don't let the Freudians coax it out of you. Whatever it is, hold it dear, for when you lose it you go over by that much to the others. You begin to cease to be."[82]

The dreams forwarded by activists like Martin Luther King also found validation and support—of a kind—from the very extremists who opposed the methods of peace and nonviolence. Malcolm X, who ridiculed the March on Washington as the "Farce on Washington" because of its diluted radicalism and because of its cooptation by whites and moderates, nonetheless believed that the advocation of violence by radical blacks helped to spread and foster the dreams and successes of nonviolent activists like Martin Luther King.[83] According to Coretta Scott King, Malcolm X told her that he was "trying to help. . . . He said he wanted to present an alternative; that it might be easier for whites to accept Martin's proposals after hearing him [Malcolm X]."[84] Malcolm X also told Alex Haley, who assisted Malcolm X with his *Autobiography,* that "it was us extremists who made it possible" for the peaceful civil rights activists to realize their moderate dreams and goals.[85]

In constructing a new set of values the countercultural revolution of this awakened era followed the suggestions that had appeared in the aroused culture from the earliest years of the decade. Imbibing the spirit of King's dream, the cultural revolt also relied on exhortations for change that had circulated at the time of the Berlin and Cuban missile crises, exhortations like those of Rabbi Dresner, who had urged a "change in man's heart," or of Lewis Mumford, who had insisted on the creation of "a new myth of life" that would reveal "a passionate religious faith in man's own capacity to transform and perfect his own self and his own institutions in co-operative relation with all the forces of nature, and, above all, with his fellow men."[86] Mumford predicted that it was the young in America who would be in the forefront of the movement forging this new myth of life, and it was in fact the amorphous "youth culture" of the sixties and seventies that carried forth the countercultural rebellion. From its sexual revolution and its peaceful antiwar protests to its embrace of human communality and a respect for the environment and nature, the youth culture embraced the dream of human brotherhood and a new myth of life.

Although diverse, the counterculture that spread in these years was nonetheless expressive of the new and imaginative alternatives being adopted against the ruling and authoritative values of the American system. Rejecting the styles of life and styles of expression of the establishment, the youth culture experimented with sexual liberation, communal living in nature, drugs, music, clothing, and hairstyles—all in an attempt to differentiate youthful life and morality from the traditional status quo in America.[87] "Hippie" culture rebelled against the stultifying expectations of the establishment and against the technological, dehumanized, and desensitized culture of the atomic age. The renewed respect for human sexuality and for nature in particular embodied the spirit of the youth culture, and from the "Summer of Love" in San Francisco in 1967 to the creation of the "Woodstock Nation" at the Woodstock Music and Arts Festival in upstate New York in August 1969 the counterculture developed the sensibilities of a new myth of life.

The principles of love and respect for both human beings and nature and the willingness to explore new avenues to each, including rock 'n' roll, communes, and drugs, constituted the central features of the counterculture. In recrafting a new sexuality of freedom the counterculture rebelled against the unnatural human constraints against love and sex which characterized the devalued human relations of the atomic age. Barriers against premarital sex collapsed and the young in America freely used sex to create closer human relations and to break down the limits on love and life in an emotionally repressed society. Rock 'n' roll music, especially from a group like The Doors, exploded with the new sexual openness of the culture. Lead singer Jim Morrison, like Elvis before him, exuded sexuality, and songs like "Light My Fire" (1967) and "Touch Me" (1969) demonstrated the new sensuality characteristic of the liberated counterculture. Sexuality became a symbol for the renewed values of love and respect in the counterculture, and connected with this renewed respect for human life was a renewed respect for all natural life, the natural life that had been subverted, as had human life, by the bureaucratic and technological system of America.[88] The symbol for this new environmental ethos and concern for nature, of course, was the flower.

Hippies, likewise called "flower children," had demonstrated their concern for peace and nature with their use of the flower, whether by placing flowers in the gun barrels of soldiers during protest marches or by adopting a style of life consistent with flowers—a return to nature. In an article entitled "The Flowering of Plants and Men" (1968) Lewis Mumford had the task of discussing the dangerous ecological imbalance existing in America and the "challenge of survival, for men and plants," within this imbalanced society. He looked to the "flower children" of the counterculture for a solution:

Not by accident, the young, who are in revolt against our power-stricken and machine-regimented society, have seized upon the symbolism of the flower, and call themselves "flower children." In a very innocent, simple-minded, sometimes downright silly way, they have used the flower symbol to express their rejection of this automated and computerized and life-hostile technology. We, too, must learn to be flower children again, and rejoin the old procession and pageantry of life.[89]

As usual, Mumford was warning of the apocalyptic dangers to life threatened by the American society of "lopsided technology," which, while best represented by the atomic bomb, was certainly not limited to that ultimate threat of annihilation, given the widespread pollution of America's air and water, for example.[90] In his conclusion to "The Flowering of Plants and Men," Mumford again returned to the young and their "flower power" as the means for avoiding the imbalanced and destructive and unnatural future:

> It is against this miscarriage of science and technology, this wholesale curtailment of the possibilities of life, this continued threat of collective extermination by nuclear bombardment that might wipe out all higher life on this planet, or by slower but equally deadly modes of poisoning, that the young today are in revolt. In their use of the flower as the symbol of vitality and creativity, of unashamed sexuality and love, they are reminding us of the terms upon which men and plants have not only survived but prospered together—with the aid, of course, of all the other species and orders whose combined activities have produced a living environment. Unless we change our minds, as the young are doing, and alter our whole routine of living, we shall not need a nuclear war to bring the whole evolutionary process to a halt.[91]

The countercultural concern for nature, for human sexuality, and for a "living environment" in general found its best representation in the one striking event that symbolized the alternatives and the possibilities of life proposed and practiced by the youth culture: Woodstock. Billed as "Three Days of Peace and Music," the Woodstock Music and Arts Festival was a massive gathering of the young at a three-day rock concert held in the countryside on Max Yasgur's dairy farm on the outskirts of Bethel, New York, in mid-August 1969.[92] With approximately a half million young Americans in attendance, the various facilities of the festival were strained and inadequate, yet the possibilities for disaster under such circumstances were transformed into an apparent miracle of youthful harmony, cooperation, and peacefulness. Woodstock was a microcosmic display of the best of the counterculture: its rock music, its human sharing and caring, its communalism and brotherhood, and its embrace of human sexuality and the natural life. The young shared food, drugs, sex, and companionship in natural environs; the ideal image was summed up in one of the stage announcements made during the concert: "We must be in heaven, man!"[93]

Woodstock in fact became a symbol of hope not just to the youth culture but to society as a whole. Max Yasgur, owner of the land on which the concert was held, maintained that "if half a million young people at the Aquarian Festival could turn such adverse conditions—filled with the possibility of disaster, riot, looting, and catastrophe—into three days of peace and music, then perhaps there is hope, that if we join with them, we can turn those adversities that are the problems of America into a hope for a brighter and more peaceful future."[94] At least one commentator, Philip Tracy of *Commonweal,* saw the proof of a "new culture" in Woodstock. As he noted in "Birth of a Culture," the youth at Woodstock "became a distinct society with their own rules, rituals, costumes, and standards of behavior. Mobs riot, cities don't, and Woodstock was the first city of the new culture."[95]

If Woodstock youth had become an alternative society or "city" with a culture distinct from that of mainstream America, it was certainly a very natural city. Along with the other ideals represented by Woodstock, the desire to return to nature, to recapture the quality of life associated with more natural surroundings, was central. Joni Mitchell's "Woodstock" (1969), which had immediately memorialized the event in song, reflected the symbolic importance of nature at Woodstock and in the counterculture in general. Mitchell immortalized Woodstock's children of God, who congregated at Yasgur's farm in a quest to find their souls and inhabit the natural land. The golden youth of Woodstock's America fused rock 'n' roll and a return to nature.[96]

The "back to the garden" sensibility of the counterculture signified the withdrawal of the youth culture from the out-of-balance American system of technology and signaled the countercultural desire to restore the balance in relations both in human society and between humans and nature. While Woodstock symbolized the coming together of the diverse new values and life-styles of the counterculture, the alternatives of love and respect for both human and natural life offered in the counterculture spread far beyond Woodstock, influencing and intensifying the cultural demands for peaceful change. Music in particular expressed youthful desires for peace and change as well as the young's growing concerns about the environment. In his impressive thematic album

What's Going On (1971) Marvin Gaye gave voice to a number of these countercultural imperatives. His "Mercy, Mercy Me (The Ecology)" served as a plea to save the earth from the type of devastation so characteristic of this era:

Ah, mercy, mercy me
Ah, things ain't what they used to be, no no
Where did all the blue skies go
Poison in the wind that blows from the north and south and east . . .
Ah, mercy, mercy me
Ah, things ain't what they used to be, no no
Radiation under ground and in the sky
Animals and birds who live near by are dying
Oh, mercy, mercy me
Ah, things ain't what they used to be
What about this over crowded land
How much more abuse from man can she stand . . . [97]

Gaye's sympathies encompassed humanity as well as nature, and his title song, "What's Going On," highlighted the means that the counterculture used to combat the imbalances in nature and among human beings: "You know we've got to find a way / to bring some lovin' here today." While the song held that "only love can conquer hate" and suggested that America's war, crying, dying, and brutality could be tamed by love, Gaye felt enough danger for the culture to ask plaintively in "Save the Children": "Who's willing to try to save a world / That's destined to die?"[98] Despite the persistent perils facing America, the counterculture—with its dedication to love and life—remained resolved in trying to save its world. Even as the American establishment continued to wage war in Vietnam, in spite of growing public discontent, the counterculture continued to cherish its new myth of life and to insist on its alternative to the deadly American system of cold war power: life.

The black comedy *Harold and Maude* (1971) provided a countercultural demonstration of what was in fact needed in America, a resurgence of life and love. What made the film particularly appropriate for its time was its central belief that this renewal of life and love could in fact follow from death. The film focuses on the rather strange relationship between the young Harold and the elderly Maude. Harold is obsessed by death and he torments his mother by staging spectacular, but fake, suicide scenes. He spends his leisure time attending funerals, and it is at one such funeral that he meets Maude. Through death, then, Harold meets the eccentric woman who inspires his love and his life. She shows him how to respect nature and living things and to reject material possessions; she counsels him, "Don't get attached to *things*," and she steals other people's cars to teach them the same lesson.[99] Harold comes to life as a result of his "immaterial" and spiritual relationship with Maude and he absorbs her lesson about life: "Reach out, take a chance. Get hurt even. . . . Give me an L, give me an I, give me a V, give me an E. L-I-V-E. *Live*."

When Maude decides on her eightieth birthday to commit suicide, Harold is horrified—he loves Maude. She soothes him and tells him, "That's wonderful. Go out and love some more," and she passes on her love of life to Harold, who will go out and live and love. It was in the end precisely this message that the counterculture produced in the 1960s and early 1970s. Together with the impulse for violent protest in the culture of dissent, the countercultural development of an alternative system of values sealed the cultural awakening to the dehumanized and demoralized moral legacy of the atomic age and completed the cultural revolt against the American authorities responsible for that legacy. That new life did in fact come from this cultural awakening and revolt was demonstrated in the early seventies, when America witnessed the symbolic but significant defeat of its cold war system of power and authority.

While a variety of historical and cultural circumstances combined to end America's involvement in the Vietnam War and to end the presidential career of Richard Nixon, the cultural revolution of the 1960s and early 1970s had certainly contributed to the social turmoil that culminated in America's extrication from Vietnam in 1973 and in the resignation of Nixon in 1974.[100] Social and cultural rebelliousness had escalated along with the Vietnam War, and one measure of the successful dissent of these years was its increasing persuasiveness even among those in the establishment or the government. Senator J. William Fulbright, who had voiced his support for "the regenerative counterforce of protest," represented growing congressional discontent and cynicism about the war and America's "arrogance of power" which mirrored the dissenting culture's protest. Another such defecting "insider" was Daniel Ellsberg, whose release of *The Pentagon Papers* (leaked to Congress in 1969 and published in the *New York Times* in 1971) reinforced the already widespread antiwar sentiment in the culture. Ellsberg noted his own conversion to dissent in his *Papers on the War* (1972), commenting, "There are some who have been resisting for years, by a variety of means, what they saw clearly as an unjust war, a brutal fraud, a lawless imperial adventure. I deeply respect their courage, their insight, and commitment; I have, belatedly, joined them in spirit and action."[101]

Some of Ellsberg's statements on the war and on the American policies that directed it revealed the extent to which the atomic age culture of dissent had influenced the larger culture and society, including inside officials like Ellsberg himself. In "The Responsibility of Officials in a Criminal War" Ellsberg examined his own actions concerning Vietnam—given his "service in the Marines, in the Defense Department, the State Department, service in Vietnam, the Rand Corporation"—in the context of "war criminality," and in doing so he expressed the necessity of recognizing and resisting an evil system, a necessity long held in the dissenting culture.[102] He traced the roots of American trouble in Vietnam to America's initial atomic arrogance in World War II, and he discussed how the bomb remained central to understanding the brutality of the Vietnam War. He claimed that "the obvious fact that in any given situation we could annihilate an opponent with nuclear weapons, or even with conventional weapons, produces an almost inevitable feeling among what Richard Barnet calls our 'national security managers' that we cannot be doing anything so very wrong as long as we refrain from that [annihilation]." He also pointed out how this atomic option thus allowed the immorality and brutality of America's war against Vietnam to develop, even among presumably "liberal, humane" men in the presidential administrations.[103]

Those administration officials, like Robert McNamara, for example, who had moral qualms about using heavier bombing, including nuclear bombing, in Vietnam, had to hide their qualms, said Ellsberg: "It was seen as dangerous to lend substance to the active suspicions of military staffs and their Congressional allies that there were high Administration officials who didn't love the Bomb"; thus they proposed the "lesser evil" brutalities of the war in Vietnam.[104] It was this sense of "restraint" that allowed administration officials to ignore the deaths resulting from their policies, and it was this kind of moral recognition by Ellsberg, along with his use of the very language of *Dr. Strangelove or: How I Learned to Stop Worrying and Love the Bomb,* which suggested the impact and influence of the culture of dissent. When an administration official's own sense of war guilt and his understanding of the bomb's place in the American system are shaped by popular cultural products of rebellion and by popular conceptions about the bomb in the culture of dissent, the cultural revolt against the American system and its authorities had been achieved.

While cultural dissent and the new cultural values of life spread to the highest levels of government, thereby helping to ensure an end to America's involvement in Vietnam and an end to the death and violence of that war, so too did the moral challenging and questioning of authority spread to the highest level of the system, ultimately resulting in the first deposition of an American president. Lyndon Johnson had voluntarily retired from politics in the face of the opposition he stirred with his Vietnam policies and his credibility gap, but Richard Nixon was forced to resign in disgrace as a result of his criminality and his loss of legitimacy and authority. Vietnam served in its way as the ultimate undoing of both Johnson and Nixon; Johnson's Great Society was unreconcilable with the corrupting war, and Nixon's desire to protect his secret extension of the war into Cambodia first spurred the illegal domestic wiretapping that also characterized the paranoid behavior exposed in the Watergate scandal. The fall of Richard Nixon, however, took on larger cultural connotations in the atomic age, if only because he had been associated with political authority throughout much of this era. The widespread alienation from American authority represented by Nixon reflected the consummation of the long-term cultural suspicions about the American atomic age system of power and its figures of authority. The Watergate scandal gave true credibility to the cynicism and disdain for corrupt and immoral authority which had developed in the awakened and rebellious culture of the 1960s and early 1970s.

With the conclusion of America's war in Vietnam and with the resignation of Richard Nixon, a troubling and turmoil-ridden era in America's history came to something of a conclusion. Two paramount symbols for America's system of death and violence had receded from public view, their disappearance testament in part to the influence of America's atomic age culture of dissent and to the impact of the revolutionary cultural awakening that had taken place on America's "eve of destruction." President Gerald Ford, on assuming office after Nixon's resignation, proclaimed to America that "our long national nightmare is over," and in a sense this was accurate.[105] With the cessation of the worst everyday evidence of death and violence and with the collapse of the most corrupt representative of American power and authority, the cultural imperative to dream and imagine, to live with a new myth of life, appeared to have triumphed. The nightmare, however, did not disappear along with Vietnam and Nixon. Given the continued existence of nuclear weapons and the persistent power of America's cold war system, the possibility of a nightmarish future always remained an option in America.

Of course, the cultural revolution of the 1960s and early 1970s had not succeeded in completely overthrowing the ruling systems of belief and authority in America, but it had succeeded in exposing and limiting the most violent manifestations of American power and authority in these years. The culture of dissent, whether with a violent or peaceful counterforce of protest, had kept the tension in American culture and society high and had ultimately promoted the alternative peaceful and humanist values that helped to control the destructive values of the system. Life in Dr. Strangelove's America meant living with the bomb, but it did not mean loving the bomb or accepting the bomb's promise of an apocalyptic future. When American authorities risked the survival of civilization as Kennedy did in the early 1960s, the dissenting culture awakened to the threat and prevented the complete failure of the "human element" in American society.

The enduring accomplishment of this cultural revolution in the 1960s was its permanent alteration of the nature of cultural and political debate and its extension of the boundaries of dissent in America. When President Ronald Reagan in the early 1980s once again threatened a revival of cold warriorism and atomic diplomacy, the aroused antinuclear culture of those years demonstrated patterns of dissent similar to those that had emerged from the revolutionary era and sensibility of *Dr. Strangelove*. The history and culture of recent America is then to a significant degree the history and culture of Dr. Strangelove's America. The central and historical dynamic tension between cultural dissent and the atomic age political status quo, aroused and openly expressed in the cultural revolution of the sixties and early seventies, has persisted in keeping a tenuous balance between American dreams and myths of life and American nightmares and visions of apocalypse.

Notes

PREFACE

1. *2001: A Space Odyssey,* dir. and prod. Stanley Kubrick (MGM, 1968). All scenes taken directly from the film.

2. Brigadier General Thomas Farrell, quoted in Martin J. Sherwin, *A World Destroyed: The Atomic Bomb and the Grand Alliance* (New York, 1975, 1977), 312.

3. "The Bomb," *Time,* 20 August 1945, p. 19.

4. Albert Einstein, quoted in Paul Boyer, *By the Bomb's Early Light: American Thought and Culture at the Dawn of the Atomic Age* (New York, 1985), 36.

5. Robert Jay Lifton and Richard Falk, *Indefensible Weapons: The Political and Psychological Case against Nuclearism* (New York, 1982), ix.

6. Jonathan Schell, *The Abolition* (New York, 1984), 9.

7. Boyer, *By the Bomb's Early Light,* 334.

8. Paul Brians, *Nuclear Holocausts: Atomic War in Fiction, 1895–1984* (Kent, Ohio, 1987), 3.

9. Ibid., 3–4.

10. Allan M. Winkler, *Life Under a Cloud: American Anxiety about the Atom* (New York, 1993), 9.

11. Ibid., 3–4.

12. Ibid., 4.

13. This was, however, not the intent of Winkler's work. His aim, as he stated, was "to explain why deep-rooted and corrosive fears of nuclear destruction have failed in the past fifty years to bring atomic weaponry under effective control." Winkler, *Life Under a Cloud,* 4. In fact, Winkler paid a fair amount of attention to some of the cultural products reflective of the fear and activism that he otherwise did discuss.

14. Robert Jay Lifton and Greg Mitchell term traditional justifications of the bomb's use "the official narrative" in *Hiroshima in America: Fifty Years of Denial* (New York, 1995). See "Part I: Explaining Hiroshima—The Official Narrative," 3–114, and elsewhere.

15. Lifton and Mitchell, xi; Barton Bernstein, "The Struggle Over History: Defining the Hiroshima Narrative," in *Judgment at the Smithsonian,* ed. Philip Nobile (New York, 1995), 238. Both works provide in-depth coverage of the controversy at the Smithsonian, among other issues.

16. The concept of "nuclear winter" was developed in Paul R. Ehrlich, Carl

Sagan, Donald Kennedy, and Walter Orr Roberts, *The Cold and the Dark: The World after Nuclear War* (New York, 1984). For a very good treatment of American atomic activism in the 1980s, see Winkler's chapter 8, "A Resurgence of Concern," in *Life Under a Cloud,* 187–208. Other academic works that suggested the increased interest in the atomic bomb and nuclear issues in the 1980s include Richard Rhodes, *The Making of the Atomic Bomb* (New York, 1986); Spencer R. Weart, *Nuclear Fear: A History of Images* (Cambridge, Mass., 1988); and Peter Wyden, *Day One: Before Hiroshima and After* (New York, 1984).

17. Indeed, as Paul Brians's work in *Nuclear Holocausts* suggests, it is even necessary to abandon an exclusive focus on only those cultural works that deal explicitly with the bomb. Given the lack of sources in a genre defined around the bomb (atomic fiction), it seems wise to gauge atomic age cultural change from a broader perspective. This is not to imply that direct cultural responses to the bomb were negligible in number; Brians himself examines over eight hundred stories and novels (although he notes that "stories of the atomic holocaust have never rivalled in number stories of other conflicts such as the American Civil War or World War II"). See Brians, *Nuclear Holocausts,* 3.

18. Nathanael West, *Miss Lonelyhearts and the Day of the Locust* (New York, 1962; orig. pub., 1933, 1939), 30–31.

19. *Film Noir: An Encyclopedic Reference to the American Style,* ed. Alain Silver and Elizabeth Ward (Woodstock, N.Y., 1979), specifically documents film noir as part of the atomic age. On page 2 the editors note that

> foremost in the list of socio-political developments that influences the post-World War II film industry are McCarthyism and nuclear weapons. The effect of the former has been well documented. . . . The potential hazards of the atomic bomb and, after 1949, the threat of nuclear war may have been depicted most explicitly in the scores of radioactive monsters raised from the depths or the visions of Armageddon produced in the science fiction genre; but such concepts also altered the narratives of film noir. In fact, McCarthyism and the specter of the Bomb became the unspoken inspirations for a leitmotif of fear or, more specifically, paranoia that resounded through the noir cycle after the war.

While film noir predated the war, the number of "black films" produced both before and after the war confirms the appropriateness of film noir for the atomic age. Between 1929 and 1945, 44 films noirs were produced, while between 1946 and 1959, 234 films noirs appeared. The years between 1946 and 1951 were especially good ones for the genre, accounting for 160 of the 234 films released during these years. See Silver and Ward's appendix B, 333–336, for the chronological listing of these films.

20. *Sunset Boulevard,* dir. Billy Wilder, prod. Charles Brackett (Paramount, 1950). All scenes and dialogue taken directly from the film.

21. For a full treatment of *Dr. Strangelove* and its rebellious spirit of black humor, see below, chapter 8, "Judgment Day: Dr. Strangelove's Cultural Revolution."

1. F. Scott Fitzgerald, *The Great Gatsby* (New York, 1953; orig. pub. 1925), 182.

2. Henry F. May, *The End of American Innocence: A Study of the First Years of Our Own Time, 1912–1917* (New York, 1959).

3. Ezra Pound, "Hugh Selwyn Mauberley" (1920), in *The Norton Anthology of American Literature,* ed. Ronald Gottesman et al. (New York, 1979), 2:1059.

4. Nancy Arnot Harjan, in Studs Terkel, *"The Good War": An Oral History of World War Two* (New York, 1984), 560.

5. J. Robert Oppenheimer, quoted in Richard Rhodes, *The Making of the Atomic Bomb* (New York, 1986), 676.

6. Trinity director Kenneth Bainbridge, quoted in Rhodes, *The Making of the Atomic Bomb,* 675.

7. The larger context of Oppenheimer's 1948 statement is as follows: "In some sort of crude sense which no vulgarity, no humor, no overstatement can quite extinguish, the physicists have known sin, and this is a knowledge which they cannot lose." His comments on sin in physicists appeared in J. Robert Oppenheimer, "Physics in the Contemporary World," *Bulletin of Atomic Scientists,* March 1948, p. 66. This issue of sin is also addressed in Allan M. Winkler, *Life Under a Cloud: American Anxiety about the Atom* (New York, 1993), 38.

8. Oppenheimer, quoted in Rhodes, *The Making of the Atomic Bomb,* 676. This speech was from 1946.

9. Philip Morrison, in Terkel, *"The Good War,"* 512.

10. Stanislaw Ulam, quoted in Rhodes, *The Making of the Atomic Bomb,* 677.

11. For a more in-depth treatment of scientists' responses to the atomic bomb and of their efforts toward the control of atomic energy, see Winkler's chapter "The Question of Control" in *Life Under a Cloud,* 34–56. Richard Rhodes also deals extensively with views of scientists in *The Making of the Atomic Bomb.*

12. Frank Keegan, in Terkel, *"The Good War,"* 37.

13. Truman, quoted in Paul Boyer, *By the Bomb's Early Light: American Thought and Culture at the Dawn of the Atomic Age* (New York, 1985), 193.

14. Henry May, *The End of American Innocence,* 397 and 398.

15. Oppenheimer, from a January 1953 advisory group report to President Eisenhower, quoted in Robert C. Williams and Philip L. Cantelon, eds., *The American Atom: A Documentary History of Nuclear Policies from the Discovery of Fission to the Present, 1939–1984* (Philadelphia, 1984), 73.

CHAPTER ONE

1. Paul Edwards, in Studs Terkel, *"The Good War": An Oral History of World War Two* (New York, 1984), 573.

2. Harry Truman, *Memoirs of Harry S. Truman, 1945 Year of Decisions* (New York, 1955), 1:437.

3. *It's a Wonderful Life,* dir. and prod. Frank Capra (Liberty Films/RKO Radio Release, 1946). All scenes taken directly from the film.

4. Truman, *Memoirs,* 1:462–463.

5. Ibid., 1:537.

6. James F. Byrnes to Truman in an April meeting on the atomic bomb, as reported in Truman, *Memoirs,* 1:87.

7. For a variety of historical interpretations on the use of the atomic bomb, see Gar Alperovitz, *Atomic Diplomacy: Hiroshima and Potsdam,* expanded and updated ed. (New York, 1985); Herbert Feis, *The Atomic Bomb and the End of World War II* (Princeton, 1961, 1966); and Martin J. Sherwin, *A World Destroyed: The Atomic Bomb and the Grand Alliance* (New York, 1975, 1977).

8. Truman, *Memoirs,* 1:524.

9. Ibid.

10. Ibid., 1:531.

11. Ibid., 1:523.

12. Ibid., 1:510.

13. Truman, quoted in Stephen Ambrose, *Rise to Globalism: American Foreign Policy since 1938,* 5th rev. ed. (New York, 1988), 85–86.

14. For detailed accounts of official American anticommunism and its internal security network, see David Caute, *The Great Fear: The Anti-Communist Purge under Truman and Eisenhower* (New York, 1978); Victor Navasky, *Naming Names* (New York, 1980), which focuses on Hollywood's experience but nonetheless provides an in-depth treatment of the workings of the system; Nora Sayre, *Running Time: Films of the Cold War* (New York, 1982), which offers a brief overview in "Prelude," 3–29; and Stephen J. Whitfield, *The Culture of the Cold War* (Baltimore, 1991).

15. *White Heat,* dir. Raoul Walsh, prod. Louis F. Edelman (Warner Bros., 1949). All scenes and dialogue taken directly from the film.

16. William Styron, "Echoes of Distant Battle" (reprint of the 1968 "My Generation"), *Esquire,* June 1983, p. 71.

17. Ibid., 72.

18. Ibid.

19. Ibid.

20. Erhard Dabringhaus, in Terkel, *"The Good War,"* 474. See his entire oral testimony (pp. 471–477) for the story of America's involvement with Barbie.

21. Ibid., 477.

22. Telford Taylor, in Terkel, *"The Good War,"* 462.

23. Mike Royko, in Terkel, *"The Good War,"* 137.

24. Ibid., 137–138.

25. Ibid.

26. Robert Lekachman, in Terkel, *"The Good War,"* 68.

27. *The Stranger,* dir. Orson Welles, prod. S. P. Eagle (RKO Radio Picture, 1946). All scenes and dialogue taken directly from the film.

28. *Notorious,* dir. and prod. Alfred Hitchcock (RKO Radio Picture, 1946). All scenes taken directly from the film.

29. *The Third Man,* dir. and prod. Sir Carol Reed (London Films, 1949). All scenes and dialogue taken directly from the film.

30. *Crossfire,* dir. Edward Dmytryk, prod. Adrian Scott (RKO Radio Picture, 1947). All scenes and dialogue taken directly from the film.

31. Ibid.

32. Ibid.

33. In *Homeward Bound: American Families in the Cold War Era* (New York, 1988), historian Elaine Tyler May also discussed the dislocation of veterans and the fears aroused in the culture as a result. See especially pp. 65–66 and 87–88.

34. Dialogue taken directly from *Crossfire.*

35. *The Best Years of Our Lives,* dir. William Wyler, prod. Samuel Goldwyn (Goldwyn Productions, 1946). All scenes and dialogue taken directly from the film.

36. *Till the End of Time,* dir. Edward Dmytryk, prod. Dore Schary (RKO Radio Picture, 1946). All scenes and dialogue taken directly from the film.

37. *Suddenly,* dir. Lewis Allen, prod. Robert Bassler (Libra Productions/ United Artists, 1954). For the other Korean era veteran films see *Where the Sidewalk Ends,* dir. and prod. Otto Preminger (Twentieth Century-Fox, 1950), and *Niagara,* dir. Henry Hathaway, prod. Charles Brackett (Twentieth Century-Fox, 1953). All scenes and dialogue taken directly from the films.

38. Sloan Wilson, *The Man in the Gray Flannel Suit* (New York, 1955), 77.

39. Norman Mailer, *The Naked and the Dead* (New York, 1981; orig. pub. 1948), 3.

40. Ibid., 85.

41. Ibid., 702.

42. James Jones, *From Here to Eternity* (New York, 1975; orig. pub. 1951), and *From Here to Eternity,* dir. Fred Zinnemann, prod. Buddy Adler (Columbia Pictures, 1953).

43. Herman Wouk, *The Caine Mutiny* (New York, 1951), and *The Caine Mutiny,* dir. Edward Dmytryk, prod. Stanley Kramer (Columbia Pictures, 1954). A number of commentators have seen *The Caine Mutiny* not as work tarnishing war or naval officers but rather as a work that upholds the ideal of authority. The basis for this interpretation lies in the dramatic closing speech given by Lieutenant Greenwald, the lawyer who successfully defends the mutineers. At their celebratory party Greenwald chastises the men for their actions, claiming that Queeg had deserved their loyalty and sympathy, and he makes it clear that he only defended the men because the real "author" of "The Caine Mutiny" was not on trial—the contemptuous and cowardly intellectual, Lieutenant Tom Keefer. Representative of this interpretation are Stephen Whitfield in *The Culture of the Cold War,* 60, where he argues that "authoritarian ideology" and "military esteem" are upheld, and Michael P. Rogin, *Ronald Reagan, the Movie and Other Episodes in Political Demonology* (Berkeley, 1987), 255–257. Others, though, see the relative weakness of this claim, especially in the film. One film analyst noted that "a more serious flaw in the film is the poorly defined perspective in the end. Greenwald's attempt to salvage the deportment of an obvious neurotic by appeal to his patriotism does not make Maryk's [the executive officer and major mutineer] action seem any less necessary." See the *Magill Movie Guide* review of *The Caine Mutiny,* 1993.

44. *Mister Roberts,* dir. John Ford and Mervyn LeRoy, prod. Leland Hayward (Warner Brothers, 1955). All scenes taken directly from the film.

45. *The Bridge on the River Kwai,* dir. David Lean, prod. Sam Spiegel (Columbia Pictures, 1957). All scenes and dialogue taken directly from the film.

46. Stephen Whitfield in *The Culture of the Cold War,* 149, also sees *The Bridge on the River Kwai* as an effective antiwar film that questioned "the high price of military values during World War II."

47. The Rivers and the Leutze versions of George Washington can be viewed and contrasted in Sidra Stich, *Made in U.S.A.: An Americanization in Modern Art, The '50s & '60s* (Berkeley, 1987), 15.

48. The Lichtenstein and the Kienholz appear in Stich, *Made in U.S.A.,* 18 and 33.

49. See Stich, *Made in U.S.A.,* 20–21, for *Flag* and *Flag on Orange,* and Trewin Copplestone, *Modern Art* (New York, 1985), 211, for *Three Flags.*

50. Styron, "Echoes of a Distant Battle," 71.

CHAPTER TWO

1. Frank Conroy, "America in a Trance" (reprint of the original 1968 *Esquire* article), *Esquire,* June 1983, p. 116.

2. Plans for the international control of atomic energy are discussed in "Atomic Energy in a Postwar World," in Robert C. Williams and Philip L. Cantelon, eds., *The American Atom: A Documentary History of Nuclear Policies from the Discovery of Fission to the Present, 1939–1984* (Philadelphia, 1984), 71–74; the Baruch Plan is reprinted in full on pp. 92–97. See also Allan M. Winkler, "The Question of Control," in *Life Under a Cloud: American Anxiety about the Atom* (New York, 1993), 34–56.

3. Philip Morrison in Studs Terkel, *"The Good War": An Oral History of World War Two* (New York, 1984), 515–516.

4. John Hersey, *Hiroshima* (New York, 1981; orig. pub. 1946), 114.

5. Ibid., 24.

6. In *Life Under a Cloud* Winkler discusses how the American government orchestrated the news that reached the public about the atomic bomb in the earliest days of the atomic age. See especially the discussion on p. 26.

7. Hersey, *Hiroshima,* 64–65.

8. In *By the Bomb's Early Light: American Thought and Culture at the Dawn of the Atomic Age* (New York, 1985) Paul Boyer suggests that *Hiroshima* ultimately offered "implicit expiation for Americans" because Hersey also recorded the Japanese fatalistic acceptance of the bomb's use under the circumstances of war (p. 210). While persuasive in its own right, this view presumes that Americans felt a guilt that required expiation. If anything, Hersey's account served to irritate consciences and arouse doubts through the force of its horrific descriptions, which certainly overwhelmed other aspects of the work. Even so, overt recognition of atomic guilt remained the problem of a minority of Americans. See pp. 203–210 for Boyer's complete analysis of *Hiroshima* and its reception among Americans.

9. Henry L. Stimson, "The Decision to Use the Atomic Bomb," *Harper's Magazine,* February 1947, p. 107.

10. United States Atomic Energy Commission General Advisory Committee Report on the "Super," 30 October 1949, in Williams and Cantelon, eds., *The American Atom,* 125–126.

11. Ibid., 127.

12. Advisory Group Report, January 1953, quoted in "Atomic Energy in a Postwar World," in Williams and Cantelon, eds., *The American Atom,* 73.

13. Eisenhower, quoted in "Atomic Energy in a Postwar World," in Williams and Cantelon, eds., *The American Atom,* 73.

14. President Dwight D. Eisenhower, "Atoms for Peace" Address to the United Nations General Assembly, 8 December 1953, in Williams and Cantelon, eds., *The American Atom,* 110–111.

15. Ibid., 111.

16. Winkler also discusses Eisenhower's "Atoms for Peace" speech in *Life Under a Cloud,* 145–146, and he details some of the results of this plan.

17. "The Real Power of the Super-Bomb," *New Republic,* 8 November 1954, p. 3. *Newsweek* reported the fate of the Japanese fishing boat in "Panic After 'Sunrise,'" 29 March 1954, p. 23. One of the *Lucky Dragon*'s crew members eventually died from radiation complications. Winkler notes in *Life Under a Cloud,* 94, that this incident helped to arouse opposition to fallout and nuclear testing, and Paul Brians in *Nuclear Holocausts: Atomic War in Fiction, 1895–1984* (Kent, Ohio, 1987), 18, also identifies this incident as one that aroused American interest in and attention to atomic issues.

18. Strauss, quoted in Winkler, *Life Under a Cloud,* 94.

19. Marnie Seymour, in Terkel, *"The Good War,"* 520.

20. Incoming Confidential Telegram from Tokyo to the Secretary of State, 12 May 1955, reprinted in John Hersey, "Hiroshima: The Aftermath," *New Yorker,* 15 July 1985, p. 61.

21. Ralph J. Blake secret diplomatic message, reprinted in Hersey, "Hiroshima: The Aftermath," p. 61.

22. Joseph McCarthy, quoted in Nora Sayre, *Running Time: Films of the Cold War* (New York, 1982), 14.

23. United States Army, *How to Spot a Communist* (1955), quoted in David Caute, *The Great Fear: The Anti-Communist Purge under Truman and Eisenhower* (New York, 1978), 296.

24. Nevada senator, quoted in Sayre, *Running Time,* 29.

25. Detailed accounts of HUAC in Hollywood can be found in Victor Navasky, *Naming Names* (New York, 1980), and Caute, *The Great Fear.* Stephen J. Whitfield's chapter "Reeling: The Politics of Film," 127–151, in *The Culture of the Cold War* (Baltimore, 1991), also examines the anticommunist impact on Hollywood and its films.

26. Tiba Wilner, interviewed in the documentary "The Legacy of the Hollywood Blacklist," dir. and prod. Judy Chaikin (One Step Productions/KCET, 1987).

27. Ibid.

28. For more on the Hollywood blacklists and their impact on the content of films, see Navasky, *Naming Names*; Sayre, *Running Time*; and the Judy Chaikin documentary "The Legacy of the Hollywood Blacklist."

29. Jean-Paul Sartre, quoted in Caute, *The Great Fear,* 68.

30. Julius Rosenberg letter, 1951, quoted in Caute, *The Great Fear,* 68. See Caute's chapter 3, "Espionage Fever: Myth of the Vital Secret," for an account of the Rosenbergs.

31. Lewis Strauss to Harry S. Truman, 25 November 1949, in Williams and Cantelon, eds., *The American Atom,* 129.

32. K. D. Nichols to J. R. Oppenheimer, 23 December 1953, in Williams and Cantelon, eds., *The American Atom,* 146.

33. "The Oppenheimer Paradox: Sense and Senselessness" and "The Fifty Years of Dr. Oppenheimer," *Time,* 26 April 1954, pp. 28–29.

34. Both Nixon and McCarthy are quoted in "The Oppenheimer Paradox," *Time,* 26 April 1954, p. 28 and p. 29, respectively.

35. K. D. Nichols to the USAEC, "Findings on the Case of J. Robert Oppenheimer," 12 June 1954, in Williams and Cantelon, eds., *The American Atom,* 170–171.

36. Whitfield offers a less sympathetic account of Oppenheimer's fate in *The Culture of the Cold War,* 181. He does not see Oppenheimer as any kind of martyr and in fact claims he was "scarcely a hero." Recent allegations suggesting that Oppenheimer was a Soviet agent also call into question his status as a victim of political repression, but these charges concerning Oppenheimer's involvement in atomic espionage have yet to be substantiated—and in fact have been vigorously questioned and challenged. Pavel Sudoplatov (with Anatoly Sudoplatov and Jerrold L. and Leona P. Schecter) in his autobiography, *Special Tasks: The Memoirs of an Unwanted Witness—A Soviet Spymaster* (Boston, 1994), claims that not only Oppenheimer but also Enrico Fermi and Leo Szilard served as sources for Soviet intelligence. Sudoplatov's own credibility is, however, questionable. For an analysis of the credibility problems in Sudoplatov's autobiography, see Timothy Naftali, "Pavel Sudoplatov: Assassin's Tales," *Boston Book Review,* Fall 1994, pp. 4, 31. In her article on Sudoplatov's charges against Oppenheimer and the others, Priscilla Johnson McMillan declares simply in her title: "They Weren't Spies." She undermines Sudoplatov's claims and notes: "That Oppenheimer, stripped of his security clearance in 1954 by a government board which nonetheless attributed to him 'an unusual ability to keep to himself secrets,' should again be accused without documented evidence is a bitter injustice." She points out as well that these scientists, all dead, cannot defend themselves. See Priscilla Johnson McMillan, "They Weren't Spies," *Washington Post,* 26 April 1994, p. A15. Other evidence has been marshaled to clear Oppenheimer's name; see "Oppenheimer No Spy, Says Former KGB Officer," *Washington Times,* 24 April 1994, p. A9, and Walter Pincus, "Book Saying U.S. Scientists Aided Soviet Atom Bomb Effort Is Faulted," *Washington Post,* 26 April 1994.

37. *The Day the Earth Stood Still,* dir. Robert Wise, prod. Julian Blaustein (Twentieth Century-Fox, 1951). All scenes and dialogue taken directly from the film.

38. Klaatu's moral goodness and superiority are underscored by his resemblance to Christ. He adopts the name "Carpenter" when he escapes from Walter Reed Hospital, and he is later resurrected, albeit with the aid of advanced technology. In *Running Time,* 196, Sayre comments of *The Day the Earth Stood Still:* "The movie also asks how we would behave if Christ returned to earth: the answer is that we would shoot him."

39. *The Thing,* dir. Christian Nyby, prod. Howard Hawks (RKO Radio Picture, 1951). All scenes and dialogue taken directly from the film.

40. *Invaders from Mars,* dir. William Cameron Menzies, prod. Edward L. Alperson (Twentieth Century-Fox, 1953), and *Invasion of the Body Snatchers,* dir. Don Siegel, prod. Walter Wanger (Allied Artists, 1956). An extended analysis of these films can be found in chapter 4 below.

41. *The Beast from 20,000 Fathoms,* dir. Eugene Lourie, prod. Hal Chester and Jack Dietz (Warner Brothers, 1953). All scenes and dialogue taken directly from the film.

42. *Them!* dir. Gordon Douglas, prod. David Weisbart (Warner Brothers, 1954). All scenes and dialogue taken directly from the film.

43. *Godzilla,* dir. Terry Morse, prod. Tomoyuki Tanaka (Toho, 1956). All scenes and dialogue taken directly from the film. The film was made originally in Japan and released in 1954, and it was thereafter reworked for American audiences. *Godzilla* was the first popular Japanese film in America.

44. *Above and Beyond,* dir. and prod. Melvin Frank and Norman Panama (MGM, 1952); *Strategic Air Command,* dir. Anthony Mann, prod. Samuel J. Briski (Paramount Pictures, 1955); and *Bombers B-52,* dir. Gordon Douglas, prod. Richard Whorf (Warner Brothers, 1957). All scenes and dialogue taken directly from the films.

45. Dialogue taken directly from *Above and Beyond.*

46. Oppenheimer, quoted in Richard Rhodes, *The Making of the Atomic Bomb* (New York, 1986), 676.

47. *The Fly,* dir. and prod. Kurt Neumann (Twentieth Century-Fox, 1958). All scenes and dialogue taken directly from the film.

48. Walter B. Miller, Jr., *A Canticle for Leibowitz* (New York, 1982; orig. pub. 1959), 245. Paul Brians notes in *Nuclear Holocausts: Atomic War in Fiction, 1895–1984* (Kent, Ohio, 1987), 14 and 80, that the three novellas that constituted the later novel were actually published between 1955 and 1957. His analysis of the work appears on pp. 80–83.

49. Miller, *A Canticle for Leibowitz,* 255–256.

50. In *The Culture of the Cold War* Whitfield examines the difficulties of criticizing law enforcement officials and figures of authority in general. On p. 58 he discusses the overall high prestige of the military and the FBI that discouraged negative evaluations of members of these elites, and on p. 183 he notes, "When the dangers of Communism loomed larger than the value of the Bill of Rights, any exposure of police methods as resembling those of the enemy was unwelcome."

51. *Strangers on a Train,* dir. and prod. Alfred Hitchcock (Warner Brothers-First National, 1951), and *North by Northwest,* dir. and prod. Alfred Hitchcock (MGM, 1959). All scenes taken directly from the films.

52. *The Asphalt Jungle,* dir. John Huston, prod. Arthur Hornblow, Jr. (MGM, 1950). All scenes and dialogue taken directly from the film.

53. *Where the Sidewalk Ends,* dir. and prod. Otto Preminger (Twentieth Century-Fox, 1950). All scenes and dialogue taken directly from the film.

54. *Pick Up on South Street,* dir. Samuel Fuller, prod. Jules Schermer (Twentieth Century-Fox, 1953). All scenes and dialogue taken directly from the film.

55. Scenarios taken directly from *Suddenly,* dir. Lewis Allen, prod. Robert Bassler (Libra Productions/United Artists, 1954).

56. Jim Thompson, *The Killer Inside Me* (New York, 1983; orig. pub. 1952), 93.

57. Ibid., 187.

58. Mickey Spillane, *Kiss Me Deadly* (New York, 1952), 35–36.

59. Ibid., 36.

60. Ibid., 101–102.

61. Ibid., 170. The filmed version of *Kiss Me Deadly,* dir. and prod. Robert Aldrich (United Artists, 1955), ends on an apocalyptic note appropriate to the atomic age culture of dissent, even as it departs from the novel. In the film Mike is after the "great whatsit," which turns out to be a stolen box of radioactive material; the novel's theme of domestic corruption is thus transformed in the film into a concern for international intrigue and atomic destruction. At the end of the film a woman opens this new Pandora's box and is consumed by flames. Although the film is ambiguous about the fate of Mike and Velda, who are with the woman, the woman and the house in which she releases the atomic demon are consumed by a mushrooming cloud, presumably betokening the end of the world. See also Michael Rogin, *Ronald Reagan, the Movie, and Other Episodes in Political Demonology* (Berkeley, 1987), 249, for a discussion of the film.

62. Harry Whittington, *Forgive Me, Killer* (Berkeley, 1987; orig. pub., 1956), 76.

63. Ibid., 122.

64. In *Running Time* Nora Sayre discusses Carl Foreman's intent for *High Noon.* Foreman was subpoenaed by HUAC during production of the film, and he was later blacklisted. See p. 176 for Foreman's story. Whitfield also analyzes the film and Foreman's point of view in *The Culture of the Cold War,* 146–151. On p. 147 he notes that Foreman claimed to have "felt 'morosely pleased' that his political message had been widely comprehended at the time." Whitfield also believes that *High Noon,* "better than any other film of the 1950s, exemplified political criticism in the shadow of the blacklist" (p. 146).

65. *High Noon,* dir. Fred Zinnemann, prod. Stanley Kramer (United Artists, 1952). All scenes and dialogue taken directly from the film.

66. Winkler provides information on the "doomsday clock" in *Life Under a Cloud,* 40. Initially the clock was meant to be permanently fixed at a given time (it began at seven minutes to midnight), but later the minutes to midnight shifted back and forth according to the levels of atomic danger in the world.

67. John Wayne, quoted in Whitfield, *The Culture of the Cold War,* 149.

68. *Shane,* dir. and prod. George Stevens (Paramount, 1952). All scenes and dialogue taken directly from the film.

69. Arthur Miller, *The Crucible* (New York, 1953); *I Confess,* dir. and prod. Alfred Hitchcock (Warner Brothers-First National, 1953). All scenes taken directly from the film.

70. *I Want to Live!* dir. Robert Wise, prod. Walter Wanger (United Artists, 1958). All scenes taken directly from the film.

71. These television programs were showcased on "The Golden Age of Television," KOFY, San Francisco, 24–26 October 1986.

72. See Nora Sayre's chapter "Penance and Assault," 79–99, in *Running Time* for an account of these films. For another intriguing and intelligent interpretation of cold war films, see Michael Rogin's "Kiss Me Deadly: Communism, Motherhood, and Cold War Movies," in his *Ronald Reagan,* 236–271.

73. *On the Waterfront,* dir. Elia Kazan, prod. Sam Spiegel (Columbia Pictures, 1954). See Sayre's "Behind the Waterfront," 151–172, in *Running Time* for a full analysis of the film's meaning and making.

74. For a similar interpretation of these films, see Whitfield, *The Culture of the Cold War,* 134–136, for *I Was a Communist for the F.B.I.,* and 136–140 for *My Son John.* Michael Rogin also discusses these films in his chapter on cold war films "Kiss Me Deadly: Communism, Motherhood, and Cold War Movies," in his *Ronald Reagan,* 236–271. See pp. 250–252 especially for an incisive analysis of the "sexual politics" of *My Son John.*

75. All scenes and dialogue taken directly from *I Was a Communist for the F.B.I.,* dir. Gordon Douglas, prod. Bryan Foy (Warner Bros., 1951).

76. All scenes and dialogue taken directly from *My Son John,* dir. and prod. Leo McCarey (Paramount, 1952).

77. Telford Taylor, in Terkel, *"The Good War,"* 462.

78. Ibid., 463.

79. Whitfield, in *The Culture of the Cold War,* 28, also sees the Hiss case as central to the demise of liberalism and the Democratic party in these years.

80. Leslie A. Fiedler, *An End to Innocence: Essays on Culture and Politics* (New York, 1972; orig. pub. 1955), 24.

81. *Vertigo,* dir. and prod. Alfred Hitchcock (Paramount, 1958). All scenes taken directly from the film.

82. President Dwight Eisenhower in his 1961 "Farewell address," reprinted as "President Eisenhower Warns of the Military-Industrial Complex," in Robert Griffith, ed., *Major Problems in American History* (Lexington, Mass., 1992), 166–167. Stephen E. Ambrose also discusses this address in *Eisenhower: The President* (New York, 1984), 612.

PART TWO

1. J. D. Salinger, *The Catcher in the Rye* (New York, 1964; orig. pub. 1951), 1.

2. Ibid., 14.

3. Ibid.

4. Ibid., 141.

5. Ibid., 173.

6. Ibid., 202.

7. Ibid., 204.

8. *Psycho,* dir. and prod. Alfred Hitchcock (Paramount, 1960). All scenes and dialogue taken directly from the film.

9. "The Bomb," *Time,* 20 August 1945, p. 19.

10. Dorothy Thompson, quoted in Paul Boyer, *By the Bomb's Early Light: American Thought and Culture at the Dawn of the Atomic Age* (New York, 1985), 280–281.

CHAPTER THREE

1. Don McFadden in Studs Terkel, *"The Good War": An Oral History of World War Two* (New York, 1984), 148.

2. In her impressive study of postwar families, *Homeward Bound: American Families in the Cold War Era* (New York, 1988), historian Elaine Tyler May outlines the multiform cultural ideals and social stresses that upheld this ideology of "togetherness," or what she terms "domestic containment."

3. President Dwight Eisenhower, quoted in William E. Leuchtenburg, *A Troubled Feast: American Society since 1945* (Boston, 1979), 84.

4. In *Make Room for TV: Television and the Family Ideal in Postwar America* (Chicago, 1992), Lynn Spigel analyzes the process by which television became accepted and absorbed into postwar American family life. While this image of television promoting family fun and togetherness was one touted by the television industry and the culture at large, Spigel also documents the familial divisions that resulted from television's arrival in the home—especially for women, even more isolated in the home after television replaced other types of social outings. Spigel notes on p. 69 that "while television was primarily shown to be an integrating activity in the first few years of diffusion, in the 1950s it came to be equally (or perhaps even more) associated with social differences and segregation among family members." This type of challenge to the ideal of family togetherness is variously discussed in chapters 4 and 5 below.

5. Leslie Fiedler, "Italian Pilgrimage: The Discovery of America," in his *An End to Innocence: Essays on Culture and Politics* (New York, 1955), 96.

6. Lynn Spigel points out in *Make Room for TV,* 178, that these family-oriented situation comedies became particularly popular toward the end of the decade, having replaced shows that offered somewhat more controversy (however subdued that controversy was). Milton Berle's bawdy humor, images of bumbling men and less than satisfied housewives, were homogenized into the bland, nationally acceptable sitcom by the late 1950s. According to Spigel, "the realist suburban family sitcom flourished at the end of the 1950s, with programs such as *Father Knows Best, Leave It to Beaver,* and *The Donna Reed Show* drawing on codes of verisimilitude to present portraits of everyday life in the white middle-class suburbs. . . . [T]hese programs worked to 'naturalize' family life, to make it appear as if this living arrangement

were in fact the only one possible." See also pp. 142–154, "Addressing the Family Audience," for information on changes in the nature of television programming to make it less controversial or regional. Gerard Jones in *Honey, I'm Home! Sitcoms: The Selling of the American Dream* (New York, 1992) also charts this transformation in sitcoms, showing for example how the freedoms of an early show like *I Love Lucy* (which featured housewife dissatisfaction, nascent female rebellion, and ethnic mixing) were lost as television "mythologized" the American family in shows like *Ozzie and Harriet* and *Father Knows Best.* See his chapter 5, "Why Love Lucy?" (pp. 62–75), and chapter 7, "Inventing America" (pp. 87–102). In *The Culture of the Cold War* (Baltimore, 1991), 155, Stephen J. Whitfield argues simply that there was no dissent on television.

7. Spigel in *Make Room for TV,* 178, discusses the launching of Ricky Nelson's singing career in a 1957 episode of *Ozzie and Harriet* entitled "Ricky the Drummer." She also notes of Ricky Nelson and other such teen television singers (notably Shelley Fabares and Paul Peterson from *The Donna Reed Show*) that "rather than fracturing domesticity, these teen idols seemed to repair it by bringing the new youth culture, with its threatening Elvis Presleys and Little Richards, into a domestic world where children sang the latest hits under the watchful gaze of their parents." See *Make Room for TV,* 178–179, for this analysis.

8. Frank Conroy, "America in a Trance" (reprint of the original 1968 *Esquire* article), *Esquire,* June 1983, p. 116. Conroy also highlights the fun and faddish aspects of 1950s culture in pictures and words on pp. 116–117.

9. For examples of photographs illustrating Eisenhower's sporty and playful image, see the photographs in Stephen E. Ambrose, *Eisenhower: The President* (New York, 1984), between pp. 230 and 231.

10. Television also kept atomic and hydrogen fireballs in the public's eye, particularly because of the industry's cooperation with civil defense programs. Live broadcasts of nuclear tests were a regular feature of the networks. Whitfield notes this in *The Culture of the Cold War,* 154. For many the television was meant at its best to be a "window to the world," including the atomic world. As Gary Simpson, NBC director, said in 1955: "Mr. Public views that television set in his home as a twentieth-century electronic monster that can transport him to the ball game, to Washington D.C., to the atomic blast in Nevada—and do it now. The viewer is inclined to accept it as his window to the world, as his reporter on what is happening now—simultaneously." Simpson, quoted in Spigel, *Make Room for TV,* 99.

11. John Foster Dulles, quoted in Stephen E. Ambrose, *Rise to Globalism: American Foreign Policy since 1938,* 5th rev. ed. (New York, 1988), 138–139.

12. Jules Masserman, quoted in Paul Boyer, *By the Bomb's Early Light: American Thought and Culture at the Dawn of the Atomic Age* (New York, 1985), 277.

13. *The Challenge of Atomic Energy,* quoted in Boyer, *By the Bomb's Early Light,* 281.

14. Joseph Barth, quoted in Boyer, *By the Bomb's Early Light,* 276.

15. Boyer discusses David Bradley's *No Place to Hide* on p. 91 of *By the Bomb's Early Light.*

16. See Allan M. Winkler, *Life Under a Cloud: American Anxiety about the Atom*

(New York, 1993), 109–125, for an account of early civil defense measures and their social and cultural impact.

17. Eugene Rabinowitch, "The Realities of Atom Bomb Defense," *New Republic,* 25 September 1950, p. 21.

18. Ibid., 22.

19. This segment of Rabinowitch's article was reprinted as "Can We Atom-proof America?" *Science Digest,* February 1951, p. 71.

20. Ibid.

21. "Civil Defense: No Take-to-the-Hills," *Newsweek,* 11 December 1950, p. 25.

22. "Civil Defense: Plans and Uncertainties," *Newsweek,* 18 December 1950, p. 19.

23. Winkler discusses the creation of the FCDA in *Life Under a Cloud,* 111–112. After reorganization in 1958, the FCDA became the Office of Civil and Defense Mobilization (OCDM).

24. "How U.S. Cities Can Prepare for Atomic War," *Life,* 18 December 1950, p. 77.

25. Ibid.

26. Ibid., 79.

27. Ibid.

28. "Mental First Aid," *Science News Letter,* 27 January 1951, p. 53.

29. Ibid.

30. Ibid.

31. Murray S. Levine, "Civil Defense *vs.* Public Apathy," *Bulletin of Atomic Scientists,* February 1953, p. 27.

32. Ibid.

33. Ibid., 28.

34. Ibid.

35. Ibid.

36. "The Bill for CD," *Newsweek,* 30 March 1953, p. 32.

37. Ibid.

38. Robert W. Stokley, "Civil Defense and the Budget," *Bulletin of Atomic Scientists,* September 1953, p. 256, and Michael Straight, "Defending the U.S. against Atomic Attack," *New Republic,* 21 September 1953, p. 7.

39. Cartoon included in the "Top of the Week" summary of contents, *Newsweek,* 5 April 1954.

40. "H-Bomb Odds: 1 Million to 1—and That's What May Save Us," *Newsweek,* 5 April 1954, p. 28.

41. Ibid., 33–34.

42. Ibid., 28.

43. Val Peterson, quoted in "H-Bomb Odds," 28–33.

44. Eugene Rabinowitch, "Must Millions March?" *Bulletin of Atomic Scientists,* June 1954, p. 194.

45. All comments from ibid.

46. Ibid., 238.

47. In *Life Under a Cloud* Winkler discusses the issue of fallout and the fear and activism it aroused, in "Fear of Fallout," 84–108.

48. Ralph E. Lapp, "Civil Defense Faces New Perils," in Robert C. Williams and Philip L. Cantelon, eds., *The American Atom: A Documentary History of Nuclear Policies from the Discovery of Fission to the Present, 1939–1984* (Philadelphia, 1984), 189–190.

49. Ibid., 190.

50. "The Real Power of the Super-Bomb," *New Republic,* 8 November 1954, p. 4.

51. President Dwight Eisenhower, quoted in Ambrose, *Eisenhower,* 314. See pp. 312–314 for an account of the early conflict over the "missile gap."

52. Eisenhower, quoted in Ambrose, *Eisenhower,* 314.

53. "Scientific Blueprint for Atomic Survival," *Life,* 18 March 1957, p. 147.

54. Willard Bascom, "Difference between Victory and Defeat," *Life,* 18 March 1957, p. 150.

55. Ibid.

56. Ibid., 154.

57. Ibid.

58. Ibid., 162.

59. Donald Robinson, "If H-Bombs Fall . . . ," *Saturday Evening Post,* 25 May 1957, p. 25.

60. Ibid., 105.

61. Ibid.

62. "False(?) Alarm," *Harper's Magazine,* November 1957, p. 25.

63. Robinson, "If H-Bombs Fall," 105.

64. Ibid., 108.

65. Ibid., 111.

66. Ibid., 113.

67. Ibid.

68. "Civil Defense Is Dead," *Nation,* 28 September 1957, p. 186.

69. Ibid.

70. Eisenhower, quoted in Ambrose, *Eisenhower,* 423. See pp. 423–435 for Eisenhower's measured responses to the panic over Sputnik.

71. Merriman Smith, quoted in Ambrose, *Eisenhower,* 429.

72. Eisenhower, quoted in Ambrose, *Eisenhower,* 429.

73. "Civil Defense Shelters: An Interview with Congressman Chet Holifield," conducted by Ralph Lapp, *Bulletin of Atomic Scientists,* April 1958, pp. 130–131.

74. Ibid., 134.

75. William Leuchtenburg includes these statistics in *A Troubled Feast,* 104.

76. Film of Nixon proclaiming Mental Health Week is included in *The Atomic Cafe,* dir. and prod. Kevin Rafferty, Jayne Loader, and Pierce Rafferty (The Archives Project, Inc., 1982).

77. This informational film on civil defense was presented in *The Atomic Cafe*; for information on tranquilizer prescriptions, see Leuchtenburg, *A Troubled Feast,* 104.

78. This cartoon was featured in *The Atomic Cafe.*

79. William M. Lamers, "A Civil Defense and Disaster Program," *Safety Education,* January 1959, p. 2.

80. *The Atomic Cafe* illustrates all of these civil defense drills for children and includes segments from the educational films (see n. 68 this chapter).

81. W. Gayle Starnes, "Schools and Civil Defense," *School Board Journal,* August 1957, pp. 21–22.

82. Lamers, "A Civil Defense and Disaster Program," 3.

83. Ibid., 13.

84. Ibid.

85. Ibid.

86. Marnie Seymour, in Terkel, *"The Good War,"* 521.

87. Todd Gitlin, *The Sixties: Years of Hope, Days of Rage* (New York, 1987), 22.

88. Ibid., 22–23.

89. Michael Carey's findings, originally published as "Psychological Fallout," in the *Bulletin of Atomic Scientists,* January 1982, are reported here by Robert Jay Lifton in Robert Jay Lifton and Richard Falk, *Indefensible Weapons: The Political and Psychological Case against Nuclearism* (New York, 1982), 49. See pp. 48–56 for a full description of the study, in which Lifton occasionally participated.

90. Lifton details these common psychological threads in *Indefensible Weapons,* 51–52.

91. Ibid., 54.

CHAPTER FOUR

1. *Newsweek* cover, 5 April 1954.

2. Elaine Tyler May, *Homeward Bound: American Families in the Cold War Era* (New York, 1988), 10.

3. Ibid., 11.

4. Ibid.

5. Ibid., 14.

6. Both May's *Homeward Bound* and Stephen J. Whitfield's *The Culture of the Cold War* (Baltimore, 1991) discuss the dangers of and the pressures against domestic dissent and open discontent in this era.

7. May, *Homeward Bound,* 14.

8. Ibid., 27. See May's chapter "Hanging Together: For Better or Worse," 183–207, for an account of the failings of both domestic containment and the therapeutic approach. She notes on p. 207 that American homes contained "enormous discontent." This was especially true for women.

9. Dialogue taken directly from *Crossfire,* dir. Edward Dmytryk, prod. Adrian Scott (RKO Radio Picture, 1947).

10. J. D. Salinger, "A Perfect Day for Bananafish," in *Nine Stories* (New York, 1986; orig. pub. 1948–1953, 1958), 6.

11. Ibid., 18.

12. *Spellbound,* dir. Alfred Hitchcock, prod. David O. Selznick (Selznick International Picture, 1945). All scenes and dialogue taken directly from the film.

13. *Miracle on 34th Street,* dir. George Seaton, prod. William Perlberg (Twentieth Century-Fox, 1947). All scenes and dialogue taken directly from the film.

14. Psychologist Michael Fleming and film expert Roger Manvell argue that *The Snake Pit* marked a significant departure in American film treatment of insanity, focusing critical attention on the dramatically new post-World War II public concern for psychological troubles and mental institutions, "largely due to the prospect of serious overcrowding by World War II veterans with various neuropsychiatric disorders." Also, "the plight and symptoms of those confined in psychiatric institutions" gained new visibility in postwar film. See Michael Fleming and Roger Manvell, "Hollywood and Madness: Troubled Visions on the Silver Screen," *San Francisco Examiner/Chronicle,* 13 September 1987, "This World," p. 10.

15. *The Snake Pit,* dir. and prod. Anatole Litwak (Twentieth Century-Fox, 1948). All scenes and dialogue taken directly from the film.

16. Arthur Miller, *Death of a Salesman* (New York, 1949), 56.

17. Ibid., 126.

18. Dialogue taken directly from *Sunset Boulevard,* dir. Billy Wilder, prod. Charles Brackett (Paramount, 1950).

19. Jim Thompson, *The Killer Inside Me* (New York, 1983; orig. pub. 1952), 169–170.

20. Ibid., 179. An earlier American film also made this point about the mobility and widespread appearance of the insane. *The Devil Thumbs a Ride,* dir. Felix Feist, prod. Herman Schlom (RKO Radio Picture, 1949), featured a hitchhiking psychopathic killer who catches a ride with an unsuspecting driver and takes his insane violence on the road.

21. Jim Thompson, *A Hell of a Woman* (Berkeley, 1984; orig. pub., 1954), 21–22.

22. Ibid., 93. From this point in the novel Dillon uses a reversal of his name, and the final pages of the novel present a spectacular schizophrenic dialogue of his dual personas.

23. Sloan Wilson, *The Man in the Gray Flannel Suit* (New York, 1955), 1.

24. Ibid., 24 and 41–42.

25. Ibid., 64–69.

26. Ibid., 98.

27. Ibid., 158.

28. Ibid., 164.

29. Ibid., 251–252.

30. Ibid., 272.

31. *The Three Faces of Eve,* dir. and prod. Nunnally Johnson (Twentieth Century-Fox, 1957). All scenes and dialogue taken directly from the film.

32. Wilson, *The Man in the Gray Flannel Suit,* 267.

33. *The Man in the Gray Flannel Suit,* dir. Nunnally Johnson, prod. Darryl F. Zanuck (Twentieth Century-Fox, 1956). All scenes and dialogue taken directly from the film.

34. See Trewin Coppleston, *Modern Art* (New York, 1985), 182–188, for an account of Pollock's methods and for reproductions of his paintings.

35. William Leuchtenburg discusses and reproduces *The Subway* in *A Troubled Feast: American Society since 1945* (Boston, 1979), 105.

36. Charles Addams, *Monster Rally* (New York, 1950), 88.

37. Ibid., 36.

38. Ibid., 81.

39. *House of Strangers,* dir. Joseph L. Mankiewicz, prod. Sol Siegel (Twentieth Century-Fox, 1949). All scenes and dialogue taken directly from the film.

40. All scenes and dialogue taken directly from *Strangers on a Train,* dir. and prod. Alfred Hitchcock (Warner Bros./First National, 1951).

41. All scenes and dialogue taken directly from *The Big Carnival,* dir. and prod. Billy Wilder (Paramount, 1951).

42. All scenes and dialogue taken directly from *Clash by Night,* dir. Fritz Lang, prod. Harriet Parsons (RKO Radio Picture, 1952).

43. Jim Thompson, *A Swell-Looking Babe* (Berkeley, 1984; orig. pub., 1954), 63–64.

44. Ibid., 86.

45. Vladimir Nabokov, *Lolita* (New York, 1984; orig. pub. 1955), 7.

46. Ibid., 43.

47. Ibid., 122 and 125.

48. Ibid., 258 and 268.

49. Ibid., 272.

50. Ibid., 280.

51. *Rear Window,* dir. and prod. Alfred Hitchcock (Paramount, 1954). All scenes and dialogue taken directly from the film.

52. *Dial M for Murder,* dir. and prod. Alfred Hitchcock (Warner Bros./First National, 1954). All scenes taken directly from the film.

53. *The Man Who Knew Too Much,* dir. and prod. Alfred Hitchcock (Paramount, 1956). All scenes taken directly from the film.

54. *The Wrong Man,* dir. and prod. Alfred Hitchcock (Warner Bros./First National, 1956). All scenes and dialogue taken directly from the film. In his biography of Hitchcock, Donald Spoto confirms that Hitchcock's intentions in *The Man Who Knew Too Much* and *The Wrong Man* involved tracing the widespread loss of mental and family stability in a variety of locales. Of *The Wrong Man,* he noted:

> What intrigued Hitchcock was not only the confusion of innocence and guilt: . . . there was also . . . enormous emotional potential in the situation of the wife's breakdown—an element that had been added, late in the writing, to the script of *The Man Who Knew Too Much.* Hitchcock said he would stress an innocent man's terror and his wife's trauma, the loss of mental health and stability in a family not on vacation (as in the previous film) but in familiar neighborhood settings. In the new film he would again detail the threat to a household and to sanity, but not in an exotic foreign locale, amid international assassination plots and mysterious governments; instead, the disorder and madness would enter the living room.

See Donald Spoto, *The Dark Side of Genius: The Life of Alfred Hitchcock* (New York, 1983), 396.

55. Examples of other 1950s films upholding the sane necessity for suspicious paranoia included *All about Eve,* dir. Joseph L. Mankiewicz, prod. Darryl F. Zanuck (Twentieth Century-Fox, 1950), and *Niagara,* dir. Henry Hathaway, prod. Charles Brackett (Twentieth Century-Fox, 1953). In *All about Eve* the veteran stage actress Margo Channing takes a star-struck younger woman, Eve, under her wing, but she soon finds herself doubting the sincerity and trustworthiness of Eve. Margo's friends believe she is being cruel and paranoid, to the point that Margo throws an emotional fit about them being ready to drag her screaming to "the snake pit," but her paranoia about the true viciousness and ambition of Eve proves more than justified. In *Niagara* a psychologically disturbed veteran appears insanely jealous of his wife and unreasonably paranoid about her movements, but his mental torment has a basis in reality: his wife is having an affair with another man and the two are in fact plotting the husband's murder. Other science fiction films, like *The Beast from 20,000 Fathoms, Them!* and *The Fly,* also contain incidents in which those who warn of real danger are considered insane and paranoid.

56. All scenes and dialogue taken directly from *Invaders from Mars,* dir. William Cameron Menzies, prod. Edward L. Alperson (Twentieth Century-Fox, 1953).

57. All scenes and dialogue taken directly from *Invasion of the Body Snatchers,* dir. Don Siegel, prod. Walter Wanger (Allied Artists, 1956).

58. For an excellent analysis of *Invasion of the Body Snatchers,* see Stuart Samuels, "The Age of Conspiracy and Conformity: *Invasion of the Body Snatchers* (1956)," in John E. O'Connor and Martin A. Jackson, eds., *American History/American Film: Interpreting the Hollywood Image* (New York, 1977, 1988), 203–217.

59. Lewis Mumford, "Social Consequences of Atomic Energy" (1953), in his *Interpretations and Forecasts: 1922–1972* (New York, 1979), 307.

60. Ibid.

61. Ibid., 308 and 310.

62. Lewis Mumford, "Post-Historic Man" (1956), in his *Interpretations and Forecasts,* 376.

63. Ibid., 377.

64. Ibid., 379.

65. Ibid., 382.

66. Ibid., 383.

67. Ibid., 387.

CHAPTER FIVE

1. Louisa Randall Church, "Parents: Architects of Peace," *American Home,* November 1946, pp. 18–19, quoted in Elaine Tyler May, *Homeward Bound: American Families in the Cold War Era* (New York, 1988), 135.

2. May, *Homeward Bound,* 135.

3. Ibid., 135–136.

4. William March, *The Bad Seed* (New York, 1954), 7.

5. Ibid., 6.

6. Ibid., 22.

7. Ibid.

8. Ibid., 11 and 27.

9. Ibid., 27–28.

10. Ibid., 38.

11. Ibid., 47.

12. Ibid., 51. See pp. 50–60 for Rhoda's suspected past crimes.

13. Ibid., 104 and 114.

14. Ibid., 166. In the more conservative film version of *The Bad Seed,* dir. and prod. Mervyn LeRoy (Warner Bros./First National, 1956), it is Rhoda who dies while Christine is spared. Christine had attempted the murder/suicide, but both had been rescued. When Rhoda is released from the hospital, she goes out during a storm to retrieve the penmanship medal from the lake where her mother had thrown it. She is struck by lightning while trying to fish out the medal.

15. March, *The Bad Seed,* 122.

16. *Storm Center,* dir. Daniel Taradash, prod. Julian Blaustein (Columbia Pictures, 1956). All scenes and dialogue taken directly from the film.

17. *Red River,* dir. and prod. Howard Hawks (Warner Brothers, 1948). All scenes and dialogue taken directly from the film.

18. *The Boy with Green Hair,* dir. Joseph Losey, prod. Stephen Ames (RKO Radio Picture, 1948). All scenes and dialogue taken directly from the film.

19. *The Boy with Green Hair* was subjected to a fair amount of censorship and change because of its antiwar message; owner of RKO Howard Hughes ordered the pacifism toned down in consideration for his own and others' strict anticommunist attitudes. The original producer, Adrian Scott, one of the Hollywood Ten, was replaced and the director was later blacklisted.

20. *Rope,* dir. and prod. Alfred Hitchcock (Transatlantic Pictures, 1948). All scenes and dialogue taken directly from the film. This film was based on the Leopold and Loeb case, and these disturbed youths received yet more treatment in these years. *Compulsion,* dir. Richard Fleischer, prod. Richard Zanuck (Twentieth Century-Fox, 1959), also presented the story of "the mad act of two sick children who belong in a psychopathic institution" but used the story as a plea against capital punishment as well.

21. Arthur Miller, *Death of a Salesman* (New York, 1949), 16.

22. Ibid., 121.

23. Ibid., 132–133.

24. Ibid., 138.

25. Jim Thompson, *The Criminal* (Berkeley, 1986; orig. pub., 1953), 2.

26. Ibid., 49.

27. Ibid., 57.

28. Ibid., 64.

29. *The Wild One,* dir. Laslo Benedek, prod. Stanley Kramer (Stanley Kramer Company, 1953). All scenes and dialogue taken directly from the film. In a late

1950s article sympathetically explaining the beat mentality, John Clellon Holmes noted society's confusion at youths' celebration of the ugly and violent self-portraits presented in such films as *The Wild One:*

> Critics constantly express amazement at the willingness, even the delight, with which this generation accepts what are (to the critics) basically unflattering images of itself. It was noticed, for instance, that the most vociferous champions of the film *The Wild One* (which gave a brutal, unsympathetic account of the wanton pillage of a California town by a band of motorcyclists), were the motorcyclists themselves.

See John Clellon Holmes, "The Philosophy of the Beats," *Esquire,* June 1983 (reprint of February 1958 *Esquire* article), 164.

30. *Rebel Without a Cause,* dir. Nicholas Ray, prod. David Weisbart (Warner Brothers, 1955). All scenes and dialogue taken directly from the film.

31. Holmes, "The Philosophy of the Beats," 162.

32. Ibid.

33. Ibid., 163–164.

34. *The Blackboard Jungle,* dir. Richard Brooks, prod. Pandro S. Berman (MGM, 1955). All scenes and dialogue taken directly from the film. Fred Bronson discusses the importance of "Rock Around the Clock" as the first number-one rock hit on the *Billboard* charts in *The Billboard Book of Number One Hits* (New York, 1985), week of July 9, 1955, no. 1.

35. The reaction to *The Blackboard Jungle* and its "Rock Around the Clock" theme is traced by Bronson, ibid. He also notes that Clare Boothe Luce denounced the film as "degenerate," which prompted withdrawal of the film from the Venice Film Festival.

36. In his prologue to *Mystery Train: Images of America in Rock 'n' Roll Music* (New York, 1975), Griel Marcus conveys a sense of the refreshing rebelliousness of early rock which helped to counter the deadened aspects of 1950s culture:

> Listening now to Little Richard, to Elvis, to Jerry Lee Lewis, the Monotones, the Drifters, Chuck Berry, and dozens of others, I feel a sense of awe at how fine their music was. I can only marvel at their arrogance, their humor, their delight. They were so sure of themselves. They sang as if they knew they were destined to survive not only a few weeks on the charts but to make history; to displace the dreary events of the fifties in the memories of those who heard their records . . . (p. 4).

The rebelliousness and alienation evinced in rock music stem in part from the music's roots in the black musical culture of rhythm and blues—and from the major role black Americans played in creating and disseminating rock 'n' roll. It is not surprising that disaffected American youth, black and white, appreciated a music that emanated from a culture with a long history of alienation and disaffection from the repressive mainstream American society and culture. The same observation pertains to the beat attraction to jazz.

37. For the full text of the song, see Elvis Presley, "Heartbreak Hotel" (1956), from *Elvis Presley Commemorative Issue: The Top Ten Hits* (RCA, 1987).

38. In *The Elvis Catalogue* (Garden City, N.Y., 1987), Lee Cotten includes samples of the 1956 "Elvis Presley Personal Appearance Contract," where Elvis is touted as "the nation's only atomic-powered singer" (p. 16). The phrase was also used on other Elvis memorabilia from 1956.

39. Lee Cotten reports on the adult criticism and legal surveillance of Elvis variously throughout *The Elvis Catalogue,* but see pp. 54–59 for specific incidents.

40. Elvis Presley, quoted in Cotten, *The Elvis Catalogue,* 38 and 54.

41. "I Like Elvis" buttons are pictured in Cotten, *The Elvis Catalogue,* 59, and in a documentary on the early years of rock 'n' roll, *Rock 'n' Roll: The Early Days,* dir. Patrick Montgomery and Pamela Page, prod. Patrick Montgomery (Archive Film Production, 1984). Film footage of Elvis's fans show them wearing the buttons.

42. For the full lyrics, see Elvis Presley, "All Shook Up" (1957), from *Elvis Presley Commemorative Issue: The Top Ten Hits.*

43. See the complete text in Elvis Presley, "It's Now or Never" (1960), from *Elvis Presley Commemorative Issue: The Top Ten Hits.*

44. The documentary *Rock 'n' Roll: The Early Days* features a film clip from Steve Allen's television show in which he ridicules the meaninglessness of rock lyrics, showing little respect for or understanding of the impulses behind the music and its lyrics. To the amusement of his audience Allen announces that he will read a popular song as poetry, to get at the "simple beauty and the profundity of sentiment," and then he slowly recites the lyrics: "Be-bop-a-loo-la / She's my baby / Be-bop-a-loo-la / I don't mean maybe / She's the one that's got the beat / She's the one with the flying feet."

45. Jerry Lee Lewis, "A Whole Lotta Shakin' Goin' On" (1957) and "Great Balls of Fire" (1958), *The Essential Jerry Lee Lewis* (Charly Records, U.K., 1978).

46. *Rock 'n' Roll: The Early Days* includes film footage and statements of the media and the adult authorities regarding the evil of rock 'n' roll as well as coverage of local and national government investigations into the music.

47. Holmes, "The Philosophy of the Beats," 158.

48. Ibid., 160.

49. Ibid.

50. Allen Ginsberg, quoted in Ronald Gottesman et al., eds., *The Norton Anthology of American Literature* (New York, 1979), 2:2397.

51. Allen Ginsberg, *Howl* (1955–1956), in Ginsberg, *Howl and Other Poems* (San Francisco, 1956, 1959), 9.

52. Ibid., 9–11.

53. Ibid., 12.

54. Ibid., 17–18.

55. Ginsberg, "Footnote to Howl," in his *Howl and Other Poems,* 21.

56. Ginsberg, "Howl," in his *Howl and Other Poems,* 14.

57. Jack Kerouac, *On the Road* (New York, 1957), 5.

58. Ibid., 9.

59. Ibid., 11.

60. Ibid., 38–43.

61. Ibid., 46.

62. Ibid., 89–90.

63. Ibid., 95.

64. Ibid., 107, 99, and 111.

65. Ibid., 111 and 123.

66. Ibid., 161.

67. Ibid., 191 and 217.

68. Ibid., 225–226.

69. Ibid., 229.

70. Ibid., 241.

71. Ibid., 246.

72. Ibid., 250.

73. Ibid., 253.

74. Allen Ginsberg, "America," in his *Howl and Other Poems,* 31.

75. Ibid.

76. All scenes and dialogue taken directly from *Psycho,* dir. and prod. Alfred Hitchcock (Paramount, 1960).

77. Alfred Hitchcock, as stated in *The Men Who Made the Movies: Alfred Hitchcock,* dir. and prod. Richard Schickel (Directors Guild of America Presentation/ American Cinematique Production, 1973).

PART THREE

1. For the visual and written text of *The Twilight Zone* introduction, see the opening pages of Marc Scott Zicree, *The Twilight Zone Companion* (New York, 1982). The opening narrations varied over different seasons, but all adopted this same tone and theme of an open imagination.

2. Ken Kesey, *Sometimes a Great Notion* (New York, 1983; orig. pub. 1963, 1964), 505.

3. Ibid.

4. John F. Kennedy, "Inaugural Address," 20 January 1961, in Ronald Lora, ed., *America in the Sixties: Cultural Authorities in Transition* (New York, 1974), 32.

5. Kurt Vonnegut, Jr., *Cat's Cradle* (New York, 1988; orig. pub. 1963), 21. Vonnegut alludes to Oppenheimer's comment "The physicists have known sin." (See part 1, p. 6, above.)

6. Kennedy, "Inaugural Address," 34.

7. "Gun Thy Neighbor?" *Time,* 18 August 1961, p. 58.

8. "Letters," *Time,* 1 September 1961, p. 4.

9. *Time,* 8 April 1966.

10. What made this malaise and questioning of God and religion in the 1960s even more striking was that it followed the religious revival that had characterized spiritual life in the 1950s. For an account of this religious revival in the 1950s, see Stephen J. Whitfield's chapter "Praying: God Bless America," 77–100, in *The Culture of the Cold War* (Baltimore, 1991). Just as the spiritual malaise in the 1960s was

tied to the perils of the atomic age, so too was the revival of religion apparently tied to fears of the new atomic age. Whitfield notes that it is "tempting" to interpret the popularity in the 1950s of a preacher like Billy Graham and his pro-Christian, anticommunist message as "little more than an escape route from the post-Hiroshima world" given that Graham was fond of "mixing the fear of Armageddon with the assurance of redemption" (p. 78).

11. Barry McGuire, "Eve of Destruction," *Eve of Destruction* (ABC Dunhill Music, 1965).

12. Harold E. Fey, "Fifteen Years in Hell Is Enough" (1960), in *God and the H-Bomb*, ed. Donald Keys (New York, 1961), 67.

CHAPTER SIX

1. "The Great Illusion," *Nation*, "Editorials," 11 March 1961.

2. Ibid.

3. "Wanted—A Peace Movement," *Nation*, 11 March 1961.

4. *Newsweek* referred to the "Armageddon attitude" that had developed even before the Berlin crisis, defining it as the belief that no one and nothing would survive an all-out nuclear war. See "Civil Defense: Who'd Survive?" *Newsweek*, 7 August 1961, p. 48. The article also credited the novel and film versions of *On the Beach* with helping to establish and spread this attitude.

5. Nevil Shute, *On the Beach* (New York, 1983; orig. pub. 1957), 36.

6. Ibid., title page.

7. Ibid., 268.

8. Freeman Dyson credits *On the Beach* with creating an enduring atomic age myth about nuclear war, a myth that "pictures nuclear war as silent inexorable death from which there is no escape." Dyson details the technical and scientific inaccuracies in Shute's end-of-the-world scenario, but he sees the human truth of the novel: "On the fundamental human level, in spite of all the technical inaccuracies, it spoke truth. It told the world, in language that everyone could understand, that nuclear war means death. And the world listened." See Freeman Dyson, *Weapons and Hope* (New York, 1984), 33–34.

9. "Time Enough at Last," written by Rod Serling, dir. John Brahm, prod. Buck Houghton, *The Twilight Zone*, CBS, 20 October 1959. All scenes and dialogue taken directly from the episode. Marc Scott Zicree's *The Twilight Zone Companion* (New York, 1982) also includes an account of this episode, 66–70.

10. See Fred Bronson, *The Billboard Book of Number One Hits* (New York, 1985), for the week of February 8, 1960, for information on "Teen Angel."

11. For the full text of the song, see Mark Dinning, "Teen Angel" (1959), *Teenage Tragedy* (Rhino Records, Inc., Santa Monica, Calif., 1984).

12. All these teen death songs are collected on the album *Teenage Tragedy*.

13. Even though there is no specific reference to the bomb in these songs, there is a general recognition of the songs' belonging to the atomic age. In *The Rolling Stone Encyclopedia of Rock and Roll*, ed. Jon Pareles and Patricia Romanowski (New

York, 1983), 140, the entry for "Death Rock" notes that "perhaps songs about death made listeners feel more alive. Or perhaps they were a manifestation of the A-bomb generation's anxieties."

14. Fred Bronson discusses the reluctance of radio stations to play songs like "Teen Angel" in *The Billboard Book*. See this in his account "Teen Angel," February 8, 1960.

15. Walker Percy, *The Moviegoer* (New York, 1980; orig. pub. 1960, 1961), 83.

16. Ibid.

17. Ibid., 99.

18. Ibid., 180.

19. Norman Gottwald, "Nuclear Realism or Nuclear Pacifism?" (1960), in *God and the H-Bomb*, ed. Donald Keys (New York, 1961), 44.

20. Ibid.

21. "Wanted—A Peace Movement," *Nation*, 11 March 1961.

22. Kennedy's 25 July 1961 speech on civil defense is quoted in both "Civil Defense: The Sheltered Life," *Time*, 2 October 1961, p. 21, and Walter Karp, "When Bunkers Last in Backyards Bloom'd," *American Heritage*, February/March 1980, p. 85. This speech is also discussed in Allan M. Winkler, *Life Under a Cloud: American Anxiety about the Atom* (New York, 1993), 126, and Winkler notes that international affairs analyst Michael Mandelbaum called the speech "one of the most alarming speeches by an American President in the whole, nerve-wracking course of the Cold War."

23. Kennedy, from the July 25, 1961 speech, quoted in Stephen E. Ambrose, *Rise to Globalism: American Foreign Policy since 1938*, 5th rev. ed. (New York, 1988), 189. See Ambrose, *Rise to Globalism*, pp. 188–192, for an account of the events and issues involved in the Berlin crisis.

24. Khrushchev, quoted in "The World," *Time*, 18 August 1961, p. 20.

25. Ambrose discusses the Soviet tests in *Rise to Globalism* (p. 191) and claims the fifty-eight megaton weapon was three thousand times more powerful than the original atomic bomb, and *Time* magazine reported on the Soviet boast that the "superbomb" was five thousand times the size of the Hiroshima bomb, "The Cold War: Response to a Power Play," *Time*, 8 September 1961, p. 19.

26. Kennedy, quoted in "The Cold War: Response to a Power Play," *Time*, 8 September 1961, p. 20.

27. *Time*, 8 September 1961.

28. Kennedy speech (May 1961), quoted in *Newsweek*, "CD—The Weak Spot," 31 July 1961, p. 14.

29. "CD—The Weak Spot," *Newsweek*, 31 July 1961, p. 14.

30. *New York Times*, 27 July 1961, quoted in Karp, "When Bunkers Last in Backyards Bloom'd," 85.

31. "Civil Defense: Who'd Survive?" *Newsweek*, 7 August 1961, p. 48.

32. Ibid.

33. Walter Karp presents these numbers in "When Bunkers Last in Backyards Bloom'd," 86.

34. OCDM official, quoted in "Civil Defense: Who'd Survive?" 48.

35. Ibid.

36. Herman Kahn, quoted in "Civil Defense: Who'd Survive?" For more on Kahn's views, see Herman Kahn, *On Thermonuclear War,* 2d ed. (Princeton, 1961), especially "Alternative National Strategies," 3–39.

37. "Gun Thy Neighbor?" *Time,* 18 August 1961, p. 58.

38. Ibid.

39. Ibid.

40. Ibid.

41. Ibid.

42. "Letters," *Time,* 25 August 1961, p. 3.

43. Both letters in ibid.

44. "Letters," *Time,* 1 September 1961, p. 4.

45. Ibid.

46. *Life,* 15 September 1961.

47. Surviv-All, Inc. advertisement, in Karp, "When Bunkers Last in Backyards Bloom'd," 88.

48. Karp includes pictures and commentary on some of these civil defense companies in Karp, "When Bunkers Last in Backyards Bloom'd," 90–91, and *Time* includes a picture of a bomb shelter display at the Dallas Fair, "Civil Defense: The Sheltered Life," 20 October 1961, p. 22.

49. "The Power and the Honor," *Life,* 15 September 1961, p. 4.

50. Letter from President Kennedy in "Fallout Shelters: A New Urgency, Big Things to Do—and What You Must Learn," *Life,* 15 September 1961, p. 95.

51. "Fallout Shelters: A New Urgency, Big Things to Do—and What You Must Learn," *Life,* 15 September 1961, p. 96.

52. Ibid.

53. Ibid., 98–104.

54. Ibid., 105.

55. Ibid., 106–107.

56. "Civil Defense: The Sheltered Life," *Time,* 20 October 1961, p. 22.

57. Virgil Couch, quoted in "Civil Defense: The Sheltered Life," p. 21.

58. "The People: Ready to Act," *Time,* 29 September 1961, p. 13.

59. "Civil Defense: The Sheltered Life," 21.

60. "The People," *Time,* 29 September 1961, p. 14. A photograph of the truck carrying the bomb shelter accompanies the article on the same page.

61. The "Foam-Ettes" advertisement is included in Karp, "When Bunkers Last in Backyards Bloom'd," 89, and the burial suit description is in "Civil Defense: The Sheltered Life," 23.

62. "The People," 14.

63. "Letters," *Time,* 13 October 1961, p. 7.

64. Ibid.

65. "Aristotle & The Bomb: Red, Dead or Heroic?" *Time,* 13 October 1961, p. 29.

66. All quotations from ibid.

67. Ibid.

68. "Civil Defense: The Sheltered Life," 23.

69. Father McHugh's position is outlined and quoted in "Civil Defense: The Sheltered Life," and in Karp, "When Bunkers Last in Backyards Bloom'd," 92.

70. This portion of Bishop Dun's reaction is quoted in Karp, "When Bunkers Last in Backyards Bloom'd," 92.

71. "Civil Defense: The Sheltered Life," 23.

72. While the culture's general opposition to civil defense and thermonuclear bravado found its fullest expression in these early years of the 1960s, there was also some organized protest offered to a variety of nuclear policies during the late 1950s and early 1960s. In *If I Had a Hammer: The Death of the Old Left and the Birth of the New Left* (New York, 1987), Maurice Isserman devotes a chapter to the development and actions of these groups in the mid- to late 1950s; see "Radical Pacifism: The Americanization of Gandhi," 125–169. Here he discusses civil defense protests against New York City's annual drill (which began in 1955 but gained great popularity in 1960 and 1961), resulting in the drill being abandoned (pp. 144–147); the formation of the National Committee for a Sane Nuclear Policy (SANE) in 1957 (pp. 147–149); and the founding of the group Non-Violent Action against Nuclear Weapons (NVAANW) in 1957 (pp. 149–150). Winkler in *Life Under a Cloud* also addresses similar issues, especially the origins and goals of SANE (pp. 105–106) and civil defense and its critics in the early 1960s (pp. 125–135). Contemporaneous with the culture's overall arousal was the Women's Strike for Peace, on November 1, 1961, which Elaine Tyler May analyzes in *Homeward Bound: American Families in the Cold War Era* (New York, 1988), 218–219. This strike gathered together fifty thousand housewives who protested America's nuclear policies, and its leaders were subjected to FBI surveillance and grilling by HUAC. One of these leaders pointed out to the committee in 1962 "that saving children from nuclear extinction was the essence of 'Americanism'" (p. 219). May concluded that "the familial-cold war consensus was beginning to lose its grip."

73. In "When Bunkers Last in Backyards Bloom'd" Karp discusses the widespread religious criticism leveled at Father McHugh (p. 92).

74. All quotations from "Civil Defense: Who'd Survive?" 49.

75. Opening narration for "The Shelter," 29 September 1961, taken from the synopsis of the episode in Zicree, *The Twilight Zone Companion*, 227.

76. Closing narration for "The Shelter" in Zicree, *The Twilight Zone Companion*, 227.

77. Paul Brians in *Nuclear Holocausts: Atomic War in Fiction, 1895–1984* (Kent, Ohio, 1987), 46, briefly discusses this episode of *The Twilight Zone* as part of "the shelter fad," and he notes that "a good deal of debate went on about the morality of fallout shelters." He also documents (on pp. 21–22) the large number of science-fiction stories about shelters which appeared in 1961 and 1962. He concludes from his analysis of nuclear literature that nuclear fiction, like the culture, rejected shelters:

> Fallout shelters have been used in a number of ways in fiction: as a high-pressure environment for the blossoming of love affairs, as a refuge for religious

cultists, as emotional pressure cookers providing violent conflict, and even as time-travel machines. Indeed they have served every purpose except that for which real bomb shelters are ostensibly designed: the protection of their inhabitants from blast and radiation. Whatever their perspective, all but a handful of authors writing about shelters view them as metaphors for racial suicide, a symbol of the self-defeating nature of nuclear weapons, which make us our own prisoners of war (pp. 49–50).

78. Eisenhower, quoted in Karp, "When Bunkers Last in Backyards Bloom'd," 92.

79. "Survival: Are Shelters the Answer?" *Newsweek,* 6 November 1961, p. 19.

80. Ibid.

81. Ibid.

82. Ibid., 19–20.

83. Ibid., 23.

84. Ibid.

85. Margaret Mead, "Are Shelters the Answer?" *New York Times Magazine,* 26 November 1961, p. 29.

86. Ibid.

87. Ibid.

88. Ibid., 29 and 124.

89. Ibid., 124.

90. Ibid., 124–125.

91. Ibid., 125.

92. In "Civil Defense: The Sheltered Life," *Time* included a photograph of William Walker building his shelter, and his front window contained a sign reading "He Who Laughs Last" (p. 23).

93. The shelter contractors and manufacturers are cited in Karp, "When Bunkers Last in Backyards Bloom'd," 92.

94. In *Weapons and Hope* Freeman Dyson corroborates the idea that Americans' rejection of shelters was an essentially moral stance. On p. 89 he explains:

The antipathy toward shelters in the United States has a strong ethical component. Shelters are not merely unpopular; they are perceived by the public to be unethical. . . . The evil reputation of shelters arises from two main sources. First, the building of private shelters created an image of the rich home-owner sitting comfortably in his shelter and locking his doors against the homeless refugees dying of radiation sickness outside. Second, the building of public shelters, by a government heavily armed with nuclear missiles, created an image of a country setting out to massacre its enemies while keeping its own population safe from retaliation. Both images are exaggerated nightmares, but both also contain an element of truth. If rich people have shelters and poor people have none, or if governments build shelters while simultaneously building offensive missile forces, then shelters are inextricably linked in our imagination with murderous intentions. Shelters have lost their innocence.

95. Herman Kahn, *On Thermonuclear War*, 2d ed. (Princeton, 1961), 20.

96. Ibid., 20–21.

97. Ibid., 21.

98. Robert Moore Williams, *The Day They H-Bombed Los Angeles* (New York, 1961), 5.

99. Ibid., 6.

100. Ibid., 9.

101. Ibid., 10.

102. Ibid., 35.

103. Ibid., 40.

104. Ibid., 49.

105. Ibid., 51.

106. Ibid., 89.

107. Ibid., 89–90.

108. Ibid., 96.

109. Ibid., 31.

110. Ibid., 110.

111. Steve Allen, foreword, in *God and the H-Bomb*, ed. Donald Keys (New York, 1961), 7.

112. Bishop James A. Pike, "Survival by Shelter or Sanity?" in *God and the H-Bomb*, 140.

113. Ibid., 140–141.

114. Ibid., 140.

115. Ibid., 142.

116. Ibid., 142–143.

117. Ibid., 143–144.

118. Ibid., 144.

119. Israel Goldstein, "The Road to Sanity," in *God and the H-Bomb*, 156–157.

120. Samuel H. Dresner, "Man, God and Atomic War," in *God and the H-Bomb*, 129.

121. Ibid., 132.

122. Ibid.

123. Ibid., 133.

124. Ibid., 134.

125. Ibid., 134 and 137.

126. Ibid., 136.

127. The "Open Letter" was reprinted in the *Bulletin of Atomic Scientists*, February 1962, p. 28.

128. Ibid., 29.

129. Ibid.

130. Ibid.

131. Letter to the Editor, *Science*, 16 February 1962, p. 603.

132. Gerard Piel, "The Illusion of Civil Defense," *Bulletin of Atomic Scientists*, February 1962, p. 2.

133. Ibid., 7.

134. Ibid., 8.

135. Ibid.

136. Ibid.

137. Gerard Piel, "On the Feasibility of Peace," *Science*, 23 February 1962, p. 648.

138. Ibid.

139. Ibid.

140. Ibid., 650–651.

141. Ibid., 648.

142. Ibid., 651–652.

143. Ibid., 652.

144. Ibid., 648.

145. Editor's introduction to Roger Hagan, "Community Shelters," *Nation*, 24 February 1962, p. 160.

146. Hagan, "Community Shelters," 164.

147. Irving Brant, "Who Shall Be Saved by Shelters?" *New Republic*, 5 March 1962, p. 7.

148. Ibid.

149. Ibid.

150. Stanley L. Newman, "Civil Defense and Congress: The Quiet Reversal," *Bulletin of Atomic Scientists*, November 1962, p. 35. The statistics on civil defense appropriations appear on pp. 33–34.

151. Ibid., 35–36.

152. Ibid., 36.

153. Ibid., 37.

154. Asher Brynes, "Where's Civil Defense Now?" *New Republic*, 1 December 1962, p. 16.

155. Ibid.

156. "Civil Defense: Helter Shelter," *Newsweek*, 11 June 1962, p. 32.

157. In *Life Under a Cloud*, 132, Winkler credits the 1963 Limited Test Ban Treaty with halting concern for civil defense: "The Limited Test Ban Treaty, signed by the United States, the Soviet Union, and Great Britain in 1963, squelched the most serious agitation for civil defense in the postwar years." It seems somewhat evident that the waning of civil defense came a bit earlier and can be credited to the public's disenchantment.

158. Fey, "Fifteen Years in Hell Is Enough," in *God and the H-Bomb*, 67.

159. *The Day the Earth Caught Fire*, dir. and prod. Val Guest (British Lion-Pax Production, 1962). All scenes and dialogue taken directly from the film.

160. Todd Gitlin, *The Sixties: Years of Hope, Days of Rage* (New York, 1987), 98.

161. "Showdown-Backdown," *Newsweek*, 5 November 1962, p. 27.

162. D. G. Green, "Imagining the Bomb," in "Letters," *Nation*, 18 April 1981, p. 450.

163. "Showdown-Backdown," 34.

164. "Top of the Week" and "Showdown-Backdown," 21 and 27.

165. "The Lessons Learned," *Newsweek*, 12 November 1962, p. 21.

166. "Danger . . . Doubt . . . Determination—and Hope," *Newsweek,* 5 November 1962, p. 33.

167. "Showdown-Backdown," 30.

168. The partial text of Khrushchev's October 28 letter appears in "Showdown-Backdown," 27, and Bertrand Russell is quoted in "Danger . . . Doubt . . . Determination—and Hope," 33.

169. "Statement by the President Following the Soviet Decision to Withdraw Missiles from Cuba," October 28, 1962, as reprinted in Robert C. Williams and Philip L. Cantelon, eds., *The American Atom: A Documentary History of Nuclear Policies from the Discovery of Fission to the Present, 1939–1984* (Philadelphia, 1984), 251.

170. Gitlin, *The Sixties,* 96.

171. Ibid., 97–98.

172. Barrington Moore, Jr., quoted in Gitlin, *The Sixties,* 100.

173. Paul Potter, quoted in Gitlin, *The Sixties,* 102.

174. Dresner, "Man, God and Atomic War," in *God and the H-Bomb,* 132.

CHAPTER SEVEN

1. In his preface to *If I Had a Hammer: The Death of the Old Left and the Birth of the New Left* (New York, 1987), xvii, Maurice Isserman notes that the emergence of radicalism in the 1960s was "produced by a complex interaction of demographics, economics, and politics (both mainstream and radical)." He thereafter suggests the broad character of revolt in the 1960s and its connection to nuclear issues after the Cuban missile crisis in his list of "factors" explaining the changing atmosphere of the early 1960s:

> The political climate would probably have remained much the same as in the previous decade had it not been for the following factors: the baby boom and the resulting postwar expansion of American higher education; the redistribution of the black population from the rural South to the urban South and North and the resulting increase in potential black voting strength; the general prosperity that prevailed in the early 1960s and the resulting willingness on the part of politicians and opinion makers to consider the plight of the 'other America'; and finally, a lessening of the immediate prospects for nuclear confrontation, resulting in a greater public willingness to question or at least to tolerate questions about the direction of American foreign policy.

Both Elaine Tyler May in *Homeward Bound: American Families in the Cold War Era* (New York, 1988) and Stephen J. Whitfield in *The Culture of the Cold War* (Baltimore, 1991) also see the early 1960s as the time when cracks in the cold war consensus appeared. See May's "Epilogue: The Baby Boom Comes of Age," 208–226, and Whitfield's "Thawing: A Substitute for Victory," 205–230.

2. Lewis Mumford, "World Culture" (1956), in his *Interpretations and Forecasts, 1922–1972* (New York, 1979), 443.

3. Accounts of this anti-HUAC demonstration are included in Todd Gitlin, *The*

Sixties: Years of Hope, Days of Rage (New York, 1987), 82, and in Isserman, *If I Had a Hammer,* 188–189.

4. Isserman, *If I Had a Hammer,* 188, notes that "it was the first time in its nearly three decades of existence that the committee had ever been met with such a mass public protest."

5. Whitfield points out that by the late 1950s the blacklist was "enfeebled" (but still in operation); in 1957 alone numerous blacklisted writers were working, if without credit, and were making Academy Award-winning films. See pp. 149–150 in *The Culture of the Cold War.*

6. Whitfield in *The Culture of the Cold War* examines the radical context of *Spartacus* (pp. 218–219), reminding readers not only that Spartacus "was long included in the pantheon of Communist heroes" but also that President-elect Kennedy and Robert Kennedy crossed American Legion picket lines to view the film.

7. *Spartacus,* dir. Stanley Kubrick, prod. Edward Lewis (Universal International, 1960). All scenes and dialogue taken directly from the film.

8. Joseph Heller, *Catch-22* (New York, 1977; orig. pub. 1961), 116.

9. Ibid., 117.

10. Ibid., 119–120.

11. The subversive and oppositional character of laughter is suggested, albeit in a far different historical and cultural setting, in Mikhail Bakhtin, *Rabelais and His World* (Bloomington, 1984). See especially the introduction, pp. 1–58. The specific connection between black humor and the changing culture of the 1960s is addressed in chapter 4, "Black Humor and History: The Early 1960s," in Morris Dickstein, *The Gates of Eden* (New York, 1977).

12. Heller, *Catch-22,* 275.

13. Ibid., 47.

14. Ibid., 17.

15. Ibid., 30.

16. Ibid., 180.

17. Ibid., 176–177.

18. Ibid., 127.

19. Ibid., 107.

20. Ibid., 311–312.

21. Ibid., 46–47.

22. Ibid., 416.

23. Ibid., 193.

24. Ibid., 60.

25. Ibid., 334–337.

26. Ibid., 259.

27. Ibid., 260.

28. Ibid.

29. Ibid., 262–263.

30. Ibid., 266.

31. Ibid., 184–185.

32. Ibid., 424. There are earlier images in the novel that add to this Christ-like

vision of Yossarian and that create the basis for a reborn Yossarian. Even though Yossarian only later comes to understand the deeper meaning of Snowden's death on the Avignon mission, he is nonetheless greatly affected by it at the time. He sheds his clothes after the mission and appears naked at Snowden's funeral, sitting in a tree a small distance from the cemetery. Yossarian considers the tree "the tree of life . . . and of knowledge of good and evil, too." This, and his nakedness, suggest the genesis of his desire to begin life anew; and, as Milo arrives to sit with him in the tree, there is a contrast between devilishness and angelicism as well. The chaplain views this scene and, never considering that it could be an actual event, believes it is "a secret, enigmatic vision," "a revelation" (see pp. 267–276).

33. Ibid., 430.

34. Ibid., 431.

35. Ibid., 434–437.

36. Ibid., 449. The entire Snowden scene appears on pp. 446–450.

37. Ibid., 450.

38. Ibid., 455.

39. Ibid., 458–463. Joseph Heller defended Yossarian's choice of desertion against its critics as the only solution with "integrity," as the only solution consistent "with the moral viewpoint of the book." According to Heller:

> Now, in Yossarian's situation—his environment, his society, the world, and it's not just America, it's the world itself—the monolithic society closes off every conventional area of protest or corrective action, and the only choice that's left to him is one of ignoble acceptance in which he can profit and live comfortably—but nevertheless ignoble—or flight, a renunciation of that condition, of that society, that set of circumstances. The only way he can renounce it without going to jail is by deserting it, trying to keep going until they capture him. I like to think of him as a kind of spirit on the loose.

See the 1962 interview with Paul Krassner, "An Impolite Interview with Joseph Heller," in Robert M. Scotto, ed., *Catch-22: A Critical Edition* (New York: Dell, 1973), 471–474.

40. Heller, *Catch-22*, 414.

41. Ken Kesey, *One Flew Over the Cuckoo's Nest* (New York, 1986; orig. pub. 1962), 38.

42. Ibid., 124.

43. Ibid., 20.

44. Ibid., 39.

45. Ibid., 8.

46. Ibid., 11.

47. Ibid., 68.

48. Ibid., 89.

49. Ibid., 121.

50. Ibid., 123 and 141.

51. Ibid., 226.

52. Ibid., 227–228.

53. Ibid., 181.

54. Ibid., 66–67.

55. Ibid., 180.

56. Ibid., 271.

57. Ibid., 275.

58. Ibid., 276.

59. Ibid., 277.

60. Ibid., 304.

61. Ibid., 305.

62. Ibid.

63. Ibid., 307.

64. Ibid., 308.

65. Ibid., 310.

66. Ibid., 198.

67. The novel's appearance in 1959 points to the roots of open rebellion in the late 1950s, and Condon's work was linked by Paul Krassner to both *Catch-22* and *One Flew Over the Cuckoo's Nest* in "An Impolite Interview with Joseph Heller." Krassner questioned Heller about "other writers' approaches to the insanity of our time," and he included Kesey and Condon in the group of writers who, like Heller, dealt with this subject. Heller noted both the "serious" and "burlesque" qualities in *The Manchurian Candidate*, a contrast intensified in the film version. See pp. 461–462 in Scotto, ed., *Catch-22: A Critical Edition* for the Krassner and Heller comments. The film and the novel differ most clearly as a result of the film's simplification and tightening of characters and action. The somewhat "extraneous" detail of the novel is stripped away in the film to allow a starker and "blacker" presentation of the story's ironies and incongruities. For example, in the brainwashing sequences, in which the American soldiers are convinced through mind control that they are at a women's garden club when in reality they are being tested and examined by communist officials, the film's ability to make the contradiction between brainwashed illusion and reality visible, by fading back and forth between images of old women in flowery dresses and communist officials in uniform, increases the strangely humorous and bizarre nature of the experience.

68. *The Manchurian Candidate,* dir. John Frankenheimer, prod. George Axelrod and John Frankenheimer (United Artists, 1962). All scenes and dialogue taken directly from the film.

69. The sexual perversion of Mrs. Iselin is even more explicit in the novel. She seduces her son while he is in his brainwashed trance (and he is thus unaware of her as his mother, although his later deprogrammed memories of this "affair" help to push him toward her assassination); moreover, she is presented throughout as a heroin addict as well as a communist agent. See the entire characterization of her in Richard Condon, *The Manchurian Candidate* (New York, 1959).

70. For other interpretations of *The Manchurian Candidate,* see Whitfield, *The Culture of the Cold War,* 211–213, and Michael P. Rogin, *Ronald Reagan, the Movie and Other Episodes of Political Demonology* (Berkeley, 1987), 252–254. Rogin claims that the film "aims to reawaken a lethargic nation to the Communist menace"

(p. 252), an analysis Whitfield finds "dubious" (p. 212). Whitfield cites director Frankenheimer's memory that at one point both the Communist party and the American Legion wanted to picket the film and that he loved it because "after all, the whole point of the film was the absurdity of any type of extremism." Whitfield concludes that "when the Communists felt free to picket again, when a movie director could welcome such controversy, and when the American Legion was considered as 'extremist' as the Communists, the 1950s were going into remission" (p. 213).

71. Daniel Bell, "The Dispossessed," in Daniel Bell, ed., *The Radical Right: The New American Right* (Garden City, N.Y., 1962), 2.

72. Ibid., 5 and 45.

73. Steven Allen, foreword, in *God and the H-Bomb,* ed. Donald Keys (New York, 1961), 8.

74. Ibid., 8–9.

75. Kurt Vonnegut, Jr., *Mother Night* (New York, 1981; orig. pub. 1961, 1966). In the introduction added by Vonnegut in 1966, he suggests a nonfictional correlation between Nazi and Allied methods of mass death by discussing the firebombing of Dresden, which he witnessed as a prisoner of war in Germany. He noted how "one apocalyptic flame" grew forth from the bombings, and he commented on what remained after the bombings: "Everything was gone but the cellars where 135,000 Hansels and Gretels had been baked like gingerbread men" (see pp. vi–vii). Clearly troubled by the firebombing of Dresden, "the largest massacre in European history, by the way," Vonnegut returned to this subject in *Slaughterhouse-Five* (1968).

76. Vonnegut, *Mother Night,* xii.

77. Ibid., 133.

78. Ibid., 141.

79. Ibid., 45.

80. Ibid., 80–81.

81. Ibid., 60–61.

82. Ibid., 119–120.

83. Ibid., 162–163.

84. Ibid., 192.

85. Ibid., 108.

86. Ibid.

87. Ibid., 122.

88. Ibid., 123–124.

89. Ibid., 124. Hannah Arendt, *Eichmann in Jerusalem: A Report on the Banality of Evil* (New York, 1963; rev. ed., 1964).

90. Vonnegut, *Mother Night,* 124.

91. Arendt, *Eichmann in Jerusalem,* 48–49.

92. Ibid., 50 and 54.

93. Ibid., 54–55.

94. Ibid., 22.

95. Ibid., 115 and 116.

96. Ibid., 103.

97. Ibid., 289.

98. Ibid., 276.

99. Ibid., 294–295.

100. Ibid., 232–233.

101. Ibid., 276.

102. Ibid., 273.

103. Ibid., 287.

104. Timuel Black, in Studs Terkel, *"The Good War": An Oral History of World War Two* (New York, 1984), 281–282.

105. Donald Robinson, "If H-Bombs Fall . . . ," *Saturday Evening Post,* 25 May 1957, p. 110.

106. Langston Hughes, "Harlem," from *Montage of a Dream Deferred,* excerpted in Langston Hughes, *Selected Poems* (New York, 1959), 268.

107. Langston Hughes, "Lunch in a Jim Crow Car," from *Words Like Freedom,* excerpted in Hughes, *Selected Poems,* 280.

108. James Baldwin, *The Fire Next Time* (New York, 1977; orig. pub. 1962, 1963), 141.

109. Ibid., 73.

110. Ibid., 73–74.

111. Ibid., 74–75.

112. Ibid., 76.

113. Ibid., 76–77.

114. Ibid., 79–80.

115. Ibid., 80.

116. Students for a Democratic Society, "The Port Huron Statement," in Ronald Lora, ed., *America in the Sixties: Cultural Authorities in Transition* (New York, 1974), 259. For more background information on the SDS, see Isserman's chapter "Toward a New Left," in *If I Had a Hammer,* 202–219 especially.

117. SDS, "The Port Huron Statement," 260.

118. Ibid.

119. Ibid., 261.

120. Ibid.

121. Ibid.

122. Ibid., 264.

123. Ibid., 267.

124. Ibid., 262.

125. Ibid., 263–264.

126. Ibid., 265.

127. Lewis Mumford, "The Human Prospect" (1962), in his *Interpretations and Forecasts, 1922–1972* (New York, 1979), 462.

128. Ibid., 463–464.

129. Ibid., 466.

130. Ibid., 467.

131. Ibid., 467–468.

132. Ibid., 472–473.

133. Ibid., 473.

134. Rod Serling, introduction to "Mr. Bevis," *The Twilight Zone,* written by Rod Serling, dir. William Asher, prod. Buck Houghton, CBS, 3 June 1960, included in Marc Scott Zicree, *The Twilight Zone Companion* (New York, 1982), 124.

135. Rod Serling's conclusion to "The Brain Center at Whipple's," *The Twilight Zone,* written by Rod Serling, dir. Richard Donner, prod. William Froug, CBS, 15 May 1964, included in Zicree, *The Twilight Zone Companion,* 405.

136. There was, of course, some continuity in the presentation of the "normal" American family; not only did the Nelsons, Andersons, and Cleavers stay perpetually alive in reruns, but shows like *The Donna Reed Show* (1958–1966) bridged the gap between the 1950s and the 1960s. Nonetheless, even in the television shows dedicated to traditional family values, including *The Andy Griffith Show* (1960–1968) and *My Three Sons* (1960–1972), the family was not conventional, lacking the presence of a mother. See Tim Brooks and Earle Marsh, *TV in the Sixties* (New York, 1985), for listings and brief descriptions of television shows in the 1960s, or see Tim Brooks and Earle Marsh, *The Complete Directory to Prime Time Network Shows 1946–Present,* 5th ed. (New York, 1992).

137. General information on these shows, the characters, and the air dates can be found in Brooks and Marsh, *TV in the Sixties,* which also identifies the genre of "ghoul comedy" (p. 4). For an in-depth treatment of *Bewitched,* see Herbie J. Pilato, *The Bewitched Book* (New York, 1992). Gerard Jones in *Honey I'm Home! Sitcoms: The Selling of the American Dream* (New York, 1992) discusses many of these shows in chapter 12, "Fantasyland," 163–180. For an insightful analysis of *The Beverly Hillbillies* and its place in sixties culture, see David Farber, *The Age of Great Dreams: America in the 1960s* (New York, 1994), 52–55.

138. Mumford, "The Human Prospect," 463.

139. These works of Thiebaud and Oldenburg are presented in "American Food and American Marketing," in Sidra Stich, *Made in U.S.A.: An Americanization in Art, The '50s & '60s* (Berkeley, 1987), 78–87.

140. The Wesselmann and Watts pieces are pictured in Stich, *Made in U.S.A.,* 107–108 and 83.

141. Warhol's *Soup Cans* (1962) and *210 Coca-Cola Bottles* (1962) also appear in Stich, *Made in U.S.A.,* 90–92.

142. Andy Warhol from an interview with Gene R. Swenson, "What Is Pop Art?" November 1963, quoted in Stich, *Made in U.S.A.,* 91–92.

143. Thomas Pynchon, *V.* (New York, 1979; orig. pub. 1963), 264–265.

144. Ibid., 265.

145. Ibid., 266–267.

146. *The Birds,* dir. and prod. Alfred Hitchcock (Universal, 1963). All scenes and dialogue taken directly from the film.

147. Alfred Hitchcock, quoted in Donald Spoto, *The Dark Side of Genius: The Life of Alfred Hitchcock* (New York, 1983), 479.

148. Hitchcock made these comments in the documentary by the Directors Guild of America, *The Men Who Made the Movies: Alfred Hitchcock,* dir. and prod. Richard Schickel (The American Cinematique, 1973).

149. François Truffaut, *Hitchcock/Truffaut* (New York, 1983–1984), 285.

CHAPTER EIGHT

1. Malcolm X and Alex Haley, *The Autobiography of Malcolm X* (New York, 1988; orig. pub. 1964–1965), 300–301.

2. The text of the "Memorandum of Understanding between the United States of America and the Union of Soviet Socialist Republics Regarding the Establishment of a Direct Communications Link," 20 June 1963, is included in Robert C. Williams and Philip L. Cantelon, eds., *The American Atom: A Documentary History of Nuclear Policies from the Discovery of Fission to the Present, 1939–1984* (Philadelphia, 1984), 251–254.

3. "Treaty Banning Nuclear Weapon Tests in the Atmosphere, in Outer Space, and Under Water," 5 August 1963, in Williams and Cantelon, eds., *The American Atom,* 203. The complete text appears on pp. 202–205.

4. See Allan M. Winkler, *Life Under a Cloud: American Anxiety about the Atom* (New York, 1993), 178–182, for an evaluation of the Limited Test Ban Treaty.

5. John F. Kennedy, quoted in Stephen E. Ambrose, *Rise to Globalism: American Foreign Policy since 1938,* 5th rev. ed. (New York, 1988), 198 and 200.

6. Stephen Ambrose discusses the quickened pace of the arms race after the Cuban missile crisis in *Rise to Globalism,* 201.

7. Lawrence Suid outlines LeMay's position on this film in "The Pentagon and Hollywood: *Dr. Strangelove or: How I Learned to Stop Worrying and Love the Bomb* (1964)," in John E. O'Connor and Martin A. Jackson, eds., *American History/American Film* (New York, 1977, 1988), 224. According to Suid, LeMay knew that two films on accidental nuclear war—*Dr. Strangelove* and *Fail-Safe*—were being prepared for release in 1964, so he supported the making of this earlier positive film on the military service responsible for the delivery of nuclear weapons.

8. *A Gathering of Eagles,* dir. Delbert Mann, prod. Sy Bartlett (Universal International, 1963). All scenes and dialogue taken directly from the film.

9. Robert A. Heinlein, *Farnham's Freehold* (New York, 1983; orig. pub. 1964), 35.

10. Goldwater's campaign for American escalation in Vietnam, including the potential use of nuclear weapons, is outlined in Ambrose, *Rise to Globalism,* 211. Daniel Ellsberg also identified the "most salient issue" of the 1964 presidential campaign as "who should have his finger on the nuclear button." Given his perspective as an administration insider and as a Rand analyst, he was as well in a position to see how refraining from using nuclear weapons released American officials and advisers under Kennedy and Johnson from a sense of moral responsibility or remorse when urging a less than apocalyptic application of American power, as in Vietnam. See his article "The Responsibility of Officials in a Criminal War," in Daniel Ellsberg, *Papers on the War* (New York, 1972), 304–306.

11. Kurt Vonnegut, Jr., *Cat's Cradle* (New York, 1988; orig. pub. 1963), 11.

12. Ibid., 14.

13. Ibid., 13.

14. Ibid., 14 and 21.

15. Ibid., 15–17.

16. Ibid., 13–14.

17. Ibid., 113–114.

18. Ibid., 18–19.

19. Ibid., 21.

20. Ibid., 34–35.

21. Ibid., 36.

22. Ibid., 40.

23. Ibid., 41.

24. Ibid., 36.

25. Ibid., 52–53.

26. Ibid., 164.

27. Ibid., 168.

28. Ibid., 74.

29. Ibid., 143 and 157.

30. Ibid., 118.

31. Ibid., 118 and 189.

32. Ibid., 177.

33. Ibid., 182.

34. Ibid., 188.

35. Ibid., 190–191.

36. Stanley Kubrick, quoted in Suid, "The Pentagon and Hollywood," 226.

37. In *Nuclear Holocausts: Atomic War in Fiction, 1895–1984* (Kent, Ohio, 1987), 3, Paul Brians comments that finding atomic war "absurd" was a feature common to many literary accounts of nuclear war as well. He notes, "Even those few writers who try to establish that atomic war might be purposeful [as opposed to the more relied upon 'accidental' cause for war] or beneficent seem led by its internal logic to depict it as absurd." Later, in the context of discussing *Dr. Strangelove* and other works of satire, he points out that "there is something to be said for the argument that the concept of nuclear war is so irrational that only a satirical treatment of it is adequate" (p. 85), but he goes on to challenge the wisdom of his observation when he criticizes *Dr. Strangelove*'s satire for promoting fatalism and avoidance of thinking (p. 86).

38. Kubrick, quoted in Suid, "The Pentagon and Hollywood," 230.

39. Vonnegut, *Cat's Cradle,* 53.

40. All scenes and dialogue taken directly from *Dr. Strangelove or: How I Learned to Stop Worrying and Love the Bomb,* dir. and prod. Stanley Kubrick (Columbia, 1964), unless otherwise noted.

41. Brians demonstrates in *Nuclear Holocausts,* 59, that in contrast to *Dr. Strangelove*'s merging of sex and death, most writers on the subject of nuclear war "seem to be battling atomic thanatos with eros" by going to real extremes in order to

incorporate sex into their stories. Yet Brians does also document the existence of sexist and misogynist characters in nuclear fiction who mirror the characters in *Dr. Strangelove*, if in a much different context. See pp. 61 and 90–91. Brians relates this violent trend (and others) in science fiction works on nuclear war to the almost exclusively adolescent male readership of the genre.

42. The written and published screenplay of the film charts Dr. Strangelove's past as a Nazi scientist in more detail: "He was a recluse and perhaps had been made so by the effects of the British bombing of Peenemünde, where he was working on the German V-2 rocket. His black-gloved right hand was a memento of this." See Stanley Kubrick, Peter George, and Terry Southern, *Dr. Strangelove or: How I Learned to Stop Worrying and Love the Bomb* (New York, 1963), 35.

43. The published screenplay again offers a more emphatic account of Dr. Strangelove's Nazi orientation. The president wonders whether mine-shaft dwellers, traumatized by the massive deaths of those outside the mines, will even want to live, and Dr. Strangelove counters with an argument for the adaptability of man and for the acceptable conditions of life in the mines: "After all, the conditions would be far superior to those of the *so-called* concentration camps, where there is ample evidence most of the wretched creatures clung desperately to life." Kubrick, George, and Southern, *Dr. Strangelove,* 141.

44. Joan Didion, "I Can't Get That Monster Out of My Mind" (1964), in Joan Didion, *Slouching towards Bethlehem* (New York, 1968), 154–155.

45. Homer Jack, "The Strange Love of *Dr. Strangelove*: A Movie Review," adapted from a sermon delivered at White Plains Community Church, 23 February 1964, and published as a public service by the National Committee for a Sane Nuclear Policy, p. 2.

46. Nora Sayre, *Running Time: Films of the Cold War* (New York, 1982), 217 and 219.

47. *Newsweek,* 3 February 1964, pp. 79–80, as quoted in Suid, "The Pentagon and Hollywood," 232.

48. Lewis Mumford, quoted in Suid, "The Pentagon and Hollywood," 231.

49. Bosley Crowther, quoted in Jack, "The Strange Love of *Dr. Strangelove*," 3.

50. Mumford, quoted in Suid, "The Pentagon and Hollywood," 231.

51. Bosley Crowther, quoted in Suid, "The Pentagon and Hollywood," 231–232.

52. Crowther, quoted in Suid, "The Pentagon and Hollywood," 232.

53. Robert Brustein, quoted in Jack, "The Strange Love of *Dr. Srangelove*," 4.

54. Jack, "The Strange Love of *Dr. Strangelove*," 3.

55. Ibid., 4.

56. Also touting *Dr. Strangelove* as emblematic of the changing atomic age and cold war consciousness are Elaine Tyler May, *Homeward Bound: American Families in the Cold War Era* (New York, 1988), 219–220; Stephen J. Whitfield, *The Culture of the Cold War* (Baltimore, 1991), 218–225; and Allan M. Winkler, *Life Under a Cloud: American Anxiety about the Atom* (New York, 1993), 177–178. In *Nuclear Holocausts* Brians documents nihilism as the "dominant mood" of nuclear writers in the 1960s,

and he concludes: "At last science fiction found a fictional voice appropriate to the nightmare of nuclear war" (pp. 22–23).

57. Eugene Burdick and Harvey Wheeler, *Fail-Safe* (New York, 1962), 7–8.

58. *Fail-Safe,* dir. Sidney Lumet, prod. Max Youngstein (Columbia Pictures, 1964). All scenes and dialogue taken directly from the film.

59. Bosley Crowther, from the *New York Times,* 16 September 1964, quoted in Suid, "The Pentagon and Hollywood," 233.

60. Max Youngstein, quoted in Suid, "The Pentagon and Hollywood," 233.

61. John Frankenheimer, quoted in Edward Guthmann, "Assassination Movie Predicted History," *San Francisco Chronicle-Examiner,* 17 February 1986, "Datebook," p. 23.

62. *Seven Days in May,* dir. John Frankenheimer, prod. Edward Lewis (Paramount Pictures, 1964). All scenes and dialogue taken directly from the film.

63. The Khrushchev comment appears in Ambrose, *Rise to Globalism,* 196, as do the comments on Lyndon Johnson (p. 231). Eugene McCarthy termed LBJ a "wild man," and Ambrose reports that "doves" as a rule saw LBJ as a "monster." The rival 1964 campaign slogans appear in Frederick F. Siegel, "From the Great Society to Black Power," in Allan M. Winkler, ed., *The Recent Past: Readings on America since World War II* (New York, 1989), 157.

64. Richard Nixon, quoted in Stanley Karnow, *Vietnam: A History* (New York, 1983), 582.

65. In his article "The Pentagon and Hollywood," Lawrence Suid concludes that "it was the defeat in Vietnam, not the General Rippers or Turgidsons that forced the American people to reexamine their unquestioned acceptance of the military establishment" (p. 234); there is a general historical and cultural agreement about Vietnam's role in fomenting and symbolizing the chaos of the 1960s, such as is reflected in the comment of a graduate student who participated in the Vietnam "teach-ins" at the University of Michigan in the mid-1960s: "Vietnam was for some, then, a symbol for the deeper ills of American society." This comment, by James Gilbert, is quoted in Godfrey Hodgson, "The Great Schism," in Winkler, *The Recent Past,* 218.

66. In Charles S. Maier, "Revisionism and the Interpretation of Cold War Origins" (1970), in Richard Abrams and Lawrence Levine, eds., *The Shaping of Twentieth-Century America* (Boston, 1965, 1971), 574–575, Maier opens his evaluation of revisionism with the following comments about Vietnam's impact:

> Few historical reappraisals have achieved such sudden popularity as the current revisionist critique of American foreign policy and the origins of the Cold War. Much of this impact is clearly due to Vietnam. Although the work of revision began before the United States became deeply involved in that country, the war has eroded so many national self-conceptions that many assumptions behind traditional Cold War history have been cast into doubt.

Clearly, however, revisionists found cause for reappraisal of American policies long before Vietnam: William Appleman Williams, respected "father" of revisionism, published works from the early 1950s forward.

67. Maier terms Gar Alperovitz "the revisionist *enfant terrible*" in "Revisionism and the Interpretation of Cold War Origins," in Abrams and Levine, eds., *The Shaping of Twentieth-Century America,* 579, and Alperovitz's argument can be traced in *Atomic Diplomacy: Hiroshima and Potsdam* (New York, 1965) or in the revised and updated edition released in 1985, where he includes further corroboration of his original argument and defends his thesis against its many critics. See especially the introduction to the 1985 edition, "The Bombing of Hiroshima and Nagasaki," 1–60. Alperovitz's argument remains controversial and heavily criticized, yet more evidence supporting his claims keeps emerging, and even more popular treatments of the bomb and its early use have incorporated elements of Alperovitz's arguments. See Robert L. Messer, "New Evidence on Truman's Decision," *Bulletin of Atomic Scientists,* August 1985, reprinted in William H. Chafe and Harvard Sitkoff, eds., *A History of Our Time* (New York, 1991), 8–19, and see Peter Wyden's *Day One: Before Hiroshima and After* (New York, 1984) for a popular work's absorption of this revisionist argument.

68. Alperovitz first quotes Truman on the "master card" in *Atomic Diplomacy,* 11.

69. Ibid., 110.

70. "No Time Like the Past," written by Rod Serling, prod. Herbert Hirschman, dir. Justus Addiss, *The Twilight Zone,* CBS, 7 March 1963. All scenes and dialogue taken directly from the episode.

71. Ken Kesey, *Sometimes a Great Notion* (New York, 1983; orig. pub. 1963, 1964), 415–416.

CHAPTER NINE

1. *Lady in a Cage,* dir. Walter Grauman, prod. Luther Davis (Paramount Pictures, 1964). All scenes and dialogue taken directly from the film.

2. See the full lyrics to the song in Barry McGuire, "Eve of Destruction," *Eve of Destruction* (ABC Dunhill Music, 1965).

3. "On Evil: The Inescapable Fact," *Time,* 5 December 1969, p. 26.

4. Ibid., 27.

5. Ibid.

6. From the oral history of a Vietnam veteran, included in Mark Baker, *Nam: The Vietnam War in the Words of the Soldiers Who Fought There* (New York, 1981), 196.

7. Sylvia Plath, *The Bell Jar* (New York, 1971; orig. pub., London, 1963). Plath spent time in mental institutions as a result of her sense of "suffocation," and the novel seems to make clear the connections between the social constraints (particularly severe in the 1950s) imposed on women and their mental health.

8. Betty Friedan, *The Feminine Mystique* (New York, 1963, 1974). Sara Evans in *Personal Politics: The Roots of Women's Liberation in the Civil Rights Movement and the New Left* (New York, 1979) provides an incisive and moving analysis of how the modern women's movement was sparked by the multiform radical activism of this era.

9. Malcolm X, "Message to the Grass Roots" (November 1963), in Ronald

Lora, ed., *America in the Sixties: Cultural Authorities in Transition* (New York, 1979), 69.

10. Ibid., 68.

11. Ibid., 72.

12. The declaration is included in Harold Jacobs, ed., *Weatherman* (Berkeley, 1970), 509. For a blistering account of the failings of the Weatherman faction of SDS, see Peter Collier and David Horowitz, *Destructive Generation: Second Thoughts about the Sixties* (New York, 1989), especially chapter 2, "Doing It: The Rise and Fall of the Weather Underground," 67–119. A more balanced view of Berkeley in the 1960s is W. J. Rorabaugh, *Berkeley at War: The 1960s* (New York, 1989), and an intelligent assessment of the 1960s generally and radical movements specifically is David Farber, *The Age of Great Dreams: America in the 1960s* (New York, 1994). See especially chapter 9, "Stormy Weather," 190–211.

13. The events of the Altamont concert are recounted in Jonathan Eisen, *Altamont: Death of Innocence in the Woodstock Nation* (New York, 1970).

14. The name under which Charles Manson was booked is quoted in "Manson," *Newsweek,* 3 July 1989, p. 54.

15. Joan Didion, "The White Album" (1968–1978), from Joan Didion, *The White Album* (New York, 1978), 15.

16. Ibid., 41.

17. Ibid., 18–19.

18. Ibid., 46.

19. Ibid., 15. Didion's vertigo and nausea were ultimately diagnosed as symptoms of a serious illness, multiple sclerosis, but she herself sees the attack as not "an inappropriate response" on a wider social and cultural level.

20. Truman Capote, *In Cold Blood* (New York, 1965), 15.

21. Ibid., 102.

22. Ibid., 86–87.

23. Ibid., 95.

24. Ibid., 105.

25. Ibid., 277.

26. Ibid., 275 and 288.

27. Ibid., 326–327.

28. From the *Garden City Telegram,* quoted in Capote, *In Cold Blood,* 305–306.

29. Ibid., 361–362.

30. Cover, *Time,* 8 April 1966.

31. "Theology: Toward a Hidden God," *Time,* 8 April 1966, p. 82.

32. Ibid.

33. Ibid., 82–83.

34. Ibid., 83.

35. Ibid., 82.

36. Ibid., 85.

37. Ibid., 84.

38. Ibid., 87.

39. Ibid., 84 and 87.

40. John Lennon, quoted in "The Beatles," in Jon Pareles and Patricia Roman-owski, eds., *The Rolling Stone Encyclopedia of Rock and Roll* (New York, 1983), 34.

41. The American reactions to Lennon's comments are reported in Pareles and Romanowski, eds., *The Rolling Stone Encyclopedia*, 34.

42. "Theology: Toward a Hidden God," *Time*, 82–83.

43. Ibid., 82.

44. J. W. Fulbright, "The Great Society Is a Sick Society," *New York Times Magazine*, 20 August 1967, p. 30.

45. Ibid.

46. Ibid.

47. Ibid., 30 and 88.

48. Ibid., 88.

49. Ibid., 90.

50. Ibid., 95.

51. Ibid., 90 and 92.

52. Ibid., 95.

53. Ibid., 95–96.

54. Ibid., 96.

55. *Bonnie and Clyde,* dir. Arthur Penn, prod. Warren Beatty (Warner Brothers, 1967). All scenes and dialogue taken directly from the film, unless otherwise noted.

56. Bonnie's poem is quoted in Pauline Kael, "Bonnie and Clyde" (October 1967 review in the *New Yorker*), in Gerald Howard, ed., *The Sixties* (New York, 1982), 324.

57. Bosley Crowther, quoted in Lawrence L. Murray, "Hollywood, Nihilism, and the Youth Culture of the Sixties: *Bonnie and Clyde,*" in John E. O'Connor and Martin A. Jackson, eds., *American History/American Film* (New York, 1977, 1988), 245–246. The contours of the controversy about the film can be traced in this article.

58. Andrew Sarris, quoted in Murray, "Hollywood, Nihilism, and the Youth Culture of the Sixties," 246.

59. Kael, "Bonnie and Clyde," 329.

60. Ibid., 332.

61. Ibid., 333–334.

62. Ibid., 341–342.

63. Murray, in "Hollywood, Nihilism, and the Youth Culture of the Sixties," 245, makes this same point: "The brutality of their execution exceeds anything done by the gang and the film closes, as it had opened, with the audience being drawn to the principals. The previous confusion of emotions is resolved in the final frames."

64. Malcolm X and Alex Haley, *The Autobiography of Malcolm X* (New York, 1988; orig. pub. 1964–1965), 366–367.

65. Cover of the *New Left Notes,* 30 June 1969, published by the Progressive Labor faction of the SDS, quoted in Richard Hofstadter, "Reflections on Violence in the United States," in Richard Hofstadter and Michael Wallace, eds., *American Violence: A Documentary History* (New York, 1970), 29.

66. The purposefulness or destructiveness of violence and radicalism in the 1960s remains open to debate, particularly in regard to the radicalism of the New Left. The 1980s witnessed a fairly harsh backlash against the 1960s and the accomplishments of the New Left, and representative of this reaction is Collier and Horowitz's work, *Destructive Generation*. The authors disavow their own radical pasts in the New Left and offer a scathingly critical backward glance at the New Left and radical violence of all sorts in the 1960s. Their impetus for writing appears to have been the "riptide of a Sixties revival" (p. 217) they perceived in the 1980s, and they go on to tie the ills of the 1980s to the 1960s past: "In the inchoate attack against authority, we had weakened our culture's immune system, making it vulnerable to opportunistic diseases. The origins of metaphorical epidemics of crime and drugs could be traced to the Sixties, as could literal ones such as AIDS" (p. 16). This retrospective attributing of eighties horrors to the sixties also occurred in *Newsweek*'s coverage of the twentieth anniversary of the summer of 1969. In its article "The Summer of 1969," 3 July 1989, pp. 47–59, the magazine tied events from 1969 to the late 1980s—Woodstock gave birth to MTV, the "lunatic lethality" of Charles Manson fed into the crack and drug crisis, and gay activism at Stonewall (and by extension the entire sexual revolution) led directly to the AIDS epidemic. In *If I Had a Hammer: The Death of the Old Left and the Birth of the New Left* (New York, 1987), Maurice Isserman questions the extremism of this reassessment, particularly its tendency "to take the most violently apocalyptic moments in the history of the New Left and present them as the sum and substance of the movement." He notes that "there are marked similarities between 'the politics of revenge' of the 1950s, with its preoccupation with the preceding 'twenty years of treason,' and the analysis that now scorns the twenty years of 'adversary culture' that preceded the Reagan administration" (p. xiv). He concludes his thoughts on the radicalism of the New Left with moderation: "The New Left's radicalism consisted not in any inherent propensity for violence, irrationalism, or sympathy with totalitarianism (though all three became far too prevalent among sections of the New Left by the end of the 1960s) but rather in the attempt to understand the interconnection of such diverse issues as the danger of nuclear annihilation, the war in Southeast Asia, and racial injustice" (p. xvii).

67. Hofstadter, "Reflections on Violence in the United States," 30.

68. Ibid., 30–31.

69. Capote, *In Cold Blood,* 105.

70. John Lennon, "Imagine," *Imagine* (Capitol-EMI, 1971).

71. *Planet of the Apes,* dir. Franklin J. Schaffner, prod. Arthur P. Jacobs (Twentieth Century-Fox, 1968). All scenes and dialogue taken directly from the film.

72. *Beneath the Planet of the Apes,* dir. Ted Post, prod. Arthur P. Jacobs (Twentieth Century-Fox, 1970). All scenes and dialogue taken directly from the film.

73. This was the recurring opening narration for every episode of *Star Trek* (1966–1969). The series, a Desilu Production, was produced by Gene Roddenberry and Gene L. Coon.

74. The conceptualization of the future in *Star Trek* can be abstracted from the shows themselves or from the published accounts of the series, including Stephen

E. Whitfield and Gene Roddenberry, *The Making of Star Trek* (New York, 1968), and Allan Asherman, *The Star Trek Compendium* (New York, 1981).

75. In an article written for the twentieth anniversary of the "Summer of Love" in 1967, Michael Dougan headlined this point: "Something was happening, but it wasn't on TV." He pointed out that "in 1967, the status quo ruled the waves," and he excluded television as a medium of change in 1967: "Little on the networks warned TV fans that, in the summer of '67, long-simmering social changes would erupt, eventually leading an entire generation into rebellion." See Michael Dougan, "Something Was Happening, but It Wasn't on TV," *San Francisco Examiner,* 5 August 1987, p. E-3.

76. Martin Luther King, Jr., "I Have a Dream," in Allan M. Winkler, ed., *The Recent Past: Readings on America since World War II* (New York, 1989), 275.

77. Ibid., 276.

78. Ibid.

79. Ibid.

80. Ibid., 276–277.

81. Ibid., 277.

82. Thomas Pynchon, *The Crying of Lot 49* (New York, 1966), 103.

83. Malcolm X discussed the "Farce on Washington" in *The Autobiography of Malcolm X,* 278–281.

84. Coretta Scott King, quoted in Alex Haley's "Epilogue" to *The Autobiography of Malcolm X,* 427.

85. Ibid., 423.

86. Samuel H. Dresner, "Man, God and Atomic War," in *God and the H-Bomb,* ed. Donald Keys (New York, 1961), 134, and Lewis Mumford, "The Human Prospect" (1962), in his *Interpretations and Forecasts, 1922–1972* (New York, 1979), 472–473.

87. For a concise treatment of the sixties counterculture, see chapter 8, "The War Within," in David Farber's *The Age of Great Dreams,* 167–189.

88. In *Personal Politics* Sara Evans correctly notes that the new sexuality of the sixties was often less than ideal for women, even those intimately engaged in radical movements. She discusses how the open sexuality of this era neither translated into liberation for women in the civil rights movement and the new left nor augured sexual equality. She points out that the old left had a better record on gender issues than did the new left, and she offers a trenchant feminist critique of the new left and its sexual politics:

> Although the new left was engaged in a cultural revolt, championing openness and honesty, sexual freedom, and the end of campus regulations *in loco parentis,* it reflected more than it challenged the underlying sexual stereotypes of these early years. While SDS was certainly no worse than the society as a whole, it was only marginally freer for women. A few strong women in the inner circles, frequently married to key men, helped to shape SDS's politics, and chapters on women's campuses were very active. But the new left embodied the heritage of the feminine mystique far more strongly than the older left had. Its oblivi-

ousness to the issue of women's oppression was a sign, in fact, of how thoroughly the "new" left represented a break with the old (p. 116).

89. Lewis Mumford, "The Flowering of Plants and Men" (1968) in his *Interpretations and Forecasts,* 487 and 493.

90. Ibid., 490.

91. Ibid., 496.

92. The various Woodstock promoters billed the festival "An Aquarian Exposition" and "Three Days of Peace and Music." The promotional slogans are discussed in "Woodstock," *Newsweek,* 3 July 1989, p. 50.

93. Hugh Romney, "Stage Announcements," *Woodstock Soundtrack* (Cotillion, 1970).

94. Max Yasgur, quoted in Robert Spitz, *Barefoot in Babylon* (New York, 1979), 489.

95. Philip Tracy, "Birth of a Culture," *Commonweal,* 5 September 1969, p. 532.

96. For the full text of the song, see Joni Mitchell, "Woodstock," *Ladies of the Canyon* (Reprise, 1969).

97. Marvin Gaye, "Mercy, Mercy Me (The Ecology)," *What's Going On* (Motown, 1971).

98. "What's Going On" and "Save the Children," in *What's Going On.*

99. *Harold and Maude,* dir. Hal Ashby, prod. Colin Higgins (Paramount Pictures, 1971). All scenes and dialogue taken directly from the film.

100. Collier and Horowitz in *Destructive Generation* do not see America's withdrawal from the Vietnam War, or the role played by 1960s radicalism in that withdrawal, in such a positive light. See especially chapter 4, "Divided Loyalties," 143–150. The authors focus in particular on the totalitarian and brutal character of the later victorious Vietnamese regime in order to criticize those who protested America's involvement in Southeast Asia.

101. Daniel Ellsberg, *Papers on the War* (New York, 1972), 1.

102. Ibid., 291.

103. Ibid., 305 and 307.

104. Ibid., 308.

105. Gerald Ford, quoted in William Leuchtenburg, *A Troubled Feast: American Society since 1945* (Boston, 1979), 271.

Index

doomsday clock, 68; and reasons for establishment of, 94

Burdick, Eugene, 331

Butch Cassidy and the Sundance Kid (1969), 367

By the Bomb's Early Light: American Thought and Culture at the Dawn of the Atomic Age (Boyer), xvii

Caine Mutiny, The (Wouk), 34

Caine Mutiny, The (1954), 34–35, 393 n.43

Cambodia, 349

Canticle for Leibowitz, A (Miller), 57, 60–61

Capote, Truman: on imagination, 373; and *In Cold Blood,* 356–359; and new journalism, 356; on the sky, 374

Capra, Frank, 13

Carey, Michael, 110

Carmichael, Stokely, 352

Castro, Fidel, 194

Catch-22 (Heller), 245–256; as black humor attack on past and system, 245; and the capitalist imperative (Milo Minderbinder), 251–253; and definition of the enemy, 247–248; and evolution of "Catch-22," 249–250; and "flies in the eyes," 246; and the "Glorious Loyalty Oath Crusade," 243–245; and imperative of rebellion, dissent, 256; and insanity, 248–249; and military's insanity, 247–251; and prevalence of death, 247; and time, 246; and World War II, 256; and Yossarian's desertion of God, 253; and Yossarian's rebirth and desertion of system, 253–256

Catcher in the Rye, The (Salinger), 83–85; and Holden Caulfield as symbol of atomic age youth, 149

Cat's Cradle (Vonnegut), 188, 309–317; black humor in, 309, 317; and bomb's centrality in revolutionary culture, 309; and "cat's cradle" as symbol, 310–311; and cultural rebellion in 60s, 309; and the deadly

ethos of science and technology, 312–314; as encapsulation of spirit of dissent in 60s, 309; and "dynamic tension," 315; and the end of the world and absent sex urges, 316; and the moral void in the atomic age, 188, 312; and scientific "truth" in opposition to human principles, 313, 315

Caulfield, Holden, 83–85, 149. *See also The Catcher in the Rye*

Central Intelligence Agency (CIA), 18

Challenge of Atomic Energy, The, 92

"Chantilly Lace" (Big Bopper), 170

Chaos: cultural, as emblematic of bomb's impact, xxi; images of in 60s culture, 347

Checker, Chubby, 168, 171

Children: as not bulwarks against but mirrors of age's terror, 150; and civil defense in schools, 108–110; as deviants in counterculture, 157; and the psychological impact of the atomic age, 108; and no sanctuary for in atomic age, 151

China, 18

Church, Louisa Randall, 149–150

Civil defense: apathy about, dispelled, 203, meaning of, 200, 234; aroused interest in after Kennedy's 1961 speech, 202–212; as atomic fatalism, 94; concerns raised in debate on, encompassed in culture of dissent, 241; debate on after Berlin crisis and bomb shelter craze, 218–234; establishment of national program of, 95; as forum on psychological and physical dangers of living with the bomb, 92; and government spending on in 1950s, 98, in 1960s, 233–234; as "mania" and "illusion," 193; "mental," 96; and mental anxiety, 108, 111; as metaphor for

"split" or "schizoid" American life, 93; and morality, 227–228; as novel idea introducing Americans to atomic age insecurity, 93; opposition to as kernel of cultural revolution, 234, and forcing government abandonment of plans for, 231–234; programs in, reevaluated with each new nuclear development, 92; as promoted by popular periodicals during bomb shelter craze, 206; proposals for as barometers of American insecurity, 94; and its psychological impact on children, 109–110; and the reduced value of human life in, 93–94; and schools as conduits for information on, 108–109; as threat to black community, 283; and the vulnerability of American cities, 95–96

"Civil Defense Is Dead" (*The Nation*), 105

"Civil Defense vs. Public Apathy" (Levine), 97–98

Civil rights, restrictions on during cold war, 19

Civil Rights Act (1964), 352

Civil rights movement: the impact of the cold war and atomic bomb on, 282–284; the impact of World War II on, 281–282; increasing violence in, 351–352; and its links to atomic age culture of dissent, 281–286

Clash by Night (1952), 133–134

Cleaver, Eldridge, 353

Clift, Montgomery, 158

Climate of hate, 305

Cold war: and apparent Democratic moderation under Johnson, 308; and confusion of identity during, 74–75; debate over polarizing in 60s, 200; as given definition in the early postwar years, 16–18; intensification of its risks under Kennedy, 187; official American policy in, unchanged after Cuban missile crisis, 307; and the rejection of liberalism in,

Family (continued)
in 60s, 294–297; as undermined by psychological alienation in films and novels, 127–137
Family Fallout Shelter, The, 203
Family Food Stockpile for Survival, 203
Fantl, Kurt, 96
Farewell to Arms, A (Hemingway), 33
Farnham's Freehold (Heinlein), 307–308
Farrell, Thomas, xv
Father Knows Best, 90, 295
FBI. *See* Federal Bureau of Investigation
FCDA. *See* Federal Civil Defense Administration
Federal Bureau of Investigation (FBI): and its role in internal security, 19; and its methods as questionable in anticommunist films, 70–74
Federal Civil Defense Administration (FCDA); creation of, 95; criticized for stumbling procedures, 105; and new civil defense policy with hydrogen bomb, 99; on school civil defense, 108; and urged to forego "secrecy" in policies, 97–98
Feminine Mystique, The (Friedan), 351
Fermi, Enrico, 43
Fey, Harold, 191
Fiedler, Leslie, 75–76, 89
"Fifteen Years in Hell Is Enough" (Fey), 191
Film noir: as atomic age genre, xxii; the blurring of good and evil in, 62, 63; as emblematic of dissent in 40s and 50s, xxii–xxiii, xxv, 390 n.19; and its imagery in *White Heat,* 23–24; and the mirroring process linking criminal and police worlds, 62; and the presentation of family and community discord, 129; women in, as outside of traditional gender boundaries, 133
Final Solution, 29, 270, 271
Fire Next Time, The (Baldwin), 284–286

Fitzgerald, F. Scott, 3–4, 24
Flag, demythologized images of in pop art, 36–37
Flag (Johns), 36
Flag on Orange (Johns), 36
Floor Cone (Oldenburg), 297
Flower, as symbol of nature, 381–382
Flower children, 381–382
"Flowering of Plants and Men, The" (Mumford), 381–382
Fly, The (1958), 59–60
Folger, Abigail, 354
Ford, Gerald, 387
Foreman, Carl, 66, 398 n.64
Forgive Me, Killer (Whittington), 65–66
Frankenheimer, John, 245, 264, 336
Freed, Alan, 171
Free speech movement, 352–353
French Fries and Ketchup (Oldenburg), 297
Friedan, Betty, 351
From Here to Eternity (Jones), 34
From Here to Eternity (1953), 34
Fulbright, J. W., 363–366; and American arrogance of power, 363; and his critique of the Great Society, 363–366; and the regenerative counterforce of protest, 366, 371; on the sickness of the Vietnam War, 363–366; as symbol of dissenters in government, 385; on violence as part of protests, 371–372; on World War II as genesis of sick system, 364; and on the young as a "regenerative generation," 364–366
Future, and conflicting cultural images of in space, 374–377

Gaither, H. Rowan, Jr., 106
Gaither Report, 106
Gargarin, Yuri, 194
Gathering of Eagles, A (1963), 307
Gaye, Marvin, 384
Genocide, black American fears of after World War II, 281–283

Gentleman's Agreement (1947), 29
Germany, division east and west, 18
Ginsberg, Allen, 86, 171, 172; and "America," 178; and *Howl,* 171–172, 173–175
Gitlin, Todd: on American power as a "menace" during Cuban missile crisis, 239; on childhood civil defense drills, 109–110; on the Cuban missile crisis and its fueling of student radicalism, 238–239; on "time" during the Cuban missile crisis, 236
Glenn, John, 374
God: at center of spiritual awakening about the bomb, 188–191; fate of in 60s and 70s, 339; and questioning of existence, meaning, 356, 359–363; and the questioning of spiritual and political authority, 189; as a spiritual force to rebuild American morality, 223, 363
God and the H-Bomb (Keys, ed.), 223–227; and its comparison of the Holocaust with potential nuclear annihilation, 271
Godfather, The (1972), 367
"God's Judgment of White America" (Malcolm X), 304–305
Godzilla (1956), 57, 58
Goldstein, Israel, 225
Goldwater, Barry, 194, 308, 340
Gottwald, Norman, 199–200
"Great Balls of Fire" (Lewis), 82, 171
Great Depression, xxi
Great Gatsby, The (Fitzgerald), 3–4
"Great Illusion, The" (*Nation*), 193
Great Society, 352, 363–366
"Great Society Is a Sick Society, The" (Fulbright), 363–366
Green Berets, 307
Guilt: as evoking remorse over Hiroshima and Nagasaki, 116; as nourished by Hiroshima and Nagasaki, 39; and redemption

from by relinquishing power, in pulp crime novels and westerns, 66
Guns, in shelters, 203–205; ethics of, 204–205, and continued controversy over, 211–212
"Gun Thy Neighbor?" (*Time*), 189, 203–205

Hagan, Roger, 231
Haldeman, H. R. "Bob," 340
Haley, Alex, 380
Haley, Bill and the Comets, 167
"Harlem" (Hughes), 283–284
Harold and Maude (1971), 384–385
Harris, Lou, and poll on Americans' belief in God and their religious practices, 360
"Heartbreak Hotel" (Presley), 169
Heinlein, Robert, 307
Heller, Joseph: and *Catch-22,* 245–256; and his ridicule of anticommunism, 243–245; and his use of World War II in *Catch-22,* 245–247
Hell of a Woman, A (Thompson), 121
Hell's Angels, 354
Hemingway, Ernest, 33
Hendrix, Jimi, 353
Hersey, John, 41–42
High Noon (1952), 66–68; and clocks as atomic age symbol, 68; and critique of HUAC and internal security system, 66, 67–68
Hippies, 381
Hiroshima (Hersey), 41–42; and promotion of American guilt and remorse, 42, 394 n.8; and similar impact of Hiroshima Maidens, 45
Hiroshima: as hell on earth, 362; and its historical and ethical ties to the bomb shelter craze, 217
Hiroshima and Nagasaki: as evoked in *Godzilla,* 58; fiftieth anniversary of and debate over bomb's use, xviii; as inspiration of American guilt, 39; and official justifications of,

to counter moral criticism, 42–43; and the rise of the culture of dissent, 341
Hiroshima in America: Fifty Years of Denial (Lifton and Mitchell), xviii
Hiroshima Maidens, 45–46
Hiss, Alger, 76
Hitchcock, Alfred: and *The Birds,* 300, 302; and his cycle of films noirs, 129; and *Dial M for Murder,* 138; and films on family and community corrosion, 137–139, 406 n.54; and *I Confess,* 69; and his images of a corrupted America, 61–62; and *The Man Who Knew Too Much,* 138; and *North by Northwest,* 61–62; and *Notorious,* 28; and *Psycho,* 85, 179, 181–182; and *Rear Window,* 137–138; and *Spellbound,* 116; and *Strangers on a Train,* 61, 127, 129; and the theme of lost innocence in films, 77; and *Vertigo,* 77; and *The Wrong Man,* 138–139
Hofstadter, Richard, 372
Holifield, Chet, 106
Holly, Buddy, 168
Hollywood Ten, 47, 48
Holmes, John Clellon, 167, 172–173
Holocaust, 270–271
Homeward Bound: American Families in the Cold War Era (May), 113–115, 150
Hook, Sidney, 211
Hot line, 305
"Hound Dog" (Presley), 169
House Committee on UnAmerican Activities (HUAC): criticism of in *Spartacus,* 242–243; in Hollywood, 47–48; less inspiring of terror in 60s, 186; and open protest against, 242; as presented in *I Was a Communist for the F.B.I.,* 70; revival of, 19; and silencing dissent, 47–48. *See also* Internal security; Law and order
House of Strangers (1949), 127
Howl (Ginsberg), 172, 173–175
How to Spot a Communist, 47
"How U.S. Cities Can Pre-

pare for Atomic War" (*Life*), 95–96
Hughes, H. Stuart, 211
Hughes, Langston, 283–284
Hydrogen bomb: development of, 18, 43; and impact on civil defense, 92, 99–101; and odds for survival in attack using, 99; and Oppenheimer's opposition to and resulting loss of security clearance, 49–50; and scientist opposition to its development, 43; and testing of on Bikini atoll, 45, 99

ICBMs. *See* Intercontinental ballistic missiles
I Confess (1953), 69
I Dream of Jeannie, 295
"I Have a Dream" (King), 377–379
I Led Three Lives, 69, 74
"Illusion of Civil Defense, The" (Piel), 228–229
"Imagine" (Lennon), 373–374
In Cold Blood (Capote), 356–359; and being told there is no God, 357, 359; and the ease of killing, 358–359; and the frequency of mass murder, 359; and the idea of "who's safe?" 357; and imagination, 373; and the implications of sudden, irrational death, 356; and a vision of the sky, 374
Indefensible Weapons: The Political and Psychological Case Against Nuclearism (Lifton and Falk), xvi
Informing: as condemned in *Spartacus,* 243; criticism of, 69; as demanded by HUAC in Hollywood, 47; as patriotic duty, 69–70
Innocence: and Americans' notions of and fears about their, 2–3; and the atomic age loss of, 75–77; as lost in *Vertigo,* 77; and resistance to admitting the end of, 9; and World War II, 2; and youths' loss of, 82
Insanity: as an appropriate response to dangers of atomic age, 111, 113; in counterculture visions of

Killer Inside Me, The (Thompson), 63–64, 120–121
King, Coretta Scott, 380
King, Martin Luther, Jr.: assassination of, 348; and Christian nonviolence, 351; and fomenting moral rebirth and a new myth of life, 377–380; and his "I Have a Dream" speech, 377–379; influence on counterculture, 379–380; and the Montgomery bus boycott, 283; and his relationship with Malcolm X and radical protest, 380
Kiss Me Deadly (Spillane), 64–65
Kiss Me Deadly (1955), 398 n.61
Knowing sin: among Oppenheimer and the scientists, 6–7; in the culture of dissent, 20
Korean War, 18; and disillusion as result of, 27–28; and its impact on civil defense, 93; and shifting postwar alliances, 27
Kramer, Stanley, 194
Kubrick, Stanley: on black humor in *Dr. Strangelove,* 318; and *Dr. Strangelove,* xiv, xxiii, 190, 309, 319; and *Spartacus,* 242; and *2001: A Space Odyssey,* xiv, 374

LaBianca, Leno and Rosemary, 354, 355
Lady in a Cage (1964), 346–347
Lapp, Ralph, 100–101
Laughter, as subversive attack on American system, 245, in *One Flew Over the Cuckoo's Nest,* 258–259. See also Black humor
Law and order: and enforcement officers as indistinguishable from criminals and communists, 62; idealized representations of forces of, 69–70; increased presence of forces in America, as in *White Heat,* 24; and the preservation of atomic secrets, 46; and tainted images of its forces in 40s and 50s, 61–66; in television shows, 69. See

also House Committee on UnAmerican Activities; Internal security
"Leader of the Pack" (Shangri-Las), 198
Leave It to Beaver, 90; as model overturned by bizarre families in 60s television, 294, 295
Lee, Dickie, 198
LeMay, General Curtis, 307
Lennon, John: on the Beatles and Jesus Christ, 362; and "Imagine," 373–374
Levine, Murray, 97–98
Lewis, Jerry Lee, 82, 86, 168, 171
Lichtenstein, Roy, 36
Life magazine: and criticism by *Newsweek* of its optimistic survival odds in nuclear war, 215; and optimistic predictions of survival in a sheltered America, 207; and its promotion of shelter plans, 206–208
Life Under a Cloud: American Anxiety About the Atom (Winkler), xvii–xviii
Lifton, Robert Jay, xvi, xviii
"Light My Fire" (The Doors), 381
Little Richard, 168, 171
Lolita (Nabokov), 135–137
"Love Me Tender" (Presley), 169
Lucky Dragon, 44, 58, 100
"Lunch in a Jim Crow Car" (Hughes), 284
Lymon, Frankie and the Teenagers, 171

MacArthur, Douglas, 19
McCarthy, Joseph, 46–47; and his opinion on Oppenheimer's loyalty, 49; parody of in *The Manchurian Candidate,* 265–266; and revulsion for and censure of after Army-McCarthy hearings, 77
McGuire, Barry, 190, 347
Machine guns, controversy over as items to stock in shelters, 189; their planned use to repel evacuees in nuclear war, 105
Machines, and attacks on: in literature, 298–299; in Mumford, 292–293;

in pop art, 297–298; on television, 294–295
McHugh, Father L. C., 212, 223
Madmen, language of, associated with American leaders, 340–341
Mailer, Norman, 33
Malaise: in *Bonnie and Clyde,* 367; as expanding in 60s, 197; in *The Moviegoer,* 198–199; as nihilistic, in 60s, engendered by violence and religious crisis, 189, 411–412 n.10; and violence, as one extreme of cultural rebellion, 342–343
Malcolm X: assassination of, 348; on black power and revolution, 351–352; and "God's Judgment of White America," 304–305; on Kennedy's assassination, 304–305; and the limits on violence, 371; on the March on Washington, 380; and "Message to the Grassroots," 351–352; on the relationship of his radicalism to King's nonviolent protests, 380
"Man, God and Atomic War" (Dresner), 225–227
Manchurian Candidate, The (Condon), 264, 422 n.67, 422 n.69
Manchurian Candidate, The (1962), 265–269; as a black humor attack on the American system, 245; and the collapse of communist/anticommunist distinctions, 265, 268–269; and the corruption of authority figures, 268; and the enemy within, 264–265, 268; and Johnny Iselin as a parody of Joseph McCarthy, 265–266; and *My Son John* and bizarre mother sexuality, 268; and its parody of cold war modes of logic, 265; and its satiric reversals of anticommunist films, 268; and the surrealism of brainwashing sequences, 266
Man in the Gray Flannel Suit, The (Wilson), 32, 107, 121–124, 125–126

Nihilism, in *Bonnie and Clyde,* 367; as one extreme of cultural rebellion, 342–343. *See also* Malaise

1960: and the meaning of the new decade, 184–185, 190–191; and the urgency of change in, 199–200

1980s atomic awakening, xvi, xix, 388

Nixon, Richard M.: and his criminality, 386–387; and his declaration of "Mental Health Week" as Vice President, 107; and the impact of cultural rebellion on his presidential career, 385, 386–387; and leaving office in disgrace, 340; and the "Madman Theory," 340; and his opinion on Oppenheimer's loyalty, 49; and his resignation, 385, 387; and the Vietnam War, 349

Nonviolence, 351

No Place to Hide, 92

North Atlantic Treaty Organization (NATO), 18

North by Northwest (1959), 61–62

"No Time Like the Past" (1963), 343–344

Notorious (1946), 28

Nuclear arms race, acceleration after Cuban missile crisis, 307

Nuclear attack warnings, ignored by Americans, 104

Nuclear-freeze movement, xix

Nuclear Holocausts: Atomic War in Fiction, 1895–1984 (Brians), xvii

Nuclear numbing, xvi–xvii, xx

Nuclearosis, 107

Nuclear weapons, and refraining from using as "moderation" in foreign policy, 308

Nuclear winter, xix

Nuremberg trials, 26–27

Office of Civil and Defense Mobilization (OCDM), 402 n.23; and concerned calls to after Kennedy's speech, 202

Oldenburg, Claes, 297

One (Pollock), 126

"On Evil: The Inescapable Fact" *(Time),* 349–350

One Flew Over the Cuckoo's Nest (Kesey), 256–264; and the benefits of movement 259; as black humor attack on American system, 245; and the Chief's rebirth and McMurphy's sacrifice, 261–264; and "The Combine," 256–257; in comparison to *The Catcher in the Rye,* 264; and the enemy within, 264; and escaping the system, 264; and "fog," 257–258; and resistance to the system, 257; and system's naked forms of control, 261; and the threat of nonconformity, 260–261

"Only the Lonely" (Orbison), 170

On the Beach (Shute), 57, 194–196; and the Armageddon attitude, 194–196, 412 n.8

On the Beach (1959), 194

"On the Feasibility of Peace" (Piel), 229–231

On the Road (Kerouac), 175–178

On the Waterfront (1954), 69–70

On Thermonuclear War (Kahn), 218–219

"Open Letter to President Kennedy," 227–228

"Operation Candor," 44

Oppenheimer, J. Robert: and atomic remorse, 6; defense of in Rabinowitch, 99–100; as head of the AEC's General Advisory Committee on the H-bomb, 43; and his moral qualms concerning atomic and hydrogen bombs, 49; and "Operation Candor," 44; and "the physicists have known sin," 6; and the revocation of his security clearance as the final defeat of scientist activism, 50; as a "security risk," 48–50, 396 n.36; and his sense of knowing sin in science fiction, 59; on im-

ages of United States and U.S.S.R. as "scorpions," 10

Optimism: and spiritual regeneration, as one extreme of cultural rebellion, 342–343; after World War II, 88

Orbison, Roy, 170

Papers on the War (Ellsberg), 385–386

Paranoia, as operational in 50s, 139, 407 n.55

Paris summit, 194

Parks, Rosa, 283

Past: and a new understanding of and rejection of menacing system developed in, in 60s counterculture, 241; as opened to new critical observation in 60s, 186; and rethinking of as hallmark of cultural rebirth, 242

"Patches" (Lee), 198

Peace Race, The (Melman), 215

Pentagon Papers, The, 385

Percy, Walker, 198

"Perfect Day for Bananafish, A" (Salinger), 115–116

Periodicals, and the promotion of civil defense information and education, 206

Perkins, Carl, 168

Peter, Paul and Mary, 353

Peterson, Ray, 198

Peterson, Val, 99

Philbrick, Herbert A., 69, 74

"Philosophy of the Beats, The" (Holmes), 172–173

Pick Up on South Street (1953), 62–63

Piel, Gerard: and "The Illusion of Civil Defense," 228–229; and "On the Feasibility of Peace," 229–231; and his opposition to civil defense, 228–231; and his recognition of World War II as a starting point for American immorality and insanity, 230, 245

Pike, Bishop James A., 224–225

Planet of the Apes (1968), 374–377; and an apocalyptic, nightmarish future, 374–375; and its contrast to *Star Trek,* 375–377

Plath, Sylvia, 351

SDS. *See* Students for a Democratic Society

Serling, Rod: and the introduction to *The Twilight Zone,* 184; as writer and narrator of "The Shelter," 213–214; as writer and narrator of "Time Enough at Last," 196–197

Seven Days in May (1964), 331, 336–338; and its comparison to *Fail-Safe* and *Dr. Strangelove,* 338–339

Sexual revolution, 380–381; as often less than ideal for women, 434 n.88; as symbol of renewed values of love and respect for life, 381

Shane (1952), 66, 68

Shangri-Las, 198

"Shelter, The" (1961), 213–214

Shelters: blast and fallout, 93; and ethics, 212, 217; as the heart of civil defense, 92–93. *See also* Bomb shelter craze; Civil defense

"Shout" (Isley Brothers), 171

Shute, Nevil, 57, 194

Silent generation, 39, 90–91

Sit-in, 242

Smithsonian National Air and Space Museum, xviii

Snake Pit, The (1948), 118–119

"Social Consequences of Atomic Energy" (Mumford), 144–145

Soft Fur Good Humors (Oldenburg), 297

Sometimes a Great Notion (Kesey), 185, 344

Soviet Union: and its atomic bomb, its influence on American internal security, 46, and civil defense, 92; and early cold war American perceptions of, 16–17; and the easing of overt tensions with after Cuban missile crisis, 305–306; as "evil empire," xix; and its expansionism fueling American interventionism in cold war, 18; and Kennedy's willingness to confront, 187; and its rapid

transformation to enemy, 26

Space, as futuristic cultural terrain, 374–377

Spartacus (1960), 242–243

Spellbound (1945), 116–117

Spillane, Mickey, 63, 64

Sputnik: and Eisenhower's response to, 105–106; and hysterical American response to, 105; and its illustration of the psychological value of satellites and missiles, 102; and Kennedy taking advantage of panic over to reinvigorate cold war, 187

Standardization, critique of: in Mumford, 291–294; in *One Flew Over the Cuckoo's Nest,* 257, 260–261; in pop art, 297–298

Starr, Edwin, 353

"Star Spangled Banner" (Hendrix), 353

Star Trek (1966–1969), 375–377

Still Life #24 (Wesselman), 298

Still Life #30 (Wesselman), 298

Stimson, Henry L., 42

Storm Center (1956), 151, 154–157

"Strange Love of Dr. Strangelove: A Movie Review, The" (Jack), 328, 330–331

Stranger, The (1946), 28, 40–41

Strangers on a Train (1951), 61, 127–129

Strategic Air Command (1955), 59

Strategic Defense Initiative ("Star Wars"), xix

Strauss, Lewis, 44, 49

"Street-Fighting Man" (Rolling Stones), 353

Students for a Democratic Society (SDS): and the "Port Huron Statement," 286–290; and the purposes of violence, 371; and violent trends in, 352–353

Styron, William: on Hiroshima as the defining moment for loss of innocence, morality, 25, 37; on the Korean War and an "un-

hinged cosmos," 25; on the place of World War II and its impact in his generation's outlook, 24–25; and his "unhinged cosmos" imagery in *Vertigo,* 79

Suburbia, 89; its connection to civil defense, 96; on television, 90

Subway, The (Tooker), 126

Suddenly (1954), 32, 63

Summer of Love, 381

Sunset Boulevard (1950), xxiii–xxv, 85, 119–120

"Survival: Are Shelters the Answer?" (*Newsweek*), 214–216

"Survival by Shelter or Sanity?" (Pike), 224–225

Survivalism, radical ethos of during shelter craze, 203–204; in *Farnham's Freehold,* 307

Swell-Looking Babe, A (Thompson), 134–135

Swenson, Gene, 298

"Sympathy for the Devil" (Rolling Stones), 353, 354

System (or establishment): destroyed in order to build anew, in *Cat's Cradle* and *Dr. Strangelove,* 309; evil and violence committed by, 350; and its image revised in the 60s, 270; as open to critical judgment of many kinds, 305; as responsible for climate of violence, 371–372; symbolic defeat of in early 70s, 385–387

Tanimoto, Kiyoshi, 45, 46

Tate, Sharon, 354, 355

Taylor, Telford, 26–27, 75

Technology: and cultural change, xiv–xv; increased use of by internal security forces, as in *White Heat,* 24; twentieth-century destructiveness of, 3

Teenage death songs, 197–198, 412 n.13

"Teen Angel" (Dinning), 197–198

Television: and its celebration of nonconformity, 294; and its challenge to the cold war consensus, 294–297; and dehumanization,

Designer: Seventeenth Street Studios
Compositor: Prestige Typography
Text: 10/14 Bembo
Display: Syntax
Printer & Binder: Edwards Bros.